MW00776631

Unpublished Fragments

from the Period of *Thus Spoke Zarathustra*

(Summer 1882–Winter 1883/84)

Volume Fourteen

Based on the edition by
Giorgio Colli & Mazzino Montinari

First organized in English by Ernst Behler

The Complete Works of Friedrich Nietzsche

EDITED BY ALAN D. SCHRIFT AND DUNCAN LARGE

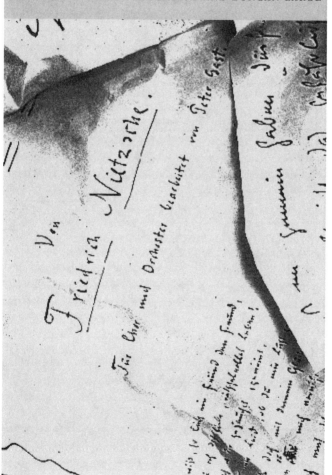

Friedrich Nietzsche

Unpublished Fragments

from the Period of *Thus Spoke Zarathustra*

(Summer 1882 – Winter 1883/84)

Translated, with an Afterword,
by Paul S. Loeb and David F. Tinsley

STANFORD UNIVERSITY PRESS

STANFORD, CALIFORNIA

Stanford University Press
Stanford, California

Translated from Friedrich Nietzsche, *Sämtliche Werke: Kritische Studienausgabe*, ed. Giorgio Colli and Mazzino Montinari, in 15 vols. This book corresponds to Vol. 10, pp. 7–664.

Critical edition of Friedrich Nietzsche's *Sämtliche Werke* and unpublished writings based on the original manuscripts.

Printed in the United States of America on acid-free, archival-quality paper

CIP data appears at the end of the book.

Contents

Reference Matter

A Note
on This Edition

This is the first English translation of all of Nietzsche's writings, including his unpublished fragments, with annotation, afterwords concerning the individual texts, and indexes, in nineteen volumes. The aim of this collaborative work is to produce a critical edition for scholarly use. Volume 1 also includes an introduction to the entire edition, and Volume 19 will include a detailed chronology of Nietzsche's life. While the goal is to establish a readable text in contemporary English, the translation follows the original as closely as possible. All texts have been translated anew by a group of scholars, and particular attention has been given to maintaining a consistent terminology throughout the volumes. The translation is based on *Friedrich Nietzsche: Sämtliche Werke. Kritische Studienausgabe in 15 Bänden* (1980), edited by Giorgio Colli and Mazzino Montinari. The still-progressing *Nietzsche Werke: Kritische Gesamtausgabe*, which Colli and Montinari began in 1963, has also been consulted. The Colli-Montinari edition is of particular importance for the unpublished fragments, comprising more than half of Nietzsche's writings and published there for the first time in their entirety. Besides listing textual variants, the annotation to this English edition provides succinct information on the text and identifies events, names (except those in the Index of Persons), titles, quotes, and biographical facts of Nietzsche's own life. The notes are numbered in the text and are keyed by phrase. The Afterword presents the main facts about the origin of the text, the stages of its composition, and the main events of its reception. The Index of Persons includes mythological figures and lists the dates of birth and death as well as prominent personal characteristics. Since the first three volumes appeared, important corrections to the 1980 edition of the *Kritische Studienausgabe* have been noted, and these corrections have been incorporated into the translation that appears here.

ERNST BEHLER AND ALAN D. SCHRIFT

Unpublished Fragments

from the Period of *Thus Spoke Zarathustra*

(Summer 1882–Winter 1883/84)

Preliminary Note to Volume 14

Volumes 14 and 15 of the *Complete Works of Friedrich Nietzsche* (Volumes 10 and 11 of the *KSA*) together comprise Nietzsche's unpublished fragments from July 1882 to Autumn 1885, which correspond to Part VII of the *KGW*. The fragments are preserved in thirty-six manuscripts, specifically in twenty-one notebooks in larger format, twelve notebooks, and three loose-leaf binders.

The organizing principles that govern the publication of Nietzsche's unpublished fragments are set forth in the Preliminary Note to *CW* 10.

In addition, the following comments concerning Volumes 14 and 15 of *CW* should be noted. The manuscripts from the period July 1882 to Autumn 1885 include preliminary work on the four parts of *Thus Spoke Zarathustra*; drafts, outlines, and fragments that have to do with parts of this work that were not included; extensive collections of sayings that in many cases relate to work on *Z*; and notes that — in literary terms — have no relation to *Z* (the latter make up approximately half of the complete material; they were published as a small part of the notebooks related to *Beyond Good and Evil* [and included in *CW* 16]). All of these notes are being published as *Z*-fragment literary remains, which precede the actual early drafts and final clean copies of each part of *Z*. Yet since Nietzsche, each time after completing a part of *Z*, recopied a large number of the previous notes that he hadn't used into new notebooks, often without changing anything, it was impossible to avoid the repetition of certain notes — although in differing contexts.

Volume 14 of *CW* corresponds to Volume VII/1 of the *KGW* (Berlin / New York: Walter de Gruyter, 1977) and thus contains the fragments from July 1882 to Winter 1883–84. Nietzsche's Tautenburg Notes for Lou von Salomé (July–August 1882) are published with the kind permission of Dr. (Honorary) Ernst Pfeiffer (Göttingen).

There is no Afterword by Giorgio Colli for Volume 14.

MAZZINO MONTINARI

Editorial Note to Volume 14

Unless another volume in the *CW* is cited, all cross-references to fragments in the notes are references to fragments in this volume. In cases where a cross-reference to a fragment is followed by a number (e.g., 5[1] 22), this indicates that the reference is to the sentence or paragraph numbered 22 in fragment 5[1]. In cases where a cross-reference to a fragment is followed by an underline and a number (e.g., 22[1]_547), this indicates that the reference is to a passage in fragment 22[1] that appears on page 547 of this volume.

In cases where the format of a fragment in this volume differs significantly from the format of the fragment as it appears in *KSA*, we have chosen to follow as closely as possible the format of the fragment as it appears in Nietzsche's handwritten notebooks.

ALAN D. SCHRIFT

[1 = N V 9a. N VI 1a. Tautenburg Notes for Lou von Salomé. July–August 1882]

1 [1]

"*solitudo continuata dulcescit*"[1] Madonna del Sasso. (Locarno)[2]

1 [2]

Refutation of Morality? —

Morality is what matters to those who *cannot* free themselves from it: it is for that very reason one of the "conditions
of existence" for them. It is impossible to refute conditions of
existence: We can only — *not have them*![3]

1 [3][4]

Basic Principles

The *final* physical state of force we unlock must necessarily
also be the *first*.

The dissolution of force into *latent* force must be the cause
of the emergence of the *most vigorous* force. The state of the
highest position must follow the one state of negation.

Space, like matter, is a subjective form. Time is *not*.

Space first emerged through the assumption of *empty space*.
This doesn't exist. Force is everything.

We are incapable of conceiving simultaneously what is
moved and what is moving, but that is what makes matter and
space. We *isolate*.

The development of a thing allows retrospective conclusions
about its emergence.

All development is an emergence.

Matter, material is a *subjective* form.

We cannot conceive of anything except as being *material*. Even thoughts and abstractions obtain from us a very refined materiality, which we perhaps *deny*: nevertheless they do have it. We have accustomed ourselves to overlook this sophisticated materiality and to speak of "the immaterial." Just as we have *distinguished* dead from alive, logical from illogical, etc. To unlearn[5] our *oppositions* — is the task.

1 [4]

Even *concepts* have *emerged*. From where? — There are *transitions* here.

1 [5][6]

People who were employed for an enterprise which has *failed* should be doubly compensated.

1 [6][7]

If you want to stay young for a long time, become young late.

"Anyone who is too strict in his judgment of others is bad in my opinion" — I say with Demosthenes.

1 [7]

"*Suaviter in re, fortiter in me.*"[8]

1 [8][9]

What all the resurrected believe. — It is highly unlikely that someone who has died early once will die a second time.

1 [9][10]

Life after death. — Those who have reason to believe in their "life after death" must learn to endure their "death" during their life.

1 [10]¹¹

    Late youth. — Late youth sustains long youth.

1 [11]¹²

    The ideal. — The eye sees everything as outside itself: and thus we still see our ideal *before us*, even if we have already reached it!

1 [12]

    Concept and feeling of "noble" has a different prehistory than concept and feeling of "good."

1 [13]¹³

Vademecum. Vadetecum¹⁴
By F. Nietzsche
First Complete Edition

Contents:
Human, All Too Human. With Appendix
The Wanderer and His Shadow
Dawn
The Joyful Science.

1 [14]

The Plowshare.
*A Tool for the Liberation
of the Spirit.*

First complete edition
in two volumes

Contents:
Human, All Too Human. With Appendix:
Mixed Opinions and Maxims.
The Wanderer and His Shadow.
Dawn. Thoughts on the Presumptions of Morality.
The Joyful Science.

1 [15][15]

To – – –

Friend![16] — spoke Columbus — do not trust
a Genoese ever again!
He's always staring into the blue,
What is most distant draws him all too much!

*

Courage! I am on the open sea,
Behind me lies Genoa.
And in league with you I will win
Lands of gold and America.

*

Let us stand on our own two feet!
For us there is no more turning back.
Look outward: greeting us from far away
One death, one fame, one fortune![17,18]

1 [16]

a largely or exclusively vegetarian diet
People of strong affects, ambitious invidious lascivious people may in fact wish to ask themselves whether for them a little
meat is already too much, although for me the much more
important question than *what* they should eat, is that other
question: how much, which here means: *how little*.

1 [17]

As when a friend tears himself away from a friend's bosom.
Go ahead! You will still have your pain![19]

1 [18]

What is my book worth if it cannot at least endure the scru-
tiny *sub specie trecentorum annorum*?[20]

1 [19]²¹
  Free spirits.
  Style.
  Moral and *organic.*
  Selfishness and neighborliness.²²
  Heroism.
  The effect of the thought on the future of the world.
  God and *devil.*

1 [20]

                  On the Morality of the "I."

The difficulty of making oneself *understood.* This is impossible to do with many people.

Every action is misunderstood. And in order *not* to have continual encounters, it is necessary to have a *mask.* Also in order to *seduce* . . .

Better to associate with people who consciously lie, for only they can also be consciously truthful. Usually, truthfulness is a mask that is *not conscious of being a mask.*

The "I" subjugates and kills: it works like an organic cell: it pillages and is violent. It wants to regenerate itself — pregnancy. It wants to give birth to its god and to see all of humanity at its feet.²³

The I's that have been liberated fight for mastery.

1 [21]
  This is no book: what use are books!
  What use are coffins and shrouds!
  This is a will, this is a promise,
  This is a last burning-of-bridges,
  This is a sea breeze, a weighing of the anchor,
  A roaring of the paddlewheels, a setting of the tiller,
  The cannon roars, its fire a white steam
  The sea laughs, the monster —²⁴

1 [22][25]

to give selfishness a beautiful name, after it is supposed to
be evil

1 [23]

I believe G. I. Ascoli and E. Rénan when they say that the
Semitic race was Indoeuropean.

1 [24][26]

The lives of heroic humans contain the abbreviated history
of multiple generations in regard to the deification of the
devil. They experience in turn what it is to be heretic, witch,
prophet, skeptic, weakling, believer and what it is to be
overwhelmed.

1 [25][27]

Those who themselves possess the will to suffer are differently disposed to cruelty; when they inflict hurt, they do not
believe hurting to be in and of itself damaging and bad.

1 [26][28]

"Jesus saw someone working on the Sabbath and said to
him: *if you know what you do, then you are blessed*; but if you
know not what you do, then you are cursed and a violator of
the law."

Luke, 6,4. ancient ms.

1 [27]

The existing world of forces leads *back* to a most simple state
of these forces: and in the same way *forward* to a most simple
state, — could and must *both* these states not be *identical*? No
infinite number of states can be derived from one system of
specific forces, that is, from one *measurably stable* force. Only
with the false assumption of an infinite space into which force
dissipates, as it were, is the final state an *unproductive, dead*
state. The simplest state is at once – and +

1 [28]

If we adopt the strictest standpoint of morality, e.g., sincerity, then any interaction with things, all of the articles of faith within our usual sphere of action, are already immoral (e.g., that there are bodies.

Likewise, suppose that human = human in place of the atomism of individuals.

In this way everything becomes *dishonesty*. And assuming we acknowledge that life is dishonesty, thus immorality — *in this way life can be denied.*

In the same way, unconditional justice brings the insight that life is essentially unfair.

Consequence of the most extreme morality of knowledge: demand for annihilation.

But now the critique of morals and morality makes its redemptive arrival: *it does away with itself.*

Therefore: life is not to be denied, for morality does not stand above it, morality is dead. The excess of morality has shown that its antithesis, evil, is *necessary and useful*, and is a source of what is good.

Having done that, should we *give up* what is good? No, *absolutely not*! For our honesty *no longer needs to be so strict.* Good people certainly are *not*.

1 [29][29]

Emotional needs should not be confused with the need *for* emotions: that a few extremely cold people possess.

1 [30]

Dogs respond to benevolence with submission. Cats enjoy themselves in its presence and have a lascivious feeling of power: they give nothing back.

1 [31][30]

In explanation of the so-called "spiritistic phenomena." A portion of the intellectual functions of the medium[31] occurs in him unconsciously: his condition is thereby hypnotic (separation of a waking and sleeping intellect) The nervous energy is concentrated in this unconscious portion. — An electric current must then pass among the people holding hands in the direction of the medium, allowing each person's *thoughts* to pass over into the medium. A current of thoughts like this is no more marvelous than the message carried from the brain to the foot within a person when he stumbles. The questions are answered through the intellectual capacity of the participants: whereby memory often contributes and offers something that *usually* seems to have been forgotten. Result of nervous emotion. — There is no forgetting. — Even unconscious deception is possible: I mean, a deceptive medium operates with any number of deceptive manipulations, without knowing it: his kind of morality finds instinctive expression in these actions. — Ultimately, this is *always* the case, with all of our actions. The most essential things occur unconsciously in us, and ninety times out of hundred and even more often the con artist is more unaware of *himself* as a con artist than aware.

Electrical phenomena, *cold* chills, sparks are all possible in such cases. Feelings of being touched may be the products of trickery, hallucinations of the senses: whereby it is possible that *several* people share the same hallucina(tion). (Such as with the ancient orgiastic cults)

The belief in being reunited with the dead is the presupposition of spiritism. It is a kind of freethinking. Truly *pious people* do not need this belief. (Buckle[32] on immortality)

1 [32]
Advocatus diaboli[33]
New representations of God and devil. Unconditional knowledge is a form of madness from the era of virtue; with it, life would perish. We must *sanctify* lies, delusions and faith, injustice. We must liberate ourselves from morality, *to be able to live morally.* My free **choice,**[34] **the ideal I myself created**

demands this or that virtue from me, i.e., *downfall as a result of virtue.* This is *heroism.*

1 [33]

The principle of nations will free the Mohammedans the Indians from their bonds.

1 [34]

So what makes, e.g., prostitution, so destructive, sneaky, unsure of itself? Not "the evil in itself" within it, but rather the bad opinion in which it is held. This against statisticians. In the case of **good people** what should be *taken into account* is that the *more direct* and *more subtle aftereffect* of their judgments is what *constitutes* the inner and outer misery of humanity. And then they use this misery as *evidence* that they are right, as evidence of nature and force! Bad conscience poisons good health.

Marriage as the sanctioned form of satisfying lust.
War as the sanctioned form of murdering your neighbor.
School as the sanctioned form of training.
Justice as the sanctioned form of revenge.
Religion as the sanctioned form of the drive for knowledge.

Good people as Pharisees, evil people living with bad consciences and oppression. So what is *debauchery* of any kind other than the consequence of the *dissatisfaction* of so many with *sanctioned forms?* What is most *criminality* other than the inability or unwillingness to participate in the *hypocrisy* of "good people"? Lack of training of the *strong* drives? There are only opponents and despisers of such thinking.

1 [35]

On the happiness of the *Pharisees*.

Their self-overcoming. Producing "**ethical**" actions in all circumstances and training themselves to keep only such motives in their awareness and to falsely label their *real* motives (namely as ethical).

This is the ancient practice within the *herd*: the actual *dishonesty*, to *see* in themselves only the *sanctioned* judgments and feelings. *This* practice, common to all good people, gives rise to the *uniformity* of common actions: it gives them their monstrous *power* to *acknowledge* so *few* motives in themselves and their neighbors, and only *good ones*.

The Pharisee is the prototype of the preserving human, always needed.

Antithesis:

the *strong evil ones*

and the *weak evil ones*, who *feel* this way.

From them there occasionally emerges the *one-who-is-good-to-himself*, the devil who has become God.

1 [36]

To minimize suffering and to remove oneself from suffering (i.e., from life) — this is supposed to be moral?

To create suffering — for oneself **and for others** — to make them fit for the highest form of life, that of the *victor* — would be my goal.

1 [37]³⁵

It is *nauseating* to see great humans *venerated* by Pharisees. *Against* this sentimentality.

1 [38]

Even *reversal and decline*, in the individual and in humanity, must engender their *ideals*: and the belief in *progress* will always endure. The *"ape"* ideal could at some time stand before humanity — as a goal.

1 [39]

My virtuosity: to endure what is unpleasant to me, to do justice to it, yes even to oppose it playfully — humans and knowledge. In this I am the most practiced.

1 [40]³⁶

I have a tendency to allow myself to be robbed, exploited. But as soon as I realized that everything was meant to *deceive* me, I moved into *egoism*.

1 [41]

Having emerged from the old, perfected morality I felt compelled toward selfishness.

1 [42]

Why do I love **free-spiritedness**? As the final consequence of morality up to now. Treat everything *justly*, rise above compulsion and repulsion, become a part of the order of things, be *above oneself, overcoming and courage* not only in regard to one's personal enemies, embarrassments, but also in regard to the evil in things, to *honesty* even as an opponent of idealism and piety, yes even of passion, even in regard to honesty itself; *loving attitude* toward anything and everything and the good will to discover its *value*, its justification, its necessity. *To refuse to act* (quietism) out of the inability to say: "it should be otherwise" — to rest in God, as it were, in a God who is *becoming*.

I recognized *selfishness* as a **means** to *this* free-spiritedness, as necessary in order not to be devoured by things: as restraint and refuge. That completion of morality is only possible in an *I*: insofar as it acts in a lively, constructive, demanding, creative manner, and in every moment resists being absorbed in things, it reserves its power for itself in order to force ever more things to be taken up and absorbed into itself. In relation to the self and to selfishness, free-spiritedness is therefore a becoming, a struggle between two opposites, with nothing resolved, nothing perfected, no state:³⁷ it is *the insight of morality,*

*which can preserve itself in its existence and in its development
only by means of its opposite.*

1 [43]

1. Dissatisfaction with ourselves. Antidote for remorse.
   The transformation of the temperaments (e.g., through
   inorganic entities). The *good* will toward this dissatisfaction. To let *the good will's* thirst grow and reach its
   peak in order to discover *its* wellspring.[38]
2. To reshape death[39] as the means to victory and
   triumph.
3. Sexual love, as the means to the ideal (longing to be
   submerged in its opposite.) Love for the suffering
   godhead.
4. Illness, and response to it, freedom until death.
5. Reproduction as the most holy of circumstances.
   Pregnancy, the creation of the woman and the man,
   who want to enjoy their *oneness* in the child and to
   create *a monument to this oneness.*[40]
6. Compassion as danger. To create conditions, so that all
   could help themselves and so that it is up to them
   whether they should be helped.
7. The education into *evil*, into *one's own* "devil."
8. The inner *war*, as "development."
9. "Preservation of the species" and the thought of eternal
   recurrence.
10. To what degree every created god in turn creates a
    devil for himself. And this devil is *not* the god from
    whom he emerged. (This devil is the *neighboring* ideal,
    with which this god must *struggle*)

1 [44]

The state has forced the i⟨ndividual⟩ to incorporate its
morality.

Choice[41] perhaps once the most exalted name for morality

1 [45]⁴²

Style

The first thing needed is *life*: style should *live*.

Your style should fit *you* every time in regard to one person in particular, to whom you wish to communicate yourself.

We must first know precisely: "I would say and state this in such a way" — before we may begin writing. Writing should only be a kind of imitation.

**

Because writers *lack* many tools enjoyed by speakers, they must in general have as their model a *very expressive* kind of speech: the written reproduction of it will necessarily come across much less colorfully (and much more naturally to you).

Wealth in life reveals itself through wealth of gesture. We must *learn* to feel everything, length brevity of sentences, punctuation, choice of words, pauses, the order of arguments — as gestures.

*

Careful with periods! Only those people with real stamina, also in speaking, have the right to use periods. For most people the period is an affectation.

Style should demonstrate that we *believe* in our thoughts, that we not only think them, but also feel them.

**

The more abstract the truth we want to teach, the more we have to seduce the senses into embracing it.

The tact of good prose writers consists in approaching the boundaries of poesy as closely as possible without ever crossing the line. It is impossible to have this tact without the finest feeling for and abilities in poetry itself.

*

It is not good form, nor is it smart, to anticipate the more obvious objections of our readers. It is very good form and smart, to leave the expression of our essential wisdom to the readers themselves.

1 [46]

G. Sand, Letter of 1868 to Maxime Du Camp.

"*Faites un mariage d'amitié pour avoir des enfants. L'amour ne procrée guère. Quand vous verrez devant vous un être, que vous aimerez plus que vous-mêmes, vous serez heureux. Mais ce n'est pas la femme que l'on peut aimer plus que soi-même, c'est l'enfant, c'est l'être innocent, c'est le type divin, qui disparaît plus ou moins en grandissant, mais qui, durant quelques années, nous ramène à la possession d'un idéal sur la terre.*"[43]

1 [47][44]

Behind all the feelings a man has for a woman there still lies *contempt* for the female sex.

1 [48]

Against moral outrage.

The same cruelty as in religious wars. "Contempt for fellow humans" as the object of Christ's indignation (he came to treat the Pharisees unjustly.)

(Evil must be *preserved*!)

1 [49][45]

Anyone who has the ideal of a person perceives the real person as its *caricature*.

1 [50]

1. *Female* assessment of the *affects*.
   — of the individual virtues and vices of men and women.
   women and work

women and state
women and fame.

2. Female judgment and women's faith in the accuracy of their judgment.

3. The hidden reality and — — —

4. To proclaim as true the unreality to which women feel themselves obligated.

5. Seducing others into having a high opinion of us, and then bowing before this opinion as an authority.[46]

6. Tempo of female affects.

7. *Pregnancy* as the quintessential condition, which has gradually shaped the essence of women. Relation of all modes of female thought and action to this.

8. Child raising partly educationally regressive — partly all too *deinfantilizing*. Female *rationalism*.

9. The difference between female and male imperiousness.[47]

10. The female feeling of perfection – in obedience.

11. What is felt to be unwomanly. History.

12. Denying destroying hating taking revenge: why women are more *barbaric* in these things than men.[48]

13. Sensuality different in men and women.[49]

1 [51]

On the Reemergence[50] *of the World.*

A position emerges from two negations, if the negations are forces. (Darkness emerges from light against light, cold from warmth against warmth etc.)

1 [52][51]

Throw your words out ahead of your deeds: obligate yourself through shame at the broken word.

1 [53]

Only people who are unrelenting may be silent concerning themselves.

1 [54]

We are fairer to others than to ourselves.

1 [55]⁵²

In regard to all truth, things work the same way for us as they do in regard to our inner organs.

1 [56]

Originally a lie was moral. The opinions of the herd were *simulated*.

1 [57]⁵³

In order to have a good conversation, some seek a midwife for their thoughts, while others seek someone they can help.

1 [58]⁵⁴

In every *three-way* conversation one voice is superfluous and thereby keeps the conversation from getting *deep*.

1 [59]⁵⁵

Those who do not make us productive will surely leave us indifferent. Those *we* make productive still do not give us a reason for loving them.

1 [60]⁵⁶

How good people imagin⟨e⟩ *great* humans. Against their sentimentality.

1 [61]

To formulate ideals, i.e., to *re-create* our devil as *our* god. And *to do that*, we must have created our devil in the first place.

1 [62]⁵⁷

Everything good came out of something evil.

1 [63]⁵⁸

People who strive for greatness find quantitative reasons for their perfection and satisfaction. *People of quality strive for something puny.*

1 [64]⁵⁹

The state of becoming absolutely cold to all previously held values precedes the state of *warming up* to them.

1 [65]⁶⁰

I am the *advocatus diaboli*⁶¹ and God's accuser.

1 [66]⁶²

The human being is too imperfect a thing. Love for a human being would *destroy* me.

1 [67]

Cruelty in enjoying compassion. Compassion is strongest, the deeper we come to know and love the other. Consequently those lovers who are cruel to the ones they love will get the most *enjoyment* from cruelty. Assuming we love *ourselves* the most, then the highest enjoyment found in compassion would be cruelty *to ourselves*. **Heroic** = this is striving for an absolute downfall into one's opposite, the reshaping of the devil into God:⁶³ this is *that degree of cruelty.*

1 [68]

The *conditions of existence* of a being, as soon as they represent themselves as an "*ought*," are its *morality.*

1 [69]⁶⁴

How the devil becomes God.

1 [70][65]

On the Philosophy of Recurrence

on heroic greatness as the only state of those who are preparing the way.

(Striving for absolute downfall as means of enduring ourselves.)

Wanting to become a function: feminine ideal of love. The masculine ideal is assimilation and overwhelming domination or compassion (veneration of the suffering God).

absolute indifference to the opinions of others (because we know them through and through[66]): but compassionate *in* our opinion of ourselves.

We must not want *a single* state, but must rather *want to become repeating* beings[67] = *similar* to existence.

I deliberately chose to live out my days in complete **opposition** to the life of *someone* with a **religious nature**. I know the *devil* and **his** *plans for God*.[68]

"Good" and "evil" as sensations of pleasure and displeasure. Indispensable. But for each *his* evil.

Those who do *not* find the way to their ideal live more frivolously and more brazenly than those who have no ideal at all.[69]

To hurt those we love — is the real devilry. In regard to ourselves it is the state of the heroic human being — the highest abuse of power. To strive for the opposite is part of this.

1 [71]

"Idealist" as the opposite of the *honest* and fearless one who knows. The judgments of idealists disgust me, they are completely useless.

1 [72]⁷⁰

Joy in others being hurt is something other than cruelty, the latter is *delight* in compassion, and reaches its height whenever compassion is at its highest (at the point that we love the one we are tormenting).

If another were to hurt the ones we love, then we would become insane with rage, compassion in that case would be wholly *painful*. But we love them: and *we* hurt them. In that way compassion acquires a monstrous allure: it is the *contradiction* of two strongly opposed drives, which functions here as the *highest allure*.

Juxtaposed, self-mutilation and sensuality are the same. Or the clearest consciousness and torpor and lethargy after opium.

1 [73]

General question: how do contradictory feelings function, in other words, a duality? How do they relate as duality? (*Weakening?*)

The *highest love for the I*, when it expresses itself as heroism, is accompanied by lust for self-destruction, that is, cruelty, self-violation.⁷¹

Those who loved humanity *have hurt it the most.*⁷²

The *beloved's* unconditional surrender and *delight in suffering*, the desire to be mistreated. Surrender becomes *defiance against one's self.*

On the other hand, the man who is loved, who torments what loves him, enjoys his feeling of power, and even more so, the more he tyrannizes himself in the process: it is a *doubled* exercise of power. Here will for power⁷³ becomes defiance against one's self.⁷⁴

1 [74]

The freethinker as the most religious person that now exists.

1 [75][75]

God killed God.

1 [76][76]

Morals died from morality.

1 [77][77]

A person of faith[78] is the opposite of a religious person.

1 [78][79]

Precondition of procreation should be the will *to want* to have an image and a legacy of the beloved person: and a monument to oneness with that person, indeed a *consummation of the drive for oneness*, through a new being. — A *matter* of passion and *not* of sympathy.

1 [79][80]

The preeminent and honest form of sexual relations, that of passion, is now accompanied by *evil* conscience. And the basest and the most dishonest by *good* conscience.

1 [80]

The confusion of the means used to preserve marriage: the woman believes that she is *predestined* only for *this one marriage*. In truth everything is mere chance, and a hundred other men would be just as good for her. She wants to obey: she works for the man and thinks and says: "what haven't I done for *you*!" — but this was not done for "you," but rather for someone or other, who came within range of her drives. — The spouses *are separated* by career and daily work, which keeps things bearable. — Because men and women[81] have not experienced *earlier what friendship* really is, they are not disappointed by the interaction: they know *neither* love *nor* friendship. Marriage is designed for *atrophied* half-humans.

1 [81]

   Vain — insulted
   cautious — take heed
   immoral — despise.

1 [82]

   He kills when he cannot live otherwise.

   He robs when he needs an object or a person (marriage).

   He lies when he wants to remain concealed for the sake of his goal.

1 [83][82]

Noon and Eternity
Outline of a *heroic philosophy.*

1 [84][83]

   Humans who strive for greatness are usually evil humans: it is the only way they can live with themselves.

1 [85][84]

   How long (how many centuries) it takes before greatness becomes *visible* to humanity as greatness and *shines* — is my measure of greatness. It has probably been the case up until now that **all** the greatest ones are exactly the ones who have remained concealed.

1 [86][85]

   Anyone who no longer finds greatness in God no longer finds greatness *anywhere* and must deny its existence or — *create it* — help to create it.

1 [87][86]

   The enormous expectations that women[87] bring to sexual love blind their eye to all broader perspectives.

1 [88][88]

Heroism — this is the mentality of human beings who believe that they count for nothing in comparison to their goals. Heroism is the *good will* toward absolute self-destruction.[89]

The opposite of the heroic ideal is the ideal of harmonic total development: a beautiful opposite and one very much worth wishing for! But an ideal only for good human beings!

1 [89]

All h⟨uman⟩ interaction revolves *solely* around pregnancy.

1 [90][90]

When five people speak together, a sixth always has to die.

1 [91][91]

All girls believe that a man makes friends with a woman only because he couldn't get any further with her.

1 [92][92]

Anyone who does not see what is superior in p⟨eople⟩ will focus too much on what is base and with all too sharp an eye.

1 [93][93]

When talents fade, a p⟨erson's⟩ moral qualities become more visible.

1 [94]

Men are considered cruel, but women are cruel. Women are considered kind-hearted, but men are kind-hearted.

1 [95]

Ah, I'm so fed up with *tragic faces and phrases*!

1 [96]

Schilling, *Span⟨ish⟩ Grammar*, Leipzig, *Glockner*.[94]

1 [97]⁹⁵

> Should a bond not tear,
> you must try biting into it.⁹⁶

1 [98]

   Occasionally I feel enormous disdain for good people —
their weakness, their wanting to experience nothing, their
wanting to see nothing, their capricious blindness, their banal
wallowing in what is routine and comfortable, their pleasure
in their own "good qualities" etc.

1 [99]⁹⁷

> Hitzig Untersuchungen über das Gehirn Berlin 1874.⁹⁸
> Animal Depravity (Quarterly Journal of Science⁹⁹ 1875
> 415–430.
> Lilienfeld Gedanken über die Socialwissenshaft.¹⁰⁰

1 [100]

> *Cosa bella e mortal,*
> *passa e non dura!!!*¹⁰¹

1 [101]¹⁰²

                      *Columbus novus.*¹⁰³

> That's the way I want to go, and I trust
> Myself from now on and my grip!
> Open is the sea: into the blue
> Sails my Genoese ship.
>
>   **
>
> Everything becomes new and newer to me
> Behind me lies Genoa.
> Courage! You yourself stand at the helm,
> Dearest Victoria!^{104,105}

                                              (Summer 1882)

1 [102][106]

The tree speaks.

Too alone I grew and too high:
I wait: but what am I waiting for, anyway?

**

Too near to me is the throne of clouds:
I wait for the first lightning bolt.[107]

1 [103]

To the Ideal.

Whom have I loved as I love you, beloved shadow!
I pulled you to me, into me — and ever since
I have almost become a shadow, you a body.
It's only that my eye is unteachable,
Accustomed to seeing things outside itself:
For it, you will always be the eternal "Outside-of-myself."
Alas, this eye is making me feel beside myself![108,109]

1 [104][110]

"Joyful Science."
(Sanctus Januarius)[111]

This is no book: what use are books!
These shrouds and coffins!
The past is the prey of books:
Yet in them lives an eternal *today*.[112]

1 [105]

In the Mountains.
(1876.)

No way back? And no way forward?
Not even a path for mountain goats?

**

So I wait here and *hold on*[113] tightly,
To whatever hand and eye will let me hold![114]

**

Earth five feet wide, dawn,
And *below* me – world, humans and — death![115]

1 [106]

To Friendship.

Hail to you, friendship!
My highest hope's
First dawn!
Alas, trail and night often
Seemed endless to me,
All life
Aimless and despised!
I want to live twice,
Now I gaze into your eyes'
Morning splendor and triumph,
You most beloved goddess![116,117]

1 [107]

The Phrase.[118]

I'm a friend of the lively phrase:
That jumps out at us with such good faith,
That greets us with an artful curtsy,
Endearing even in its clumsiness,
Has blood within, can sniff heartily,
Creeps even into deaf ears,
And circles and flutters even now,
And what it does — the phrase delights.
Yet the phrase remains a delicate creature,
Quickly ill but just as quickly healed.
If you wish to let it live its fleeting life,
Then your grip must be refined and light,
Don't crudely grab and crush it,
It often dies under an evil eye —
And then lies there, so shapeless,
So soulless, so poor and cold,
Its tiny corpse terribly transformed,

Mutilated by death and dying.
A dead phrase — an ugly thing,
A bone-on-boney cling, cling, cling.
Shame on every ugly business,
Through which phrases and words die![119,120]

[Tautenburg Notes for Lou von Salomé][121]

1 [108][122]

I.

Humans who strive for greatness are usually evil humans; it is the only way they can live with themselves.

2.

Anyone who no longer finds greatness in God, no longer finds greatness *anywhere* and must either deny its existence or — create it (help create it)

⟨3.⟩

[+++]

4.

The enormous expectations that women[123] bring to sexual love blind their eye to all long-range perspectives.

5.

Heroism — this is the mentality of human beings who believe that they count for nothing in comparison to their goals. Heroism is the good will toward absolute self-destruction.

6.

The opposite of the heroic ideal is the ideal of harmonic total development — a beautiful opposite and one very much worth wishing for! But an ideal only for basically good human beings (e.g., Goethe)

Love is completely different for *men* than for women.[124] For most men, love is a kind of *avarice*; for the rest, love is the veneration of a suffering and shrouded deity.[125]

If friend Rée ever read this, he would think I'm crazy.

How is it going? — There has never been a more beautiful day in Tautenburg than today. The air clear, mild, bracing: just as we all should be.

Cordially
F.N.

1 [109][126]

On a Theory of Style

1.

The first thing needed is life: style should *live*.

2.

Your style should fit *you* in regard to one person in particular, to whom you wish to communicate yourself. (Law of *double relation*.)

3.

We must first know precisely: "I would say and *state* this in such a way" — before we may begin writing. Writing must be a kind of imitation.

4.

Because the writers *lack* many *tools* enjoyed by speakers, they must in general have as their model a *very expressive* kind of speech: the written reproduction of it will necessarily come across much less colorfully.

5.

Wealth in life reveals itself through *wealth of gesture*. We must *learn* to feel everything, length and brevity of sentences,

punctuation, choice of words, pauses, the order of arguments
— as gestures.

6.

Careful with periods! Only those people with real stamina,
also in speaking, have the right to use periods. For most people the period is an affectation.

7.

Style should demonstrate that we *believe* in our thoughts,
that we not only think them, but also *feel* them.

8.

The more abstract the truth we want to teach, the more we
must first seduce our *senses* into embracing it.

9.

The tact of good prose writers in selecting their methods
consists in approaching the boundaries of poetic style *as closely
as possible* without *ever* crossing the line.

10.

It is not good form, nor is it smart to anticipate the more
obvious objections of our readers. It is very good form and
very smart to leave the *expression* of our essential wisdom to the
readers *themselves*.

F.N.
A good morning to you,
my dear Lou!

[110]¹²⁷

"Yes, a weaker sex!" — this is the way men talk about women,¹²⁸ this is also the way women¹²⁹ talk about themselves: but who believes that they are thinking the same thing when they use the same words? But let the men think whatever they like for now; what does a woman usually mean when she speaks of the weakness of her sex? —

To feel weakness — this means not only to feel a lack of power, but rather: to feel *a need for power*.¹³⁰ She looks for power, she looks outside of herself for it, she wants support, she is a cornucopia of everything that she could possibly lean on, she coils herself demandingly around things that are not capable of giving support and attempts to hold on to them, yes she likes to delude herself about the power of everything different from or foreign to her — she believes *just as strongly* in the power outside herself as she does in the weakness within herself. The feeling of weakness, felt at its most extreme, finds strength everywhere and projects power into everything outside of itself with which it comes into contact: and whenever the eye should contradict this, then the eye is — *shut*!

Such in fact is the state in which the weaker sex finds itself, and not just in relation to the men of its acquaintance, but also in regard to religion and custom: the weak woman believes in her inability to stand without support and turns everything that surrounds her physically and spiritually into *props* — she does not want to see *what* all this really *is*, she does not want to test whether the balustrade along which she crosses the river will really *hold up*, she believes in the balustrade, because she believes in her own weakness and fear. Whatever a woman in her situation leans on is in all cases not the power *she knows*, but rather the power she expects, wishes for and projects: and the greater her feeling of weakness, the more power she will want *to feel* in whatever "gives her support." The weakest woman will make a god out of every man: and similarly something holy, inviolable, final, worshipful out of every precept of custom and religion. It is obvious that the weaker sex is more important for the emergence of religions than the stronger. And given how women are, if they were left to their own devices, they would consistently create out of their weakness not only "men" but also "gods" — and both, one would presume, would resemble one another —: *as monsters of power*!

1 [111]^{131}

On Women.

1. Female *judgment* and women's *faith* in (superstition about) the accuracy of their judgment.
2. Fem⟨ale⟩ assessment of the affects,
      of the individual virtues and vices,
3. Fem⟨ale⟩ judgment concerning
      men and women,
      state and nature,
      work, leisure, etc.
4. What part of reality women *conceal* from themselves.
5. In what way they feel obligated to claim as *real*
      something they nevertheless know to be unreal.
6. Tempo of female affects
7. Child raising partly educationally regressive and
      retarding, partly all too *de*infantilizing. (fem⟨ale⟩
      rationalism)
   To what extent women treat men like children.
8. To what extent women *seduce* others into holding them
      in high regard and
   nevertheless bow before this regard (as before an
      authority)
9. The history of what is perceived by women to be
      unwomanly, — according to peoples and prevailing
      customs.
10. The fem⟨ale⟩ faith in some *supreme* fem⟨ale⟩ virtue,
      which *must* exist, so that a superior nature of
      women may be achieved — and the act⟨ual⟩ change
      of these "supreme virtues."

11. Feeling of perfection and completion of her being e.g., while serving, obeying

12. Pregnancy as the quintessential condition, which has gradually, in the course of time, fixed the essence of women. Relation of all modes of female thought and action to this.

13. Denying, destroying, being alone, fighting, despising, taking revenge: why women are more *barbaric* in all of these things than men etc. etc. etc.

2 [1][1]

Metteyya

2 [2]

Carus, vergl⟨eichende⟩ Psychologie[2]

2 [3][3]

Vogt[4] 19185
Lindau[5] 18772
Wilbrandt[6] 18761

2 [4]

The morality of the chosen or the free morality.
We as the preservers of life.
Inevitably contempt and hatred for life are emerging. Buddhism. The European drive to achieve will cause mass-suicide. In that regard: *my* theory of recurrence as the most terrible burden.

If we do not survive, then everything is finished. *Our survival by means of an organization.*
The friends of life.
Nihilism as a small prelude.
Impossibility of philosophy.
Just as Buddhism makes us *unproductive and good*, so under its influence Europe also grows: **tired!**

Good people, this is the weariness.
Reconciliation, this is the weariness.
Morality, this is the weariness.
Proper customs (e.g., marriage) this is the weariness.
Against idealists.

2 [5]

That which is to come.

True striving into *nothingness*.
Wars over the principle of better-not-to-be-than-to-be.
(A)
First consequence of morality: *life is to be denied*.
Last consequence of morality = morality itself is to be denied.
(B)
Therefore: the first consequence falls away
    liberation of selfishness,
    liberation of evil,
    liberation of the individual.
The new good people ("I will this") and the old good people ("I should").[7]

Liberation of art as rejection of unconditional knowledge. Praise of the lie.

Reclaiming religion.

(C)

Through all this liberation the *allure* of life continues to grow. Life's innermost denial, moral denial, is *set aside*. — And with this the downfall begins. The necessity of barbarism, to which, e.g., religion also belongs. Humankind must live in *cycles*, the *only* lasting form. Not the longest lasting culture, but as brief and high as possible. — **We** at **noon**: *epoch*.

(D)

What determines the *highest of heights* in the history of culture? The moment when the allure is the greatest. Measured by the fact that the mightiest thought is borne, yes even loved.

2 [6]

That which is to come.
A Prophecy.

A. Victory of morality over itself.
B. Liberation.
C. Middle and beginning of the downfall.
D. Characteristic features of noon.
E. Freely-chosen death.

2 [7]

Serpent, spoke Zarathustra, you are the most clever animal under the sun — you will know what strengthens a heart — my clever heart — I do not know. And you, eagle, you are the proudest animal under the sun, take my heart and carry it wherever it demands — my proud heart — I do not know.

2 [8][8]

P⟨eople⟩ who do not need to lie a lot make much of the fact that they only lie a little.

2 [9][9]

And yet proclaim to me, you animals: Is the sun already at its noon height? Is the serpent called eternity already coiling itself? Zarathustra goes blind.[10]

For me everything always turns to *death*. Who wants to be my destiny? I love every destiny. Zarathustra grows blissful!

Zarathustra knows nothing more, Zarathustra deciphers nothing more.

2 [10]

Always give back: never accept anything as a gift, other than as a *commendation* and as a sign that we *recognize* those who love others by such signs and compensate through **our** *love*.[11]

2 [11]

Taking away morality from humans because they are making *such poor use* of it: and *forcing* brutal *feelings* into them — "thou shalt" — *like soldiers* —

2 [12]

Commit yourself to **something** e.g., "I want to be just." Only one sin: cowardice.

2 [13]¹²

Lack of love likes to disguise itself as the absence of someone worth loving.

2 [14]¹³

A man uses love to search for an unconditional slave, a woman for unconditional slavery — love is the longing for a vanished culture and society.

2 [15]

When faced with independent people who hate being bell-wethers, the moral person harbors a suspicion that they could be wide-rang⟨ing⟩ predators.

2 [16]¹⁴

Iron hates the magnet when the m⟨agnet⟩ can't draw it completely toward itself.

2 [17]¹⁵

What we hate the most is not what keeps us from being loved, but what keeps us from loving fully.

2 [18]¹⁶

Those who conceal nothing about themselves provoke outrage.

2 [19][17]

"Unfortunate one, your God has burst and shattered, and serpents dwell within him. And now for his sake you love even these serpents."

2 [20][18]

We do not want to be spared by our enemies — any more than we want to be spared by those we love deeply.

2 [21][19]

Watch out for that one: he speaks only so that he may listen afterwards: — and you only listen because it will not do to keep speaking forever — i.e., you listen badly and that one listens well.

2 [22][20]

That bitch sensuality, who only wants to carve herself a bite of flesh, knows all too well how to beg for a bite of spirit.

2 [23][21]

It never gives, it does not even pay back — it only replies.

2 [24]

There are natures that give, there are those that give back.

2 [25][22]

It is impossible to give gifts to truly just people — they give everything back.

2 [26][23]

In the communication of knowledge there is always some betrayal.

2 [27][24]

There is shamelessness in all writing.

2 [28][25]
Anyone who loves God chastises him.

2 [29][26]
Superficial people always have to lie because they have no substance.

2[30][27]
To educate: i.e., educating someone to lie in all circumstances.

2[31][28]
Those who are truthful end up realizing that they always lie.

2[32][29]
Those who lie contradict not only what they know, but also what they don't know.

2[33][30]
It is nobler to admit wrong than to be in the right.

2[34][31]
A lie is the philanthropy of the one who knows.

2[35][32]
Suicide

2[36][33]
Justice only *possible* with respect to things.

2[37]
Our influence as a *nec*essary[34] *deception*.

2[38][35]
Injustice shared is justice halved.[36]

2[39][37]

    p. 200 Hum⟨an⟩, All T⟨oo Human⟩

    p 77 Dawn

    167,8 J⟨oyful⟩ Science

2[40]

    Terrible consequence, when human beings are loved *only for the sake of God*.

2[41][38]

    "But how could you do such a thing! said a friend to a very clever p⟨erson⟩ — it was stupid." It hasn't been easy for me either, replied the latter.

2[42][39]

    Those who want to ascend to ultimate knowledge[40] must also leave truthfulness behind. The wall of knowledge[41] definitely cannot be scaled from the starting point of morality.

2[43][42]

    "Life for the sake of knowledge," wanting-*to-stand* on one's head is perhaps somewhat insane — but when it is a sign of joy, this wanting may continue, it doesn't look so bad an ele⟨phant[43] that is trying to stand on its head.⟩

2[44][44]

    The price of a good reputation is usually too high: namely ourselves.

2[45][45]

    The danger for the wise is that they fall in love with the irrational.

2[46][46]

    Love for a woman! If it is not compassion for a suffering god, then it is an instinct for the beast concealed in women.

2[47]⁴⁷

The touchstone for a person's nature is not the way it loves, but rather how all its vulgarity or superiority comes to light when it knows that it is loved.

2[48]

I am more surprised by blame than by praise; I have more contempt for praise than for blame.

2[49]⁴⁸

Mor⟨al⟩ outrage is the most insidious kind of revenge.

2[50]⁴⁹

I like compassion only in the faces of the victorious. When these miserable people, whose appearance is painful, even so make compassionate faces, — — —

Compassion may be something for gods, but it suits heroes better to be cheerful about the misery that surrounds them.

3 [1]

On the High Seas.
A Book of Sentences
by
Friedrich Nietzsche.

"That's the way I want to go! And I trust
"Myself from now on and my grip.
"Open is the sea, into the blue
"Sails my Genoese ship.
"Everything becomes new and newer to me,
"Space and time shine far into the distance —
"Hail to you, ship! Hail to your helm!
"Around you roars eternity!" —[1,2]

Silent Speeches
A Book of Sentences.

"Beyond Good and Evil."
Book of Sentences.[3]

"il sait goûter sa vie
en paresseux sensé qui pond sur ses plaisirs."[4]
(Duc de Nevers.)

1. A: What is the meaning of justice? B: My justice is love with open eyes. A: But think of what you are saying: this justice would acquit everyone except those who judge! This love bears not only all punishment but also all guilt! B: This is the way it should be![5]

2. Becoming youthful late keeps us young longer. We do not have to look for youth among the young.[6]

3. When talents fade, a person's moral qualities become more visible; and it is not always stars that become more visible with the approaching night.[7]

4. Anyone who cannot see superior qualities[8] in people will for that reason alone look with eagle-eyes for their base qualities.[9,10]

5. There is also an intrusiveness in those who know: this intrusiveness is condemned to see only the foreground of all things.[11]

6. When five people speak together, a sixth always has to die.[12]

7. God choked to death on theology; and morals on morality.[13]

8. Those who have loved humanity the most have always hurt humanity the most: they have asked the impossible of it, as all lovers do.[14]

9. So spoke a saint: "I love God — for a human being is too imperfect a thing. Love for a human being would destroy me."[15]

10. The time has come when the devil must be God's advocate: at least if he himself wants to continue to exist.[16]

11. "You have become cold to everything that previously had value, colder than ice — but those who touch you now claim that you are red hot: and pull their fingers quickly away in the belief that you have burned them. And soon there will be people who seek you out in order to *warm* themselves on you."[17]

12. It is treasonous when someone strives for greatness. People of the finest quality strive for something puny.[18]

13. Those who do not make us fertile will surely leave us indifferent. Yet making others fertile does not come close to giving us a reason for loving them.[19]

14. The third person is always the cork that keeps the conversation of two from sinking into the depths: which in certain circumstances is an advantage.[20]

15. Throw your words out ahead of your deeds: obligate yourself through your shame for the broken word.[21]

16. It is the way of women to *seduce* their neighbors[22] into having a high opinion of them and then to *believe* in this opinion as if it were an authority.[23]

17. In denying, destroying, hating, taking revenge women are more barbaric than men.[24]

18. The sacrifices we offer only prove how much less we come to value everything else when we *love* something.[25]

19. Whatever we love to do the most, we would like this to be regarded as the thing we find most difficult to do.[26]

20. Behind all their female ambition women still have contempt for "women *as such*."[27]

21. What we recognize in other people, is also what we kindle in them; and anyone who recognizes only the base qualities in people also exerts an attraction on these qualities and brings them to release. The affects of those closest to you that are directed against you are the critique of your knowledge, based on superiority[28] and lowliness.[29]

22. Giving our affects names is already a step beyond the affects. The deepest love, e.g., does not know what to call itself and probably is asking itself, "am I not hatred?"[30]

23. Masculine and feminine affects differ in their tempo: for this reason men and women will never stop misunderstanding each other.[31]

In getting to know other people better we do not move outside ourselves, but rather ever further into ourselves.

24. We do the same thing awake as we do in our dreams: always, we first invent and poetically imagine the people with whom we associate — and immediately forget that they are invented and poetically imagined.[32,33]

25. We are also punished for our virtues.[34]

26. Emotional needs should not be confused with the need *for* emotions that several extremely cold people possess.[35]

27. Those who do not need to lie make much of the fact that they do not lie.[36]

28. Women understand children better, but men are more childlike than women.[37]

29. People of faith[38] find their natural adversaries not in free-thinkers, but rather in religious people.

30. Those who create are the most hated: for they are the most thorough annihilators.[39]

31. Phariseeism is not a kind of degeneracy in good people, but rather a condition of their being good.[40]

32. We love life, not because we are alive, but because we are used to life.[41]

33. From time to time even our virtues should be allowed to sleep.[42]

34. You believe in your "life after death"? Then you must learn to be dead during your life.[43]

35. Our flaws are our best teachers: but we are always ungrateful to our best teachers.

36. "Let's not speak of it!" —"My friend, *this* is something we shouldn't even be quiet *about*."[44]

37. What do people know of love who have not been forced to despise precisely what they have loved![45]

38. Seeing beyond ourselves is necessary in order to *see* well.[46]

39. "People are *not equal*!" — So speaks — justice.[47]

We do not believe in many things only because we do not believe in the conventional way they are explained.[48]

40. Those who are passionate about justice experience even their most painful affect as a kind of relief.

41. Ponderous, melancholic people become more lighthearted and rise to the surface through the very things that make others heavy-hearted, like hate and love.[49]

42. Soap bubbles and butterflies and their human equivalents seem to me to know best what happiness is: to see these airy foolish agile dainty little souls fluttering about — this moves me to tears and poetry.[50]

43. "Did you see your devil?"— "Yes, ponderous serious profound thorough pathetic: he stood there just like the *genius gravitationis*[51] by which all beings and things — fall."[52]

44. Anyone who would have compassion for the entire human race would have to be seen by each individual as hardhearted and tyrannical.[53]

45. A thing that is brought to light[54] ceases to interest us. So take care that you don't become too enlightened about yourself![55]

46. We must know how to be a sponge if we want to be loved by a person who is filled to overflowing.[56]

Here lies the most frequent form of dishonesty among those who know: they deny the facts.

47. Anyone who has seen the ideal of a person perceives the real person as its *caricature*.[57]

48. Some seek a midwife for their thoughts, others someone they can help: this is how a good conversation arises. But watch out if two midwives run into each other! They don't carry forceps for nothing![58]

49. Those incapable of finding the way to *their* ideal live more frivolously and more brazenly than those who have no ideal at all.[59]

50. The devil has the best perspectives on God: that's why he stays so far away from him — he is, after all, a friend of *knowledge*.[60]

51. "Should a bond not tear,
      You must try biting into it."[61]

Marriage, the most dishonest and hypocritical form of sexual relations, may be right for those incapable of either love or friendship and for those who would like to deceive themselves and others about this deficiency: to this end, state and religion have declared marriage to be holy, and it also may be right for those who cannot be disillusioned by marriage because they have no experience in either love or friendship.[62]

52. The danger for the wise is that they are most easily seduced into falling in love with the irrational.[63]

53. Love for a woman! If it is not compassion for a suffering god, then it is the instinct that seeks the beast concealed in women.[64]

54. Moral outrage is the most insidious kind of revenge.[65]

55. To remain cheerful amid universal misery defines heroes: and not out of compassion, but out of abundance, they reward others and "sacrifice themselves," — as we say.[66]

56. Self-interest and passion are married to each other: this marriage is called selfishness: this unhappy marriage!

57. What? you do not want to be judged by your effect, but rather by your intentions? But your intentions are themselves derived from your effect.[67]

58. Anything questioned for a long time becomes questionable.[68]

59. Terrible experiences lead us to speculate whether those who experience them aren't also something terrible: maybe even without knowing it.[69]

60. Marriage is the most dishonest form of sexual relations; and for that very reason has good conscience on its side.[70]

61. We usually sacrifice too much for our good reputation: namely ourselves.[71]

Those wanting to become leaders must want to be regarded by their followers, for a while at least, as their most dangerous enemy.[72]

62. People will chase after anyone who knows how to deceive them into thinking they have lost their way: it flatters them so much to hear that they *have* a way at all.[73]

63. The great thoughts that come "from the heart," the petty ones that come from the underbelly: both are badly conceived.[74]

64. "Great thoughts"? My friend, those are thoughts that puff you up and make you big: a windbag is not great![75]

It is not *how* people love that reveals either the vulgarity or the superiority of their inner nature — for love is in all respects much more of a liar than a traitor! But it pays to look more closely at how people behave when they *are loved* ! — And for a few who had reason to remain unknown, it was a subtle aspect of their destiny never to be loved.[76]

65. Life for the sake of knowledge is perhaps an insane thing: but still a sign of exhilaration. Watching someone who wants it is about as amusing as watching an elephant that tries to *stand* on its head.[77]

66. "But how could you *do* such a thing! — said a friend to a very clever person — it was stupid!" — It hasn't been easy for me either, replied the latter.[78]

67. Jesus of Nazareth loved evil people, but not good people: the sight of their moral outrage moved even him to curses. Wherever judgments were rendered, he sided against those judging: he wanted to be the annihilator of morality.

68. Jesus said to the people: "love God as I love him, as his son: what do we sons of God care about morality!"[79]

69. You think you seek "the truth"! You seek a leader and what you really want is to have someone command you!

70. Why so apart? —"I found no person I could still obey and no one I would like to command."[80]

71. A shepherd always has need of a bellwether, too.[81]

72. Love brings to light the lofty and rare qualities in people; in this way love is deceptive about them (most of all to themselves). But anyone who does not want to be deceived, pay attention to what happens when people know themselves to be loved but *do not love*: there the soul unwillingly reveals its sediments.[82]

73. No one has ever arrived at complete knowledge by means of truthfulness.[83,84]

74. We have rendered lightning *harmless*: but that is not enough, it should also learn to work on our behalf. — This is how I think of all the "evil" in you and me.[85]

75. The Christian god, the god of love and cruelty, is a person who has been conceived very cleverly and without moral prejudice: just the right God for Europeans who want to subjugate the earth.

76. Whatever a particular era perceives to be evil, wherever it recognizes a contradiction with its ideal, is in truth only an echo of what earlier times have held to be good and, as it were, the atavism of an older ideal. Original sin — this is in all circumstances = original virtue.[86]

77. Out of the eye of all who judge gazes the executioner.[87]

78. When we have raised ourselves above good and evil, we see merely unintended comedy even in tragedy.[88]

79. Philosophical systems are the most mundane form through which some people can talk about themselves — an unclear and stammering form of memoir.[89]

80. To see tragic natures perish and *still be able to laugh*, surpassing the deepest understanding, feeling and compassion for them — is divine.

81. "There is no doubt that much lying and deceiving is done by those who believe in this cause: therefore everything about this cause is deception and lies" — this is the conclusion drawn by superficial people. But anyone who knows humans more deeply will draw the reverse conclusion: "therefore there must be something true about this cause: its believers only reveal through this how secure they feel and how for them any bait will do, as long as it is effective in luring someone to their cause."

82. The innocence of a lie is the sign of sincere belief in something.[90]

83. It is essential to have seen someone asleep: otherwise it is impossible to know how that person looks. The face of your best friend that you think you know is *your* face in an imperfect and roughly polished mirror.[91]

84. What difference does it make whether you are flattering a god or a devil, or whether you are whining to a god or a devil? You are merely flatterers and whiners![92]

85. Anyone who is a coward through and through is usually clever enough to take on so-called lovable qualities.[93]

86. The consequences of our actions grab us by the scruff of the neck,[94] quite indifferent to the fact that we have "bettered" ourselves in the meantime.[95]

87. Commanding people will also command their God, however much they believe they are serving him.

88. A supremely moral mendacity would be conceivable by which people become aware of their sexual drive merely as the obligation to produce children.

89. He calls it party loyalty: but it is only his complacency which no longer lets him climb out of this bed.

90. When a particular virtue finally becomes habitual for us, we should at least have the good taste no longer to call it virtue, but rather "taste."

91. There is camaraderie: may there be friendship as well![96]

92. When the compassionate become shameless and tell us compassion is virtue itself: then they arouse our compassion.[97]

93. Noble human beings always stand in the way of good people: the good often marginalize them merely by saying that they are good.[98]

94. In the presence of a hero everything turns into tragedy; in the presence of a demigod — everything turns into satyr play.[99]

95. Cruelty is a displaced and more spiritualized sensuality.

96. Criminals are treated by moral people as an appendage[100] to a single action[101]— and criminals treat themselves the same way, especially if this single action was the exception in their existence: it works like a chalk line drawn around a hen.[102] — In the world of morality there is a lot of hypnotism.[103]

97. You call them "lofty feelings," "sublime mentality": I see nothing more than lust for the heights and the spasms of a moral ambition.[104]

98. Your stride reveals that you are not yet walking your path, your eagerness to dance would have to be evident. Dance is the proof of truth.[105]

99. "Serious," "strict," "moral" — that's what you call him. To me he seems evil and unjust to himself, always ready to punish us for that and to play our executioner — and indignant that we do not allow it.

100. "Lofty feelings!" — Upon the heights there is no feeling of elevation, but rather of depths and of finally reaching solid ground for the first time: as long as the innocence of heights has really been attained.

101. By being willing to help, by commiserating, by subjugating themselves, by forgoing personal demands, even insignificant and superficial people may become somewhat bearable to look at: indeed they should not be disabused of the notion that this willingness to help is "virtue itself."

102. Morality is now the excuse for superfluous and random people, for worms that are weak in body and spirit who *should* not be alive — In this respect morality is mercy: for it says to everyone "you are really something very important": which of course is a lie.

103. That "a foolish woman with a good heart stands high above any genius," this sounds very good — in the mouth of a genius. It is his way of being polite — it is also a sign of his cleverness.

104. We do not find the vanity of others distasteful until it competes with our own.[106]

105. We always love only our desire and not what we desire.[107]

106. The natural consequences of an act are seldom deliberated as long as such consequences include public punishment and denunciation. Here flows the great spring of all superficiality.

107. Women direct their love toward those who inspire fear in them: this is their kind of bravery.[108]

108. "One person is really still too many to have around"[109] — thinks the solitary person. One times one is two.[110]

109. We love utility only as the vehicle for our inclinations: and actually find the noise of its wheels intolerable.[111]

110. "Just being yourself": this may be the distinction we reserve for our best friend — with the result that they wish we would go to the devil.[112]

111. People may often be equal to what they do but not to their *image* of what they've done.[113]

112. The most beautiful colors with which the virtues shine are the invention of those who lacked them. For example, where does the velvet sheen of goodness and compassion come from? — Certainly not from good and compassionate people.

113. Only great criminals have any significance in world history, including those many who were capable of a serious crime but through some chance did not commit it.

114. "Religious person," "fool," "genius," "criminal," "tyrant" — these are pejorative names and details in place of something unnamable.

115. Bad conscience is the tax that the invention of good conscience levies on human beings.

116. You want to be just? Unfortunate one, how do you propose to give *to each his own*? — No, I don't want that. I will give *to each my own*:[114] that will be enough for everyone except the wealthiest people.[115]

117. Solitude makes us harder on ourselves and makes us yearn more for people: it builds character through both.

118. People are strictest with their God: *he* is not allowed to sin![116]

God devised the teleology of pregnancy: then he devised women.

119. "I do not believe in anything anymore." — This is the proper mindset for a *creative* person.

120. La Rochefoucauld stopped halfway: he denied the "good" qualities of human beings — he should have denied the "evil" ones as well.

When moral skeptics have reached the point of mistrusting morality, then they still have one more step to take — skepticism of their mistrust. *Denial* and *trust* — here they shake hands.

121. Belief inside the form, disbelief inside the content — here lies the allure of the maxim —therefore a moral paradox.

122. We forgive our opponents most completely their — failures.[117]

123. What? You want to know yourself? Learn rather to know what makes you happy!

124. I want wishes, nothing but wishes: and always a new wish instead of fulfillment.[118]

125. The most expensive luxury that humanity has so far bestowed upon itself is the belief in something unreal, in selflessness. For this devalued what is most real, selfishness. — Since then all happiness is yearning.[119]

126. Intense hatred is also an idealist: whether in hating we transform our opponents into gods or into devils, either way we give them too much credit.

127. Even in hatred there is jealousy: we want to have our enemy for ourselves alone.

128. The solution for the riddle "woman" is not love but pregnancy.[120]

129. Our faith in others reveals *where* we would like to have faith in ourselves.[121]

130. "The heart is one of the entrails" — Napoleon once said. The entrails of the head lie in the heart.[122]

131. Every strong expectation outlives its fulfillment when the fulfillment comes sooner than expected. This friend arrived two days too early: his presence is unbelievable to me.

132. Knowledge would have little allure if we did not have to overcome so much shame on the way to acquiring it.[123]

133. "Knowledge for its own sake" — this is the last snare laid by morality: with this there is once again complete entanglement in morality.[124]

"All women[125] are either birds or cats or cows" — the look in their eyes shows which one.[126]

What is the best life? To be tickled to death.

134. Wherever the tree of knowledge stands is still paradise.[127]

135. "Morality itself was the first fall into sin: morality itself is the original sin" — everyone who knows thinks this way.

136. He has learned to express himself — but since then he is no longer believed. Only those who stammer are believed.

137. I would only believe in a God who knows how to dance.[128]

138. Pangs of conscience teach us how to bite.[129]

139. We do not believe that cold people are capable of foolishness.[130]

I spit on the educated rabble who are ashamed to say to themselves: "Here I feel nothing!" "Here I know nothing."

The one who knows lives among human beings not as if among animals, but rather as among animals.[131]

140. The inclination toward the tragic increases or decreases along with sensuality: it is part of every adolescence and young manhood.[132]

141. There is much more intrusiveness in praise than in blame.[133]

142. Abundant good will to live — but too little will to suffer — this is what makes people complacent.[134]

143. Objections, mistrust, infidelity are signs of health: all unconditional striving is a kind of pathology.[135]

144. Anyone who *feels* the unfreedom of the will is mentally ill; anyone who *denies* it is stupid.

145. What is done out of love, this is *not* moral, but rather religious.

146. It is not enough to have talent: we must also be allowed to have it.[136]

147. Be wary of people with moral outrage: they have a stinger-like cowardly viciousness that they conceal from themselves.

148. The Christian God who is "love" emerged at a time when love was still not divine enough.

149. Good and evil people — it's all the same to me: but I despise cowardly and loveable people.[137]

The strength of good people does not lie in their goodness, but rather in the fact that their evil is strong.

150. Those who are teachers through and through only take seriously those things that have to do with their students — even themselves.[138]

151. "At least be my enemy": thus speaks true reverence, which does not dare beg for friendship.[139]

If you do not inspire fear in the first place and in all circumstances, then no one will take you seriously enough to finally come to love you.

152. All rights of ownership cease to apply for the one who knows.

When good people moralize, they arouse disgust: when evil people moralize, they arouse fear.

153. The intoxication of victory is always followed by a feeling of great loss: our enemy, *our* enemy is dead! We mourn even the loss of a friend less deeply — and therefore more loudly!

154. People of knowledge must not only love their enemies but also be able to hate their friends.[140]

155. It is in poor taste when people of knowledge make themselves out to be "moral people": anyone *looking at* them should be able to tell that they "have no need" of morality.

156. Everything about him is ripe for the harvest: but he lacks the sickle — and so he rips off the tassels and is annoyed.[141]

157. Some travel in order to find themselves, others because they would like to lose themselves.

158. Killing not through wrath but through laughter.[142]

159. Insanity seldom occurs in individuals — but in groups, political parties, peoples, ages, it is the *rule*: — and that's why historians have yet to speak of insanity. But at some point physicians will write history.[143]

160. When we love we create people in the image of *our* God: only then do we begin to hate *our* devil most completely.[144]

161. It is not easy to find a book that would teach us as much as the book we produce.

162. Those who know "readers" certainly don't write for readers any more — but rather for themselves, the writers.[145]

163. In the mountains the shortest route leads from peak to peak: but for that you need long legs! — Maxims *are* peaks.[146]

164. It is not enough to make amends for something, we must also remake ourselves, be good to ourselves again, for example, by means of some small, superfluous mischief or good deed.[147]

165. Giving to each his own: that would mean wanting justice and achieving chaos.

166. Here both these people have basically the same bad taste: but one of them would like to convince himself[148] and us, too, that his is the best. And the other is ashamed of his taste and would like to convince himself and us, too, that he has a different and better kind of taste — ours. All intellectual philistines belong to one of these two types.

When people freely take suffering upon themselves, they also have the free will to do themselves good: and whoever denies this — — —

167. Beware of good people, the eternal Pharisees, practicing history! They paint over the great people of the past until they look just as fat and well-behaved as good people.[149]

Morality struts around pretending to be the antagonist of evil — — —

168. Another century of newspapers — and all words will stink.[150,151]

169. The one who knows dislikes wading into the water of truth, not when it is dirty, but when it is shallow.[152]

170. *To skeptics.* — Those who grow too tired eventually lie down to sleep even in the snow — take care not to go too far.[153]

171. Anyone who climbs high mountains laughs at all tragic gestures.[154]

172. The air thin and pure, danger nearby — and the spirit full of cheerful malice: they go well together.[155]

173. Courage destroys ghosts but creates goblins.[156]

174. The thought of suicide is a very strong source of comfort. It is a good way of getting through the "evil night."[157]

175. There are feelings that want to kill us; but if they don't succeed, they must die themselves.[158]

176. Not only our reason, but our conscience, too, submits to our strongest drive, the tyrant within us. If we possess no such tyrant among our drives, then our individual drives *compete* for the favor of reason just as much as for the favor of conscience —: and reason and conscience become almost sovereign.[159]

177. Those who commit suicide among us are giving suicide a bad name — not the other way around![160]

178. It is nobler to admit wrong than to insist on being in the right — especially when you are right.[161]

179. A lie *can* be the philanthropy of the one who knows.[162]

180. Those who are truthful end up realizing that they always lie.[163]

181. As in the case of the hypnotized, in many women[164] the intellect only appears suddenly and sporadically and with unexpected force: the spirit then comes "over them" and apparently not out of them. Hence their three-eyed[165] cleverness in interrelated matters — hence also their faith in inspiration.

182. There is much about evil people that disgusts me, but also much about good people: and, truly, it has nothing to do with their "evil"![166]

183. "It is not enough to punish criminals, we should also reconcile with them and bless them: or did we not love them as we caused them pain? ⟨Did we not⟩ suffer by *being forced* to use them as a means of deterrence?"[167]

184. Wherever friendship just won't turn into love, isn't the reason a natural opposition like that between dogs and cats?

185. We *must* repay good and bad things: but why particularly to the person who has done something good or bad to us?[168]

186. A punishment should be devised in such a way that after a violation we will accept it as our right and our honor.[169]

187. Lying involves contradicting what you know, but even more so contradicting what you don't know. — The second kind of lie is so common that it is no longer a stumbling block: human interaction is shaped by it.[170]

188. To educate: that usually means, "teaching someone to lie."[171]

189. Anyone who loves God chastises him.[172]

190. It is impossible to give gifts to truly just people: they give everything back. Which is why those who love them find them horrifying.[173]

191. We no longer love our knowledge enough as soon as we communicate it.[174]

192. That bitch sensuality, who only wants to carve herself a piece of flesh, knows all too well how to beg for a piece of spirit.[175]

193. Poets are shameless about their experiences; they exploit them.[176]

194. Whether you betray yourself or me, you are a traitor. *To writers.*[177]

195. Watch out for that one: he speaks only so he will be allowed to listen afterwards — and you listen only because it will not do to keep talking forever: i.e., you listen badly and he listens only too well.[178]

196. We do not want to be spared by our true enemies: any more than we want to be spared by those whom we love deeply.[179]

197. Unfortunate one, your God has burst and shattered, and the serpents dwell within him — and now for his sake you still love even these serpents![180]

198. Those who conceal nothing about themselves provoke outrage.[181]

199. Iron hates the magnet when the magnet can't draw it completely toward itself — and yet still *attracts*.[182]

200. Not what keeps us from being loved, but what keeps us from loving fully, is what we hate the most.[183]

The thing we hate about our neighbors is that they cannot have our ideals.

201. When we become tired of ourselves and no longer like to love ⟨ourselves⟩, then loving thy neighbor is advisable as a cure: insofar as our neighbors will very soon require that we *believe* in our own "lovability."

202. "Our neighbor doesn't live in the neighborhood": this is how all politicians and peoples think.[184]

203. This virtue would lead to your downfall, my friend: but heaven gave you a second virtue, which sometimes makes you unfaithful to the first.

204. Through loving someone we want to get past our envy of that person.[185]

205. We all pretend to be more naïve than we are — and in fact even to ourselves.[186]

206. Substantial obligations don't make us grateful but vengeful.[187]

207. We like to call in witnesses when we want to talk about ourselves: this is what is called "human interaction."[188]

208. We grow accustomed to scorning evil when we live only in the company of weak and petty people: evil in great people has something inspiring about it.

209. Lack of love likes to disguise itself as the absence of someone *worth* loving.[189]

210. A man uses love to search for an unconditional slave, a woman for unconditional slavery — love is the longing for a vanished culture and society — it harkens back to the Orient.[190]

211. Injustice should only be taken on by someone who can bear it: that's what humaneness calls for.[191]

212. Injustice shared is justice halved.[192]

The most poisonous arrows are shot at a friend who severs ties without even giving insult.

213. *After a break-up.* — "Say what you will to hurt me: you know me too little to know what will hurt me most."

214. Monogamous love is a kind of barbarism, perpetrated at the expense of all others and damaging to knowledge. Rather, you should love many: — then love forces you to be just to each lover: and thus to know each lover. Loving many is the way to knowledge.[193]

215. The cruelty of those who feel nothing is the opposite of compassion; the cruelty of those full of feeling is compassion raised to a higher power.

216. What we have learned to believe without justification is the hardest thing to unsettle by means of reasons.[194]

217. Anyone who is chaste by nature does not think highly of chastity, with the exception of a few vain fools. Their idolizers are those who have reason to wish that they could be or could have been chaste — the swine of Circe.

218. Certainly, anyone who finds chastity very difficult should certainly also be advised against it.[195]

219. *Needs of the heart.* — Animals that go into heat do not so easily confuse what is in their hearts with their lust: in the way that people and especially females[196] do.

220. A woman doesn't want to admit to herself how much "manliness" (any manliness) she really loves in her beloved: that's why she idolizes "the humanity" in him — to herself and to others.

The "I" subjugates robs kills and commits every act of violence: by doing all of that it wants nothing but to nurture its pregnancy: so that it may bear a god and see all of humankind at its feet.[197]

221. With these people, what is fabricated is not their outward appearance but rather their inner world: they abhor appearing to be semblance and surface, but that is what they are.[198]

222. Heroic humans with knowledge deify their devil: and in the process experience what it is to be a heretic witch prophet, skeptic, sage, to be inspired and overwhelmed, and drown at last in their own ocean.[199]

223. Once we have the will to suffer, then we are just one step away from having the will to cruelty — and in fact as a right as well as a duty.[200]

224. It takes a long time to die for the second time: this is true of everyone who has come back to life after death.[201]

225. Even when a people goes backwards, it is pursuing an ideal: it always believes in a forward.[202]

226. The tendency to let ourselves be disparaged, robbed lied to and exploited, in short, humility can be the shame of a god among humans.[203]

227. Anyone who, like a god, creates a new good has always been taken for a devil by the guardians of the old good.

228. Only vice-ridden people are unhappy when their need for vice merges with their disgust with vice — and their disgust never outgrows their need.

229. We have been poor observers of life if we have failed to notice the hand that in a *merciful* way — wanted to kill.[204]

It is not everything you have done in life but rather your accompanying opinion of what was done that determines whether you now feel satisfied or dissatisfied with yourself.

230. A little revenge is in most cases more humane than no revenge at all.

231. Those who despise themselves nevertheless still flatter themselves with the thought that at least now they are not lying to themselves.

232. Friend, everything you have loved has disappointed you: this disappointment has in the end become your habit: and your last love, which you call the "love of truth," is perhaps just the love of disappointment.

232. The inability to lie is in no way the same as the love of truth. In fact, in every love there is the ability to lie — in the love of truth as well.

233. He shakes himself, looks around, runs his hand over the top of his head — and he is always called someone who knows. But freedom from fever is still not knowledge.[205]

234. "Where is there an ocean in which it is really still possible to *drown*? namely, a human being!" — this cry resounds through our time.[206]

Possessing the truth is not awful, just tiresome, like every possession.

235. Malice is where presumptuous and weak people meet: but they misunderstand one another.[207]

236. Those who feel an aversion to the sublime regard not only a yes but also even a no as too overwrought: — they are not to be counted among negative people, and whenever they stray onto this path, they stop abruptly and flee — into the bushes of skepticism.

237. In battle we obviously risk our lives; but the victors are tempted *to throw* their lives *away*. In every victory there is contempt for life.

238. "I do not shun human contact: it is precisely the distance, the eternal distance between any two human beings that drives me into solitude."

Insatiable need for something and at the same time disgust toward that thing — this is what constitutes the *feeling of those who are vice-ridden.*

239. Even truth, like all women, demands of her lovers that they become liars on her behalf — yet it is not her vanity that demands this, but rather her cruelty.

240. "I did that," says my memory; "I could not have done that" says my pride and remains adamant. In the end, memory gives in — [208]

241. To look at things coldly, so that they lie there naked and without plumage, — this is called "love of truth," and is only the incapacity to lie.[209]

242. Those who are sick with fever see only ghosts of things, and those without fever see only shadows of things: and both require the same words.[210]

243. "I listened for an echo — and I heard only praise."[211]

244. Discovering that we are loved in return should actually have a sobering effect upon us with regard to the being that is loved: how can this being be so foolish as to believe in you?[212]

245. "Why is it always necessary also to hate whatever must be loved? Is not love the greatest of all agonies?" That is why humans must be overcome.[213]

246. If you have seen the dull indifference with which the black man endures the kind of severe internal illnesses that would almost certainly bring you to despair: this should cause you to consider just how *little pain* is really present in human-kind, aside from the ten thousand people who have superior spirits.[214]

247. "My happiness *begins* when I see myself beneath myself, as a being among other beings."

248. Our era is a tumultuous era, and for that reason not an era of passion; it keeps itself constantly overheated because it senses that it is not warm — basically, it is freezing. I do not believe in the greatness of all of these "great events" you speak of.

249. The one who knows feels like God become animal.[215]

250. These days events do not acquire greatness until there is an echo — the echo of newspapers.[216]

251. Poor artists! So what does the nervous rabble demand of you? It does not wish to be reeducated but rather to be *amazed*![217]

252. Not the intensity but rather the *duration* of lofty feeling[218] makes superior human beings: they should not be confused with human beings who are having moral spasms![219]

253. *And once again.* — Honest with ourselves and with anyone else who is a friend to us, courageous against the enemy, generous to the vanquished, courteous to all.[220]

254. Those who have no will of their own want at the very least to be know-it-alls.

255. Originally herds and herd-instinct; the self as exception, perceived by the herd as nonsense, madness.

256. The sage as astronomer. — As long as you feel the stars as something "above you,"[221] you still lack the knowing gaze: there is no longer any above and below with respect to knowledge.[222]

257. It is possible to be so closely related to someone that in our dreams we see them doing and suffering everything they really do and suffer: because it would be possible to do and suffer the same thing ourselves.

258. Those who have character also have their typical experience that always recurs.[223]

People fall into two categories, those who are capable of terrible deeds and those who are not.

259. There are two fundamentally different kinds of people: the ones who feel ashamed about the ebb of their feelings (in friendship or love), and the ones who are ashamed of the flood.

Precisely because one lover's passion reaches its climax and recedes, the growing passion of the other lover tends to last somewhat longer than it would have otherwise: the curve of the longer-lasting lover.[224]

260. Whether people count as good or evil is in no way determined by their actions, — but rather by their opinion about these actions.[225]

261. Only when selfishness has become greater cleverer subtler more inventive, will the world begin to *look* "more selfless."

262. Anyone who can meet the eye of a thinker directly is struck by the kind of horrible impression that some creatures make when their eyes slowly *extend out* of their heads, as if on stalks, as they look around.

263. Even saints require the annihilation of morality: so that they can do whatever they *want*.

264. Those who attain their ideal are thereby already — transcending it.[226]

265. People of genius are intolerable unless they possess at least two qualities: gratitude and purity.

266. That which love gives can never be given back and reciprocated: any drive to reciprocate should be drowned in the ocean of love.

267. Why would you want to treat me justly? — said the saint. I already embrace your injustice as *my* due.[227]

268. At the sight of the sublime, sublime humans become free, firm, expansive, serene, cheerful: but the sight of the perfectly beautiful jolts them and bowls them over: in its presence they negate themselves.

269. Anyone who does not feel at home in the sublime will perceive the sublime as something uncanny and false.

270. Many a peacock hides its tail from all eyes: and calls this its "pride."[228]

271. Strange! As soon as I want to conceal a thought from myself and keep it at a distance, then you can be sure that this thought will approach me in bodily form, as a person, and now I must deal deftly with this "angel of God"!

272. To offer blessings when we are cursed is inhuman. So better to join in the cursing for a bit![229]

273. I have seen the triumph of many a truth, but never without the well-meaning support of a hundred errors.[230]

274. Whenever skepticism and yearning mate, mysticism emerges.

  Those whose thought has crossed over into mysticism, even once, do not escape without a stigma on all their thoughts.

275. Degree and kind of a person's sexuality reach up to the highest pinnacle of that person's intellect.[231,232]

276. With our principles we want to tyrannize our habits, or to justify, or to venerate, or to castigate, or to conceal them. Nevertheless, people with the same principles probably want to use them for something completely different.[233]

277. Will — this is an assumption which to me explains nothing. For the one who knows, there is no willing.

278. We have yet to see La Rochefoucauld inverted: someone who shows how the vanity and selfishness of good people have twisted certain human qualities and in the end *have rendered* them — evil and harmful.

279. Do not repay evil with good: for this would shame the recipient, but rather show that something good was done to you.[234]

280. All admiration involves some fearing and running away from ourselves — yes, with even some self-denial, self-disavowal mixed in.

281. Those who despise themselves may want consider that they are not only despised but also despising: they may thus admire themselves as despisers![235]

282. In so much as you know what you do, you are blessed. In so much as you do not know, you are cursed and a sinner before the law — said Jesus to someone who broke the Sabbath — advice for all breakers and lawbreakers.[236]

283. A sudden outburst of revulsion toward ourselves can just as well be the result of a more refined taste — as of a corrupted taste.

284. "Will to truth!" Let us stop speaking so simplistically and bombastically! We want to make the world conceivable to ourselves, to make it observable where possible — yes, *to make*! — All of physics is directed toward making-observable.

285. Will and intellect (or, as is said, heart and head) — this is man and woman; their interactions always have something to do with love, procreation, pregnancy. And mind you, the *heart* is in this case the man and the *head* the woman!

286. He is alone and has nothing but his thoughts: it is no wonder that he often caresses them and teases them and tweaks their ears! — But you rubes say that he is a skeptic.

287. "God's love for humans is *his* hell" — said the devil. "But how is it possible to ever fall in love with humans in the first place!"[237]

288. In routinely conditioning ourselves to tolerate the presence of all kinds of fellow humans, we unconsciously condition ourselves to tolerate our own presence: which is actually humanity's most incomprehensible achievement.

289. The magnitude of human egoism is not the sword that hangs over humankind, but rather the reverse, the feebleness of its egoism, whereby humankind could too easily become fed up with itself.

290. Under peaceful conditions warlike people attack themselves — for lack of other enemies.[238]

291. To create: this means to move something out of ourselves, to make ourselves emptier, poorer and more loving. Once God created the world, he became nothing more than a hollow concept — and love for what was created.

292. "Here is the island of the solitary one. And here I welcome everything that is becoming wandering seeking fleeing! Hospitality is my only remaining form of friendship! I love all that becomes!"

293. The love of life is almost the antithesis of the love of a long life. All love thinks of the moment and of eternity — but *never* of "the length."

294. "My love is so demanding that it instills fear! I cannot love without believing that the one whom I love is destined to do something immortal. And he guesses what I believe — what I demand!"

295. Those who know avoid self-knowledge and let their roots sink into the earth.

296. The most comprehensible part of language is not the word itself, but rather tone, force, modulation, tempo, with which a series of words is spoken — in short, the music behind the words, the passion behind this music, the person behind this passion: thus all of those things that cannot be *written*. So there is no point in being a scribbler.

297. *Gait and kind of gait.* — I *learned* to walk: since then I have allowed myself to run.[239]

298. *The free spirit.* — Those who can fly know that they do not have to be given *a push* in order to take off; as all you entrenched spirits need to do in order to "progress" at all.[240]

299. To be ashamed of our immorality: this is a step on the way that ends with being ashamed of our morality as well.[241]

300. We reserve our most profound and enduring love for our children or our works alone: and our love for ourselves is always a symptom.[242]

301. We will never discover some natures unless we first invent them.[243]

302. "Human interaction corrupts character, particularly when character is absent" — Timon said.[244]

303. "You know nothing about w⟨omen⟩: how is it that sometimes you are right about them?"— With w⟨omen⟩ nothing is impossible.[245]

304. Selfishness is still lacking everywhere.

305. Whoever writes maxims does not want to be read, but rather to be memorized.[246]

306. Most humans[247] act like cattle in a herd and not like persons especially when satisfying their lust (for food women possessions, honor power) — even when they are persons.

307. Everything turns out the best for me: who has the desire to be my destiny? I love every destiny.[248]

308. The age of greatest events will in spite of everything be the age of smallest effects if people are made of rubber and all too elastic.

309. "Before every action I am tormented by the fact that I am only a dice player — I no longer know anything about freedom of the will. And after every action I am tormented by the fact that the dice fall in my favor: am I then a cheater?" — Scruples of the one who knows.[249]

310. Unlearning revenge would also have to mean unlearning gratitude, but not love.

311. Wanting-to-love reveals weariness with the self and pure satiation, yet wanting-to-be-loved reveals demand-for-self, selfishness. Lovers give themselves away; those who want to be loved would like to receive a gift of themselves.

312. The reasons used to justify the punishment for a crime can also be used to justify the crime.

313. Maturity in a man: this means to have rediscovered the seriousness that we had as children at play.[250]

   "*Ella guardava suso, ed io in lei*"[251] Dante. And I in her![252]

314. I've never been lonely before: I felt a longing for people, I looked for people — always I found only *myself* — and now I no longer feel a longing for myself!

   Puny people are incapable of evil: consequently they are incapable of becoming either good or evil people. (But good is a kind of diminished evil?)

   To want something and to make it happen: is taken to be the mark of strong character. But not to want something in the first place and still to make it happen is characteristic of the strongest, who feel themselves to be fate made flesh.

   Anyone who remains a child forever also remains an innocent egoist and, as the object of envy and hatred for "guilty" egoists, is hated more.

315. I love human beings: and never more so than when I can resist this compulsion.[253]

316. A woman attempts to love whenever she feels compelled to obey and serve: it is her work of art, created so as to bear her yoke more easily.

317. "Love me!" — a god who speaks with humans like this has gone mad — out of jealousy.[254]

318. We do not hate something when we think that it is inferior, but only when we think that it is equal or superior.[255]

319. The idea of being suddenly frightened is frightening.

320. It is not the criminals' crime, but rather their cowardice and foolishness after the crime, that allows us to think contemptuously of criminals at all.

321. Evil acquires a bad reputation only after being confused with what is low and disgusting. Until then it is attractive and encourages imitation.

322. All women for whom sexual satisfaction has been forbidden by customs and shaming find religion to be something irreplaceable, as a more spiritual release of erotic tension.

⟨323.⟩ My love for human beings ebbs and flows: and every single individual whom I love is only an occasion for this love. To realize this is depressing.

324. We occasionally embrace an individual out of love for humanity because we cannot embrace everyone: but we should never reveal this to the individual![256]

Good is puny evil: that is why puny people so easily become good people.

325. Those to whom we feel closest are always loved at the expense of those from whom we feel more distant.

"The weaker person is the better person" — say our moralizers.

Weak people say "I have to" strong people "it has to."

Women commit ten times fewer crimes than men — thus they are ten times more moral: according to statistics.

326. The innocence of egoism is characteristic of a child: and if you do not become like children then you will never enter *this* heavenly kingdom.[257]

327. We should take leave of life the way Odysseus left Nausicaa —blessing it more than loving it.[258]

328. We do good deeds for our neighbors, but we don't create for them: thus speaks the honesty of all who create.[259]

329. The love for those who are distant, those to come, is superior to loving thy neighbor: and the love for things is superior to all love for persons.[260]

330. I want to say "enemy," but not "criminal": I want to say "vermin," but not "scoundrel": I want to say "sick," but not "monster"; I want to say "fool," but not "sinner."[261]

331. Denying procreation to all cowards: this should be the negative morality of women.

332. Solitary people love what it is to be human — but they don't love human beings: and when this love-of-what-it-is-to-be-human has accumulated and become dammed up within them, it then cascades forth like a torrent on whoever comes to mind, regardless of whether it is an enemy or a friend.

333. You say, "I love *myself*," "I despise *myself*," "I pity *myself*" — my friend and denier of God, I do not want to challenge your "I," but this *myself* of yours is just as poetic and invented as any god — you must deny it, too.

334. Making compassion and sensitivity toward our neighbor a part of morality (or even morality itself) is a sign of vanity, *assuming* we are compassionate and sensitive by nature — which means lacking pride and nobility of soul.

The cult of compassion is only *proper* for people who did not come to know it from their own experience.

335. If we train our conscience properly, it kisses us at the same time as it bites.[262]

336. Morality is the posturing of humans in the face of nature.[263]

337. "Perhaps a devil invented morality in order to torment humans with pride: and then sometime a second devil will take morality away in order to torment them with self-contempt."

338. "There are no humans, for there was no first human": this is how animals make inferences.[264]

339. The familiarity of superiors is embittering because it may not be reciprocated. Courtesy is advisable instead, i.e., the enduring impression that there might be something for superiors to honor.[265]

340. I do not understand why we find it necessary to slander others. If we want to hurt people, we only need to say something true about them.[266]

341. We always know a little too much about everyone.[267]

342. We praise only what appeals to our taste — i.e., when we praise, we always praise only our own taste — which also goes against all good taste.[268]

343. Only human beings resist the pull of gravity: they would like to fall constantly — *up*.

344. The ladder of my feelings is long, and I do not at all mind sitting on its lowermost rungs, precisely because I often have to spend too much time sitting on the highest ones: for there the wind is biting and the light is often too bright.

345. Jealousy is the most inspired passion and nevertheless still the greatest folly.[269]

346. Like the scorpion, those who burn with jealousy turn the poisonous stinger against themselves — yet without the scorpion's success.[270]

347. Not that you lied to me, but rather that I no longer believed you, this is what has shaken me.[271]

348. I should forgive? But I don't blame you for the same reasons you blame yourself: how *could* I then forgive you?[272]

349. Talking a lot about ourselves is also a means of concealing ourselves.[273]

350. It is easier to forgive our enemies than our friends.[274]

351. The hatred of evil is a ceremonial robe that Pharisees use to disguise their personal antipathies.[275]

Music is for women[276] a form of sensuality.

Women are much more sensual than men, precisely because compared to men they become far less aware of sensuality as such.[277]

352. In today's music there is an audible synthesis of religion and sensuality: and consequently more of woman than has ever existed in music before.

I and Me are always two different persons.[278]

353. Ever since I saw the storm-tossed ocean and above it a pure shining sky, I am no longer fond of all the sunless, overcast passions which know no light other than lightning.

354. All successful people understand the difficult art of knowing the right time to — go.[279]

Those who give a taste of their minds are liked: but those who devour minds are feared. The moment you are liked, consider how near the moment is when you — — —

355. It is not their love of humanity, but rather their impotent love of humanity, that stops today's Christians from erecting stakes for the burning of heretics.[280]

356. You believe, so you claim, in the necessity of religion! Be honest! You believe only in the necessity of police and live in fear of robbers and thieves stealing your money and your tranquility![281]

357. How moral and sublime people become every time they have a good chance of using these qualities to inflict pain![282]

358. Nobility in obedience, freedom under coercion and law, contempt for the rebellious desires of slaves: these are the marks of the first caste "human."

359. Eleven-twelfths of all great men in history were merely representatives of a great cause.

Until now humanity's perception has been too dull to recognize that the most powerful humans were great actors.

360. Only those who dramatize their virtues become famous in their lifetimes.[283]

361. "I don't like him." — Why? — "I am no match for him." — Has any person ever answered in this way?[284]

362. When hungry for people we look above all for *comfort* food, even if it is not especially nourishing: like potatoes.

364.[285] Rebellion is the slave's noblest attitude.[286]

365. When you taste best, that is when you must stop letting yourself be eaten — this is the secret of women who are loved for a long time.

366. Dramatizers of greatness who are unaware of their play-acting have the same effect as the truly great and even surpass them — in brilliance.

367. You are going to be with women? Don't forget the whip![287]

We always *create* a distance around ourselves through what we admire and how we admire it.

368. It isn't what he does and how he schemes against me during the day that bothers me: but that I appear in his dreams at night — gives me chills.[288]

369. Through music the affects take pleasure in themselves.[289]

370. The test of a strong character consists in remaining impervious to even the best rational objections once a decision has been made: in other words, a periodic madness.[290]

371. "What is freedom? — Your good conscience" — said Periander, the seventh sage.

"I could do this or that or something else, anything would be instructive, particularly if it would lead me astray and cause me distress" — this is how free spirits think and speak, the lovers of knowledge: for this reason they laugh when they are accused of weak will and irrationality.

372. Have I ever felt a pang of conscience? — My memory is completely silent in response to this inquiry.

373. Morality is a proto-scientific method of coming to terms with the explanation for our affects and states. Morality has the same resemblance to a future pathology of general feelings[291] that alchemy has to chemistry.

374. There are no moral phenomena at all; but rather only a moral interpretation of certain phenomena (— an erroneous interpretation!)[292]

375. Criminals are usually no match for their deeds, they recant and *slander* them.[293]

376. "Better to lie in bed and feel sick than to have to *do* something" — all self-tormenters live by this secret principle.

377. Recognizing that I agree with others makes me slightly suspicious of whatever it is we agree upon.

378. The one who knows finds the *pia fraus*[294] even more tasteless than the *impia fraus*.[295,296]

379. Beware the *sancta simplicitas*:[297] she is the one who always had the task of building a fire around the stake.[298]

380. At one time the religious explanation supported the scientific one: and even now the moral explanation supports the physiological one. Those who think very little and have learned very little trace everything back to morality, their mood swings under the influence of the weather, digestive problems, anemia, their urinary needs or the equivalent, their lack of success, ennui, dissatisfaction, insecurity.

381. If you wanted to say out loud all the things that you have already done in your thoughts, then everyone would scream: "away with this disgusting vermin! It befouls the earth" — and they would have all forgotten that they had also done the very same thing in their own thoughts. — This is how candor makes us moral.[299]

To speak in physiological terms, the drive of the weak to be assimilated by the strong finds expression in morality.

382. "I love her and *that is why* I wish she loved — but why me in particular? I do not love myself enough for that" — this is how divine love speaks out of the mouth of a man.

So you wish to beguile him? Then pretend to be embarrassed around him.[300]

383. Demanding to be loved in return is vanity and sensuality.

384. People who mistrust themselves want more to be loved than to love, in order, if just for a moment, to be allowed to believe in themselves.

A god who loves is not worthy of letting himself be loved: he prefers to continue to be hated.

385. The love for superhumans[301] is the antidote to compassion for humans: the latter would cause the very rapid downfall of humankind.

386. A little more compassion among humans, and despair over life would knock at the door.

387. "Love your neighbor" — that means above all: "leave your neighbor alone!" — And precisely this part of virtue is the most difficult!

388. Trivial suffering makes us small, great suffering makes us great. The will to suffer greatly should therefore be a requirement of selfishness.

389. Better evil companions than puny ones![302]

390. An enchanting work! Yet how unbearable that its creator constantly reminds us that it is *his* work. Doesn't he know that "the father" is always a comical figure?

391. Happiness in frequent, small doses rewards us with misery in frequent, small doses: and thereby corrupts character.

392. All creature comforts should be used as a sick person uses a bed: for convalescence.[303]

393. We do not find the embarrassment of very clever people believable.[304]

394. H⟨umans⟩ are the animals with red cheeks: all too often they have had to be ashamed of themselves.[305] "I am predestined to see and not to believe, to me all people of faith are something foreign and noisy."

395. There is a kind of arrogance in goodness that manifests itself as malice. Our vanity becomes most difficult to wound precisely in those moments when our pride has just been wounded.[306]

396. These two wenches, past and future, are making so much noise that the present is running away from them.

397. To make a "thou shalt" out of an "I feel like," to reshape habit into virtue, customs into ethics: this is a subtle old ancient form of second-rate counterfeiting — and I still see through it today.

398. "Thou shalt" sounds sweeter to most than "I will this": the herd-instinct still lingers in their ears.

399. In a certain state of illness it is impossible to be anything but miserly. Miserliness is an affect. You love my levelheadedness too much: even this miserliness is illness.

400. We become mistrustful not because we find a reason to be so, but rather "we always find a reason" to be mistrustful when we become mistrustful.

401. Under certain circumstances the overall damage is less when people unleash their affects on others than when they unleash them on themselves: this is especially true of creative people, whose usefulness extends into the future.

402. We would be in big trouble if people did not have their malicious petty thoughts! How much more pleasure do they have then, how much less pain do they inflict upon us then![307]

403. A human being is still more of an *ape* than any ape.[308]

404. It is the heart that inspires: and it is the mind that heartens us and keeps us cool when we are in danger. Oh language![309]

405. What? A great man? I see in him only a dramatizer of his own ideals.

Selfishness in the case of thieves, robbers, usurers and speculators is fundamentally unambitious and unassuming enough: certainly there is nothing easier than merely wanting people's money.

406. Faust, the tragedy of knowledge? Really? Faust makes me *laugh*.

407. The supremely tragic motifs have up to now remained unused: poets know nothing from experience about the 100 tragedies of conscience.

408. People speak of the causes of affects and mean the occasions for them.

409. He has sacrificed people for the sake of his knowledge and is proudest of nothing so much as this cruelty against himself.

410. In those who know, compassion seems almost laughable, like sensitive skin on a giant.[310]

411. Enduring and deep physical pain is a school for tyrants.[311]

412. Being compassionate as well as cruel is necessary for being either.

413. More than a few who wanted to exorcise their demons have thereby driven themselves into the swine.[312]

414. "Those who praise" mostly portray themselves as giving something back: in truth they want to be given a gift.[313]

415. Human beings are not revealed in their affects, only their affects are revealed.[314]

Our eyes hear more subtly than our ears: we have better understanding and taste when we read than when we hear — with books as with music.

416. Keeping a mistress is corrupted by — marriage.[315]

417. Christianity poisoned Eros: while he did not die of it, he did degenerate into "vice."[316]

Full of passion but heartless and playful: that's how the Greeks were, even Greek philosophers, like Plato.

418. Intimacy is genuine only in heartless people and for them almost a shameful thing.[317]

419. A bit of envy at the start — and afterwards a great love? That's how an explosion happens by striking a match.

420. If the goddess of music wanted to speak in words rather than tones, we would cover our ears.

421. Responding to praise with delight is in some people intellectual vanity, in others a sign of a courteous heart.[318]

422. We lie with our tongues, but we tell the truth with our mouths and faces[319] — this is how physiognomists see it.[320]

423. Sensuality hastens the growth of love so that the root stays weak and the whole plant is easily torn out.[321]

424. Some people feel a deep need for *their* enemies: for them alone they also feel hatred at first sight.[322]

425. My eyes see other people's ideals, and I am often transported by what I see: but you nearsighted people then think these are *my* ideals!

426. The morality of every society says that isolation is guilt.

427. In almost every living thing there hides a parasite.

428. When we are forced to see people in a new light, there is a tendency to blame them harshly for the inconvenience they cause.[323]

429. In kindness there is no trace of hate for people, but for that very reason all too much contempt for people.[324]

430. Always remaining "a pupil" poorly repays the teacher.[325]

431. Like a tree: the more it wishes to grow upwards into height and light, the more strongly its roots must reach in the opposite direction: its will goes inwards, downwards, into the darkness, the depths, outwards — into so-called "evil."[326]

432. You call it God decomposing himself: yet it is only him shedding his skin: — he sheds his moral skin! And you are supposed to see him again soon, beyond good and evil.

433. A people is a detour of nature, on the way to 5, 6 great men.[327]

434. At patriotic festivals even the spectators are among the performers.[328]

435. Even the ugly has its ugly little ceremonial robe: it is called "the sublime."[329]

436. What is good? — "That which is pretty and moves us at the same time" — answered a little girl.[330]

If God is a God of love, then conscience's bite would have to be God's bite and consequently a bite given out of love.[331]

437. Courageous, heedless, mocking and even somewhat violent: that's how wisdom wants us: she is a woman and — only ever loves the warrior.[332]

438. Many soldiers and yet so few men! Many uniforms and even more uniformity.[333]

439. "Once again the time of harvest is past: the wind blows over the empty fields, and now even the most bountiful crop seems to me a monstrous loss" — this is the way every creative person feels.

440. A real man wants two things: danger and play. That is why he desires a woman as the most dangerous plaything.[334]

441. The responsibility of a woman is to discover and preserve the child in a man.[335]

442. To want the emancipation of women achieves only the emasculation of men.

443. Man should be trained for war and woman to help the warrior's recovery: anything else is foolishness.[336]

444. The word "scholar" refers not only to soldiers of the mind but — unfortunately — also to those who darn its socks.[337,338]

There is no more pitiful group than scholars: with the exception of those few who have been scarred by war in body and mind.

There are too few men: and that is why women are becoming manly.[339]

445. What a subtlety it is that God learned Greek when he wanted to become a writer; just as subtle, that he did not learn it better![340]

This thinker is colder than ice; for that reason he burns the fingers of those who touch him and is easily regarded as red hot.[341]

3 [2][342]

Pine and Lightning.

High above human and beast I grew;
And I speak — No one speaks with me.

**

Too alone I grew and too high:
I wait: but what I am waiting for, anyway?

**

Too near to me is the throne of clouds, —
I wait for the first lightning bolt.[343]

**

3 [3][344]

Portofino

Here I sit waiting — waiting? Yet for nothing,
Beyond good and evil, and lusting no more
For the light than for the darkness,
Friend of noon and friend of eternity.

**

3 [4]³⁴⁵

On the High Seas.

Friend — spoke Columbus — do not trust
a Genoese ever again!
He's always staring into the blue,
What is most distant draws him all too much!

**

Whomever he loves, he likes to lure
Far beyond space and time — —
Stars beyond stars shine above us,
Eternity roars all around us.³⁴⁶

**

[4 = N V 9c. N VI 1b. N V 8.
November 1882–February 1883]

4 [1]

We are about to encounter *the greatest excitation* — and behind it, *the backlash*! the yearning toward nothingness! — And **we** do not want to perish, either in this excitation or in this yearning — we friends of life.

4 [2]

I have the *most extensive* soul of all Europeans now living or who ever lived: Plato Voltaire — — — it depends on conditions that do not entirely depend on me, but rather on the "essence of things" — I could become the European Buddha: which admittedly would be a counterpart of the Indian one.

4 [3][1]

In all first encounters there is luck and some kind of good omen.

4 [4][2]

A false saying goes as follows: "those who do not redeem themselves, how can they redeem others?" If I have the key to your shackles, why would your lock and mine have to be the same?[3]

In war you are holy and even when you murder and burn.

"Uni-form" is what they call it, the thing they wear: uniformity is what they cover with it.[4]

You should go back to sleep — and dream better.[5]

This cruelty sits in my guts. See, I am evil.

You say: it is the cause that justifies the war? The war is what justifies the cause![6]

Herds are no good, not even when they follow you.

The shepherd is a gilded tool of the herd.

4 [5][7]

Reason is the exception even in the wisest person: chaos and necessity and whirling of the stars — this is the rule.

We must make our death into a festival and thereby be a little malicious toward life: a woman who wants to leave us, us!

As for heroes, I do not have that high an opinion of them: but still: it is the most acceptable form of existence, namely, when there is no other choice.

4 [6][8]

We both have something for each other: you the affects I the reasons.

I make balsam for my wounds from my own vitriol.

I milk your udder, beloved misery!

Many god-humans[9] have existed on earth: and all god-humans created their god.

There is no greater enmity on earth than between god-humans and their gods.

You brothers, I have exposed myself: I am not ashamed to show myself naked.

Shame is the ghoul who became a companion of humans when they were seized with the desire to transcend animals.

People are free to believe in Zarathustra: what does Zarathustra care?

4 [7]
    Demigod.
    Hero.
    Man.
    Child.
    Am I not after all a comrade of companion-animals.

4 [8]
    I come to help you — and you complain that I don't want to weep with you.[10]

4 [9]
    I have known this for a long time: people like my m⟨other⟩ and s⟨ister⟩ must be my natural enemies — nothing can be done about this: the reason lies in the essence of all things. Being with p⟨eople⟩ like them poisons the air for me, and I require a lot of self-overcoming.[11]

4 [10]
    To men. This is the doctrine of holiness.
    To women. Beyond good and evil.
    To children. Noon and eternity.
    Zarathustra among animals. The seven solitudes.

4 [11]
    Any single one of my affects would have brought about my downfall. I have always played one off against the other.

4 [12]

There should not be any people who instill disgust or hatred in me.

4 [13][12]

"Like Brahma, men live alone; like gods, they live in twos; like a village, they live in threes; where there are more, there is bustle[13] and turmoil."[14]

Do not speak as a human does to animals, you say, — — —

My strongest trait is self-overcoming. But I also have the greatest need for it — I am always on the edge of the abyss.[15]

I am speaking and a child is playing: is it possible to be more serious than we both are right now?[16]

4 [14]

I am not great enough *not* to have these feelings: but I am great enough not to be ashamed of them.[17]

4 [15][18]

There is no one alive who would be worthy of praising me.

For man "I will this" for woman[19] "I must"

I belong to the race of berserkers, of libertines, of those obsessed with revenge, of religious fanatics — I myself almost forgot it.

4 [16]

Morality has been taken to its pinnacle by freethinking and it has been **overcome**.

I am addressing men, spoke Zarathustra — tell the women to go away.[20]

4 [17] [21]

A fool spoke in this way: make the old sacrifices to a new spirit, transform the old soul by means of a new body.

Blood justifies nothing; blood also redeems nothing. I dislike those love me⟨a⟩ls,[22] — — —[23]

4 [18] [24]

The best man is evil, the best woman is bad.

It was the love of shepherd and herd that from this time on conceived benefit as good and holy:

It was the love of children and race: this love was rage against the betrayers of the love of all, and guilt was a betrayal of the love of all.

They conceived good and evil out of love: and not out of prudence, for love is older than prudence.

What universal love demanded was once useful: and whoever felt the strongest love was made by the herd into its shepherd.

Loving thy neighbor was still insignificant, the I despised: and the herd was above all else.

4 [19]

I honor all h⟨umans⟩ I despise only the Pharisees.

4 [20][25]

One morning Zarathustra climbed up a mountain: when he was alone with himself he glorified himself in this way: you, my book, — — —

Humankind has no goal: it can even *set* a goal for itself — *not* for the end, *not* for *preserving* the species, but rather for **abolishing** it.

And the people should all speak: this criminal is holy.

The creator (the one who knows), the communicator (the artist), the simplifier (the lover).

Bear my *virtue*! (as a superpower).

State and society are not *necessary* for some: but they must *endure* them and withdraw as much as possible.

Austerity of the one who cannot love.

4 [21]
An uncanny and inglorious goal.

4 [22] [26]
(One day Zarathustra glorified himself and spoke in this way)

They must combine three characteristics: to be authentic, to want and to be able to make themselves understood, and to be privy to knowledge (into one)

the disciples of sacred selfishness
or one of the three
or to be able to be merely a tool[27] of the three.

he should say: I am evil, I preserve the force of evil.

All people should turn their existence into the goal of the plan.

Up to now there has been no goal: onward, so let's *seize* one for ourselves.

Speaking *on behalf*: of vain people, of cruel people, etc.

The supreme pleasure: that which we *must* do, even that which we want. In this way to integrate *ourselves* into the grand *plan*.

4 [23]

All creation is communication.

The one who knows the one who creates the one who loves are *one*.

4 [24]

1000 formulas for the recurrence (is the threat).

4 [25]

The birth of the *superhumans*.[28]

4 [26] [29]

Good people as the necessary *Pharisees*.

Here, too, there is a contrast like the one between *religious people* and *people of faith*.

Those who create what is good find their *opposite* in those who preserve what is good.

The point where people find the courage to perceive their evil as their good e.g., Christians their "cowardice."

4 [27][30]

Good people now almost worthless.

It all depends on *evil people with religious intentions*! And it has always been that way!

4 [28][31]

I have to be an angel if I want to live: you do not have such hard conditions.

4 [29]³²

At the same time, let your enlightenment also be a dawn.

Error in crime.

it is not pleasant feelings that are called good — but rather states *of fullness of power*

She was aroused by what they once revered.

you must newly redefine your need: that which already is should be a necessity for you.

4 [30]

Anyone who lives at the foot of the highest Alps does not see their peaks: excuse me — — —

4 [31]

We are also punished for our virtues.[33]

4 [32][34]

They call it a love meal when their redeemer is devoured out of love.

Churches are founded on blood and reason-shunning.

4 [33]

But what are you not saying about the faithful of the correct faith? What does your silence mean? — Zarathustra smiled and said only the words "All honor to the vanquished!"

4 [34][35]

If compassion does not have to break through a hard shell — —

I presuppose compassion: to be cruel is a disease of the brain and of the nerves.

We can only be silent when we have bows and arrows: otherwise we babble and — bicker.

I would like to remove from the world its heartbreaking character

4 [35]
It is not the finger of God that is crushing your windpipe. Long ago, they say, God did approach the dying: then he became anguished and horrified.

4 [36][36]
Actors have little intellectual conscience: they believe in whatever lets them instill the strongest belief.

Only the appraisers and the inventors of new values are creative:[37] the world revolves around them alone. Anyone who instills belief in new values is known among the people as "creative" —

4 [37][38]
Anyone who sees the *base* qualities in a person also usually feels a certain attraction for these qualities and triggers their release.

As one who creates, you run away from yourself — you cease being your contemporary.

Disgust at filth can be so great that it prevents us from cleaning ourselves.

Fools want to have it better than good.

4 [38][39]
What must I do to become blessed? Be blessed[40] and do what you must do.

Something becomes dear to us: and no sooner do we love it with all our hearts, than the tyrant, the higher self, speaks to us: "give me that very thing as a sacrifice!" — and we give it to him.

I urge you to battle, not to work — I urge you to victory, not to peace. May your work be a battle, your peace a victory.

I awoke you from your sleep, for a nightmare oppressed you. And now you say: "what should we do now! Night is all around us." — you ungrateful ones![41]

Everything about women is a riddle — everything about women has one solution: pregnancy.[42]

If you want to have an easy life, then always stay with the herd. Lose yourself in the herd! Love the shepherd and honor the fangs of his dog!

If you know how to bark and bite, then — be the herd's dog: then you will make life easy for yourself.

I know everything that is good and everything that is evil: I also know what is beyond good and evil.

Good and evil are God's prejudices — said the serpent. But even the serpent was one of God's prejudices.

The Church is the stone on the grave of a God-made-human: it does not want him to be resurrected.

I love myself as I love my God: who could forgive me a sin? I know only sins against my God: yet who knows my God? —

4 [39][43]

Noon and Eternity.
Thus spoke
Zarathustra.

4 [40][44]

What keeps me alive? Pregnancy: and every time a work was born, life hung by a thin thread.

I have hidden myself away. I want to keep my disgust from them, these puny people. This has become most difficult for me: but they are blameless, like grass and weeds.

We are only ever pregnant with our own child.[45]

You say "this is dark." I placed a cloud in front of your sun. But look how the edges of the cloud are shining and becoming bright!

Don't look at the sun! The moon is still too bright for your nocturnal eye!

You should love peace as a means to a new war!

In war, revenge is silent; in war, what is person⟨al⟩ dies.

4 [41][46]

Lies and dissimulation — how all education works.

How should I make fun in a terrible way?

"You have overcome me" See to it that I become wings for you and not a stumbling block!

4 [42][47]

There once was an ancient[48] righteous god; he had substance and also a heart: and much anger and love were in his vitals.

And behold, love played a trick on him and he fell in love with humans: so that this love became hell for him.[49]

What did this ancient righteous god do? He convinced a human woman to bear him a son: and this son of God gave humans only this advice: "love God! as I love him! What do we sons of God care about good and just people!"

And like a jealous lover the ancient righteous god persecuted humans with his love.[50]

Do you think he succeeded? In time, he convinced precisely those among humans he did not like, good and just people.

They called themselves "Church" and the chosen: and babbled a lot about their love for God — love-deprived people!

Then they broke the ancient righteous god's heart: and he suffered the same fate as his son: he died on the cross of compassion. In truth these good and just people are corrupters of the zest for life and not just of the ancient righteous gods.

"Three things should always accompany us — they were always saying — truth, money and virtue: this is how we love God."

"We are chosen and the most superterrestrial ones on earth."

4 [43][51]

Whatever we *most love* to do, we would like this to be regarded as the thing we find most *difficult* to do: and be regarded as such *by ourselves*.

Our sacrifices prove only how little every thing means to us when we love something.[52]

Moral states and strivings are only *means to knowledge*, immoral ones as well.

The pleasure in knowing is an extremely intensive *faith*. If we do not achieve this, then there is still a wanting-to-know in response to stimuli, e.g., as desire for security or novelty or desire for something worth desiring, yet to be discovered.

Since the ones who know spoke only of knowledge, this involves much mendacity — they had an interest in letting knowledge appear to be the most valuable state.

Lovers of knowledge! And you have never even killed a human being in order to see how it feels!

The perfect knowledge of necessity would abolish[53] every "should" — but to understand even the necessity of "shoulds" as a consequence of *ignorance*.[54]

4 [44][55]
As happy as an elephant when it tries to stand on its head.[56]

You lack the courage to burn yourself up and to perish: and you will never become something new in this way. That which today gives us wings color fashion and force will be ashes tomorrow.

Marriage might be right for those incapable of either love or friendship — for almost everyone then — and perhaps even for those very rare people who are capable of both at the same time.[57]

4 [45]
There is another kind of virtue, a mercenary one, and it wants to be paid well, either here or in a not-here-place and it calls this "justice."
Oh you friends of gift-giving virtue, let us dance in mockery of all mercenary virtue.

But you have not yet learned this from me: how to dance in mockery.

4 [46]
That which is to us warmth or light or noise or array of stars — may seem somewhat different to senses other than human ones: yet it will never be goodness or wisdom or love.

Loving thy neighbor. When utility is the driving force.[58]

4 [47]
all around you is a meaning that makes things degenerate, and "distress[59] is absent in everything"

4 [48]
Community (not herd)
his *overcomings*
tablet
difficult

That my animals without [—] willingly [—] escort[60] to me.

4 [49][61]
The interpretations 1) Error of the first cause, a god conceived as opposite (— — —

Your life is wasted: you are like a sycophant.

where your poverty and sobriety cried out to heaven

let a lightning bolt lick you with its tongue!

they shot an arrow of flaming love into the universe.

It is not the ignorance of people that is pitiful: what is pitiful is the people themselves!

Science only as a kind of asceticism.

exploitation of the accidental — ambiguity as the condition for life in many species — consequently indifference to essence

How is it possible that you narrow souls can keep up with my thinking?

4 [50]
Don't get incensed! They are taking your money away from you! and there are more important things that poorer people also have access to. Jesus as nonmonetary *sacrifice*!

4 [51][62]
Asceticism of the intellect as *preparation for creating*. Intentional *deprivation* of the creative drives.

4 [52]
There are preachers: they teach suffering. They serve you, even if they hate you at the same time.

I do not address you as I would address the people. For them, the *best thing* is to despise and destroy themselves: the next best thing is to despise and destroy each other.

4 [53]
Every effect is followed by an effect — this belief in causality is anchored in the strongest of the instincts, the instinct for revenge.[63]

Let's not confuse these things: the downfall of an actor is not being praised, the downfall of a genuine person is not being loved.

The antithesis of an actor is not an honest person, but rather a secretive self-deceiving person.
(most actors belong to this group)

4 [54]⁶⁴

"Evil has its heroes just as good has its heroes"⁶⁵ — in the mouth of a La Rochefoucauld this is complete naïveté.

Seeing and still not believing is the cardinal virtue of the one who knows.

In striving *not* to know themselves ordinary people are very subtle and devious.

In G⟨ermany⟩ aspiration is admired much more than ability: it is the right place for unaccomplished and pretentious people.

4 [55]

The sight of naïve people is a delight, as long as they are evil by nature and have an intellect.

Sly people are usually simple and not complicated people.

Labyrinth.
Labyrinthine people never seek the truth, but rather always only their Ariadne — whatever they might say to us.

4 [56]⁶⁶

When we feel comfortable around p⟨eople⟩, we like ascribing this comfort to their and our morality.

Skepticism regarding all moral values is a symptom of the emergence of a new moral code of values.

When we no longer feel ashamed even about our own evil, this is a *step forward* in intellectual taste.

To have no phrase at the ready that would corrupt his philosophy —

Contempt for what I do, and contempt for what I am.

The Church is nothing but a profoundly mendacious kind of st⟨at⟩e.

The masculine animal is cruel to what it loves — not out of malice, but because when it is in love it feels itself too strongly and no longer has any feelings at all left over for the feelings of others.

4 [57]⁶⁷

Those who are lacking in love are stingy even with their courtesy.

In matters of honor, women are coarse and clumsy.

If we want to have friends, we must be willing to go to war for them, i.e., we must *be able* to be an enemy.

Today they had the good intention of being friendly: but how miserable they were at it, what little inventiveness!

I divide philosophical people into two categories: those always pondering their own defense and those pondering attacks against their enemies.

The hero is cheerful — this displeases writers of tragedies.

With sarcastic people, feelings seldom spill forth, but always very loudly.

It is astounding to what foolishness even sensuality can be led when corrupted by love, how as soon as love speaks to it, sensuality loses all good taste and calls what is ugly beautiful.

4 [58]

So-called lovable people know how to spend the small change of love on us.

All those who have not yet forgotten how to digest their experiences have also not yet forgotten the slothfulness of digestion: they become indignant about it, in this time of haste and stress.[68]

For women there is only one single point of honor; they have to believe that they love more than they are loved. Just beyond this point lies prostitution.

Cruelty toward the man she does not love.

Will to self, selfishness is a subtle and a later evolved refinement of the will to pleasure: insofar as that will to pleasure is a self.

"You" is older than "I" and yet *still* survives in the *I*.
"I" — this is a working hypothesis for the purpose of making the world conceivable — just like matter and atom.

4 [59][69]

As soon as prudence says, "don't do that, it will turn out badly for you" — I have always disobeyed it.

A bad reputation

The *utile* is always just a means, its end in any case is the *dulce*.[70] Utilitarians are stupid.

They do not love me: is this a reason not to bless them?

Behold! The world has just now become perfect.

4 [60]

sit tibi terra levis:[71] to wish people in Germany well it is necessary to wish that they might find the earth rather heavy.

4 [61]

Basic tenet

It could *not be tolerated*: therefore the following *things that make life easier* are *required*.

Away with good and evil!

Highest degree of self-satisfaction!

Tragic people step back!

Avoiding the strong affects!

The liberation of *multifaceted* people.

Do not act differently, but rather think differently of your self!

The vanity of sublime people!

against the cruelty of the heroic.

all these life improvements are *useless* because our value judgments have not changed, e.g., health.

against "all-too-hasty" people.

4 [62][72]

Petty thieves, petty backbiters, petty cynics and detractors should be *wiped out* — not murderers

there should be no compassion for mosquitoes[73] and fleas

Contemptible and terrible people.

The forests should be preserved, evil people should be preserved.

4 [63]

Do people who know have ownership? Truly, I forgot it — or did I unlearn it?

4 [64][74]

Our evil affects also have a conscience and become annoyed when they have let themselves be overcome.

Conscience is a ventriloquist, when it speaks, we cease to believe that its voice comes from us.

Religion wants to make people happy and to put "I must" in place of "thou shalt": it wants to free us from what is impossible for humans in morality.

Now I am just — means in many cases "now I am avenged."[75]

The filthiest thing about "good people" is how they interpret their inclinations and disinclinations as their duty.

The pride of the unhappy lover tells him that his beloved does not deserve to be loved by him at all. But a superior pride says to him: "No one deserves to be loved. — You just do not love her enough!"

4 [65]
The unhappiness of the unhappy lover does not end when love is returned, but rather when love is increased.[76]

If we want to be rid of people then we only need to diminish ourselves in their eyes — this touches their vanity immediately and they run away.

As long as you remain on hostile terms, your time together is not yet at an end — she should not be allowed to see you at all, that is how superior and distant you should be toward her.

4 [66]
The less he is accepted, the more Zarathustra keeps giving.
"I was stingy — you were right to disparage me!"
Sequence of themes to be arranged according to their philanthropy.
he is being **exiled**.

4 [67]

Conquering our affects means in most cases temporarily inhibiting and damming them up: thus increasing the danger.

Most people who rescue some unfortunate person from danger were driven not by compassion but by *courage* and danger.

Recklessness has done more great deeds than loving thy neighbor.

Humans are only now making the world conceivable to themselves — and we are still in the process of doing so — : and once they have understood it, and they feel that it is completely their *work* — alas, and now they must *love* their work, like every creator![77]

Men, as long as there are men, will be trained for war and hunting: that is why they now love knowledge as the most extensive opportunity for war and hunting. What a woman *could* ever love about knowledge would have to be something else — — —

4 [68]

We take the bitterness that we feel toward people and use it to justify our moral outrage — and we admire ourselves in the process: and the fading of our hatred to justify our forgiveness — and we admire ourselves once again.[78]

If we have enough of the truth, we no longer need lies to interact with people: with these lies we can deceive and lead others astray any way we like.

4 [69]

The highest form of courage in those who know is not revealed when they provoke wonder and horror — but rather when they have to be *perceived* by those who do not know as superficial, lowly, cowardly, irrelevant.

Those who know must also understand how to place the crown of victory on their own heads: they cannot wait because it is this that drives them to new transformations.

4 [70][79]

The passion of two people for one another — this is in all circumstances two passions, and with different arcs peaks speeds: their lines can *cross*, nothing else.

We say pleasure and think of lusts, we say sense and think of sensuality, we say body and think of underbellies — and in this way we deprive three good things of their dignity.

Bourgeois and courtly virtues do not understand each other and malign each other.

Even our ability to learn and our industriousness have to do with talent.

That everyone is permitted to learn to read and reads, this will eventually ruin not only writers but even minds in general.

4 [71][80]

He wronged me — this is bad. But that he wants to go so far as to beg my pardon, this drives me crazy![81]

It requires very good character not to attribute the unpleasant consequences of some trivial folly to our character.

To actually attribute the unpleasant consequences of our own folly to folly and not to our character: this requires more character than most people have.

No sooner do we progress even one step beyond average hu⟨man⟩ goodness, than our actions are reprimanded.

You say, "I like this" and think you are praising me! — Oh you fools, how I like this!

Scientific people share the fate of rope-makers: they weave their strand longer, but in the process they themselves move — backwards.

4 [72][82]
Life is hard to bear: it requires defiance in the morning and surrender in the afternoon

I am absent-minded: I don't have any appetite until after a meal.[83]

Truly, the refutability of a theory is not the least of its charms.[84]

Constitutional monarchs were thought to be virtuous — they can no longer "commit injustice" — but in return they were stripped of their power. Since then they have wanted nothing but war — why is that?

Those fortunate enough to remain obscure should also take advantage of the freedom that darkness affords and espe-cial⟨ly⟩ "whisper well."[85]

4 [73][86]
I hate honorable men[87] far more than sinners!

Do I love music? I don't know — too often I also find my-self hating it. Yet music loves me — and as soon as someone leaves me, music jumps into my lap and wants to be loved.

How long until fame arrives?[88]

One moment he squares his shoulders as if the whole weight of the world were to be laid upon us — and the next moment he trembles like a rosebud that is weighed down by a mere dew drop. My brothers and sisters, do not act so gently toward me! we are all comely sturdy male and female donkeys, and we are certainly no trembling rosebuds.

4 [74][89]

In order to need brakes,[90] it is first necessary to have wheels.

I have lived close to death for too long to have any fear of life.

I call such p⟨eople⟩ "totalities"

4 [75]

I call them actors (*those who communicate*)

Out of overflowing life, superhumans have an opium smoker's hallucinations and madness and Dionysian dance: they do not suffer from the pains that follow.

Illness now leads to much that is not *in itself* a symptom of illness: to a *vision*.

Not your sin — your sobriety cries to heaven.[91]

Save us from sin and give us back our arrogance!

The pale criminal in a dungeon and by contrast *Prometheus*! Degeneration!

"We want to create a being" we all want to have a part in it, to love it, we all want to be pregnant — and *therefore* to honor and respect ourselves.

We must have a *goal* that makes us all love one another! **All** other goals deserve to be annihilated![92]

4 [76][93]

To have *understood* a philos⟨opher⟩ and to be *convinced* by him.

Today I turn everything into gold, give me what you will — destiny!

Don't let yourselves be deceived! The most active peoples are now the most fatigued! They no longer have the strength to be lazy!

The *only* happiness lies in creating: you all should *join me in creating* and in every action you will have *this* happiness!

You should preserve chaos within you: those who are yet to come want *to form* themselves from it!

Redemption from the eternal flux.

4 [77][94]

We often perform our actions as an opiate against the past.

To do our favorite thing without describing it in lofty phrases — can be heroism. To be ashamed of sublime gestures.

"I follow" — not "I will this."

"I couldn't *spare* anything when I created superhumans. All of your evils and falsehoods, your lies and your ignorance — everything is in their semen."

(Contra strict vegetarianism) Do we really want to create lamb-souls and visionary virgins? Lions are what we want and monsters of force and love.

Let humans be the impetus for something that is no longer human.

Not to become unworldly — but rather to overpower the world and ourselves within it.

I want to turn *procreation* and *death* into a festival.

4 [78][95]
We must be as good at being cruel as we are at being compassionate: let us guard against becoming smaller than nature!

I teach not only compassion but also cruelty: however, I also teach that intellect is part of both, and a goal.

We must prepare the earth for the superhumans and animals and plants
I inoculate you with the madness

Your excess love is there for the puny people.

You see her on stage, but you must see her in life and not in any way slight her.

Your best things amount to nothing without a performance.

Moral people feel smug about their pangs of conscience.

4 [79]
You are waging war? You fear one of your neighbors? So remove the border markers — then you will have no more neighbors.[96]

4 [80]
To begin with funeral rites.

I *fore*see something terrible. Imminent chaos, everything in flux.

1. Nothing that has value in itself — nothing that commands "thou shalt."

2. It is intolerable — we must counter the spectacle of this annihilation by *creating*.

3. We must counter these shifting goals with a single goal — create it.

4. As material we have everything that has been incorporated, in this we are not free. *To grasp* this material, *to comprehend* it (through science).

5. To create *superhumans* after we have thought about all of nature in relation to ourselves, *made* it conceivable.[97]

6. We can only love something that is wholly related to us: we have the most love for a being we have conceived. When it comes to a work and a child, love doesn't need to be commanded. Advantage of superhumans.

4 [81]

I do not want life *again*. How have I endured it? Creating. What makes me endure the sight of it? a glance at the superhumans who *affirm* life. I have tried to affirm it *myself* — Alas!

4 [82][98]

Thinking of life should be the focus of recuperation: otherwise thinking only of responsibilities.

Mémoires:[99]

I grasped *primum vivere*,[100] and *everything* that has to do with *vivere*!

to know in order to *live* — *earlier*: in order to deny life.

4 [83]

The dissolution of morality has as its practical consequence the atomistic individual and eventually the fragmentation of the individual into pluralities — absolute flux.

This is why, now more than ever, one goal is needed and love, a *new love*.[101]

4 [84][102]

There is a danger of turning back into *animality*. We create a posthumous justice for all of the dead and give their lives a meaning when we shape superhumans out of *this* material and give all of the past a *goal*.

If I did not love humans, how could I stand Zarathustra?

Honor actors for my sake and seek the best ones offstage!

Whip.

4 [85]

When Zarathustra had said this, a mom[103] waved to him and spoke: "Now I gladly want to die, for my mouth has nothing more to teach Zarathustra."

Do not fear the flux of things: this flux turns back into itself: it flees itself not just twice.[104]

All "it was" becomes an "it is" again. The past bites all that is future in the tail.

Where "should" is no longer felt, —

Emergence of *love* — *love as consequence of morality.*

4 [86]

I still have all these wild dogs at ⟨my place⟩, but in my cellar. I do not want to ever hear them bark.[105]

Then a mom waved to him and said: Now I die in peace I have experienced Zarathustra.

4 [87]

No one comes to see me. And I myself — I went to see every-one and *found no one*.[106]

4 [88][107]

On the penultimate day Zarathustra sent home the disci-ples who had accompanied him and spoke thus to them:

The location Zarathustra laughed at, *must* [— —]

Everything has 2 faces: one of passing away, one of becoming.

The more there is to the individual, the more the herd to which it belongs will advance.

The *bon goût*[108] of knowledge reaches up to the highest level of morality.

If you had any idea of the *agony* of responsibility that *superior humans feel*!

4 [89]

On the Morality of Superior Humans.

Everything that is otherwise moral has become love here.[109]

Yet now a new "thou shalt" begins — the knowledge of the free spirit — the inquiry into the supreme *goals.*

4 [90][110]

Just as we no longer need morality, so — we no longer need religion either. The "I love God" — the single ancient form of the religious — is converted into the love of *an ideal* — has become creative — nothing but God-humans.

Morality is needed: by what standards are we to act, since we still must act? And we must *evaluate* what we have done — by what standards?

Finding errors in its genesis is no argument against morality. Morality is a condition of life. "Thou shalt"

On the sanctification of the passions.

He obeys as much as he can.

I have lived on the narrowest stoop of life.
Suffering such as mine is the suffering of someone who is *buried*.

Every *superior* act is a many-sided violation of *ethical law*.

To teach *utility* and reason?[111] We are not nearly reasonable enough for that.

4 [91][112]
To acknowledge the value of *all passions* one by one, but *to sanctify* them.

I wanted to know, now I am struck by my fate (vivisection) and my pain at the silent stare of the dog.

The ones who create should be treated humanely, they are lacking in loving thy neighbor.[113]

Someone profound.[114] — You forgive today what was done to you. But you have not yet experienced it at all: after half a year you will never again forgive and forget it.

4 [92][115]
No sooner does the intellect collide with morality than all hell breaks loose.

H⟨umans⟩ began by taking morality for themselves, we, too, can *give* ourselves a morality!

"What is most difficult?"

I did all this, spoke Zarathustra, and today I offer it cheaply — for a girl's smile.

And have you nothing more to say to human beings?

No, said Zarathustra, the cup is empty. And when he ha⟨d⟩ said this, he went on his way and alone. Yet his disciples wept.[116]

Beware of hurting a hermit. A hermit is like a deep well: it is easy to toss a stone into it, but how do you propose to retrieve it? A hermit never forgives.[117]

sticking yet another arrow of contempt into his quiver.

plucking

4 [93][118]

Don't reveal yourself! And if you must, then in rage but not in shame!

Do I have to tell you how to defend yourselves against burglars and cutthroats? I speak to those who are tired of their virtues and enjoy being robbed and maligned just once so that they can make a festival out of their virtue. —

4 [94][119]

Do not forget this about me! I told h⟨umans⟩ to create superhumans, I taught noon and eternity and redemption from flux, and my doctrine is: the For All is older and was called good sooner than the "for me"; the "for me" must still be sanctified by you.

You should not kill your senses but rather sanctify them — make them innocent.

Then all the people said: we must destroy the destroyer of morality —

If we want to become perfect as human beings, we must also become perfect as animals.

You will always have only as much morality as your strength allows.

Superhumans, solitary wanderers, timid ones — — —

4 [95]

a disciple — this is neither a child nor a creative work," here Zarathustra was silent and, transformed, stared intensely into space. His disciples approached him anyway and as⟨ked⟩ him: "do you have nothing more to share with us — that we can take home with us?"

Zarathustra went onwards until he came to his cave and mountains: there he also found his eagle and his serpent. Yet when ⟨he⟩ had greeted the cave and the animals, all at once he became very old.

At the time it was said among the people: the worst thing is not falling into Zarathustra's hands but dreaming of him at night.[120]

He reflected for a long time and said no word while his animals waited before him and the morning strolled through the mountains. Suddenly his eyes took on a different look. It was around the hour of noon as he groped about and said: — — —

4 [96][121]

Injustice should be taken on by someone who ⟨is⟩ c⟨apable⟩ of it.

Dangers of the solitary person.

Pine

I did all that and I will bear it — Smile of a *child*

4 [97]

Here wafts the spirit of a hero — pass by quietly. He suffered too much; for that very reason he is still determined to inflict suffering.

4 [98]

May he himself have mercy on his soul.

4 [99]

I demand of you every act of self-sacrifice, of goodness, of sacred selfishness, and you should say in response to all that: "think nothing of it! It suits my taste and no one else's!" And I demand in addition that you pursue knowledge because I know it goes against your taste, so that you say: "we probably have to be this way," but this compulsion of ours should not be a law nor become a shadow and an irritation to others.

4 [100]

My brothers, I know of no greater consolation for a woman than to tell her: "you, too, can give birth to superhumans."[122]

What do you have in common with wolves and cats? who just keep taking and don't give and who prefer to steal rather than take?

You are the ones who keep giving gifts.[123]

4 [101]

All of your weaknesses and vices are still following you within your knowing! A book is difficult to read: but anyone who has eyes to see — — —

4 [102]

It is your fate to be mistreated: no one fears your revenge. At least you will not be completely eclipsed in time.[124]

4 [103]

Compassion in regard to superhumans (Disciples — Chap⟨ter⟩).

(Chap⟨ter⟩) if I could see superhumans! they do not see me, they see their vision.

(Chap⟨ter⟩) The *good* — no God gave it to you, and none will lead you into a better beyond; this cannot be proven; and is idle error. Therefore only: "I will this!"

To describe the love for a contemporary (for a genius) — what torment! but when we place the genius at a distance and then see the distorted image! **(Chap⟨ter⟩)**

4 [104]¹²⁵

You say you believe in Zarathustra. But what does Zarathustra care? You are my brothers: I do not love you that much: a brother, this is neither a child nor a creative work.

I love freethinkers when their hearts are free as well. To me the head is like the entrails of the heart. Whatever a heart accepts, this must be digested by the head and turned into thoughts.¹²⁶

Still better for you to rage than to shame!

And when you are cursed, I don't like it that you then want to bless: it is better to join in the cursing for a bit. May the devil take me!¹²⁷

I recommend that all martyrs consider whether the obsession with revenge has driven them to extremes.

4 [105]

your poets books actors are supposed to anesthetize you against your *lack of visions* — they impoverish you even more! They are not *my* visions! And poets are supposed to lie!

I want to have nothing to do with art — except for that which brings joy! Out of pleasure and super-pleasure! The lie in art is the evil that comes from arrogance!

I don't want to hear your *screaming*! Yes, now you are "true"! Overthrow!

4 [106]

This is a counterargument, and I am grateful to you. But now, friend, refute the counterargument for me!

I am delighted to see you, spoke Zarathustra, and yet you are ⟨not⟩ what delights me, rather for me you are a — — —

This is the hour of summer, an hour and no more. To me you are a mountain range: solid as ice, many storms and clouds. . .

4 [107]

I do not want to be hating and loving with them: I cannot bear their cries and their happiness.

4 [108]

N.B. **To be accomplished with supreme passion:** lovers (deceived) are *foolish* and they are *not* able *to communicate* their love.

Those who know are without love and uncommunicative.

Actors are without love and foolish.

4 [109]

they do not understand me — but it is eerie that they run to my favorite spot.

to turn to the courts is already a sign of contempt.

4 [110][128]

We are proud to worship when we cannot be idols.

when a w⟨oman⟩ goes into heat and she pictures m⟨en⟩ —
Look at that pale woman; I would rather fall into her hands,
although she has murderous hands, than into her dreams.[129]

Whom does Zarathustra *first* encounter? He is happy to
tolerate them again.

(Chap⟨ter⟩) I went into solitude because I wanted to love *the*
human being, but I could only ever hate them. Finally, I came
to love the superhuman being — since then I have *tolerated*
humans. I want to bring them a new hope! And a new fear —
said Zarathustra.

4 [111]
There was a time when I was overcome with *disgust at myself*: summer 1876. The danger of insanity, a scholar's bad conscience about the interference of metaphysics, the feeling of
exaggeration, the ridiculousness of "sitting in judgment" —
therefore to restore reason, and, with the greatest austerity, *to
try* to live without metaphysical assumptions. "Freethinking"[130]
— above and beyond *myself*!

4 [112][131]
when I was young
Today I will gladly give all of this up — in return for the
smile of a child. You must overcome your youth, too, if you
want to be a child again.

Am I truly the one you honor? And if I am — be careful
that a falling pillar does not kill you.

4 [113]
Now murderers appear to be *sick*: this shows how much
moral *judgments* have been *incorporated*.[132]

to collect captivating things.

4 [114]
   Hard-heartedness is a *virtue* in compassionate people.[133]

4 [115]
   Blood is a bad witness for a truth: blood poisons a doctrine
so that it becomes hatred.[134]

4 [116][135]
   When I was young, I was inclined to inflict pain on myself:
people called it my inclination to the sublime.

   To nurture ourselves with the grass and acorns of knowledge.

   Humans should be the midpoint between plants and ghosts.

   I love all these heavy drops, how they fall one by one from
the dark cloud that conceals lightning within itself: the name
for this lightning is the superhumans.

4 [117][136]
   The child within us should overpower even the lion within
us — spoke Zarathustra.

   I do not give alms — I am not poor enough for that — says
Zarathustra.

   I am a support and a balustrade along a mighty river —
grab onto me whoever can! I am not a crutch

   to humiliate ourselves and to injure our arrogance: to con-
fess our folly in order to mock our wisdom.

   I forbid you to *believe* in these metaphysical things: here
mistrust is appropriate and insight into *where* the valuation of
these questions came from in earlier times. *Our mode of
thought must be thoroughly human!*

4 [118][137]
> *Moldenhauer*[138]
> *Mainländer*[139]

4 [119]

but since you want to listen to me, then take from what is mine everything that belongs to you.

4 [120]

The hermit gritting his teeth — he opened his mouth reluctantly.[140]

How is it possible to communicate? How is it possible to be heard? When shall I emerge from my cave into the open? I am the most hidden of all hidden ones.

4 [121]

Look away! Lift yourselves into a higher light! No **compassionate person** loves superhumans!

4 [122]

> Here I sat waiting —
> Beyond good and evil, enjoying the light
> Then enjoying the shadows: nothing but play
> Entirely ocean, entirely noon, entirely time without goal.[141]

4 [123]

Alas for our goodness! — we honor our ancestors.

4 [124]

Your themes always resound with something like despair.
H⟨einrich⟩ K⟨öselitz⟩

4 [125]

Chap⟨ter⟩: on the rejection of martyrdom.

4 [126]

A human a group of atoms completely dependent in all its movements on all distributions and alterations of force in the universe — and on the other hand, like every atom, unpredictable, a something in-and-for-itself.[142]

We become conscious of ourselves only as a heap of *affects*: and even sense perceptions and thoughts belong among these revelations of the affects.

4 [127]

The most tragic of all stories with a heavenly resolution.

Zarathustra growing progressively greater — his teaching progressively unfolding along with this increasing greatness.

The "return" shining above the last catastrophe like a setting sun.

4 [128][143]

helpless, lacking the intellect to help free themselves from their *sins* — their condition remains "fixed"

When we suffer a lot, we become humble enough to be vain.

"I do not know of any reason against it" — but this "I do not know" is unfortunately not a reason for it! There is so much I do not know —

4 [129][144]

When we praise, we always praise ourselves: when we blame, we always blame others.

I am lying down below, shrouded in heavy melancholy — my life hangs on small coincidences.

(Chap⟨ter⟩) Keep your souls fresh *cool* (against compassion)

Compassion, when strong, is a hellish feeling.

Murder, out of supreme love for humans.

4 [130]
How well you heal, savior.[145] These were her words. For the woman loved Zarathustra.

4 [131]
We are not writing poetry here: we are doing calculations. But we first had to write poetry in order to be able to calculate.

I no longer experience anything: I am sublime, even beyond experience.

You cold-hearted and levelheaded people, you do not know the delights of cold-heartedness!

I remove your chains: die! — and the woman was seen smiling as she died.

When Zarathustra had heard the woman's words, he covered his head and braced himself.

Isn't this compassion a kind of hell? Isn't this fervor a kind of flame?

the judges said in unison: this man suffers from madness: let him go wherever he wishes: and don't let him stay. Then Zarathustra decided on his own to return home to his cave and to his animals.

4 [132]
having taught "recurrence" — "I *forgot* misery." His compassion increases. He sees that the doctrine is unbearable.

Climax: the holy murder. He invents the doctrine of superhumans.

Return home: sojourn at the hermit's "why do you not teach hard-heartedness? And hatred of what is puny?"

Zarathustra: *you* teach that! I *am* no longer that person! I was that way when I first arrived among humans. I have grown too *poor* for that, — I gave away everything, even my hard-heartedness. — Hermits think this way: I swear to you with quivering lips and with the lines that agony has chiseled on my brow, with the smiles of the dying — he weeps. (May God live in this way) God is dead: and it is time for superhumans to live.

4 [133]
To elevate to reform the concept of justice — or to prove that human actions are necessarily unjust.

it is possible to take a position outside a *particular* valuation, but not outside *all* valuations.

to evaluate morality — *by what standard?*

4 [134]
It is certainly possible to tolerate ourselves: but what about our neighbors? they suffer too much.

I didn't know how poor they are — I didn't know that it is more beautiful to take than to give. —

Isn't compassion God's hell? And perhaps he died of this fervor?

4 [135][146]
With blood feuds: basic feeling like all those who represent the state: respect for the profound suffering of a kin-group and concession to this feeling.

if we combine what is harmful with horror or disgust, then the feeling evil, bad, emerges.

There are always people who love serving in dangerous posts: and without examining here the motives for this love or just praising them any further — the free spirit — —

4 [136]¹⁴⁷

With morality above us, life *cannot to be endured at all* — if we are not Pharisees and are able to see freely — that is why I destroyed morality.

A pile of emotions, a *primum mobile*,¹⁴⁸ but retarded in its movement and crushed by everything that moves.

in order to affirm *myself,* I destroyed morality: I showed that there are *creators* and *tyrants* everywhere *at the same time*. But this *simultaneity* is not needed, because the herd — — —

4 [137]

All *goals* are destroyed. Humans must *give* themselves one. It was an error that they *had* one: they have given themselves all of them. But the *presuppositions* for all earlier goals are destroyed.

Science shows the flux, but not the goal: yet it does provide *presuppositions* to which the new goal must correspond.

4 [138]¹⁴⁹

Every human being is a creative cause of occurrences, a *primum mobile* with an original movement.

4 [139]

When God understood himself, he created himself and his opposite.¹⁵⁰

You have indeed made the journey from worm to human! and much within you is still worm and a mcmory of your journey.

4 [140]

Icepacks. — My disgust with people had grown too great. Likewise my counter-disgust with the moral arrogance of my idealism. I was becoming like the people I despised, I searched within myself for everything that I despised: I wanted to dampen my ardor. I took up the cause *against* all the *accusers* of humankind — I wrested from them and *from myself* the right to *exalted* words.

The drive to criticize wanted *life* —

Heroism of living on *as little as possible*: the desert.

Heroism of debasing our own intellectual drive, to think it through as affect.

I discredited the affects in order to say *afterwards*: I *had* an affect, nothing more!

Life *under* morality not to be endured at all. (Significance of Wagner *early on*)

4 [141]

W⟨agner⟩, who will endure as a h⟨uman being⟩ who took tasteless arrogance to the furthest extreme.

4 [142][151]

I deny moral drives, but *all* affects and drives are *colored* by our *value judgments*; completely *different* judgments are competing within us. *Result*: to *comprehend* the multiplicity of moralities.

a constant *praising* and *blaming*.

our affects speaking morally

our general feelings speaking morally

our intellectual pleasures ⟨speaking morally⟩

our illnesses show up as moralistic phenomenon

everything in people is a crime, which we like or dislike

all utility

landscape

bed

a kind of *illness moralis*[152]

other moral affects foregrounded on bad days

4 [143]¹⁵³

Everything we don't feel *in that way* makes little difference to us. We constantly forget it.

The praise and blame of our affects, in other words *valuation*, is what I call "morality."

Explaining the sounds is not enough to explain music — let alone *to refute* it.

There are ages in which there is appalling indifference to human life. The opposite of this is the *blood feud*.

Unburdening ourselves: this is the only way we are able to endure ourselves — and then we go *mad* with compassion.

4 [144]¹⁵⁴

With shoulders squared it stands braced against the void: and where there is space, there is being.

4 [145]

Entirely ocean, entirely noon, entirely time without goal¹⁵⁵
A child, a toy
And suddenly one becomes two
And Zarathustra walked past me.

4 [146]

as judge and executioner I bring about my own *downfall*.

4 [147]

"Good for something," "bad for something": *originally* all moral judgments are judgments about *means to ends*.¹⁵⁶ But gradually the ends have been forgotten, and "good" "bad" remained — as if there *could* be something good in itself. Praise and blame have always been given *with an end in mind*: but eventually the end was denied in order *to be able to praise and blame* **fully completely**, namely when feelings like respect love or disgust were immediately perceived in these *means.*

And so it is *affect* that created "good in itself" and "evil in itself."

However things might stand now with these incorporated "moral feelings" — it is apparent from the *history* of moral feelings that *no codes of goodness,*[157] no *final end* remains standing — everything is refuted. We have a monstrous force of moral feelings within us, but *no end* for anyone. They stand in contradiction with each other — they **derive** from *different* codes of goodness, — — —

There is a monstrous moral force, but there is *no* longer *a goal* toward which all this force could be expended.

4 [148][158]

What can all people do? Praise and blame. This is the madness of humans, the mad animals.

I say that the fuzz goes with the peach,[159] I say that lies go with life.

We commit many injustices — and not only when we *inflict pain* but also through our praise charity compassion — we *do not retaliate* when it *would be necessary*!

4 [149]

There is only one rationality. And is there only one sensibility?[160] A perfectly human interpretation of the world's process *must* simultaneously — or: a comforting interpretation of the world's direction has been possible for each phase of human emotion.

4 [150]

It is terrible to see how unjust things are. But at least there is consolation in knowing that we are the creators of justice and that we *suffer on account of ourselves.*

4 [151]
Morality — the epitome of all of our incorporated value judgments: what is to become of this monstrous accumulation of force? This is the only thing that interests me about the question of how these valuations emerged.

4 [152][161]
What do you know of the love that a lunatic has for reason?

4 [153]
(Chap⟨ter⟩) speech to those who are *most intellectual*.[162]
(Chap⟨ter⟩) *the veiled life.*

4 [154]
They have never experienced a moment that said to them, "we are pitiful"

this ancient God-made-human could not laugh.

A Hebrew named Jesus was the best at loving until now.

4 [155][163]
I didn't repudiate this p⟨erson⟩ that I had always admired: but rather, the reasons why I had always admired this person.

4 [156]
Conclusion of the section. And I chose for myself even this *suffering* on the basis of *truthfulness*.

4 [157]
You have seen their ideals — now shatter them yourself and be hard-hearted! Compassion.

4 [158]
Form: this p⟨erson⟩ landed on top of a box that has no floor and no walls.

4 [159]

What! You want to *immortalize* these miserable people? To chain them together? Just let them perish! Socialists what do we care about the rich and the poor!

4 [160][164]

When this *timelessness*[165] gazes into the world, everything crooked becomes straight[166]

If you see blue, what good does it do you to convince yourself and say: it is gray!

to despise

4 [161]

It is difficult to say something false about women: with women nothing is impossible — answered Zarathustra.[167]

4 [162]

The last humans — they wheeze and enjoy their happiness.

4 [163]

Humans are determined to stay put as super-apes, images of the last humans who are the eternal ones.

4 [164][168]

There are enough of these people: they know nothing better on earth than to lie with a woman.

4 [165][169]

H⟨umans⟩ are something that must be overcome: what have you done to make this happen? What do I care about your good evil h⟨umans⟩?

4 [166]

What use is it to free the mind if it then has no wings to fly away?

4 [167]

Last conversation with the hermit.

— I praise you for not becoming my student.

Hermit: I have too much contempt for humans, I love them too much — I cannot stand them — for both, I have to *dissimulate* too much.

I bring them a new love and a new contempt — superhumans and last humans.

I do not understand you — they will not accept what you bring them. Let them first beg for alms!

Zarathustra: — — —

But they need only alms, they are not rich enough to be able to need your treasures.

I write songs and sing them, I laugh and weep[170] when I make my songs.

I have nothing more to teach this man.

4 [168][171]

Some want to throw dice and others want to calculate and count and still others are always wanting to see waves and dances of waves — they call it science and sweat while they do it.

But they are children who want to have their game. And truly, it is beautiful infantile nonsense, and some laughter would not hurt the game

4 [169][172]

Purpose of *asceticism*: to become as thirsty as possible, the creative flow must be blocked.

4 [170]

There are many things to figure out about the world: but to figure out the world — this is tedious.

4 [171][173]

The antithesis of *superhumans* is *last humans*: I created one[174] at the same time as the other.

Everything superhuman appears in humans as illness and madness.

We must already be an ocean in order to absorb a filthy stream without getting filthy.

4 [172][175]

When I considered *purpose* I also considered chance.

It has to be possible to explain the world through purposes and to explain the world through chance: through thought as much as will, through movement as much as tranquility: through God as much as the Devil. For, all of this *is* the I.

These perspectives from which we see things are not *our own*; they are the perspectives of a being of the same kind as us, a *greater being*: *whose images we gaze into.*

4 [173]

In order to learn this, I decided to hate those I loved, to blame what I had been praising up to now and to see what in the first place was good about evil and what was evil about good. I called this justice.

I finally discovered what was most difficult: not to love and not to hate, not to praise and not to bla⟨me⟩ and to say: there is no good and there is no evil.

When I had discovered this, I went into the desert.

4 [174][176]

The world stands there finished, a golden bowl[177] of goodness — yet the creative mind wants to continue creating what has already been created— the mind invented time, and now, spinning, the world breaks apart and then, turning in great rings, spins back together again — as the becoming of good by means of evil.

4 [175][178]

You are too crude for me: it is impossible for minor experiences to be your downfall.

4 [176][179]

"And indeed everything speaks quite differently to me than to you."

At the point where your honesty stops looking, your eye no longer sees.[180]

4 [177]

History = *evolution of purposes in time*: such that ever higher forms grow out of lower ones. To be explained, why ever *higher forms of life* have to emerge. The teleologists and Darwinists are *in agreement* that this happens. But the whole thing is a **hypothesis** based on *value judgments* — and indeed, comparatively recent value judgments. The reverse, that everything until us is *decline*, is equally demonstrable. The human and especially the wisest human as *nature's greatest blunder* and self-contradiction (the being that suffers the most): nature has *been descending* until now. The organic as degeneration.

4 [178]

In my eyrie and forest. Zarathustra 4.

4 [179]

Determining value, this means the same thing as determining *disvalue*. In order to have the happiness of value judgments, we must also bring along all *evil* and all the displeasure of contempt.

This person says: the whole world is thought — will — war — love — hate: my b⟨rothers⟩ I say to you: all these taken singly are false, all these taken together are *true*.

4 [180]

Humankind must set its goal beyond itself — but not in a false X-world, rather in its own *continuation*.

The question: how something *becomes* is only meaningful for me because of the question of what it *should* become.

4 [181]¹⁸¹

What apes are to us, objects of painful *embarrassment* — so shall *we* be to superhumans.

4 [182]¹⁸²

How would someone have to speak to you so that you would understand! It would have to make you *sick*!

4 [183]¹⁸³

As soon as the will takes the stage, feeling experiences a sense of *liberation*. This is called freedom of the will. For feeling is *imprinted through suffering* — and as soon as the will takes the stage, feeling *is suspended* and does not suffer

4 [184]¹⁸⁴

No sooner are you born than you have already begun to die.

4 [185]

Compassion and love *opposite* of morality. No justice involved! No obedience, no duty! No love of truth and no honesty! In addition, abandoning our own way — the **character of** *passion* — and its *irrationality*.

4 [186]¹⁸⁵

Did I not invent a new smell and a new color? — Thus spoke Zarathustra.

The ocean carried you: — — —

Who among you has the most extensive soul
putting tightrope walkers on the lowest level.[186]

4 [187]
And no matter where I climb, my dog follows me everywhere, the dog called "I."

4 [188]
No I prior to the herd. Opposite of this: within *superhumans*,
over millennia, the You of many I's has become one. (thus the
individuals have now become one[187]

4 [189]
The *I* also contains a *number of* entities (as in the herd) no
contradiction. Likewise a plurality of *forces*. Occasionally
pausing — invisible, like an electric current.
   Striving toward *compaction*, it is at its strongest like a diamond, at its most creative? Really? As a people even more so?

4 [190]
They go to the charcoal burners[188] and speak to them of
eternal torment.

4 [191][189]
Conversation with a King (Chap⟨ter⟩).

4 [192]
The history of *great moments* — this includes even teaching
in front of charcoal burners.

4 [193][190]
And if you are not able to squash what is small, if you do
not want to be a shoo-fly:[191] then go into ⟨solitude⟩.

4 [194]

our eye sees things falsely, it contracts things and merges them together: is this a reason for rejecting sight and saying: it is worthless?

4 [195]

But do you believe that Zarathustra found what he was seeking? Do you believe that a blind man walks a straight path? — And so it came to pass that this time Zarathustra did not perish.

4 [196][192]

Illness is a clumsy experiment for the sake of good health. Cut this experiment short!

4 [197]

the feeling of power, the competitive urge of all I's to find the thought that will stay fixed above humankind as its star — the I a *primum mobile*.

4 [198]

Goal: for a moment, to *reach* superhumans. **For this** I will suffer *everything*! That triad!

The most peaceful external life because so much is *happening*!

4 [199][193]

Is it not a matter of indifference that as many p⟨eople⟩ as possible live as long as possible?

Isn't the happiness of these many a despicable thing and no justification for existence?

Let the meaning of your life be to justify existence — and for this you will not only have to become the devil's advocate but also even God's intercessor before the devil.

4 [200][194]

He loved humans because God loves them. He wanted to redeem them in order to redeem God.

Love for humans was the cross to which he was nailed; he wanted to deliver God from his hell: which is the love of God for humans.

4 [201]

For people are hard of hearing: and anyone who is clever beats their ears to such a pulp that they begin to hear with their eyes.

they quit laughing instead they stared at Zarathustra.

and surface everywhere, — — —

4 [202][195]

Speech to the cliff — I love that it does not speak. Its silence is *dignified* (Everything is moral)

4 [203]

The I knows nothing of itself in plants: it splits itself when procreating; in many it is one (herd) it is extinguished here — what's the significance? The coincidence[196] of the *I* (in different entities) irrelevant.

4 [204]
(*the veiled life*)
a pale youth
you will never discover many of them
Pine

(the last human being: a kind of Chinese)

As often as his spirit moved him, Zarathustra went up a mountain and on the way wrote down his sayings. And once, when he was alone with himself, he glorified himself and spoke[197]

You should be like trees that hang over the ocean and bend from — — —

He walks alone; for his figures surround him, figures that he alone sees. And should he meet his equal, then their minds embrace and with 4 eyes they see the very same figures.

whatever is just lies in my attempts to create justice for everything abhorrent to me

a *tree*: to shake loose the leaves and to give them small movements and to give the roots and branches the same etc.

The hermit looked at him for a long time — — —
Zarathustra, said the hermit, you have grown poor — and if I wanted alms from you, would you really give them to me?

4 [205]

All morality has to do with **inventing** or **seeking** *higher corporeal states* where it is possible to bring together previously *separated* abilities.

4 [206]

Pay no attention to what is good and evil — follow the path to your good and create your evil and good. There are still 1000 paths not yet taken!

4 [207]

Many minds[198] are housed within humans like creatures of the sea — they battle one another for the mind "I": they love it, they want it to climb on their backs, they hate one another on account of this love.

— the I, the frisky kitten with a silver sense of animal joy.

When has a drowning man ever suffered from thirst!

and again the kitten I squeals and again someone is happy
and again all the others are envious.

A lovely consolation for those young enough for it, said a
little old lady.[199]

Was I born to be a preacher of repentance? Was I born to
rattle on like a priest and a drum?[200]

4 [208][201]
I teach you about the superhumans:[202] the great contempt
you'll have to teach yourselves.

4 [209][203]
(Chap⟨ter⟩) The *Brotherhood of Justifiers.*

4 [210][204]
In good and evil they lack the shame of the spirit: and
praise and blame as if
    and in their spirit they lack the shame of good and evil:
They overturn icons and say: there is nothing exalted and
worthy of worship — because they themselves can create neither icon nor god.
    Just listen to the contempt of their rage against icons — the
great contempt for themselves!

I love souls that squander: they do not give back and do not
want thanks because they are always giving gifts.[205]

there they go forth on their own

4 [211][206]
I am explaining even your virtues by what is to come.
It's not your virtues I'm rejecting, it's the virtuous among you.

The friend as the best despiser and enemy.

How few are worthy!

To be a friend's *conscience*. To note every humiliation. To understand conscience not only in a moral sense: also taste, also to stay within one's limitations.

Friends as demons and angels. They hold the key for each others' chains. In their presence a chain falls away. They *elevate* each other. And as an I composed of the two, they approach superhumans and rejoice at possessing friends, because each provides for the other a second wing, without which the first would be useless.

4 [212]²⁰⁷

It is cool, the meadow lies in shadow, the sun has departed.

Is it not absurd to live? Wouldn't we have to have more reason in order to make something reasonable out of life?

My brothers, forgive the soul of Zarathustra for the fact that it is evening.

4 [213]²⁰⁸

The invention of *conditions*

It is high time that humans set themselves a goal. They are still rich and wild enough for the most exalted goal. I say to you: you still have the chaos and world-collisions within you that are needed to give birth to a dance of the stars.

But someday humans will become too poor, someday they will no longer have enough momentum and drive even for the fury of contempt.

4 [214]²⁰⁹

Our contempt for h⟨umans⟩ drove us beyond the stars. Religion, metaphysics, as symptom of a desire to create superhumans.

4 [215]²¹⁰

Humankind is walking around pregnant, how quaint the pregnant are!

4 [216]

(Chap⟨ter⟩) Prove yourself to me! Which duty is yours?

4 [217]

1. The *emphasis* on **states** and the striving for them. Significance for the body.

2. This particular *attitude of the I toward itself* emerges, in which the *herd-type* remains preserved.

3. Nausea and evil.

The outbreak of entire reform movements as correctives of the *body*.

What does asceticism mean?

Buddhism and monasticism as the production of *healthy bodies* (countering the destructive and debilitating affects).

Morality as a language of metaphors about an unknown region of *corporeal states*. — Here the talk ⟨is⟩ still entirely of will and purpose and *of nothing else at all*.

1. The adaptation of corporeal desires to each other.

2. The *adaptation* of the *body* to a *climate* brings about the manifestation of moralities.

3. The body of the *ruling* caste brings about a morality.

4. The body for the necessary labor and diversity of labor.

5. The preservation of the type brings forth a morality. That which is the perishing of the type and immorality.

thus altering the body *apparently* without *chemical* means — — in truth, morality is ⟨about⟩ changing the *chemical composition* of the body.

Monstrous *detour*. In what way might it be possible to proceed more directly?

"Concept of health and ideal of health *dependent* on the goal of human beings" — ? but the *goal* itself is an expression of a particular *composition* of the body and its *conditions*.

The body and morality.

4 [218]

And he did not know how to overcome his virtue.

The lion within him tore apart the child within him: and finally the lion devoured itself.

This hero was cruel and wild — — —

Behold, I teach you the love for superhumans.

— — — he took it upon himself and shattered under the burden.

4 [219]

Passions = states of our organs and their aftereffect on the brain — along with *seeking release*.

4 [220]

He was called a sage, but he was nothing of the kind.

4 [221]

In earlier times, the position of religion in relation to nature was reversed: religion reflected the *popular understanding* of nature.

Now the *popular* understanding is the materialistic one. Therefore whatever there is of religion must now speak *the same way* to the people: materialistically.

4 [222]

squarely built, with a strong neck
using the lion to kill the lion tamer

4 [223][211]

You should not want to have many virtues — you are not rich enough for that. One virtue is already a lot of virtue: in order for it to live, you must already be perishing.

4 [224]²¹²
   I live so that I know: I want to know so that superhumans may live.

   We experiment for them!

4 [225]
   The thoroughly *creative character* of everything that happens — — —

   The freedom of the will is much more convincingly demonstrated than cause and effect (in truth cause effect is only a *popular conclusion*)

4 [226]
   We are too tolerant of bad air: and you yourself are bad air for other people.

   Three or 2.

   Whoever does not make us fertile²¹³

4 [227]
   A quest for whatever it is about the truth that hurts *me*, and sacrificing everything, a monstrous tension
   nothing in my head but a personal morality: and to establish my right to it is the meaning of all my historical questions about morality. (For it is terribly difficult to establish this *right* for ourselves!)

4 [228]²¹⁴
   I love humans who bring²¹⁵ about the downfall of their virtue.
   behold, I show you the bridge to the superhumans!
   ⟨I love those⟩ who squander their souls, who do not thank and never give back because they are always giving gifts.²¹⁶

4 [229][217]

Those who justify the people of the future and redeem the people of the past.

And those who are compassionate should create out of this their duty and doom, and those who are loyal should let loyalty become their duty and their doom — and you cannot have enough ingenuity[218] for your virtue.

Let your life be an experiment — let your failures and successes be proof: but take care that people know how you have experimented and what you have proven.

they said: let us make ourselves dead to the world, they sought their salvation beyond the stars — they have not heard a word about superhumans.
They maligned their health, — — —

There is so much about your good people that disgusts me, and truly not what is evil about them.[219]
I wish they had a madness that would mean their downfall, as the pale criminal's madness meant his,
I wish their madness were called compassion or loyalty or justice.
But they have their virtue in order to live a long time, — — —

back then there was doubt, the search for justice, compassion for friends — — —

4 [230][220]
And his scholar should be a *penitent of the mind.*

And his speech displeased everyone except for one person.

Interaction.

Scholars

A call to stand alone and to talk your way out of things!

4 [231]
The right to my own *values* — where did I get this? From the rights of all old values and from the limits of these values.

4 [232]
The point of marriage: a child that represents a type *superior* to the *parents*.

NB. they must despise you as you move above and beyond them — they do not understand what it is to be above ourselves.

You yearn for love — but, no, you must learn to endure contempt.

You set your hearts on money and you yourselves are losing your hearts. Railroad and *state are to the advantage of many and are their doom.*

For those who do **not** belong to the many.
You are losing your caution, your lynx eyes and your bear claws.

4 [233]
Value terminology is a banner planted where a *new blissfulness* was invented — a new *feeling*.

4 [234][221]
Sometimes I want from you: that you be profoundly clever and that you be profoundly proud: then your pride will always accompany your cleverness. You will walk the paths of foolishness: yet I call even upon your foolishness, that it may always take pride as its escort. But if you want to be foolish — — —

Do I recommend to you loving thy neighbor? I much prefer to recommend fearing thy neighbor and loving those far away.

I discovered a new land in humans
where the soul overflows

you show me a brush and a j(a)r full of paint and say: we have refuted the picture.

Society is decaying.

the dreaming future

You are fleeing yourselves: and always you move out of the frying pan of self-contempt into the fire[222] of loving thy neighbor.

Cats and wolves should also be my role models: they are more self-possessed.

(*Shoo*-flies) for the little *annoyances* of daily life.

4 [235]

A god who proves his existence poorly is as good as a god who does not prove his existence at all.

This is a god who proves his existence either not at all or poorly.

When 100 stand together, all of them lose their minds and acquire different ones.

Oh these impoverished friendships! Whatever they do for their friends, I promise to do for my enemies — and I do not want to have become poorer.

4 [236]

And just as a child uses his little foot to push a glass shard in front of him, so life propels us foolishly forward.

4 [237][223]

Yes, laden with heavy burdens, I hurried into my desert: but there I found for the first time my heaviest burden of all.

to be the smith and anvil of our own virtue, the judge and touchstone of our own worth.

There are many heavy burdens and when I was young I did a lot of searching for the heaviest one.

Yes, I fled into the desert — and there in the most isolated desert, I found for the first time my heaviest burden of all.

This heaviest burden — this became what was most precious to me, like a god I taught that my heaviest burden should be revered.

sighed deeply and spoke no more.

4 [238][224]

And when someone does you a great injustice, then see to it only that you also do that person a small injustice in return, it's humane that way.

4 [239]

And you believe that justice will already be limping along after you?

4 [240][225]

There is more reason in your body than in your reason. And even that which you call wisdom, — who knows why your body needs just this wisdom?

4 [241]

I realized that shepherds and breeders of herds created these codes: in this way they gave a foundation to the life and continuation of their herds.

4 [242]²²⁶

Yes, I bore all of this burden! I knelt down and loaded all of this burden upon myself, like a camel I bowed my head and hurried away into the desert.

Where are the truths that cause suffering? I exclaimed.

The first one was the dragon and he spoke: "The worth of all things is worthless," "Contradiction is at the heart of all values"

At that point I recognized the origin of good and evil: and that humankind lacks the goal.

To give myself the right to name things with new names and values, was the heaviest burden.

I envied all plants — I envied even all ghosts.

To shatter the tablets of values with *superior values*

my own tablets I set beside the others — how much courage and fear it took!

4 [243]

you are the despisers of the body

4 [244]

I looked into the eyes of these greatest ones and crawled into their souls. Alas!!! — Depiction of *geniuses* and *saints*. Concerning the question *whether* {they}²²⁷ have existed already! — If they did, then the earth knew nothing of it.

4 [245]²²⁸

The preachers of the slow death are venerated the most.

4 [246]

(Chap⟨ter⟩) What became Zarathustra's **heaviest burden**? *To disengage himself from the ancient morality.*

4 [247]

Chap⟨ter⟩. Do you want a *reward*? **What** you want as a reward is for me the measure of your *virtue.*

4 [248]

I gave a new color to ⟨the⟩ earth — I spread the veil of a new hope across the earth.

4 [249]²²⁹

Blood founds churches: what does blood have to do with truth! And if you want my approval, then prove it to me with reasons and not with blood.

4 [250]

(Chap⟨ter⟩) *Puny people.* Go forth into solitude, you cannot endure a *small shower of raindrops.*

4 [251]

and suddenly it opens its eyes, the eyes of a child and of a blossom. What happened? The hand of a creative one touched it. The sun of a creative one revealed the god that was concealed.

4 [252]

I brought those lost in flight back down to earth and to their huts: at the heights I taught them depth.

4 [253]²³⁰

Tell me, where have they gone, these dear sages? Do their eyes not grow heavy? — Here and there a few such sages are still around you: they preach good and evil in soft voices.

Blessed are these sleepy ones.

4 [254]

Have there already been superhumans? Value of our culture.

4 [255]

they spin on the edge of earthliness and their keen eyes grow blind in this twilight.

4 [256]

To invent a thousand new ways to live — no longer just for herds!

4 [257][231]

She is betraying lock, stock and barrel[232] — that's what's so vile! We must learn to ennoble what is vile.

4 [258]

yearning and questioning and only shedding tears etc. — *Against religious people.*

it is no longer *honest*. It *is not sufficient* for faith!

Therefore: **after this position**,[233] *renunciation*!

4 [259]

I want to hear your dominant thought and not only that you have escaped a kind of insanity.

Are you the sort of people who are allowed to escape from a kind of insanity? Or did you toss aside your last value when you threw away your servitude . . .

Free, from what? — why should this even matter to Zarathustra when you squint at the question: free *for what*?

I want to hear your dominant thought, so that it may exonerate you in my presence! — or I will have my thoughts strike your ears like scourges.

4 [260][234]

A sun, with the serpent of knowledge coiled in rings around it.

4 [261]

"that which is earthly" — you must learn to *perceive* it differently.

Lay aside the false measures of value that were taken from an unknown world

Humans stand tall — — per⟨haps⟩ *superior* beings will *suddenly* be achieved!

4 [262]

(Chap⟨ter⟩) The alleged love of God and "everything to our advantage"

4 [263]

The *good* it wants to preserve itself by means of the ancient

4 [264]

They dearly wish to *escape*: yet they cannot find any way to other stars, so they believe that there are subterranean ways — of a completely different kind and as it were secret ways. — *Rare* conditions were felt to be superterrestrial. Delight and convulsions combined.

To me your love is not abundant enough to be a love of the universe!

Our feelings — this is the *entire* human past up until you and me: the values that have been created.

Our more lofty feelings — we would have *to eradicate* them if we don't give them a new goal!

If it weren't for this dreary cloud in the sky, you wouldn't have dreary knowledge either!

4 [265]

My direction for *art*: don't continue writing poetry in the *margins*! the *future* of humanity instead! There must be many *pictures* out there that can model ways to *live*!

4 [266][235]

Against hinterworlders.

Your life an experiment and monument to your experiment.

Artists helped to ensure that life was not improved. In most cases artists themselves the victims of their works.

penitents of the mind[236]
the one who creates

4 [267]
Some *sacrifice* is involved in *giving up* this hinterworld. Manliness!
What is earthly is not enough for us — therefore what is heavenly — flawed conclusion.

Nature *denies* you this intrusion!

In the beginning a wrinkled tuber, and a noxious[237] root drenched with many poisons — *every* feeling.

4 [268]
someone who creates is someone who creates new values. But not the artist!

4 [269]
the gathering of individuals (festival)

4 [270]
Gods, I have a bow! What a bow — a good bow against gods themselves!

4 [271][238]
The *great test: are you ready* **to justify** *life*? *Or your own death?*
At the lowest level still enduring it.
Illness led many to take this *second* way.
Renunciation.

The great *halfway point.* — The decision about wanting to live or die.

4 [272]
State and church, and everything that is founded on lies, serve the preachers of death.

4 [273]
you think the solution to your riddle must be in the dark! But consider the destiny of a worm. The solution lies in your goal and in your hope: *it's your will!*

No God has ever *intervened*! But you have *subjugated* yourselves too much to convention, even to nature.

But the knowing one[239] sees how every love and sun has bowed down to ugly weeds.

4 [274]
Many an ostrich has buried its head in the thinnest layer of sand.

4 [275][240]
Whenever you stepped from a lower virtue up to a higher one — — —
I want to be the first to give you your dignity: you ought to be *penitents of the* mind!

Ruins should not be destroyed: grass and roses and tiny herbs and whatever residue of life decorates these ruins, all of this destroys even what is dead.

This I has been most convincingly demonstrated, this I that contradicts itself.
Truly the world is well concealed from h⟨umans⟩. The belly of existence[241] will never speak to h⟨umans⟩!

For what reason did I tell you this? In this way the *liar* has become the signpost of the superhumans.
Separation

4 [276]
The decision. There must be countless *sacrifices*. An experiment.

4 [277]
Even the sweetest woman tastes bitter.

4 [278]
If the good[242] of the many is our good, then we should not call it virtue when we do good for the many. *On loving thy neighbor.*

4 [279]
So punch your way out of this false stargazing nonsense!
The belly of existence will never speak to you.

4 [280][243]
3 Transform⟨ations⟩
Sleep and Virtue
1001 goal
the despisers of the body.
Hinterworld.
our own virtue.
On the Pale Criminal
the tree on the mountain
Reading and Writing.
Preachers of Death.
The New Idol.
Z⟨arathustra's⟩ Solitude 1.
Friend.
Soldiers.
Loving thy Neighbor.

Chastity.
Path of Those Who Create.
Women.
Viper's Bite.
Marriage.
Death.
on holy *selfishness*.

5 [1]¹
1. Will to live? I have always found only will to power in its place.²

2. The constant zeal for a cause, even the highest, our own, betrays a lack of spiritual refinement, as do all things that rest on unconditional faith: for the emblem of this is always — a cool gaze.

3. I consider all people harmful who are no longer capable of opposing that which they love: this is how they corrupt the best things and persons.

4. There are persons who would like to force everyone into a yes or no with respect to their entire character: Rousseau was one of them: the megalomania they suffer from originates in their insane mistrust of themselves.

5. We must overcome even the youth in ourselves in order to become children again.³

6. It is with our intentions that we rationalize our incomprehensible drives to ourselves: as, e.g., murderers do when they justify to their reason their actual compulsion to murder, namely, by deciding to commit a robbery or to take revenge.

7. The pleasure that all morality has conveyed up to now and still conveys — in other words the pleasure that morality has accumulated up to now — lies in the right it gives everyone to praise and blame, without extensive evaluation. And who could bear life without praising and blaming![4]

8. This is the crux for moral pessimists: if they were serious about wanting to help their brothers toward redemption, then they would have to decide to make their brothers' existence miserable, in other words ⟨to⟩ be their unhappiness; out of compassion they would have to — become evil!

If it were true that life does not deserve to be affirmed, then moral people would be *abusing* their neighbors precisely by using self-denial and helpfulness — for their most personal gain.

9. I want to know whether you are a *creative* or a *productive* person in any particular way: as a creative person you belong among free people, as a productive person you are their slave and their tool.

10. As much as possible and this as quickly as possible: this is what is demanded by the great intellectual and emotional malady that is sometimes called "the present," sometimes "education," in truth it is nothing but a symptom of consumption.[5]

11. Women and geniuses don't work. Up until now women have been humankind's greatest extravagance. In those moments where we *do* our best, we don't work. Work is only a means to these moments.

12. We are most unfair not toward that which displeases us, but rather toward that which does not concern us at all.[6]

13. No sooner do we take even one step beyond average human goodness than our actions arouse suspicion. For virtue rests "in the mean."[7]

14. You say "we like this" and think you are praising me. Oh you fools! How *much* I like it when you do this![8]

15. Of everything that has been written I love only what people write with their blood. This is why I love books.[9]

Affects are nothing to be ashamed of, they are too irrational for that.

16. The affects are a relief for those who are frequently burdened by their rationality; namely, as a kind of irrationality.

17. This century loves to ascribe to its most intellectual men a taste for immature, mentally deficient and modest little girls of the people, Faust's taste for Gretchen — this speaks against the taste of the century and of its most intellectual men.

18. As if that weren't bad enough! The time for marriage comes much earlier than the time for love: the latter regarded as the measure of maturity, in men and women.

19. When a woman attacks a man, it is only to defend herself against a woman. When a man becomes friends with a woman, she thinks he's doing it *because* he can't get any further with her.[10]

20. It is impossible to suffer without having someone pay for it; every single complaint contains revenge.[11]

21. My brothers and sisters, do not act so delicately toward me! We are all comely sturdy male and female donkeys and truly no trembling rosebuds for whom a mere dew drop seems too much![12]

22. Life is hard to bear: but why else would we have our defiance in ⟨the⟩ morning and our surrender in the afternoon?[13]

23. I am astounded: I often don't get hungry until after a meal.[14]

24. Truly, not the least of a theory's charms is the fact that it is refutable.[15]

25. These constitutional monarchs were thought to be virtuous: since then they can no longer "commit injustice" — but in return they were stripped of their power.[16]

26. Those fortunate enough to remain obscure should also take advantage of the freedoms that darkness affords and, especially, "whisper well."[17]

27. To actually attribute the unpleasant consequences of our own folly to folly and not to our lack of character — this requires more character than most people have.[18]

28. Scientific people share the fate of rope-makers: they weave their strand longer and longer, but in the process they themselves move — backwards.[19]

29. For me, the worst thing is not to fall into his hands: but into his thoughts.[20]

30. To experience a lot: a lot of the past included; to experience a lot of our own and others' experiences as an integrated whole: this shapes the most superior humans; I call them "totalities."[21]

31. Death is near enough that we need not be afraid of life.[22]

32. In order to need brakes, it is first necessary to have wheels. Good people are brakes: they obstruct, they preserve.[23]

⟨33.⟩ "Honorable men"[24] are offensive to my taste.[25]

⟨34.⟩ To become illustrious in 300 years — that is my thirst for glory.[26]

⟨35.⟩ Do I love music? I don't know: too often I also find myself hating it. And yet music does love me, and no sooner does someone leave me than music jumps into my lap and wants to be loved.[27]

⟨36.⟩ They do not love me: is this a reason not to bless them?[28]

37. "Behold! The world has just now become perfect": that's what every woman thinks when she obeys out of total devotion.[29]

38. Evil should be preserved, just as forests should be preserved. It is true that the earth became warmer when the forests were thinned out and cleared — —[30]

39. There should be no compassion for mosquitoes and fleas. Justice would be done if petty thieves, petty backbiters and detractors were hanged.[31]

40. We shouldn't use one word to categorize contemptible people together with terrible people.[32]

41. Affects that are evil and great shake us to the core and overthrow everything that is rotten and small within us: you must first experiment with the possibility of not being great.

42. Our delicate feelings keep us deluded and make us depressed, let's say this *openly*: "I **like** it this way — I don't care why!"

43. In regard to most truths, women have the feeling that someone wants to look *under their skin*.[33]

44. In addition to our ability to judge we also have our *opinion* of our ability to judge.

45. You lack the courage to burn yourself up and to become ashes: and so you will never become new and never become *young* again![34]

46. Marriage is designed for average people who are not capable of either extraordinary love or extraordinary friendship, in other words, for most people: but also ⟨for⟩ those very rare individuals who are capable of both love and friendship.[35]

47. You lovers of knowledge! So what have you done up until now out of love of knowledge? Have you ever stolen and murdered in order to know how it feels to be a thief and a murderer?[36]

48. Lies have also been told about the value of knowledge: those who know have always cited it in their defense — they always found themselves extremely marginalized and almost criminalized.[37]

49. To become as close to a friend as possible without surrendering to the friend entirely! We ⟨should⟩ honor even the enemy in our friends.[38]

50. The more abstract the truth you want to teach, the more you have to seduce even the senses into embracing it.

51. The subtlety of compassion consists in discerning whether the sufferer really wants compassion.

52. "Obedience" and "law" — these ring out from all moral feelings. But, in the end, "choice" and "freedom" could still become the death knell of morality.

53. A child as the monument to the passion of two persons; a twosome's will to oneness.[39]

54. We must endure *our* thirst and let it become acute: otherwise we will never discover *our* wellspring, which can never be another's!

55. You must raise even your devil to greatness: that way you rid yourself of petty deviltry.[40]

56. The great epochs of our life are to be found wherever we find the courage to rebaptize our evil as good.[41]

57. Even truthfulness is just one of the means to knowledge, a ladder — but not the ladder.[42]

58. The will to overcome an affect is, in the final analysis, only the will of another affect.[43]

59. Those who themselves possess the will to suffer are differently disposed to cruelty: they no longer take it to be in itself damaging and bad.[44]

60. Persons who were employed in an enterprise that has failed should be doubly compensated.[45]

61. Heroism — this is the mentality of people who pursue goals that, logically speaking, they have no chance of achieving. H⟨eroism⟩ is self-destruction in good faith.[46]

62. The enormous expectations that women bring to sexual love ruin for them all additional perspectives.[47]

63. Those who no longer find greatness in God no longer find greatness at all — they must deny it or create it.[48]

64. Unconditional love also contains — the desire to be mistreated: in that case love defies itself, and out of devotion there grows at last even the wish for self-destruction: "Perish in the depths of this ocean!" [49]

65. Lust and self-mutilation are neighboring drives. Even among those who know there are self-mutilators: they do not want to be creative at all.[50]

66. There are temperaments[51] that can find no way of living with themselves except by striving for their own downfall.[52]

67. The closer you come to being completely coldhearted in regard to everything that was previously valued, the closer you also come to a new warmheartedness.[53]

68. Every good is the transformation of an evil: every god has a devil for a father.[54]

69. "What must I do to become blessed?" I don't know, but I say to you: be blessed[55] and then do whatever you want.[56]

70. Something becomes dear to us: and no sooner have we come to love it with all our hearts than that tyrant within us calls out: "give me that very thing as a sacrifice" — and we give it.[57]

71. I urge you to battle, not to work, I urge you to victory, not to peace. May your work be a battle, your peace a victory.[58]

72. I awoke you from sleep: for I saw that a nightmare was oppressing you. And now you are out of sorts and tell me: "what should we do now? Night is still all around us!" — you ungrateful ones! You should go back to sleep and dream better![59]

73. Every church is the stone on the grave of a God-made-human: the last thing it wants is for him to be resurrected.[60]

Everything about women is a riddle, everything about women has one solution: it is called pregnancy.[61]

74. Good and evil are God's prejudices — said the serpent. But even the serpent itself was one of God's prejudices.[62]

75. What's the point! Apparently you don't understand anything other than barking and biting — so at least be my dog — said Zarathustra.[63]

76. I know everything that is evil and everything that is good — I also know what is beyond evil and good — said Zarathustra.[64]

77. Today I love myself as I love my God: who could forgive me a sin today? I know only sins against my God; yet who knows my God?[65]

78. Do you want to have an easy life? Then always stay with the herd and lose yourself in the herd. —[66]

79. In war, personal revenge is silent.[67]

80. You should love peace as the means to new wars![68]

81. Don't look at the sun! The moon is still too bright for your nocturnal eyes![69]

82. You say: "this is dark." And in truth: I placed a cloud in front of your sun. But don't you see how the edges of the cloud are already shining and becoming bright?[70]

83. We are only pregnant with our own child.[71]

84. There they stand over there, the puny people, like grass and weeds and undergrowth — blameless in their pitifulness. And now I creep through them and crush as few as I can — but at the same time disgust eats away at my heart.[72]

85. What sustained me, you ask? Always pregnancy and nothing else. And every time a work was born, my life hung by a thin thread.[73]

86. Disgust at filth can become so great that it discourages us from cleansing ourselves.[74]

87. As one who creates, you live above and beyond yourself — you cease being your contemporary.[75]

88. Alas, you wanted to have it better than good! This is your folly.[76]

89. We can only be silent when we have bows and arrows: otherwise we babble and bicker.[77]

90. I assume that you are compassionate: to be without compassion means to be sick in mind and body. But we must have a strong mind before we are allowed to be compassionate. For your compassion is damaging to you and to all.[78]

91. I love compassion that is hidden under a hard shell: I love compassion that makes people bite so hard they break off their teeth.[79]

92. A false saying goes as follows: "those who cannot redeem themselves, how could they redeem others?" But if I have the key to your shackles, why would your lock and mine have to be the same?[80]

93. Once war begins, you will become holy, even if you are brigands and cruel.[81]

94. ("A uniform" is what they call it, what they wear: uniformity is what they mean by it.)[82]

95. I love something: and no sooner do I love it with all my heart than the tyrant within me says: "I want that very thing as a sacrifice." This cruelty is in my guts. You see: I am evil.[83]

96. You say, a good cause is that which justifies even war? I say: war is that which justifies every cause![84]

97. Reason is an exception even in me, said Zarathustra: chaos and necessity and whirling of the stars — this is the rule even in the wisest of worlds.[85]

98. We should make our death into a festival, even if only out of malice toward life: toward this woman who wants to leave us — us![86]

99. We both have something for each other: how wonderful it is to disagree in this — you have the passion, I the reasons![87]

100. I am not great enough — not to have these feelings: but I am great enough not to be ashamed of them.[88]

101. "There is no one alive who would be worthy of praising me. And whom may Zarathustra not praise?"[89]

102. I make balsam for my wounds from my own vitriol: and I milked the milk out of the udder of my misery.[90]

103. I have exposed myself and am not ashamed to stand here this naked. Shame is the name of the ghoul who became a companion of humans when they were seized with the desire to transcend animals. ("Speech to the Animals")[91]

104. People are free to believe in Zarathustra: but what does Zarathustra care?[92]

105. I came to help you, and you complain that I don't want to weep with you.[93]

106. All god-humans created their own gods: and there is no greater enmity on earth than that between gods.[94]

107. Acknowledge your own will, and say to us all, "this is the only thing I *want* to be": set above yourself your own law of punishment: we want to be the ones who carry it out!

108. If you are too weak to make laws for yourselves: then a tyrant should lay his yoke on you and say: "obey, grind your teeth and obey" — and everything good and evil should drown in obedience to him.

109. Give back and pay back; pay back richly, good and bad — be modest in accepting, let your accepting be a mark of distinction.[95]

110. Be careful with cats: they never give, they do not even pay back — they only reply and purr in the process.[96]

111. Tell me, you birds, who travel widely and see many who are concealed: who among humans has the most extensive soul? the most extensive souls are like small countries[97]

112. You are still perfectly innocent in your admiration: you do not believe that you can ever be admired.[98]

113. I am speaking and a child is playing: who can be more serious than the both of us?[99]

114. You have overcome yourself: but why are you showing yourself to me merely as someone who has been overcome? I want to see the victor: throw roses into the abyss and speak: "A gesture of thanks to the monster because it did not know how to devour me!"

115. There you sit on the beach, freezing and hungry: it is not enough to have saved your [100] life!

116. Who would believe it of me, spoke Zarathustra, that I belong to a race of berserkers, and to a race of libertines, of religious fanatics, of those obsessed with revenge? But war has justified me.[101]

117. Happiness for men lies in "I will this," happiness for women in "I must."[102]

118. Even the best man is fundamentally evil below: even the best woman is fundamentally bad below.[103]

119. I have to be an angel if all I want is to live: but you live under other conditions.[104]

120. Those who say to their god: I want to put all my evil too at your service — are the most pious people.[105]

121. You say I should be your teacher! See to it that I am your wings and not your stumbling block.[106]

122. How can I be fun in such a terrible way?[107]

    What do I care about the purring of those who, like cats, are incapable of love?

123. Many a deed is done in order to forget another deed: some actions work like opium. I am here so that another is forgotten.[108]

124. I am doing what I love best and for that very reason I am loath to describe it with fancy words: I don't want ⟨to⟩ dare to believe that it is a sublime compulsion, a law that I obey: I love what I love best too much to want to show myself as being compelled to do it.

125. Not your sin — your sobriety cries to heaven.[109]

126. In my view, you have become too life-impoverished: now you want to make austerity into virtue itself.

127. Golden era, when arrogance was considered to be the wellspring of evil![110]

128. You should preserve chaos within you: all those yet to come must have material out of which they can form themselves.[111]

129. Don't let yourselves be deceived! The most active peoples feel the greatest fatigue, their discontent is weakness — they no longer have the substance required for waiting and for laziness.[112]

130. Just for today, destiny, give me the unluckiest roll of your dice. Today I turn everything into gold.[113]

131. No one comes to see me anymore. And I myself: I went to see everyone, but I *came to see no one*![114]

132. Thinking of life should be the focus of recuperation: otherwise thinking only of the work we have to do![115]

133. We must be as good at being cruel as we are at being compassionate: let us guard against becoming poorer than nature![116]

134. "I could *spare* nothing when I *created* superhumans. All of your evil and falsehood, your lies and your ignorance, are still in their semen."[117]

135. Let humans be the impetus for something that is no longer human! You want species-preservation? I say: species-overcoming![118]

136. Do I really want to create lamb-souls and visionary virgins? Lions are what I want and monsters of force and love.[119]

137. The point must be reached[120] where humanity's greatest festivals are procreation and death![121]

138. We must prepare not just the earth for superhumans but also the animals and plants.[122]

139. The best things amount to nothing until an actor has "performed" them.[123]

140. "You must be inoculated with the madness" — said Zarathustra.[124]

141. I still have all these wild dogs at my place, but in my cellar. I do not want to ever hear them bark.[125]

142. Thinking of life should be the focus of recuperation: otherwise we should think only of the work we have to do.[126]

143. Honor actors for my sake and don't ever look for the best ones on stage![127]

144. If I did not love humans, how could I stand Zarathustra?[128]

145. You are waging war? You fear your neighbor? So remove the border markers: then you will have no more neighbors.

But you want war: and that's why you set up the border markers in the first place.[129]

146. "This is how I want to live, illuminated by the virtues of a world that has yet to exist."[130]

147. Every thing has two faces, one of passing away and one of becoming.[131]

148. This good discerning exacting sense found in knowledge, which you in no way want to make into a virtue, is the flowering of many virtues: but the "thou shalt" from which it sprang is no longer visible, its roots lie beneath the earth.[132]

149. Love is the *fruit* of obedience: but often generations lie between the fruit and the root: and freedom is the fruit of love.[133]

150. The freer and more grounded individuals are, the *more demanding* their love becomes: in the end they yearn for superhumans because nothing else *quenches* their love.

151. Don't reveal yourself! And if you must, then in rage and not in shame![134]

152. Did I come to teach you how to defend yourselves against burglars and cutthroats? I speak to those who are tired of their virtues and who will allow themselves to be robbed or killed to experience it just once.[135]

153. And have you nothing more to say to human beings? his disciples asked. "No," said Zarathustra, "the cup is empty." And when he had said this, he went on his way, alone. Yet those who saw him go, wept.[136]

154. Beware of insulting hermits: they never forgive. A hermit is like a deep well: it is easy to toss a stone into it: yet how would you propose to retrieve it once it reached the bottom?[137]

155. Be humane toward those who create! It is their nature to know little of loving thy neighbor.[138]

156. Before we can forgive, we must first experience being wronged: and with profound people all experiences last a long time.[139]

157. Each action by a superior human being breaks your moral law a hundred times.[140]

158. I can still stand on the narrowest stoop of life: but who would I be if I showed you this skill? Do you wish to see a tightrope walker?[141]

159. Ah, what a lap of luxury you live in! You have a law — and a nasty look for anyone who even *thinks* about opposing it. For our part we are free: what do you know of the agony that results from taking responsibility for oneself —[142]

160. I teach you redemption from eternal flux: the flux also flows back into itself again and again, and you always step into the same flux again and again, as the same people.[143]

161. I taught myself this: humans gave themselves all of morality: although they now believe that they merely received it. Well then! We, too, can still *give* ourselves a good and an evil![144]

162. What is it that humans find most difficult to do? To love those who despise us: to abandon our cause when it is celebrating its triumph: to renounce reverence for the sake of truth; to be ill and turn away anyone who wishes to comfort

us; to wade into cold and dirty water; to make friends with doves; to extend a hand to a ghost who terrifies us: — all of this, said Zarathustra, I have done, and I carry it with me: and all of this I give away today at a bargain price — for the smile of a child.[145]

163. I wanted to know: I had to be cruel. Did I flee from revenge? Didn't I know of the speechless eyes of all the injured?

164. Even as animals we should be perfect — said Zarathustra.[146]

165. We are proud to worship when we cannot be idols.[147]

166. I love free minds when their hearts are free as well. My head is like the stomach of the heart — but we should have a good stomach. What the heart accepts, the head must digest.[148]

167. It is not enough to have a talent: we must also be allowed to have it![149]

168. Compassion a hellish feeling: *compassion* is itself the *cross* to which those who love human beings are nailed.[150]

169. Keep your souls *fresh* and *cool* and *raw*! May you remain far from the lukewarm air of those people full of feeling, from the stale humid air of sentimental people![151]

170. "Shrouded in heavy sadness: my life hangs on small coincidences." The hermit.[152]

171. When we suffer a lot, we might finally become humble enough to be vain — said the hermit: he opened his mouth reluctantly, he usually preferred to grit his teeth.[153]

172. "I do not give alms — I am not poor enough for that" — said Zarathustra.[154]

173. I am a support and a balustrade along a mighty river: grab onto me whoever can! — I am not a crutch.[155]

174. "Humans should be the midpoint between plants and ghosts."[156]

175. Blood is a poor witness for truth: blood poisons a doctrine so that it becomes a kind of hatred.[157]

176. Hard-heartedness is a virtue in compassionate people.[158]

177. Murderous desire, hatred, mistrust are now phenomena that accompany bodily illness: this is how much moral judgments have been incorporated in us. — In barbaric times, cowardice and compassion might appear to be symptoms of illness. Perhaps virtues can also be symptoms; — — —[159]

178. This is how humans are: a new force, a first movement: a self-revolving wheel; if they were strong enough, they would make the stars revolve around themselves.[160]

179. With shoulders squared, space stands braced against the void. Where there is space, there is being.[161]

180. You told me what a sound is and what an ear is: but what does this have to do with artists of sounds? Have you explained music by saying this — or refuted it instead?[162]

181. There are no moral drives,[163] but *all* drives are *colored* by our value judgments.

182. What is life? A constant praising and blaming.[164]

183. When horror consorts with what is harmful, evil emerges; when disgust consorts with it, bad emerges.[165]

184. Zarathustra: "As long as your morality hung over me, I breathed like someone suffocating. And so I strangled this serpent. I wanted to live, that's why it had to die.[166]

185. What is a human being? A pile of passions that reach out into the world through the senses and the mind: a tangle of wild serpents seldom growing tired of the struggle: then they gaze out into the world to find their prey.[167]

186. It is impossible to live without assigning value: but it is possible to live without assigning value to what you *value*.

187. Now the lead weight of their guilt lies upon them: they are so ponderous, so stiff: if only they could shake their heads, it would roll off. But who will move these heads?[168]

188. I want to force you to think like a human being: a necessity for those human beings who can conceptualize human beings. The necessity of having gods would not be *true* for you.[169]

189. The force of praise and blame is monstrous: but where is the goal that could devour this force?

190. And what was too foul to feed to your dogs — this is precisely what you threw to your God. Perhaps he died from your diet?

191. Your souls lack the frankincense of shame: but even a good peach has its fuzz.[170]

192. When storm clouds gather, you should lay your resolutions to rest.

193. We should question gods only in cases where gods alone can answer.

194. Before destiny strikes us, we should lead it around like a child and — not spare the rod: yet once we meet it, then we should seek to love it.

195. It seemed godless to our ancestors and insatiably greedy that we should grub around for treasure in the bowels of the earth.[171]

196. Beware of waking the dead, lest lightning strike you.[172]

197. The greatest sacrilege is the sacrilege against humans after there are no more gods: and of devaluing what is human in favor of the entrails of unknowable things.[173]

198. Become necessary! Become lucid! Become beautiful! Become well![174]

Some love a bird in flight and others see only dawns and oceans.

199. Beware of damaging the coffins of the living[175]

200. to become active on behalf of great matters and otherwise to be slow and — — —

201. Do I love the past? I destroyed it in order to live. Do I love my contemporaries? I look away from them in order to be able to live.

202. Incapable of believing in something for long!: knowledge[176] loses its value the moment it is acquired. Therefore create!

203. To create a being superior to ourselves is *our* essence. *Creating* **above** *and beyond ourselves*! This is the drive of procreation, this is the drive of deeds and of works. — Just as all

willing presupposes a purpose, *so do human beings presuppose beings* who ⟨are⟩ not there, but who supply the purpose of their existence. This is the freedom of all willing! In *purpose* lies love, reverence, seeing completely, longing.

Praise of the *forest*. Blessed be this tree where I thought of you

Becoming accustomed to gratitude.

you should not kill before the animal is not dozing.[177]

Sentenced to be executioners, you scholars!

204. I was afraid when I was among humans: something demanded that I join them and nothing gave me rest. Then I went into solitude and created superhumans. And as I created them, I arranged for them the great veil of becoming and let the noon shine all around them.

205. The moment in which I fathered the recurrence is immortal. For the sake of this moment, I *endure* the recurrence.

206. What is it that imparted sense, worth, meaning to things? The creative heart that desired and created out of desire. It created pleasure *and pain*. It wanted to *satiate* itself even with pain. We must take upon ourselves, and affirm, *all* suffering that has ever been felt by humans and animals, and we must *have a* goal *whereby* **suffering** *preserves reason*.

207. There is no redemption for those who suffer on account of their existence except that of no longer suffering on account of their existence. How do they attain this? Through *sudden death* or *through enduring love*.[178]

208. *Every* action continues to create *us*, it weaves our cloak of many colors. Every action is free, but a cloak is necessary. Our *experience* — this is our cloak.

209. Desire is happiness: satiation as happiness is merely the last moment of desire. To be entirely a wish is happiness and to be a new wish again and again.[179]

210. I converse with you, my wisdom, just the two of us: *I will*, *I desire*, *I love* — and this is why I *praise* life. If I didn't create, but I only *knew*, I would hate life.

211. *Not* doing, letting go, *not creating*, *not destroying* — this is *my* evil. The one who knows *also* as the one who does not desire.

212. Emptiness, oneness, motionlessness, fullness, satiation, not-willing — this would be *my* evil: in short: sleep without dreams.[180]

213. Knowing is a desire and thirst: knowing is a procreation. Love for the corporeal and for the world is the consequence of knowing as willing. As creating, all knowing is not-knowing. *Seeing through things* would be death, disgust, evil. There is no other form of knowing than that of first creation. To be a subject —[181]

214. The *greatest danger* is *faith* in knowing and faith in being known,[182] i.e., faith that creating has ended. This is the great fatigue. "It is nothing."[183]

215. All knowing, as creating, never ends. To each person there would have to correspond an explanation of the world that would belong to that person completely: to that person as a first movement. We never want to admit this to ourselves and we look to the herd.

216. Injustice has not been done until we do something to help someone: justice and injustice do not have to do with *helping* and *hurting*, but rather with *advantage* and harm.[184]

217. You will be called destroyers of morality: but you are merely the inventors of yourselves.

218. These are my enemies: they want to overthrow things and not to develop themselves. They say: "all of this is worthless" — and do not want to create any value themselves.

219. I am "the awakened one": and you — no sooner are you born than you have already begun to die.[185]

220. What can all people do? — Praise and blame. This is the virtue of humans, this is the madness of humans.[186]

221. *Injustice is always being committed* — says justice — and not only when you hurt yourselves but also when you help, love, and serve each other. Nothing is remedied by praise and love, they are harmful because they do not remedy anything.[187]

222. What do you know of the love that a lunatic has for reason, like the love someone burning with fever has for ice![188]

223. In science, in knowing, drives have become *holy*: "the thirst for pleasures, the thirst for becoming, the thirst for power." The humans who know have *far surpassed themselves* in holiness.[189]

224. I was in school: I lived for knowledge. There my soul purified itself, all desires became holy. It is the *preschool*: the solitude of the one who knows. *You should deal with humans the way you deal with objects*: your love should be above all individual objects and individual humans.

225. *The will to suffer*: once in a while you must live in the world, you who create. You must *almost* perish — and afterwards *bless* your labyrinth and your stray paths. Otherwise you cannot *create*, but only *die off*. You must have your triumphs and your downfalls. You must have your evils and once in a while take them up again. You eternally returning ones, you yourselves must make of yourselves a return.

226. Creating is redemption from suffering. But suffering is necessary for those who create. Suffering is self-transformation, in every birth there is a death. We must be not only the children, but also the ones who give birth: as those who create.[190]

227. We must want to pass away in order to be able to emerge again — from one day to the next. *Metamorphosis* through a hundred souls — let this be your life, your destiny:
      And then finally: to want this entire sequence once again!

228. Look at him to see if he has a clear eye and a mouth free of contempt. Look at him to see if he walks like a dancer.[191]

229. Often you have to abandon everything, your woman, your land, your usefulness: you must tell the sun in your life to stand still.[192]

230. Your life of pleasures is a kind of self-mortification: and both are illnesses and degradations.[193]

231. We should serve those whose spirit, self-overcoming, and invention of new projects will be expanded through your service: — in this way, as a servant, you will have been most useful to yourself.

232. Don't be angry at those who think in the way that perishing people tend to think: they are grasping at their straws

of life and know little of life other than grasping and that it makes little sense to do so: perishing people aren't worth much — this is the kernel of their "wisdom"[194]

233. You have not yet decided to live, but rather you are afraid and tremble like children at the water they are supposed to dive into. And meanwhile your time slips away, and you search for teachers who tell you: "be afraid and tremble at the ocean called life" — and you call this teaching good and die early.

234. The *value* of *life* lies in value judgments: value judgments are *something created*, not something taken, not something learned, not something experienced. What has been created must be destroyed to make room for the newly created: a value judgment's *ability to live* includes its capacity to be destroyed. The creator must always be a destroyer. Yet valuation itself cannot destroy itself: *for this is life.*[195]

234. "Life is suffering?" — If you are right: well then, it is *your* life that is suffering! — so *make sure* that you stop; make sure that life, which is nothing but suffering, stops. Your morality is: "thou shalt kill thyself," "thou shalt steal away."[196]

235. And even those who turned their backs on life and *found* joy and peace in the process — — — they found it by *creating* an image of such a life, as *ones who create*! — — — as ones who create, you brought your suffering to an end! And *in this way* loved your life!

236. You imagine that you are free from the maxims of those who know: but you are incapable of doing anything without grasping for *our* valuations, you helpless people! Much less ever creating! This delusion of being free is part of the *happiness of deprivation*! A consolation for prisoners! A good deed on behalf of those born blind!

237. Animals don't know anything about themselves, they don't even know anything about the world.[197]

238. I am too full:[198] in this way I forget myself, and all things are in me, and there is nothing more than all things. Where am *I headed*?

239. The tightly interwoven sensations that always return ("holding a time together in a relative sense") are regarded by us as raw materials and realities: in the first instance, our bodies. But "all the properties of these things consist of our sensations and representations."[199]

240. We should be a mirror of being: we are God in miniature.

241. What is to come is just as much a condition of what is as of what has been. "What should be and what must be is the basis for what is."[200]

242. Am I supposed to have created the whole universe? Was it the movement of *my* I that brought this about, just as it brought about the movement of a body? Am I merely a *droplet* of this force?

243. I *comprehend* only a being that is simultaneously one and many, that changes and stays the same, that knows, feels, wills — this being is my *primordial fact*.

244. Once when I wanted to find *pleasure in truth*, I *invented lying* and *illusion* — proximity and distance, what is past and what is to come, that which is perspectival. Then I projected obscurity and deception into myself and made myself into something that deceived myself.[201]

245. There is much to love about humans: but humans should not be loved. Humans are too imperfect a thing: love for humans would kill me.[202]

246. I did not repudiate these humans that I loved: but rather the very thing that made me love them, that's what I repudiated.[203]

247. Look into the world as if time were missing: and all that is crooked will become straight for you.[204]

248. If you see blue, what good does it do you to overcome yourself and to say to yourself: you should not be seeing blue![205]

249. Some want to throw dice and others want to count and calculate, and those over there want to see dancing: they call it science and it makes them sweat. But they are children who want to have their game — and truly, it is a kind of beautiful childishness, and some laughter would not hurt the game.[206]

250. All signs of the superhuman appear as illness or madness in humans.[207]

251. We must already be an ocean in order to absorb a filthy stream without getting filthy.[208]

252. When I considered purpose, I also considered chance and folly.[209]

253. You are too crude for me: it is impossible for minor experiences to be your downfall.[210]

254. Your eye doesn't go blind at the point where it can no longer recognize things, but just at the point where your honesty ceases, that's where your eye sees nothing more.[211]

255. What apes are to us, a laughing stock or a painful embarrassment: so shall humans be to superhumans.[212]

256. How would someone have to speak to you so that you would understand! You must first get sick before you have ears to hear.[213]

257. As soon as the will takes the stage, feeling experiences a sense of *liberation*. For feeling suffers — and as soon as the will takes the stage, feeling is suspended and does not suffer. This is called freedom of the will.[214]

258. How heavy the world became for me then — like a creature that has lived in the sea and was now forced to crawl up on land: now how is it supposed to drag its own body along![215]

258. Have I not invented a new color and a new smell?[216]

259. You should not live in places where you are forced to have puny feelings. There is no worse way to waste your life than in puny settings.

260. If you are too soft and squeamish to kill flies and mosquitoes, then go into solitude and fresh air where there are no flies and mosquitoes: and be solitude and fresh air yourselves![217]

Your poor body — ignorance of the laws of nature.

261. Illness is a clumsy experiment at achieving good health: our minds must come to the aid of nature.[218]

262. My brothers, nature is stupid: and insofar as we are nature, we are all stupid. Even stupidity goes by a nicer name: it calls itself necessity. Let us definitely come to the aid of necessity![219]

263. What is it about the fact that as many people as possible live as long as possible? Is their happiness a justification of all existence? And not actually a despicable thing?[220]

264. And if you wish to justify existence, you must not only become the devil's advocate, you must also be God's advocate with the devil.[221]

265. Speech to the *cliff*. I love that you do not speak. Your silence is dignified. (Perceiving everything in nature morally: all value lies in that)[222]
    Speech to a king.

266. The world stands there, finished — a golden bowl of goodness. But the creative spirit also still wants to create what is finished: so it invented time — and now the world spun apart and spins in great rings back into itself again, like the emergence of good through evil, like a mother giving birth to purposes out of chance.[223]

267. There are enough of these people who do not know anything better on earth than to lie with a woman. What do they know of happiness![224]

    Invisible ties bind most tightly.

268. Whenever I honor a feeling, the feeling becomes infused with honor.

269. What use is your virtue if you have yet to experience the moment when you come to deeply despise *what is human within you* out of love for superhumans? And despise your virtue along with it?

270. In the history of humankind, the *moments of great contempt*[225] are the events: as the source of the great desire for superhumans. Don't let yourselves be fooled — hasn't there always been a desire to journey into the beyond or into nothingness or to become one with God!? All these colorful phrases served to express how tired humans were *of themselves — not of their suffering*, but rather of their usual ways of feeling.

271. To await the hour of the great contempt: this is the *commendation*. The other hours exist merely for the sake of cultivating the *last humans*.

272. Thoughts are merely signs, as words are merely signs for thoughts.

273. At one time the I was hidden in the herd: now the herd is still hidden in the I.[226]

5 [2][227]

I teach you two things; you should overcome humans, and you should know *when* you have overcome them: I teach you war and victory. (Chap⟨ter⟩)

5 [3][228]

It is cool, the meadow lies in shadow, the sun has departed. Is it not absurd to live?

Wouldn't we have to have more reason in order to make something reasonable out of life?

My brothers, forgive the soul of Zarathustra for the fact that it is evening.

5 [4][229]

Am I really rejecting your virtues? I am rejecting the virtuous among you.

5 [5]²³⁰

I am explaining even your virtues by what is to come.

5 [6]

As soon as feeling grows and swells within the herd, feeling comes closer to the herd.

First "for all" became sacred, then "for someone else" finally "for my God."

5 [7]²³¹

I love souls that squander: they do not give back and do not even want thanks — because they keep giving gifts.

5 [8]

I teach you about the superhumans: where is my brother who teaches them²³² the great contempt?

5 [9]²³³

They overturn icons²³⁴ and say: there is nothing exalted and worthy of worship — because they themselves can create neither icon nor God.

Have mercy on them! Just listen to the contempt of their rage against icons — the great contempt for themselves!

5 [10]²³⁵

⟨chap⟨ter⟩⟩ "the brotherhood of justifiers."

5 [11]²³⁶

It is terrible to die of thirst in the middle of the ocean: must you then salt your wisdom so much that it doesn't taste like pure water?

5 [12]²³⁷

Humankind is walking around pregnant, how quaint its labor pains.

5 [13][238]

Our contempt for humans drove us beyond the stars and allowed us to search around for a god.

5 [14][239]

The scholar should be a *penitent* of the *mind*

5 [15][240]

They said "let us make ourselves dead to the world," they sought their salvation beyond the stars, they did not find news[241] of the superhumans.

5 [16][242]

Let your life be an experiment with a hundred permutations: let your failures and successes be proof: and take care that your experiments and what you have proven become known.

5 [17][243]

I love those who justify the people of the future and redeem the people of the past: even as they perish because of the people of the present.

I love those who make virtue into their duty and their doom.

I love those who do not spare a drop of spirit and who are entirely the spirit of their virtue:

I love those who squander their souls, who do not want thanks and do not give back because they are always giving gifts.[244]

I love those who take upon themselves the injustice suffered by those who cannot bear it[245]

I love those who live to know and who want to know so that the superhumans may live.

I love those who do not want to become dead to the world and who do not seek their salvation beyond the stars: those who have understood the news of the superhumans.

I love those whose souls are deep even when wounded and who can perish as a result of one minor experience.[246]

I love those who are so full that they forget themselves, and all things are in them: but they will perish.

I love those whose minds are free just as their hearts are free: and let their heads be merely the entrails of their hearts.

I love those who are so compassionate that they make hard-heartedness into their virtue and their god.[247]

I love those who strew golden words before their deeds and still always deliver more than they promise.

I love those who are ashamed when the dice always fall their way and who ask themselves: am I then a cheater?

I love those who forgive their opponents not only their failures but also their victories.[248]

I love those who chastise their god because they love their god.

I love those who do not expect rewards from their virtue, but rather punishment and downfall.

I love those who see the suffering god hidden in their neighbors and who are ashamed of the animal that was visible in their neighbors.[249]

5 [18][250]

You should not want to have too many virtues. One virtue is already a lot of virtue: and we must be rich enough even for just a single virtue. You should perish so that it may live.

5 [19][251]

I entreat you, my brothers, remain true to the earth and don't believe those who speak to you of hopes beyond this earth:[252] they are poisoners and despisers of life: whether they know it or not, they are the ones who are dying off and have poisoned themselves.

At one time, sacrilege against God was the greatest sacrilege: but God died, and then even the people committing sacrilege died with him. Sacrilege against the earth is now the most terrible thing, and reverence for the entrails of unexplorable things more than for the meaning of the earth.

5 [20][253]

Let your life be an experiment with a hundred permutations: let your successes and failures be proof; and take care that your experiments and what you have proven become known.

5 [21][254]

There are libertines of the mind: there are penitents of the mind.

5 [22][255]

The eye doesn't go blind at the point where it can no longer distinguish things, but rather at the point where your honesty ceases, that is where the eye sees nothing more.

5 [23][256]

Some want to throw dice and others want to count and calculate, and those over there want to see dancing: they call it science and it makes them sweat

But they are children who want to have their game — and truly, it is beautiful infantile nonsense, and a bit of laughter would make the faces of the players more lovable.

5 [24][257]

When you consider purpose, you must also consider chance and folly.

5 [25][258]

Objections, mistrust, adultery are signs of a healthy spirit. Everything unconditional reveals[259] a sick person.

5 [26][260]

Once, when I wanted to find pleasure in truth, that's when I invented lying and illusion, proximity and distance, what is past and what is to come; then I internalized deceit and twilight.

5 [27][261]

I was in the desert, I lived merely as one who knows. The soul of one who knows purified itself, and all desires and the thirst for power became sacred to that person. As one who knows I ascended far above and beyond myself in sanctity and virtue.

5 [28][262]

Human existence is uncanny and still without meaning: a clown[263] can bring about its doom.

For what purpose does this person live? For what purpose does that person die? No one can know, because there is no for-what-purpose in these matters.

Formerly, when death approached, people used to lift up a hand and say, "a gift from above."

This giver did not exist at all, a roof tile was the gift: in death, ignorance was as far as reason went.

I want to teach humans the meaning of their existence: which is the superhumans.

5 [29][264]

Let yourself be schooled by love for things and justice for things.

5 [30][265]

You shroud your souls: nakedness would be scandalous for your souls. Oh when will you learn why gods are naked! They have nothing to be ashamed of. They are more powerful naked!

The body is something evil, beauty is the work of the devil; emaciated, ghastly, starving, black, dirty, that's how the body should look

Sacrilege against the body is for me a sacrilege against the earth and against the meaning of the earth. Pity those unhappy people for whom the body seems evil and beauty diabolical!

5 [31]

Your body and your embodied self stand behind your thoughts and feelings: the *terra incognita*.[266] *What is the purpose of* you having *these* thoughts and these feelings? Your embodied self *wants* to do something with them.

5 [32][267]

The asceticism of the mind (addressed to the most intellectual)
the friend (the ideal company)
solitude
the body philosophizes
the one who creates
danger in the sermon on suffering
Against the devaluation of life
in knowledge, the drives are justified
the goal of humankind has been missing up until now
justification of the entire past
the one who communicates as fragment
the one who loves as fragment
the one who knows as fragment
not to value contemporary culture too highly!
for once, the passions as good health
chastity
teaching peace and inner effort. Against "effort."
the criminal.
retribution
moral outrage and forgiveness.
the one who praises
women
means of self-overcoming
the scientific ones
death
the recurrence
herd and I
slowly accumulating fame
critique of morality and its meaning

judgment in pleasure
contradiction in your ideals
we must also want our counterpart, the Pharisee.
the hidden human
the last human
speech to a king.
superhumans

invention of festivals
penitents of the mind — as purifiers of their affects
great decision between death and life[268]
actors and those who create.
the new art form as 1000 ways to live (independence *first*! a
thought that *compels* those who follow it freely)
life an experiment by those who know
to ennoble what is common, nearest, earthly! (cuisine diet)
solitude and life — sleep and waking (life as will to suffer
(— to create —)
the supreme knowledge: the new *evaluator*.
slowly accumulating fame
critique of morality and its meaning: we want to lift ourselves above praise and blame!
madness as *pre*figuring.
retribution — you want compensation?
without a homeland.
to turn humility into pride.
new wars.
whether there have already been superhumans

5 [33][269]
It is not enough to make amends for something: we must
also remake ourselves, be good to ourselves again, e.g., by
means of some small superfluous mischief or good deed.
Before we can forgive, we must first experience being wronged.
And with more profound individuals all experiences last a long
time.[270]

It is easier to forgive our enemies than our friends.

I should forgive? But I don't blame you for the same reasons you blame yourself: how could I then forgive?

Not that you lied to me, but rather that I no longer believed you, this is what has shaken me.

We take the bitterness that we feel toward people and use it to justify our moral outrage — and admire ourselves in the process; and we justify forgiveness through the fading of our hatred — and admire ourselves once again.[271]

He wronged me, this is bad. But that he now wants to go so far as to beg my pardon, this is worse, this drives me crazy.[272]

Beware of insulting a hermit! He never forgives! A hermit is like a deep well — it is easy to toss a stone into it. But how do you propose to retrieve it once it has reached the bottom?[273]

5 [34][274]

All goals have been destroyed: value judgments are turning against themselves,

those who follow their heart are called good but also those who are merely alert to their duty

unassuming, forgiving people are called good, but also brave unbending austere people.

those who make no demands on themselves are called good, but also heroes of self-overcoming

unconditional friends of truth are called good, but also pious people, the glorifiers of things

those who obey themselves are called good, but also pious people

noble, genteel people are called good, but also those who do not despise and condescend

good-natured people who avoid battle are called good, but also those who lust for battle and victory

those who always want to be first are called good, but also those who never want to take advantage of anyone.

5 [35]²⁷⁵

I do not understand why we find it necessary to slander others. If we want to hurt people, we only need to say something true about them.

We always know too much about everyone.

We praise only what appeals to our taste i.e., we praise only our own taste.

the most inspired passion

to make a virtue out of antipathy for someone

In the flam⟨es⟩ of jea⟨lousy⟩ we turn the poisonous stinger against ourselves, like a scorpion — yet without ⟨its⟩ success

When I notice that people are lying to me, I don't complain that they are lying to me, but rather that they are lying at all.

6 [1][1]

Asceticism:[2] to cultivate *only* reason

> to admit to oneself the small joys that knowledge
> > brings — to keep all others
> > away.

> cruelty in admitting to ourselves the *dirty*
> emergence of all supreme things

> attempt to look away from human beings and to
> fix them as points in becoming — not to model
> everything on them.

> on behalf of little certain hard truths — military
> discipline simplicity

> mocking the blissful effect of "truths," likewise
> mocking the beautiful form. Religion morality
> and art concerning the *surface* of things

> metaphysics as related to the belief in spirits and
> ghosts: also to poor interpretation

> the perspective of happiness as harmful to science

> where does the *value* of metaphysics come from?
> From errors and passions.

> Not to allow ourselves to become dependent upon
> the *most uncertain things*

> to admit to ourselves the weakness of our
> reasoning: dreams.

a strong feeling proves nothing about the truth of
what is believed.

Attempt to look at things in such a way that
substance and *freedom* of the will are errors: even
the I regarded as having become. The world as
error.

Mistrust of the metaphysical world because of the
difficulty of the problems.

All tranquility ceases with the belief in eternal
basic truths, we no longer care about anything
beyond our future because by then *other* things
will become necessary.

Era of comparison: a choice from among the
various ethics. Downfall of lowly ethics.

Cult of error: it made humans so sensitive, deep,
inventive. The world as error is so rich in
meaning and full of wonder.

we are, from beginning to end, illogical and
unjust beings — there is no life without this.

all initial approaches to the value of life false.
Final purposelessness. Squandering.

universally successful renunciation: always to
know better, the only consolation to float above
evaluations.

Result: I don't need to believe in anything
Things are unknowable.
I don't need to suffer on account of my injustice.
despair purged through skepticism

I acquired the right to *create*
the right to call things *good*
the right not to make connections to the past
finally: within all the activity of the drives I discovered
living morality, *driving* force. I had only *imagined*
that I was beyond good and evil.

Freethinking was *itself a moral act*
    1) as honesty
    2) as bravery
    3) as justice
    4) as love
I held *myself* apart as *one who posits values*
I did nothing other than criticize the *practice* of morality up until now. The establishment of moral judgments is itself a *piece* of this practice.

the determination of purposes as a *condition of existence*,
                                as a condition for one[3]
                                        existence **merg**ing into
                                        another.
                            herd — individual.

6 [2][4]

> 1. *Asceticism* — attempt to live without morality.
> 2. *Result*: we ourselves have practiced morality, *continued to* practice it — the life within us required it of us.

Everything that   3.   The *one who creates* and the
happens does not   *one who posits values*. Herd
correspond to the   and individual.
judgment of value. 4.   Attempt at a standpoint
                          beyond good and evil.

6 [3]
Asceticism: attempt to liberate ourselves from morality
    Change, indeed, opposition of moral judgments (no eternal norm)
    there have never ever been any moral actions: if they are characterized as free and as unegoistic.
    what *we* take to be evil (injustice) is a condition for existing.

in critiquing our best actions, we find it absolutely *necessary*
to use elements that belong to evil.

all moral systems have been *refuted*: and in any case their
value is dependent upon the truth of their last assertions:
these assertions are *uncertain*.

A *multitude* of opposing moral systems are contained in
our valuations themselves.

> (our judgments *underlying* the feelings
> are contradictory.)

In the end there *is* no longer any goal: morality is no *longer*
the way to heaven: no longer even the way to heaven on
earth (agony of pangs of conscience) Morality no longer
stands or falls with states and peoples.

Terrifying look back at the *agony* of humankind. They
were close *to renouncing*[5] life because of their moral
dissatisfaction.

6 [4]

1) Ascetic attempt to liberate ourselves from morality:
why?
initially, as practical consequence: a soldier's poverty,
nearness of death. Freethinker.

2) But now we recognize freethinking itself *as morality*.
In what way.
All feelings are morally tinged. What we did was a
therapy, a means to *life*. Morality appeared as a
condition of existence.

3) the new *freer* view of morality as a condition of existence
in life and progress in life.
Herd — evolution of the I. No retribution etc.

4) Attempt at a beyond good and evil.

[7 = M III 4b. Spring–Summer 1883]

7 [1][1]

Concerning the introduction.

Absolute *honesty* — missing up to now in moralists. Every character weakness will announce itself in the course of the investigation.

Thereafter historical *meaning.*

Bravely resisting our own inclination to make value judgments.

Ancient goal: the breeding of *superior* humans, using the masses as a means of doing so.

Concerning the Plan.

Every objective obligation is lacking. Universal agreement a principle hostile to life.

There are commands from individuals: an unconscious form of slavery

honesty requires that whatever we do for the sake of utility is also designated as such.

Motives for honesty etc. are found in the impulses of the powerful: the emancipation from morality also spreads *within the same sphere.*

To turn irresponsibility into something positive: we want to make our image of human beings *prevail.* Because we **can**! — is the point! Anyone who *feels oppressed* belongs in the inferior order. There must be "slaves."

Up to now we overlooked the creative aspect of individuality: we noticed only criminals etc. we overlooked *arch-criminals* Homer Michelangelo.

Greatest possible diversity of individuals! Let the struggle begin!

We *want* to move toward an ethics: and since we do not believe that we can find our way to it from egoism, we flee toward authority, toward tradition.

ethical taste is a thing without basis — but it emerged at one time as *compulsion*, as a result of other *drives* which *demanded* a particular judgment and valuation.

Where we no longer know how to trace our feelings back to their origins due to the *complexity of their emergence, we posit them as something different*: this is how aesthetic ethical moral metaphysical drives are to be understood.

We perceive a *name* and think that it corresponds to something new.

NB. The moral(istic) way of thinking **accords** with our behavior but *does not guide it*!

When there is no *drive* to obey, then a "thou shalt" has no meaning.

Given the way we are — we then become resistant to a "thou shalt." Our morality has to mean "I will this."

7 [2]

In fact, the egoism of the individual reaches as far as it can and as far as its strength permits —: it is nonsense to fear the consequences of the egoist(ic) principle.[2] No one is constrained by principles!

7 [3]

It would be very *superficial* to write *without* asking how long everything that is being written today will endure!

7 [4]

The confidence with which we act is completely *un*related to the *goodness* of our motives for acting *in this or that way*!

7 [5]

from Socrates onward, virtue *without shame* (in competition) and, as a subject of *cleverness,* virtue has no need of shame! A kind of self-abasement of virtue —

7 [6]

Critique of "*good people,*" indeed of the *best people*! Skepticism very justified!

My entire approach doesn't involve *morality*— what was formerly consciousness of sin, I also direct these things against the intellect, virtue, happiness, human strength.

On the basis of essentially *extramoral* considerations, I came to consider morality *from a distance.*

To discern the conditions under which future humans will live — because such *discernment* and *anticipation* have the **force** *of a motive*: the *future,* as something that we *will, acts* upon our now.

The immorality of our age at its best (e.g., the lack of reverence in regard to nature)

7 [7][3]

Speeches to My Friends.

I have always made an effort to prove to myself the *innocence* of becoming:[4] and probably I wanted to attain in this way the feeling of complete "irresponsibility" — to make myself independent of praise and blame, of all todays and traditions: in order to pursue goals that concern the future of humankind.

The first solution for me was the aesthetic *justification of existence.* However: "justifying" should not itself be necessary! Morality belongs to the realm of appearance.

The second solution for me was the objective lack of value of all concepts of *guilt* and the insight into the subjective, *necessarily* unjust and illogical nature of all life.

The third solution for me was the *denial* of all purposes and the insight into the *unknowability* of causalities.

redemption through illusion: the *principium individuationis*,[5] along with all morality, a redemptive *vision* for the individual.

Morality a means of *remaining within* individuation and of not being sucked back into primordial suffering.

art as the "genuinely metaphysical activity of human beings."[6]

that "at the foundation of things, in spite of all the changing appearances, life is indestructibly powerful and pleasurable" p. 54.[7] as tragedy's consolation.

Art saves him (from denying the will): and through art life saves him for itself.

A protest against pessimism: from the standpoint of the Greeks. The Greek, "deeply sensitive and singularly capable of the most tender and the most severe suffering"

Music as by far the *most vital* **art form**.

The task of *music* in an age *analyzed to death*, an age that is *tired of thinking*:

p. 82 Science, *led ever again to its limits, must be transformed into art* — that which leads it is the illusion that it could *correct* existence.[8]

Socrates relieved of his fear of death through knowledge and reasons.

the determination of science, to *make* existence *appear intelligible* and *thereby justified*: and when the reasons prove insufficient, *myth* too must be made to serve — it is fundamentally intended for this!

Were that sum of force *not* applied toward knowledge, but rather toward the practical aims of a people and of human beings, the desire for life would be so weakened that an ethic arising out of compassion could emerge (The Indic peoples too *weak* and *passive* even in their *com*passion)

tragic knowledge **needs** *art* "which stares into the inscrutable"[9]

Art represented as *dependent* upon the development of knowledge: it bursts forth wherever knowledge devours itself.

We should seek pleasure not *in* appearances, but *behind* them.

p. 92 Quintessence.[10]

p. 102. the self-destruction of *knowledge* and the insight into its ultimate limits was what excited me about Kant and Schopenhauer. From this dissatisfaction I came to believe in *art.*[11]

I thought that a new age *had arrived for art*. I experienced the outcome of philosophy as a *tragic event*: **how to endure it!**

W⟨agner⟩ seemed to me a means of alienating the G⟨ermans⟩ from Christianity

his old and tired work, Parsifal, doesn't refute this either, even less his blindly inflamed admirers with their skinned knees and brains.

Belief in the rebirth of the Greek world p. 117.[12]

"another being and a higher pleasure, for which the battling hero is prepared not through his victories, but through his downfall" p. 120.[13]

"Only a horizon rearranged by myth culminates in an entire cultural movement toward unity" p. 132.[14]

p. 136 *antichristian* — in this sense,[15]

p. 142 "   "   " *German* hope[16]

7 [8]

The entire 18th century held **Gothic** *architecture* in the deepest contempt Lecky I 199.[17]

This century *had* its own taste. The Milan Cathedral as object of derision.

Our century must *have recovered many of those feelings* from which those churches emerged —

The misidentification of *Homer* cf. in — — —
Winckelmann's critical evaluation of *Laocoön*.[18]

7 [9]

Compassion. Initially **reproduction of another's pain**. Now
a *reaction* **to it** must follow
either a powerful purging from the senses, fleeing from it (as
at the sight of a disgusting wound
or positive pushing aside and elimination of what hurts us,
in other words, an intervention in the sphere of the sufferers,
interpreted by *them* as help, etc.

We are *outraged* by each act of suffering, when it is senseless,
"*undeserved*" (our custom of blaming and punishing functions
here as a *wounded* drive: the image of the sufferer[19] is an assault
on the foundations of this drive) We react to this outrage with
"help" etc.

Thereafter: — we shiver, we ourselves feel the danger, insecurity sudden misfortune "it's unbelievable!" — our sense of
harmony and logic is outraged.

where we feel that we can help, our *feeling of power* awakens,
hence the zeal for duty, the excitement, the heroism while res-
cuing victims; the pleasure at the opportunity to be brave etc.

Love, tenderness are not *necessary* in such situations!

7 [10]

Hartmann[20] p. 776. the *sovereignty of the individual*, according
to him, merges with the *egoistic attention to prudence* that puts
limits on choice! This is typical!!

7 [11]

Our neighbors as our *progeny*
having given them the traits to which our drives **react**. The whole
image, a progeny that is useful *to us*: that is beneficial *to us*, harmful etc. is *swept away* — for the *purpose* of assimilation or flight.

What then is "loving thy neighbor"?

Our neighbors are in themselves unknowable, except by inference in relation to us, and this according to the subtlety or crudity of our observations: our overhastiness in deciding (it's a matter of fear or longing) etc.

We battle what seems harmful *to us* in our enemies: whatever hinders our growth, our survival, what poisons our *air*: hence we battle **our** *drives* of *mistrust*, of *tension* — i.e., one kind of drive pushes aside another.

7 [12]

The Jews *corrupted* by the Egyptian captivity.

7 [13]

Architecture: to bring *what is distant* nearer (St. Peter's Basilica)

another principle: the greatest possible striving for the distant.

7 [14]

We hate those people most who seduce us back into feelings that we have conquered with the greatest effort: those who betray us to our enemies *after* our triumph: this is how it is for those like us who are seduced into revenge even after we have forgiven someone.

7[15]

our conscience adapts ⟨itself⟩ to the environment in which we live; inasmuch as drives like fear, skepticism, reticence, stealth etc. are generated by the feeling that our valuations are not in agreement: these drives gradually *immediately* discharge themselves at the time of our impulses and transform our conscience into an *evil* conscience.[21]

7 [16]

Wagner received many favors from his contemporaries: but he was of the opinion that fundamental injustice toward benefactors was part of a "grand style": he was always living as an actor and under delusions of cultural sophistication, as actors typically do. I myself have been perhaps his most generous benefactor. It is possible that in this case the image will outlive the man on which it is modeled: this has to do with the fact that there is still plenty of room in my image for a host of real Wagners: and above all for those much more richly gifted and more single-minded in purpose.

7 [17]

Those who live among Germans should count themselves lucky if they find a single individual who keeps a distance from that idealistic self-delusion and color-blindness that the Germans adore and revere almost as virtue itself. (The French with their Montaigne La Rochefoucauld Pascal Chamfort Stendhal are a much *purer* intellectual nation) This was my joy when I got to know Rée:[22] he spoke of morality only to the extent that he knew it and without conjuring up something based on his moral drives. To be sure: he didn't know much about it and even this was based only on hearsay: and in the end he thought that morality itself was hearsay.

7 [18]

Since Kant, all talk of art, beauty, knowledge, wisdom has been mangled and muddied by the concept of "disinterest."

What strikes *me* as beautiful (from the viewpoint of history): that which becomes visible about the most-admired people of an era, as an expression of what **most deserves** admiration.

7 [19]

It was Helvétius's accomplishment, a matter of *fortitude*, to take *pleasure* (*intérêt*[23]) seriously (just as Socrates did with *utility*):

just like Epicurus (as opposed to taking pleasure in the paradoxical, like Mandeville): and to say *plaisir*,[24] as Stendhal wished,
was perhaps already too *damaging* to Helvétius (given the moral
taste out of which he himself grew)

7 [20]

Just as optics limps along behind sight, so, too, moral theory[25]
behind morality.

Individual observations are by far the *most valuable thing*.

A mor⟨al⟩ theory of fundamental error is most often the
origin of great philosophical systems: something must be
proved which *agrees* with the praxis of the philosopher (e.g.,
Spinoza) (Schopenhauer the exception — *noblesse*[26] therein)

7 [21]

My demand: to produce beings who stand sublimely above
the entire species "human being": and who sacrifice themselves and "their neighbors" for this goal.

Morality up to now has had its boundaries dictated by the
species: all moralities up to now were useful for establishing
first and foremost the unconditional stability of the species:
when this has been achieved, the goal can be set higher.

The *one* movement is unconditional: the leveling of humankind, giant ant hills etc. (Dühring to be characterized as
extraordinarily impoverished and typically *narrow*, despite his
lofty words)

The *other* movement: my movement: is conversely the intensification of all oppositions and divisions, elimination of
equality, the creation of the superpowerful.[27]

The *former* generates last humans. *My* movement, superhumans.

The goal is **not** *at all* to conceive of the latter as the masters
of the former: but rather: the two species should exist alongside one another — as segregated as possible; the one, like *the
Epicurean gods, having no concern for the other.*

Principles: there *have* never *been* any moral actions. And every morality is *impossible: just like every moral action*.

But the history of what has *been accepted* up to now as moral action: and the true *meaning* of the acceptance. And the history of the emergence of this *acceptance*.

They all proceed from the belief that morality itself is *there*, at least as a conscious *measure* (as with Kant), that we *know* what good and evil are.

The essential unknowability.

Something is necessarily *achieved*: but already *knowledge* of it is *impossible*, therefore even *foreknowledge of it*!

The most important standpoint: *to attain the innocence of becoming, in that purpose is excluded*. Necessity, causality — all gone! And always to brand as mendacity any mention of "purpose" wherever a *necessary result* appears! History can never prove "purpose": for, one thing is clear, that what peoples and individuals have **wanted** has always been essentially different from what has been *achieved* — in short, that *everything that has been achieved* is absolutely *incongruent* with *what has been wanted* (e.g., *chewing* as "intention" and "action")

History of "intentions" is something other than history of "facts": — in morality. It is the **crudest form of prejudice** *to see nothing more than what is congruent* with its *intended purpose*. This *attention to purpose* is a sign of a *low* level of intellect — everything essential, *the action itself and the result are* **overlooked**!

7 [22]²⁸

While wandering through the many subtler and cruder moralities, I found certain traits in a consistent pattern, always recurring with each other and connected to each other: so that finally two basic types were revealed to me: there is master-morality and slave-morality. I would add that, in times of higher culture, attempts at mediating between both moralities come to light, even more frequently their intermingling, indeed occasionally a bitter coexistence — even in the same person, within a single soul.

First question: where did moral value judgments emerge? In general, among aristocrats, among a ruling kind that becomes conscious of how it differs from the ruled.

In general, making moral value judgments means that a superior kind of human being becomes conscious of its superiority to a lower kind.

The need to form a superior kind of human being initially existed in relation to the subjugated, then in relation to virtue. In the first case, the exceptional, unique, noble, distinguishing qualities are emphasized, in the second case, the difficulty in attaining and maintaining a noble type, in short, in working toward virtue.

Second question. What follows in general from the fact that the rulers are the ones who determine the concept "good"?

There are in fact a number of traits that *return* in drastically differing moralities: the reason for this lies in the fact that the traits of the *powerful* are contained in these moralities.

An immoral person is in general a contemptible person (*not* an "evil" person).

This extends as far as the ultimate consequence: those who, like me, devalue moral value judgments by comparing them to each other, want to distinguish themselves as superior human beings from those who can bear to live according to conventional value judgments.

The sublime loftier states are the ones that are called "good":[29]

Contempt for those who are cowardly, anxious

Contempt for those who think of strict utility, for petty people

Contempt for the mistrustful, who want to have oaths

Contempt for the poor, for beggars, self-denigrators, slave- and dog-like people, who let themselves be mistreated.

By contrast, all honor to feelings of fullness and of over-flowing: rich enough to help the unfortunate,

All honor to those who have control over themselves, who understand when to speak and when to be silent, who understand when to command and when to obey

All honor to wisdom that knows how to keep long-term utility in mind and that can stand by its long-term decisions

All honor to those who don't *want* to be liked, because they like themselves: the proud.

Reverence for elders

       for ancestors

reverence for *women*[30] is modern:[31] respect for the *elderly* is somewhat *lacking*.

ἀμύνεσθαι "defense" as a part of revenge.[32]

capacity for long-term gratitude and revenge.

Restitution as a delusion of justice. —

anyone indifferent to a grave personal offense is contemptible . . . but: "the best man is the one who can bear the most insults" Menander.[33]

but *not* inclined to bear a grudge! —

complete distinction between judging actions directed at equals and actions directed at beings of lesser rank.

the *friend*

The enemy is *not* regarded as contemptible: hence *evil* actions have a different value than the enemy's actions.

Inasmuch as enmity *is necessary*, the point of it must be kept in mind, thus in a certain sense *cultivated*.

(like deception among the Spartans)

hardness of feeling, cruelty, etc.

Enemies are needed as lightning rods for affects like jealousy, contentiousness — in order to be a good *friend*.

the **powerful ones** judge: anyone who harms *me* is *harmful by nature*. They are the supreme determiners of value.

What would the *commonalities in morality* have to look like when the weak, the *subjugated* and the oppressed moralize?

When those who are victimized, oppressed, suffering, unfree, unsure of themselves, exhausted, moralize: what will be the commonalities in their moral distinctions? Probably a suspicion will be expressed; perhaps a condemnation of humans along with their situation.

A denigrating view of the virtues of the more powerful: subtle skepticism and mistrust of everything "good" will be honored there and also a decrease in the happiness of the powerful and a diminishment of life.

Foregrounding of the qualities by means of which those who suffer can make their lives easier: renown of *compassion*, but for different reasons than those given when the powerful celebrate it (utility is the reason)

Renown of *humility* and refinement of this viewpoint through universal subjugation to the laws of existence: predilection for "unfreedom of the will"[34] — human beings dependent through and through.

There is a kind of *revenge* in the foregrounding of competing virtues: thus *abstinence*, capricious mortification, solitude, intellectual poverty are praised: and the future is associated with apathy.

In Europe this entire moral pivot is *Jewish*.

Granted, this kind of mentality gradually achieves dominance and people who have it become the rulers: thus the result is a monstrous *moral mendacity* (or shamelessness).

(the plebeian quality in the Greek moralists Socrates)

This happened among the European clergy. In English utilitarianism, in Kant, Schopenhauer.

(value of the French: their *tact* in regard to shame)

Now a second twist is possible: that of *shamelessness*: the universal pleasure in the human beast, in the *fact* that there are illusions

*Among the ruled, evil becomes "**bad**."*

Imagining a grand *revenge* (Tertullian)[35,36]

7 [23]

That which is logical, time, space would have to be produced by us: nonsense! When the mind obeys its own laws, this is

because they are *actually true*, true in themselves! That we *believe* in
this truth, absolutely, is the consequence of the abnormal people
dying out: *an error with respect to these truths avenges itself.*[37]

7 [24]

   Since Rée proceeds from the principle that good is solely
what people do not do for their own sake: then when he wants
to give society the right to make use of the maxim "the end
justifies the means," he has, in a most laughable fashion, provided the rope for his own hanging.[38] This is because, with all
its punishment of criminals, society seeks *its own* preservation
and advantage — there is no doubt about this. Consequently,
there is nothing good, nothing holy about society's end: consequently, its end cannot justify its evil means.
   Anyone who remains fixated on "good" and "evil" cannot
punish: the same is true of anyone who believes in "deserved"
and "undeserved": against all of this, absolute causality must be
established. — Only when power is seized by a superior kind of
human being to oppress a lesser kind, to keep it reined in, in
any case to oppose it on all fronts: do I understand everything
having to do with "punishing." It is *oppression* — using the
word justice is Phariseeism. I wouldn't know from where to derive
the notion that the stronger, the superior *are allowed* to use their
power against the lesser: much less why they should *not* be
allowed to.
   In any place where that which is superior is *not* that which
is more powerful, *something is lacking precisely in that which is
superior*: it is only a fragment and a mere shadow.

7 [25][39]

   Pain and pleasure are only *accompanying phenomena*.
   Hunger does not have as its goal satisfying the appetite: but
rather, the process, the *distinguishing feature* of that which we
call hunger, is in no way a drive or a state of feeling: it is a
chemical state in which the affinity for other things is perhaps
greater.

How impoverished is our insight into everything that is real if we are bound by *pleasure* and *displeasure* as *the only language for it*!

"Drive" is only a translation from the language of nonfeeling into the language of feeling:

"Will": this is what is communicated to our feelings as a *result* of that process — in other words already an *effect*, and *not* the beginning and cause.

Our speech is a *mishmash* of two spheres.

"End and means" — is only taken from the language of *feeling*.

Thus every single function *goes its own way*: but how little of it we notice! — And still we think that we can *explain* our actions with "ends," with striving for bliss!

7 [26]⁴⁰

Not "happiness follows virtue" — but rather the more powerful people *initially determine their state of happiness as virtue*.

Evil actions are the province of the powerful and the virtuous: bad base actions are the province of the subjugated.

The most powerful people have to be the most evil, inasmuch as they force their ideals on all people *in opposition to* all those people's ideals and reshape these ideals in their image — the ones who create.

Evil means here: hard-hearted painful imposed

7 [27]⁴¹

Humans like Napoleon must continually return and reinforce faith in the self-glorification of the individual: yet he himself was corrupted by the means he *had to* employ and *lost* the *noblesse* of character. In establishing himself among a different kind of human being, he could have used other means, and so it would not have been *necessary* that a Caesar *would have had to become a bad person*.

7 [28]

To help the common masses achieve a ruling position is clearly the only means of *ennobling* their kind: but hopefully not in their struggle for domination, but rather once they *have begun to rule*. Instead, the struggle unleashes their most profound baseness.

Hence the Jews ruling for a while is the only means of *ennobling* them.

7 [29]

"We act according to 'ends'" (according to *representations* that accompany expected pleasurable *feelings*) — or so we say. In truth, something *completely different*, unconscious and unknowable, is happening: with the phrase "ends and means," we fix our gaze on the tiniest part of what happens — and *we initially interpret* even that *as ends and means*.

We speak as if feelings *were causes* and **could** be causes in the realm of nonfeeling people.

The *images and reflexes* of a process are understood and interpreted by us as the process itself.

This is our greatest error, to think that the *reality* of a process is **proved** through pleasure and pain, to think that here everything is most real.

Feelings as accompanying phenomena can certainly teach us the *sequence of processes* of which they are images: but **not** the **causality of this sequence**.

7 [30]

Those who are useful to others, why should they be better than when they are useful to themselves? But only when the utility they provide others is superior in an absolute sense to the utility they provide themselves. If others are *worth less*, then the useful act rightly when they are useful to themselves, even at the expense of others.

All this chatter about "utility" already presupposes that what is useful to people has been defined: in other words, useful **for**

what! i.e., the *people's purposes* are *already taken for granted*. Survival, making people happy, etc., if these are purposes: but then there are also circumstances under which their opposites are the higher purposes, e.g., as with a pessimistic view of life and suffering.

Thus, a *belief* is already presupposed — when praising those who are not self-interested:[42] that the ego *does not deserve* to take precedence over the ego of another? Yet *this* is contradicted by the *higher* appraisal of those who are not self-interested: indeed, they are certainly assumed to be a rarer type. For what reason, then, *should* the rarer superior people lose sight of themselves? — They certainly shouldn't, it is stupid, but they do it: and others *profit by it* and are grateful to them for it: they *praise* them. — Thus do egoistic people praise those who are unegoistic, because they are stupid enough to put *their* advantage ahead of their own advantage: because they act as egoistic people would not — but to *their* benefit.

7 [31]

According to Spinoza: "insofar as humans make use of reason, they consider **useful** only *that which leads to knowing*."[43]

7 [32]

The *supreme ruler* and the *slave* (the former elevated into a god, the latter sinking by the same measure)

7 [33][44]

That in all "sense-impressions" we are not only passive but rather *very active*, choosing, connecting, completing, interpreting — it has to do with sustenance, as with a *cell*: with assimilation and adjustment of what is disparate.

7 [34]

the limited *means of knowledge* "he is calmed, subdued, renouncing, patient, collected"[45] the more proximate means of knowledge: study of the Vedas, sacrifice, alms, penitence, fasting — a *means* of *achieving knowledge*.

7 [35]

Spinoza took *revenge* on *Jewish law* through his ethics: "individuals can do what they *want*":[46] similar to Paul.

7 [36][47]

In repudiating all eudaimonism, Kant sought the most extreme expression of *moral pride*: absolute *obedience*: the ideal of a *subjugated* and *oppressed person* who assigns all value wherever the obedient have the best training — and no "pleasure," no matter what!

7 [37]

"Illusions are necessary, not only for happiness, but also for the preservation and enhancement of humans: in particular, no action at all is possible without illusion. Even each step forward in knowledge is not possible except through illusion: *consequently*, the source of the illusion must *be maintained* if we want to know, behave correctly and grow" — that's what I once thought.[48]

If there were an *absolute morality*, it would demand that the truth be followed *unconditionally*: consequently, that *I and human beings would perish as a result.* — This my interest in *destroying morality*. In order to be able to live and to become superior— in order to *satisfy* the *will to power*, every *absolute commandment* would have to be *abolished*. For the *most powerful* human beings, even *lying* is *an acceptable means* when creating: this is exactly how nature works.

7 [38]

The morality of *prudence* developed in oppressed natures: to the point that the crime that remains concealed is regarded as virtuous and has beneficial consequences for the perpetrator.

The *extreme pursuit of pleasure as a goal of morality* is already characteristic of oppressed and suffering natures. With the powerful, things are appraised according to the *pleasures* **of the moment**: here *lofty feelings* become intellectual.

Eudaimonism hedonism utilitarianism as signs of unfreedom, just like every prudential morality.[49]

Heroism as sign of freedom. "Hints of a heroic philosophy."[50]

Heroism includes, then, even a heartfelt involvement in the trivial, the idyllic.

7 [39]

We don't have to look for morals (even less, morality!) in those who write about morals, the vast majority of *moral theorists* are oppressed suffering impotent vengeful — they are drawn to a little happiness: sick people who think that convalescence is everything.

7 [40]

A very *noble* way of thinking shines forth in La Rochefoucauld, characteristic of the society of that time: he himself is a disappointed idealist who under the *inspiration of Christianity* seeks out *nasty* names for the impulses of his time.

7 [41]

The moral *complexity* of the soul throughout Christianity and the time of chivalry is suited to the character of Louis XIV and his era: the Greeks (Homer) seem too simple and straightforward, even with respect to their souls.

7 [42]

With freedom of trade, *groups of similar* people can band together and establish associations in common. *Overcoming of nations.*

Predators and the primeval forest show that *evil* can be quite healthy and helps to build magnificent bodies. If predatory species of animals were plagued by inner struggles, they would long ago have atrophied and degenerated.

Dogs (who whine and whimper so much) are degenerate predators, just like cats. Huge numbers of good-hearted oppressed people show that *good-heartedness* is *accompanied* by a decline in vitality: fearful feelings *predominate*! and control the organism.

Therefore we do not have to foreground the kind of evil that shows up as overly refined and stimulating, as a result of physical degeneration (cruelty-induced-lust etc.) and the moral *mindlessness* that comes with moral insanity![51]

To observe *goodness*, how it shows up as a *sign of degeneration* — as religious lunacy e.g., as philanthropy etc.: wherever there is a decline in healthy egoism and a pursuit of apathy or asceticism. The "saint" as ideal of the atrophied body, even the entire Brahmin-philosophy a sign of degeneration.

a) the superior kind: — — —
b) the inferior kind: — — —
c) the degenerates: their "good"
                          their "evil."

7 [43]
"No one wants her as a gift: so she needs to sell herself!"[52] — I said

7 [44]
I consider Greek morality to be the supreme morality up to now; what this consideration shows me is that its *bodily* expression made ⟨it⟩ the supreme morality up to now.

Yet *by that* I mean the actual *people's morality — not the one espoused by the philosophers*: the *decline of morals* begins with Socrates: there are exclusively one-sided elements in the different systems that in earlier times were parts of a whole — it is *the disintegrated older ideal*. In addition there is the predominantly plebeian character, there are people without power, marginalized, oppressed etc.

In more recent times the Italian Renaissance brought human beings to their highest level: "*the Florentines*" — for similar reasons. *Isolated conditions* are also evident there **alongside** perfect and *whole* human beings, like *fragments*: e.g., "the tyrant" is such a fragment: the art aficionado.

Perhaps the Provençal had already achieved such an apogee in Europe — *very rich*, multifaceted, and yet self-possessed human beings, who were not ashamed of their drives.

7 [45]

Luther's kind of *enmity* betrays his peasant heritage and baseness, his lack of nobility.

Napoleon corrupted in the struggle for power, like Bismarck. I am hoping for puny "tyrants" in the coming century.[53]

7 [46]

From offstage Stendhal cites as a proverb: "*Telle trouve à se vendre, qui n'eût pas trouvé à se donner.*"[54]

7 [47][55]

"*Morality as sign language.*"

7 [48]

We cannot conceive the beginning of moral judging (in other words, morals —) modestly enough, a beginning which came late, perhaps millennia later than morality: that is why I took pleasure in watching R⟨ée⟩ attempt to construct the entire, wonderful gothic edifice of morals upon a few clever assertions, a few errors, a few forgettable assertions! I myself had other foundations: but we both had in common the tendency to think that the foundations had to be as bad as possible.[56]

7 [49]

Everything works so shoddily and unscientifically these days — see the first page of Lecky![57]

7 [50]

Competent in war and competent in giving birth: this is immediately and supremely decisive.

7 [51]

Noblesse demands repaying like with like, *even in revenge*: the concern of those who still *place limits* even on their own affects — it is just the same with gratitude. But what business does the state have with this *noblesse*!

7 [52]

The *most free action* is one where our truest strongest most subtly integrated nature springs forth and in such a way that *our intellect simultaneously* shows its *controlling* hand. — Therefore the *most arbitrary* and yet *most reasonable* action!

7 [53]

the argument against revenge grounded in unfree will would also be an argument against gratitude: the fact that the doer is *unfree* has nothing to do with our repayment of good deeds.

7 [54]

Reward and *punishment* corrupt our ability to see the natural consequences of every action.

7 [55]

How *can* the state *take responsibility for* revenge! First, it is coldhearted and does not act through affects: which someone taking revenge does. Next, it is not a person, much less a noble person: therefore it also cannot demonstrate its *noblesse* and self-discipline in the process of keeping things in *proportion* (as in "like for like"). Third, it robs revenge of precisely *that* which leads to the restoration of *injured honor*: the voluntary forsaking of life, danger for the sake of honor. It would therefore offer satisfaction only to the *ignobly* thinking injured party, while, on the contrary, *robbing* those who are noble of the opportunity *to restore their honor.* — Finally: it presupposes the shamelessness of the injured parties: who must speak publicly of their injuries! The "complaint" is, after all, a demand made by the state! But the noble person suffers *in silence.* — Thus only base natures are able to see the state as *a tool of retribution.* Hence the bitter struggle *against* the state *on behalf of* the vendetta. — Pasquale Paoli was forced for this reason to portray the surrender to the whole as *something nobler* — as a sacrifice! — and to demand the renunciation of vendettas as a *superior* kind of self-overcoming: for this reason he *denounced* anyone who takes revenge.

The state affords *protection* to those who are weaker, who are incapable of defending themselves against evildoers: punishments are therefore initially security measures, also insofar as they deter. The state does not want **us to defend ourselves** — it does *not* fear revenge, but rather *sovereign mentality*!

Therefore: subjugation to *state justice* is a **self-sacrifice**, of no benefit to more noble people. Given this, the state itself must have functioned as something that was felt to be *superior*: in short, *faith in the sanctity* (venerability) of the state must be **older** than subjection under the exercise of state justice: older and *stronger*! The nobility maintains for a long time its *high status* in regard to children and slaves: thus its sovereignty. — The *impulses of heroism,* not the standpoint of prudence, were crucial to the *emergence of the state*: the faith that there is something superior to the sovereignty of the individual. Here respect for the extended family and for the elders of a particular extended family plays a part: the younger generation makes offerings to it. The veneration of the dead and the transmitted wisdom of ancestors: people of today make offerings to it. — Here homage to someone who is intellectually superior and victorious plays a part: the delight at encountering our own idol in the flesh: here oaths of fealty emerge. — It is *not coercion, and not prudence,* that hold the early forms of the state together: but rather the outpouring of more noble impulses.

Force would be impossible to impose, and prudence is perhaps still *insufficiently* developed in the individual. — A common *danger* probably provides the *impetus* for coming together: and the feeling of new *collective power* is something *compelling* and is a source of more noble decisions.

7 [56]⁵⁸,⁵⁹

At one point there was a *theory* of the state as a calculable utility: *now we have the practice* of it! — The time of kings has passed[60] because the people are no longer worthy of them: they do not *want* to see in their king the archetype of their ideals, but a means to their utility. — This is the whole truth!

7 [57]

Human beings *would certainly like to have something* like supreme purpose, ultimate goal, absolute duty, ⟨absolute⟩ ought: the demand for these is the cause of the many moralities. But *what is the cause of these demands*? Probably many factors, e.g., — once it has *taken control of the intellect, every single* human *drive* probably demands to be recognized as the *ultimate lord* and goal-setter of all human matters. *The most disparate drives have erected their monuments in moralities.*

7 [58]⁶¹

There are moralities which are meant to *legitimate* their creators in the eyes of other people: other moralities are meant to *pacify* and satisfy the creators; with other moralities they want to *nail* themselves on the *cross*; with others they want to *take revenge* on other people; with others they want to *conceal* themselves; with others they want to *glorify* themselves, whether in their own eyes or in the eyes of other people; with others they want to *elevate and improve themselves*; with others they want to exercise power and *creativity* on humankind; with others they want to obey, with others to *rule and humiliate*. With others they want to *forget* or *be forgotten*. Enough, moralities are nothing but a sign language of the affects.

7 [59]

not the *intention of an action*, but rather precisely *what is unintended* about it, determines its value or disvalue.

7 [60][62]

Moralities as sign language of the affects: the affects themselves, however, a sign language of the functions of everything organic.

7 [61]

Quite apart from the value of such assertions: such as "there is a categorical imperative!" it can still be asked: what does such an *assertion* say *about the person who is asserting it.*

7 [62]

It is just now dawning on people that music is a sign language of the affects: and eventually we will learn clearly to recognize musicians' systems of drives by analyzing their music. They certainly wouldn't think that *they were revealing themselves in this way.* This is the *innocence* of these self-confessions, as opposed to that of all written works.

But there is also this innocence in the great philosophers: they are not aware *that they are speaking of themselves* — they think it has to do "with the truth" — but really it has to do with them. Or rather: the most powerful drive within them forces itself to the surface, with the greatest shamelessness and innocence of a fundamental drive — *it* wants to be master and, wherever possible, the purpose of all things, of everything that happens! The philosopher is only a kind of occasion, and enabling means, whereby the *drive speaks for the first time.*

There are many more languages than we think: and people reveal themselves much more often than they would like. What doesn't speak! — yet there are still so few of those who hear people babbling forth their confessions, as it were, into empty rooms: people are squanderers with their "truths," as the sun is with its light. — Isn't it a shame that empty rooms have no ears?

There are viewpoints that make people feel: "this *alone is true and right* and truly human; anyone who thinks differently is wrong" — these are called religious and ethical viewpoints. It is clear that *a sovereign drive is speaking here* which is stronger than the person. Here, each time the drive believes itself to be in possession *of the truth and of the highest concept "human."*

There are probably many p⟨eople⟩ in whom one drive has *not* become *sovereign*: they have no convictions. This is therefore the first characteristic: Every philosopher's closed system proves that in this philosopher *one* drive is the ruler, that *a fixed order of rank exists*. This then calls itself: "*truth*." — The feeling here is: with this truth, I have reached what it means to be "human": the other is *of a kind inferior to me*, at least as the kind of person who knows.

With primitive and naïve people, convictions even rule in regard to their customs, indeed in regard to their tastes: it is the *best possible* thing. With cultured peoples, tolerance rules in regard to such matters: but in that case there is an *even more strict* adherence to their highest standard of good and evil: whereby we want to have not only the *most subtle taste* but also the *sole legitimate taste*.

This is the universally *dominant form of barbarism*, *not* yet knowing that *morality is a matter of taste*.

Incidentally, in this area we find the most *lying* and *deceiving*: *moralistic* and *religious literature* is the *most mendacious*. The ruling drive, whatever it may be, employs *deceit and lies* against the other drives in order to maintain its superiority.

Alongside religious wars there persists a *moral war*: i.e., one drive wants to *subjugate* humankind; and the more that religions die off, the more *bloody* and *visible* this struggle will become. We have just begun!

7 [63]

Apperception is first and foremost only activity ("voluntary" movements!)

7 [64]

My theory: in *every action* of a person, the *entire development* of psychic life is experienced[63]

even sense perceptions are actions: in order that something can be perceived, an *active force* must already *be functioning*, a force that registers the stimulus, *allows* it to work and *adapts* to a stimulus like that and *modifies* it.

It is a fact *that something absolutely new is continually being generated*. "Cause and effect" is merely the popular generalization of "means and end" i.e., of another popular logical function to which *nothing* in reality corresponds. There are no *final* appearances, except to a being that has already created a *beginning* and an *end*.

There is also always something *new* being generated in the development of the mind. Feelings[64] and representations are absolutely *not derivable from each other*. Thought and feeling![65]

7 [65]

The "voluntary" movement of the lowest organisms is — — —

7 [66]

First: how can people be made capable of ruling themselves? second: how — — —

7 [67]

Digesting everything that the past has produced is certainly not what is most desirable: that's why I wish that *Dante* would offend our tastes and appetites in some fundamental way.

7 [68]

To regard *Hamlet* as the pinnacle of the human intellect — that's what I call not judging intellect and pinnacles harshly

enough. This is above all a *failed* work: its creator would probably laughingly admit this if I said it to his face.

7 [69]
Why has a judicial reward not developed alongside judicial
punishment? Why has the state not also taken responsibility
for the individuals' gratitude toward others?

"Justice," according to Ihering, *securing the conditions of life
within society by means of compulsion.*[66]

An act is *not* evil *in itself*, but only insofar as etc.[67]

e.g., a troublemaker can be *killed* without penance
    martyring and *torturing* on behalf of the state
    stealing among Egyptians
Collective conscience and *collective responsibility.*
It is not the guilt that is *punished.*
Crime as *misfortune.*
To distinguish between bad (contemptible) and evil.
Morality among the powerful and the subjugated.

Tremendous *complexity* of the emergence of current moral
value determination: but **unity** as *feeling.*

Anyone who refuses to punish on account of freedom of the
will is also not entitled to praise, to thank, to be angry: the
fundamental belief of *all affects while interacting* is — — —

7 [70]
Desire for revenge[68] is awareness of *being injured, first* as a matter of fact, *second with respect to our belief in our power* (rationality,
formidableness etc.) Both require a counterresponse, thus: *1) defense,
2) substitution*, and *3) generating a feeling of power*: **leaving aside
completely the belief in the perpetrator's guilt**. The *desire for
revenge has nothing to do with belief in the freedom of the will.*

7 [71]
    Organic — moral.
    Freedom of the will.
    Evil as the preliminary stage of a good.

7 [72]

"What is *good* for me is good in itself" is only the judgment of someone powerful who is *accustomed to assigning value*.

7 [73]

Perhaps it has never been seen as a problem *that* moralizing happens at all. Is it *necessary* that human beings will always moralize?[69] Or couldn't morality die out, just as astrological and alchemical speculation has died out or is dying out? Necessary for what? For life? But it is possible to live without judging morally, as plants and animals show. Or necessary for a happy life? The abovementioned animals show that in any case it is possible to live more happily than human beings — even without morality. Therefore morality cannot be necessary either to life as such or to becoming happier: without going so far as to make morality responsible for the fact that human beings suffer more than animals: — suffering more in this way could certainly have other causes and morality could perhaps be a means of warding off a great deal more suffering. But it is certainly the case that if becoming happier and becoming more free of suffering were the goal we had to set for ourselves: a gradual bestialization would be rational: which would in any case also have to include refraining from moral judgments. So, if humans want not just to live and not just to live more happily: what do they want? Now, morality says: we should act this or that way — why "should"? *Therefore morality must know this*: this why, this goal, which is neither life as such nor becoming a happier person. — But it doesn't know this! it contradicts itself! **It gives orders**, but it is incapable of justifying itself. — *Giving orders is the essence of what it does!*

So what purpose does morality serve? Away with every "thou shalt"!

7 [74]

The feeling of "*being bad*" is completely different at that level where guilt is not actually connected to intention: Oedipus (more *disgrace* and unhappiness)

Actually, there is no "badness" in *noble* morality: yet "evil" still has something about it that inspires reverence or compassion.

7 [75]

Actions e.g., stealing are *accompanied* by completely different categories of feeling and judgment once they are seen as allowed.

It is possible to show, through the comparison of peoples, that *this* is perceived as *good* in one place and *bad in another*: but the *opposition* itself of "good" and "bad" is present everywhere: it is just that actions are *classified* otherwise. — *And yet* there are also differences in the universal judgment good and bad!

7 [76]

Animals follow their drives and affects: we are animals. Do we do anything else? Perhaps it is merely an *illusion* when we follow morality? In truth, do we follow our drives, and is morality merely a *sign language* of our drives? What is "duty" "justice" the "good," the "law" — which drive-life corresponds to these abstract signs?

When morality says: "you should become *better*" — why "better"? — Neither life nor the prospect of a happier life can demonstrate this. Hence the *indemonstrable imperative* the commandment without purpose — this is supposed to be morality?

Yet "better" — is in no way *conceivable* without purpose.

7 [77]

What is the source of actions? That is *my* question. For what purpose? to what end? is something secondary. Either *from pleasure* (*overflowing* feeling of force, which must exhaust itself) or from *displeasure* (restraining the feeling of power, which must free itself or ensure compensate for itself) The question: how should we act? is posed: as if something could not be accomplished until an action has taken place: but what is most proximate is *the action itself as success*, as what is accomplished, *apart* from the consequences of the action.

Therefore, people do not act *for the sake of happiness* or *utility* or in order to avoid displeasure: but rather a *certain amount of force* is released, seizes something on which it can vent itself. That which is called "*goal*," "*purpose*," is in truth the *means* for this involuntary explosive process

And *one and the same amount of feeling-of-force can be discharged in a thousand ways*: this is "freedom of the will" — the feeling that a hundred different actions serve just as well in relation to the necessary explosion. The feeling of a certain *choice* of actions in regard to this release of tension.

My solution: the degree of feeling of force makes the mind fertile; it displays many goals, chooses one goal for itself which, when pursued, is tension-relieving for the feeling: thus, there is a double discharge: once in *anticipating* a tension-relieving goal, then in the action itself.

"if I did that, I would despise myself, and then I would be unhappy." This would therefore mean: not to do a deed *because of the consequences for my feelings*.[70]

Helvétius thinks that *when the possibility of an action arises in us*, we basically ask "what will be the consequences of this action for my feelings?"[71]

Stendhal *sur l'amour* v. p. 252.[72]

Yet the *first* fact is *that* this possibility appears to noble people: they see something about which simple souls have no idea.

An overflowing charged feeling of force is there: the goal set for the action provides an *anticipation* of tension relief and thereby *pushes even more toward discharge*; the resulting action provides the actual tension relief.

So it is! *The goal that is set brings the desire for discharge to its peak.*

Therefore: **happiness**, "*le plaisir*"[73] as a goal of action, is only a means of increasing the tension: it must not be confused with the *happiness that lies in the action itself.* The final happiness is very determined; the happiness in the action could be expressed through a hundred such precisely determined images of happiness.

Therefore: the "in order that" is an illusion: "I am doing this *in order to* harvest the happiness from it." This is not the way it is. The person who acts *forgets* the actual *driving force* and *sees* **only** the "motive."

"The happiness in reaching a goal" is itself an *offspring* of *the tension of forces*: an analogical anticipation and self-escalation. *Eudaimonism* is therefore a result of *imprecise observation*. We do *not* act for the sake of enjoyment: *yet that is the illusion of the person who acts.*

7 [78]
Dühring Cursus p. 147, "the mechanical state of the body is a partial condition of cosmological mechanics"[74]

7 [79]
"I must not punish him — for he can't help it" — this "I must not" means: I would act *irrationally*, as if I wanted to punish a tree that had fallen and killed someone.

7 [80]
Fearful people, with vivid imaginations, who would be ready to subjugate themselves and to reconcile very easily — become increasingly obsessed with thoughts of endangerment that spring out of fear and imagined fear and *for this reason* easily *take disproportionate, deadly* **revenge** — revenge for suffering that they had mostly only *dreaded*.

7 [81][75]
Organic beings have 1) the force to bond chemically 2) particular explosions that regulate these chemical processes. When

both of these conditions *coincidentally* happen in conjunction with each other and simultaneously, so that the temporal joining and ⟨the⟩ force of these explosions work to regulate the bonding and dissolution processes, then there emerges an organic being. This is therefore the result of *these two older kinds of beings*: such regular exploding and such growth processes.

7 [82]

Accusers do *not* want *to admit to themselves* how *useful* the pain was to them. Their *drive for revenge* is revealed in this way: with words they wish to hurt and to exert their power over whatever wounded them.

7 [83]

How much more we live with a *sense of well-being* is revealed by the fact that pain is felt so much **more strongly** than a single pleasure.

7 [84][76]

Truth and courage only in those *who are free* (truth *a kind* of *courage*)

The *evildoer* as *an unhappy person*: form of *humanity*.
Servitude makes someone *bad*.

we don't *react to most injuries*, rather we *submit*. (Missing in Dühring!)

7 [85]

noble — good
Characteristics of *persons* — later *applied* to actions.

7 [86][77]

1) Struggle of the parts for space
   for nourishment
   whether with or without stimuli[78]
2) direct struggle with destruction or assimilation of the weaker[79]

3) the stronger produce more offspring than the weaker[80]
the advantage always belongs to those who have a greater tendency to more easily regenerate themselves and to consume less.

greater capacity for self-nourishment and less consumption for their own needs — applying this morally! — favorable preconditions for growth and, with it, autocratic rule.[81]

When nourishment is lacking, the first to die out and starve will be those who *consume* the most nourishment.[82]

Advantage to those who, under stimulation, use up their own resources the least rapidly, even more so where assimilation of nourishment and regeneration thereby become stronger, indeed are *made stronger* by the stimulus to the point of overcompensation.[83]

Morally: the value of **pain**, of *injury*
Ability to resist pressure gives advantage

7 [87]
In themselves, *courage, shame, anger* have nothing to do with concepts
physiological facts, the name of which and the *psychological* conception of which, are mere symbols
What does language express about the *names of the affects*? *ira*[84]
What does it mean: to change a person through morality? therefore physiologically through chronic fear or extreme agitation exhaustion
To study the effect of illnesses on the *affects*.

7 [88][85]
my task: to position the good drives so that they get hungry and have to activate themselves.

7 [89][86]

Concerning the existence of highly perfected mechanisms of adaptation Roux p. 43 Emergence of animals out of the water

7 [90][87]

The *characteristics that are typical in a family* first become fully visible in the man; the least visible in easily stimulated, excitable adolescents. Tranquility must have set in first and the *number* of external stimuli reduced: or on the other hand the *excitability* must have significantly subsided. — That is why peoples *past their prime* are so eloquent concerning *their typical characteristics* and make them more clearly known than they did in the *bloom of their youth*.

7 [91]

Struggle leads to the *survival of the best*.

7 [92]

Rivalry among citizens, it's always the most industrious who achieve an *enduring* influence: thus the state continues to exist.[88]

Relative autonomy of the parts even in the highest organisms Roux p 65.

7 [93]

Concerning the inequality[89] that really exists Roux. 69.

7 [94]

In the same way that, physiologically, cell borders cell, so, too, drive borders drive. The most comprehensive image of our being is *a socialization of drives*, with continuing rivalries and individual alliances among them. The intellect object of the competition.

7 [95]

When a quality of the cell is chemically constituted such that assimilation outweighs decomposition, therefore over-compensation for what is consumed, *growth* appears: this important feature thus establishes *dominance* over the other q⟨ualities⟩.

We don't know of any organism, any cell, that would not have this force in one stage of its life: life would *not* be able *to propagate* without this force.

The struggle for nourishment and space takes place in the cell as soon as there is an inequality of constituent parts.[90]

Processes which increase their capacity for life, namely for assimilation, through additional *stimuli*: where therefore the stimulus has a *trophic, nourishment-increasing effect* — funda-mental condition for plants, the nourishment of which is entirely dependent on sunlight and warmth (even electric light produces rapid unfolding and fructification.[91]

Thus, influence of stimuli on more rapid assimilation — in morality: increase in power at the place where a plethora of the *most subtle injuries* occurs and, with that, an increase in the need for *appropriation*. (Even more so with exotic foreign ideas — Greeks.)

The more easily *reactive substance* accommodates *more stimulus*.[92]

7 [96]

Justice — the will to perpetuate a particular power relation-ship. Satisfaction with this is the prerequisite. Everything wor-thy of honor is added in order to allow justice to appear as something eternal.

7 [97]

Practical consequence. Transformation of character. Breed-ing instead of moralizing.

to work with direct influence on the organism instead of the indirect influence of ethical breeding. Then another kind of corporality *is* already *creating* for itself *another* soul and ethos. So *reverse it*!

in Socrates, a *plebeian* mistrust of the affects: they are ugly, wild — therefore to be repressed — that's why *Epicurus* is ahead of the *Stoics* in terms of *nobility*. Yet *they* are more *understandable on a popular level*.

In much the same way, the Christian saint is a plebeian ideal.

7 [98]

Processes emerge where a stimulus becomes necessary, *becomes a stimulus to life*: otherwise deterioration and decline set in.

These are the *supreme processes*.[93]

All of this occurs *without* the struggle among individuals.[94]

Selection in the struggle among individuals will *choose* those characteristics for lasting preservation that prove to be *useful* for the *whole individual*.[95]

Therefore: many kinds of morality must emerge — the struggle among their supporters and their triumph result in *lasting preservation* for the kind of morality that is *useful* and indispensable for the *life* of the most powerful.

Innumerable *attempts* at moral value judgments must have already been made, depending on the development of separate *strong basic feelings*:

Absolute requirement that the best *morality* must be associated with the *most powerful individuals*: who are they?

All states and communities are *inferior* compared to the individual, but are *necessary* forms[96] of the individual's *higher education*.

7 [99]

The "*real meaning*" behind[97] **accusations** is that people always *intensify* their pain: so that they do not let it go too quickly — thus drawing upon even *superior* forces, the sculptors of themselves!

7 [100]

To have a subtle knowledge of what hurts us and of how easily others hurt us, and as it were to influence their thoughts in advance so that they do not act in ways that are painful to us: this is the main thing for many amiable people: they bring joy and allow the joy in others to pour forth — because they *are so frightened of pain*. This is called *"sensitivity."* — Those with a reclusive hardened nature have no need to put themselves in other people's shoes and *often hurt* them; they do not *assume* such a great susceptibility to pain.

7 [101]

the self-enhancing aristocratic principle is always inventing superior types among superior people. Powerful people gain ever more *power over themselves*, exude ever greater force: we see that nobility has many levels — and something in the individual person *is growing* on its own.

7 [102]

Power as imagined by those who *have had to fear* it.

7 [103]

The pleasure we take in people who are similar to us, as our duplicates, is only possible if we take *pleasure in ourselves. Yet the more this is the case, the more our taste is offended by what is foreign: hatred and disgust for what is foreign are as great as our pleasure in ourselves.*

This hatred and disgust result in our *destroying* and remaining *cold* to everything that is *foreign*.

But if we take *no pleasure in ourselves*, this can be *used* as a *bridge* to *universal human compassion* and becoming closer 1) we demand the presence of others so that we forget about ourselves: conviviality in many people 2) we assume that others also take no pleasure in themselves: and once we perceive this, they no longer provoke envy "we are equal" 3) as we come to tolerate each other, despite feeling displeased with ourselves, we get used to tolerating even "those similar to ourselves." We no longer feel contempt; hatred and disgust *dissipate*: becoming closer. In this way the doctrine of universal sin and depravity *brought* people *together*. Even the truly powerful are imagined differently: "*basically* they are poor miserable people."

7[104]

    people who are walking legislation

7 [105]

    the judgment "good" appears within us as taste: as tyrannical and certain as a taste for sour pickles or as when I can't stand to be in the presence of someone spitting.

7 [106]

    do not lose the affect of distance!

7 [107]

    Conquering — is the natural consequence of *excess* power: it is the same as **creating** and **procreating**, in other words the *incorporation of one's own image* into foreign material. That is why superior humans must *create* i.e., impose their *superiority* on others, whether as teachers *or even as* **artists**. For artists want to **communicate** *themselves* or, more specifically, *their* taste: artists for their own sake is a contradiction. It is the same with *philosophers*: they want to make their taste *dominate* the world — *that is why they teach and* **write**. Wherever excess power exists, it wants to conquer: this drive is often called *love*, the love for those *with whom* the conquering instinct would like to have its way. — *Vain people* want to please, they want to exist *according to the taste of others*: in this they show their lack of creative force — they are "empty." Dissemblers hypocrites, even clever, cautious people fear the taste of others: a lack of surplus force is the prerequisite here. Whereas imprudent reckless defiant unconcerned straightforward hasty incautious qualities are more easily found in the presence of a quantity of force, which increases the tension too much and quickly explodes into action — *in opposition to utility. This* also explains why *attention to prudence* is not respected by the powerful: being prudent can easily be an indication of lack of force. On the other hand, in some circumstances *imprudent* actions are noble: and this is perhaps why *unselfishness* is praised: unselfish people i.e., those who do **not** act out of *prudence* and *caution* but like those who *spill over* — what do they care about *the direction*? Calculating people are despised: *but those who* **calculate** *for the entire community* **are all the more admired**. For we assume that people are *not superfluously* "prudent".[98] *thinking is regarded as difficult.* — — —

Thus emerges the **praise of wisdom**: as the praise of someone who thinks, calculates, deliberates often well and easily, and not out of prudence for the sake of utility, but rather out of love for the community, out of love for *perpetuating* its thoughts and institutions. This is something *rare*!

7 [108]

Fear of power as productive violence. Here is the realm of religion. On the other hand, becoming **one** *with the most powerful thing that exists* appears to be the *supreme human striving*. This is the origin e.g., of Brahmanism: generated within the imagination of the ruling caste as a fantasized expansion of the need for power, probably because this need *has no* release in *wars*.

The *union* with the godhead can be desire for supreme sensual satisfaction (feminine hysteria in many saints) or desire for supreme tranquility and stillness and spirituality (Spinoza) or desire for power etc. Or even as the consequence of the most desperate fearfulness: the only salvation and escape is to flee into God. The most refined form of this union may well be "overcoming grace" in the mystics.

7 [109]

Conscious intention in a harmful action is not considered "evil" in itself, but rather insofar as it allows *foreigners, enemies* to appear more *dangerous*. "They have evil intentions toward me," or "they have evil intentions."

As long as enemies are felt to be present, features of the ignominious contemptible are still lacking in evil actions. Only when evildoers show themselves to be simultaneously *harmful* and *pitiable*, does an action become *morally suspect*. Thus, morality begins with *contempt*.

7 [110]

Those who lie often and knowingly and live under conditions where it is dangerous and difficult to lie, are, for that very reason, sensitive to the *truth*, even to an extraordinary degree: whereas idealists and do-gooders constantly live in a fog concerning themselves and their desires and basically *can never* speak the truth: — their "taste" is not subtle enough for this.

7 [111]

Those who, as poets, want to pay with pure gold must pay with *their* experiences: for this reason, though, poets refuse to tolerate having their closest friends as interpreters — their closest friends figure things out by giving them *feedback*. Yet these closest friends should be amazed at **where** those poets *emerge* on the paths of their suffering — they should learn to look ahead and above and not backwards, below. —

7 [112]

Granted, that *punishments* should inflict pain in proportion to the severity of the crime, then they would also have to be determined in proportion to every criminal's sensitivity to pain, i.e., there should *never be a predetermined punishment for any offense*!

7 [113]

"Good people" emerge only when there is a *feeling of opposition*: these are people who are simultaneously *harmful to them and yet* **contemptible**. Lawgivers make an effort to endow many actions with this character, so that they *appear contemptible*, associated with disgrace: so that an action and its accompanying disgrace occupy a single feeling. — In general, it is our custom[99] to regard all criminals in the same way. It is otherwise where lawbreakers are admired or win *excessive* favor through great heroism and disdain for danger. E.g., *heretics* and all sectarians often win *admiration* as opposed to the contempt that initially greets them. It is evident: there is *power involved*.

7 [114]

Public-spiritedness[100] is older than *selfishness*, in any case it has been stronger for a longer time. The differences in mentality were in fact not great: and so the value of actions was not judged at all according to mentalities, but rather according to *consequences*. The *species* believed in itself *and its mentality* as a *fact of nature*: people readily expected to find their own mentality in all their neighbors —actions were simply not weighed any further, "they were all self-evident."

7 [115]

People say one thing and do something completely different: even moralists do this. **So what's the point** of moralizing? Be honest for once! The main point is, that we have to do it. Every "*what's the point*" is nothing but shadow-boxing and embellishment.

7 [116]

"representative virtue"

7 [117]

Nature wants nothing but always achieves something: *we* want something and *always achieve something else*. Our "intentions" are only "coincidences." —

7 [118]

When human beings do everything for the sake of their happiness and yet devote very little thought to what makes them happy: the result is that, for them, *reflection* brings *great displeasure*.

7 [119]

Great men[101] like Caesar Napoleon are a living species! *Every other form* of ruling is *imitation*.

7 [120]

39) Our actions *reshape us*: in every action certain forces are exercised, others are *not* exercised, thereby eventually falling into neglect: an affect always affirms itself at the expense of other affects, from which it drains some force. The actions that we *perform most often* eventually become like a *thick shell* around us: they readily make use of the force, it would be *difficult* for other intentions to prevail. — Not doing something on a regular basis reshapes a person in the same way: eventually we can tell whether others have *overcome* themselves a few times *every* day or have always let themselves go. — This is the **initial consequence of every action**, *it continues to sculpt us — our bodies* as well, of course.

40) Now *opinions* about these actions, generated *by us* **concerning ourselves**, are also a part of each action. *Our opinion about ourselves is just as much a consequence of each action* — it adds to the total assessment we have made of ourselves, whether weak, strong etc. praiseworthy blameworthy, whether we should avoid the judgments of others, whether we can show ourselves in any light. Perhaps self-deception becomes a habit: the *consequence* of this, intentionally flawed *appraisal* and squinting of the eye, seeing falsely, must of course ultimately reveal itself again in our actions. Deceit used against us, lack of trust in us, fear of us, contempt for us — *all of the affects belonging to impotent natures* progressively alter the *body* as well. The awareness of a lack of self-control, **un-noble**[102]

expressions creep in — and even if someone were living on a desert island.

7 [121]
38) Completely leaving aside all other people, the value of a human being undergoes constant change, becoming better or worse:

1) because every action builds on a person's system of affects

2) because the appraisal associated with each action builds on it and becomes in turn the cause of subsequent actions.

That which is *base, un-noble grows* — or dissipates etc.

Baseness corresponds to a completely corporeal *substrate*, and certainly not just in facial features!

7 [122]
NB. Absurdity of all praise and blame

7 [123]
the pride of the weak is so fragile because they fear that no one *believes* in their energy and force.

7 [124]
It seems like only yesterday Kant proposed in all seriousness that we should only perform actions etc.!

7 [125]
As for me, I have grown accustomed to observing a primitive kind of sign language in all moral judgments, through which certain physiological facts about the body *would like to* make their presence known: to those who have ears to hear it.[103] But who has had ears to hear it until now![104]

Now in fact that there were no ears to hear it, or wrong ears, and false interpretations ⟨existed⟩, and that for millennia, consciousness continued such vain attempts and *interpreted itself* — this proves it.

And so I believe that the understanding of morality does have a future and that hopes for improving the human body might come with this better understanding.

7 [126]

37) Anyone who has developed some idea of the body — how many systems are working simultaneously there, how many things are done for each other and against each other, how much subtle accommodation, etc. is there: will conclude that all consciousness is meager and limited by comparison: that no mind is even remotely capable of reaching what was supposed to have been accomplished here by the mind and perhaps, too, that the wisest ethicist and lawgiver would have to feel clumsy and amateurish in the middle of this mechanism of warring duties and rights. How little we are aware of! How much this limited awareness leads to error and confusion! Consciousness is but a tool: and considering the amount and significance of what is accomplished without consciousness, neither the most essential nor the most worthy of admiration. On the contrary: there is perhaps no organ so poorly developed, no other that is deficient in so many ways, no other that malfunctions so much: it is after all the organ that emerged last and is therefore still a child — let us forgive it its *childish tantrums*! These include, among much else, *morality* as the compendium of all previous value judgments concerning human actions and mentalities.

Therefore we must reverse the order of rank: everything conscious is only *of secondary importance*: that it is *nearer* and *dearer* to us would not be a reason, at least not a moral reason, for appraising it differently. That we take *what is nearer to us* to be *more important* is nothing but *age-old prejudice*. — So *learn to see things differently*! in major evaluations! That which is mental is to be preserved as sign language of the body!

7 [127]
Morality an attempt by the affects to become conscious of each other.

7 [128]
34) The recognition of *authority* increases in proportion to the decrease in creative powers

7 [129]
35) *False oppositions.* All stages still exist alongside one another (or many) — but the *higher stage* does not want to recognize the lower stage as way and means — it should be its opposite! This is the *affect of distance.* Anyone who does not possess or show it provokes the greatest confusion e.g., Epicurus.

7 [130]
36) *The same thing* e.g., self-control in some people leads someone else to think "you have to watch yourself around them, they only consider, coldly, what is to their advantage and ulterior advantage"[105] — and someone else might think "you can let yourself go in their presence and show yourself as you are — they will not go to extremes" *plurality* of all characteristics, depending on the degree of prudence, or considerations of beauty-nobility.

7 [131]
                    The Future of the *Science of Morality*
In bidding farewell to moral problems for a while, in order to avoid the danger that I myself will no longer find the time to come back to this subject, I want to provide a few hints to those etc.

7 [132]
so whether the *superior* species might not be better and more quickly achieved by means other than the terrible game of wars between peoples and revolutions? —

whether not through nutrition
                     selective breeding
                     elimination of certain experimental
                        groups

7 [133]

Our body is something far superior more refined more complicated more perfect more moral than all of the human organizations and communities known to us: the small size of tools and servants at its disposal is not a fair argument against it! In matters of *beauty* its achievement stands supreme: and our *works of art* are shadows on the wall compared to this not merely illusionary but also *living* beauty!

7 [134]

The *expansion within a state of pleasure* (in Mainländer,[106] p. 64). It wants to "show its state and expose itself to others — if it were possible, to the entire world" hugging, hopping, dancing, jumping, laughing, screaming, cheering, singing, speaking — I see an overflowing force that *wants to expend* itself

In displeasure, approximately this way: "the gleam in the eyes is extinguished, the countenance becomes white, the limbs motionless or contracted. The skin of the forehead wrinkles, the eyes close, the mouth grows silent, the hands make fists, the persons cower, collapse into themselves."[107]

The temperature changes: the extremities become cold: hotter in pleasure and in anger.

7 [135]

Key questions: can temperaments be changed?
33) The *qualities of the will* are "comparable to scorings into which the will flows at the slightest stimulus: they have expanded themselves into channels" "But infants already show great depths under mere scorings: character (its *form* of temperaments)"[108]

7 [136]   *Qualities of the Will.*

envy	magnanimity
greed	generosity
cruelty	mercy
miserliness	prodigality
infidelity	fidelity
pride	humility
defiance	pusillanimity
imperiousness	mildness
immodesty	modesty
baseness	noblemindedness
rigidity	flexibility
cowardice	temerity
injustice	justice
obduracy	openness
trickery	honesty
brashness	bashfulness
sensuousness	moderation
vileness	desire for honor
vanity	saintliness.[109]

   "moods"
  states of the will
  "movements that are felt"
  sense of life (equanimity) — its *modifications*:
    joy
    courage
    hope
    love
    hate
    despair
    fear
    sorrow.[110]
  Double movements
Wrath, rage (first the will flows back, concentrates itself (hate),
and then suddenly flows to the periphery, in order to destroy)

7 [137][111]

30) *The starting point of praise and blame*: *weak* people praise and blame *because* this and that are praised and blamed: *strong* individuals present *themselves* as the standard. The same applies to the moralists and their *own* feeling of power — depending on whether they feel themselves to be *lawgivers or teachers* of *laws that have been given.*

In the utilitarianism debate[112] both sides are in agreement —?
Bentham feels himself to be a lawgiver, Rée a ruled subject.

7 [138]

"The condition of our muscles determines in large measure our kinesthetic feeling of health and strength, fatigue, illness and weakness — with every movement of our body we know enough to estimate with incredible exactness (as with the act of seeing) the degree of contraction that we have to force our muscles to achieve. We also know the different positions that our muscles assume, even when they are at rest: we acutely *feel* a fatigued limb and especially a lame limb."[113]

7 [139]

Cold objects appear to weigh more than warm ones of the same weight (according to Weber)[114]

When 2 sensations follow each other at close enough intervals at the same place, they tend to melt into each other: the same thing happens when sensations occur in very close proximity on the skin.[115]

7 [140][116]

Love: the most powerful outpouring, the will would like to break out of its sphere, to become the entire world.

Love as based in the quality of will imperiousness
    as based in the heart
    as based in quality desire for fame (as pleasurable feeling of intellectual superiority)
    as based in fidelity (as friendship)

7 [141]

Erroneous *simplifications*: e.g., seeing something as a means while overlooking 100 things.

7 [142]

NB. *a moral feeling something very complex.* It has to do *with the fact* that saying "good" has such a different effect than saying "useful," because 50 additional ingredients are mixed in.

7 [143]

The *unconditioned* is only logically derived from the conditioned, like *nothingness* is from being. — As "unconditioning" —

7 [144]

27) All of the *wonder* we have invested in *nature* up to now we must also learn to feel when observing the *body*: it is pathetic to let ourselves be tyrannized by "big" and "little" like this! What the forest, the hills, would have to say to us — and the distant heavenly bodies "which call us to solitude"[117] (Emerson) — "these delights are good for us, they make us sober."[118]

7 [145][119]

28) The meaning of our gardens and palaces (and similarly, too, the meaning of all desire for wealth) is, *to remove disorder and coarseness from our sight and to build a homeland for the aristocracy of the soul.*

Of course most people believe that their *natures* become *superior* once such beautiful serene objects have had an effect on them: that explains the mania for Italy and travel, etc. all reading and going to the theater. *They want to be shaped* — this is the meaning of their labors on behalf of culture!

But the strong powerful want *to do the shaping and want to have nothing foreign in their presence anymore*!

29) This is why people go into the great outdoors, not to find themselves, but rather to lose themselves in it and forget themselves. "*To be outside oneself*" as the wish of all those who are weak and dissatisfied with themselves.

7 [146]

Advantage enjoyed by *cold* natures: they pursue their interests as a colder thing.

7 [147]

To accept nothing when we have nothing to give back and the *shame and pleasure* we experience in the presence of everything good — is noble. "Allowing oneself to be loved" is common.

7 [148]

The mother's compassion for her child is almost like the compassion we feel for ourselves: artists feel the same thing for their work and their fates. There's nothing noble about it: there is also *compassion for ourselves* — it is something completely different from suffering itself!

7 [149]

With "ends and means" we are speaking a *sign language*: but in this way we indicate *only* **what is peripheral about actions** (their relationship to the *accompanying phenomena* pleasure and pain)

7 [150]

24) *Contempt for the body* is a consequence of dissatisfaction with it; and the overvaluation of the mind and of moral *laws* is the state of those who habitually want to *become* something superior and who believe they can become greater by strolling around among "eternal values." All this demand for the everlasting[120] is the consequence of dissatisfaction — such is the will *to* culture, as a demand of "people dissatisfied with themselves."

7 [151]

25) The *body's* beauty — this has been understood too *superficially* by artists: this superficial beauty would have *to be followed* by a beauty in the whole inner workings of the organism

— in this way the greatest sculptors *provide inspiration* for *creating beautiful human beings*: this is the point of art — it provokes *dissatisfaction* in those who feel shamed by it and inspires creativity in those who have sufficient force. The result of a *dramatic performance* is: "*that's just how* I want to be, like this hero" — stimulation of the creative force, turned back on ourselves!

Epicurus is to the Stoa as the beautiful is to the sublime: but we would have to be Stoics at the very least in order to be capable of seeing this beauty in the first place! in order to be able to be envious of it!

7 [152]¹²¹

26) Our age with its striving to remedy accidental difficulties, to prevent them and to combat unpleasant possibilities in advance, is an age of the *poor*. Our "rich" — *they* are the poorest of all! The real *purpose* of all wealth is *to forget*!

7 [153]

Teichmüller p. 204 the I *compares* its imaginary representative content and finds the awareness of *something that happened before* (or of a content given in memory)

Thus, in all perceptions of time the I is *active*. "To atemporally bring *together* and compare the acts {of} *memory sensation* and *anticipation* — this is the activity of the I."¹²²

7 [154]

Against Kant. Of course I feel connected, even to the beautiful that appeals to me, through an interest in it. But this interest does not appear in its naked state. The expression of happiness perfection stillness, even that aspect of the artwork that is silent, that lets itself be judged — everything speaks to our *drives*. — In the final analysis I perceive as "beautiful" only that which corresponds to an ideal ("*the happy person*") of my own drives e.g., wealth, celebrity, piety, an outpouring of power, for different peoples, capitulation can become the feeling "beautiful."

7 [155]

20) Great enough to gild what has been despised: intelligent enough to understand the body as something superior — this is the *future of morality*!

In our intentions and will we must *fervently seek* the sublimity that we so *worship* in nature — we should be the redeemers of nature and not its deifiers! "Deification of nature" — this is the result of poverty, shame, anguish, stupidity!

Our actions *should* be **mis***understood*, as Epicurus is misunderstood! It is characteristic of all prophets that they were understood *soon* — it diminishes them! *We must first have human beings whose* **significance** *becomes* *evident after centuries* — our "fame" has thus far been something wretched! — I do not want to be understood for a long time.

On the other hand, we must endure *misunderstanding things* and seeing more than what is there: oh you who do nothing more than *understand* "great humans"! Your force should be such that you see superior beings that are a hundred miles *above* them! And this is what I call idealization: to see a sunrise where — a candle is lit!

Death would shine most brilliantly if it *led* us *further* into the other world, if we took *pleasure* in everything that is becoming and for that reason even in our passing away!

7 [156]

21) *Noble feeling* is what **forbids** us from being merely *people who enjoy* existence: it rebels against hedonism — we want to **accomplish** something *in opposition to it*! But the masses believe in their hearts that life must be lived for nothing — this is their *vulgarity*.

7 [157]

Judging *humans* from the standpoint of *animals*! Are we not their parasites?

7 [158]

22) The *parasitical* as essential element of the vulgar mentality.

the feeling *of receiving nothing without giving something in return* or *of thereby receiving something in return* is the *noble* mentality. Nothing for nothing! No "favors"! But also no sufferings, no — — —

7 [159]

23) "For the wise person, nature transforms itself into a tremendous promise" Emerson.[123] Now, you yourself are nature and you promise, along with it, something tremendous and you are probably careful not to reveal your own secret too quickly!

7 [160]

18) The gods as the cause of evil (sin and suffering) I 232[124]

So how did badness come into being where there are "good people"?

Because of fading insight — and this is often the work of the gods.[125]

7 [161]

19) *Aidos*[126] is the impulse and inhibition against injuring gods, human beings and eternal laws: therefore the instinct of *reverence* as habitual among good people. A kind of *disgust* at *injuring* what is worthy of being revered.[127]

The Greek aversion to *excess*, in the joyful i⟨nstinct of⟩ hubris, ⟨against⟩ any transgression of *their* boundaries, is *quite noble* — and *highborn*! The injury of *aidos* is something terrible to behold for someone accustomed to *aidos*.[128]

κόρος = ὕβρις[129] satiety, to be intoxicated with *happiness*

Hubris and rage are mutually exclusive (*Eudem. Ethics* 1149b), for *hubris* presupposes a *joyful* condition, rage a painful one.[130]

Those who were *free, moderate* invented *competition* as an ever more sophisticated refinement of the need for the exercise of power: through *competition* hubris was *averted*: which emerges when the lust for power is not satisfi⟨ed⟩ for a long time.

Envy — pain over present or past happiness of *friends*: an entirely Greek concept![131]

If *rage* is "sweeter than honey"[132] — sweeter than rage — — —

7 [162]

The devil becomes envious of anyone who *suffers* terribly and banishes this person into heaven.

7 [163]

14) When slaves do philosophy

What are slavish natures? The ones that do not know what is good and just, Socrates says. According to Theognis, betraying a friend is a sign of slavish mentality.

Their dependence makes it impossible for them to be *truthful* I, 266[133]

7 [164]

Quite remarkable. Plato, *Timaeus* p. 86 etc. (I 281) mental illnesses brought on by faulty disposition of the body: the task of the educators and the states is to provide *healing* in such cases. If healing cannot be achieved in time, then the educators and the states, and *not the sick, are to be held responsible*.[134] — — —

7 [165]

"Pathological tendency to loot temples"[135] Greek.

7 [166]

How little imagination we have for the suffering we inflict on others!

7 [167][136]

16) *Present-day slavery*: *a barbarism*! Where are those *for whom* they work? — We cannot expect that both complementary castes will always *exist at the same time*.

Utility and fun are *slave-theories* of life: the "blessing of work" is a self-glorification. — Incapacity for *otium*.[137]

7 [168]

[15] Way of thinking *common to old people*: according to Aristotle, mistrust, lack of strength of feeling,[138] fearfulness, inquiring about the utility of everything and not the moral worth.

The true joy of old age consists in *being revered* says Pericles. (Simonides thought it was pleasure in profit.)[139]

7 [169]

The Origin[140] *of Morality.*

The moralists themselves are among the facts of morality.
When noble people employ morality
When slaves and women   retribution
When the aged
When sick and degenerate people
When inactive people
Development and downfall of a morality, conditions
Mor⟨al⟩ *instinct.*
organic function of good and evil
Conscience

7 [170]

Struggle *between different moralities* a means of cultivating them. Stagnant moralities (Chinese)

7 [171]

12) **Compassion**: traced back by me to involuntary imitation of *signs* that are observed.

7 [172]

13) The actions that constitute the well-being of the community, of the organism, did not emerge *for the sake of this purpose*: all moral customs have a prehistory — every kind of action *originally* had *another* purpose and *meaning.* — Just as seeing was not the goal in the emergence of the eye, and just as eyes have in turn been used for the *expression* of *feelings*:[141]

7 [173]

Means of self-expression, of self-disclosure — *originally* however the intention of self-disclosure was absent, rather all *communication* is actually a wanting to acquire something, a *grasping* and *wanting to appropriate* (mechanical). To incorporate the other — later to incorporate the *will* of the other, to appropriate it, this has to do with *conquering the other. Self-disclosure* is thus originally *extending our power over the other*: an ancient sign language underlies this drive — the *sign* is the (often *painful*) *imposition of one will upon another will*

to make ourselves understood by blows (ants)

NB. Even the *injuries* done to others are a *sign language* of the *stronger*

Thus, *understanding* is originally a sensation of pain and the recognition of a foreign power. Yet *quick, easy understanding* becomes very advisable (in order to receive as few blows as possible)

the quickest mutual understanding is the *least painful way of relating to each other*: that is why it is *so sought after* (

negative sympathy — originally the creator[142] of the *herd*.[143]

7 [174]

8) A moral way of looking at actions — the *organic functions* of individuals for whom the i⟨ndividual⟩ is not the purpose but rather a *superior principle* (the superior principle can be a community): or even more so: attempt at conversion into organic functions. Wherever living things come together, there continually arises a mutual influence and a gathering together in the attempt to see whether an organism can be formed. Similarly h⟨uman⟩ to h⟨uman⟩.

Yet even bad actions should be examined *as having functional characteristics*! their usefulness in this non-individual sense! The organism exists by means of *struggle*!

10) NB. The accompanying phenomena have *been transformed* in many respects: some things are now associated with displeasure, formerly with pleasure. Even great moments of *cleverness*

may in earlier times have given the impression of *inspiration*: an entirely different *appraisal* of cleverness, as demonic.

11) *The pleasure* in *doing damage*; malice, defamation, estrangement because of *passion*. Murderous intent. Under what circumstances *natural*? When pathological? Atavism?

7 [175]

9) So are laws made against wicked people? Against *innovators* and *not* against wicked and bad people!

The "bad person" is first generated as a contrast to the good person.

So even *moral conscience* is something relatively *late*, *bad* conscience at the same time as *good* conscience (*continuous* **delight** in its impulses!) therefore **active**!

7 [176]

Striving for happiness is foolishly interpreted by people as striving for *enjoyment*; and the *crippling capacity to enjoy things* is considered to be an argument against *egoism*. Hartmann p 591.[144]

7 [177]

Complexity of *today's mor⟨al⟩ feeling*. In *today's feeling*: "ethical" is present: the *drive* of reverence, helpfulness, nobility, devotion, courage, piety, the drive for advantage purposefulness, for the common good

7 [178]

4) *On moral instinct.* Most prevalent in very ancient unchanged peoples.

We do not inherit our ancestors' *knowledge* as animals do: as a result of great changes in lifestyle Roux 37 [145] — but something of the kind is present in all nonmigratory peoples, precisely the *moral instincts* are the result of many similar experiences among less migratory peoples. If a *great migration* ensues, then the instincts are soon lost. There are a number of *time-tested behavioral rules* (initially attitudes and gestures, like those of defense, reverence etc.) that are instinctively chosen.

7 [179]

Epicurean theory. Pain ensues when a *desire*, a *wish* is inhibited in its satisfaction. Pleasure, the clearing away of the obstacle — negative. To seek pleasure — would be nonsense, would be to seek something negative! Not to suffer would be the goal instead! Where there is pleasure, an earlier displeasure can be presupposed.[146]

7 [180]

6) Where the means of power are not great enough, *intimidation* appears, *terrorism*: thus any punishment for the sake of deterrence is a sign that the positively *outflowing virtue* of the powerful is not great enough: a sign of skepticism regarding its own power.

7) A power must stand solidly on its own two feet and have its *center of gravity. Counterpart* to that: Schmidt, II 269.[147] To this there corresponds a kind of morality. —

7 [181]

5) *Inactivity*: Just to take a breath is the highest thing there is! *Otium* in the best case — not creating!

7 [182]

NB. *Egoism is not a moral principle*, is not "Thou shalt"! for it is the only "You must."[148]

7 [183]

The problem of the competition[149] among different moralities: the Hellenic concept in competition with the Athenian. The *community* and the *superpower*. II p. 273.[150]

1) Competition among moralities

The *masculinity* of the nation is disappearing p. 274:[151] how that is manifested in the culture. Epicurus.

7 [184]

Beauty imparts the intuiting soul with the *impetus* that makes it capable of **conceiving** *noble thoughts*. Plato.[152]

7 [185][153]

II 353 it is **disgraceful**, according to Socrates, when *a good deed cannot be repaid*. Thus there is no "innocent acceptance" in Greek friendship. *To* **base** *our friendships on* **bestowing good deeds**! Pericles — Athens. important!
2) *Power*-morality.

7 [186]

There is a continuous *chain* of *injuries in response to injuries*, even on a small scale: in war, we can no longer know who the evildoer is. Blood feud is merely the strongest expression of all such interactions among *equals*.[154]
3 Retaliation

7 [187]

It is *not unjust* to rejoice at the suffering of *enemies* — Socrates II p 357.[155]

7 [188]

Diogenes: attaining virtue requires either *staunch friends* or fierce *enemies*.[156]

7 [189]

Hatred moral, envy *not*.[157]
Happiness in the harm done to enemies p 362.[158]

7 [190]

Struggle among tissues must lead to a balance among the parts, or else the whole perishes.

Tissues which are too *vital*, no matter how beneficial, bring destruction upon the whole. *Tumors*, e.g., are a kind of tissue endowed with abnormal vitality: they expand to other tissues at the cost of nourishment and space and destroy the whole.

One tissue can achieve *dominance*, merely through the abnormal **weakening** of another tissue.[159]

The lack of balance between tissues quickly leads to the death of individual tissues and to the *elimination* of them and of their *disadvantageous qualities from the ranks of the living*: only the conditions of balance remain: in this way a *harmonic unity of the entire organism* would be *engendered* by the self-elimination of the deviant tissue.[160]

Struggle among tissues becomes a *regulating principle*: principle of *functional self-design of the most suitable proportions*.[161]

7 [191][162]

Among the most powerful factors governing the development of a state are not only the struggle with neighboring peoples and the development of defensive capabilities: but also the competition among members of a social class and the *competition among the social classes* themselves.

7 [192]

Falling silent in the presence of the beautiful is a profound **expectation**, a wanting-*to-hear* the most delicate, distant sounds — we act like someone who is all ears and eyes: beauty has *something to say to us*, **that's why** we fall **silent** and think *none of our usual thoughts*. The silence, that introspection, patience is thus a **preparation, nothing more**! This is the case with all contemplation: —

But the *serenity involved, the sense of well-being, the freedom from tension*? Evidently a very **steady** *stream of force emanates from us* during the process: we *adjust* as it were to the high colonnades through which we stroll, and we impart the kinds of movements to our soul, that through peace and gracefulness, are *imitations* of what we see. Just as a noble gathering inspires us to noble gestures.

7 [193]

First, assimilation into the work, **later** *assimilation into its creator* who spoke only in signs!

7 [194]

"Up to now all good characteristics of an organism have been derived solely from selection among individuals in the struggle for existence!"[163]

7 [195]

Resisting the foreign, not allowing its allure to become *formative* — but rather setting a thick skin, hostile feelings against it: is for most people a *necessity* for survival. Yet the *saintliest of saints* live *among criminals* as if in their element.

— the open-mindedness[164] of morality therefore finds its limits wherever someone perceives the allure of the foreign to be only *harmful*, not *stimulating*.

Those who are rich in saintliness are at home among the most evil people: and all nay-saying is the province of impoverished people.

7 [196]

just as the active quantitative and qualitative *variety of nutrients* determines the entire development of cells so, too, does the human being *choose from* among the events and stimuli, thus working actively among all the random intrusions — thereby *repelling* many of them. Roux p. 149.[165]

7 [197]

The parasite forces the host to encase it in a cocoon and a larger surrounding container p. 151.[166]

7 [198]

Drives are *superior organs*, according to my understanding: actions perceptions and states of feeling growing more entwined in each other, organizing themselves, nurturing themselves — — —

7 [199]

Evil people as *rudimentary* Schneider p 29.[167]

7 [200]

Vanity and the drive for distinction *have opposite origins*.

Just as words were considered to be congruent with things, so too what we said about people was considered to be congruent with them: we did not *doubt* a person's ability to know absolutely (*be known absolutely*)[168] of a person. That's why an opinion about someone was absolutely decisive: and why vanity is now only an *atavism*: originally this drive was not yet so *debased* (vain people today are skeptical about themselves) *In earlier times, the thought did not even exist* that people could have a value for themselves, a concealed value. To be concerned about the good opinion of others — was identical with "being good." — Vain people *subordinate themselves* and want to please; those who strive for distinction want people to see *them ranking themselves higher*, they want to be *admired*.

7 [201][169]

Morality for Moralists.

Up to now, moralists can be distinguished from each other according to their prevailing biases, in this way: some are fixated on how people act toward each other; others on how people should act toward each other. But what both these kinds have in common is evident as soon as we allow them to explain the little word how? "What motives determine actions? That is what we ask": this is what some people say. "What motives should determine human actions? This is what *we* ask" so say other people. That *motives determine actions* wherever there is action, this is their common presupposition: this is their common error; they have all done a poor job of examining the *foreground* of the entire moral landscape, indeed overlooked it — the fact *that* there is action, and that there has to be action, and that so-called motives do not provide the explanation *for this*.

7 [202]

Actual morality is infinitely more subtle, more complicated, more thoughtful than *theoretical* morality; the latter still stands awkward and embarrassed at the starting point.

7 [203]

All *conservative* powers have in themselves a kind of *Jesuitism*: they believe the truth is *there*, seeking it is forbidden. "Justice" e.g., should be there!![170]

7 [204]

Utility an exalted principle! Indeed, not to be underestimated! But it concerns itself with means ("*subordinate purposes*") — the valuation and the code of values must already be *there*![171]

7 [205]

Due to hunger, preferring poisoned bread to not eating at all!

7 [206]

Will as *striving for pleasure*: presupposes that willing itself desires its own end. Hartmann.[172]

7 [207]

That which an action achieves is what catches the eye: the motive should lie in the *representation of the result of the action* (e.g., an emotional state that is achieved)

7 [208]

"What people want, without reflection, and nothing further, is pleasure: '*happiness*' a multifaceted, depleting and lasting pleasure." (Hartmann).[173]

7 [209]

With *Epicurus* everything depends on *finding the proper balance* of pleasure and displeasure: therefore φρόνησις[174] is the chief virtue, the basis: *morality of prudence.*

The significance of sensual pleasure is to free us from desires and needs which disturb the ἀταραξία[175] of the soul.

Bliss as *ultimate purpose of the individual life.* Aristotle and everyone else![176]

So it is the *predominance of the concept of purpose* that has corrupted all moralists up to now. "Life must really have a 'for what?'"!

That even the *rational conscious life is a part* of the development of *life without purpose* — ego.

7 [210]

The actual *assessment* of life depends on generally prevailing moods: when they came to South Asia, the Aryans perceived all actions as suffering and all feelings likewise: profound serenity in the shadow of the highest balsam. It is a *mistaken decision about where to settle,* refined to the highest degree and made into a decision about the value of life. (Even the emergence of the *state* a matter of *fatigue!*)

7 [211]

Superior organs develop on the basis of drives and these organs *struggle* with one another for nutrition, stimuli — — —

The hand of the pianist, the pathway to it, and an area of the brain, together make up an organ (which must *close* itself *off* to be able to contract strongly enough). *Separate parts of the body telegraphically connected — i.e., drive.*

Schopenhauer added the *unconscious purpose* to this!

7 [212]

What is essential about all actions is purposeless or indifferent with respect to a multitude of purposes.

7 [213]
Renunciation of earthly bliss in favor of the thousand times greater heavenly bliss is *good business*. Christianity and its *cleverness*!
   good in Hartmann p 26.[177]
   Reward and punishment with Christ.
   It is *folly* not to accept Christianity.

7 [214]
   We should do good in secret *so that it* is *not rewarded here* Luke 14 (12–14) — otherwise the heavenly reward might slip away from us.[178]

7 [215]
   The more hopeless and wild the conditions on earth, the more fervent the belief in heavenly reward: since a person cannot *count* on earthly happiness. The more superstitious the people, the more fervent the belief in hell.[179]

7 [216]
   Punishment meaningless in the case of unfree will? But then we could not promise anything, could not take on obligations etc., could *do nothing*. Since we *can* confidently *expect* a lot of ourselves,[180] i.e., *advantages* are given to us. We are disadvantaged when we *cannot do what we have promised*: or else we are *belatedly* compensated for the advantages that were given to us earlier. (Punishment here as the delayed *compensation* of advantages that were granted to us, a *revocation* of social security etc., *displaced into a state of enmity*. Society is deceived in its assessment of punishment: it *takes as much as it can* from the power of the evildoer as remuneration, e.g., forced labor etc.)

7 [217]
   Today I said "oh, this is a good person!" At the same time I had a feeling as if I were holding in my hand a beautiful ripe plump apple with soft skin: a feeling of tenderness, as if I were

drawn to this person: a feeling of security, as if I were allowed to rest here under a tree: a feeling of reverence, as if an object were present that could only be grasped with the cleanest hands: a feeling of satiation, as if I were liberated from dissatisfaction at a single stroke. Thus, *a state* corresponding to the moral judgment "good" arose in me when I thought of a certain person. It is the same as when I call a rock "hard."

7 [218]

When bliss is *impossible* (Hegesias), then the absence of suffering becomes the goal of life: *without purpose, the goal of life was not understandable!*[181]

7 [219]

Common striving of all ancient philos⟨ophers⟩ for freedom of thought and for casting off all the *chains of slavery*. It is the atavistic nobility of *idle people* who have nothing more to do and let themselves decay.[182]

7 [220]

Taking the avoidance of the causes of pain to its logical conclusion — this is the practice. Here we preserve the completely **empty** *life* and the thinking about this emptiness. Here the question arises: so there is no redemption from life?[183]

7 [221]

This belief in *purpose* leads to *pessimism*.

Conversely: the purpose is not to feel happy; people are led back from the false paths of life; the more we suffer, the *true purpose* is achieved "There is an unmistakable touch of intentionality in all of this." Schopenhauer.[184] Hartmann p. 42 "Morality a palliative against choosing a radical cure" p. 43 "the *evil* deeds done to us actually a *blessing*."[185]

7 [222]

In cynicism the *worthlessness* of life is recognized, but has not yet been turned *against* life.

No: many minor triumphs and a big mouth are *satisfying* here![186]

7 [223]

Teichmüller: feelings of pleasure or displeasure are *signs* of the position that the I takes as a whole, over and against individual activity: all of this is *will*, insofar as we consider the I as the single point of reference: the two opposing basic forms: *desire* and *loathing*. If we consider *another* point of reference, then the activity itself, as such, remains *unconscious*, yet its accompanying *what* becomes conscious every time, and so this *what* becomes a sign of that which we want to designate. We call the accompanying ideational point of reference an *evil* or a *good*, corresponding to loathing or desire, and designate it by means of the content of accompanying sensations or intuitions. *All images of our intuition* and all our activities stand in particular regular relations to one another e.g., the intuition-image of the rose and the sensation of its fragrance. In this way, even a child designates one thing a *means*, another thing an *accomplishment*.[187]

7 [224][188]

First absurdity: all life is willing of a purpose

egoism is the will to our own happiness

Second absurdity: it is moral to serve a foreign *will* and self-denial.

thus the purpose of life does not lie in happiness: first insight!

the purpose of the ethical life should lie in the will of another.

But what then is this will of another other than a will to satisfaction?

My opinion: intentions wishes purposes are *secondary* — "striving for happiness," in general, doesn't actually exist at all, but even striving for the happiness of others and *not* striving for our own happiness ("*renunciation*") *is* **not** *at all* **possible** *in the first place*, whereas a partial striving for personal happiness *is possible*.

All actions yield a lot, even for others!

The individual will pursues the purpose: happiness — impossible to find it!

Thus, the individual will must adopt another will as its purpose, it is the means to another person's purpose —

But, Mr. von Hartmann! As soon as it **promotes** a *will at all*, whether our neighbor's or of the world-process — then it is certainly working to *prolong misery*: and indeed after it has already comprehended that all will is essentially miserable! Hence its promotion is either madness or *evil*.

Yet there is a second absurdity presupposed *here*, that an *unegoistic action is possible*.

The first absurdity: *all action is a willing of satisfaction*

the second absurdity: there is an unegoistic action an action as *not-willing of our own self, but* **willing** *of a foreign self* !

7 [225]

The setting of *goals* is itself a pleasure — a quantum of intellectual force is expended in means-end thinking!

7 [226]

Willing, a pressing feeling, quite pleasant! It is the accompanying phenomenon for all *outpouring of force*.

much the same for *all wishing* in itself (entirely apart from fulfillment)

7 [227]

Let us not fail to recognize the profound lack of *noblesse* of feeling in Christ, his *Jewishness*, the tidy profits and the irritation at the stupidity of missing out on them! The Europeans have *read* so many nobler feelings *into this*![189]

7 [228]

We *select* the *facta*,[190] we interpret them — unconsciously. The wishes that stick with us —

Running counter to our *purposes* and all *conscious willing*, there exists a greater kind of *reason*, in all our actions, much more harmony and subtlety than we consciously imagine ourselves to possess.

7 [229]

We still have not freed ourselves from the logical mania of antiquity, they prized nothing more than the dialectic — likewise "intentions" "purposes."

7 [230]

Most people are completely incapable of experiencing anything: they haven't lived in solitude enough — an event is immediately washed away by something new. Deep pain is *rare* and a mark of distinction. In everyday life there is more *prudence* than in Stoicism. — Avoiding pain.

7 [231]

all our *purposes*, seen from a certain distance, become exceptional as tests and throws of the dice — there is *experimenting* going on.

We must preserve whatever is arbitrary illogical about our best purposes!

We would never act if we *imagined* all the consequences.

7 [232]

Weakness-of-will as consequence of disorganization and as sign of decline.

7 [233][191]

Kant says: I endorse these sentences of Count Verri (1781 *sull'indole del piacere e del dolore*)[192] with complete confidence

il solo principio motore dell'uomo è il dolore. Il dolore precede ogni piacere

il piacere non è un essere positivo.[193]

7 [234]

"To feel our life, to take pleasure in it — to feel ourselves continually driven to abandon our present circumstances, pain which for that reason must be as frequent as it is chronic."[194]

7 [235]

"The rational will may only lessen pain and repress needs." —[195]

7 [236]

Cardanus concluded, we must seek out as much suffering as possible in order to create a greater sum of pleasure through its elimination.[196]

7 [237]

"Shortly before the pupal stage, all actions of the larvae are directed at the preservation of the final insect, rather than at its own preservation, they do not correspond to the needs of the larval stage, but rather to those of the completely developed creature" etc. Schneider I p. 58[197]

7 [238][198]

The highest principle[199] *of* **Jesuitism** also that of socialism: *Ruling* humankind for the purpose of *satisfying* it
Satisfying humankind by maintaining illusion, faith
In response my countermovement: —

Ruling humankind for the purpose of **overcoming** *it.*
Overcoming through teachings that bring about the downfall of humankind, **except for those who survive them**[200]

Fundamental error up to now: "all human actions are *consciously purposeful.*"

"the purpose of the human being is the *preservation of the species* and *only incidentally* the preservation of the person" — *current* theory.

This is the case, too, with people who are very individualistic, we take care of our *future needs*!

7 [239]

Original form of all protective movements, *upon unpleasant contact drawing itself together, drawing all parts into itself.* What is the psychological equivalent? In *summary*: pain *makes us concentrate.*

The drive *to conceal something* is *shame*, a protective drive: also wanting to conceal ourselves, when hummingbirds e.g., become red in the process (is an effect of fear!)

Human beings are guided by their instincts: *purposes* are *chosen* only to serve the *instincts*. Yet *instincts* are ancient habitual actions, *ways* of *expending* their available *force*.

The *result achieved by* an instinct should not be called "purpose"!

To give our drives completely free rein: yet often they *come in conflict* with one another. Actual life is a *wrestling match* of instincts, a growth of some, a waning of others.

"Use of stored up nervous energy."

"Which *idea* leads to action? That which awakens the *strongest* drive. Which is that? That which *promises* the greatest comforts, the *most pleasant idea*. This is not a rule which allows exceptions, but is rather *a law*, and the *dependence* of the human will rests on it" Schneider p. 75

!! But the *drive itself* first *called* forth **this** idea! — I say.

Thus: *drives* decide the *expenditure* of accumulated force, *not that* **action is undertaken in the first place**. The how? is the province of the drives.

Thus: when we become aware of a drive, *it promises pleasure*. *Promised pleasure* as the cause of action? — Not of action in the first place, but only of the specific *direction* of the agent! So, too, Stendhal.

Thus: wherever ideas lead to action, there the person *must* follow the idea that *promises the most pleasure*: the strongest drive *decides* the *choice*.

Accordingly, morality must be changed 1) first, the *accumulation of force* must be considered 2) second, the *expenditure of force*, the how?

The first principle, overlooked up to now.[201]

7 [240]

First fact: society kills, tortures, robs[202] freedom, robs property: commits violence through restrictions on education; through schools; lies, deceives, harasses (as police) — therefore all of this cannot be regarded *as bad in itself.* — Society desires its preservation and advancement — this is not a sacred purpose: it fights for this against other societies. — Thus all of this happens for the sake of utility. But *mad*! Precisely *these* actions should be accorded special veneration and respect: as "justice," ethics, preservation and cultivation of the good. That here the needs of the many are prioritized over those of the few, this would only make sense if we assume that the individual *cannot* have more value than all of society! Yet the *intention* here, from the start, is to prevent such individuals from emerging at all: the image of human beings that is used as the measuring stick for the preservation of the common good is already available. The assumption of *society must be* that it represents the *supreme type* "human," and *from this* it derives its right to fight against all that is hostile *to it* as what is hostile in *itself.* — Without this faith in itself, society is "*immoral*" in every sense. Yet *until it has* faith, it does not determine *what should* be moral. — it makes sense this way!

7 [241]
                    (End Justifies the Means.)
There are actions that we will never allow ourselves to engage in, not even as means to the *noblest*[203] end e.g., betraying a friend.

Better to perish and trust that there will be more favorable circumstances for achieving our noblest end. — But what sort of noblest end is involved in preserving a community, a state! The action of one person *who sacrifices the state in order not* to betray his ideals can be the *noblest accomplishment of all*, whereby the entire existence of this state becomes a matter for posterity!

7 [242]
Presupposition made by the *state up to now*: "*the human being should not develop further*, the *mold* is *there*!" The Catholic Church (the oldest of all forms of the state in Europe) now best represents the ancient state!

7 [243]
Trade requires a *patriciate*: therefore a *counterweight*.

7 [244]
The point of *punishment* is the *elimination of parasitic* humans.

Birds that keep parasites away from a buffalo, live off it — thankful that they signal to him the arrival of an enemy. — Meaning of the *police*. Espinas p. 159.[204]

7 [245]
Incessantly busy listening and paying attention to one another and thereby the feeling of security — p 162.[205]

7 [246]
Affection the consequence of a *fervent need*[206]

7 [247]

Tracing *punishments* in their kind and essence back to *war or* to *sacrificial cults* (human sacrifice)

In one case, the fundamental thought behind punishment is return to precommunal conditions, in another case, *mockery* of the *gods*. Post I, 201[207]

A punishment meted out to unfree people becomes *demeaning* **for that reason** e.g., lashes as pun(ishment). The punishment meted out to free people has long been regarded as ennobling **for that reason**. Post I 214.[208]

7 [248]

"— the *only direct value judgment* we presuppose is that of *sensualistic well-being,* and we believe everything else to be *indirectly* realizable through a connection to this direct willing. Observance of laws, morality, religion is supposed to be induced by reference to well-being in this world or the next" Baumann p. 32.[209]

Universal belief in the *value of sensualistic well-being*: every action should be a path or a detour to this.

7 [249]

Legal prohibitions only make sense when there is no need to achieve something in *this way* that is prohibited: in other words, if there *is another way* — i.e., very specific promises and concessions are a part of all prohibitions.

7 [250]

The *center of gravity*[210] *shifts* in word, in use, in respect —

7 [251]

"the good of all with *exclusion* of the *individual.*" Hartmann p 605[211] pathetic hypocrisy!

7 [252]

That the difference between a scoundrel and an honorable man does not consist only in a few differently convoluted brain movements —

7 [253]

Strength of character. To take in very many stimuli and to let them have a *deep* effect, to allow oneself to be distracted almost to the point of being lost, to suffer very much and — nevertheless to persevere in our *general direction*.

Typical strong character types are cold, shallow and devoid of sympathy: they also do not take possession of other people. *Plastic force.*

7 [254]

Our *choice* is greatest wherever our practice and our spontaneous energy is greatest: it is the readiest docility and agility in the one who obeys (*free will perceived most strongly*, wherever we are the least creatively restricted) Baumann p. 18.[212]

7 [255]

A book of sayings and quotations
a book of anecdotes.
A book of facts.
Jokes.

7 [256]

Egoism is not a principle, but rather the one fact.

7 [257]

From the standpoint of purpose, as much is squandered in every action as from the heat of the sun radiating into the universe.

7 [258]

The individual as *fruit* of the communal entity, not always as means.

7 [259]

Every condition may be considered as if it had been *purpose*, or as means *or* as a misstep in an experiment.

7 [260]

Satisfaction of a drive is *not* to be sought in the result of an activity, but rather in the *performance* of it.

Happiness would be the *equilibrium of the triggering activities of all drives*.

7 [261]

Experimentation as true character of our lives and of *every* morality: something voluntary[213] must be involved!

7 [262]

Origin of Christianity among collectives of the poor. Baumann p. 22[214] divine aid and mutual support.

7 [263][215]

The *idea* of an action's joyful beneficial *result* brings joy, exhilaration, blood flows more freely. In this way the *purpose* of an activity has an additional exhilarating, pleasurable force *during* the action.

Thus: the *activity* of the drive is tied to pleasure. The *goal* of the activity is imagined and causes pleasure in the same way that increasing the activity does (the *goal is the activity of* **another** drive). But the drive itself does not will a result of what it does. Our *drive to understand* certainly takes pleasure in *determining the purpose* — this is its activity; just as it does in devising the means — *logical pleasure* in all actions.

In every action many drives are active.
At the very least
1) the one that finds satisfaction in doing
2) the one that finds satisfaction in setting end and means
3) the one that finds satisfaction in anticipating success.

The drive *finds satisfaction* i.e., it is *active* when it *takes control* of stimuli and *transforms* them. In order to take control of them, it must struggle: i.e., it must *hold back* another drive, subdue it. In truth, *it always exists as an active drive*: but nourishing it engenders *larger* amounts of force, so that even its output of force must be different. Yet the drive itself is nothing other than a *particular way of being active*: a personification.

7 [264]
   Effect of reward and punishment p. 31 Baumann.[216]

7 [265]
   A stimulus is in itself neither pleasure nor displeasure, but it can certainly be accompanied by pleasure or displeasure there cannot be a *middle ground* that would be *neither pleasure nor displeasure*! — what is "*not* pleasure" is just not *pleasure*!

7 [266]
   Will as the form-giver?

7 [267]
   Satisfaction: the word presupposes *discord* and awakens prejudice.

7 [268][217]
   1. *Innocence of becoming: without purpose.*
   2. *Action, drive, pleasure, free will.*
      in the meantime the economy of our drives far outstrips our insight.
      the essentially erroneous self-observation within all agents has turned into morality.

3. *The type of morality among the powerful.*
4. *The type of morality among the unfree.*
5. *The individual and the community.*
   "Individual as result." Collective conscience.
6. *Punishment, revenge, the responsibility.* (End justifies means)
7. *The two movements in the future.*
   Morality as sign language of the body.
8. Taking possession of *history* under the guidance of stimuli and drives — there is no "objective history."
9. *Evil* a precursor of the good: *that which is creative and those who create*: the *new* value judgment and its history. *The organic function of evil.* (Humankind as mass of force which increases and must expend itself)
10. "Living for others" and the "unegoistic"
    Hartmann, p. 593

7 [269]
Much less intention in our deeds than we *pretend* (vanity in assuming purpose!). Emerson, p. 99.[218]

7 [270]
The future of humanity not that delicate a concept. *Against this* p. 599.[219]

7 [271]
With an "in order to" an action is deprived of its *value.*

7 [272]
"Good" "bad" corresponds to the states of those who judge.[220]

7 [273]
The individual as multiplicity.

7 [274]
Point of departure: the denial of moral significance — Birth of Tragedy.

[8 = Mp XVII 1a. Summer 1883]

8 [1]

The Tonga-islanders cut off their little fingers as a sacrifice.[1]

In the Orient a woman covers her face when surprised while bathing — in this way decency is maintained!

Shame prohibits women in China from showing their feet, among the Hottentots they merely need to cover the backs of their necks.[2]

White is the color of mourning in China.[3]

The ancient civilized peoples of the Americas were not familiar with *milk*.[4]

The Chinese eat very many dishes in very small portions.

No. 29.

People do not want to take on the flaws of animals e.g., the cowardice of the stag (in Borneo) — women and children are permitted to eat them.[5]

Even bats frogs worms larvae caterpillars are eaten. Rats that have been fattened up a delicacy of the Chinese. "Eating tiger hearts makes you headstrong" (Java) Dog livers make you clever.

The Siamese, e.g., eat incredible amounts of rice.[6]

8 [2]

— just as the bald eagle sits proudly and serenely above the falls of the Niagara and frequently dives into its churning mist[7]

— just as the albatross abandons itself to the ocean for weeks at a time: the king of the birds

— just as the condor of the Andes at soundless heights (it can glide through the air for over an hour without beating its wings)[8]

Serenity of the one who flies[9]

8 [3]

What a difference we observe in walking swimming and flying! And still it is one and the same motion: it is merely that the carrying capacity of the earth differs from that of water which in turn differs from that of air! Thus we should also learn *to fly* as thinkers — and not suppose that when we do this we are becoming fantasizers![10]

8 [4][11]

The authority of Sir Andrew Aguecheek in Shakespeare: "I am a great eater of beef, and I believe that does harm to my wit"[12]

8 [5][13,14]

Punishments among the Germanic tribes: to have a millstone dropped on someone's head (mythical), quartering by horses, trampling by horses; to be boiled in oil or wine (14th and 15th century); similarly in the Middle Ages being buried alive, walled in, starved. The rack (purely Germanic), flaying alive (cutting strips out of skin). To abandon someone smeared with honey to the flies and the hot sun. To hack off the right leg and the left arm. Nose, ears, lips, tongue, teeth, eyes, private parts.[15]

8 [6][16]

Matrilineage: children do not belong in the father's family, but in that of their mother's brother. The father belongs to another family: father and son in a hostile relationship. The father marries into a foreign family and in it he is solely a breeder, and little more than a slave. — Patrimony is nothing self-evident but rather a late-attained legal institution. The moral bond between father and child *is lacking*! The father is not considered related to his children by blood. The *umbilical cord* is the family bond.

In associations of blood relatives there is neither *individual* crime, nor individual property, nor marriage. Only the extended family has rights and privileges. Women are communal property like children. Yes there are situations where there are no personal relationships, instead only groups are related. — *Group marriages.*

Legal subjects are *now* so-called "natural persons," the individuals: they are the bearers of rights and obligations.

An old Chinese man said, he heard that when kingdoms are about to perish they have many laws.

Marriage with a bad conscience: before they marry, women must undergo a time of concubinage, they must be deflowered. They must give themselves to members of the tribe before belonging to one man. Last vestige the *jus primae noctis*[17] of chieftains or even priests (as with the Buddhists in Cambodia)

Concubines enjoy high standing in some parts of Africa, in India and in Java, they have remained true to the gods of the people. —

In this place, a husband supports, along with his wife, all of her sisters, in that place all brothers have *a single* wife.

Among animals the young females[18] are unadorned, beauty is the province of males — those who desire and fight become beautiful.

in our culture,[19] women make "conquests"

The superior *beauty* of women among humans proves that here women are the ones who fight and feel desire; they easily understand how to conquer men. Among animals masculine intelligence is enhanced by the sex drive. —

In Athens the men were more beautiful than the women — according to Cicero: yet this is probably a consequence of the great dedication to beauty, under the influence of pederasty.

With the emergence of *individual* marriage a *new obligation* emerges, by which brothers and sisters, father-in-law and daughter-in-law, mother-in-law and son-in-law, brother-in-law and sister-in-law, may not speak, eat with one another, indeed, may not even see one another. — In earlier times the mother and daughter were often married off together. — Hostility and coldness are among the obligations wherever *individual* obligations emerge. Animosity immediately appears whenever love does. Human love in general has yet to exist without intense hatred.

For a long time, marital fidelity had the appearance of being immoral.

Women as property, which the stronger man can take away from the weaker at any time. A test of strength decides the matter. Only the chieftains and priests have the beautiful women. Young people must be satisfied with insignificant old women. — *Abduction* the customary means of acquiring a woman.

the engagement ring as a remnant of the chains in which the abducted woman was dragged away

Originally absolute "coldness and indifference" between spouses. The woman has been bought or abducted. In addition, the secret reproach of conscience concerning marriage as something unnatural and immoral: spouses live essentially *apart*, not sharing table and bed. Separation of the sexes the basic idea behind *Chinese* marriage. The house ⟨has⟩ two parts: the husband lives in the outer part, the wife in the inner part. The door should be carefully secured. Each must die *alone*. It is the *separatio quoad thorum et mensam*[20] carried to completion.

Higher associations of lineal collectives: Many small communities with no contact at all with each other, often separated by large forests, owing fealty and levies to a chief who does not interfere in the internal administration of the small communities (as today in India and Sumatra). This kind of community is as closed as possible from within: the Greek πόλις.[21]

Oldest division of classes according to *age*: **piety**.

The Tupinambazis fattened up their prisoners of war secured with long ropes and provided them with sex slaves, until they were fat enough to be eaten.

8 [7]²²

Joking and high-handed treatment of other people used to have a dreadful meaning for us: namely of prisoners of war. Of the insane: even old Don Quixote!²³ *Laughter is originally* the expression *of cruelty*.

8 [8]²⁴

One person originally: priest sorcerer doctor judge chieftain. Rain peace good weather good harvests fat calves — but also birth defects plague misfortune in war or the hunt, bad weather.

Contempt for old age because of weakness in war and hunting.

Killing of twins, at least of one of them. Twins are seen as proof of *adultery* (e.g., among the Caribs) Even the Germanic tribes had this way of thinking. — This multiplicity regarded as bestial, similar to rats and bitch-dogs.

Here and there it is still considered shameful to bear daughters.

Ancient Germanic custom: the baby lies on the ground until the father declares whether he will allow it to live or not. *If he does not pick it up*, it is left to die — just as among Fiji-Islanders

The chieftains are liable for the conduct of women and children, for damages done by slaves and animals. For blood debts²⁵ incurred by one of his own; he must pay their debts. Dowries. A completely different *conscience emerges in such people*. Even *now* still the case in princes and statesmen.

For a long time, responsibility separated from conscience!

8 [9]

Type of primitive family collective: a group of relatives descended from the same ancestral mother, living with women, children and property completely in common, so that there is no marriage between individuals, no individual patrimony or parenthood; all members *equally* closely related, all property, movable and immovable, as communal, all work communal; all production consumed communally, all debts communal debts of the collective, all blood relatives active in every blood feud and obligated by the blood guilt of a blood relative. Foreigners taken in through adoption.

Kin-groups and tribes take precedence over lineage. *House-kinships* fundamentally different from this as associations of descendants from the same ancestral father. Hardly a primitive construct: corporate group of men and women, children and slaves, united under the patriarchal authority of a chieftain or house father. With its own gods, justice-system government, inalienable land. Not bound to the existence of individual members, *preservation* of the house-community *first* duty: and pressure to divorce an infertile woman: celibacy as punishable: when the husband was impotent, the wife had the duty to conceive a child with one of his male relatives.[26]

Any place where the organization depends on blood ties, there are blood feuds: the collective life of the association comes to be expressed as force that is incomprehensible and transcends the individual, object of religious reverence. Basic tendency: the balance is restored **between two families**; individual guilt is irrelevant, it is war between families. As the state apparatus develops, the line blurs between blood feuds and acts of revenge against the perpetrator.[27]

Presupposition for blood feuds is initially that it is a family matter: to begin with, the territorial overlordship or the state does *not* get involved.[28] But it already *pre*supposes *the superior organization*: it is a duel between equals, belonging to a single whole. Enmity toward the family of someone with blood guilt is fundamentally different from enmity toward anything *not* belonging to the superior communal organization. Absent is the contempt, the belief in the inferior race of the enemy: in the blood feud there is *honor* and *equal status*.

Outlawing: a member is expelled from the social collective; he is now completely without rights. Life and property can be taken ⟨from him⟩ by anyone. The evildoer can be killed by anyone without retribution. Basic feeling: *deepest contempt, unworthiness* e.g., still in Islamic law in cases of heresy or blasphemy against the Prophet: while in cases of murder and corporeal injury it acknowledges only blood feud and compensation within the social collective. It is *ostracism*: hearth and home are destroyed, women and children and whoever lives in the house are killed, e.g., in the Peruvian empire of the Incas whenever a sun virgin transgressed with a man her entire family and relatives had to pay for it with their lives, the house of her parents was razed to the ground etc. The same in China when a son kills his father.[29]

Therefore: offenses that put the existence of the community at risk provoke outlawing: the rotten offshoot is eradicated. *What* is regarded as such an *irrevocable and fundamentally contemptible act* varies according to what is regarded as a condition of the community's existence — and therefore can be very different in different communities.[30]

In practice all kinds of mitigation emerge, e.g., the offender is allowed time to withdraw by fleeing. Exile and confiscation of property are its furthest branches. In particular, punishments *involving denunciation* have their origin here.[31]

Social collectives: associations for protection and defense in which the members guarantee each other's lives and property, in which disturbers ⟨of the⟩ peace are expelled from the peace, in which children, women, goods and guilt are held in common — *most ancient* form.

Formation *of the state*: a kingdom severed from the basis of blood relations, a public state justice-system, individual property, individual arrest for crime and debts — *most recent* form. —

The more surely an organic entity, e.g., a community herd comes to self-awareness, the stronger its *hatred of what is foreign*. Sympathy for those who belong and hatred of what is foreign grow in tandem.

In regard to the continuity of *communal* life and the quantity of thoughts which it calls forth: how limited is the extent of the role played by purposes and images related to the essence of the individual self! Social drives far outweigh individual ones. Animals perform self-destructive acts that benefit the group.[32]

To use the current language of morality (but corresponding to fundamentally different feelings), animal societies are based upon love, constancy of affection, education of the young, work, frugality, courage, obedience by the weak, solicitude by the strong, sacrifice by all.[33] No society can survive without such qualities, and these drives are inherited by the society that survives: at a certain level of strength they would make society dull: but *internal antagonistic forces* arise in proportion to *increasing external* security. And once a condition of external peace is achieved, then society *dis*integrates into *individuals*: tension develops that had previously existed between communities. Only then does *compassion* come into existence — as feelings between individuals who perceive themselves as such. (The altruistic acts of those unified primitive societies presuppose an I-feeling, but a collective-I, and differ fundamentally from compassion.) Maybe *one family* first felt something like compassion and respect for another family within a larger collective, thus *not* for individuals. Here is the origin of compassion. My opinion: blood feuds are the oldest form of this respect for another family: as opposed to the absolute feeling of enmity.

8 [10]

Even "savages" are indescribably advanced humans, when measured in the longest span of time.

8 [11][34]

Human beings originally *altruistic*, more than any animal — hence their slow development (children) and sophisticated training, hence also the extraordinary ultimate kind of egoism. — Predators have much more *individuality*.

8 [12]

Atavism: joyful feeling, for once being able to obey unconditionally.

"Thou shalt allow thyself to be exploited, robbed, lied to" —
the fundamental feeling of the Catholic priest-state, especially
perfected in Jesuitism. *sacrificio dell'intelletto*[35] ancient and
original — yet not perceived as sacrifice, but rather as the *opposite*, as *agony*

8 [13]

Yes, the philosophy of right! This is a science which, like all
moral sciences, is not even in diapers yet! E.g., the oldest *meaning* of punishment has yet to be recognized, not even by jurists
who imagine themselves to be freethinking — it is completely
unknown: and as long as jurisprudence fails to establish itself
on new ground, namely in history and comparative studies of
peoples, it will remain trapped in dreary battles between thoroughly false abstractions that fancy themselves these days to be
"philosophy of right" and that are completely derived from
contemporary h⟨umans⟩. Yet contemporary h⟨umans⟩ are such
a convoluted web, even in regard to their leg⟨al⟩ valuations, that
this philosophy allows for the most varied *interpretations*.

8 [14]

My *first solution*: **Dionysian wisdom.**
Dionysian: temporary identification with the principle of
life (including the sensuality of martyrs).
Delight in the destruction of the noblest people and at the sight
of *how* they gradually come to grief
  as delight in **what is to come, the future,** *which triumphs
over what* **is there, still so good**[36]

8 [15][37]

    The Greeks as Connoisseurs of Human Nature.
The simplifying, the aversion to what is complicated, and to
minor details
The logicizing, the *presupposing* of something logically comprehensible even with respect to character

The idealizing ("beautiful and young"), the aversion to the atypical, the unconscious lying (taking sides against oneself, a certain generosity, is lacking)

The political necessity of *making* ourselves commonly understood: the lack of hidden individuals II 398, of restrained feelings (those called disreputable because of aversion to action II 401).[38]

The competition. Feelings, with which every philosopher wanted to beat down his opponents — through the practical proof that *he* was the happiest. "Virtue is happiness" — from Socrates onwards, all psychological observation has refuted[39] this; they defend *themselves* (the "feeling for facts" *only* developed as reaction in agon with the mythical sensibility, not as an original force).

(Perhaps they *were* simpler? — But the *enormous abundance of* different *individuals*.)

The nobility (γενναῖος meaning roughly "naïve"!): *instinctive* action and judgment are *good* form; self-gnawing and self-decomposition is ignoble.

Their will to the "universally human," even initially to the universally Greek — their sense of being the opposite of barbarians

Evil people encounter part reverence, part compassion; they themselves are not yet consumed by worms — the whole destructive churning self-contempt is lacking.

The "useless" waste of energy (in any kind of agon) as ideal to which the state aspires (*as opposed* to the Romans); they have little understanding for impetus arising out of pressing circumstances, while the Indians (Brahmans), through lack of initiative, feel "all action is suffering."

Stoicism would not have been possible at all in a morally *enlightened* world. — Every word of B. Gracián[40] or La Rochefoucauld or Pascal has the *whole of Greek taste* **against** it.

they complain and leave it at that (the pessimism of Homer Sophocles Epicurus — "evasion" perceived as "divine").

thus: they *suffer* to the greatest degree, but they react to it with such intense self-satisfaction in creating and also in speaking of things that *are beneficial*.

they are the people most susceptible to *pain*, but their formative power in *using* the pain is extraordinary: this also involves moderation in *avenging* pain, in wallowing in pain: a need for a *victorious* attitude, as cure. Consequently they are inclined to be *dishonest* about suffering: and in this way "their sensibility" became less visible in proportion to the increasing visibility of the *conquering* affects, brilliant intellectuality and courage. Obsession with slander required the concealment of passions.

Thucydides as the greatest example of sidestepping the national aversion to anatomical treatment.

During the period of greatest productivity in forms, *reflection is still missing* from opposites (like Dionysian-Apollonian): the *facts are there*.

The fine arts develop much later. To which can be added philosophy from Socrates onwards: — a drive *to return* from multiplicity back to *a few* types.

goal of the philosophers lively *portrait of the most superior humans*.

Among the philosophers absolute lack of a history of moral value judgments.

Antipathy to allowing *another type* to gain legitimacy.

(let's consider Plato: he denies *greatness in everything else*! Homer, the fine arts, prose, Pericles — and in order to tolerate Socrates, he *re*constructs him!)

General impression: a certain *superficiality* in the psychological (as opposed to Shakespeare and Dante and Goethe, as opposed to all of the French from Montaigne to Balzac, as opposed to Gracián (Christian skepticism) Italians J⟨acob⟩ B⟨urckhardt⟩ even the Indic peoples are more profound in their analysis of the suffering human being).

But perhaps they *were* indeed simpler human beings? This idea fits with "the youth of humankind" etc.

Precisely here is the danger of a *major error and mistaken conclusion*. Suppose that the fine arts of the Greeks had perished and we had been limited to the *judgments* of the philosophers: what a mistaken conclusion!

And likewise: all of their aesthetic judgments are far below the level of their creations.

So a discrepancy might be **possible**: that the Greeks' knowledge of human nature lagged way behind the actual wealth of types and individuals: that they might have been only faintly aware of their "humanity."

It is probably the case that never have so many different individuals gathered in such a small space and allowed themselves to perfect their peculiarities through competition.

Yet if we examine the national peculiarities of their intellect: then it seems *probable* that their knowledge of human nature remained *hampered*. *All their great powers worked to hamper this.* This is *my* thesis.

Plato's unconstrained approach to Socrates (like his bust in Naples)

The unconstrained approach for coming to grips with Socrates (just like Xenophon)

in types, the decline of the individual (Homer Orpheus etc.)

Antipathy toward *exactness*. Poetry far superior to history: the latter treats human beings in general, the former their particularities. For that reason, poetry better suited for gaining knowledge of human beings. "The essential things repeat themselves, there is nothing new, there is no development" — this is authentically Greek. Absent is all reflection about different futures. What do anachronisms matter! hundreds of characteristics fly at great persons and they stick.

Conclusion. The whole Hellenic essence is *deeper* than supposed. Little can be done with testimonies. Historical *facts, actions* are more important, e.g., for their ethics, than all their *words*. We have yet to *decipher* the Hellenic essence: it is still essentially *alien*.

we would offend their taste
>   our knowledge of human nature *shameless*
>   our technology ὕβρις[41] opposed to nature
>   our science petty-hucksterish
>   untruthful, because so much about us is imperceptible II 399.
> universal suffering of modern people: "self-diminution" p. 399.

Introduction

Drives of their intellect and their senses	1) The simplifying (they are so *comprehensible*), delight in overlooking secondary features, energy to make one feature the focus.
	2) The logicizing: a kind of enchantment (dialectic as something divine. Antigone's verse).
	3) The idealizing ("beautiful and young") the feeling that we satisfy in the great outdoors they satisfy *among people.*
Drives and feelings from the political sphere	4) The feeling of nobility they[42] trusted themselves to determine correct self-worth II 397. Unfair to the humble. Nemesis: to think oneself worthy of great things of which others are not worthy.
	5) The atmosphere of *political* clarity, the necessity of *making* themselves commonly understood.
	6) The *agonal* feeling that wants to triumph
the best developed instinct of their entire *morality*	before an audience and that must be understandable by this audience. (Which is why such different individuals *excessively* profess to be "universally human."

Judgment of the awakening "*factual sense*" as itself a consequence of the agon. Praise of Thucydides.

In the mouth of a Greek it was paradoxical to claim to see the epitome of perfection in the sphere, they don't like curvature and roundedness.

The feelings they have for nature are much more closely related to a religious sensibility than ours are. In our case, the main thing is always that we are *liberated* from humans — we seek feelings that we *do not* have among humans.

I discovered what it means to be Greek: they believed in the *eternal recurrence*! This is the *mystery-faith*!
(passage in Cratylus)
Plato believes the dead in Hades are *true philosophers, liberated from the body.*

γνῶθι σαυτόν,[43] but not humans
to read for subtext[44]
πρόσθε Πλάτων, ὄπισθέν τε Πλάτων μέσση τε Χίμαιρα.[45]

Purposes.

Their weakness points to their strength.
They are actors. For their intellect, willing and being converge.

8 [16]

Superior humans,
their self-redemption and self-preservation.

8 [17]

the appreciation of truth among the *powerful* (among the oppressed as revenge, vindication — Spinoza).
Self-overcoming of morality.

8 [18]

the *preservation of the species* reminted as moral principle!

8 [19]⁴⁶

To completely *emancipate* absolute necessity *from purposes*: otherwise we may not even experiment and sacrifice ourselves and let ourselves go! It is the innocence of becoming[47] and nothing else that gives us the *greatest courage* and the *greatest freedom*!

8 [20]

I write for myself: and what's the point of writing in this age that has been written to death? little: for, apart from scholars, no one knows how to read anymore, and even scholars — — —

8 [21]

Our age has implanted new eyes in order to see suffering everywhere: and with a monstrous hypnotic fixed gaze which has had its equal just once before in history and which forces the gaze of beholders in the same direction — — —

When I was young, I was essentially one of the world-deniers and pessimists; which is understandable and forgivable in an age that seems tailor-made for driving youth to despair. The more a young man suffers on account of his own becoming, the more he wants to fit into the whole, complete and finished; he wants security above all, *stability*: yet this age has been thought to death by the thoughts of all ages, it is mistrustful, with a mistrust that has never yet existed among humans, and for that reason this age is often tired of thinking, often tired of mistrusting, often senile and "*tentative*" in its yes and in its no: for this age presumes ⟨a⟩ yes in every case, where — — —

Here, then, the decisive protest of an individual like Schopenhauer *against* the whole of existence as a redemption: it simplifies

8 [22]

Every human being we meet stimulates certain drives in us (fear trust etc.) Uninterrupted movement of our drive-life through the outside world (nature): entirely apart from the uninterrupted registering and absorption of electrical atmospheric effects.

8 [23][48]

good people[49]

Since every drive is unintelligent, "utility" is not a consideration for it at all. Every drive, by being active, sacrifices force and other drives: it is eventually constrained; otherwise it would ruin everything, through dissipation. Thus: that which is "unegoistic" sacrificial imprudent is nothing special — it is common to all drives — they do not think about the benefit of the whole ego (*because they don't think!*) they act "contrary to our benefit," against the ego and often *for* the ego — innocent in both!

8 [24][50]

In philosophy we seek an image of the world that makes us feel freest; i.e., in which our most powerful drive feels free in its activity. This will be the case even with me!

8 [25][51]

The nonsense of all metaphysics as a derivation of the conditioned from the unconditioned.

The nature of thinking includes *conceiving*, inventing the unconditioned *as an addition to* the conditioned: just as thinking conceives, invents the "I" as an addition to the multiplicity of its processes: it measures the world with benchmarks posited solely by itself: in connection with its basic fictions like "unconditioned," "means and ends," things, "substances," with logical laws, with numbers and shapes.

There would be nothing called knowledge if thinking had not first *re-created* the world into "things," self-identicals.

It is *due to* thinking that there is *untruth*.

Thinking is *underivable*, so too are *perceptions*: but that is *far from* proving them to be original or "existing in themselves"! rather, this only establishes that we cannot get *beyond them*, because we *have* nothing but thinking and perceiving.

8 [26]⁵²

*The Innocence of Becoming.*⁵³
A Guide to Liberation from Morality.⁵⁴
By
Friedrich Nietzsche.

Introduction.

I. The Fundamental Errors of Morality.

II. Morality as Sign Language.⁵⁵

III. The Overcoming of Morality and its Replacement.

8 [27]⁵⁶

Anyone who advances rationality thereby also infuses new energy into forces that oppose it, into mysticism and folly of every sort.

In every movement to distinguish

1) where it is *partly* fatigue from a preceding movement (satiation from it, malice of the weakness toward it, illness

2) where it is *partly* a newly awakened, long dormant, accumulated force, joyful, arrogant, violent: good health.

9 [1]¹

Your spring pours forth too mightily; it empties the cup at the same time it wants to fill it.²

Peels and clamshells and whatever other playful things fall from the table of life³

Your good deeds should fall like dew on the grass, then, when the night is most secretive.⁴

I expect and want goodness especially from you, who I think is capable of any evil⁵

You should call advantage and need what advantage and need are and keep the name of virtue holy.

What makes your actions good is not their reason or purpose, but rather whether your soul trembles and shines when you do them.⁶

How could any act of mercy be performed if it did not mean: taking injustice upon *ourselves*?

If your shoulders are broad enough for the task, then don't hesitate, add the injustices of others to your own: and your mercy will be praised.

Knowing: this means: understanding all things as being to our best advantage!

"I will this," "thou shalt," "he must" — that's how they understand I you and he.⁷

Experience approaches me imperiously: but no sooner has it been experienced than it is already on its knees.⁸

Do you feel the thirst and the hot breath of the sun? It wants to be nursed by the ocean. Do you see the ocean's lust rise with a thousand breasts? It wants to be kissed and nursed by the thirst of the sun[9]

9 [2]

To believe in Schopenhauer's will — this requires a very strong *will to believe*!

9 [3][10]

Midnight's brilliance was all around me, solitude looked at me with drunken tired eyes.
— my voice screamed out of me —
Deathly silence slept and snored[11] in its sleep.
There lay sleeplessness and midnight with drunken eyes.
There lay solitude and deathly silence at its side: both slept and snored.

9 [4][12]

God stopgap.
Onward to immortality

9 [5][13]

On the shame of the gift-giver.
About justice (proletarians).
On intoxication.
The newer convents etc.
Historical education — "I speak freely."
Honesty of the pitiable.
Genius's!
"Punishments" as enmity toward the enemies of our ideals.
Temporary "marriage" —

9 [6][14]

slamming the door

how ridiculous it would be if you wanted to convert to *my* cause![15]

You come to me, and I don't *want* you: but as I must give, so you *must* take!

"Party liner"[16] — I want to turn this into an insult.

I want to be a white steer and pull the plow: wherever I lie, there should be serenity and the earth should smell of earth.

Wildly the eagle beats its wings: but its surge[17] founders on my will.

They no longer experience anything: their skin is barely scratched. Events sit on their skin like mosquitoes. — Thus h⟨umans⟩ remain heavy and the same, like a stone in the sun.

Church: simulated light, sweetened seriousness of the incense, being seduced into false fears, I can't stand the soul who — kneels to its God above.

I looked into life as into an eye.

Monk in the moon, you wet-cheeked one! I'll never call you the "man" in the moon! Lecherously you creep from window to window around all dark corners! you most jealous tomcat of all, jealous of all lovers, you grin through each window into the room within.

9 [7][18]

They want to use their virtues to claw out the eyes of their enemies.

They engage in vice because they cannot create.

They — — —

9 [8]

The dances of Zarathustra.

9 [9]

I wanted to be the philosopher of *unpleasant truths* — for six years!

9 [10]¹⁹

For too long I belonged to solitude: thus I have unlearned silence.

I have become nothing but mouth and the roar of a stream from high cliffs: I want to send my words cascading into the valleys.

I hate all nightwatchmen and guardians of the graves and anyone else who blows a dismal horn.

I long for something and I watch — and now you come, my eagle: did you see no one, — — —

I laugh at your free will and even at your unfree will: there is no will. A delusion is born out of pain and contemplation — that's what we call "will."

9 [11]²⁰

I look down into the ocean: it lies placidly and out of it an image looks treacherously back at me.

In its arms the ocean holds a priceless image with white breasts: it steals languidly and treacherously across the sand, so that — — —

in this way, ocean and an image of the future lure me

Languidly and treacherously the ocean moved away from its white breasts.

The sand has covered half the image and the jealousy of the wave the other half.

9 [12]

Determinism is to be eliminated *in this way*:

I *want* to submit myself to the judgment of certain h⟨umans⟩: it should be my education, spur me on and discourage me — all as a means of *getting* an *ideal to prevail* and making it dominant.

Organic = moral, is the *solution* to the problem of morality.

Initially, individuals are *honored* insofar as they evoke a *type*: e.g., "the priest," "the hero" etc. — only later, insofar as they are "a person alone."

There are moralities which make a virtue out of becoming *not* an individual, *but rather a type*! finally, *becoming one* in feeling with a revered type of the people.

9 [13][21]

The ring's thirst to reach *itself* again — I thirst for it.[22]

9 [14][23]

Your minds were not yet a source of worry and heartache: your bread of life is not yet soured by thoughts.

As a hunter Zarathustra set forth, to hunt ugly truths.

The hand moved forward and the clock of my l⟨ife⟩ took a breath: then it spoke: now the hour has come to preach redemption from redeemers.

9 [15]

How I sought to understand everything that is human, at one point even wretched and mediocre people

Now and then even the wretched become honest: then it is advisable to listen to their voices and to climb into their swamp.

And at one point I, too, sat down among the reeds and heard the frogs of wretchedness make their confessions.

You people claim to be of sturdier stuff? I say to you, you are only better at deluding yourselves.

He came to us, he lived among us — *we* ourselves were his underworld.

Believe me, Z⟨arathustra⟩ died and is no more. A star burned out in barren space: but its light — — — [24]

9 [16][25]

Destroy for me these godly grinning masks! was I made to play the fool by a godly grin and did ⟨I⟩ forget the entrails with which the masks were stuffed?

Rip up for me the skins on which a god's soul seemed to play!

Serpent entrails and serpent filth ooze from the hidden
body of the lizard: the coiled-up ringed putrid-smelling thing
  a horrid ringed worm has crept into the mask of a god.
  holy laughter

9 [17]²⁶

You see only my sparks: but you do not see the anvil that I
am.

And I prefer to sleep on ox hides than on the bed of your
complacency and love, — — —

You are tools and watches to me: thus I want to wind you
up with my ridicule and you shall purr with contentment as I
do it.

I do not want to turn you into stone with serpent locks of
fear: I protect myself from you with my shield "Beauty." My
image of the most beautiful shall strike you dumb.

I do battle with the dragon of the future: and you puny
people, you shall do battle with earthworms.

9 [18]

You are adept and have clever fingers: but you have no idea
how to make a fist!

Not until your clever fingers creep back into a fist will I
want to believe in your power.[27]

His eye flashes golden: a golden bark[28] floats there upon
dark waters:[29]

In his eyes ⟨he⟩ crouches low and leaps high again in dance
and you, who carry him — — —

To me you are arid grass and steppe: but I want to make
wildfires of you and heralds with tongues of flame.[30]

When this moon rose, I thought that it wanted to give birth
to a sun: it lay there on the horizon so wide and heavy with
young.

But to me the moon is a liar, this barren one, with its pregnancy, and it is neither woman nor man.[31]

9 [19]

a strange cock, pecked at by hens[32]

he rose like a moon, but stayed lying languidly on the horizon.[33]

Anyone who knows horses also knows what it means to be in the saddle.[34]

9 [20][35]

Did I cause you the greatest pain when I did what I liked to do the most?

I did penance for my injustice: my admiration was even more unjust than my contempt.[36]

With vigils I did penance for the admirer's 1000 lies and for his eye's desire to be blind.

With 1000 acts of evil I took revenge on all prettification and nonsensical fantasy.

I despise you oblivious liars far more than I despise those who know they lie.

Because you lie about the way things are, no thirst will emerge within you for the way things ought to be.

9 [21][37]

they were choking on their nothingness: I gave them their nothingness to feed on.

They were rotting away at the sight of themselves: I held up my mirror to their ugliness

Just as they perished from their own nothingness and were unable to bear the sight of themselves, they experienced their highest moment.

And I would need gloves of glass in order to poison you.

9 [22]

La vie est une tragédie pour ceux qui sentent, et une comédie pour ceux, qui pensent.[38] *Horace Walpole.*

9 [23]³⁹

You don't want to hear that someone is strolling around above your heads. And so you place wood and earth and refuse above your heads: that's how you muffle the speech of my steps. You put all human error and obtuseness between yourselves and me: you call this a dead floor in your houses. But in spite of this I stroll around above your thoughts, and they themselves should stroll around on top of my mistakes.

You shame yourselves with broad stairways for those who would rise like gods: and as the arches break above you and play off against each other — — —

you put your longing into the mouth of the faraway moon: your longing stretched beyond the words and above as well!

Whatever contradicted them they called God: their kind of heroism, to destroy what is human within them in this way: but the time is past for human beings to nail themselves to the cross.

All those who create seek new languages: they have grown tired of their thin used-up tongues: the mind has been walking on these soles for far too long.

As long as beauty is not one of your needs, what do I care about your obsession with the beautiful!

Not satisfaction, but rather beauty, should be the end of desire

The way you are, you are only to be tolerated as ruins: and that which destroys you, lightning and downpours and weeds: your unhappiness and adversity justify your existence.

You must learn to build with mountains: merely removing mountains⁴⁰ means little.

Your sayings — "puny truths" near the swamps: and some cold frog is sitting in there.

9 [24]⁴¹

May my eagle always be a danger to small white sheep and be known as a raptor!

Are you familiar with the terror of people falling asleep? They are shaken to the depths of their being, for the dream is beginning — and often their terror shakes them awake.

Your virtue should serve and honor only that for which you despise yourselves the most. This alone should be the service and the benefit provided by your virtue!

What are your father- and motherlands to me? I love only my children's land, through my children I wish to make up for the fact that I am my father's child.

I wanted to catch a fish and threw a net into the sea — but I drew forth a god's head instead: the sea gave me, the hungry one, a stone.

nature is a divine puppet show.
ashes and embers blow upon me
wildfire
dry grass
crackling

9 [25]
Many things must come together for a *moral* action
1) a strong spontaneity
2) the most extreme tension of the willing I
it is the *highest form of organic functions*.

9 [26][42]
I also demand *grace*[43] even from *those inclined to greatness*.

9 [27]
the *Dionysian* as the aspect of antiquity that is most accessible for me.

9 [28]
Genius and bungling

9 [29][44]
Corsica and Italy.

Democracy as decline of the state.

Taking away the Jews' money and giving them another direction.

the Dionysian as access to the Greeks.

an enormous mass of lofty feelings, for which thoughts are still lacking and goals

to raise humans above themselves, as with the Greeks, not disembodied phantasms.

9 [30]⁴⁵

Your Great Flood still oppresses the earth

I come from there like a strong wind and that's why I advise those who despise me: when facing the wind, be careful not to — spit.

The monster of the body has scarcely raised itself out of the darkest slime

I call this festival the cleansing and sanctification of the earth

to be your only contemporary!

You want to sap the strength of sickness and, for me, in the process you are sapping the strength of the sick, you witch doctors and saviors!

Whenever those who could command attempt to persuade and hide their kingly hands beneath their robes: I call this courtesy.

My savage wisdom got pregnant atop lonely mountains: it brought forth its young on bare stone. Now it runs foolishly through the harsh desert and seeks soft grass for its youngest, my old savage wisdom.

9 [31]⁴⁶

I believed myself to be the richest one of all: now I have made a gift of myself.

I do not even touch their souls' skin anymore!

Ever more solitary and exiled: ever more ardent in love and wanting to go among the people.

The 7 solitudes.

All typical *sufferings* of the reformers; and their *consolations*.

1) Consolation: I will lay my hand on the next millennium.

2) I live as if I were living in another age: my eminence gives me contact with solitary and misunderstood people in all age⟨s⟩

3) I do not hate I defend myself with beauty.

9 [32][47]

With many small doses it is possible to turn a brave man into a coward: but also a coward into a brave man.

Cosmic dependence

Pass by these enemies quietly and with a sleeping sword: those who attack them sully themselves.

Like the buffalo I live near the sea and even nearer to the forest.

9 [33]

Drives should be denied as long as possible — **principle** of moral-physiolog⟨ical⟩ research.

Whatever *makes* us value a human being **now** has always done so. H⟨uman beings⟩ came to be honored first and *only then* actions[48]

9 [34][49]

How would I endure it if I didn't love superhumans more than you?

For what purpose did I give you the 100-faceted mirror?

I also overcame love for you with love for superhumans.

And as I endure you, you must endure yourselves, out of love for s⟨uperhumans⟩.

For me, you are the stone in which the most sublime of all
statues sleeps
And as my hammer swings at you, you should swing at
yourselves for my sake: the call of the hammer should awaken
the sleeping statue.

People who wanted to conceal themselves, and were shamed
by the clear sky, created for themselves these sweet-smelling
caves.
I do not want to become enamored again of these places
until grass and red poppies flourish on ruined walls.

9 [35]⁵⁰

Dirges at the volcano's edge
Nature's stillness — thunder.
Golden casket.

9 [36]

§ Redemption from redeemers is what Zarathustra teaches.
§ generous to the earth? no, just.
§ "I acquit: for **I** also would have acted in the very same
way" — a ghastly historic formulation! it means "I am tolerant
of myself — consequently!"
"Thou shalt? I will this"

9 [37]

Every time I put on a good pair of glasses, I am amazed at
how ugly h⟨umans⟩ are and how anyone could stand to be
around them.

9 [38]

The meaning of causality becomes ever *weaker* when looking backwards (e.g., myths) *Consequently* conceptions about
what is inner must be especially *lacking* in reason.
The *oldest* assumptions must bc thc dumbest

9 [39]

"Will" is a concept for unifying all of our passions.

Passions are feelings for identifying particular bodily states that are *not* attributable to the body.

"Common feelings"

Moral feelings are passions transformed by *value judgments*.

The influence of *judgment* on *feeling* (even with pleasure and pain)

Pleasure and pain are value judgments

9 [40]

How *superficial* and *impoverished* is everything *that is inner*:

    e.g., purpose (image of chewing and actual chewing)

    e.g., a concept of horse in comparison to a horse,

    e.g., the feeling of warmth in comparison to what happens

    e.g., the I in comparison to the "self"

    e.g., seeing in comparison to the mechanics of seeing,

    e.g., the feeling of a heartbeat in comparison to its mechanics

9 [41]

There are *only* **bodily** states: mental states are consequences and symbolism.

To separate outer and inner world, as metaphysicians do, is already a sensory judgment.

Eye ear are also "outer world."

Feelings *and the outer world* are given to us: and even the feelings *localized in this world*.

I call all sense impressions "stimuli."

"Illusion" only makes sense for the *eye*.

To show "*the metaphysics of metaphysics*"!

We are in the process of figuring out the being of things: consequently we must already have an *opinion* as to what *being* is. **This can** *be* an *error*! e.g., I.

9 [42]

The silliness of morality in its assessment of value according to *difficulty*.

The "*inner* world" is much thinner and shorter than the mechanical world. Overestimation!

Unegoistic acts as self-deception and shortsightedness. "Shortcut"

Purification of the inner world.[51]

At some point religious aesthetic and moral attitudes must have been *one and the same*.

Designation and valuation of our bodily states — how to do it?

9 [43]

I had to *abolish* morality in order to have my moral will prevail.

Supposing morality is valid, then I must not overwhelm my neighbors with the power of my judging. So I *also* must not terrorize (unnerve) them

Yes, they are innocent

Struggle for power! To make my ideal prevail *in a manner* derived from my ideal!

Human actions can in no way *be explained* by reference to human *motives*.

Individuals *continue* to have an effect inside their *impulses*.[52]

The superior intellect bound to a weak nervous character — is to be eliminated.

Contempt for the accumulation and influence of power runs *counter* to the principle of the organic.

9 [44]

1. Passions = virtues and vices.

2. Measures of value (the scientific measure *lacking* up to now)

Herds and individuals.

Fear or hope accompany a feeling of pain or pleasure — *as with all passions.*

Anger (and all affects) *initially* a bodily state: which is interpreted. Later the interpret⟨ation⟩ freely generates the state.

9 [45]⁵³

not necessary and not even superfluous

they shoot off their mouths; we are supposed to think that this is out of the abundance of their hearts.⁵⁴

A star went under and disappeared — but its light is still on its way, and when will it cease being on its way?

Are you a star? Then you, too, must wander and be homeless.

§ The murder-of-God-penitents and their festival⁵⁵

You have yet to be taught *hunger* for your knowledge.

Dancers have their ears in their toes.

It is also sweet to resist ourselves and to comb back the hair of bushy feelings.

§ to *wean* h⟨uman beings⟩ from feelings of "punishment" and "guilt"⁵⁶

9 [46]

Everything organic must be *overcome*. Little and often!

How could I want to live if I did not look *ahead* — beyond you!

Fear the one who has withdrawn! The tiger prepares to spring![57]

Reverence is itself a passion: just like verbal abuse. Through *reverence* the "*passions*" were turned into *virtues*.

I can only rarely recall an unconditional "should": thus no authority! Kant's "moral sense" is nothing! This is the *vanity* that *wants* one "should" to be the "should" for all the world!

9 [47]

Corporations — apart from the state.

Our thoughts come as stimuli from somewhere. (Nothing to do with "pleasant" and "unpleasant.")

In the weak, I appraise the good and bad alike.
Stronger people as nobler people.

For the education of individuals.

Workers should for once live like the bourgeois now live: but **above** them the **higher caste**, distinguishing themselves through lack of needs! thus poorer and simpler, yet in possession of power.[58]

Right to design your *own* entirely *individual* approach to *punishment*.

If you do **not** want to *advocate* the *individuum* in *what most belongs to you*, but rather to contradict it, then the *contradiction* is **part** of the individual "responsibility" —

9 [48][59]

The most influential people are the most hidden.

Culture is just a thin apple skin over a glowing chaos.

People *not* equal: thus speaks justice.[60]

Not utility but gravitas determines value: a noble person is the result of much labor.

Individuum est aliquid novum:[61] actions are not shared in common with anyone.

The[62] will a delusion.

The truth hurts because it destroys a *belief*: not in itself.

Inventors of new states of the soul are the true inventors: people seek *to mimic* these states[63]

Dühring: no one would wish for such a bitter soul. That is why his philosophy is not attractive.

Feeling of power. — Happiness is *not* the goal: but rather a monstrous force in humans and in humankind wants to *expend* itself, wants to create, it is an ongoing chain of explosions that in no way have happiness as the goal.

So you want to be paid?

"like a sweet smell" — but she had to die.

9 [49]⁶⁴

Purification from revenge is *my* morality. §
"When has such a flame ever burned? (as Zarathustra)
I hate anyone who limps along in front of us.
Those who walk forward with their heads turned backward—

The ocean that delights in spreading its peacock train upon soft sand.

[50]

§ the proletarian ("Dühring")

§ *Intoxication.* Its *common* form in convulsive atonement. Warn about Dionysus!

9 [51]

Within different people we find the *same number* of passions: yet these are given different names, evaluated differently and in the process *adjudicated* differently. *Good* and *evil* are distinguished by the differing orders of rank of passions as they relate to one another and by the dominance of goals.

9 [52]⁶⁵

You think everything is the wild play of giants? Yet a single word, arriving on the wings of doves, directs the will of these wild ones: The still source

9 [53]⁶⁶

It is night —now
all gushing fountains speak more loudly
— and you, too, my soul
are a gushing fountain.
It is night — and all songs of those who love
just now awaken.
And you, too, my soul, are
the song of someone who loves.⁶⁷

9 [54]
    Incense of someone being burned at the stake.

9 [55]
    The very best knowledge[68] is barely sufficient for faith.

9 [56][69]
    —the dream
    —proletarians
    —intoxication. Its most common form in convulsions of
conscience
    —redemption from redeemers
    —"I acquit: for I also would have done the same thing."
    —generous to the earth? no, just!
    —Do you want to be paid?
    —Annihilation and resurrection of morality.

9 [57]
    Daniel *Darc, bréviaire du Parisien* (Ollendorf *éditeur*)[70]
    Brehm
    Moldenhauer

9 [58]
    Collection of *sublime* states and objects.

9 [59]
    No. 343 M⟨ixed⟩ O⟨pinions⟩ and M⟨axims⟩

[10 = N VI 3. June–July 1883]

10 [1][1]

by striving upward against my burden, I rejuvenated myself: and just when I became more hardened within myself, I learned grace, too.

inventive in small stratagems and lusting for buyers, they waited: with emaciated souls and meager in hope.

10 [2][2]

My stream threw itself wildly in wrong directions and into impassable canyons: but how should it ever come about that a stream failed to reach the ocean?

I found a lake, a hermit and a self-satisfied person: but my stream threw itself into this lake ⟨and⟩ swept it along into the ocean.

10 [3][3]

like Caesar. immovable.

You don't know me

I gave you the heaviest burden — so that the weaklings would perish from it — for *breeding*.

No compassion!

I want to form and *transform* myself and you

how would I bear it otherwise![4]

when my I[5] *dreamed* **you**

10 [4][6]

Pity the humans and superhumans who do not have a pinnacle that is even above compassion!

The smallest gap stands between me and you: but who has ever built bridges across the smallest gaps!

Conversation with the *hound of hell*.[7] (volcano)

On ashes I stride up the mountain of ashes at dusk: my shadow grows long and longer.

A boat floats far away in the violet-blue sea: the sailor who sees me striding along crosses himself

Now Zarathustra is journeying to hell — he says, shuddering: I had always figured it would end this way!

You are completely wrong, fisherman! The devil is not taking me: instead, Zarathustra is now taking the devil as his own.[8]

10 [5][9]

your knees worship, but your heart knows nothing of it.

to **bring** *redemption*

There lies the island of tombs, there, too, the tombs of my youth: I want to carry an evergreen wreath of life there.

I thought of my youth today I walked up my street of tombs I sat on ruins between red poppies and grass — on my own ruins.

traveling to the island of the departed on sleeping seas

You still live, old patient heart of iron: and in you, too, what is unredeemed, unspoken from my youth, still lives.

10 [6][10]

Jesus — like a sweet smell.

The preservation of the species is *guaranteed*: but what does it **involve**!

Redeemers
Philosophers. Those who know. Scientists.
Genius
Free spirits.
Romantics.
Artists.
Conquerors "strong willed" mocked
Statesmen
Saints:

Fidelity
Truthfulness
Compassion.
Justice.
Bravery
Obedience.

And if you aren't a bird, be careful not to camp above an abyss.

I can no longer descend to you: my eye itself blurs and becomes blind to the upward path that I traveled.

10 [7]¹¹
The art of the tarantula is black and blackening: yet I call tarantulas the teachers of the "worst world"

10 [8]¹²
I had renounced life: I had become nightwatchman and guardian of the graves in death's mountain fortress.
Up there I guarded his coffins in musty vaults: they stood full of such victory emblems: life that had been overcome stared at me from glass coffins.

I myself am like the wind that shatters the gates to the chambers of the dead. I myself am like the coffin filled with colorful malicious words and angeli⟨c⟩ grimaces, I myself am the laughter of life in the midnight chamber of the dead.¹³

10 [9][14]

one person rejoices that justice still includes taking revenge: and another person rejoices that revenge still means that justice is being done. (Dühring and the Corsican[15])

If there were gods: how could I stand not being a god! But there are no gods.

10 [10][16]

Long ago, this happened to me: I dreamed my most burdensome dream, and while dreaming I composed my darkest riddle.

But, behold, my life itself interpreted this dream. Behold, my today redeemed my yesterday and the meaning imprisoned within.

And so, too, this happened recently: thunder boomed three times through the night in my direction, the vaults howled three times.

Alpa, I called, Alpa, Alpa. W⟨ho⟩ ⟨is⟩ c⟨arrying⟩ ⟨his⟩ a⟨shes⟩ t⟨o⟩ ⟨the⟩ m⟨ountain⟩? Which of those lives that have been overcome approaches me, the nightwa⟨tchman⟩ and guardian of graves?

When I dreamed *you*, I dr⟨eamed⟩ my most burdensome dream.

This is why I want to be your horror — your fainting and your awakening.

10 [11][17]

Praise of Cool Reason[18]

the one who creates praises poverty of the intellect and skepticism

sweet smell

midsummer

The courage to demand the extraord⟨inary⟩ is rarer than the courage to achieve it.

Strength and duration of resolve and frugality (insight into earthly imperf⟨ection⟩

10 [12][19]

Sweet and stale like the smell of aging virgins[20] you scholars.

You redeemers, what do you know of human beings!

And why don't you want to make yourselves into bait — alongside me?

But no voice responded.

Alas, you do not know how much I, a solitary man, am comfortable with human voices which a wind or a bird carried to me. I have even gotten drunk on ugly voices.

Alpa! I screamed, so let your voice be heard already. Alpa! my fear and longing screamed forth from me.

10 [13]

How easy it is for us to take on the burden of an apol⟨ogy⟩, as long as there is no responsibility.

But I am responsible.

10 [14][21]

You compassionate ones, when you throw yourselves from the *heights* at the people below, what price do you put on broken limbs!

10 [15][22]

But there was silence, terrible silence redoubled. Alas, you are not familiar with it, the redoubled silence, the one that ties our hearts in knots!

Alpa! I screamed. Alpa! Alpa! The fear of redoubled silence screamed forth from me.

10 [16]²³

Stooped over, working in dim gloomy shafts, this is the prisoners' hardest lot.

10 [17]

Where did he go? Who knows?
But it is certain that he met his downfall.
A star burned out in barren space.²⁴

The intransitory — this is only a symbol, and poets lie too much.²⁵

They also know too little and are bad learners: so they must already be lying.

And what is most dear to them is the kingdom in the clouds: they enthrone their colorful brats up there and call them gods,

And when they lie in a garden under trees or give speeches by themselves in front of the flowers by a precipice, then they think that their tend⟨er⟩ feel⟨ings⟩ are knowledge.

They all believe that nature is in love with them and are always listening in to its accolades.

10 [18]²⁶

Dare to believe in yourselves no matter what! How else should anyone believe in you otherwise! Those who do not bel⟨ieve⟩ in themselves are always lying!

Willing liberates! — thus do I teach you f⟨reedom⟩ ⟨of⟩ t⟨he⟩ w⟨ill⟩

10 [19]²⁷

This laughter shattered me, and ripped apart my guts, and slit open my heart.

Strong will? An enduring will is what I need, a hard-hearted eternal resoluteness.

10 [20]²⁸

All creation is transformation — and wherever creative hands are working there are many deaths and downfalls.

And only this is dying and disintegration: without pity sculptors hammer away at the marble.

That they may free the sleeping image from the stone, this is why they must be without pity: — this is why we must all suffer and die and turn to dust.

But we ourselves are the sculptors, serving the sculptor's eye: we ourselves often tremble at the creative savagery of our hands.

10 [21]²⁹

Who among you poets has not adulterated his wines? Many a poisonous mishmash lies hidden in your cellars.

Do you want to see the rainbow and the bridge of the superhumans? Right now is the time.

The storm cloud is still rumbling, but already the sun shines again.

10 [22]³⁰

Prophecy.

Someday I will have my summer: and it will be like a summer in the high mountains.

A summer near the snow, near eagles, near death.

10 [23]³¹

This is the most unforgiveable thing about you: you have the power and you don't want to rule.

You see, don't you, the one they all need the most. This is the one who can command.

Will — — —

10 [24]³²

You have hungry minds: so take this truth quickly from me as a snack: the intransitory — this is only a symbol.

10 [25]

superhumans completely beyond all previous virtue, *hard-hearted* due to their compassion, — those who create, who *unsparingly hammer* their marble.

For Zarathustra's last speech.

10 [26]

To play the great game — to wager the existence of human-kind on the poss⟨ibility⟩ of achieving something higher than the preservation of the species.

F⟨or the⟩ l⟨ast⟩ spee⟨ch⟩

10 [27]

I will reach you *late* — just as the Greek artists are reaching you only now.

Aesch⟨ylus⟩

10 [28]³³

Conversation with the *hound of fire*
Mockery of his pathos
against the revolution

10 [29]

Mockery of revolutions and Vesuviuses. Something from the surface

10 [30]³⁴

You are not yet driven by any strong wind or will
You are still too stiff for me and your neck is too stiff³⁵
Alas, that you would walk across the sea, already full and rounded like a sail, trembling in the storminess of your will!
Only then shall I call you beautiful and properly prepared!

10 [31]³⁶

These are heated times right now, the air is on fire — now everyone is walking around *naked*, good and evil people! this world without clothes is a festival for those who know.

States burst apart
Earthquakes
everything becomes visible
Taine³⁷
What makes the earth *quake*: the silent words of the saints
Storm of malice.
Rejoicing that everything is becoming visible and bursting.
I feel so wonderful!
End of all customs and secret dealings.
Twilight of the gods —³⁸
There is nothing eternal!

10 [32]³⁹

Deep knowledge flows cold, its deepest wellsprings are ice-cold: that's why it is refreshing to hot hands and to anyone eager for action.

10 [33]⁴⁰

I love the turbulence of a bad reputation, like a ship, the wake that the ship creates. I tread more lightly, when the way around my keel — — —

10 [34]⁴¹

But just as I was awakened by you and came to myself, so you, too, should be *awakened by yourselves* — and come to *me*!

Redeemers? I call you the ones who bind and tame!

to approach the wellspring with humble hands

10 [35][42]

Truly, I say to you: wherever there are tombs, there have also always been resurrections!

Speak your word[43] and founder on it. What do you matter!

10 [36][44]

I am well disposed to all that is pure:

I say to you, mediators and equivocators, to you half-and-halfers: you are not pure

how could I be well disposed to you conciliators!

10 [37][45]

There haven't been any superhumans yet. I saw them both naked, the greatest and the puniest humans: and I found both of them still — all too human!

10 [38][46]

You play and you want your play to be watched — I call all of you actors.

Whether you call yourselves poets or dancers or public servants and the voice of the people —

Whether you teach or paint or compose or play "Black on White": — you want to make a name for yourselves.

Mother Vanity

The opposite of those who would like to erase their names and stick their heads in the sand — so that their *task* will not see them and will pass them by.

10 [39]

and only when I am a burden to *myself*, do you weigh heavily on me.

10 [40][47]

1 Laughing at the ethical world-order. "paid for"

2 Dance song

3 Dream.
4 Hound of fire
5 Mediators.
6 Praise of cool reason
7 Penitents of the mind.
8 Many societies (to the conquerors = founders)
9 Poets geniuses actors
10 Scholars
11 to stroll among fragments!
12 Philosophers
13 Socialists for equality
14 Those who speak freely[48]
15 Pessimists

10 [41][49]

    On the Hucksters
        the Curious
            Frugal (Mystics)
    on the *Vanity of the Pure*
    On the *Sculptors of Idols.*
    On *Necromancers*
        Free-speech advocates.
        Reconcilers. Mediators
    There haven't been any superhumans yet.

10 [42][50]

    Pleasure of the mistral wind
            of the plowshare
            of the heights
            of life
            of the change in seasons (ring) Organic
            of the stream
            of the dawn
            of the clear sky
            electricity.
    Pleasure as mother of pain.

10 [43]
   Main doctrine: nature is *like a human being: errs* etc.
   Anthropomorphizing of nature.

10 [44]
   Therefore, I conclude, a belief in time is good for our health.
(pessimists last of all)

   There are three solitudes: that of the one who creates, that
of the one who waits and that of shame.

   I know the word and the sign of the superhumans: but I do
not show it, I do not show it to myself.

   What did *you* do? ("Festival of Life") — — "This is how
things are, coming from the mind of Zarathustra"

   The doctrine first *called* good by the **rabble**, in the end
called good by the most superior humans.

   We want to live like Z⟨arathustra⟩, ashamed in the face of a
great truth.

10 [45]51
Act I. The temptations. He does not consider himself ripe.
        (Chosen people)
        Solitude on account of being ashamed of himself
Act II. Zarathustra attending the "great noon" incognito
        Is recognized
Act III. Catastrophe: *everyone* abandons him after *his* speech.
         He dies from the pain.
Act IV. Funeral rites
        "We killed him"
   countering the arguments

10 [46]

Concerning 1). He refuses. Finally the children's choirs bring him to tears.

A *fool*!

2 kings lead the donkey.

Concerning 2) When the procession does not know where to turn, the messengers arrive from the plague city. Decision. As in the *forest*. Fire in the marketplace symbol⟨ic⟩ purification.

Destruction of the *big city* the end

I want to lead the *pious* astray.

10 [47]

Zarathustra sitting in the ruins of a church Act 4

the gentlest person must become the most hard-hearted person — and perish in the process.[52]

Gentle to humans, hard-hearted for the sake of superhumans **Collision**.

apparent *weakness*.

he prophesies to them: the doctrine of return is the *sign*.

He **forgets himself** and teaches return **as derived from the** *superhumans*: the superhumans *withstand the doctrine* and *use it to punish.*

As he returns from his vision, he dies from it

[11 = N VI 4. June–July 1883]

11 [1]
sleepless agony, *bleeding*

11 [2][1]
On Scholars.
On the Land of Education.
On the Rabble.
The Funeral Rites.

11 [3]
Which of the two of us is the bigger fool?
Zarathustra answered: the one of us who thinks that of the other.

What is the most fertile mother of tragedies?
Wounded vanity.[2]

Which of the two of us is the happiest?
⟨The one⟩ whose unhappiness has gone wrong in the best way.

This is my abyss and my danger, that I plummet into these heights — and certainly not into your depths!

11 [4]³

Let's see whether or not the lioness is learning to roar gently!
—

Alas, if only I knew how to lure you back to me with shepherds' flutes! Alas, if only the lioness would learn to roar gently!

11 [5]

Frustration at the fact that *necessity is iron* and that the retroactive will is denied to us:

Rage at the fact that time flows away into the future and does not allow itself to be forced into the mill of the past!

That something suffers, refreshes us —: this is our most ancient folly.

11 [6]

W⟨agner⟩ turns to those who are made mistrustful by arguments but are convinced by sublime gestures.

11 [7]

I never take people completely seriously. My enemies don't have to make a lot of amends to me because it's too easy for me to start laughing at them. But I could easily kill on impulse.

11 [8]⁴

There is something fundamentally flawed in human beings — they must be overcome. Attempt it!

11 [9]⁵

Dühring. He is satisfied when he has added a few angry and arrogant words: that's what he calls "witty"

11 [10]⁶

III Zarathustra includes:
the Penitent of the Mind
*The Murderer of God.*⁷
weary people
The Beehives

11 [11]

When the house is burning, even dinner is forgotten —
said the hound of fire.

Yes, and the hound finishes it later amidst the ashes.[8]

11 [12]

This is true virtue, which does not know about itself — this
is how you taught me the doctrine.

ever since then, I have found true modesty on heaths and
hedges and everywhere:

everywhere it grows like huckleberries, where nothing else
grows that is good.

11 [13][9]

   a The Funeral Rites
   b On the Hound of Fire
   c the stillest hour

11 [14]

With every action a lot is *accomplished* that we don't think
about.

11 [15][10]

Your will is still too proud and timid. If you want to have
good —

They will build beehives like Towers of Babel.

11 [16][11]

And may everything shatter that can be shattered by our
truths! There are still many worlds to build!

11 [17][12]

   On the Rabble
   On Tarantulas
   the pro⟨phet⟩
   The Funeral Rites

11 [18][13]
  Ill Humor of the Gift-Giver
  On Good and Evil.
  Conversation with the King
  On Great Events
  The Stillest Hour

11 [19]
  Victory over the *spirit of gravity*

11 [20]
  an architectural style for this soul

11 [21]
  strange saints are coming along, one by one, even a fool.

[12 = Z I 3. Summer 1883]

12 [1][1]

"*Wicked Wisdom.*"
Maxims and Mottos
by
Friedrich Nietzsche.

Barbs.
Maxims and Mottos
by
Friedrich Nietzsche.

1. Public opinions — private laziness.[2]

2. Convictions are more dangerous enemies of truth than are lies.[3]

3. Many people are stubborn in regard to a path once they have entered upon it, few in regard to the goal.[4]

4. The serpent must first become a dragon so that someone can become a hero against it.[5]

5. Not to speak of ourselves at all is a very refined form of — hypocrisy.[6]

6. Truth is least likely to find advocates, not when it is dangerous to speak the truth — but when it is boring to do so.[7]

7. We are so glad to be out amid nature because it has no opinion about us.[8]

8. The irrationality of a thing is no argument against its existence, but rather a condition for it.[9]

9. The iron necessity of which people speak is usually neither iron, nor necessary.[10]

10. When we have a lot to put into it, a day has a hundred pockets.[11]

11. Anyone who hears poorly always hears something more.[12]

12. We are in the most danger of being run over when we have just gotten out of the way of some vehicle.[13]

13. Waiting makes people immoral.[14]

14. The disciple of a martyr suffers more than the martyr.[15]

15. The advantage of a bad memory is that we can enjoy the same good things for the first time many times.[16]

16. A profession is the backbone of life.[17]

17. A marriage proves its worth by being able to put up with an occasional deviation.[18]

18. If you don't have a good father, you should find one.

19. Those who have never learned to do proper work don't get bored.[19]

20. Some men have sighed over the abduction of their wives, many more because nobody wanted to abduct them.[20]

21. It is doubtful whether a much-traveled person will have found any parts of the world uglier than those in the human face.[21]

22. We persuade courageous people to undertake some action by representing it as more dangerous than it is.[22]

23. The best means of coming to the assistance of people who are embarrassed is to praise them with conviction.[23]

24. We can speak very much to the point and yet in such a way that everyone in the world shouts the opposite: when, that is, we are not speaking to everyone in the world.[24]

25. The visionaries deny the truth to themselves, the liars only to others.[25]

26. Everyone who finds enjoyment thinks that the fruit is what mattered to the tree; but what mattered to it was the seed.[26]

27. Anyone who has seen someone's ideal is that person's unrelenting judge and guilty conscience as it were.[27]

28. The followers of a great man like to blind themselves in order to be better able to sing his praises better: poor songbirds![28]

29. What is genius? Wanting both a lofty goal *and* the means for attaining it.[29]

30. What is bad gains prestige through imitation, what is good loses it, especially in art.[30]

31. We must know how to dim our lights in order to get rid of mosquitoes and admirers.[31]

32. That you are trying to identify the exceptions ranks you far below someone else, especially when that person is trying to identify the rule.[32]

33. Every master has only one pupil: a pupil who will be unfaithful to just that master. For that pupil is also destined for mastery.[33]

34. It says nothing against the ripeness of a spirit[34] that it has a few worms.[35]

35. In solitude, solitary people consume themselves, amid multitudes, they are consumed by many. Now choose.[36]

36. Differently from a journeyman does a master love the master.[37]

37. We won't get the crowd to cry hosannas until we ride into town on an ass.[38]

38. Our supporters never forgive us if we take sides against ourselves.[39]

39. Women are the idleness of the creator on every seventh day.[40]

40. We must take care not to become prematurely sharp, because then we become prematurely — dull.[41]

41. Anyone we leave standing for a long time in the anteroom of our favor begins to ferment and becomes sour.[42]

42. Vanity is for proud people the mask of politeness.[43]

43. Wit is the epigram upon the death of a feeling.[44]

44. A good maxim is too hard even for the teeth of time.[45]

45. A good book enriches even the spirits[46] of its opponents.[47]

46. In art, a sanctified means can sanctify a vile end.[48]

47. When your work opens its mouth, you should shut up.[49]

48. What has to be given to you in pieces need not be fragmentary for that reason.[50]

49. Good ideas that follow too quickly after one another block each other's "view."[51]

50. Self-sacrifice is present in every action, in the best as well as in the worst.[52]

51. Whether we have a serpent's tooth is something that we do not know until someone has put their heel upon us.[53]

52. Those who find even one grain of humiliation in a sack of advantages that have been given to them will still make the worst of a good thing.[54]

53. We know a little too much about everyone.[55]

54. The mother of excess is not joy, but joylessness.[56]

55. Still better to wash with dirty water than to remain unclean.[57]

56. All that is gold does not glitter: it is too soft for that.[58]

57. We should remove the scaffolding once the house has been built.[59]

58. A bit of good health now and then is the best remedy.[60]

59. The most dangerous supporter is the one whose defection would annihilate the entire party — hence the best supporter.[61]

60. The greatest dispenser of alms is cowardice.[62]

61. People press toward the light, not in order to see better, but in order to shine more brightly.[63]

62. Before we "go looking for the right person," we must have found the lantern.[64]

63. Every word is a kind of prejudice.[65]

64. The style that has been found is a pain in the ear to any friend of the style that has been sought.[66]

65. When virtue has slept, it will arise refreshed.[67]

66. The ascetic makes a necessity out of virtue.[68]

67. Scoundrels are not to be sought among law-breakers but rather among those who do not "break" anything.[69]

68. The wittiest authors raise a barely perceptible smile.[70]

69. Antithesis is the narrow gate through which error prefers to creep toward truth.[71]

70. With one talent more, we stand less secure than with one fewer.[72]

71. We forget our guilt when we have confessed it to another.[73]

72. "Should a band not tear loose — you must try biting into it."[74,75]

73. The higher we soar, the smaller we appear to those who cannot fly.[76]

74. How good bad music and bad arguments sound when we march off after an enemy![77]

75. Part of the masters' mastery is warning their pupils about themselves.[78]

76. Why don't people see things? They themselves are standing in their own way: they *cover up* things.[79]

77. Those who want to kill their enemies should consider whether this act will immortalize their enemies for them.[80]

78. In most cases, the best cure for love is still that age-old radical medicine: requited love.[81]

79. Some people have the greatest right to act in such and such a manner. But once they start defending that right, we no longer believe in it.[82]

80. For people in need of solace no means of receiving it is more comforting than the assertion that for their situation there is no solace.[83]

81. Lively natures lie for only an instant: afterwards they lie to themselves and are convinced and upright.[84]

82. To rush into the midst of the enemy can be a sign of fear and cowardice.[85]

83. Fearful people don't know what it means to be alone: enemies are always standing behind their chairs.[86]

84. We no longer want to turn the causes into sinners and the consequences into executioners.[87]

85. We ought to do away with beggars: for we feel annoyed giving to them and annoyed when we don't.[88]

86. Scholars: this is what the soldiers of the mind are called today, as are — unfortunately — also those who darn the socks of the mind.[89]

87. It is the heart that inspires: and it is the mind that heartens us and keeps us cool when we are in danger. Oh language![90]

88. We lie with our tongues but we still tell the truth with our mouths and maws.[91]

89. Humans are the animals with red cheeks: humans are the animals that have often had to feel ashamed of themselves.[92]

90. Talking a lot about ourselves is also a means of concealing ourselves.[93]

91. You believe, so you claim, in the necessity of religion? Be honest! You believe only in the necessity of police.[94]

92. Women[95] are more sensual than men, but they know less about their sensuality.[96]

93. Morality is human posturing in the face of nature.[97]

94. We praise what appeals to our taste: i.e., when we praise, we are praising our taste: doesn't this go against all good taste?[98]

95. There are no h⟨umans⟩ at all: for there was no first h⟨uman⟩ — this is how animals make inferences.[99]

96. God, too, has his hell, said the devil: this is his love for humans.[100]

97. Those who attain their ideal are thereby already — transcending it.[101]

98. Many a peacock hides its tail from all eyes and calls this — its pride.[102]

99. Occasionally the truth will finally triumph, there is no doubt: some kind of error was fighting on its behalf.[103]

100. The one who knows feels like God — become animal.[104]

101. I listened for an echo and I heard only — praise.[105]
    Many people become great only after death — by means of the echo.

102. Poor artists! You wanted to reeducate this rabble and they want only — to be amazed![106]

103. Faith brings bliss, especially faith in ourselves.[107]

104. "Our neighbor doesn't live in our neighborhood, but rather in theirs" this is how all peoples think.[108]

105. Substantial obligations do not inspire gratitude, but rather vengefulness.[109]

106. Those who go too far eventually lie down, exhausted, to sleep even if they are in the snow: like skeptics.[110]

107. Pangs of conscience teach us how to bite.[111]

108. There is much more intrusiveness in praise than in blame.[112]

109. We do not believe that cold people are capable of stupidity.[113]

110. The one who knows lives among humans not as if among animals, but rather — as among animals.[114]

111. We forgive our opponents most completely — only their failures.[115]

112. Out of the eyes of all who judge gazes the executioner.[116]

113. The consequences of our actions grab us by the scruff of the neck,[117] quite indifferent to the fact that we have "bettered" ourselves in the meantime.

114. "But how could you do such a thing? It was stupid!" — "It hasn't been easy for me either."[118]

115. Alas! You have seen his ideal! From now on you will see in him merely the caricature of his ideal.[119]

116. Humans would take themselves for gods if it were not for the lower half of their bodies.[120]

117. Compassion for humankind — that would be tyranny against every individual.[121]

118. Seeing beyond ourselves is necessary in order to — see well.[122]

119. "All people are *not* equal!" — Thus speaks justice.[123]

120. Whoever does not see superior qualities in people sees their base qualities[124] from much too close a distance.

121. Once talent grows dim in people, their moral qualities become more visible: and it's not always stars that thereby become visible.

122. When fatigued, we are even attacked by concepts that we have long since overcome.

123. That forgetting exists has never yet been demonstrated: but only that many things do not occur to us when we want them to.[125]

124. The belief in cause and effect is anchored in the strongest of the instincts, that of revenge.[126]

125. If people make us feel comfortable we judge their morality more positively.[127]

126. In striving *not* to know themselves even ordinary minds are still very subtle.[128]

127. Seeing and still not believing — is the primary virtue of those who know; visual appearance is their greatest temptation.[129]

128. What is "church"? — A fundamentally mendacious kind of state.[130]

129. Carrying our gold around unminted is uncomfortable; this is what thinkers do who have no formulas.

130. Whoever intends to treat people honestly is stingy even when it comes to courtesy.[131]

131. "The hero is cheerful" — this has not yet occurred to writers of tragedies.[132]

132. The *utile*[133] is only a means; its end is always some kind of *dulce*[134] — now be honest, my dear Sirs Dulciarier![135]

133. Our bad qualities allow *us* to be rewarded whenever they have allowed themselves to be overcome by virtue.[136]

134. "Now I am just" — "now I am avenged": this sounds similar and not merely similar.[137]

135. We never have: because we never *are*. We are continuously winning or losing.

136. Better evil deeds than puny thoughts![138]

137. Circe's swine worship chastity.[139]

138. We can die of thirst in the middle of the ocean and just as easily in the midst of truths that are too salty.[140]

139. For the sake of health, digestion requires a kind of slothfulness. Digestion of an experience, too.[141]

140. It is often more blessed to steal than to receive.[142]

141. In every complaint there is revenge.[143]

142. Not that you lied to me, but that I no longer believe you, this is what has shaken me.[144]

143. All people think themselves "experts" on good and evil, and are mistaken.[145]

144. Those who praise mostly portray themselves as giving something back: in truth they want to be given a gift.[146]

145. Women stop being childlike by constantly passing themselves off as educators when they are with children.

146. We reserve our most profound love for our children or our works.[147]

147. Whoever does not make us fertile will certainly leave us indifferent.[148]

148. "We do good deeds for our neighbors but do not create for them": this is the thinking of all those who create.[149]

149. Anger does not reveal what is in a person, but rather just anger.[150]

150. When the age has turned against us, we have either not yet transcended it enough — or we lag behind it.

151. "Where is there still an ocean in which it would be possible to drown?" — this cry runs through our times.[151]

152. There are many cruel people who are just too cowardly to be cruel.

153. We must overcome even our youth in order to become children again.[152]

154. "Only those who are hot can know the delights of cold-heartedness": thus spoke a free spirit.[153]

155. We are most unfair, not toward that which displeases us, but rather toward that which does not concern us at all.[154]

156. It is certainly not the least of a theory's charms that it — is refutable.[155]

157. "Good and evil are God's prejudices" — said the serpent.

158. We should question gods only in cases where gods alone can answer.[156]

159. Many people do not find their hearts until they — lose their heads.

160. Things: they are merely the limits of human beings.[157]

161. Many things become transparent to us: but this doesn't mean by a long shot that we can — get through them.

162. Learning to command is more difficult than learning to obey.

163. Not our actions, but rather our opinions and the opinions of others about our actions — make us into good or evil people.[158]

164. That the truth is simple is what error claims. *error veritate simplicior*[159]

165. *Ubi pater sum, ibi patria.*[160]

166. Refusing a request is preferable to refusing a thank-you.[161]

167. Here where we live,[162] the punishment sullies even more than the crime.[163]

168. In itself, truth is no power: if it does not join sides with power, then it will certainly perish.[164]

169. This is what shows who the masters are, that they neither err nor hesitate.[165]

170. What has disturbed h⟨umans⟩ so much? Not things, not opinions about things — but rather opinions about things that do not exist at all!

171. The intransitory is only a symbol.[166]

172. There is a hard-heartedness that would like to be understood as strength.

173. When people have just been honored highly and have eaten well, then they are at their most benevolent.

174. We notice more closely whether other people perceive our weaknesses than whether we ourselves notice the weaknesses of others.

175. It is the wearer who makes the outfit.[167]

176. Improving style — this means improving the ideas — and nothing more![168]

177. The weakest side of a classic book is that it is predominantly written in the mother tongue of its originator.[169]

178. We first begin to place special value on possessing a certain virtue when we have noticed its absence in our opponent.

179. All minor happiness should be used as a sick person uses a bed: for convalescence — and otherwise not at all.[170]

180. Taking pleasure in malicious petty thoughts saves human beings from many great evil acts.[171]

181. Enduring and deep pain makes us tyrannical.[172]

182. If we do not raise our devil to greatness, petty deviltry makes us — petty.[173]

183. We should be a resting place for our friends, but it should be a hard bed, an army cot.

184. When something goes wrong, assistants should be paid double for their help.[174]

185. Be modest in accepting things! Let your accepting be a mark of distinction![175]

186. Anyone who keeps giving easily becomes shameless in the process.

187. When has any great person ever looked as fat and well-behaved as a good person![176]

188. "I forgive you for what you did to me: but how could I ever forgive *the fact that* you did it to yourself!" — thus spoke a lover.

189. You say "I like this" and think you are praising me. But *I* don't like you —![177]

190. The love of oneself is characteristic of pregnancy.[178]

191. Very solitary people find even noise to be a comfort.

192. In the presence of demigods even heroes become a laughing stock.[179]

193. "How many more decades will it take before he starts to shine?" This question helps to measure a person's distance and superiority.[180]

194. The enormous expectations that women bring to love ruin their vision for all other — distances.[181]

195. "We are only pregnant with our own child": thus speaks the selfishness of all those who create.[182]

196. He still is perfectly innocent in his admiration: i.e., it still has not occurred to him that he himself could be admired one day.[183]

197. Many an existence has no meaning, beyond forcing another existence to be forgotten. And in the same way there are actions that work like opium.[184]

198. A solitary person spoke: "I gladly went to see people, but I never arrived!"[185]

199. Whoever wants to justify existence must also be capable of being God's advocate[186] with the devil.[187]

200. Those incapable of love or friendship will most certainly find their just deserts — in marriage.[188]

12 [2]
    Stupidity often goes by a nicer name and calls itself necessity.[189]

12 [3]
    There is much foolishness and clumsy groping in what you call nature: yet your mind is definitely a part of this "nature."

12 [4]
    Everything that feels, suffers, and is in prisons: but willing comes as liberator and bringer of joy — therefore *I* am teaching you "freedom of the will."[190]

12 [5]

Just at the point where your honesty ceases, your eye sees nothing more: oh, I know your will to blindness![191]

12 [6][192]

If you want to make crooked all that is straight: then think that time is gone and that transitoriness is a lie.[193]

Thinking this is the worst form of madness: your bones will think they are awhirl and your stomach that it is vomiting.

12 [7][194]

They want to play dice with the tiniest of dice or to see things dancing that are hard to see: the dwarves of existence, the delightful elementary particles: but they call it science and it makes them sweat.

But to me they are children who want to have their game: and if there were some laughter in their game, I would want to endorse their "joyful science."

12 [8][195]

Knotted taut feelings that you no longer regard as knots: and that which often returns, in whose eternal recurrence you believe: this is your "reality," your best superstition.

It wasn't until I invented pleasure in the truth that I also invented deception and illusion: for the sake of such pleasure I projected proximity and distance into things.

12 [9][196]

All valuations have been created: every valuation destroyed. But valuation itself, how could this be destroyed! This is life itself, no matter what you say — to value things!

To value is to taste.

There is no arguing about taste? Oh, you fools, all life is tasting, and taste and disagreements about taste and tasting!

12 [10]

You fancy yourselves to be free: but you pirouette at the end of our wires. Values and opinions live above and within you: we who evaluate have made you what you are, you clockworks!

12 [11]¹⁹⁷

And if you want to be free, then you must not only throw off your burdensome chains: the hour must come when you flee from those you love the most.

You must be able to abandon your woman, your land, your profits, your most precious beliefs: and for a time the sun of your life shall set for you.

12 [12]¹⁹⁸

And those who invent themselves will be regarded as lost for a long time.

12 [13]¹⁹⁹

Sleep without dreams — for me, that would be the greatest evil. And I call all ultimate knowledge my greatest danger.

12 [14]²⁰⁰

Knowing: for me, this is desire and thirst and calculation and struggle of values. Yet, as creating, all knowing must also be an unknowing.

To see through things, through the ephemeral net and the ultimate veil — this would be the great weariness and the end of all who create.

But believe me, my friends: there is nothing that is intransitory: it is only a symbol!

12 [15]²⁰¹

To be a wish in every way and to soar like an eagle toward faraway coasts: this is what I call happiness.

12 [16]²⁰²

There are two ways to deliver yourselves from suffering: sudden death and enduring love.

12 [17]

Once I had created superhumans, I wrapped them in the great veil of becoming and let the sun stand over them at noon.

12 [18]²⁰³

Become lucid! Become well! Become necessary!

12 [19]

The drive toward procreation, toward a purpose, toward a future, toward something superior — this is the freedom in all willing. Only in creating is there freedom.

12 [20]²⁰⁴

You sages, be careful that you do not founder on shame! For fuzz is also part of a good peach.²⁰⁵

12 [21]²⁰⁶

To our ancestors it seemed godless to grub around for treasures in the bowels of the earth: now there are new insatiable people!

12 [22]²⁰⁷

When you felt horror while doing something harmful, then you said: this is "evil": but when you felt disgust, then "that which is bad" emerged.

12 [23]

Virtue as the final result of much expended work and effort; yet later on appearing for the first time in individuals. "Talent" is the same — a well-trained mechanism.

12 [24]

To judge: this is to affirm a feeling — i.e., to *recognize* a feeling again (which presupposes comparison and memory).

12 [25]

To clean up the inner world! There are still false entities there! For me, feeling and thinking are sufficient. "*Willing*," as a third something, is a fantasy. In general, all drives, demands, aversions etc. are not "unities," but rather *seemingly* "simple states." Hunger: this is an unpleasant feeling and knowing how to end it. It can even have developed unknowingly out of a series of movements by the organism which are instrumental in eliminating the hunger: the *stimulus* of this mechanism is *felt at the same time as* the hunger.

12 [26]

The image *prior to* an action is not a concept of it, but rather an *ideal* — — — —

12 [27]

How the organs develop diversely out of a single organ, e.g., the nervous system and brain out of the skin: in the same way, all feeling and representing and thinking must also have originally been *one thing*: therefore sense impressions a *late* unique phenomenon. This *unity* must be present in the inorganic: for the organic *begins* already with separation. The *effect* of inorganic entities on each other should be studied (it is always an *effect at a distance*,[208] thus some "knowing" is necessary prior to any effect: what is distant must be perceived. The sense of touch and the sense of muscle movement must have their analogues:)

12 [28]

The movements of the foot during walking and slipping — are they really the results of conscious purposeful placements like this and like this? But even all conscious *exercise* is not what we think it is. Most of the movements during practice are experiments, and the intellect *affirms* the successful ones, it does not produce them. This affirmation is very superficial, because the intellect's image of the process is very vague. — The innumerable subtleties cannot be explained in this way: they would have to have been practiced, tried out and *affirmed* by an infinitely more subtle intellect and *observed* by entirely different sense organs than we possess. — Hence intellect does *not* explain those adaptations; nor does "*exercise*."

12 [29]

All morality is really just a refinement of the measures that all organic entities take in order *to adapt* and while still *nourishing* themselves and *gaining power*. The relationship of one human being to another can be mechanistically expressed as an *alteration* of the arc of the motion[209] of its being.

Even the most subtle alterations in consciousness must first be mechanistically possible before they can occur. In this way, even expressions of the will are dependent on mechanistic preconditions.

12 [30]

But let us pause at the feeling of will! What are we *conscious* of as "will"? Here we recognize that will is merely a hypothesis. It could be true — or maybe not.

There is no "will" beyond that of which we are *conscious*. I.e., we have *poetically asserted* the will *as an addition* to certain appearances of consciousness: like "matter" as an addition to other things.

12 [31]

Everything organic differs from the inorganic (in that) it *collects experiences*: and is never identical to itself in its processes. — In order to understand the essence of the organic, we must not regard its *smallest* form as its *most primitive form*: instead, *every smallest* cell is **now** heir to the entire organic *past*.

12 [32][210]

The quantity of compensatory systems in the body p. 195.

12 [33]

Consciousness localized on the *surface* of both hemispheres. — Every "experience" that we have is a mechanical and chemical fact that cannot stand still but rather "*lives*": yet we *know* nothing about it!

12 [34]

Wherever we have life, we presuppose "mind": but the mind that is known to us is completely incapable of doing anything. How impoverished is every image of consciousness! *It is probably itself* only the *effect* of a change that now draws after itself a further change (action). Every action that we "*will*" is in every way imagined by us merely as the *illusion of* an *appearance*. —

All consciousness merely a **secondary** *manifestation*[211] *of the intellect* (?) What we are conscious of cannot *provide the cause for anything.*

Just compare *digestion* and what we perceive of it!

12 [35]

Will is only known to us as something conscious. Yet those sudden explosions are made *obscure* and unclear when we supply them with such an "inner world."

12 [36]

Cherubini influenced by Gluck and Haydn, Spontini by Gluck, Beethoven, as dramatist, by Cherubini: Gluck by Lully and Rameau. Wagner by Euryanthe[212] (whereas he *pretends* that it's Gluck).

12 [37]

Our intellect can definitely not grasp the multiplicity of clever interplay, much less produce it, e.g., the process of digestion. It is the interplay of *very many intellects*! Everywhere that I find life, I find this interplay already happening! And there is even a ruling intellect is there among the many intellects. — Yet as soon as we think of organic actions as performed *with the help of many intellects*: they become completely incomprehensible to us. Instead, we must think of the intellect itself as an ultimate consequence of those organic actions.

12 [38]

The nature of heredity is completely obscure to us. Why is an action "easier" the second time around? And "who" feels this greater ease? And does this feeling have something to do with the fact that the action is done the same way the second time around? In that case, the feeling of different *possible* actions would certainly have to be *imagined* prior to the deed!

12 [39]

The powerful organic principle impresses me so much, especially the ease with which it incorporates inorganic material. I don't know how this functionality is to be explained simply by *increase*. I would rather believe in the existence of eternally organic entities. —

12 [40]

Listen to me for a bit, oh Zarathustra — said a pupil one day — there is something whirling around in my head; or, I would almost like to think, my head is whirling around something in such a way that it is spinning.

What then is this, our neighbor? Some facet of us, changes in us, that we have become aware of: our neighbor is an image.

But what are we ourselves? Are we ourselves not also merely image? A facet of us, changes in us, of which we have become aware?

Our self that we know: is even this not merely an image, something outside of us, something outside, something outer?

We are always coming into contact merely with the image and not with ourselves.

Are we not just as foreign to ourselves and just as close as a neighbor?

Truly, we have an image of people — we created it out of ourselves. And now we apply it to ourselves — to understand *ourselves*! Oh yes, to understand!

The state of our self-understanding is bad, so absurdly bad!

Our strongest feelings: insofar as they are feelings, are something outside us, something outer, image-like: they are similes.

And what we have called inner world elsewhere: alas, it is for the most part impoverished and deceptive and hollow and poetic!

12 [41]

I'm tired of the happiness of human virtue and reason: of their great human beings, their redeemers, liberators, poets, sages, their just good compassionate serene conciliatory enthusiastic people.

12 [42]²¹³

Scientific people

Asceticism of the mind — addressed to the most intellectual. "Penitents"

Herd and I. Responsibility.

the Pharisee.

Inventor of festivals.

to ennoble what is nearest

Critique of morality: in order to make us independent of praise and blame

Compensation in the beyond? You want to be paid?

Homeless.

Purification from revenge, *my* morality.

The most influential people lived in the greatest concealment.

Culture —that thin little apple skin!

People *not* equal![214]

the noble person a result of much work

Inventors of new states of the soul the true inventors. They are imitated.[215]

Power wants to expend itself: not happiness.

"like a sweet smell"

the weak are the danger

the higher caste, mightier yet poorer.

To bring about the triumph of our ideal — struggle for power in a *manner* that follows from the ideal.

Individuals live on within their impulses. Fame.

The need to purify the inner world and to learn!

The murder-of-God penitents and their festival.

To wean human beings from feelings of "guilt" and "punishment"!

12 [43][216]

I don't want to be mixed up and confused with others

There are those who preach my doctrine of life: but at the same time they are preachers of equality: I don't want to be mixed up and confused with them

People are *not* equal: thus speaks justice. I will tell you such things another time.[217]

Yet life, when it proclaimed its law to me in total secrecy, added: "and people should not be equal either!"

Humans should keep becoming ever more unequal — for the sake of the superhumans! — that's the way my love itself wants it!

Whatever the father kept quiet, the son speaks of openly. And often the son is merely the father's madness revealed.

A careworn conceit, a suppressed envy: this bursts forth in the son as flame and madness of revenge.

This is what justice means to me — so says this madness — that I take revenge and curse all those who are not my equals.

And "will to equality" — this should become the name for virtue: may my screaming about virtue rise up against everything that has power!

He preaches life in order to hurt those who themselves turn away from life: for they are mightier than he and purer of heart.

But he himself sits in his cave turned away from life: and spinning webs and eating flies like a spider is not what I call life.

His wellspring of revenge always flows too strongly: and he always empties the cup at the same time he wants to fill it.[218]

This courtliness should also be present in speech: he who could command conceals his kingly hands beneath his robe, he persuades through his beauty, instead of commanding.[219]

"Everything about the world displeases me: this is how he thinks — but most of all how I displease everyone." That is why he speaks of the future.[220]

Finally:

He offends my taste: this is the argument I use to fight against him.

There is no fighting about taste? Oh you fools, all of life is fighting about what is tasty and what is taste and this must be the case.[221]

And I myself, my foolish friends! — what then am I if not something to fight over: a taste![222]

This advocate of life sits in the belly of a whale: the whale that he preaches against keeps him swallowed up.[223]

I want to bring his secrets to light: then I will laugh my laughter of the heights into his envious countenance.[224]

Not with serpent locks of fear do I want to defend myself against what you teach, you preachers of equality: I protect myself from you using only beauty as my shield![225]

What I love about the wind is its invisibility: and only in this way would I like to become visible, as a flame on the mast becomes visible: — full of astonishment, solitary voyagers see the good sign[226]

He would like to be regarded as a god: but for that to happen he would have to conceal his face and shroud himself in the veil of Isis.

But I say to you: those who make an enemy of their age have yet to transcend it fully enough.

The tyrant's will cries out of him, demanding equality: his word "equality" is a tyrant's lie and seduction

That humans be redeemed from revenge — this, truly, is the rainbow of the superhumans and a bridge to the highest hope.[227]

12 [44]

"We have the task of teaching bears to dance: but must we ourselves be dancing bears to do it?"

So you want to tell me, you teachers: "we want to be educators: but we ourselves are not educated."

The last thing I want to do is to injure your vanity, you teachers! I have already seen too much tragedy grow out of injured vanity.

12 [45]

Contest of the affects.

12 [46]

History of value judgments concerning food.

What is the value of having done (eaten) such and such — and not something else?

12 [47][228]

Scholars.
Poets.
Great events.
Prophets.

On redemption.
Human prudence.
stillest hour.

12 [48]
It has nothing whatsoever to do with the right of the stronger, but rather the stronger and the weaker are all equal in that they extend their power as far as they c⟨an⟩

12 [49]
Superior h⟨umans⟩ like Napoleon
Affects in them
Mutual appraisal
Compassion and a sense of community

[13 = Z I 4. Summer 1883]

13 [1]¹

Zarathustra's
Holy Laughter.

The hand moved forward, the clock of my life took a breath: never have I heard such stillness surround me: so much so that it startled me.

Then life spoke to me without language: the hour has come for you to preach redemption from redeemers.[2]

Your minds were not yet a source of worry and heartache: your bread of life was sour, but not yet completely soured by thoughts.[3]

As a hunter Zarathustra set forth, hunting ugly truths: he would often return home from the forest in a dark mood.[4]

Oh human, this is what your knowing is: to spin and construe all things to your best advantage. To me, you all are spinners and construers, you who know!

Experience came imperiously, but my will spoke to it: then it was already on its knees, pleading.[5]

Don't you feel the thirst and the hot breath of the sun? It wants to be nursed by the ocean and drink its depths up to itself in the heights.

And now the ocean's lust rises with a thousand breasts. It wants to be kissed and nursed by the sun's thirst: it wants to become air and height and the path of the light. And for this reason, like the sun, the ones who know love life: they want to carry the profoundest things back up to their heights.[6]

Don't dancers have their ears in their toes?[7]

Are you a star? Then you also must want to wander, you inconstant one, and to be without a home.[8]

My ocean floor is still: who would have guessed that it conceals playful monsters!

My depths are unshakeable: yet they shine with swimming riddles and with laughter.

See how the woman struggles against herself and how she runs the comb against the defiance and will of her golden hair!

They shoot off their mouths: and now we are supposed to think that it is out of the abundance of their hearts.[9]

I don't take you too seriously, you contemporaries: to me, you are thin and transparent: torn veils, through which eternity gazes. And how could I ever want to live among you if I couldn't look upon what is behind you and ahead of you!

I did not find you necessary: you don't even seem superfluous to me. Truly, there is little about you that is capable of overflowing.[10]

A star went under and disappeared: but its light is still on its way. And tell me, will you: when will it cease to be on its way?[11]

Is the ocean not the greatest peacock of all? It rolls out its silver train upon soft sand, its topmost plumes of silver and of silk: when will it ever grow weary of itself? Life is in love with itself in the very same way.[12]

Midnight looked at me with drunken eyes: solitude cowered next to her and the gasping stillness of death, the worst of my girlfriends.[13]

And the thirst of the ring, eternally the same, is also my thirst for myself: to reach itself again, every ring twists and coils itself.[14]

You make me laugh, you who limp along! But beware of those who have the will and are in a hurry: that you don't feel the weight of their heels!

Do you want to be a stumbling block to all those who stride ahead? Then go to meet them and keep your head turned backward![15]

Fear those who have withdrawn! Fear the tiger who prepares himself to spring![16]

Up to now your spring poured forth too mightily: it always immediately emptied the cup in the very act of wanting to fill it.[17]

Stillness. Modesty at the heights.

I wish to adorn myself with the garbage that falls from the table of life: and with peels and clam shells and thistles I want to be more beautifully adorned than you![18]

Your good deeds should fall like dew upon the grass, then, when the night is most secretive.[19]

I think I am capable of any evil: that's why I demand, especially of myself, that which is good![20]

Whether you sing your own praises as poets or as dancers: whether you call yourselves the voice of the people and the servants of the public good.

Whether you teach or paint or compose or play the game "Black on White":[21]

To me, you are children, all devoted to one principle and one obsession: which says "thou shalt — *make* a name for thyself."

Yet there are others, less common, who *have* a name: but they would like to be rid of it and erase it from all tablets.

They hide their heads in the brush and in caves or they baptize themselves with false names: so that their terrible queen[22] fails to recognize them and hurries by them in her wrath.

Who is the terrible queen by whom they do ⟨not⟩ wish to be found?[23]

I call it mercy and merciful disposition, to take another's injustice on our shoulders and to gasp under a double burden.[24]

What makes your actions good is not their reason or purpose: but rather that your soul trembles and shines and overflows when you do them.[25]

"the scholar"[26]

Now there you stand, so gaunt in your ribs that you are astonished at yourself.

And thus do you speak: did a god secretly steal away with something of mine while I slept? Truly, he did steal away with enough to make a mere woman[27] out of it.

Wondrous is the poverty of my ribs![28]

See him, how he swells and overflows with compassion for everything that is called human: his mind is already completely drunk with compassion; soon he will be doing incredibly foolish things.

I come from there like a strong wind; and to those who despise me I give advice like this: when facing the wind, be careful not to — spit![29]

You wanted to sap the strength of sickness and, in my view, you have sapped the strength of the sick, you witch doctors and saviors![30]

Where I live is too high and too steep for you: I built my nest in the tree "Future,"[31] I have become my only contemporary.

Whenever those who could command, persuade and hide their kingly hands beneath their robes: I call this courtesy.[32]

My savage wisdom got pregnant atop lonely mountains: it brought forth its young, the youngest of all, on bare stones.
Now it runs foolishly through the harsh desert and seeks and seeks for soft grass — my old savage wisdom.
On the soft meadow grass of your hearts, my friends! — on your love it would like to take to bed what is most dear to it! But what is happening to me?[33]

What everyone knows is being forgotten by everyone; and if it weren't for the night, who would still know what light is!

Truly I say to you: Intransitoriness is only a symbol. (The thirst of the ring[34]

We despise everything that can be explained. A bit of stupidity let itself be surprised and stood there naked before the person explaining it.

Have you ever really seen people who did things to their own advantage?

A god who loved us would have had to do a few foolish things for our sake! What do I care about your praise of your god's "wisdom"!

Your happiness is still young: be patient with it!

Bad air surrounds you: this is caused by thoughts that are floating around right now.[35]

Not long ago I saw an image in the sea, the image of a goddess: languidly and treacherously the wave crept around her white breasts.

The sand has covered half of her and the jealousy of the wave the other half.[36]

For too long I belonged to solitude: thus I have unlearned silence.

I have become nothing but mouth and the roar of a stream from high cliffs: I want to send my words cascading into the valleys.[37]

I cannot abide any of you, you nightwatchmen and tomb-watchers and anyone who does nothing but blow a dismal horn.[38]

I laugh at your free will and even at your unfree will: to me, everything you call will is a delusion, there is no will.[39]

This delusion that you call will gave birth to itself in pains and thoughts. And because there is no will, there is also no absolute obligation.[40]

I probably drew this conclusion: yet now it's drawing me![41]

Humility has the thickest pelt.

Even what we have left undone weaves the fabric of the entire future: even nothingness itself is the master weaver of all weavers.[42]

Many grow weary of themselves: and only then does their happiness begin.[43]

If you want to drive well, then hitch a little donkey in front of the stallions of your will!

I have been wounded by my happiness: all those who suffer ought to be my doctors!

Those who do not believe themselves are always lying.[44]

When your hatred and your envy finally grow lazy and stretch their limbs: your sense of justice awakens and rubs its sleepy eyes.

"those who know"
With their virtues wasted away to nothing and their fragile souls, they have been sitting for far too long in the shadows: therefore — they starved to death from their expectations.

"*the great one*"
As I turned away from myself, only then did I jump over my own shadow: and truly, my friends, into the middle of my sun!

Am I not modest? I live at the foot of my heights and I have never seen my peaks: my humility cannot be convinced of anything. Every intellect comes to — me: I love it because it wishes to be my intellect.[45]

I was robbed of whatever I loved completely: now my love overflows in torrents, down to the evening and the morning; out of taciturn hills and thunderstorms of pain, my soul roars into the valleys.[46]

("those who know")

You have been haggling with your own minds, you have poisoned your blood with haggling: only by bleeding to death can you find an antidote for your poison!

"Genius" Has a superhuman ever lived?

A horrid ringed worm has crept into the mask of a god: for all too long I was made to play the fool by godlike skins: serpent-coils were the entrails with which they were stuffed!

And I believed I saw a god's soul at play: serpent-filth and foul odor concealed the disguise from me. A salamander's trick was sneaking around inside the mask of a god![47]

To sanctify laughter and to stretch it like a multicolored tent across the world — that's why I have come: to create a new sky with stars and new wonders of the night, and I was able to reach you by creating blacker nights for you.[48]

I yearn and I look into the distance: on you, my eagle, I lay my hand, now tell me what was the most distant thing that eagle eyes saw!

"It is showing itself" you tell me? No, my brothers, it is withdrawing, and it will withdraw more and more![49]

(Contemporaries)

And anyone who knows how to remove mountains will also remove the valleys and the lowlands.[50]

My drink should make you sneeze, and my sparkling wines should tickle your noses and fill you with lust.[51]

The wave roared through, and the child is crying because the wave swept his toy into the abyss: but the very same wave has poured a hundred other toys out into the soft sand for him. So don't cry over me, my brothers, about my passing through.[52]

There should be no fighting about taste? Oh you fools, all of life is fighting about what is tasty and what is taste, and this ought to be the case![53]

I smell the smell of your dust, your souls have not been aired out for so long.

I do not direct my teaching at your ears: but rather at your hands. Do as I do: only doers learn: and only as a doer will I also be your teacher. Better to be a poor imitation of me than to sit on your hands and worship![54]

Truly, I have as little love for hot, moist minds as I do for chilled ones: yet if they ever come together, then something emerges that I love — a brisk blast of wind.

I thought I had landed on an island: but it was a monster that was sleeping.

I have yet to see a downfall that was not a procreation and a conception.

That a bolt of lightning would strike your feed, and your maws would have to feed on fire! —[55]

I have not yet walked through fire for the sake of my teachings: but my teachings walked forth out of my fire.

It was a human being who hung on the cross for two millennia: and a ghastly god had his cruel way with him and called it love.

"Everything about the world displeased me: yet most of all I was displeased that everything displeased me."

I have already bid many a farewell: but I did not slam the door — and that's why your dull ears never heard a thing.

How ridiculous I find everyone who *wants* to convert anyone![56]

You come to me whether I want you or not: yet just as I *must* give to you, so you *must* take from me — you must take *me*![57]

I want to be a white steer and go before the plowshare snorting and bellowing: and just as my serenity lies down in the sun, so should my happiness smell like the earth.[58]

Wildly my eagle beats its wings against my will: but its surge founders on this cliff.[59]

What does "experience" still mean to them? Events sit on them like mosquitoes, their skin is still being pierced, but their hearts are no longer aware of it.

I don't like this pale, fat moon: in truth, I have never thought him to be the "man" in the moon. He is only a monk to me, with wet cheeks, a lecher: lecherously he creeps around all dark corners and peers into half-closed windows — he, the most jealous of all tomcats who wander the rooftops at night! He is jealous of all lovers, the pale fat monk in the moon!

It is night: once again above the rooftops
The moon's plump face in promenade.
The most jealous of all tomcats, he
Looks jealously down upon all lovers
This pale fat "man in the moon."
Lecherously he creeps around all dark corners,
Leaning, braced against half-closed windows,
Like a lecherous fat monk he treads
Impudently at night on forbidden paths.[60]

Oh beyond this simulated light, this sweetened sickly air! Here where the soul is never allowed to fly to its heights, but rather is supposed to merely kneel — to the heights above.

Oh life! I look into you as into an eye.

What I can see of you is this, that *you* look at me: what I can figure out about you is this, that *you* have figured me out!

It is winter, today I want to dance. I have enough warmth for this snow; I want to climb the mountain, there my warmth can wrestle with the cold winds.

Am I not the meteorological divide? Don't all winds come to me and want to know my will? I will lay my hand on everything that is to come.[61]

You think everything is the wild play of giants and the clumsiness of giants' fists? Yet a single word arriving on the feet of a dove guides the will of these wild ones — a word of value: and such words come from the most profound stillness.[62]

It is night: now all gushing fountains speak more loudly: and my soul, too, is a gushing fountain.

It is night, now all the songs of those who love have just awakened: and my soul, too, is the song of someone who loves.[63]

My life is fire and burning: and the incense of my life being sacrificed lives longer than the sacrifice. Its fragrance flies far across the ocean: it shakes the solitary voyager to the core.

Here is autumn and harvest and plenty and afternoon and distant seas: but right now I must be a bird and fly onward above you toward noon: knowing your autumn, I prophesy for you your winter and your icy poverty.

Be honest: I have figured out what is the best thing for you to believe. Now I want all of your knowledge to serve *this* best belief!

My speech flows too slowly. I shall spring into your carriage, you storm, and I want to whip even you with my wickedness: we want to journey over the vast seas like a cry and like a cheer.

Perfection throws a shadow ahead of itself: I call this shadow *beauty* — the lightest and stillest of all things came to me as shadow of the superhumans.

My words should root around like the snout of a boar in the soil of your souls: I want to be called a plowshare.[64]

What is happening to me? My fountains have run dry and my ocean has receded: does my foundation want to crumble and engulf me in its own depths?

— Onward to immortality! *Via Appia.*[65]

And there, where your understanding has sprung a leak, you quickly stick the poorest of all plugs: his name is "God."

I want to vanish in a dark thunderstorm: and in my final moment I want to be human at the same time as I am lightning.[66]

My sweetest word is now becoming like sourdough to you: revenge is bringing you to fermentation for me, and when for my sake you are completely activated and risen with your malice and your revenge, only then will I find you tasty.[67]

I want to bring your secrets to light: which is why I laugh my laughter of the heights into your countenance.[68]

Your countenance is dark to me, you people eager for action: the shadow of your hands plays around your countenance, the meaning of your eyes is hidden from me.

A thought, asleep in granite, awaits the one who will awaken it.

In the belly of the whale I become the advocate of life.[69]

I have seen all of you *naked*: and how do I now separate those of you who are good from those of you who are evil!

My blissfulness arrives like the winds of a storm: and, without wanting to, it flings against hard walls those clumsy people who do not know enough to flee from it.

He is sinking, and his demons pull him down: and the more he sinks, the more intensely shines the light of his eyes and the desire to be with his god.

Contemporaries
You crash up against me, for I am striking you with my oar — and still you must carry even my boat[70] into immortality.[71]

It is life that cuts even into life: it increases its own wisdom through the agony it causes itself.

A child will hold the mirror for me, the mirror upon which the world is inscribed.[72]

He solves his riddles, but he does not liberate them: they do not fly up transformed into heavenly children.

My thoughts are colors: my colors are songs.

My knees were trembling for the very first time as I found my way and walked onward: and anyone who saw this, told me: you have unlearned the way, now you are unlearning even how to walk.

Now I have unlearned even how to will: accustomed to climbing, I am raised up and pulled aloft by the ether on golden threads.

Did I ever fall asleep on my fame? Every kind of fame has been like a bed of thorns to me.[73]

All beauty lures me away beyond you humans: all beauty lures me away from all gods: so I cast my anchor upon the open sea and said: "let the island of the superhumans be here one day!"

And when your beauty itself no longer preaches penitence, what will your words achieve!

The neck of an ox — and the eyes of an angel, these are what I want you to have!

I have become blind.
My blindness and the tapping and probing of a blind man may yet tell you of the power of the sun that I saw.

That, long ago, knowledge once learned to smile serenely and without being jealous of beauty

You stood liberated from all intellect, a sanctuary and joyful place for the intellect.[74] Yet now I want it this way: not only should my virtue occupy your city — it should possess it; you shall become possessed by my virtue.

I impatiently endured the winter: now even the malice of April is playing with my impatience, and often I foam over at its halting gloom and its — derisive snowflakes.

For the first time I once again brought together the just people, the heroes, the poets, the sages, those who know, the prophets, the leaders: I erected my vault above the peoples: pillars on which a firmament rests — strong enough to *bear* a firmament. (Superhumans should speak in this way!)

Justice appeared before me: then I destroyed my idols and felt ashamed. I submitted to a penance and forced my eye to look upon where it did not like to look: and to bring love there.[75]

the highest form of passion, the streaming passion grown still

[(Conclusion) — and all those who must someday suffer felt themselves, as sacrificial lambs, to be already anointed and to be consecrated by tears. You call it my "happiness" —

His power streams forth out of the fullness of simplicity. "Alas, must I then become a god?" — he spoke.

like a waterfall that pauses while cascading —

we want to saturate nature with what is human and liberate it from godly mumbo jumbo. We want to take from nature what we need in order to dream something *above* and beyond humans. Something shall yet emerge *more splendid* than storms and mountains and sea — but as son of man![76]

You come from there, heavy and creaking, like wagons carrying stones downhill: yet your dignity is precisely that which reveals your downhill path — the depths are drawing you to them!

with a well-worn sharpened tongue

I wanted to catch a fish and threw my net into the sea —
but there I drew forth the head of an ancient god: thus did the
sea give me, the hungry one, a stone.[77]

What are your father- and motherlands to me! I love only
my children's land, yet undiscovered, for whose sake I tell my
sail to run over the sea and search: in this way I want, through
my children, to make up for the fact that I am my father's
child.[78]

Your virtue should benefit only that for which you despise
yourselves and whatever is beneficial to yourselves. Otherwise
let contempt for whatever is beneficial occupy your virtue's
gaze.[79]

My eagle is a ripping robber and raptor: may it be called a
danger to all little white sheep![80]

Are you familiar with the terror of falling asleep? Sleepers
are shaken to the depths of their being because the floor falls
away and the dream begins — and they often awaken again
from this terror.[81]

Your sayings and puny truths flourished near the swamps,
didn't they? Yet I still hear a cold frog croaking within them.[82]

You must learn to build anew with mountains: it means
little that you can remove mountains, you who know! And
whoever removes mountains, removes lowlands as well.[83]

How would you be tolerated if your cold need and power-
lessness had not been shattered by lightning and covered with
colorful weeds! As ruins and victims of your misfortunes, you
ought to have a right to exist!

For you, beauty shouldn't be a hunger, but a taste; for you, your need should be called beauty: or I don't want you.

Your desire ought not to be silenced and sink into satiety, but rather into beauty —: the shadow of gods to come ought to make you silent.

What is it, anyway, that is sought by all those who create? They are all seeking new languages: they always grew tired of the old tongues: their minds have no desire to keep walking on these completely worn-down, thinning soles.

Your gazing at distant oceans, your desire to set foot on the cliffs and their summits — it is only a language for your longing. Your gazing and your desire are only seeking humans and that which is more than human!

Whatever contradicted them and inflicted pain, they called God: such was the way of these heroes. And they didn't know any other way of loving their God than to nail a human being to the cross.[84]

And therefore let us be enemies, my friends! Just as the arches in the vault above you break into pieces and play off against one another:

as light and shadow, in their enmity, are secure and beautiful like gods above you: in this way, your thoughts, and those of your friends, ought to be secure and beautiful like gods in their enmity.

You don't want to hear that someone is strolling around above your heads. And so you put wood and earth and refuse between him and your heads — that's how you muffle the speech of his steps.[85]

You put all human error and weakness between yourselves and me: you call this a dead floor in your houses.

But in spite of this, I stroll around with my thoughts above your heads: and even if I wanted to stroll around on my own errors and dead floors, I would still be above you and your heads![86]

And now the ice and innocence of my peaks are also still aglow.[87]

You who desecrate, do you still not understand what desecration does? The toppled ornamented column lay in the slime of your contempt: — and it is precisely out of your contempt that the column's life, and living beauties, suddenly awakened again.

It arose with more godly features and seductively suffering, you desecrators of the ornamented column! — and still it thanked you for its deification![88]

Dionysus on a tiger: the skull of a goat: a panther. Ariadne dreaming: "abandoned by the hero, I dream about the superhero." Keep quiet about Dionysus!

Every action requires interpretation: it beckons to all solvers of riddles. I gave new words and methods to the interpreters: so that they can make better forecasts of human weather.[89]

I am a seer: but my seeing is followed inexorably by my conscience: thus I am also the interpreter of my visions.

Black ponds from which the sweet gloom of a toad sings forth: this is what you are to me, you priests. Who among you could stand to show himself naked!

You do well to lay out your corpse in black, and I hear the evil-spiced dullness of death chambers resounding from your speeches.

How I hate the lying convulsions of your humility! In your kneeling I see the habits of slaves, you lickspittles of your God!

Yesterday, when the moon rose, I thought that it wanted to give birth to a sun: it lay there on the horizon so wide and heavy with young.

But it was a liar with its pregnancy: and I no longer believe either in the man in the moon or, truly, even in the woman in the moon. — I am giving you this parable, you enthusiasts and moon-children.

Barren and yellowed it rose, and it got smaller and smaller, looking paler and more deceptive as it climbed. Truly, its bad conscience shone forth from within, the old lecher.

It lusts for this earth and yet this lust makes it ashamed, it would much rather imbue its glances with holiness and abnegation.

And even if you, too, lie broad and heavy with young on the horizon: truly, for me you will not give birth to a sun! (Romantics)

Lusting for the earth: yet your bad conscience bites you in your lust: that's why you choose melancholy.[90]

To me, you are arid grass and steppe: but I want to make wildfires of you and heralds with tongues of fire.[91]

Life, I look within you as into an eye!

Gold flashes from his eyes: a golden bark floats there upon dark waters. Please look, for me: this gold dances leaps and crouches![92]

You are adept and have clever fingers. But you have no idea how to make a fist.

Not until your clever fingers have crept back into a fist will I want to believe in your power.[93]

The worm-like thing I struggle against I first created for myself in the form of a dragon: it was still so young and tiny and in this way I am fighting the fight with your future.

But if *you* wanted to fight and win, I would first have to turn the dragons of today into earthworms for you![94]

You are tools and watches to me and nothing more: thus I want to wind you up with my ridicule, and you will purr with contentment as I do it![95]

And I still prefer to sleep on ox hides than on the bed of your complacency and love.[96]

You see only my sparks, but you do not see the anvil that I am, you do not guess how cruel my hammer is.[97]

I do not want to turn you into stones and silence with serpent locks of fear: I protect myself from you, using only "beauty" as my shield.
Do you hear the sound and the laughter of this shield? It is the holy laughter of beauty: through it you are meant to be struck dumb for my sake![98]

I know how to ride you: and anyone who knows horses well also knows just what it means to be in the saddle.[99]

I still am like a cock in a strange barnyard, pecked at by hens.[100]

I want to be known as a fire and as a danger to all dried-out souls: glowing ashes ought to fly up from me.

Again I am solitary and exiled. I have been exiled into my solitude by my friends and by those who love me. For this is how I want to speak to my enemies.
I want to speak to those who hate me: perhaps I can persuade them more effectively than I can persuade my friends.
And thus today is the day I lust for my enemies, the way I once lusted for all truth. Truth is what I once called everything that caused me pain and the greatest pain possible.

I want to pour out all the evils of my soul against my friends: perhaps I would in this way seduce my enemies into that which guides me.

By your love? Alas, now it comes back to me, the ghastly knowledge — who was it who drove me into the wilderness and made me into someone wild?

All for naught! For naught! Yes, you yourselves drove out the wild one: it is the will of friends that made me into a cave bear.

Alas, who was it who made me solitary and wild and into a cave bear of the wilderness?

Alas, who exiled me among loveless stones and storms

Did not cry out No![101] three thunderclaps and three lightning bolts striking at midnight?

And when I look into my picture book, a dog and a child should be looking over my shoulder.

Grace is part of the magnanimousness of those inclined to greatness.

Like buffalo, I sense you near the sand, even nearer to the underbrush, yet nearest to the swamp.[102]

With many small doses it is possible to cure a brave man and make him into a coward.[103]

You should pass by these enemies quietly and with a sleeping sword. Be careful not to attack them! for those who attack them sully themselves.[104]

I, the earth-born one, am experiencing the ailments of the sun as my own eclipsing and as a great flood of my own soul.

I believed myself to be the richest one of all, and I still believe it: but no one takes from me. Thus do I suffer from the madness of the giver.[105]

I do not touch their soul: and soon I will not even reach their skin anymore. The last smallest gap is the most difficult to bridge. Did I not cause you the most pain when I did what was most precious to me?[106]

My love and my burning hunger for them grows with my exile, and even the insanity of my love makes me more distant from them and less understandable.

But I am in exile: they have turned their eyes from me. And I do not even touch the skin of their soul anymore.

Alas, and now my hunger for them grows, ever since I have been known as the exiled one: and this insanity of love makes me even more strange and terrible.[107]

My love of speaking. Against silent people.

With chests puffed out, and like those who are holding their breath: thus are you, you sublime ones! silent.

Beauty is what I call the revelation of what is good for the senses: of *my* good! for my — senses! And what intellect used to be now becomes only quasi-intellect for me![108]

Now my hope has become too well fed: at this point, it has ceased to hope (I am no longer one of the ones who hope).

I flew too far into the future, I was overcome with horror. When I finally looked around, behold, time was my only contemporary there. And so, I was longing for you, my *contemporaries*.

And even those who want to prepare poison for themselves must put on gloves of glass.[109]

I gave them their nothingness to feed on; then they choked on their nothingness.[110]

I held up a mirror to their ugliness: then they could not bear the sight of themselves: they came to grief on the evil eye of their own eyes.[111]

I did penance for all of this injustice, my admiration was even more unjust than my contempt.[112]

No matter how blind you already are: greater still is the will to blindness that I found in your eyes.

Alas, I know the blue evening distance of your deception: truly, I prefer the lies of those who know they are lying to your lies.[113]

And you would be even less able to put up with my modesty than with my pride, if it ever wanted to speak.

My narrow path runs between two dangers: a pinnacle called "arrogance" is my danger, an abyss called "compassion" is my danger.

"How I will want to draw a breath and stretch my limbs when I will have borne my burden to the highest pinnacle!" — the hero often thought this on his way up. But when he was at the top, and had thrown down his burden, then he did not do *this* — then he overcame even his *weariness*: and here a godlike shiver ran through his body.

The electricity of my cloud was all too great and too long-lasting: between lightning and thunder, it finally hurled showers of hail and ice into the depths: it violently puffed out its chest and violently blew its storm clear across the mountains — thus came its relief.

Truly, my happiness and my freedom arrive like a storm: But you think the evil one himself is racing over your heads!

Having laid his arm over his head: in this way the hero rests, in this way he also overcomes his resting.

Today I want to free my slaves and to be their servant and their sport: the drink of freedom should go to their heads and their hearts.

You now lie in the foreground for me, you contemporaries: if you don't want to become ruins for me, how could I bear to have you in my picture! And, for me, the best thing about you is your weeds!

The figs fall from the tree: they are sweet and good. And as they fall, their red skin rips. I am a north wind to ripe figs.[114]

Are you afraid of the fervor of your tones, you harpers and poets? All your harping-jingle-jangle is ghost-breath and keening to me: you finger your scrawny strings with scrawny hands, but when would you ever have swept away a heart? — if it hadn't been swept away by pity at your poverty![115]

See that you do not smear or wash away the woman's likeness on my behalf, you fashionable people!

How high up do I live? Never yet — whenever I climbed — did I count the flights of stairs up to where I live: — yet I know *this much* about my pinnacle: the roof over my head begins in that place where all stairways end.[116]

—those who must be hauled up by their hair into heaven![117]

You throw dust around yourselves like sacks of grain, you scholars, and without meaning to! Still, who would have guessed that your dust comes from grain and from the golden bliss of summer fields?

To the hero, the beautiful is the most difficult of all things: for the hero, more than anyone else, the beautiful is unwinnable and unreachable.

A little more, a little less: just this is a lot here, just that is the most here.

We must speak to slack and sleeping senses with thunderclaps and heavenly fireworks: but the beacons of beauty speak softly, they tiptoe only into the souls of those who are most wide awake.

You claim to be made of finer cloth, you visionaries? But I say to you, you are only better at dressing and disguises,[118] you know how to hide poor cloth beneath a cloak![119]

Now and then even wretched people become honest: it happens rarely enough! — then it is advisable to listen to their voices and to climb into their swamp.
And once I, too, sat down among the reeds and in this way I heard the frogs of wretchedness make their confessions.[120]

And so proud of a handful of justice, you commit sacrilege against all things and drown the world with the waters of your injustice.

They stand on the street for hours, watching people passing by: and others of their ilk sit idly in their parlors, watching thoughts that pass them by. I laugh at these contemplative people.

Tell them no, and spit at the same time: then they will quickly throw themselves to the ground and lick up your spittle. But among modest people every priest grows insolent: his humiliation takes revenge on all who have been humiliated. Nothing thirsts more for revenge than the humility of a priest.

With languid muscles, and beautiful, as befits a benevolent person: and truly: what is beauty, if not benevolence manifesting itself?

When excessive power becomes benevolent and its benevolence descends into the visible: such descents are what I call beauty.

The sun never rose above the turbid sea of your soul: and you know even less of the sun's bliss as it sets.

My compassion became a murderer: and when I loved humans the most, I nailed humans to the cross.

I am poorer now than any human being: the cup was emptied. My riches are gone: now truly, I myself have become human again.

I redeemed them from their redeemers. — Yet how could superhumans bear to understand humans! That's why humans must be persuaded to create them and to perish for their sake: so that the superhumans can *live*?

The danger for superhumans is compassion. Let us avoid giving them compassion! — But **my bliss** now lies in my **downfall**. (From the final speech)

They want to use their virtues to claw out the eyes of their enemies. They rise up because they want to put others down.[121]

I want to see only the gentleness in violent people as their self-overcoming, and I laugh at the weaklings who think themselves "good" because their claws are dull.

When have great people ever been their own followers and devotees? They definitely stepped away from siding with themselves when they stepped onto the side of greatness!

I truly want to be a *power*, but not some uncouth driver and beater:[122] instead, wherever a wind sweeps, I wish to sweep along within it: and even if I am otherwise invisible, I still want to become visible like a flame on the masts of solitary voyagers and explorers.[123]

You should grow like a column into the heights, ever more delicate and slender, but harder within yourself and with bated breath: thus does the column strive ever higher.

"This is how I would like to die! And to die once more! And to live in order to die this way!" And yet, the moment she died, she was smiling: for she loved Zarathustra.

A storm rumbled from out of the sky, as yet unseen.
Then thunder rolled: and afterward came a stillness — this stillness wound itself around us as if with terrible coils, and held us fast: the world stood still.[124]

Then the woman proclaims the coming of the eagle and the serpent. The sign. Everyone fleeing. The plague.

She pulled Zarathustra's arm to her breast.

And, once again, the abyss drew a breath: it groaned and roared, its fire shooting upward.

Here is the cave of the tarantula: do you want to see it? Then buzz like a fly. Its web hangs here: touch it so that it trembles.

I want to teach you to dance ecstatic dances: for, to me, you are the most melancholy of people. I want to cure your melancholy through madness.

He placed a naked image of a god there: in this way, the southernmost of all people still longs for a (second) south.

To me, you are a tarantula: and the triangle, the tarantula's identifying mark, sits black upon your back. Bite these shallow people for me, with your poisonous bite, so that for my sake their souls receive depth and melancholy and black scabs for the first time.

To the teachers of *pessimism*.

13 [2]¹²⁵

Act 1. Zarathustra among animals. The cave.
The child with the mirror. (It is time!)
The different petitions, intensifying. In the end, the children seduce him with song.
Act 2. The city, outbreak of the plague. Zarathustra's appearance,
healing of the woman. Springtime.
Act 3. Noon and eternity.
Act 4. The voyagers.
Scene at the volcano, Zarathustra *dying among children*.
Funeral rites.

Omens.

for 3.) Zarathustra saw and heard nothing, he was lost in rapture.

Then, step by step back into the most terrible knowledge. The outrage of the disciples, departure of the most beloved ones, Zarathustra tries to stop them. The serpent feels for him with its tongue. He recants, excess of compassion, the eagle flees. Now the scene with the woman, in whom the plague resurfaces. He kills out of compassion. He embraces the corpse.

Then the ship and the appearance at the volcano. "Zarathustra is going to hell? Or does he now want to redeem the underworld?" — Thus the rumor spreads, he is also the evil one.

Last scene at the volcano. Total bliss. Forgetting. Vision of the woman (or of the child with the mirror) The disciples peer into the deep grave. (Or *Zarathustra among* **children** at the temple ruins.)

The greatest of all funeral rites as the conclusion. Golden casket thrown into the volcano.

13 [3][126]

Put a saint on a ship: the ocean itself will flee before the saint and roar in fear. This is how the most peaceful of all humans brings on the storm: and anyone who was wind and wave will run away from me on quick feet.

Yes, I am a forest and a night of cypresses: but anyone who does not shy away from my darkness will also discover hanging beds of roses under my cypresses.

I want to give you clear sight and a dread of the real: in this way you should learn to float along after me into distant futures.

And do not be angry with me if I whip this puny god a little: he fell asleep on me here at the fountain, the dawdler; maybe he tried too hard to catch butterflies?

"I may have broken my wedding vows: but first my wedding vows broke *me*" said the woman.[127]

"Now I have become a lake with white roses: the winds of the heights play with me and laugh like children. What haven't I forgotten! Who hasn't forgotten me! And often I still forget even my forgetfulness." Zarathustra among children.

The distant cliff throws my word back at me and in this way mocks my forgetting — yes, I have forgotten it already, whatever I cried into the distance. Alas, what haven't I forgotten!

"He has already been in the underworld?" —
"Certainly he has been there: clearly he has been among us! Humans, humans alone are the underworld!"
"Zarathustra is dead? You don't know what you are saying! Don't we see him striding along! Truly, he still wishes to redeem the underworld and to bring it to light." — "He is going to hell, the devil will take him!" "Take my word for it, the devil will not take him — how would he manage that!, but *he will take the devil for his own*!" — The voyagers. The End.[128]

"I have thrown my intellect into a pit of snow."

And if the stars don't want to fall from the sky for you, then throw your stars into the sky: let that be the extent of your evil.[129]

"I speak: for I have seen. Now I must be nothing but mouth: for recently I have been nothing but eye and innocence of the mirror" Thus speaks the artist.

"You know it, don't you, Pana my child, my little star, my golden ear — you know it, don't you, that you are dear to me as well?"
Love for me persuaded you, I see that: but I still do not understand the will of your love, Pana! —

But as he saw his serpent's tongue touch him, then his face transformed itself ever so slowly: the gateway of knowledge reluctantly sprang open for him: like a lightning bolt the knowledge flew into the depths of his eyes and again like a lightning bolt: another moment, and he would have known — — When the woman saw this transformation, she screamed as if in the throes of distress. "Die, Zarathustra" —

With his left hand he forced back the eagle, which was beating against him with the fury of its wings: it screamed, like someone advising him to flee; it would have loved to carry him away from there. At his right hand on the rock-slab table

Those who want to be merely spectators of life should be careful not to sit there, where the sun beats down on the stairs: unless they want to become blind.

"And what should I do with your knife, Pana? Should I cut the golden grapes from the vine? Behold, what abundance surrounds me!"

And even at night he will not perish for your sake, but rather blood red, like a midnight sun, he will remain on the horizon.

People who wanted to conceal themselves, and had no choice but to be shamed by the clear sky, created for themselves these sweet-smelling caves.[130]

And only when grass and red poppies flourish on the walls, and the sky peeps through shattered ceilings, only then will I want to turn my heart toward these places of your god.[131]

How would I have endured it if I didn't love superhumans more than you![132]

For what purpose did I give you the hundred-faceted mirror in the first place? And the eternal gazes?[133]

I overcame even love for you with love for the superhumans.

And as I endure you, you must endure yourselves, out of love for the superhumans.[134]

To me, you are the stone in which the most sublime of all statues sleeps: there is no other such stone.

And as my hammer swings at you, you should swing at yourselves for my sake! The call of the hammer should awaken the sleeping statue![135]

And should I want to mount my wildest steed, my spear will get me up there the best: it is the most ready servant of my feet.

The best mask we wear is our own face.[136]

Streets of tombs: leading wherever it is most beautiful, most clear and most bright. Not to dismal places.

And when I hold a mirror to my own beauty, my soul shudders with divine desires: and veneration is still part of my vanity.

And kings should still lead the ass of my wisdom.

And as I lay sleeping, a sheep was cropping the ivy crown on my head!

In striving upward against my burden I rejuvenated myself: and just when I became more hardened within myself, I also learned what grace is.[137]

Inventive in small stratagems and lusting for those whose intelligence walks on lame feet: thus do they stand and wait before their wares, these hucksters![138]

Pity all those who love who do not also have a pinnacle that is even above love and compassion.[139]

On ashes, I stride up the mountain of ashes, at dusk: my shadow grows long and longer.

A boat floats in the depths of the violet-shrouded sea: its sailor stares up at me, his hand shading his eyes.

Now Zarathustra is journeying to hell — this is what the ferryman says shuddering and taps his cross.

Don't touch the cross on my account, you were wrong! The devil is not yet taking me, ferryman! maybe I am taking the devil as my own![140]

At the very least his hound of hell should answer to me: I want an answer from the abyss of his jaws.

He should groan and roar his fire and ashes up at me: *that's how* I like monsters to answer me.[141]

Few understand the art of staying noble even while being reverent: and I much prefer to see shameless people and their innocence than the contorted eyes of your devotion and obeisance!

Now only the smallest gap still stands between me and you: but alas! Who has ever built a bridge across the smallest gaps?[142]

Your knees pray for something and your hands are hosannas: but your heart knows nothing of it.[143]

I once threw myself with giving hands into the heights: but as I was falling, I was caught upon three lances — in this way, as a sacrifice, I made my way from the heights to the earth.

I placed my foot on the lower jaw of the wolf: that's how I ripped his jaws open.

laughing, the kings of the North die —

a ribbon woven from the beard-stubble of a virgin and from the sound of feline footsteps —

Who will hold the basin up to my countenance, so that the viper's poison drips into it?

I do not want wisdom to become a hospital and a poor-house for mediocre poets.

As if there were only one stile into the future: like sheep, they crowd around their stile:

"the one who knows made into the one who creates"!

And what do you care if my torrent throws itself into false ways and impassable chasms: for how should a torrent not find its way to the ocean?
Indeed, I have found a lake within myself: this lake is a hermit and is self-satisfied: my torrent of love threw itself into this lake: and now the torrent of my love is sweeping the lake along with it into the ocean!

"We have no opinion at all unless we are given one: and we are being given one.
We have no strength at all unless we are thought to be strong: and everyone thinks us strong" —pitiful people, contemporaries.

I tolerate you and I carry you, up to now I have always found you to be lightweights. And even when I gasp under my own burden, loaded down with myself, what difference does it make that you beetles and sea slugs take your seats on my bundle!

against "morality"

And when, instead of the pure "I will this," I heard the call "thou shalt" coming from clumsy maws, that's when my danger began: I hated my pure "I will this" coming from clumsy maws —

I have annihilated your good and evil, I have torn these nooses to pieces: only in this way did I learn to love *my* goodness.

The art of all tarantulas is black and blackening: yet I call tarantulas the necromancers of the mind, who are called the teachers of "the worst possible world."[144]

If there were gods, how could I stand not being a god? But there are no gods.[145]

His soul rejoices in secret over the fact that revenge is still being taken in every form of justice: and my soul rejoices over the fact that in every form of revenge a spark jumps from the anvil of justice.[146]

You are in love with great words the same way you are in love with colorful brats: and your foot knows how to hold festivals on carpets of lies, you milksops! (idealists)

You compassionate ones, when you throw yourselves down from the heights to the people below, what price did you put on broken limbs?[147]

But it was silent: terribly and doubly silent. Alas, you do not know it, the double stillness that ties up hearts until they shatter.[148]

Alpa! I screamed. Fear and longing screamed forth from me: I wanted to hear a voice again

A voice coming from a human being, as it is carried away by a wind or a bird.

Strong will? This is a lot, yet not enough: I need an enduring strong will, an eternal resoluteness born in hardness of heart.[149]

How this laughter broke my windows! How it ripped apart my guts and slit open my heart![150]

This is the most unforgivable thing about you: you have the power and you don't want to rule.

You see, don't you, the one they all need the most. This is the one who can command.

None of them want to bear the burden of those who don't take orders, but they accomplish the most difficult things if you order them to do so.[151]

A will that demands monstrous things is rare: you will have an easier time finding a will that does them.

There is no longer a strong wind and will driving you: you are standing too stiffly for my taste, and your backs are too straight.

Alas that, already rounded and full of air like a sail, you went over the sea, and you were trembling at the storminess and breath of a will!

Now all air is heated, the breath of the earth is fire. Now you all go naked, you good and evil people! In this way, those who know will have their festival.

Yes, this is the world without clothes. What caused the earth to move? Was it not the stillest words of a saint?

Every deep knowledge flows cold, the deepest wellsprings are ice cold: and that's why it is refreshing to all hot hands and heated doers.[152]

I love the turbulence of a bad reputation: just as the ship loves to hear the resistance of the wave through which its keel breaks. My own path seems easier when resistance foams around me.[153]

But just as I was awakened by you and *came to myself,* so I tell you to awaken and to be awakened by *yourselves.*
And why did you not want, you too — my brothers — "to come to me?"[154]

Approach the wellspring with humble hands: this is how it will fill your hands most easily.

Redeemers? You were the binders and tamers:[155] you should be given that.[156]

Today I am sick of people, today animals will be dear to me. And today I have buckets of love[157] to waste on them.
Oh, if only I could be a sower and a gardener among animals! I would certainly find an earthly realm there in which more eminent things would grow than the creatures I have grown so sick of.

Speak your word no matter what! Founder on it! What is it with you and your modesty!
My modesty is unspeakable.[158]

You wanted to show that your grandfather was right and that truth has always been on the side of grandfathers.
For a grandfather belongs more to the people than any grandchild does.

You are looking back, even if you are going forward: and people can't help running into you a lot.[159]

You really like to think you are building the city of the future: but, in addition to that, you are erecting the tombs and honors of past worlds.

13 [4][160]

"Kill him, if you have to power to do so" — Zarathustra called out in a terrifying way once again; and his gaze pierced the thoughts of the king.

I recognize Zarathustra, said the king with a smile: who else but Zarathustra would know how to abase himself in such a prideful fashion? But that which you rescinded was a death sentence.

— and ⟨he⟩ read slowly from the death sentence, with his voice half-lowered as if he were all by himself: he who deserves to die — Zarathustra, seducer of the people.

— deep in thought, he moved back a few steps, into the window bay; he didn't say a word and did not even look at Zarathustra. Finally, he turned toward the window.

You said it, King: the idol that goes before the people, the idol that turns them into idol-makers: the idol should become king to the people!

The time for kings has passed: the people are no longer worthy of having kings.

Destroy, you should destroy, oh King, the people who don't follow idols: these are humankind's worst enemies!

Trample the worm, that those who create[161] —

And if the kings themselves are of that ilk, then, oh King, destroy the kings, as you are able!

My judges and advocates of justice have reached an agreement to destroy a harmful human being; they are asking me whether I want justice to run its course or to let mercy prevail over justice.

What is more difficult for a king to choose, mercy or justice?

Justice, answered the king; for he was a man of mild disposition.

Then choose justice, and leave mercy to violent people as their means of overpowering themselves!

Yet, as he looked out toward the window, he saw something, and then his face turned a different color.

Zarathustra, he said in the polite tone of a king, forgive me for not answering you immediately. You gave me a piece of advice: and, truthfully, I would love to listen to it! — But it comes too late! — With these words, he tore up the parchment and threw the pieces on the ground. Silently they took leave of one another.

Yet what the king had seen from his window, was the *people*: the people were waiting for Zarathustra.

13 [5]

All of you are not fighting for justice, you righteous people, but rather so that your image⟨s⟩ of humans triumph.

And so that all your images of humans founder upon my image of superhumans: behold, this is Zarathustra's will to justice.

13 [6][162]

To the Teachers of Equality.

You don't want to hear that someone is strolling around above your heads. And so you put wood and earth and refuse between him and your heads.

That's how you muffle the speech of my steps.

You put all human error and weakness between yourselves and me: you call this a dead floor in your houses.

But in spite of this I stroll around with my thoughts above your heads: and even if I wanted to stroll around on my own errors and dead floors, I would still be above you and your heads!

For people are *not* equal — thus speaks justice. And what I want, you are not permitted to want.[163]

They want to use their virtues to claw out the eyes of their enemies: they rise up because they want to put others down.[164]

"Now I am in the right" "now I am avenged" — this sounds similar and often doesn't just sound similar![165]

His bad qualities allow him to be rewarded whenever they have allowed themselves to be overcome by virtue[166]

In every one of his laments there is revenge.

I want to bring all of your secrets to light: that's why I laugh my laughter of the heights into your countenances.

My sweetest word should become like sourdough to you: for my sake, revenge should bring you to fermentation.

And not until you have overflowed the pot and floated away in your malice, will I want to taste you and find you tasty.[167]

13 [7][168]

The Idol-Makers.

When your hatred and your envy finally grow lazy and stretch their limbs: only then does your sense of justice awaken and rub its sleepy eyes.[169]

My drink should make you sneeze: my sparkling wine should tickle your noses and fill you with lust.[170]

To sanctify laughter and to stretch it like a multicolored tent across the world —

and whenever I had to create blacker nights for you, then I also brought you new stars and new wonders of the night.[171]

My words should root around like the snout of a boar in the soil of your souls: I want to be called a plowshare.[172]

No matter how blind you already are: greater still is the will to blindness that I found in your eyes.[173]

Alas, I know the blue distances of your deception: and I prefer the lies of those who know they are lying to your lies.[174]

Just there at the point where your honesty ceases, your eye sees nothing more.[175]

The best mask we wear is our own face.[176]

What is the problem with them making sculptures of the gods naked? — In this way, the southernmost of all people still longs for new souths.[177]

13 [8]¹⁷⁸

The Penitents of the Mind.

Are you a star? Then you also must want to wander and to be without a home, you inconstant one!¹⁷⁹

Now there he stands, so gaunt in his ribs that he is astonished at himself.¹⁸⁰

And thus does he speak: "Did a god secretly steal away with something of mine while I slept?

Truly, he did steal away with enough to make a mere woman out of it. Wondrous is the poverty of my ribs."

Justice appeared before me: then I destroyed my idols and felt ashamed.

I submitted to penance: I forced my eye to look upon where it did not like to look — and to bring love there.¹⁸¹

And those wishing to prepare poison for themselves must put on gloves of glass.¹⁸²

My admiration was even more unjust than my contempt.¹⁸³

The figs fall from the trees: they are sweet and good. And as they fall, their red skin rips. I am a north wind to ripe figs.¹⁸⁴

And full of pride at a handful of justice, you committed sacrilege against all things and drowned the world with the waters of your injustice.¹⁸⁵

And whatever intellect once meant to me is only quasi-intellect to me.¹⁸⁶

We can die of thirst longing for water in the middle of the ocean, and just as easily in the midst of truths that are all too salty.¹⁸⁷

Those who go too far end up lying down to sleep even in the snow — out of fatigue.¹⁸⁸

Pangs of conscience teach us how to bite.¹⁸⁹

Eventually the truth will really triumph, some kind of error was fighting on its behalf.¹⁹⁰

Humans are the animals with red cheeks: humans are the animals that have too often had to feel ashamed of themselves.¹⁹¹

There are libertines of the mind: there are also penitents of the mind.¹⁹²

13 [9]^193

The Shortest Summer.

Up to now my spring poured forth too mightily: it always immediately emptied the cup in the very act of wanting to fill it.^194

This is all April still and May and June: and the way I am, near snow, near eagles, near death I will have a summer, short, hot, gloomy, and overflowing with bliss.^195

Alas at the halting gloom of my spring! Alas at the wickedness of my snowflakes in June!

It is night: now all gushing fountains speak more loudly. And my soul, too, is a gushing fountain.

It is night: and now all the songs of those who love have just awakened. And my soul, too, is the song of someone who loves.^196

If I were dark and of the night, how I would want to thirst for light and to drink the light!

I would bless you, you little twinkling stars and lightning bugs, and swallow you whole.

But now I am entirely engirded by the light and I squander it around me: alas, I do not know the pleasure of taking.

And often I have said to myself "Is it still more blessed to steal than to receive?" — thus I spoke from a great distance.

13 [10]^197

Wherever I saw life, I found will to power: and there too, in the will of someone who serves, I found will to power.

We subjugate ourselves to something greater in order to gain mastery over something lesser: this pleasure convinces us to subjugate ourselves.

Whatever is not, cannot will! Yet whatever has existence — how could this still — "will to exist!"

You believe that you know things and all things: that's why you posit value and tablets of goods. This is the superstition of all who make valuations

To me, you are only a river on which a boat floats along: yet in the boat sit value judgments in disguise, the solemn ones.

Honest science begins in this way: it asks: what is? and not: what is it worth?

Whatever is needed for human beings to remain in existence: these are our limits.[198]

Even your ideal is by no means your limit: your power extends further than the longing of your eye.

The sun went down long ago, the meadow is damp, coolness is coming from the woods: something unknown surrounds me and looks down pensively at me. What, you still live! Why do you still live?

Whatever moves us from within, this astonishes us, as something incomprehensible: now we invent sounds and words for it — and now we think, too, that it might have become comprehensible. This superstition is in everything that makes sounds: the insanity of the ear.

Will to truth? Oh, my wisest brothers, this is a will to making the world conceivable.[199]

Even the world should now be visible in its smallest dimensions: then you think you can *grasp* it: this is the folly of the eye.

Let us speak of it: even if it is bad; to be silent about it is terrible!

I saw other oceans, their blue seemed unbelievable to me, it seemed to me like makeup on rough skin: the blood flowed down gray and ghastly. But here is the ocean's blood — blue.

Nothing is more costly than a false illusion about good and evil!

"A good human being is impossible: life itself contains nothing but ill-will, delusion and injustice. And this would be the ultimate will to goodness, to deny all life!"

With your good and evil you have estranged yourselves from life, made your will weary; and your assigning value was itself the sign of a will in decline, longing for death.

13 [11]²⁰⁰

The Way through Many Souls.

I come from there like a strong wind: and this advice I give to my enemies: when facing the wind, be careful — not to spit!²⁰¹

I made my way through a hundred souls, I took my leave often, I know the heartbreaking final hours.²⁰²

Yet this is how my destiny wants it. Or to be honest with you: this kind of destiny is what — my will wants!

All who want to invent themselves must be regarded as lost for a long time.²⁰³

When were great people ever their own followers and devotees? they stepped away from siding with themselves when they stepped to the side — of greatness!²⁰⁴

I want to vanish in a dark thunderstorm: and in my final moment I want to be human at the same time as I am lightning.²⁰⁵

I probably drew this conclusion: now it's drawing me!

The wave roared through, and the child is crying because the wave swept his toy into the abyss. But the very same wave has poured a hundred other toys out into the soft sand for him. So don't cry over me, about my passing through!²⁰⁶

And endless too, like the thirst of the ring, is my thirst for myself: every ring coils and twists in order to reach itself again.²⁰⁷

Experience came imperiously: but my will spoke: then it was already on its knees pleading.²⁰⁸

I have already bid many a farewell, but I did not slam the door: that's why dull ears never heard a thing.²⁰⁹

13 [12]²¹⁰

On those who speak freely.

That a bolt of lightning would strike your feed and your maws would have to feed on fire for a time!²¹¹

You wanted to catch a fish and threw your net into the sea. But there you drew forth the head of an ancient god.²¹²

Thus did the sea give you hungry ones a stone: you left it alone there.

There the goddess lies forever: languidly and treacherously the wave creeps around her white breasts.

The sand has covered half of her and the reverence of the wave the other half.[213]

Your sayings and petty truths grew well near the swamps, didn't they? Yet I still hear a frog croaking out of there![214]

You are adept and have clever fingers, but you have no idea how to make a fist.

Not until your clever fingers have crept back into a fist, will I want to believe in your power.[215]

You are but tools and watches to me and no more! Thus I shall wind you up with my ridicule and you will purr with contentment for me as I do it![216]

"It has always been this way! And it will always be this way!"

And I would still prefer to sleep on ox hides than on the beds of your complacency.[217]

We know a little too much about everyone.[218]

13 [13][219]

Against Mediators.

I am well disposed to all pure things: how could I be well disposed to you conciliators![220]

All you mediators and equivocators, you half-and-halfers, you high-strung conciliators — you are not pure!

How much like gods the vaults and arches here break into pieces, as they wrestle: how they play off against each other with light and shadow, those who play like gods:

Therefore let us be enemies in a secure and beautiful way, my friends! Like gods — we want to play off against each other.[221]

You obscurers, you ask what will become of you if you tell the truth —

but the truth should shatter the world, so that the world may be built![222]

We should train our hearts by forcing them to do things.

Those who give their hearts free rein, soon lose sight of their heads.

It is noble to be ashamed of our best things because we alone have them.

"I am annoyed: for you are wrong" — this is how a lover thinks.

I love life: I despise human beings. But it is for the sake of life that I wish to annihilate them.

13 [14][223]

Associates and Associations.

I don't take you too seriously, you contemporaries: to me, you are thin and transparent![224]

Torn veils through which the future gazes: half-open doors, at which gravediggers wait!

And how would I ever want to live among you if I couldn't look upon what is ahead of you!

I did not find you necessary, you don't even seem superfluous to me: there is little about you — capable of overflowing.

You crash up against me, for I am striking you with my oar — and still you must carry my boat into immortality.[225]

And many a woman has said to me: "I may have broken my wedding vows: but first my wedding vows broke me."[226]

And if I am to love you completely, then you have to be my child or a work of mine.[227]

Whoever does not make us fertile will certainly leave us indifferent.[228]

We can do good deeds for our neighbors, but we cannot create for them.[229]

Your will is still too proud and shy! should you wish to drive well, then hitch a little donkey in front of the stallions of your will![230]

They will build beehives like Towers of Babel[231]

13 [15]²³²

New Ways of Life.

What are your father- and motherlands to me? I love only my children's land, yet undiscovered, for whose sake I tell my sail to run over the sea and search.

Through my children I want to make up for the fact that I am my father's child: and thus to redeem the past.

To be a wish in every way and a bird on the way to faraway coasts: this is happiness for me.²³³

Whether the truth benefits or harms you or me — what do I care! Let us create people for whom the truth is beneficial!

13 [16]²³⁴

On Actors.

Is the ocean not the greatest peacock of all? Even in front of the ugliest of all buffalo it rolls out its train, it will never grow weary of its topmost plume of silver and silk.²³⁵

The buffalo looks on obstinately, in his soul near the sand, even nearer to the thicket, yet nearest of all to the swamp: what are beauty and ocean and peacock finery to him!²³⁶

To you actors, I give this parable. Truly, your spirit is itself the greatest peacock of all and an ocean of vanity.

Your spirit wants spectators: even if they should be buffalo!

You play: and you want spectators at your games — I call all of you actors.²³⁷

Whether you sing your own praises as poets or as dancers: whether you call yourselves the voice of the people and the servants of the public good:

Whether you teach or paint or compose or play the game "Black on White," such a pathetic game:

One principle and obsession speaks from all of your doings: I want to *make* a name for myself! — that's how it speaks.²³⁸

Faith brings bliss — that's what you all say — especially faith in *ourselves*.²³⁹

I listened for an echo, but I heard only praise.²⁴⁰

I wanted to build them and build them up — but the rabble just wants to be astonished!

Talking a lot about ourselves is also a means of concealing ourselves.[241]

13 [17][242]

On Tarantulas.

Here is the cave of the tarantula: do you want to see it? Then buzz like a fly.

Its web is hanging here: touch it so that it trembles.

To me you are a tarantula: and your triangle and identifying mark sits black upon your back.

Bite these shallow people for me with your most poisonous bite, so that their soul receives depth and melancholy and black scabs for the first time.

I flew too far into the future, I was overcome with horror.[243]

And when I looked around, behold, time was my only contemporary there. In that place I was longing for you, my contemporaries!

The art of all tarantulas is black and blackening: this is what I call the necromancers of the mind, who are the teachers of the "worst possible world."

Do you want to make crooked all that is straight? Then think that time is gone and that transitoriness is a lie.[244]

Thinking this is the worst form of madness, and tarantula venom. Your bones will think they are awhirl and your stomach that it is vomiting.

13 [18][245]

On Poets.

The intransitory — this is only a symbol; and poets lie too much.

They also know too little and are bad learners: that's why they have to lie so beautifully.

And clouds are their favorite things: they put their most colorful little brats up there and call them gods.

And when they lie in the grass under the trees, and little impulses caress them: then they always claim that nature itself is in love with them.

And let it come to tell them secrets and to flatter them: yes the poets swell up and strut around on account of such intimacy beyond that given to all mortals.

He sinks and his demons pull him down: but the more he sinks, the more his eyes fill with glowing light and with lust for his gods.

I know how to ride you and how to saddle you anew. And anyone who knows horses also knows well what it means to be in the saddle.[246]

You harpers and poets, what have you known up to now about the fervor of tones!

All your harping-jingle-jangle is ghost-breath and keening to me: with scrawny hands you rip into scrawny strings![247]

And if the stars don't want to fall from the sky for you, then throw your own stars at the sky and let that be the extent of your evil![248]

We praise only what appeals to our taste; i.e., when we praise, we always praise our own taste: which really violates all standards of good taste![249]

They thought they were being bold, whenever they said: "all knowledge is nothing."

"Boredom and lusts" — from this they wrote the story of the one who knows.

eager for things that old wives[250] tell

"Praise be to the know-nothings and spiritually impoverished!"

you are making your listeners feel longing and pangs of conscience for whatever is no longer in them: yet I tell you: you must make them thirsty for whatever "has yet to be"!

Those who create, love themselves in the process: therefore they also must hate themselves most profoundly — they run riot in this hatred.

"Praise be to the spiritually impoverished, especially when they are young and female!"[251]

Who among you poets would not have diluted his wines with deception? Many a poisonous concoction was mixed in your cellars.[252]

13 [19][253]

Among Cripples.

And still I prefer to live among cripples than to live among these supposedly whole people.[254]

The achievement of perfection casts its shadow ahead: I call this shadow beauty.

The lightest and stillest of all things came to me as shadow of the superhumans.[255]

God, too, has his hell — said the devil: it is his love for humans.[256]

13 [20][257]

On the shame of the gift-giver.

On the clamor for equality, against desecrators

On intoxication (spasms of penitence) priests.

On speaking freely ("historical education")

On the honesty of the pitiful.

On geniuses.

On marriage by the hour. Adulteress

On new associations and monasteries.

On punishment as the enemy of enemies.

So you want to be paid?

Annihilation of morality.

The dream.

Cosmic dependence.[258] Anthropomorphizing nature.

Redemption from redeemers.[259]

First you have to learn to hunger for knowledge.

The murder-of-God penitents and their festival.

Purification from revenge.

On the indiscretion of priests.

Hunt for ugly truths.

Greatest funeral rite — onward to immortality[260]

The renunciation of the metaphysical as what virtue demands
— as *self-sacrifice.*
The blessed isles. "To the south."
On modesty.
Value of the pessimist.
Madness of someone who gives.
Scholars.
Contemporaries.
Laughter of the heights. Happiness of the sower.
Stillness of the saint.
The seductions (child with mirror)
Beauty.
Compassion.
Idealists.
to seduce the pious
(Die, Zarathustra!)
the funeral pyre (big city)

13 [21]²⁶¹

The typical *sufferings* of the reformer and even his consolations. — The seven solitudes.

He lives as if above the ages: his pinnacle gives him contact
with the solitary and unappreciated people of all eras.

His beauty is his last defense.

He lays his hand upon the next millennium.

His love grows as does the impossibility of doing good with
it.

13 [22]²⁶²

1. *Preface and first speeches of Zarathustra.*
Three additional parts:
   2. *The Laughter of the Heights.*
      (Happiness of the Sower.)
   3. *Zarathustra searches for those he has lost.*
      (or the 7 Solitudes)
   4. *Noon and Eternity.*

13 [23]²⁶³

The characteristics of superhumans gradually becoming more visible.

The laughter of the heights — the caves of S.A.

Concerning the last scene the appearance at Stromboli.[264]

The woman's speech. "How well you heal, savior!"

Always ten years in between. Solitude.

At the beginning of the last book a child appears with a mirror in Zarathustra's cave, as the first sign of his triumph.[265]

13 [24]²⁶⁶

Praise of reason and its coolness.

In his role as one who creates, to *praise* the fact that our wisdom is revealed as folly, our wealth as poverty.

Thirst! If my thirst were quenched, what would be the point of creating! *Justification of suffering.*

High summer in the mountains.

sweet smell, melancholy, regarding a sudden death, evening in the woods where elves walk.

the great human being "has fallen"

Hymn to the organic: Zarathustra feels himself related in his will to everything living, deepest understanding of nature and of what is moral.

Zarathustra says "I am the *pleasure*"

> of the mistral wind
> of electricity
> of the heights
> of the change of seasons (ring)
> of the clear sky
> of the dawn
> of the torrent
> of organic life
> the sun's thirst for ⟨the⟩ ocean
> plowshare

(as persuasion)

Way of life: to nurture ourselves such that we create ourselves in our own image.

Sensual hateful people like to eat plants.

13 [25][267]

First: laughter of the heights. Dream. Postlude.

Laughing at redeemers and compassionate people mediators reconcilers

ethical world order ("paid")

Idealists "idol-makers"

Revolutionaries — Deniers. Conversation with the *hound of fire*.

Poets

Geniuses. On peacocks.

Scholars

Educated people

Those who speak freely

Equality-socialists

Pessimists tarantulas "necromancers of the mind."

Metaphysicians

Those who know — "torrent"

("I am the coffin full of malicious deeds and masks of life")

Society

against "*long life on earth*" — "high summer" — "clear sky"

Priests and churches

Sublime people (for beauty)

Hucksters

Frugal people (nature mystics)

Vanity of cleanly people

Curious people

Romantics (moon). To heal "sorrowful people" by means of frenzied dances, to throw off *shame* and later to find that the bridges leading to dissimulation are broken.

13 [26]

    There have *never* yet been *any superhumans*!

13 [27][268]

    Actors.
    Tarantulas.
    Hound of fire.
    The dream.
    Those who speak freely.
    Penitents of the mind
    "Paid"
    Summer in the mountains.
    new society.
    Way of life.
    Through many souls
    wandering among fragments
    cool reason
    Organic — moral.
    Mediators.
    To one of the illustrious dead.

13 [28][269]

    The Funeral Rite.
    On the Contemplative Ones.
    On Actors.
    Redemption from the Redeemers.
    The Dream.
    On Famous Sages.
    Heroes and Beauty.
    On Tarantulas.
    High Summer.
    Conversation with the Hound of Fire.

13 [29]²⁷⁰
> Hound of Fire.
> On Tarantulas.
> Penitents of the Mind.
> Among Cripples.
> On Those Who Speak Freely.
> On Preachers of Equality.
> New Ways of Life.
> Associates and Associations.

13 [30]²⁷¹
> The Child with the Mirror.
> The Night Song.
> The Dance Song.
> The Prophet.
> The Funeral Rite.
> On Gods.
> On Famous Sages.
> On Those Who Are Sublime.
> On Contemporaries.
> On Scholars.
> On Contemplatives.
> On Good and Evil.
> The Stillest Hour.
> On Priests.
> On Poets.
> On the Compassionate.
> On the Rabble.
> On Virtuous People.
> On Great Events
> On Human Prudence

13 [31]²⁷²
> On Tarantulas.
> Conversation with the King.
> Among Cripples.

13 [32]²⁷³

On Poets.
On Contemplatives.
The Funeral Rite.
On Human Prudence.
On the Land of Culture.
On Scholars.
On Those Who Are Sublime.
The Dance Song.
The Prophet.
On Good and Evil.
Among Cripples.
Conversation with the King.
The Stillest Hour.

13 [33]²⁷⁴

Upon the Blessed Isles
On the Rabble.
On Tarantulas.
On Famous Sages.
the night song.
the dance song
the grave song.
On Self-Overcoming.
Sublime People.
⟨On the⟩ Land of Culture.
immaculate perception.
Scholars.
Poets.
great events.
Prophet
Redemption.
H⟨uman⟩ Prudence.
St⟨illest⟩ Hour.

13 [34]²⁷⁵

On Contemplatives.
On Scholars.
On Those Who Are Sublime.
On the Land of Culture.
On Poets.
On Human Prudence.
The Prophet.
On Redemption.
The Stillest Hour.

13 [35]²⁷⁶

On Immaculate Perception.
On Scholars.
On Poets.
The Prophet.
On Great Events.
On Human Prudence.
On Redemption.

13 [36]²⁷⁷

The Child with the Mirror.
On Those Who Are Sublime.
On Contemplatives.
On Priests.
On Famous Sages.
The Dance Song.
The Funeral Rite.
The Stillest Hour.

[14 = M III 2b. Summer 1883]

14 [1][1]

Philosophy of the Future.

On the Innocence of Becoming.
Body and Mind.
Moral and Organic.
A Millennium of Experiments.
Art.
The Free and the Unfree.
Education and Nourishment.
Men and Women.
Freely-Chosen Death.
The New Order of Rank.
The Greeks as Connoisseurs of Humanity.
Music and Philosophy.

etc. etc.
nothing but lectures and speeches.

14 [2]

On evil: i.e., inferior beings want to gain an advantage over
superior beings by exploiting a single trait of those who are
superior (e.g., their trust).

Evil is: *exploiting the virtue of other beings* who belong to a
superior species (parasitism).

A first-rate organizing power e.g., Napoleon, must be *related*
to the **species** that is to be organized (i.e., it matters little whether

he has "noble" feelings: it suffices that he *appreciates* completely and fully the *strongest* and most characteristic features of the many.)

Exploiting the backward characteristics of someone else who is generally more noble— parasites. (women)

Humankind has a relationship of *calculated utility* with nature as a whole: but what is it that upsets us when individuals *exploit* others for their own benefit? — The assumption is that they are not *worthy* enough. But assuming that they are considered worthy enough (e.g., as princes), then they are to be tolerated and they provide a kind of happiness ("devotion to God")

We guard ourselves against *exploitation* by beings *lower* than ourselves.

Thus I defend *myself* against the contemporary state, education, etc.

Evil is first of all a judgment about other beings: if we call something about ourselves evil, then it is a *metaphor* — we do not want to see a *drive* that we have classified as *lower* playing the ruler, — such a drive does not in any way have to be negated, but it *should* maintain its subordinate position and nothing more!

14 [3]

Superior human beings should be heads of state: all other forms are attempts to provide a substitute for the self-evident authority of *superior human beings*. (The ancient law does not become sacred until it *lacks* the power to make laws.)

All *lower* drives must be present and have fresh force if the highest ones want to exist and to exist in abundance: but control over the whole must be in firm hands! otherwise the danger is too great! — In regard to this danger, there was the desire to kill off the lower qualities completely (but with self-*deception*: Christians retained their affects, but employed them differently, just as Cynics kept running their abusive mouths)

or the desire to make them "gently" prudent and thereby to
have them no longer want to sanction the highest *impetus*,[2]
e.g., Epicureans.

14 [4]
Humankind still has so much more ahead of it— how
could we *possibly* derive the ideal from the past any longer!
Perhaps, by still deriving it from the *present*, which is perhaps
a nadir.

14 [5]
The *abuse of power* by the Roman emperors **disrupted** *moral
concepts* in Europe: the morality of the powerless achieved victory: — consequence, a monstrous counterfeiting.

The true source of lofty feelings is in the soul of the powerful. Self-evident joy in themselves and their deeds is the *origin*
of all value judgments — faith in themselves.

[15 = N VI 5. Summer–Autumn 1883]

15 [1]¹

Now clear skies of eternity seize my senses, the dew drop
Summoning the opponent.
Value of human beings
    1) abundance, multiplicity
    2) total power
    3) communicative force

15 [2]

I hate people who don't know how to forgive.

15 [3]

If only one moment of the world were to return, — said
the *lightning* — then all moments would have to return
absolute necessity *seen* as *shield covered with imagery*!
(chap⟨ter⟩) astronomical image of the *world*
(chap⟨ter⟩) beyond the midpoint of life — life has been
sacrificed.

15 [4]

Zarathustra's conclusion is that humans must form themselves *back* into animals in order not to feel the thought.
Or into superhumans (breeding through choice of *place*
lineage diet etc.) *Break with the past* (unhistorical mode of
thought **necessary** for *this*

to form a kind of "people"
not to be rid of error! as condition of life![2]

NB. To stage tragedies in life and *to enjoy* them!

15 [5]
Dissolution of "*free will*" and responsibility into a **prediction** and a degree of probability based on our knowledge of ourselves.

My horror at "guilty" people is a horror at having deceived myself in my predictions.

15 [6]
Zarathustra does not want to *lose* any of the past of humankind, he wants to throw everything into the mold. Transformation of force.

15 [7]
Zarathustra III. A) sudden clarity about himself. Why care about giving gifts! Why care about making people happy! About friends! About love! It is *pride* that makes him speak the truth! **His** *great contempt* is coming.

1 (chap⟨ter⟩) he looks for his animals and can no longer find them. Despair of the solitary one. Can no longer go back!

2 (chap⟨ter⟩) Temptation of suicide

3 (chap⟨ter⟩) *Regret*. Forgetting the past. Commanding as an *experiment* and roll of the dice.

In the *last* speech even the *death song* must be **fulfilled** — e.g., the good hour

to *join with* the ones who create, the ones who harvest, the ones who celebrate: this happens as part of the exclamation: *what have you done*?

4 (chap⟨ter⟩) thunderstorm rainbow lioness — doves

At the end: do you will this?

"Not *I* — but I would like to create the one who says: Yes."

At the end, the animals arrive from the sky (pride and cleverness return)

⟨chap⟨ter⟩⟩ IV **plan for the festival**, derived from the entire
system of world observations

Conclude every chapter in ⟨Zarathustra⟩ 3: "Zarathustra,
do you will this once again?"

15 [8]³

Moldenhauer
Scott *Monastery-Abbot*⁴
Haller *Old Span.*⁵
Pindar
Coleridge.
Zinzendorf
v⟨on⟩ d⟨er⟩ Goltz⁶
Meister E⟨c⟩khart and *mystics*
Swedenborg

15[9]

Zarathustra 3 as *volcanic eruption*.

Zarathustra 4 "I am the one to whom oaths are sworn."

Human beings are something fluid and malleable — we can
make them into whatever we want.

To stand *fast* for 30 years.

Zarathustra 4. you should be like the sun — and what does
the sun *not* do!

15 [10]

The Lawgiver Type.

his development and his sorrows.

What is the *point* of giving laws?

the general type of the l⟨awgiver⟩, who is the *herald* for
many lawgivers.

Chief doctrine: at every step, to achieve perfection and a **feeling of well-being** — *don't* jump!

First, giving laws. *After the prospect of superhumans*, the doctrine of recurrence in horrific fashion: now bearable!

15 [11]

cause and effect are lacking in mental processes (mirror)

15 [12]

To *enjoy* every penetrating sunbeam and every delight as metaphor and omen — *not in itself*!

because we should create a being who will strike everyone blind.

15 [13]

(chap⟨ter⟩) Arrange festivals

Festival of cosmic designations
Festival of the earth
Festival of friendship
gr⟨eat⟩ noon.

Graves, worm!

Oh, how I would want to curse him if he resembled — any other person!

But not even the relief of cursing!

Mockery of "trust in life"!

15 [14]

Zarathustra 4 Doctrine of *shared joy*.

Zarathustra 3. *Beginning*. My *premature* happiness created clouds and shadows for me

15 [15]

I want apostles but not quiet corners and communities.

15 [16]

Roar wind, roar! Take every comfort from me!

15 [17]

tortured by my happiness — otherwise it is immediately gone again!

I throw the fishing rod over my head, far out into the sea of the future

Zarathustra 3. *against the complacency of sages* — against "joyful science"

The downfall of the blessed isles *awakens* him! *Happiness* in his *failure*. Greatest suffering with the insight that whatever was *gained in life* up to now has been **lost**: massive failure! — Finally, he decides to teach his doctrine *hundreds of times*!

15 [18]

You have *set your mind against* what is human? But for humanity's sake, *no*!

Now I am clairvoyant, my diamond sword cuts every darkness to pieces. For too long I *was obsessed with* clairvoyance.[7]

An infinite process can be conceived in no other way at all than as **periodical**

3. Why didn't you drive them apart? They had found each other, well, it was time to look for others.

Good days must walk on good feet.[8]

15 [19]

Laws as *backbone* — working on them and developing them further

Zarathustra gives the model of **how** to behave with regard to the law, in that he *suspends* the law of laws, morality, in favor[9] of superior laws

achievability greater than before (individual access to interpretation)

NB. **it must** be **achievable** ⟨and⟩ a superior ideal and its law **must** grow out of this achievement!

15 [20]

As soon as you believe that *alongside* absolute causality there might also exist a god or a purpose — then the thought of necessity is *unbearable*.

15 [21]

Zarathustra 3. The evil demon *who comes from goodness* is a consequence of every teleology.

Zarathustra 3.

— Hym⟨n⟩ modesty

— Hym⟨n⟩ solitude

Failure and its consolation.

in **conclusion**.

Zarathustra himself has become a *sage* who delights in his own *foolishness* and a *pauper* who delights in his own *wealth*.

the fool and the happy pauper — possessing the tremendous **bliss** of *those who hope* and *long* and *prophesy*

Zarathustra 3. I have been concealing the worst objection to life: it is, in the long run, *boring*

the *new* saint *sanctifying* nature

the new artist.

The redemption of *evil people*

Zarathustra 3.

To rule? ghastly! I do not *want* to impose *my* type. My happiness is *multiplicity*!

Problem![10]

To invoke agon![11] those very people who would like to hide themselves away, *quiet, pious people*, — bid for dominance!

Solitude only a means of education!

against all *those who* merely *enjoy things*!

Even solitude falls under this perspective!

Self-overcoming *and all* virtue make no sense at all other than as a means of enhancing the *ruling force*.

15 [22]

Zarathustra 3 on the seduction of imperious people, noble people — deepest contempt for the comfortable for those obsessed with tranquility

15 [23]

My friend, you are like a cork, made for the light and for the surfaces of all seas — we called you fortunate

15 [24]

Zarathustra 3 Yes, if you could do that! Z⟨arathustra⟩ —

Zarathustra 3. he *praises* the vastness of the soul — he has been *licking* all good and evil things.

15 [25]

I love myself with a bad and fickle love — and occasionally I think I probably deserve a better love than the one I am giving myself.

15 [26]

Your false love of the past is a theft from the future (divine ancestry[12] of values)

15 [27]

Zarathustra 3. even if you want only *your* ideal, you *must force* all the world to accept it.

you debase your action when it is done only for the *sake* of a purpose

We must force the masses to be reasonable and even whip them into doing things to their own advantage

Zarathustra — I unlearned how to be empathetic with myself.

forgetting the self. Emerson p. 237.[13]

Zarathustra 3

those who give gifts, those who create, those who teach —
these are preludes to *those who rule*.

Which *unhappiness* is too much for me? We only ever experience *our own* happiness.

Zarathustra 3. against *authority*. When voices stopped speaking, you made a law out of this.

Zarathustra 4. A force that is *conceivable* to you must be finite and determinate — but intransitory.

15 [28]

We should not bless our enemies: but the time will come when we have no more friends, and then we will still bless the fact that we didn't curse them!

15 [29]

Every thought, like flowing lava, builds a fortress around itself and crushes itself with "laws."

15 [30]

It's not that my ocean is receding, it's that my land is growing, my new ardor is lifting it upward.

Blessed are those who outgrow their own success.

With this thought, I tow the future behind me.

Forming a new star from the debris of old ones.

15 [31]

Not to do good for people — to *perfect* existence itself, to see myself as perfected

3. The greatest pain: Zarathustra's useless squandering as **eternally** repeated.

Solution: try once again!

When I *suffered more than any human being*, I did not bear their sins and weaknesses, but rather all their perfections.

15 [32]

(chap⟨ter⟩) On the sages' happiness at their foolishness (*not knowing* the ultimate results —)

(chap⟨ter⟩) On the wealth of poor people (eternal longing)

15 [33]

Egoism and individualism

Egoism falsely labeled according to design, calculation, and altruism labeled as *uncalculating*, but cold calculation on the part of the statesman as well!

15 [34]

he who blasts me with invisible lightning bolts.

You wanted to give a gift with your overflowing: but as you must be someone who creates, you must give even yourself away.

And truly, you yourself are the best part of your overflowing

There lies a man who knows how ⟨to⟩ *take* what is rightfully his — of those who could give him what is rightfully his, who would be there!

How could I love humans for humans' sake!

15 [35]

3. Zarathustra I bring you my sins as a sacrifice and throw the sacrifice on top of you (*shaken*)

to the thought — God — hammer

If you stand high enough, then you **must** bring them up, bring them up to you![14]

Executing the gods.

(chap⟨ter⟩) Praise of *primordially determined* nature

15 [36][15]

Where there is danger, I am there and I am rooted in the earth.[16]

Training under the fire of cannons shooting at a distant target.

"An arms salesman impatient at possibly being detained by someone."[17]

As field commanders, we should let neither the victors nor the vanquished rest

to grow calm when the great danger comes.

"I want to do it or die"[18]

"Without wrath, there is no conquest" Aristotle.[19]

beautiful and horrible to look at Zarathustra 4 conclusion.

Behind the armies, a reasonable regime of terror.

"errors arising out of a good-natured disposition are most egregious in dangerous matters" Clausewitz[20]

courage that comes from a sense of honor and self-esteem not to be confused with organic courage: a compulsion whereby we *sacrifice* much of our ability.

"Cunning better than force."[21]

"This earth is too small for great ambition!"[22]

"love of glory the true *measure*[23] of a prince" Friedrich.[24]

15 [37]

"I am giving away all that I have — now I have nothing left but the great hope" Zarathustra 4

Zarathustra 4. Do I really need them? But they need me!

15 [38][25]

customs that keep the blood boiling and harden us to the sight of suffering, necessary for education.

drive to annihilate, unrelentingly hard-hearted

15 [39][26]

To respect the crowd's faith and spoon-feed them with it — remaining skeptical ourselves, we must *control* even faith.

Caution and mistrust in matters of personal safety does not rule out disdain for death.

"when life is at stake, we should not trust even our own mothers"[27]

This is my secret coat of armor.

"In war, deception is everything"[28] the foxes' hide.

"opinion is half of reality" Nap⟨oleon⟩.[29]

Wherever a great good is involved, we should *preserve* our reputation

Nobility cunning boldness bravery determination foresight perseverance deep contemplation

Intentionality of *delusion*, to be the favorite of the gods in order to influence the masses

To come to the aid of the gods!

"Human beings are too enlightened, nothing great can be accomplished anymore" Nap⟨oleon⟩[30]

Predetermination of all events. "All great things hang by a hair" Nap⟨oleon⟩[31]

their temperament jolts them out of the passivity of fatalism "to horse, sabre in hand, to *become* destiny themselves."[32]

15 [40]

With "in order to," we have created a compulsion and *annihilated freedom*. Concerning redemption from *purposes*.

15 [41]

Perfect people do as little deliberate good as they do deliberate harm.

15 [42]

ideal of the *physician*

Having sacrificed our lives. Like a fighter in the ring who gives his all and is not at all certain of victory

Epicurean happiness as that of *a convalescent*

15 [43]

I want to have *my* events, even if I do violence to them.

They want to be loved, these weaklings!

Not that you overturned idols, but rather that you overturned the idolater within yourself —

And if I must be guilty, then I still want all my virtues to kneel before my guilt

There is a happiness lying in the lap of things such that all my happiness casts shadows around its lights.

15 [44]

Conclusion 3. Feeling of dissipation and resignation — "you are too early"

Zarathustra 4. general outbreak of a mor⟨al⟩ sense, volcanic — Zarathustra is *needed*

15 [45]

Zarathustra is stewing in his own juices.[33]

His resolution perceived to be the *greatest decision* about the fate of humankind.

"to bring the universe into harmony into reconciliation and into knowledge" in this, the human soul is the greatest *work of art.*

Greatest awareness of the importance!

the universe does not *seek* its own redemption, but it *finds* it.

15 [46]

Zarathustra 3. Forward, lame-footed one, smuggler — or I'll jump etc.

that's how it screamed at me.

Life itself created this most burdensome thought for life, it wants to leap over its highest barrier *and away!*[34]

The *fool.*

The *king.*   fall into despair when they are great people

The *woman.*

15 [47][35]

like a child, the people can only *have faith*: *what* they should have faith in —

the solid realism of this observation also in Rée in regard to morality.

15 [48]

Zarathustra 4 the *new order of rank of human beings*
bad people (strong people
etc. (weak people
the many-faceted people, with the will to suffer and to get lost and to experiment, straying off course, returning — *not fearing* the most monstrous path
to *free up* the sky.
Light-hearted depths, where even a star becomes a speck.

3 Problem: My will to do good (even for myself!) *forces* me into complete *silence*.

But my will for superhumans tells me to speak and even to sacrifice friends.

Zarathustra 4. What we take to be *bad*, exploiting the weak, deceiving noble people into doing things they *must* be ashamed of. *Great curse on friends!*

I was lying in the sunshine: then came the blackest cloud. It floated like a funnel above me, leaning on the sun.

It was the sun itself, — — —

This thought leaps over me and away!

Zarathustra 3. After several chapters of fear and indecision, summoning up the *great thought*.

Conclusion: *I have the hammer*! — bliss!

And if vermin disgust you so much that you quickly move up a step because of them — then they should have the right to exist!

15 [49]

cold egoism — to exploit the weak: why does it run counter to feeling?

the same person is perceived differently by our different drives

15 [50]

To know,[36] a *delusion*.

Even laws of nature merely long-held *habits*.

Assuming that someone has a strong will, then a skeptical philosophy is best in order to spur this will most effectively to action.

Express trains everywhere!
the rich too warmly clothed
morality of the *weak* as *mimicry*[37] — wanting "to absorb."

15 [51]

not to want the means *only* for the sake of the end!

Conscience is the feeling whereby we become aware of the *order of rank* among our drives.

15 [52]

Unconscious memory

Comfort (as the longest-lasting happiness that is possible for ancient philosophers)

Skepticism suffices against all *metaphysics*

15 [53]

to locate all bliss in skepticism (the doubt concerning *pessimism*)

15 [54]

(chap⟨ter⟩) *dis-satisfied people* as life principle (*One* virtue!)

15 [55]

Limitations of the *mor⟨al⟩* point of view — every individual plays a part in the whole cosmic entity — whether we know it or not — whether we want it or not!

15 [56]

(chap⟨ter⟩) molding and remolding process of pious people, of priests

15 [57]
(chap⟨ter⟩) the herald's **call** to *individuals* (and their ideals)

15 [58]
law for lawgivers
We must transform *ourselves* from *those who pray into those who give blessings*!

15 [59]
imperious people
the — — —

15 [60][38]
Hartmann M⟨iscellaneous⟩ Wr⟨itings⟩[39]
Ranke Popes[40]
Wellhausen[41]
v⟨on⟩ d⟨er⟩ Goltz
Dreher[42]
Moldenhauer
Zinzendorf
Bentham-Benecke[43]

Buddhism by *Kern*
Leipzig Otto Schulze[44]

[16 = Z II 1a. Autumn 1883]

16 [1]

Nature must be imagined as analogous to human beings, as erring, experimenting, good and evil — as fighting and overcoming itself.

16 [2]

There are three solitudes, that of someone who creates, that of someone who waits, that of shame. — I know the word and sign of the superhumans; but I don't say it, I am concealing it from myself. — *To live in shame, in the face of a great truth.*

16 [3][1]

In Act II the different groups come and bring their gift. "What did you do?" — They say it. — "Then it is done in the spirit of Zarathustra."

The rabble, cold and without much inner need, will be the first to smile at the doctrine of recurrence. The most basic life drive is the first to give its approval. **At the very end a great truth wins over the most superior humans**: *this is the suffering of truthful people.*

Act I. Solitude as a result of being ashamed of himself: *An unspoken thought for which he feels too weak (not hard-hearted enough) The temptations to mislead him about this.* The messengers of the chosen people invite him to the festival of life.

Act II. He attends the festival incognito. He reveals himself when he finds himself venerated too much.

Act III. In happiness, he proclaims the superhumans and their doctrine. Everyone deserts him. He dies as the vision leaves him on account of the pain he feels at the suffering he has created.

Funeral rite. "We killed him" — Noon and eternity.

16 [4][2]

The gentlest person must become the most hard-hearted: and perish in the process. This the psychological problem.

Experience came imperiously: but my will spoke to it — then it was already on its knees, pleading.[3]

Don't dancers have their ears in their toes?[4]

Zarathustra's virtue still lives for us! A star went under in barren space: but its light is still on its way and is transformed — and when will it cease to be on its way?[5]

Do you want to be a stumbling block to those who stride ahead? Then limp along in front of whoever is in a hurry.[6]

Even what we have left undone weaves the fabric of the entire future: even nothingness itself is a weaver and master weaver.[7]

Many grow weary of themselves: and only then does the happiness begin that was reserved for *them*.[8]

My drink should still make you sneeze, and my sparkling wines should tickle your nose and fill you with lust.[9]

"It is showing itself": says your complacency? No, it is withdrawing and it will withdraw more and more.[10]

16 [5][11]

The *profound sterility* of the 19th century. I have not met a single person really capable of introducing a new ideal. For a long time, the character of German music gave me false *hopes*. A *stronger type* in which our powers are synthetically fused — my faith. Apparently everything is *décadence*. This downfall must be guided so that it makes a new form of existence possible for the strongest people.

16 [6]

Don't be impatient! Superhumans are our next step! *For this*, for this limitation, *moderation* and manliness are required.

16 [7][12]

Do as I do: only those who do, learn — only as a doer will I also be your teacher.[13]

That a bolt of lightning would strike your feed and your maws would learn to feed on fire![14]

The pride of my eagle whips my will with its wings: but the surge of pride also founders on this cliff.[15]

Am I not the meteorological divide? Don't all winds come to me and proclaim their will to me?[16]

I want to vanish in a dark thunderstorm: and in my final moment I want to be both human and lightning.[17]

You crash up against me — but to no effect! I am striking you with my oar: you still must carry my boat into immortality![18]
Did I ever fall asleep on my fame? Every kind of fame has been like a bed of thorns to me.[19]

Perhaps as Zarathustra III: *This is the book of the seven solitudes.*

"And the ice and innocence of my peaks are also still aglow."[20]

To me you are arid grass and steppe: but I want to make wildfires of you and heralds with tongues of fire.[21]

Gold flashes in his dark eyes: a golden bark floats there on black waters.[22]

You are clever and have clever fingers: not until your fingers have crept back into your fist, will I even want to believe in your power.[23]

I know how to put my checkered saddle blanket on you: and anyone who knows horses also knows just what it means to be in the saddle.[24]

I still am like a cock in a strange barnyard, pecked at even by hens.[25]

There is more injustice in admiration than in contempt.[26]

How high up do I live? Never yet when I climbed did I count the flights of stairs to where I live: *where all stairways end, that's where the roof over my head begins.*[27]

You will have to be hauled up by your hair into your heaven![28]

You claim to be made of finer cloth, you visionaries? That you don't merely know how to dress and disguise yourselves better! You know how to hide your substance beneath a cloak better![29]

If I remain otherwise invisible, then I still wish to be visible at the masts of solitary voyagers and explorers — as a flame and sign of hope.[30]

Didn't the world stand still? How this silence wound itself around me with terrible coils and held me fast![31]

A woman said: "I may have broken my wedding vows. But first my wedding vows broke me!"[32]

To seduce those who love us so that they do something that is shameful in their eyes and ours — this is the cruelest thing that cruel people do.

And if the stars don't want to fall from the sky for you, then throw your star into the sky — let that be the extent of your evil![33]

And those who throw themselves down from the heights at the people below: what price did they put on broken limbs?[34]

You are also looking back, when going forward: and people have to run into you a lot.[35]

I listened for an echo, but heard only praise.[36]

Talking a lot about ourselves is also a means of concealing ourselves.[37]

Whoever does not make us fertile will certainly leave us indifferent.[38]

We do good deeds for our neighbors, but we do not create for them.[39]

Eventually the truth will really triumph: some kind of error was fighting on its behalf.[40]

Just at the point where your honesty ceases, your eye sees nothing more.[41]

His bad qualities allow him to be rewarded whenever they have allowed themselves to be overcome by virtue.[42]

He is so convincing that he convinces the arguments themselves to run after him.[43]

16 [8][44]

That Zarathustra reaches the highest level of *distress* and that not until then does he reach his greatest *happiness*: he becomes progressively unhappier *and* happier. In the moment when the contrast between both feelings becomes most terrifying, he perishes. *For the outline.*

16 [9][45]

"These are Zarathustra's speeches on the seven solitudes" —: they are meant to describe how **distress** *grows* along with happiness. Giving gifts, like creating, shows its **other** face. *Hard-heartedness* in virtue:[46] *agony* in compassion and justice: isolation and homelessness for the friend of those who will come: *creating as a kind of enchantment that brings with it a* **disenchantment** *in regard to everything that is* **there**: displeasure felt toward the most superior exemplars alienates us from those who must be worked on: etc.

16 [10]

To seize *for myself* the total *immorality* of the artist in regard to my material (humankind): this was the work of my last few years.

To seize for myself *intellectual freedom* and *joy*, in order to be able to create and not to be tyrannized by alien ideals. (Basically, it matters little *what* I had to break away *from*: yet my favorite mode of *breaking away* was artistic in nature: i.e., I constructed an *image* of what had captivated me up until then: like Schopenhauer, Wagner, the Greeks (genius, saints, metaphysics, all previous ideals, the highest morality) — simultaneously a *tribute out of gratitude.*

16 [11]

It was necessary *to liberate* myself from the *delusion* that nature would have to *unlearn* **having goals**.

Liberation from *world-weariness*: *Now*, for sake of this goal, *my doctrine* of the *redemption of humanity from itself.*

"now they know and are too disgusted to act p 35 Birth of Tragedy. "art *saved* them — and by means of art they saved their own life."[47] **Fundamental thought**. *My life from then on is the consequence.*

To become artist (one who creates), saint (one who loves), and philosopher (one who knows) *in one person*: — *my practical goal*!

The *message*: to find space and strength and courage to create. (Restricted to the human, as opposed to "world process" and "hinterworld")[48]

To create for myself freedom from the old ideals: with the best motives, I turned in the direction of the *opposing ideals*: I looked for the best even from *this era*.

I broke away: from education, from the kind of scholars that have existed up to now

"pessimist of the intellect."[49]

emergence of "intellectual conscience": "what is true originally *more useful* and brings more *honor*.[50] Mixed Opinions and Maxims p. 13.

My mockery of the pretensions of *world-process* advocates, my disbelief in a "drive for knowledge in itself," I allowed the historical sense to develop out of only three drives. — Everything was already there.

Hatred of Kantian obscurantism, of the Kantian doctrine of disinterested pleasure and of the quietism of the will.

16 [12]

Thanks to those who are there taking![51]

16 [13]

Take pity on your foot so that it doesn't step into a morass: Don't even bother kicking those who betray their friends.[52]

16 [14]

A *history of origins*[53] was required for **overcoming** ideals
(philosopher, artist, saint) that have been held up to now.

In place of saint-lovers, I put people who reimagine all phases of
culture lovingly-fairly: *historical people of the most profound piety.*

In place of geniuses, I put people who *create human beings
beyond* themselves (new concept of art (against the artistry of
artworks)

In place of philosophers, I put free spirits, who are superior
to scholars, researchers, critics and who, existing above many
ideals, still remain alive: who, without becoming Jesuits, and
in spite of all this, lay the foundations for the illogical nature
of existence: *those who liberate us from morality.*

Schopenhauer as Educator p. 60 "Only after, in our present
or in some future incarnation, we have been taken up into that
most sublime order of philosophers, artists, and saints will a
new goal also be established for our love and our hate — *in the
meantime, we have our task.*"[54]

The value of error (delusion)
              of forgetting
finally the value of evil
                  of enmity

16 [15][55]

My differences with Rée: the basic disagreement, dependence on an origin[56] and breaking away from it — not "egoistic" and "unegoistic"

He lacks a historical sense of the extraordinary variety in
the codes of values comprising what is good.

H⟨uman,⟩ A⟨ll Too Human⟩ p. 79.[57]

Different derivation of the sense of justice and of vanity.

I am fighting against the notion that egoism is harmful and
reprehensible: I want to create a clean conscience for egoism.

I claim that the herd instinct is originally the stronger and
more powerful one: that acting individually (not acting in
accordance with lineage) has been perceived to be evil.

they say: to find something reprehensible, only out of habit — — —

Rée thinks, *utility* is *something trivial*: his entire way of looking at things is dependent on moral prejudice.[58]

p. 47 "when nothing about punishments reminds us that they are a means of deterrence, then the impression must arise that they are a kind of retribution."[59] Why? What is *retribution* anyway? He thinks that a sense of justice emerges because something appears {to be} retribution. But the concept of retribution has not been investigated. In addition, {he} overlooked the fact that all punishment emerges out of revenge.

"There *can* not be retribution for actions that are necessary" p. 49[60] Of course there can be! He thinks there *should* not be, it would be unfair! i.e., he himself is operating under moral presuppositions.

Sense of justice i.e., to demand that *retributive* suffering occurs. — According to Rée the consequence of 2 errors: 1) that punishment appears to be retribution 2) that the will is considered to be free.

He thinks that we would not undertake *retribution* if we *considered* our neighbors *to be unfree*. Now consider what retribution is here: first to prevent, to stop the harm from continuing. There cannot be retribution against a falling rock. — He is right.

Rée errs when he allows a sense of justice to emerge *from* the punishment and *as a result of* the punishment: whereas punishments emerge *from this sense of justice*.

There must be retribution for those who injure us because they have undermined our awareness of our power: it is a crime against our self-esteem.

It is in no way sufficient: only those who want the well-being of others for their own sake have a morally good purpose, but we should ask *what kind of well-being*.

He is only interested in the emergence of the *judgments* "good" and "evil" — but the precise makeup of these actions, their actual utility (in relation to their assumed utility) is what interests *me*.

Morality initially self-glorification of the powerful and of the ruling caste.

Pleasure-displeasure are *accompanying* phenomena, not goals.

16 [16]
Will-o'-the-wisp[61] in a swamp.

16 [17]
Substitute for revenge: as soon as we've grasped that it was the violation of our feeling of power that so upset us, then we should think about how we might increase our *feeling of power*. It is a failure of intellect for us to insist that we are injuring the very one doing the injuring and injuring that person even more. But this is still the case with our criminal justice system. Here the *communal feeling of power* is compromised when someone breaks the law: a brave undertaking, a noble act done in the best interest of the community, *could* quite easily be interpreted *as being directed against it*! Individuals should provide compensation for injuries that *other* individuals inflict: as something like benefactors who overcompensate. — Yet if *individuals* have been insulted, they should move to a *higher* level and thereby generate and extend their feeling of power. All the baseness of wretched people should become a spur and a ladder for the noble. — But we should not have retribution for individual actions: actions are symptoms of the whole being — there are no actions that are performed only once. As soon as I recognize: "people are capable of that" — then my entire position toward them changes: from now on I perceive them to be my enemy and I wish not only to fight against them, but also to annihilate them. — "*They are no longer part of our group*" is our *rule of thumb*.

My program: do away with punishment: for **us**. Counter-retribution as nonsense. (If something is evil, then whoever performs the counter-retribution is certainly committing the same evil.) The purpose is not to deter, but rather *to protect ourselves against further harm* (along with irritation at the fact that we were too gullible)

16 [18][62]

Contra Rée: where there is suffering, then something has been done contrary to utility — in nature, something contrary to purpose.

16 [19]

If it is true that the standpoint of the common good has determined the value of what is not self-interested: *now* we must still ask: is the judgment true, justified? *Is* a benevolent person beneficial?

16 [20]

Wherever there are living things, there are sudden explosions of force: the subjective feeling is that "free will" is involved. The number and power of these explosions initially determine the value of a living thing: then the *direction* that is given to these explosions. When we speak of "motives for action," we always mean only "motives for direction."

16 [21]

Goal: to build up the entire *body* and not just the brain!

16 [22][63]

We must think just as ruthlessly about the masses as nature does: they preserve the species.

16 [23]

The face of *Jesuitism* grins from behind my *first phase*: I mean: consciously holding on to an illusion and being forced to incorporate this illusion as a *basis for civilization*.[64] Or also: **Buddhism** and the demand for nothingness (the Schopenhauerian contradiction between theory and practice not sustainable). W⟨agner⟩ succumbed to the first danger.

16 [24]

NB! **History of superior humans**. Breeding better humans is enormously more painful. *To demonstrate through Zarathustra the ideal of the kind of sacrifices required for this*: to leave homeland, family, fatherland. Life lived under the contempt of prevailing ethics (*despised*). Agony of experiments and failures. Breaking away from all of the enjoyment offered by the older ideals (they taste somewhat threatening, somewhat foreign to the tongue)

16 [25]

Delight in causing pain, because it is accompanied by an increase in the feeling of power: most intense when preceded by some kind of diminishment — thus, in revenge.

Delight in *doing good* evolved in completely the same way — and *generosity* is sublimated revenge and for that reason a *much greater* delight.

16 [26][65]

Every living thing expands its force outward as far as it can and subjugates what is weaker: in this way, it takes delight in itself. The *increasing* "*anthropomorphism*" within this tendency consists in the ever more *subtle* perception of *how difficult* it is really to *incorporate* the other: how the extensive damage may indeed demonstrate our power over it, yet at the same time *alienate* us still further from its will — thus making it less easily subjugated.

16 [27]

Moral valuation initially refers to the distinction between *superior* and *inferior human beings* (or castes) morality is initially self-glorification of the powerful: and contempt in regard to the powerless. Not "good" and "evil," but rather "noble" and "base," is the original feeling. Only **then** are the differing *actions* and *characteristics* called *noble*, and the ones in opposition to them called *base*.

16 [28]

Thieves do not act in order to take delight in power, they do not project themselves into the effect that their actions produce in others. No more than do *robbers*, or people who kill others in order to take something from them. But they reveal that they are *afraid of us*, that's why — — —

16 [29]

In what way is injury an injustice? — The *need for retribution* emerges when injury occurs: what is this? Not to be confused with the feeling that we have recognized an enemy and that we will make it impossible for this enemy to do us further damage. Or with the intention of recovering what was taken from us or some equivalent. A *bitterness* remains. Enemies are not felt to be bad in themselves: but the person injured almost always feels *self-recrimination*: we were too careless, our weapons were not in good condition, we should have seen the warning signs long ago, etc. *This disappointment in ourselves* — thus a *diminished* self-*esteem* — is the main reason for the bitterness we feel in revenge: and even the motivation for subtlety in carrying out our revenge.

Because everything is *paid for* and some equivalent for everything exists, fantasizing has even led to inventing equivalents for harm: and to speaking of *retribution*. But basically all of this is concerned with something *else*, with **much more** *than a repayment*. Retribution is merely hypocrisy and whitewashing for those who avenge themselves. "Guilt."

The feeling of desire for revenge ceases when the injuring parties abase themselves, make restitution for the harm: at that point they are *vanquished*.

The intention to do harm is originally not even considered: rather the fact *that* someone has been harmed and how much. Punishment follows *at that point*. *The harm inflicted is paid back* — is the oldest form, *not a hostile mentality*. Outrage emerges *in response to the harm done*, and so to the enemies' success, not to hostility toward them. *It is the feeling of the vanquished* — the demand for retribution: not the feeling that wrong has been done.[66]

Revenge, the demand for retribution, is *not* the feeling that wrong has been done, but rather that I have been vanquished — and that I must now restore my standing by any means necessary.

Injustice emerges only after an *agreement* is broken, in other words, when *peace* and loyalty are violated. This is outrage about an *unworthy* action, unworthy of the assumed equivalence of feelings. Therefore, something base, something contemptible must be involved which refers to a lower level. The counter-intention can only be *to move* unworthy beings to this *lower level*: thus separating them from us, expelling them, humiliating them, disgracing them. *Meaning of punishment.*

The meaning of punishment is *not* to deter, but rather to move someone to a lower place in the social order: *this person is no longer counted among our* **equals**.

Every measure that achieves *this* is adequate. "*Ostracism.*" The system of punishment must develop in this direction!

16 [30][67]

Zarathustra 3: The *others* are allowed to **obey**: and their vanity demands that they do not appear to be dependent on great people but rather on "*principles.*"[68]

16 [31]

Bitterness *about ourselves* in matters of revenge transforms itself in lesser natures very quickly into being outraged toward enemies and into wishing to accuse them of something *contemptible*

16 [32]

How powerful people are overpowering and arrogant in regard to the subjugated: the development of prudence and anthropomorphism allows *this overpowering and this arrogance to be intellectualized more and more.* But why should power not want to take delight in itself!

The supreme relationship remains, that of *those who create toward their material*: this is the ultimate form of arrogance and dominance. In this way, the *organic form* is brought to completion for the first time: thus resembling the way in which the body is dependent on impulses of the will and takes delight in itself when it is under the most control.

16 [33]

Liberation from Morality.

Organic-moral[69] (competition of the affects and supremacy of one affect over the intellect[70])

Revenge, injustice, punishment.

Anyone who believes in good and evil can never treat evil as a means of achieving good; and every teleological worldview that doesn't completely break with ethics is *lost.*

There could be a history of value judgments concerning food: *in that case*, the basic question would still remain: *what value is involved* in this or that having been eaten? — Thus, the question remains: what is the value of things having always been done in this or that way, apart from the question: what kind of values have been assigned to the actions *up to now*? — The history of value-estimations *up to now*, and their rationale, is something other than the estimation itself.

No person will say: stones that are falling constitute morality. Well then! human beings climb — and that is also not morality!

The collective conscience. The *atavism* in the estimation of unegoistic people.

16 [34]

Weaker people give in, and subjugate themselves, when revenge is senseless.

16 [35][71]

"Whatever Zarathustra has decided, this will happen: how should his great soul be capable of changing its resolve!"

16 [36][72]

Let us hold fast to the notion that humans are the predator of all predators! It is said that humans love themselves: but this is precious little love!

16 [37][73]

Zarathustra recognizes that he is also not there for his friends "Who are my friends!" Neither for the people, nor for individuals! *Neither for the many nor for the few*! *To overcome friendship*! *Sign* of his self-overcoming at the beginning of III

Emerson p. 426[74] Depiction of the *sage*.

16 [38]

When he sees through Pana, Zarathustra dies from compassion for her compassion. Before that, the moment of supreme contempt (supreme bliss!)

Everything must be fulfilled, namely, everything from the *preface*.

16 [39]

The final circumstance, remaining silent in the most refined way hinders *all great success*: as soon as h⟨uman⟩ beings *are completely in harmony with the truth*,[75] *they move all of nature*. III Part Zarathustra

16 [40]

This has to do with more than giving gifts: *with* **creating**, *with overpowering*! Fundamental concept of the second solitude (*Beginning* of III.)

Our "gifts" are dangerous!

16 [41]

Controlling humankind for the purpose of overcoming it

Overcoming by means of doctrines that bring about its downfall, **except for those who can survive it**.[76]

16 [42]

First everyone turns away from Zarathustra (this *to be depicted in stages*!). Zarathustra enraptured, doesn't notice. Pana wants to kill him. *In the moment when she wields the dagger, Zarathustra understands everything and dies in pain from this compassion. This is to be made clear*!

16 [43]

The "truth," the "annihilation of illusions," "even of the *moral* illusion" — as *the* **great means** *of* **overpowering** humankind (of its **self-destruction**!) Part III.

NB. All the sufferings associated with Zarathustra's development as depicted *here* are to be depicted as much greater than what *superior humans suffer* on account of their visitors.

16 [44]

"*It was out of love that I caused the greatest suffering*: now I melt away at the *suffering* I caused —

16 [45]

When everyone has gone, Zarathustra reaches out his hand to the serpent: "what advice does my cleverness offer me?" — it bites him. The eagle tears it to pieces, the lion hurls itself on top of the eagle. When Zarathustra saw his animals fighting, he died.

16 [46]

No one has time for me? Very well, then I shall wait. What is the deal with a time that "has no time"![77]

16 [47]

Zarathustra's thanksgiving prayer of a convalescent.[78]

16 [48]

Zarathustra as "autumn," as "plowshare," etc. — different melodies!

16 [49]

Speech on the innocence of becoming. Beatitude[79] *sub specie aeterni.*[80]

The consecration of what is smallest.

Those who make vows.

The new kings

The breaking of the tablets. (From Part 4 beginning of Scene 3)

Great humans *as rivals of majestic nature.*

The two movements (toward the last humans and toward the superhumans).

The redemption of evil people.

As children, *a much longer youth*, encompassing *many* countries and industries and trades.

The new teachers as precursors of the greatest sculptors (imposing their type)

The most burdensome knowledge as hammer.

Praise of mercy (for the sake of those to come)

Summoning enemies! (we need them for the sake of our ideal!

To transform our enemies of equal breeding into gods and thus to raise ourselves up and transform ourselves!

Those who create, those who love, those who know, unified by power.[81]

The will to suffer — to feel suffering deeply as means of transformation.

The parasite as the bad person. We must not be merely those who enjoy existence — ignoble.

The rejoicing conscience: as prayer.

Contra praise and blame. To shine after centuries; predetermin⟨ation⟩ of the future.

Overpowering the past: and then forgetfulness that heals, the divine circle.

The holy laughter.

The song of solace (set to my music).

The teaching of return is the *turning point of history.*

16 [50]

Solitude necessary *for a time*, so that our being becomes whole and permeated — completely healed and hardened.

New form of community: to stand our ground as warriors. Otherwise the mind grows tired. No "gardens," and just "withdrawing from the masses." War (but without gunpowder!) between different thoughts! and their armies!

New nobility, through breeding. Foundations festivals for families.

A new division of the day; physical exercise for all ages. Competition as principle.

Sexual love as competition with the principle of what is becoming, what is to come, as the prize. — "Ruling" is taught, practiced, hard-heartedness as well as mercy. As soon as one condition has been mastered, it is essential to strive for a new one.

To allow ourselves to be taught by evil people and to give even them the opportunity to compete. To use those who make things decadent. — This should be the justice of *punishment,* that the offender should be able to be *used* as an experimental subject (for new nourishment): this is the *consecration* of punishment, that here an offender will be *used up* for the greatest benefit of those who are to come.

We *spare* our new community because it is the bridge to *our* ideal of the future. And we work *for it* and let others work *for* it.

Places of residence.
Kind of community.
Wars.
The new nobility.
Experiments (punishments etc.)
To redeem the woman in women.[82]
The many wanderings of the individual's soul. Long youth.
The time for solitude.

The choice of places of residence, new (Indic peoples as cautionary example!)

To redeem the woman in women![83]

Physical strength should be on the side of the greatest thoughts — that's how long the war between the different thoughts must last!

16 [51]

Plan for Zarathustra III

Zarathustra 3: the **transition** from **freethinker** and hermit *to having* **to rule**: gift-giving is transformed — from giving, there emerged the will's exercising its compulsion to take. *The tyranny of the artist initially as self-disciplining and self-tempering*!

Psychology of those who rule. (The desire for *friends reveals itself* as desire for *tools of the artist*!)

Zarathustra 3: first fleeing from the "inexpressible truth" skepticism, self-ridicule, voluntary blindness, increasing misery, feeling of weakness. The 7 solitudes — attempt to find refuge, to rest somewhere in a past worldview. *Objections* to his doctrine present themselves. The seducers as well. (To insert: "the song of solace.")

The *most profound suffering* is not for *his* own sake, but rather for the sake of those *dearest* to him who bleed to death on account of his doctrine. — But following this experience,

Zarathustra simultaneously rises to the greatest hard-heartedness against himself and against those nearest to him and *thinks only* of the "*future.*"

At the end, the *lion* as Zarathustra's third animal — symbol of his **ripeness** and **tenderness**.[84]

"*Thanksgiving Prayer of a Convalescent*": *Part 3* concludes with this.

16 [52]

The love for friends would like to force Zarathustra to withhold his *great truth*: even after he has admitted it to himself. — *This is the problem of those who rule*: **they sacrifice those they love to their ideal**.

16 [53]

The *band* of those sacrificing themselves gathered at Zarathustra's *grave*. Previously they fled: now, when they find him dead, they become the *heirs* of his soul and they raise themselves up to *his height*. (This the last scene in Zarathustra 4 — "*the great noon*" — *clear* — *unending sky*)

16 [54]

Everything *warns* Zarathustra about speaking further: omens. He is interrupted. One of them kills himself, another goes mad. Mood of divine exuberance[85] in the artist —: it *must* come to light. After he has *simultaneously* demonstrated the truth of the return and shown the superhumans, he is overwhelmed by compassion.

Exaltation increasing within him (*in this exaltation he goes through all stages of* **evil** *— but for the sake of his goal. Here he is the* **teacher** *of evil, of hard-heartedness etc.*) and "glow of the Alps" — gathering gloom among his listeners. Rain at the end etc.

16 [55]

Plan for Zarathustra 4.

1. The victory parade, the plague city, the symbolic funeral pyre. 30
2. The proclamations of the future: his disciples tell of *their deeds.* 30
3. The last speech with omens, interruptions, rain, death. 30
4. The band at his grave — those who make vows — the great noon — *forebodingly clear* and *eerie.* 30

16 [56]

"Do you want this once again?"

Clairvoyant about his gift-giving and teaching, about his love for his friends.

He feels the supreme responsibility resting on his shoulders. What happiness!

Will to suffer and the strength of character on the *path* (cold people, hard-hearted people, parasites).

Every authentic life an experiment!

Morality up to now based in weakness: we *wanted* authority and we designed leisure for ourselves.

The contradiction of goodness and creativity: this is the problem of wisdom.

16 [57]

Even the drives of future humankind are also already present and demand to be satisfied — although we are not yet consciously familiar with them. Thus, even in great individuals there is an apparent concern for as yet nonexistent needs.

16 [58]

These are the speeches of the seven solitudes, which Zarathustra spoke to his heart after he had abandoned his friends and even his animals; and at that time, he would have loved to have abandoned himself.

16 [59]

The woman in women should be emancipated![86]

16 [60]

It is not enough to proclaim a doctrine: we must also *change* human beings *by force*, so that they accept it! — Zarathustra finally grasps this.

16 [61]

To overcome *the past within us*: to combine drives in a new way and to direct them all together toward one goal: — very difficult! The evil drives are certainly not the only drives that must be overcome — even the so-called good drives must be overpowered and newly consecrated!

The temptations;

to rest in a worldview from the past.

Derisive skepticism and self-disintegration: what could you "create" then!

"you aren't strong enough! Leave it to someone stronger!" Enjoy your fatigue! Admire yourself!

convince yourself that your compassion is a virtue and that you are sacrificing your knowledge for the happiness of others.

Go ahead and admit to yourself what is meant by this will to create — imperiousness, which cannot be satisfied just anywhere. "Friends?" You want to have *tools*!

And so why tell this truth in the first place! Even if you *were allowed* to believe that it is the truth! There are really no constraints on you anymore! No "obligation to the truth"!

You destroy in all others the pleasure they take in what is before them, you are the teacher of the great fatigue itself!

you disempower virtue and cause it to be praised less, thus desired less. You yourself *rob* humankind of the force with which it could pursue the goal!

16 [62]

The degree of psychological subtlety decides whether people *interpret* their actions as good or evil. And not only subtlety, but also their desire for revenge, bad moods, good nature, frivolity etc.

16 [63]

NB. *The thought itself will not be articulated in the third part*: only prepared for.

First: *critique* of everything taught up to now.

> Which means of consolation were lost to him.
> faith and trust in a supreme wisdom and goodness
> faith in that which is good, the voice of duty etc.

Evil conscience (the best conscience is influenced by fear, mistrust of ourselves, skepticism, having to keep silent, distortion of, etc.)

> The song of those who fly.

> Humans as rivals of majestic nature.

Fear of the consequences of the doctrine: maybe the best natures perish because of it? The worst accept it?

Solution Zarathustra III: you must elevate yourself above morality, you have seen through it — all of your *misery* was the result *of it*.

there is no other way for human beings *to overcome themselves*.

Keeping the *smallest* secret *cripples* all of his strength: he feels that he has *avoided* a thought up to now, — now the thought hurls itself upon him with all of its force! It is a wrestling match: who is *strong* enough, Zarathustra or the thought?

What is the point of truth? — It has *become* the strongest drive, the will to truth! Zarathustra *can* do nothing else![87]

— and whether I count forward from now or backward from now: I hold the belt of infinity in my hand and — — —

Fools say: "but at that point infinity would certainly have been completed": yet we must be exact in the use of our words and never call something a beginning which at some other time we call an end.

His reassurance: the effect cannot be anticipated!

the greatest thought does its work in the slowest and most delayed way!

its most immediate effect is a substitute for faith in immortality: does it increase good will toward life?

Maybe it is not true: — may others wrestle with it!

16 [64]

1. Solitude in shame and weakness and silence in the face of a great thought.

What is the point of truth!

2. Solitude, in which all the old reasons for solace have been lost.

3. Solitude with temptations.

4. Solitude without friends, indeed with the awareness that we are sacrificing our friends.

5. Solitude of supreme responsibility.

6. Solitude in eternity, *beyond morality*: the creative one and goodness. No alternative solution exists except to *create* another being that does *not* suffer as we do.

Determinism:[88] "I am a *fatum*[89] for everything that is coming!" — is *my* answer to determinism!

7. Solitude of a sick person. Song of solace. Growing weary, growing silent. Sanctified through suffering.

13 p⟨ages⟩ *each*. Each time at the end, the thought that overcomes.

NB. *All concerns are signs of the will to suffer, a deepening of pain: when the pain is most intense,* **Z⟨arathustra⟩ throws it aside**:

greatest concluding moment (the lion): **I will this!!!**

Hymn at the end: *the victorious one.* (10 pages)

16 [65]

The third part is Zarathustra's self-overcoming, as a *model* for humankind's self-overcoming — for the benefit of the superhumans.

For this, it is necessary to overcome morality.

You sacrifice your friends — they are profound enough to perish as a result: and they didn't create the thought (which still occupies *me!*)

This as a last counterargument which confronts Zarathustra — the strongest *enemy. Now Zarathustra is becoming ripe.*

In Part 4 Zarathustra dies when he notices the pain of his friends: and they abandon him. — But after his death, his spirit comes over them.

Institutions as the *aftereffects* of great individuals and as a means of *planting* great individuals and of *rooting* them — until finally fruit emerges.

16 [66]

Wrestling contest for the use of the *power* that humankind represents! Zarathustra calls for everyone to join this wrestling contest. (P⟨art⟩ 4 Zarathustra's speeches)

16 [67]

The eudaimon⟨istic-⟩social ideals lead human beings *back* — perhaps they are targeting a very useful *worker-species* — they invent the *ideal slaves of the future* — the lower caste *that can't be missing!*[90]

The "happiness of those who know" and their **obtuseness** *up to now* about the fruits of knowledge — song of ridicule.

16 [68]

The short-lived force of artists' drives — they stop near the image of their ideal and they *themselves no longer even follow the ideal* — song of ridicule. Not to mention the audience![91] *They should be teachers* — these artists!

16 [69]

How much the field marshal *sacrifices*, the prince, those responsible to themselves — this is to be highly revered!

16 [70]

Actually, humans always try to use collectives to make the great individual *expendable* etc. But they are completely dependent on those role models.

16 [71]

The conflict of those who rule is the *struggle between their love for those who are more distant from them and their love for those who are closest to them.*

Being a creator and *goodness* are not opposites, but rather *one and the same thing*, yet with a *more distant* **or** *a closer* perspective.

16 [72]

The weak must obey.

16 [73]

To find the measure and the mean in striving *beyond* **humankind**: the *supreme and most powerful kind of human being* must *be found*! To continue **depicting** the supreme tendency **in miniature** — perfection, ripeness, glowing health, mild emanation of power. To work as artists do at their daily tasks, to bring us closer to perfection with each work, to be the best brother there is. Honesty in admitting motives to ourselves, as befits those who are powerful.

NB. everything can be ruined by the *madness of longing*!

16 [74]

NB. The inner difficulties of Part 3 have to appear at the end as *completely unnecessary*: when faced with the **general insight**, they must *cancel themselves out*.

16 [75]

Every sacrifice made by someone who rules is repaid a hundred times over.

16 [76]

General insight perhaps: the organic itself is the law, we *cannot* do anything else — absolute determinism. The many possibilities that we *see*, confuse us.

16 [77]

The great mass, force of the individual is wasted in this way, like that of the sun. Or?[92]

16 [78][93]

A fact, a work, is newly eloquent for every age and for every new kind of human being. History is always articulating *new truths*.

16 [79]

Zarathustra 3. This *entire* **distress**, with the *aversion to suffering*, came from the feeling that the *force was not yet sufficient* — an *instinct* of weakness that initially *hindered* action (even *hindered* the articulation of the thought!) — The *will to suffer* is *immediately* present when the *power* is **strong enough**.

"The stillest hour" was a temptress.

16 [80]

NB. Zarathustra's mood *not* madly impatient for the superhumans!

it is **serene**, can **wait**, but everything *that is done* has taken on **meaning** as the way and the means to get there — and must be done **well** and **completely**.

Serenity of the great torrent!!! Consecration of the smallest!!! all *disquiet, fervent longing, all disgust* should be depicted and **overcome** in Part 3!

(Gentleness, mildness of Parts 1 and 2), etc. *everything* a sign of a force that is *not yet* sure of itself!)

In the midst of Zarathustra's *convalescence,* **Caesar** stands there, unrelenting, benevolent — *the split between being creator, benevolence, and wisdom is annihilated*. Light, serenity, *no exaggerated* longing, happiness in a *moment that has been properly applied, made eternal*!

16 [81]

Beyond midlife — irrevocably sacrificed — no going back!

16 [82]

(4) Speeches: great *honesty* in regard to *morality* — as befits those who are powerful

Compilation of things in life that take hold of us

16 [83]

(Zarathustra 3.)

Recapitulation: to create superhumans by every means. But you fall in love with your friends and with yourself! The thought became a burden to us.

1. Clairvoyance.
   tossed about on the ocean
2. Summoning up the truth.
3. Beyond midlife — irrevocably sacrificed.
4. Song of mockery about the pessimists.
5. I as *fatum.*
6. Majestic nature and human beings.
7. Song of those who fly.
8. What it means to be a friend! Praise of friends (who perished) of the quiet world-*beautifiers* who create, praise of *hope* — not before now!

9. beyond good and evil
10. Mockery of those who have trust in life.
11. Mockery of artists.
12. Commiseration with those who rule and with their sufferings.
13. Skepticism as temptation.
14. Truth — lie.
15. Oh if only I had someone here I could curse!
16. Conversation with lightning. I myself the prophet
17. Insight that a feeling of *weakness* guides his mind.
18. In his desire for commiseration, he seeks out his animals and finds the cave destroyed.
19. Zarathustra's "great contempt."
20. Temptation to suicide. The serpent in the high mountains.
21. Illness. Forgetting.
22. Rainbow. Lioness with flock of doves. Praise of a primordially determined nature that turns everything into its own happiness.

against the nonsense of reclusiveness

16 [84]

(Zarathustra 4.)

1. The invitation.
2. The victory parade.
3. The convalescents' thanksgiving song.
4. The great noon.
5. The new community. I found that humans had become *inferior*, minor virtues, minor misdeeds.[94]
6. Where to? (Places of residence)
7. The new nobility and its education. (Multiplicity and unity) (*Powerful* and *puny people*)[95]
8. The woman in women[96]
9. Beehives and workers. *Puny people* and their virtues

10. Allocation of time and of the day. Solitude. Simple diet. Bridging "poor and rich."

11. The new wars (against those who merely enjoy).

12. Punishment and evil people. The new leniency for the sake of those who are coming. Evil people praiseworthy as destroyers, for destruction is necessary.[97] Afterward as a source of power.

13. Life as an experiment: happiness in *figuring things out* or in *experimenting* (skepticism). Death and the desire to see ourselves yield because we are inhibiting life.

14. The breaking of the tablets. The ideal "lawgiver." A herald's proclamation.

15. The I sanctified. "Selfishness" and "imperiousness" above all. Teichm⟨üller⟩ p. 131.[98] Called heretical up to now, all drives, because too strong in the wrong position, rehabilitated.[99]

16. The redemption of those who have passed away. The great noon filled to the brim with unified opposites.[100]

17. Praise of cool dialectical reason, as kingly = strongly influential for feelings. The grateful eye. Warding off the monstrous.

18. The sanctification of laughter and dance. (the body as testimony of growth)

19. The organization of festivals.

20. The innocence of becoming. The struggle with chance. the new "immortality" "will to suffer"

21. The great question.

22. Those who make vows.

16 [85]

Concerning Zarathustra's *convalescence* at the conclusion of the *third part*.

Zarathustra musing like a *god* about whether he will communicate his thought to humans. What motivates a god in relation to humans?

To reinterpret religion from this standpoint: a god in his relationship with humans.

Zarathustra 3. "*I* myself am happy" — when he has **abandoned** humans, *he returns to himself.* It *avoids* him like a cloud. *How* the superhuman being must typically *live*, like an Epicurean god.

a kind of *divine* suffering is the content of Zarathustra 3.

the *human* condition of the lawgiver is only cited as an example

his intense love for his friends seems like an illness to him — he is again at peace.

When invitations arrive, *he gently avoids them.*

Main doctrine: *It lies in* **our** *power to remake suffering into a blessing, poison into nourishment.* Will to suffer.

What it means to be human flew toward me, its shadow surrounded me, then I felt weakness.

16 [86]

To rule? To impose my type on others? Dreadful! Isn't observing a variety of *other people* precisely what makes me happy? Problem.[101]

To challenge to a contest of power precisely those who like to conceal themselves and who would like to live for themselves — even the wise, pious, silent people in our country! Mocking their *enjoyment* of solitude!

All *creative* natures fight for influence even when they live alone — "*posthumous fame*" is merely a false expression for what they want.

The enormous task of those who rule, those who educate themselves — they must *model* within themselves the kind of human beings and peoples over which they want to rule: they must already have become masters *there*!

All virtue and *self-overcoming* makes sense only as a kind of preparation for *those who rule*!

Against all *those who* **merely** *enjoy*! Solitude, too, as self-enjoyment, even the solitude of those who mortify themselves.

A diamond sword cuts every darkness into pieces for me: I have now become clairvoyant — I have certainly been obsessed with clairvoyance for far too long![102]

Good days want to walk on good feet.[103]

Demand: the new law must be capable of being *actualized* — and overcoming and the higher law must grow out of the actualization. Zarathustra makes room for the law by *canceling* the "law of laws," morality.

Laws as backbone.

to work on them and to create, as we perfect them. The previous slave mentality *on* trial!

Zarathustra himself has become a sage who rejoices in his foolishness and a pauper who rejoices in his wealth. Scene: *the fool and the pauper* in 4.

I do not want to establish a single ideal of the sage, but rather a hundred *ideals of the fool!* Zarathustra 4.

Against the ferocious theatrical stoic magnificence of the "sage."

The lawgiver type, its development and its suffering.

What's the point of giving laws at all?

Zarathustra is the herald who summons many lawgivers.

(For 4) Initially law-giving. Then, after the prospect of breeding superhumans has been broached by means of this law-giving — great gruesome moment! Zarathustra proclaims the doctrine of recurrence — which only now has become **bearable**, even for him *for the first time!*

16 [87]

If our fellow humans are *merely* one form of *our perceptions*: then it follows that ruling is merely one form of *self-rule*: and the will to be ruler is = the greatest victory over our own fear and compassion and transformation of the other into *our* function — therefore production of an organism.

16 [88]

I will not *give* to ⟨those⟩ other people the rights that I have won *for myself*: instead they should *steal* them for themselves!

as I do — and may they take them and *rip* them *away* from me! In this way, there must exist a law which is an extension of me, as if it wanted to make all people in my image: so that, in contrast to my image, individuals may discover themselves and make themselves stronger.

New appraisal of human beings: advancing the question:

how much power is in them?

how much multiplicity of drives?

how much ability to communicate and absorb?

Those who rule as *supreme* type.

To make the past fertile and to breed the future — let that be my present time!

Zarathustra himself the jester who jumps over the poor tightrope walker — for 3) self-mockery.

First scene of 3) perhaps "the wanderer" and a conversation with **lightning** *that* **suddenly** *blazes forth*: thus does his will blaze forth suddenly for him.

Mockery of the slavish *subjugation* in morality (under the ancient law of somebody or other)

To form a long-lasting individual (a *people*) in order to translate their thoughts into flesh blood and will

Those who *take* a right for themselves will not *give* this right to others — but rather will be their opponents *in the act of taking it for themselves*: the love of the father who resists the son.[104]

The great educators are like nature: they must pile up *barriers* so that the barriers may be *overcome*.

Against all who enjoy: — ignoble to confront life in only *this way*! To accept all enjoyment as *rest*! In this way, true enjoyment for the first time!

We are punished most severely for our virtues.[105]

A person makes an action valuable: but how should the action make the person valuable!

It is cool, the moon is shining, no cloud is in the sky —
there's no point in living.

16 [89]

Zarathustra 3 Beginning. Recapitulation. You want to teach
about the superhumans[106] — but you have fallen in love with
your friends and with yourself and made life into a refreshment.
The blessed isles make you soft — now you become *depressed*
and passionate and berate your enemies. Sign of weakness: you
avoid a thought.

But you should convince the world and convince humans to
crush themselves.

(The reformer languid in his own community: his enemies
are not strong enough. Thus his greatest enemy must emerge,
a thought,

The thought as an objection *to* life and to the continuation
of life)

16 [90]

Regret: this is revenge on ourselves.

and I give this advice to my enemies and to all those who
spit and spew:

as the teacher of the great contempt (The penultimate)
How could I bear it otherwise, teaching you the great contempt? —[107]

[17 = N VI 6. Autumn 1883]

17 [1][1]

And when someday you can no longer endure life, you must attempt to win its favor — for such has always been the artful strategy of the greatest sages.

Truly their most artful, boldest strategy was to believe in a god just when they felt the devil coming too close.

They learned to switch names for things: and so things became switched around in their minds — behold, this is the artfulness of the greatest sages in its entirety!

Most people are too crazy to be self-interested — their happiness makes all of them crazy.

They sacrifice everything for one thing — this is a kind of love; this willfulness and self-absorption loom over all people.

Their intense insanity bubbles forth out of their love — but it is a poor calculator and despises huckster virtues.[2]

Yet huckster virtue and the huckster's money-grubbing[3] fingers and cold eye — this is even beneath the dignity of an animal.

Everything that can be bought is worth little: I spit this doctrine into the faces of hucksters.

There are things, whether the hucksters know it or not — in whose proximity money sounds completely shameless.

Money passes through all fingers: therefore learn to handle money with kid gloves.

Praise be to puny poverty: for all hucksters scheme after great wealth.

17 [2][4]

Hucksters ⎫
Teachers   ⎬ they all deserve each other[5]
Tools   ⎪
Princes.   ⎭

Concerning *evil people* (imperious people — this is the *mark* of evil people)

17 [3][6]

Those who have always spared themselves a lot will still finally get sick from sparing themselves too much.

He speaks roughly — but not from a rough soul: every gust of wind makes him speak more hoarsely, this sensitive little thing!

Ultimately, the best, most fertile land (*concerning evil people*)

17 [4][7]

Zarathustra makes fun of previous attacks on evil and self-ish people, on passionate people (for the benefit of *weaklings*)

17 [5]

And we often teach despairing people to be strong only by telling them about their weakness.[8]

Some are *gluttons*, others *nibblers* — both contemptible![9]

Begetters and breeders[10]

17 [6][11]

Against **noise**

You can mold and remold the soul by means of nutrition with salts baths and exercise — how could you not bring healing to sick souls?

There were times when oaths and vows were made on a
mortar [12]

In order to change the soul it is necessary to change the
body.[13]

Holy iron shavings and bone fragments, Egyptian nights
locked up in canisters,

having thrown coal on the fire, I have completely smothered
it: it was too small anyway

17 [7][14]

Oh these narrow dull huckster-souls! Whenever money
jumps into the money box, the hucksters jump in along with it.

Whose souls have been a money belt and whose happiness
has been dirty pieces of paper — how could their blood ever
become clean?

It still flows lifeless and poisonous and foul smelling unto
the tenth generation.

stagnant and foamy

17 [8]

We have unlearned this: there is no virtue for all,

there are superior and inferior human beings: equal rights
for all is the most extraordinary injustice.[15]

17 [9][16]

On hucksters.[17]
On substitute teachers.[18]
On princes.
On laws.
On pious people.
On speed.
The great curse.
The city.
— On science — Visit of the fool. — Mocking.
— Zarathustra seeks the cave. Symbol.
— Hermit. — Speech.

17 [10]

And if I cannot live the way I wish,[19] then I have no wish to live — this is how the most saintly people still think.[20]

So, does a drive want to be *satisfied*? Does it want freedom and peace from itself? Has any will ever willed not to will?

That it *creates*, this is what drives all drives: and probably that it also sleeps in for a while — ⟨in order to⟩ become fully awake while creating!

But you distorted the essence of willing into unwillingness and into willing against itself

you misinterpret⟨ed⟩ the voice of the *weary* will

So, is sleep an invention in response to death? And would it be the case that whoever wants to sleep is someone who is weary of dying? The liveliest person can snuffle and snore.[21]

Scribblers and screamers, hasty idlers, those panting with ambition, pushy and shameless people.[22]

"The virtue of daily life suffices" — we must learn modesty even in virtue[23]

17 [11][24]

On diminishment.

The big city. as a stake at which people are burned:

1) the deep thought etc.

clumsy as a corpse[25]

17 [12][26]

Beware, you who are the wealthiest: your puny acts of charity bring impatience and spark more outrage than any miserliness: you drip like wide-bottomed bottles with all-too-narrow necks — bottles like these have already had their necks broken many times.

These neighbors and their puny distress, this city and its meager happiness — this slowly chips away at your strength; you are unlearning how to inflict great pain.

17 [13]²⁷

Contented sows or dying gladiators — don't you have any other options?

A lustful eye cast over a bilious soul²⁸

Whenever something dead is dug up, a lot of living things always get sick; sickness and harmful vapors live under excavated earth.

Gravediggers dig themselves into illness, — — —

We begin as imitators and end up imitating ourselves — this is the last childhood.

The compassion of the greatest people is firm,²⁹ like the handshake of a giant.

I wanted to be a light to them, but I made them blind; this is every sun's complaint, it puts eyes out.

How do I get through the city gate? said Zarathustra — I have unlearned how to be a dwarf.

The greatest thing about great people is what is maternal in them: the father is merely a matter of chance.

For them, being forced to give birth means the future; they do not understand what their happiness will be — they don't gloat about any kind of "freedom."

From my snow-capped peaks on downwards, I find every flower, I am all-too-human, I am also still almost-animal.

My fury still obeys me

and little children do not always come to him who suffers them to come.³⁰

You cough, but this is no objection to strong winds.

Your maw roars: food and drink! Your belly roars in response, lots! Your lusting eye: good!

Alas, says Zarathustra, I cannot exempt myself from hell — the underworld, where everything dead rises up *against* me, and where even the shades speak: life is torture.[31]

Your ailments set themselves against you and accuse you on account of the virtues you gloat about: and what doesn't suit your body, how should this — — —[32]

Your street talking is making you sicker than your street walkers: and precisely these are your most secret sicknesses.

There is a great hypocrisy among you: those who command pretend to have the virtues of those who obey.

Born to rule, but where would I have found a teacher who could teach me how to rule? That's why I am trying to persuade them when I should be commanding them!
Yet persuasion is the flattery that a superior shows to an inferior and that a lord shows to — — —
And not until everything goes as we will, does everything also go as we wish.

It writhes as if about to be martyred: it does not speak, it subjects itself to the martyrdom of keeping quiet.

Oh, Zarathustra advocate of life! You must also be the advocate of suffering![33]
Human beings must become *more evil*. Zarathustra 4 this is the greatest suffering for me — I must *make* them more evil!

and wherever I see the sticky fingers of a huckster, I prefer to draw the short straw.

The black sad sea lies before you — you must cross even beyond that, too![34]

to live among dwarves
I see crumpled houses — a child probably took them out of the box. Crumple⟨d⟩ souls

Time feels different in the dark than in the light.

spoiled by many puny triumphs — he has always had it easy — intimate and welcoming, but lowly like a door through which a tall person does not enter.[35]

Wise forgetfulness and the art of sailing in every wind — two new virtues.[36]

Only those who begin steering toward their goal have the wind at their back.

To outwit chance and lead it around by the hand — suffer chance to come to me, it is innocent like a little child.[37]

The doctrine of *life* Zarathustra 4 terrible-dithyrambic
Seed of life strewn from star to star.[38]

Beauty cloaks the man

— to become smooth and hard-hearted, we must bring our secret solitude into the crowd.[39]

"it hurts, therefore it is bad" — this is the oldest and most recent conclusion and the basest of all base things.
Ever since I have understood this origin of bad things, I have laughed at all this babble about good and bad.
Beyond what is good and bad

I respect virtue when it is the caution of someone who is pregnant: but what do I care about the virtue of those who are infertile!

17 [14]

sparing of ourselves, the wise forgetting, the bliss of those who hope, the generosity of those who also conceal their aloneness,[40] — — —

Fear has made humans tame: their weakness has grown out of the fear they feel of their monster "selfishness and imperiousness."

So why, then, do you howl through the night, you monster? You writhe, you torment yourself, what could bring you comfort?

You are sleeping poorly, an evil dream has come to you, you are groaning under the weight of evil thoughts.[41]

You want the best for yourselves and you still want even the best for me, now then — what would be the point of hurting you with my pain!

There would be so much of you that would be ruined because of me, and so little that would be improved: let me be silent!

I am sad for you and I have a grudge against myself on your account: alas that I am ⟨not⟩ strong enough to deliver you from evil dreams!

Your eyes stay open, they are sleepy, half-dead, sad eyes: your mouth is open, a gurgling choking sound

the fear of you had crippled them — awe lets them walk again

warm breath, limbs stretched out
drunk with sleep — an open eye and yet a vacant stare, he — lost to himself — seeking something, sullen
I trust you even more in a storm
your countless jaws and bared teeth

Thus my destiny lies before me like the sea, in dark sadness, chagrined, aged, still drunk with sleep, with open mouth, dreaming.[42]

Alas the eye open, and still a vacant stare, breathing warmly, wound around ⟨itself⟩, slurping

17 [15][43]

There is the black sad sea, like my destiny it lies before me — an open eye, but still craving sleep and still not looking in my direction.

Alas, the sea breathes with warm breath, like my destiny, wound around itself on the pillow of its crags, and groans in evil anticipation.

I am sad for you, you dark monster, and for your sake I bear a grudge against myself. Alas, that I do not possess enough strength to deliver you from evil dreams!

— What are you doing, Zarathustra? Do you want to comfort the sea with your song? Have you already become a compassionate spectator of your own future?

Alas, you are a love-sick fool and excessively trusting! even toward everything that is terrible! ⟨You⟩ go to every monster in order to pet it!

A breath of warm air, a bit of soft fur around the claws: and already seductive tones are pouring from your flute — truly ⟨you⟩ are yearning for *everything* that is alive!

Better to trust your destiny, you blissful trusting man, even if it roars like a sea from a thousand maws — better still its teeth bared against you in a storm than such a pregnant black sullenness at night!

Your tenderness toward everything that lives is your danger, oh Zarathustra! If you would have no creative will, watch out!

All those who create must become hard hammers! Come to me, you most terrible of smiths who forges even the hammer itself into hardness.

17 [16][44]

Now everything is just great! For the hucksters are wearing swords and walrus mustaches, and the regiment itself is the place of the bowlegged.[45]

Now everything is just great!

The best regents without principles, bringing joy to many — and my best friends are among them

He felt no lust for crime, his taste was too healthy and bright for such lusts.
But he also spared himself nothing and he committed crimes against crime, for now he took the shortest paths.
And if a straight line is not a path at all, then the shortest path must be the crooked one

It is a shipwreck that first spits him toward his promised land[46]

The greatest danger lies behind us — over there, where the blessed isles are

I think little of prayer, I think more kindly of cursing: and now I call upon you to curse all cowardly devils who whimper and fold their hands and want to pray.

the sea has gone mad — a snow-white mon⟨ster⟩ has just enough snow to drink its fill until mentally ill.
Now you speak to me of praying

Goats geese and other crusaders, led by the holy spirit[47]

you will be slit open, they believe that you have swallowed gold

I am Zarathustra the Godless: who is more godless than I?[48]

telling stories around the evening campfire (instead of the doctrine)

to set crowns on our own heads

with a voice like a stonemason's chisel.

they creep around everywhere like lice

lust loves twilight: adventure shuns the day.

Pity those who would want to entertain others[49] if this were no longer their livelihood!
They must fight with the wild animal, hunger, otherwise their entertainment would be that of a wild animal — aimed at us.

There are people with skills and people with jobs, there are those who can stand on their own — they have to stand up for themselves.

Thus do I praise myself for my part. Now it was your turn to praise me.

ill people and obsessed people

queasy and querulous

you soon become accustomed to what is around you: and where you customarily sit becomes the seat of customs.

and with you I will always be like oil and water — floating on top, unless we get vigorously shaken up together.

servile and supine

You call them stilts — but they are pride's strong feet

He rises and swells beyond all bounds: is it possible that his
fate soured him?

a contrarian is a bad spouse to himself

"by accident"[50] — this is not a good nobleman, even if he is
of the oldest line[51]

trumpeters and other butterflies

17 [17][52]
By all that is bright and strong and good

"wisdom is a creative labor pain" *goodness*
a means and a tool, like — — —

Next to every warehouse I saw an alehouse
that's where they look for wine
And anyone who does not find warmth in spiced wine looks
for it in spicy women.

A shipwreck spat him toward land.[53]

17 [18][54]
No **"I"** in Zarathustra 4!

17 [19]
Why are you blaspheming against yourself?

17 [20][55]
a puny community in the middle of nowhere, and their
miserably clad mystification[56]

Z⟨arathustra⟩ the Godless?[57]

You are being pursued, a price has been put on your head

Keep it up, they can pursue us all they want: until now, success has always come to those who are most relentlessly pur⟨sued⟩[58]

17 [21][59]

Where is Zarathustra coming to us from? Who are father and mother to him?[60] Destiny and laughter are Zarathustra's f⟨ather⟩ and mother: cruel destiny and loving laughter spawned a scion like that.

Cheerfulness as the secret foretaste of death.

"I am seeking Zarathustra. Zarathustra became lost to me.

17 [22][61]

the will to evil how it grows brighter and more beautiful on the contrarians[62]

origin of virtue

Did I come to vilify vice and to warn against pickpockets?[63]

17 [23]

The sky is on fire and the sea spits at me[64]

17 [24][65]

common and limited enough for the most limited advantages, they still read the rubbish of their happiness like tea leaves.

They are rich: but their eyes are still thieves' eyes.

put good clothes on them — now they are rag-pickers and vultures in disguise.

Curse — the brotherhood of hatred and lightning bolts

I went in search of origins — this alienated me from all reverence: and all around me it became strange and lonely.

But finally reverence itself blossomed secretly again — and behold! my tree of the future sprang forth for me —:

Now I sit in its shadow.

17 [25][66]

relentlessly pursued, never caught!

putrid, tepid, rancid blood

you wanted to take the wildness out of humans, but you have made them weak

you made wolves into dogs and humans themselves into the finest human pets.

17 [26][67]

On Scribblers and Screamers

17 [27][68]

to bring unity into the greatest tension of a multitude of oppositions — *goal*.

to *condemn* single drives *as heretical* and to *kill* them for those who cannot bring them into a beautiful unity — inferior moralities — their *value*.

the highest dialectic and its equal in every way, the strength of feeling.

what is *most terrible*: imperiousness and selfishness *saints*

17 [28][69]

Chorus of fools "once we were *sages*"

17 [29][70]

a movement like a storm — and one goal and serenity at every place on the route

Zarathustra discovered that human beings had become *inferior*.[71]

evil people as destroyers worth honoring — destruction is *necessary*.[72]

Self-love and self-contempt — synthesis.

"Who among us is a seducer?" said Zarathustra and smiled — for a memory had come to him.

to cram the great noon full of resolved oppositions.[73]

It is the age of puny people[74]

17 [30]
There are those who are actors without knowing it and those who are actors without wanting it.[75]

Some people will: but most are only willed.[76]

To have a better sense of justice in my little finger[77] than they have in their heads.[78]

As long as selfishness is considered to be fundamentally *evil*, you will *never* honestly be able to derive anything good from it — and you *have to* honestly derive everything from it. For that reason *I* have the organic-moral.[79]

17 [31][80]
Zarathustra 4 at the end: fulfillments
Zarathustra 1 Preface: poor people (lowly, superfluous people) as rich people, the sages happy to feel ignorant and foolish for a while (to become *fools* — **festival of fools**)
Choruses of poor people
of fools

Zarathustra 3, 1 premonition that terrible things will happen.
            3, 2 the *wanderer's* deepest *semblance of serenity to collect* the *most painful things*

17 [32]

to be burned at the stake, not for our faith, but for our *doubt*![81]

You ride quickly to your goal; but your lame foot will arrive with you at the same time![82]

You say it is moral to do good for your neighbors? But then you would already have to know what is *good for them*!

17 [33][83]
On servants
a) rich people
b) kings
Priests and merchants *now rule.*

17 [34]

There is a secret insight: great crimes are no longer needed — but rather *many small ones.*

in no way do I want "*the happiness of others*!" — I much prefer their discomfort and despair *under certain conditions*!

What! To tell the "*truth*"! I want to express my *feelings* and not **to conceal** myself.[84] Sp⟨encer⟩ D⟨ata of⟩ Eth⟨ics⟩ p. 269.[85]

Egoism not in contradiction with the *heroic mode of thought*!

Generosity, how you allow so many foreign and hostile thought processes to get power over you, you thinkers!

trapped in their *tiny* hearts[86]

17 [35][87]

Deeply mistrustful of destiny, ready for sudden decisions, badly governed

Do I love human beings? Do I love myself? But they are a part of my plan, like me.

17 [36][88]

Zarathustra 3 *On Boredom*.

17 [37]

I require a lot of altruism **for** the sake of my ego and its lust to *possess*.

ἀκρασία!![89]

17 [38][90]

This is the choice I have given myself: whatever *I did not want before, this is what* I **must want** *afterward* (putting things right, fitting things in — digesting — but checking to see *if* I can do it!

17 [39][91]

§ to make a poor person *rich* Emerson p. 383.[92]

§ Bliss within the greatest expanse of the soul, longest ladder up and down

working redemptively *against* stuffy "sages."

The world — **exuberance of a god**[93]

Sin as *enjoyment* of self-abolishing.[94]

17 [40][95]

you are overlooking what a monstrous thing *every* organic process already is, what a unity of opposites.

To hurl ourselves again into opposites, after a drunken moment of reconciliation.

the *most expansive* soul, which can err the furthest within itself[96]

the greatest sages, who hurl themselves into the ocean of foolishness

the most necessary people, who hurl themselves into coincidences

the one who is, who is *becoming*
the one who has, who *wants*
to approach each other again and again and to flee again
and again
the soul, **for which everything is a game**[97]

17 [41][98]
§ ⟨Zarathustra⟩ 4 What is *bad*?
§ ⟨Zarathustra⟩ 4 the most superior soul, depiction of
superhumans

Do you not see how time is only an audacity and space an
exuberance? And which mischief of freedom can be more mis-
chievous than my rolling wheel of reasons and conclusions?

they want no one to hurt them: that is why they come
before him and please him — these cowards![99]

17 [42]
Epictetus as **opposite**

17 [43][100]
11245 Reclus.

17 [44][101]
The one who warns: Zarathustra! Everything is ready to fall
apart.[102] Tell your people to save themselves and to give up
their self-indulgent solitude.
Zarathustra: Let my people be gathered and let heralds
summon them to come to the great noon.

17 [45][103]
Recipe for the mundane
Do what you want, but take care not to offend with it,
Do what you can, but take care not to be conspicuous about
it.

17 [46]
they want to learn how to *play* and have yet to learn how to be *serious*.[104]

It might be possible to fly — but first you have to know how to *dance* like an angel.

No leaps in virtue! But a different path for every person! Yet the supreme path is not for everyone! Still, everyone can be a *bridge* and a *lesson* for others![105]

17 [47]
Perhaps it is not permissible to think about the meaning and value of art and artists as I do here, especially not now: perhaps even less so to write about this the way I do — : perhaps I have many things to atone for.

17 [48]
A small light, but even so, a great comfort[106]

deep mistrust (of nature) *needed*

the breeding of *strong* humans.

Do what you *want* — assuming that you are the kind of people who can will and not be willed.[107]

Love your neighbors as yourselves, assuming that you love yourselves[108]

17 [49][109]
The average person today is my greatest enemy — I owe it to Rée that I have gotten to know this person.

He had no ch⟨aracter⟩: what could he do? So he had to steal one for himself.[110]

17 [50][111]

Not to *believe* in God.

Consequently things do *not* go as God wills. (Against the cowardly *submissiveness* that has made human beings **weak**: I teach a *profound mistrust* of this.)

17 [51][112]

Zarathustra 3. He wonders: what has made human beings so *puny*, anyway?

Opposite of his friends

moral *phrases* as a theatrical means of *enhancing ourselves.*

his disgust grows ever greater

how pleased I ⟨am⟩ that I have my *friends* and that my thought *lives in them*!

to fritter away

Happiness does not want to be sought, but rather to be found.

We should no longer seek what we have.

Anyone who has nothing to do is troubled by nothingness.

Whatever I want to do for you, you *can*not do for me! And whatever I do not want you to do for me, why should *I* not do this for you?

17 [52][113]

§ against the dubiousness of justice

§ against *clemency*, as if we have to spare superfluous people! "Alas, how necessary is everything that is superfluous!" you tell me

§ against *weakness*, induced by *trust*. I teach profound mistrust.[114]

§ against anxiety about *shedding blood*

in short: against all morality as *weakening*.

§ against religious communities à la Moravians[115] —
Christians.

Concerning Zarathustra 4. You must first gain *strength* as
destroyers!

17 [53][116]

they are getting weaker and *weaker* — ever since I stopped
seeing them.

Mockery of my blessed isles, where some have *fled* — after a
while *it doesn't matter*!

Concerning Zarathustra 4) It is high time *to stir up* the
flame again.

It is now necessary to give up God: humankind *would become*
too **feeble** *otherwise*.

17 [54][117]

Defiance in self-abasement, going so far that he demands
deadly revenge on *witnesses*

that's why God must *die*!

Even the animals are *new*: thus I myself am willing it once
again, *anew*.

Zarathustra 4. Widespread revolution — the sinking of the
isles as *omen*.

17 [55][118]

Zarathustra 3. The consolation of the saint outrages Zarathustra, he recognizes where weakness *comes from*.

Onward! Once again!

The saint: Do you want all this once again? and *leaves*.

After this, Zarathustra summons the most burdensome
thought.

⟨Zarathustra⟩ 3. Weakness your danger!

⟨Zarathustra⟩ 3. A devil's grimace.

⟨Zarathustra⟩ 3. Was the journey necessary?

Happiness is chasing after me: that's because I do not chase
after women — and happiness is a woman.

17 [56][119]

It is still too early for Zarathustra: up to now I was still my own precursor

The superhumans emerge around the *midpoint* of the *course.*

the success of all things that are relentlessly pursued[120]

My tombs opened: my pain which had been buried alive, rose again — it had slept well under shrouds, in order now to get in a good night's watch.[121]

not to wade through foreign slime.[122]

⟨Zarathustra⟩ 4 Supreme moment: one *more* time in the name of all being![123]

17 [57]

The thought that morality owes its origin to lawgivers and that — — —

17 [58][124]

Beware of willing anything halfway: be decisive in indolence and in action. And whoever wants to be lightning must be a cloud for a long time.[125]

You must learn the long silence: and no one should see into your depths. But not because your water is cloudy and your face is unreadable, but rather because your depths are too deep.

17 [59][126]

And anyone who woos the virtues of the strong should forgo the virtues of the weak: and let there be no contempt in your renunciation.

How can you want to learn to dance when you have not even learned to walk! And those who fly, and their bliss, are even above those who dance

Already I feel that I am dreaming: so perhaps I am almost awake?

We should only steal when we cannot rob: thus speaks the code of honor among rogues.

17 [60][127]

Prescription   1) strengthen the will
                   2) no lasciviousness
                   3) learn silence
                   4) learn solitude
                   5) profound mistrust and profound trust[128]
                   6) *seek out* your[129] enemies, yet *find* your
                      friends.

17 [61][130]

I do not want you to do anything "in order" or "because" and "so that," but rather everything for its own sake and for the pleasure it gives you.

An end is what desecrates every thing and every deed: for whatever must become the means is desecrated

17 [62][131]

Plant yourself **in the soil** — as a new duty
Praise of **chance**, as it seeks out its friends
Doctrine of *long-term willing* in place of happiness
The old values *annihilated*

17 [63][132]

So much goodness, so much weakness! It is not yet time to be benevolent.

§ *On the community of cowards*
Your stone is getting brittle!
to give the will a backbone
§ Our dignity as an *eternal* type
§ science teaches him nothing but its own *fleetingness* and *transitoriness*

17 [64][133]

My freedom's curiosity for novelty[134] took flight, even into prisons.

17 [65][135]

A curse on the fact that the best people secluded themselves without having children.

17 [66][136]

Zarathustra 3 There is a hesitation within you: this created — — —

Modestly embracing a little happiness and, in that very moment, already modestly making eyes at another little happiness.

Watch out if you wanted to buy them, but offered too little, and thereby made their virtue stronger!

17 [67][137]

At noon, my happiness loomed hot above me ⟨and⟩ sucked thirstily from my ocean, I love strong winds and also know where they go and from where they roar. Soon I will become a strong storm

to implant our will so that it will become a long-term will and a tall tree with broad branches.

§ I do not want the *virtues of the strong* to be confused with something else.[138]

17 [68]

Napoleon's speech — contempt for h⟨uman beings⟩, he drives his nation to the heights and again awakens the thought that a people may only live by finding faith in his *supreme* right.[139]

to make *hard-hearted*	instead of meek
— long-term	instead of fleeting
— proud	instead of modest

Conscience

A chiseled arrow —

Do not speak to me of events! Nothing will ever happen to you except you yourselves[140]

17 [69][141]

§ ⟨Zarathustra⟩ 4 the great contempt in the face of the *eternity* of the *individual*.

After that, *redeeming*: behold! *I teach you* about the *superhumans*

§ ⟨Zarathustra⟩ 3 none of them believe in their *supreme right* — peoples sages etc.

Conclusion of Zarathustra 3 "Arise abysmal thought! Now I am your equal!"[142] "*Make it hard as stone.* You are my hammer! —

Bliss of predetermined nature — hymn.

⟨Zarathustra⟩ 3 Beginning. You have *abandoned* many things already —

Long eulogy with mockery at the end

All honor to those with a lust for power who *took* their *contempt out* on *weak* humans.[143]

17 [70][144]

Anyone who up to now has had the most contempt for people — has this person in doing so not always been the people's greatest benefactor?

Take the child away — its gaze kills!

17 [71][145]

wrapped in a black cloud — do I bring you the plague?

eternal satisfaction hurled itself into its opposite

17 [72][146]

journalists as *corpse robbers* taking something from the half-dead and the dead

Zarathustra 4 "let them come to *me*!"[147]

"You bring good news: the swamp is moving"

If the most superior h⟨uman⟩ being is not a ruler of the people, then the hucksters will rule.

Say it mornings and evenings: I despise hucksters, I want to break their fingers.
Better more Handel than handlers![148]

against *teachers* who are not role models

Conclusion
Behold, this is unchosen bl⟨iss⟩

17 [73][149]
    A. Blanqui
            l'éternité par les astres
                                    Paris 1872.[150]

17 [74][151]
    the suffering of superior people on account of the imperfection of their inferiors
    ⟨the suffering⟩ of God on account of h⟨uman⟩k⟨ind⟩
    you have understood how to strangle ambition within them: to be the last among you — this would give them more pleasure than to be the first
    What makes superior humans suffer is not that which is inferior to them, but rather knowing that there is still something superior to them

17 [75]
    Zarathustra 3. *alone godless terrible terrifying*, Zarathustra should appear this way to the hermit —
    the predatory *lion* who finds delusion and arbitrariness in what is most holy

17 [76]

to make *enemies*, ever *more intellectual* ones — or everything becomes dull

Did I really come here to make human beings happy?

Whoever seeks pleasure will find little of it — even if seeking it for others

Pleasure is a woman: she runs after anyone who spurns her.[152]

17 [77][153]

Zarathustra 3 Beginning. ⟨Zarathustra⟩ is satisfied — the *seed is well sown*.

He has much *in store* for his disciples: first they must **ripen**.

17 [78][154]

you figure out how to be happy and in the process you forget all future generations

Miscalculation in regard to *happiness* — we must *want* unhappiness.

to sacrifice the happiness of contemporaries for *future generations*.[155]

Ask women:[156] having a good time is not the point of giving birth.

17 [79]

There will be qualities having to do with our intellect that pertain to it as an intellect, *and other qualities* that pertain to it as a human intellect: this is now the point of actual conflict, and we must not tire of sorting differentiating doubting and offering things to be learned

17 [80][157]

not to determine the value of things according to accompanying phenomena, c.g., letting labor pains dictate what birth is about! Then it would certainly be bad!

"There is something that wants to *command* me. Why are we wrestling with each other, let's see who is stronger!" this is how people become evil.

Alas for my melancholy! And even if I can still make it smile — angels should dissolve into tears when they see this smile. In the afternoon, when all light grows still.

Now no one who loves me remains alive; how could I still love life!

this thought! it only has to touch me with its fingertips and I shiver and blush — and my heart beats until I feel it in my throat.

now I know it and I have grown happy and tired along with it — now "that's enough!" — According to you — yet *I* want to *do* what I told you to think
Artists

their hearts were courteous even in the face of frustrating coincidence — they took it as wisdom for hedgehogs, to raise their quills against destiny.

Here is something that commands — and not even a living soul with eyes and eyes of lightning, but rather — — —

When the hours slip away from us on tiptoes, in the afternoon, there where even all light grows more still —

The ocean lies there, long and spread out: and without shame in its blue nakedness?

And whenever I have no ladder, then I climb on top of my own head

Zarathustra, said the helmsman, I don't like this!

To depict what was heart-wrenching about my break with W⟨agner⟩.

It got so still for me — there was no stillness before this: ⟨when⟩ no one thinks of me and everyone speaks of me.

He is unshakeable: and when he complains, it is more a concession to you and it is a cloak that he throws over his hard-heartedness.

Alas, my yoke is heavy! the yoke of supreme obsession.
The only thing I have ever sought is my home, this hits home[158] with me the hardest.

17 [81]
It is a mistake to see altruism as a *refinement* of egoism. This would mean ranking it too highly.

The drives whose effect is most emphatically called selfish are the least selfish, e.g., the urges for food sex and wealth. *Here* there is not yet any thought of a *self* but rather only of the preservation of a specimen "human."
The *control* of these urges (or *making them more difficult to satisfy!*) is a consequence of the craving for *self*, of a feeling of *self.*

the common drives want *above all* and *only* to be satisfied at the cost of the other drives.

17 [82][159]
— and the chimes of the bell are running in soft shoes —

And when the frost makes our souls crack and crunch, we rejoice: and we do not praise the land where butter and honey — flow.[160]

A costly drop of sweet spicy wine hidden in a block of ice
— this is happiness to me — yes, if there were gods they
would be envious of me on account of this drop!

And even when someone wants to lie down in *our* sunny
spot, then we laugh, full of doubts, and we ask ourselves: are
we made in order to make others happy!

For us, happiness is the great exception and source of wonder: we fear it and we fear being in it, we gently push it away
from us, as a mistrustful lover would do.

17 [83]

tricky as doors that secretly open, so that the thieving wind
whooshes through

17 [84]

Look at this clear sky, will you! Has it not swallowed up and
guzzled all of the stars — and yet it found its innocence again.

My happiness once descended into a valley in order to find
lodging, my own sweet burning happiness, there I found these
pure souls open, like welcoming gates.

Alas, it rankles me and it worms around, my silly worm and
abyss of thought!

17 [85][161]

Zarathustra, said the h⟨ermit⟩, until now I took you for a
sage, but what amazes me about you above all else is that I
now see that you are clever as well. The worst lies behind us
— yet you have escaped.

and looked at him sideways.

loutish virtues

17 [86]

Once I have overcome myself in regard to this, who then will overcome me? And that is why this victory will be the seal of my perfection!

how could I dare to call you forth and look upon you!

17 [87][162]

Only then, when Zarathustra has mastered his greatest pain, will he fight for victory against his greatest dragon.

It was refugees and castaways who discovered new lands: half-destroyed people have always been the conquerors.

Zarathustra, if we do not perish for your sake, we will make our escape for your sake. But I have never seen things this bad, and nevertheless the worst now lies *behind us.*

Yet the helmsman who had been the last to hear Zarathustra speak, uncovered his head and said reverently — — —

17 [88]

La gaya scienza[163] is absolutely necessary for someone who thinks as I do and *wants* something like this.

17 [89]

Honor and perfection to you oh Zarathustra!

18 [1]¹

If you can't pray, why can't you at least curse? Don't you see that we are fighting for our lives?

I fear you because you laugh while we fight for our lives: you look like someone who is sure that you will live.

Or die — said Zarathustra.

And if we get out of this, I want to say "God is not² — and Zarathustra taught me this."

I forgive you your mistrust, yet I give you nothing in exchange for your trust.³

I found in all things an arrogance that I called divine. And since I also found this arrogance in my soul, I also call my soul div⟨ine.⟩⁴

You believe in wonders and wonderworkers; true need would also teach you how to pray. The old counterfeiters of the mind have also minted a counterfeit of your intellect.

He lays his hand on millennia.

18 [2]⁵

On Tumult.

4. Once, as Zarathustra was shipwrecked and spit out toward land and once, as he was riding a wave, he wondered: "where

has my destiny gone? I do not know where I should go from here. I am losing myself." He hurls himself into the *tumult*. Then, overcome by disgust, he looks for **comfort** *in* **something** — in himself[6]

18 [3]

the *one who flies* (as a discoverer who lays his hand on a millennium)

18 [4][7]
    4. On *Puny People*.
    5. Hucksters
    etc.

18 [5]

That the dice might fall the wrong way for us, is this a reason not to play dice? On the contrary — that's where the spice is.[8]

18 [6]

In *painful* agitation, Zarathustra tests violent people, fools, and those who fly, in order to determine if he *finds himself in them* — *to no avail*!

Only *after* he learns of the death of friends

He does not find himself in *any* human being — so he seeks out *animals*.

§ intensely **mocking** himself as *advocate* of *life*

3. The *helmsman's* story. Zarathustra's awful night.

4. Cheerfulness.

18 [7]

I do not like sullen sneaks and salamanders. I can't stand will-o'-the-wisps either and everything that comes out of the swamp.

So is life a swamp?

18 [8]

A little song, but a great comfort for those who can sing it: and truly they must be good songbirds!

18 [9]

Suffering overflowed within him: this broke forth and poured down toward a sea of patriarchs.

He called the sea of all patriarchs, God— for this, righteous men called him a blasphem⟨er.⟩

18 [10]

Alas, my soul, how did you grow so hard-hearted toward the one who had such superabundant love for you!

18 [11]

egomaniacal, self-obsessed, still not heard — and at the same time a hero

18 [12]

Whenever gold clinks, there a whore winks. And there are more whores than gold pieces. Whoever can be bought I call a whore. And there are more who can be bought than there are gold pieces.

18 [13]

I am best at despising life: and I love life most of all: there is no paradox in this — no contradiction.

Emotional torment

18 [14]

§ My head is foolish, but my heart is wise.

§ Everything leaves and passes away — everything comes back.

— and leaving and passing away themselves come back

This now over there,[9] has already been — it has already been countless times

This doctrine has never been taught before. How's that? It has been taught countless times already — Zarathustra has taught it countless times.

18 [15][10]

Pain teaches hens and artists to cluck. Ask women: having a good time is not the point of giving birth.

I saw wood piled up for someone to be burned at the stake: brittle and pressed down, the woodpile waited for a spark: its own weight oppressed it

He breathed out his desires to the boys: he rasped[11] his words through dried-out gums, but the boys did not hear him

We must scream at boys: violently rip open the door of their ears and eyes

18 [16]

In the dumbest world, there is indescribable enjoyment to be had even in a *small bit of reason.*

Often I no longer know what I should ward off; I prefer to jump in and try things for *myself.*

The power to transform things into *myself,* always growing. Assuming there were a God, the world could never be conceived as dumb enough for him.

18 [17]

to observe pain magnanimously — often the third generation is the first one to **deal with** *our* pain i.e., a new power has grown within that generation.

magnanimous in regard to *people of the future* — and this is the magnanimity of those who create, who love their work more than their today.

satisfied people by far the most dangerous (satisfied with *given* ideals) especially the satisfied *puny sullen people.*

18 [18][12]

So have I come to vilify vice? And to warn against pick-pockets and shoplifters?

Did I not come to teach them my riches and all my full-ness's excess yearning

18 [19][13]

On *Princes*.
On *Teachers*.
On *Evil People*.
On *Fame*.
Conversation with Lightning

18 [20]

On the *Great Yearning*.
On Divine Desires[14]
On Pregnancy.

18 [21]

to force my enemies back behind their gate and to paint pale spots on the side of their gate

The way through all 7 solitudes: in the end, the serpent

18 [22]

Did I not teach you about — the superhumans?

18 [23][15]

What do you know of sensuality! What could you know of sensuality!

Sensuality is one thing, giving birth is another. Ask women: having ⟨a⟩ g⟨ood time⟩ is not the point of giving birth.

Pain makes artists and hens cluck. Sensuality is silent — hear now my words on fame.

thus she waits in the family way,[16] radiant and satisfied, the pregnant one.

18 [24][17]

If you have your virtue in your ears, just see how well you endure the noise of life. We are punished most often for our virtues.

18 [25]

My destiny, defend me from all small victories! Preserve me so that, just this once, my triumph — is as great as this destiny.

I am speaking to you, *providence of my soul*, destiny

that I will be a surprise and never be anticipated, appearing like a ghost

that I do not grasp fear, but rather require the greatest danger in order to break free of the disgust that life pours into me.

18 [26]

How many *caves* there are in life!

Being accustomed to caves, our yearning for them — a passage through dark tubes

18 [27]

You bolt of lightning, cutting diamond, gold zigzag! Answer me, so that I can see whether you are cutting and sharp only for the sake of appearance.

I often took you for a thinker — because, as with you, a thought walks through clouds: and as with you, a thought awakens the thunder that sleeps and rumbles behind the clouds.

18 [28]

I learned to walk on a day that was awake: to walk lightly on steady feet through a day that was awake.

While sleeping and dreaming — tell me, what did I learn that put me in a good mood even while sleeping and dreaming?

18 [29]
  NB whenever I climbed up the *mountain ridges*
  a herald for all brothers of the noon

18 [30][18]
  Sneaks, mousetraps

— For am I a tricky money-huckster and a jingling purse?

Even in the good old days every day brought me a bad newspaper

I have found this arrogance of wisdom in all things: that it tells all things to walk on the feet of fools.

As little reason as possible: she does not take anything more in her knapsack, this arrogant wisdom when she tills her field during the day and walks across country.

As l⟨ittle⟩ r⟨eason⟩ a⟨s⟩ p⟨ossible⟩ — this is, more delicately phrased: chance. All things run there and back on the feet of chance — — —

Happiness and innocence are the most shameful things on earth: neither wants to be sought. We should *have them* — and we should not even know that we have them.

their thoughts run counter to me: their meaning is a counter-meaning, their wit is a yes-but wit — but they do not stand and they do not walk — — —

Everything speaks, everything betrays, and today's rasping ghost is already tomorrow's trumpeting at the marketplace

My foot is a cloven hoof: and I trot and totter with it over hill and dale, day and night, across and overland, and I am the devil's own, whenever lust makes me run fast

My hand is a fool's hand: pity all tables and walls and anywhere else that saves a place for fools' truths

My mouthpiece belongs to the people: my speech is strange to all scribblers and ink-slingers

18 [31][19]

    On the Will to Suffer
    On Unchosen Bliss.
    Before Sunrise
    On Self-Diminution.
    The Wintersong
    On Passing By
    The Return Home of the Solitary One.
    The Other Dance Song.

18 [32]

Selfishness: a dirty and libelous word for the nature of everything living — that it wants to grow and to create beyond itself

that each and every thing walks around pregnant with its future — the lust of pregnant things and that, in its lust, it is often a miracle to itself

18 [33]

The powerful call their happiness virtue — their flowing overflowing happiness, their gift-giving that rules.

18 [34][20]

Everything talks, everything is talked to death; and what today still seems too hard for the tooth of time will tomorrow already be rent and ripped to pieces, hanging from a hundred maws.

Everything talks, everything goes unheard; people might try to ring in their wisdom with bells, the hucksters at the marketplace drown them out with the clinking of pennies.

Everything talks, no one wants to listen. All water roars to the ocean, every creek hears only its own roar.

Everything talks, no one wants to understand. Everything falls into the water, yet nothing falls into deep wells.

Everything talks, everything sets things right. Injustice is pursued — relentlessly pursued but rarely captured.[21]

Everything talks, no⟨thing⟩ succeeds, everything clucks, but no one wants to lay eggs.

Oh my brothers! That you are not learning silence from me! And solitude!

Everything talks, no one knows what to say. Everything runs, no one learns to walk anymore.

Everything talks, no one hears me sing: Oh that you did not learn stillness from me! And the suffering of solitude!

18 [35][22]

The time of gods was at an end long ago: they laughed themselves — to death.

This happened when the most godless word of all went out from a god himself — the word:[23] you shall have no other gods before me: thus an old graybeard of a god forgot himself.

A god has never been so pathetic in his jealousy as to command: "you should have no other gods before me!"

And back then all gods laughed and wobbled on their chairs and cried out: "Is it not the nature of divinity that there are gods but no God?"

You rogue-jester Zarathustra, how divinely you spoke to the last person who still believes in God!

18 [36]

And when I had done what was most difficult for me and was celebrating my triumphs of overcoming, blissful and exhausted, then they screamed — they claimed I had stepped thoughtlessly on the toes of their vanity.

They all want to make themselves into a statute: and those who can only climb, command: "thou shalt not fly."

I am hard on myself: and I often take revenge for being hard on myself by ignoring the injustice that others have committed — their i⟨njustice⟩ against me!

And even if it is your *guilt*: I take it upon myself and call it *my* guilt.

18 [37]
And how could I talk you out of your willing, you with the will of a lion! For I can read all of your willing in your eyes.

18 [38]
I bless you, oh Zarathustra, just as if you, along with me, belonged to one god and were a child of the same hope.

The way I see you — how could you want things to go badly? Even if I do not understand what you say right away

This is, after all, what you are saying: and I will be astounded if you should ever persuade anyone with talk like this — unless it would be corpses and buffoons

And I prefer to believe that you could win over animals rather than people: especially your own animals! that ugly serpent there and the roaring bird![24]

Thus spoke the hermit, for he was afraid of Zarathustra's animals: and when the serpent stuck out its head just a little, behold, then the hermit jumped up and ran away.

Thus they parted from one another, laugh⟨ing⟩ like 2 b⟨oys.⟩

18 [39]
This is *my* word that wanted to choke me!!
This is *my* serpent that crept into my craw

18 [40]

What was most difficult for me, I learned to do in secret: who had eyes for it, when I embarked alone into terrifying new oceans?

And when I turned my back on all beloved idols, who *saw* me go! Unseen I strode out into the burning deserts.

18 [41]
The sealing[25]

18 [42]

And always, when I thought of my solitude, truly, it was always as if I spoke from far away "oh precious solitude!"

18 [43][26]

"Humans are something that must be overcome": to my ears this sounds like a laughing dancing piece of wisdom. But they think I am calling them — to crawl to the cross!

Certainly: before we learn how to dance, we must learn how to walk.

18 [44]
To live for the sake of the future §
the breaking of the *tablets*

18 [45][27]
Redemption! I spit out the serpent's head!
Redemption! I taught the will even how to will backwards
stillest hour Zarathustra you are ripe — lioness doves

Every time the *midpoint* when the *will* to the *future* emerges: *the greatest event awaits*!

Prosperity and loving refreshment[28]
Oh loving refreshment of my heart!

18 [46][29]

Or did they fear my cursing? — for my curse is the brother-hood of hatred and of lightning bolts

They have made puny advantages puny — and now they are reading even the rubbish of good fortune like tea leaves!

Scarcely had fate soured them a bit — than they rose and swelled beyond all bounds.

These people in puny communities in the middle of nowhere, mist and conceit of all Bible-thumpers[30]
soft fleeting modest[31]

18 [47]

That I have a decent handful of courage for living: this means, I have a little key on me — which leads to nothingness.
That I have a decent handful of courage for nothingness — this means: I know that all nothingness — — —
The handful of force, my I — ridiculed by the universe of forces!
What I want? — to make *courage* into a small key for those who have failed
Courage for the few, to have their will prevail against the way-too-many
To compose and to create something *higher* than humans have been up to now
completely without responsibility, to embark into being, to teach bliss, which says: I want this one more time *for* ⟨the sake⟩ *of this moment.*

18 [48][32]

Ring of Rings

I whenever I dreamed of being the midpoint and noon of humankind.
II whenever I, like the alpenglow, brought back everything great from the past and made it shine.

III whenever I molded the future like wax.

IV whenever I broke the tablets and threw them down the mountain.

V whenever I went out — arrogance skepticism.

18 [49]

Humans are something that must be overcome: this is the doctrine of life as the great self-overcoming.[33]

18 [50]

I am a lawgiver, I write new things on my tablets: to the lawgivers themselves, I am law and tablet and herald's proclamation.

18 [51]

If I am the advocate of life — then I must also continue to be the non-advocate of its eternal change! —

A return of the greatest and the smallest things and of the entire ball and knot of reasons and conclusions.

18 [52]

My cleverness left me, this agile cat: my pride roared into the air! it seeks adventure for itself.

Now I sit here with my foolishness — the world quiet like a garden, the air tired from so many pleasant smells.

What welcome distress my foolishness causes me: it never wants to sit quietly and is always tumbling from the chair — will it ever grow tired of itself?

It does not grow tired even of its singing: but it learned the tune from children, evenings when purple bliss hangs in the sky.

I forgive my foolishness, for it knows not what it sings: and because I am so alone, I sing along with its nonsense — despairing at how often it falls from its chair in the process.

18 [53]

On my walk I found
his long jackass ears —

I also found my serpent,
which had lost its head.[34]

18 [54]
you had saved all your purple and emerald bliss
Heat lightning of my happiness

18 [55][35]
Dühring — a p⟨erson⟩ who scares people away from his way
of thinking because of who he is and who, like an eternally
yapping and viciously biting junkyard dog,[36] lay down in submission before his philosophy.

18 [56][37]
the humans who were overcome were themselves the fathers
of the superhumans.

Thus do I teach and do not grow weary of it: humans are
something that must be overcome: for behold, I know that
they *can* be overcome — I saw them, the superhumans.

18 [57]
"Do I have time to *wait* for my animals? If they are *my* animals, then they will know how to find me" Zarathustra's
silence
"you seek words of lasting peace in my place, the hermit's
place: the lasting peace of the deep world — alas, is this lasting peace a hermit's heights?
And if the word of this peace goes through my ear and bone
and marrow, does it seek and, for this reason, still find friends?"

Oh Zarathustra — the hermit replied — this is merely the
way you speak: I do not understand it: — and with this way of
speaking you will have a better chance of persuading animals
than persuading people.[38]

18 [58]
How much warmth do we know how to — withhold

18 [59][39]

One! Midnight commences — its song rises up out of the deep world through ear and bone and marrow.

Two! Deep is all woe, but pleasure is deeper still and if ⟨it⟩ lays its hand on your breast — this goes through bone and marrow.

18 [60]

So which suns would have set that once glowed *for you* on the heights and on the innocence of your pinnacle!

18 [61]

Whatever a grapevine and a storm have in common, something unspeakable — in this even you should be a grapevine and a storm.

18 [62]

almost starved by his expectations,
on dark paths over which hope flashes for me like heat lightning

18 [63]

3.
The End

19[1]

Consolation 1) that there is so much that cannot be figured out

2) that there is so much to make *amends* for.

advocating love for someone evil, someone who suffers.

ocean-paths

to break[1] old tablets

19 [2][2]

§ Do you still remember oh Zarathustra how you were in the forest among p⟨eople⟩ for the first time, how the birds were calling above you, how you felt the *great abandonment*

2) the great *abandonment* while among companions, when you grew tired of giving gifts

3) the great *abandonment* by the stillest hour
Concerning the distinction from solitude

19 [3][3]

The fabulists and dusk-dwellers and everything else that flies, crawls and limps on lame legs between evening and night.

19 [4]

Pebble-chewers is what I call those who are all too satisfied all too friendly:

Hog bellies — this is what I call these pebble-chewers
and they pray to everything as if to their God —

this is the taste of gluttons, the taste of those who stuff themselves with everything —

19[5]

Oh my brothers, out of malice, for once I want to do things the way puny hinterworlders do them: behold, I am drawing the hinterworlders in the sand here! May someone come and pick them out of the sand![4]

Some kind of faith is already bringing bliss to some hinterworlders: onward, grab them when they're like this!

Oh my brothers. There are those among you who understand how to laugh something into nothing — to laugh it *out* of the room! And truly, laughter is a good way of killing!

I tell these kinds of people to follow my example: I came to them as their prelude.

And to those who have no peace at all, unless they finally see the world from behind, I advise:

should the world not be the exuberance of a god?[5]

19 [6]

for in laughter all evil drives become holy: however, in such a way that everything heavy becomes light —

19 [7][6]

And every time the lion laughed, Zarathustra felt moved as never before, so that he felt around for his heart: for it always seemed to him as if a stone had been lifted from his heart and yet another stone and again another stone.

19 [8]⁷

Return Home.
The Other Dance Song.
Oaths.
The Convalescent.
The Old and New Tablets.
Hermits.

19 [9]⁸

You stir, you stretch? — You rasp.⁹ There is nothing new anymore — you rasp — let me sleep!

This is it: there is nothing new anymore, this is what you are
yourself, abysmal thought: now you are awake!

19 [10]

You must also *want* to triumph; therefore it is not enough to
be a fighter and a mercenary of life:

Thus do I whisper in the ear of Frisians and Saxons: to triumph you must also *want* to triumph!

Once life recruited you to be *its* mercenary — this is true:
but now I advise you to recruit life to be your servant.

19 [11]

Whatever we lack but have a need for, this is what we
should take: therefore, I took a clear conscience and made it
my own.

19 [12]¹⁰

I am in their midst like a diamond among lumps of kitchen
coal: they do not believe me when I say: Oh my brothers! We
are such close relatives!

19 [13]

Feeling good will toward the ocean and toward everything
ocean-like, I feel the most good will just when they contradict
me —

19 [14][11]

On new Kings.

"Soon a storm will arise" — thus speaks my soul, the prophet,[12] shaking: for the coming storms are already circulating within it.

(Cities and kingdoms and kings of the great contempt)

And the long dusk limps along in front of the storm, this sadness, tired and drunk with death, this sadness that speaks with a yawning mouth. "Everything is the same, everything is empty, everything has been" — thus it yawns and drags its feet and is so tired that it can neither sleep nor die.

19 [15]

Or who is it that you love?

Organ grinders!

to bless i.e., to *give* a beautiful soul to chance.

    choice: before and after
    the shaping force against what is *past*
    serenity of those who wait
    courage of those who take risks
    Pure i.e., without purpose.

19 [16]

Forest animals
On future songs
to listen to your yearning

[20 = Z II 2. Autumn 1883]

20 [1][1]

You go the way of greatness: now these are destined for you, abyss and — pinnacle in one.

Do not look around: let this be your greatest act of courage, that no trail remains behind you.

Here no one shall creep after you: wherever your foot has trod, here the path has been obliterated and above it is written "impossibility."

What previously was your greatest danger has now become your last refuge.

The time has passed when you were still allowed to be a wish: whatever you still are now, this should be hand and will and grip of willing.

Some people will, but most are only willed.[2]

And you should bestow everything good upon yourself as someone who could also do without it.

There are those who are actors without knowing it, and those who are actors without wanting it.[3]

That we could *bear* our immortality — this would be supreme.

Have I gotten to the point where I teach puny people their puny virtues? They already know how to find them for themselves and they resent it terribly that I am not made envious by what they find.[4]

20 [2]⁵

On the ocean.

Speech to his friends. I wanted to spare them, not to send them around as apostles, I became too loving toward them — now I have *annihilated* them by doing just this.

All in vain up to now!

Life, at midpoint, irretrievably sacrificed.

The most terrible thought of an eternal return of wastefulness.

Wasted humankind (and all fighting and greatness an eternally pointless *game*) (serpent and shepherd)

Unchosen bliss (the convalescent and pleasure in the superficial)

Seeing while in the great outdoors.

While demanding compassion, seeks his animals.

Clairvoyance concerning his wanting to give gifts. Wanderer, lightning.

Compassion for tyrants and for creators of peoples.

"I am trying it once again" solution. — Skepticism turned against all pessimism. — Forgetting, new beginning, as with all prophetic people.

Beyond Good and Evil (conclusion) prepared to do anything.

20 [3]⁶

Draft for Zarathustra 3.

1. On the ocean. "Let the wind blow." *Columbus-like.* Premonitions, driving forces, in what direction?

Irretrievably sacrificed. The wanderer. Late autumn.

2. *A place to rest. The happiness* of the free spirit. Not bound even to his friends (you have *set* them *free!*) What does *one person* matter! The "wanderer." Hesitate in your happiness! Mood of "joyful science" and critique.

3. The burial rites and the speech to the friends. The most tender aspect of a solitary person.

4. Driven out, fleeing, despised. To summarize all the misery of the founders of religion, misery which comes *from without.*

5. Wasted! Worthless! Misery that comes from *within*.

6. Clairvoyant about his "giving of gifts" and about his "love." — To feel like a golden lock and chain for many selves, this is his selfishness — this reveals the one who rules. — **Goal**: *to personally portray* the unity of the greatest multiplicity, the beauty of what is most ugly, the necessity of what is most coincidental. The state as *means*.

7. The only thing left for him is to tyrannize himself — with an unlimited *will to suffer*. Mockery of previous pessimists.

8. *To summon up* the most painful truth (*possibility*). What *if* you experienced this eternally again!

9. Majestic nature and human beings.

10. Mockery of those who trust life. Oh, that there were someone I could curse!

11. Beyond "good" and "evil" — the tartuffery[7] of the weak. Spencer 2 p 110[8]

12. Mockery of the artists: who *relax* in the pictures they create. — True meaning of fame: I want to be a spur and to score the flanks of all who come until they bleed.

13. Mockery of the enjoyment of those who know. "level-headed and ordinary"

14. Final escalation: wasted humankind. Compassion for those who rule and for their distress, and mockery of them.

15. He seeks his animals. Cave destroyed. Deepest isolation.

16. He rips his serpent to pieces, the shepherd dies, he fights with his eagle.

17. Illness. Fever dream "the one who flies."

18. The hermit as experimenter

19. The convalescent. On unchosen bliss.

20. The *will*: let us try it once again! Skepticism turned against pessimism.

21. The appearances: rainbow, lioness with flock of doves, the children's choirs.

22. Hymn to predetermined nature. "I as fatum."

20 [4]

As long as action *is called for*, that is, *commanded*: synthesis (the *abolition*[9] of the moral person) is not yet present. *Not being able to do otherwise*: drives and commanding reason above and *beyond* purpose: enjoying themselves in action. Teichmüller p. 55.[10]

the *will itself is to be overcome* — all feeling of freedom *no longer* created out of the opposite of compulsion!

to become nature!

Error of Aristotle p 65[11]

for lust does not move us and the commanding reason does not move us.

the will does not move us, rather it is an accompanying phenomenon.

20 [5]

Against the Epicur⟨eans⟩ — they *freed* themselves from an error and they are enjoying freedom as former prisoners do. Or they have overcome, or *believe* they have overcome, an opponent that they envied, without pity for those who did not feel themselves prisoners but rather felt themselves *sheltered*, *still* without pity for the suffering of those who were overcome.

20 [6]

To **evaluate** the *most inferior* people according to their effect on "*great people*."

1) the *freeloaders* — those who nest in the weaknesses of strong and great people

2) *people in pain*, who, like mosquitoes, inflict a lot of small pain on great people and in this way diminish them — who also cloud up the clear sky with their yammering.

3) the *well-meaning ones* who do not know how to resist and who ruin the great people who are commanders: they make them into contemptuous people.

4) the *comfortable ones*: they make life trivial with their pleasure

20 [7]

"The courageous person is the person who endures, fears or dares *what* should be done and *why* it should be done and *how* it should be done and *when* it should be done"[12] Arist⟨otle⟩

Liberator from the delusion "God" and even more from the delusion "God and humans."

Determining what it means to dwell on the earth
the eternal meaning of the *individual*.   ego.

20 [8][13]

Not complaining à la Hamlet! NB.
                    Plan for Zarathustra 3.

 1 Zarathustra on the ocean.
    2–10 Zarathustra hears of the death of the blessed isles.
         Speeches against his true *enemies*.
         The disturbing effect of his *praise* on his friends:
         the city *overthrown*, Zarathustra has to **tear**
         himself **away**: he *despises their* **weakness in this**.
         terrifying outbreak of his contempt, and praise of
         tyrants and of the most evil ones
   11–12 Z⟨arathustra's⟩ solitude. In vain! It is too late!
         Death of the youth with the serpent. — Symbol.
      13 Sick, appalled, Zarathustra seeks his cave. His
         animals flee and do not recognize him, the cave
         is utterly destroyed.
   14–20 The hermit's speech. Zarathustra sees that
         trusting in God is the ultimate source of all
         weakening. One more time! Decision.
   21–22 Summoning up the most terrible most abysmal
         thought. Predetermined nature — hymn.

Unchosen bliss (like a jealous man who pushes his beloved woman away from himself and who is still gentle in his hard-heartedness)

20 [9][14]

Zarathustra 3.

Several speeches at the "grave"

why did they have to depart from you?

In the end, compassion for all rulers and tyrants who took their contempt out on *weak people* (they exerted their own will to the extreme)

none of them (peoples, sages, good people) believe any more that they are *entitled* to a superior humankind — *I expose their* innermost *doubts*!

"I do not want the virtues of the strong to be confused with those of the weak."[15]

Curse, so that the best people *have to* withdraw!

On the Reign of Cowards.

concerning the characteristics of friends[16] (**in the end**, most stirring **praise**

   1. strengthen the will

   2. no lasciviousness

   3. learn silence

   4. solitude

   5. profound mistrust and profound trust[17]

   6. seek out your enemies, yet find your friends.

20 [10][18]

Zarathustra 4.

The king and the fool offer the notion that Zarathustra's coming is *necessary.*

Zarathustra draws ever smaller circles: great speeches in which he *excludes.* Ever smaller circles, on higher mountains.

First of all 1) the freeloaders are excluded, then 2) the hypocrites 3) the weak well-meaning people then 4) the unwitting hypocrites of morality.

Last scene: depiction of the *supreme soul*[19] that can reach down the deepest, of the most expansive soul that can err the furthest within itself, of the most necessary soul that hurls itself into coincidences, of the soul that is, that falls in love with becoming; of the soul that has, which demands and *wills*; of the soul that flees from itself again and again and overtakes itself again: that is completely self-love and for that reason complete *in everything*: of the soul for whom everything is a game; wisdom that hurls itself into the ocean of foolishness: laughter and tears: the world, exuberance of a god: redemption from all unique stuffy "sages" etc. — Sin itself as enjoyment of self-abolishing.[20]

All beings merely **preliminary exercises** in *unification* **incorporation** *of opposites*.

Redemption from chance: what I have *allowed* to happen, I know I can **make** this up **to myself** afterward: and therefore *wanting* afterward what I did not want before.

a goal all by itself

After this, *out of happiness for superhumans*, Zarathustra relates the **secret** that everything returns.

Effect. Pana wants to kill him.

He finally grasps it, goes through all transformations, up to and including the most victorious, yet as he sees her lying there broken — *he laughs*. Climbs, laughing, up onto the cliff: but having arrived there he dies happy.

Gripping effect of *death*: those who make vows.

20 [11][21]

Concerning the Single Victory.

Just as I once saw him triumph and die: the friend who hurled divine moments and lightning bolts into my dark youth —

playful and profound, storming forward toward joy while still in the storm of battle, bleeding more as he suffers, and where enemies were nearing the chosen flag, —

the most cheerful one among the dying, the most decisive one among the victors, contemplating-anticipating as he stands

atop his destiny — exhilarated that he was victorious, laughing that in dying he was victorious —

commanding through dying: — and he commanded *annihilation and no mercy* —

Oh you my will, my In-Myself, Above-myself! you my necessity! Make it so that I triumph in this way — and spare me for
this one victory!

Preserve me and spare me and protect me from all puny
victories, you destiny of my soul and cusp of all need, you my
necessity![22]

20 [12][23]

Don't I know, like you, all cheerfulness — even the cheerfulness in the anticipation of near-death: for the great burden
that I bore, let me often rejoice in times of great danger

puny community in the middle of nowhere and mist and
conceit of all Bible-thumpers — they *all* need rooms and little
chambers for their praying!

Like me, you are "by accident" this is the oldest nobility in
the world.[24]

and not to *their* promised land do I wish to follow the spirit
that they call holy: I have always seen goats and geese among
its leading crusaders

intimate and welcoming, but like gates through which only
lowly things pass.[25]

20 [13][26]

The solemn toy trumpeters,[27] who with their melodies preach
dreary doctrines and lies.

I wish I could already see the pillar of fire in which they are
being burned: for such pillars of fire must precede the great noon.

How many *caves* does life have

Before Sunrise.

20 [14]²⁸

I have found in all things an arrogance I call divine. I have found this arrogance even in my soul.

I have found this arrogance of wisdom in all things, that this wisdom tells all things to walk on the feet of fools.

As little reason as possible: this wisdom does not take more than that in its knapsack when it walks overland and tills its field in the daytime.

All things run on the feet of chance — to there and back and upward to wisdom,

— this is its blissful safety, that it lures all things to itself only by using chance.

20 [15]²⁹

Preferring most of all to be nourished by innocent things and impatient and ready to fly away from those few things: why shouldn't something about me be bird-like?

The spirit of gravity, arch enemy even to the body as well: where did my enmity not follow it! Where has my winged mortal hatred not flown and not gone astray!

20 [16]³⁰

$\left\{\begin{array}{l}\text{Prophet} \\ \text{Annihilator} \\ \text{One who creates} \\ \text{Unifier} \\ \text{Explorer (ocean)} \\ \text{Dancer — Laughing one} \\ \text{One who flies — One who triumphs}\end{array}\right.$

21 [1]¹

(*Concerning 3.*)

Summoning up the weightiest truth.

Song of mockery of all previous pessimists.

Song of mockery of religions and their attempts to flee.

Song of mockery of socialists Jesuits and Epicureans.

Song of mockery of artists up to now.

Compassion and *honor* to all great lawgivers, field marshals and conquerors.

What friends!

Overcoming nature by means of great humans.

Song of the one who flies.

The sick person's song of comfort — Tired: growing still. Will to suffer.

"I am fatum"

"beyond morality," above and beyond all praise.

skepticism as temptation²

suicide as temptation

Hymn of the convalescent.

To conquer for ourselves the country that we *deserve*, no matter in whose hands the country wants to be

21 [2]³

Plan for Zarathustra 3.

Solitude in shame and silence when facing the greatest thought.

Avoiding the animals

⟨Solitude⟩ of a single will that conceals itself from everyone,
   but that raises everyone up
Solitude
   without friends, indeed with the feeling of having sacrificed
   them.
Solitude bereft of all reasons to feel *comforted*, *song of mockery*
   of all previous forms of pessimism (well beyond all *previous*
   modes of thought).
Solitude and temptations. *Song of mockery* of previous attempts
   by religion to flee
Solitude of supreme responsibility. *Song of mockery* of socialists
   and Jesuits and Epicureans.
Solitude beyond morality, in eternal perspectives. Overcoming
   of great nature through humans. Song of the one who flies.
Solitude of the sick person. Song of comfort. Becoming tired
   and quiet. Sanctified through suffering. The will to suffer
   and to intensify the suffering.
"I will this!" Hymn of the convalescent and of the victorious
   one. *The laughing lion and the swarm of doves.* (A *temptation*
   — nothing more! he himself and his thought) The 4 animals arrive (pride with cleverness — power with gentleness)
   — they approach each other

21 [3]
Plan for Zarathustra 4.
   1. The invitation.
   2. The victory parade. The plague city. The stake (the old
      culture was burned).
   3. The spring festival with choruses.
   4. *Being called to account* before Zarathustra: "what have
      you done?" (what have you invented?)
      Kind of community (as in Corsica).
   5. Places of residence.
   6. Wars and wrestling matches.
   7. the new nobility.
   8. the temptations (with evil people, "punishments" etc.)

9. to redeem the woman in women[4]
10. slaves (beehives) learn to bear serenity. More machines.
    Reshaping the machine into the beautiful
11. time for solitude. Division of the day.
12. long youth and the transformations.

After that, Zarathustra's great speeches, similar to prayers.
       a few unusual saints arrive, who are also disciples: also a
       fool (Epicurus?)

13. The sanctification of laughter. Future of dance. Victory
    over the spirit of gravity.
14. The innocence of becoming.
15. The consecration of the smallest.
16. The breaking of the tablets. Praise of *cool* reason!
17. The redemption of evil people and the redemption from
    moral judges!
18. Summoning the enemy.
19. The new kings — as model teachers.
20. The eternal "I" and its sanctification. Determinism and
    its solution. There is no morality and no absolute respon-
    sibility, we *determine them for ourselves*
    beatification of drives
21. **Decisive moment**: Zarathustra asks all the masses at
    the festival: "do you want all of this once again?" —
    everyone says "**Yes!**"
    He dies of happiness as this happens.
    (the sky clear, low)
    (ominous, clear, eerie)
    (deepest silence, the animals around Zarathustra, he has
    covered his head, arms spread on the stone slab — appears
    to be sleeping)
    the howling dog
    something luminous terrible quiet moves above and away
    from all of their thoughts
    The speeches by those who make vows, around his corpse,
    constitute the conclusion.
                    Those who make vows.

22. etc. The great noon as turning point — the two paths. The hammer for overpowering humans: supreme development of the individual, *so that it must perish on account of itself* (and not, as has been the case so far, on account of dietary mistakes!) (*how death came into the world*!)

What happiness!

The one who creates as the self-annihilator. *Someone who is a creator out of goodness* and *wisdom*. All previous morality *surpassed*!

In the end the *vows* — *terrible oaths*!

21 [4]

Chorus of the godless (overcoming the churches)

Chorus of the honest (overcoming moral tartuffery)

Chorus of the penitents of the mind (overcoming idealistic vanity)

The order[5] of the hard-hearted (overcoming compassion)

The rogue-fools.

    1. New order of rank of humans and new distribution of rights.

    2. The necessity of slaves.

Visitors at Zarathustra's place he is asked for help

    1) universal slave-revolt

    2) softening of hearts, weakness

    3) darkening and insanity

the *happiness of the community* (but solitary people enjoy it!)

the *happiness of truthful people* (as opposed to all the effort of playing hide and seek).

    The omens.

    the burning of the large city.

21 [5]

            Finite as space: infinite as time.

with indestructibility, eternity is given and beginninglessness by being determined, a limit to the multiplicity of new forms.

21 [6][6]

Humans are that which must be overcome. *Here I hold the hammer* that will overcome them![7]

> This viewpoint *brings bliss* to Zarathustra at the conclusion of Part III

he becomes *ripe* in the process.

the previous evasions and attempts to flee in the face of the greatest thought:

> *Nirvana*, the thought of nothingness brings bliss.
>
> the wonderful *re-creation* in the beyond and then eternal life (in Christianity)
>
> *bestialization*, as *bien public*[8] — consequence of Eudaimonists socialists Jesuits.[9]
>
> *absolute skepticism about our minds* and practical letting ourselves go. "What do I know about actions!"[10]

Determinism: I myself am fate and I *have conditioned existence for all eternity.*

> Many drives fight within me for *supremacy.*
>
> in this I am a replica of everything that lives and I can explain it to myself.

Suddenly the terrible chamber of truth opens. There is an unconscious reaction of self-defense, caution, concealment, protection from the weightiest knowledge: *this* is how I have lived up to now. I kept something secret from myself; but the restless pronouncements and rolling away of stones turned my drive into something overpowering. Now I roll the last stone: the most terrible truth *stands before me.*

I. *Summoning truth up from the grave.*

We created it, we awakened it: highest expression of courage and of the feeling of power.

Mockery of all previous pessimism!

We wrestle with it — we discover that our only way to bear it is to create a being *that bears it*: unless we would freely choose to blind ourselves again and make ourselves blind to it. But we are no longer capable of this!

to bite off the head of the serpent!

We created the weightiest thought — *now let us create the being* for whom the thought is light and blissful!

In order to create, we must give ourselves greater freedom than has ever been given to us; in addition, liberation from morality and relief by means of festivals (intimations of the future! to celebrate the future, not the past! To compose the myth of the future! To live in hope!) Blissful moments! And then to draw the curtain again and to turn *our thoughts to concrete immediate goals*!

[22 = Z II 3a. End 1883]

22 [1][1]

Alone with myself and with my rejoicing conscience

You had your friends together on a tiny island and your enemies among them: how sweet it is to love and to hate!

Doesn't the father still have to resist the son even in what he does best? And anyone who has ever claimed a right for himself will not give this right even to his own son, out of love.[2]

We are punished most severely for our virtues. And thus learn to guess where your virtue lies: there, where you have been most severely punished.[3]

Lonely days want to walk on courageous feet.[4]

I have become clairvoyant: a diamond sword cuts every darkness to pieces for me.[5]

The reflection of their happiness flew over me like a shadow: and when they felt strong and sure-footed, mistrust crept toward me and its sibling, weakness.

We should redeem the woman in women![6] And let women lust for men but not for what is manly!

Still no one has time for me. But what is the deal with a time that has no time for Zarathustra![7]

I am told that humans love themselves? Is this true? I have still found humans to be the predator of all predators, even against themselves.[8]

"What Zarathustra has decided, this will happen: how should his great soul be capable of changing its resolve!"[9]

Take pity on your foot so that it doesn't step into a morass: and that's why you should not even bother kicking those who have betrayed their friends.[10]

I recognize people who are super rich by this: they thank those who take from them.[11]

For me there are no true orators and super-orators unless they can convince the arguments themselves to run after them.[12]

You are riding quickly enough to your goal; but your lame foot is mounted alongside you and will arrive with you at the same time.[13]

This is my fear on your behalf: that you will *stumble* just when you are at your pinnacle!

There are those who are actors without knowing it and those who are actors without wanting it.[14]

Some will, but most are only willed.[15]

The time has passed when you still were allowed to have wishes.[16]

Puny virtues are necessary for puny people: but who can convince me to believe that puny people are necessary![17]

You aren't envious of their virtues — they will never forgive you for that!

You go the way of greatness: now these are destined for you, abyss and pinnacle in one.

Stop looking around: let this be your greatest act of courage, that behind you no path remains.

Here no one should creep after you: wherever your foot has trod, there the path is obliterated and above it is written: impossibility.

What previously was called your final danger has now become your last refuge.[18]

This is his folly: he cannot endure all those who give warning or the voices of birds — he flees into his abyss *because* he has been warned about it.

"Chance" is what the weak call it. But I say to you: what could befall me that my gravity would not compel and draw to itself?

Look, will you, how I first stew each coincidence[19] in my juices: and when it is done, it means, for me, "my will and destiny."

Whatever it is about my chance that seems foreign to my body and will, how could I offer hospitality to that! Look, will you, only friends approach friends.

Warning birds flew up out of my happiness itself.

Experience came imperiously: but my will spoke to it — already it was on its knees, pleading.[20]

Do you want to be a stumbling block for those who stride ahead? Do you want to limp along in front of whoever is in a hurry?[21]

Those who look backward and go forward deserve to be run into: lest they punish their eyes with their lying feet.[22]

"It is showing itself" you complacent ones say: but complacency always withdraws and will keep withdrawing more and more.[23]

Even what we have left undone weaves the fabric of the entire future: even our nothingness is a master weaver and a woman spinning webs.[24]

Many have grown weary of themselves: and only then does the happiness that was reserved for them catch up with them — but they have always been running on too rapid feet![25]

My drink should still make you sneeze: my sparkling wines should tickle your noses and fill you with lust.[26]

Ask my foot whether I find your manner pleasing: dancers have their ears in their toes, do they not.[27]

I have reached the end of my humanity: I, the gentlest person, have become the most hard-hearted —

Did I ever fall asleep on my fame? Every kind of fame has been like a bed of thorns to me.[28]

Am I not the meteorological divide? Don't all winds come to me and proclaim their will to me?[29]

And the ice and innocence of my peaks are also still aglow.[30]

I still am like a cock in a strange barnyard, pecked at even by hens.[31]

There is more injustice in your admiration than in your contempt[32]

Do as I do: only doers learn; and only as a doer do I want to be your teacher.[33]

That a bolt of lightning would strike your feed! That your maws would finally learn to feed on fire![34]

You crash up against me like waves: — but I strike your heads with my oar. Behold, you bear my boat into immortality![35]

Here stands my will: the surge of my pride still founders on it.[36]

I want to make wildfires of you and heralds with tongues of fire: but until now you were only arid grass and steppe.[37]

Gold flashes in his dark eyes: a golden bark floats there, on black waters.[38]

Actors have no time to wait for justice: and often I have looked at impatient people to see whether they were not actors.

They all want to exist — and they call this justice. And "to make things equal" —
— to spare too much — some people are like this: to yield too much — other people are like that.

We should only steal when we cannot rob: thus speaks the voice of honor among rogues

Already I feel that I'm dreaming: so perhaps I am almost awake?

How can you want to learn to dance when you have not yet learned to walk? Yet those who fly, and the bliss of above and below, are even above those who dance.

And anyone who woos the virtues of the strong does not have to glance lustfully at the virtues of the weak, but rather should pass by these pretty maids without taking notice.[39,40]

Alas, it's too bad that you believe you have to despise what you have merely renounced!

One day I noticed that I had lost my patience: so I went out looking for it — and I looked high and low. But you probably think, my friends, that I found it again? Quite the contrary: yet I discovered so much in the course of my journey that I have to tell you about it — and I swear to you, just as we are setting forth for the first time, that you will lose your patience during the telling. — And don't think that I would have it any other way: for the best of everything that I have learned and discovered since then is just this: "it is time *for many people* to lose their patience."

And above all, for you, my friends!

Beware of willing anything halfway: and be as decisive in indolence as you are in action.[41]

And whoever wants to throw lightning bolts must float in the sky as a cloud for a long time.[42]

You must learn the long silence; and no one should see into your depths.[43]

And those who excel at silence are not the ones who veil their faces and cloud their waters, making them impossible to see through.

Instead, it is the bright, the brave, the transparent ones who excel at silence, whose depths are so deep that they cannot be revealed even through the clearest water.

For it is through these that silence reveals itself not to be silent.

It is still too early for me: up to now I have only been my own precursor and herald's proclamation.

You should not wade through foreign slime: rather, here your talent lies in running fleetingly across it like a look of divine contempt.

All things that are pursued relentlessly have been successful up to now.[44]

My tombs opened: my pain which had been buried alive rose again.— it had concealed itself under shrouds in order to get a really good night's sleep, — have pity on me, in order to get in a really good night's watch![45]

My happiness is chasing after me, said Zarathustra — that's because I do not chase after women: and happiness is a woman.[46]

And humans abased themselves to such a degree before God, and they carried their self-defiance so far, that now they seek deadly revenge: and so, he who saw everything had to die! Revenge on *witnesses* — —[47]

This is shame's scam: it wants to believe it is only giving way to violence; and what it would like most of all is just to[48] yield and to wallow in the despair of weakness.

Anyone who has nothing to do is troubled by nothingness.[49]

Whatever I do not want you to do for me, why should *I* not be allowed to do it for you? And, truly, that which I must do for you, precisely this you cannot do for me![50]

They all have no character: what could they do! they had to steal one for themselves.[51]

Do what you want anyway: but first be those who can will something!

Love your neighbors as yourselves anyway: but first be those who love themselves[52]

A small light, but even so a great comfort for the voyager whom the night wants to betray to the wild ocean.[53]

To forget: this is a divine skill. And those who want to rise into the heights, and to fly, must throw much that is heavy into the depths and make themselves light — that's what I call a divine lightness-skill.[54]

At a distance, we think poorly of someone else. But two people together — how could they not wish each other well!

Solitude ripens: it does not sow seeds.

Watch out if you wanted to buy some people but you offered too little, and now you have made their virtue stronger because it has already said no once.

Modestly embracing a little happiness and, in that very moment, already modestly making eyes at a new little happiness —[55]

My freedom, and its curiosity for novelty, took flight, even into prisons.[56]

I see so much goodness, so much weakness: and you treat each other properly and deftly, like grains of sand.

An end is what desecrates every thing and every deed: for what is holiness, if it does not lie in the heart and conscience of the thing and deed!

I do not want you to do anything "in order" and "because" and "so that," — but rather everything for its own sake and for the pleasure it gives you.[57]

And if up to now someone has had complete contempt for people — has that person in doing so not always been the people's greatest benefactor?[58]

"What does this dark cloud of a person want? Does he want to bring us the plague!"
"Take the children away: eyes like that scorch young souls."[59]

You speak falsely of events and coincidences! Nothing will ever happen to you except you yourselves! And what you call coincidence — you yourselves are your own incidents and accidents![60]

At noon, my happiness loomed hot above me, my sun drank thirstily from the ocean — now a night of clouds comes along and sudden winds.
I know well where winds come from and where they roar off to[61]

to implant his will so that it becomes a tall tree and still brings shade to future generations — a long-term will![62]

What is this that you call your conscience, anyway? Not a law, but rather the fact that you need a law and an arm to hold you steady, you drunken stumbling people!

"soft, fleeting, modest"[63]

should I stand there and whine about that whore, happiness?[64] Or about "Stepmother Nature"?

You are building a fence around yourself with praise and blame.

And when you cannot endure life, you must attempt to win its favor — for such has always been the artful strategy of the greatest sages.

Their most artful, boldest strategy was to believe in God whenever they felt that the devil was too near.

They learned to switch names for things: and so things became switched around in their minds. Behold, this is the artfulness of the greatest sages in its entirety!

Most people are too crazy to be self-interested: their happiness makes all of them crazy.

They sacrifice everything for one thing — this is a kind of love. This willfulness and self-absorption loom over all people.

Their intense insanity bubbles forth for them, out of their love: but it is a poor calculator and despises the cold virtues of the huckster.

For huckster-virtue, the huckster's money-grubbing fingers and lusting eye — this is even beneath the dignity of an animal.

Everything that can be bought is worth little: I spit this doctrine into the faces of hucksters.

Money passes through all fingers: therefore learn to handle money and moneychangers with kid gloves.

Praise be to puny poverty: for all hucksters scheme after great wealth.[65]

Wherever coins ring, whores rule.

Those who have always spared themselves a lot will finally get sick from sparing themselves too much.[66]

He speaks roughly but not from a rough throat: every gust of wind makes him speak more hoarsely, this sensitive little thing![67]

And we often teach despairing people to be strong only by speaking to them about their weakness.

Some are gluttons, others nibblers — both contemptible.

Begetters and breeders.[68]

Oh these narrow huckster-souls! Whenever money jumps into the money box, the hucksters' souls jump in along with it.
Whose souls have been a money belt and whose happiness has been dirty pieces of paper — how could their blood ever become clean?
It will flow lifeless and foul smelling unto the tenth generation:[69] the descendants of the hucksters are indecent.

On scribblers and screamers.[70] On substitute teachers.[71]

Get away from me, my tempter, Zarathustra said to the old man and kissed his trembling hand; he smiled at his own words, for a memory had come to him.[72]

It is the age of puny people.[73]

To have a better sense of justice in my little finger[74] than those people have in their heads.

Chorus of fools i.e., of sages who briefly feel themselves to be ignorant und foolish[75]
Chorus of the impoverished i.e., of narrow-minded superfluous people whose yoke is light. — Emerson p. 283.

To be burned at the stake, not for our[76] faith, but rather for doubting our faith —

I no longer want to conceal what I feel: why are you talking to me about truth![77]

His mind is trapped in the cage of his tiny heart.[78]

Do I love human beings after all? But they are a part of my plan — yet this is the extent of my love.[79]

Mistrustful and full of ulcers, capable of sudden willfulness, determined guard and lurker

Whatever I did not want before, this is what I must want afterward — no other choice has been given to me.[80]

Opposed to the stuffy sages, redeeming from them — the soul, to which everything *becomes a game*.[81]

They want no one to hurt them: that is why they beat all people to the punch and please them — these cowards![82]

"Do what you want, but take care not to be conspicuous about it! Do what you can, but take care not to offend with it!" Recipe for the mundane.[83]

There are no leaps in virtue.[84]

seek out your enemies, find your friends[85]

Prescription: to will for a long time, no lasciviousness, learn silence, learn solitude, learn profound mistrust[86]

the stone is getting brittle[87]

to give the will a backbone — by means of an organization[88]

A curse on the fact that the best people are secluding themselves without having children.[89]

To the murderer of God, the seducer of the best people, the friend of evil people[90]

Anyone who up to now has had the most contempt for people, has this person in doing so not been the people's greatest benefactor?[91]

— Corpse robbers who know how to steal something even from the pockets of the dead and half-dead

Better more Handel than handlers!
Say it mornings and evenings: "I despise hucksters, I want to break their sticky fingers."[92]

What makes superior humans suffer is not that which is inferior to them, but rather knowing that: "there is still something superior to me." *Propelled* into the heights, like a ball — this is what they call "climbing."[93]

You have strangled their ambition! To be the last among you would give them more pleasure than to be the first![94]

"Pleasure is a woman: she runs after anyone who spurns her."[95]

You are figuring out how all people could be happy and in the process you have forgotten future generations — the happiness *of most people!*[96]

Just ask women! Having a good time is not the point of giving birth.[97]

"It wants to command me? Come on, let's wrestle with each other: perhaps my will is stronger!" — concerning the emergence of evil people.

Now no one I love remains alive: how can I still love life!

Angels dissolve into tears when they see him smile

Tired and happy, like everyone who creates, on the seventh day.

My heart was courteous even in the face of frustrating coincidences: to raise my quills against destiny seemed to me like wisdom for hedgehogs.

Already the hours run on tiptoes across our hearts.

And whenever I had no ladder, I always climbed on top of my own head.

There was no stillness before this: no one thinks of me and everyone speaks of me.

I sought myself and a place where I might be at home — this hit home with me the hardest.[98]
I sought my heaviest yoke: that's where I found my selfishness.

He is unshakeable, and when he complains, then it is more a concession to you and a cloak that he spreads over his hard-heartedness.[99]

I do not praise the land where butter and honey — flow.[100]

"The worst lies behind us"[101]
"I thought you were a sage — but what astounds me about you more than anything else is your cleverness.[102]

loutish virtues[103]

"I want to live the way I wish or I have no wish to live" — this is how the most saintly people still think.[104]

Where I always felt fear, I will finally make a wish — oh abysmal thought, now I am still learning to love the abyss![105]

Selfishness and imperiousness have brought lies to an absolute pinnacle.

You are look⟨ing⟩ at the rock of the highest mountains, aren't you? Did it not form under the oceans?

Beware, you who are the wealthiest: puny acts of charity spark more outrage about you than extreme miserliness. You drip like wide-bottomed bottles with all-too-narrow necks — bottles like these have already had their necks broken many times.[106]

These neighbors and their puny distress, this city and its meager air — this chips away at your strength every day. How could you want to learn how to cause great pain in this place![107]

Clumsy as a corpse[108]

"Let us be modest in virtue as well! Only modest virtue can get along with comfort" —

Scribblers and screamers, those panting with ambition, pushy and shameless people —[109]

For does a drive want to be "satisfied," as you teach? Does it want to be free of itself and have peace? Has a will ever willed not to will?

What drives all drives is that they create: and if they sleep for a while, then they are only sleeping in, in order later to become — fully awake.

We have to sleep in, so as to become fully awake.

But you have distorted the essence of willing into unwilling and willing against itself, you have always misinterpreted the voice of the tired will and the snuffling and snoring of the sleeping one.[110]

For is sleep an invention in response to death? And would whoever wants to sleep be someone who is weary of dying? Even the liveliest person can snuffle and snore.[111]

Equal rights for all — this is the most extraordinary injustice: for then the most superior humans lose out.[112]

Equality was always praised most highly: it wins the praise of *most people* — of those people who were not *allowed* to have equal rights!

He broods on his misfortune like a hen on an egg.

Oh you who know, you, too, are intrusive! And this is to be your reward, that you always see the foreground of all things![113]

His mind is failing — now the good and the bad in him grow more visible: he grows darker — alas, if it were only new stars that now grow more visible!

22 [2][114]

Plan for Zarathustra 3.

At the ocean (late at night)
On unchosen bliss.
On the virtue that diminishes.
On the stake.

Zarathustra's self-knowledge (as a betrayal of friends) Now the disaster begins.

Story.

Zarathustra's defense:

    1) on lawgivers and princes

    2) on hucksters

    3) on substitute teachers

    4) on pious people

    the great curse

Story.

The fool's comfort — on science — everything the same, equal, etc.

Zarathustra seeks the last thing that loves him: in vain.

Conversation with lightning. Eternally "In vain!"

The boy and the serpent

Zarathustra sick. The saint

Z⟨arathustra's⟩ answer for the saint.

The decision.

Praise of predetermined nature as *fatum*.[115]

The way of the convalescent.

22 [3][116]

It is treasonous to strive for greatness: whoever has it, strives for goodness.[117]

The deepest love does not know what to call itself and is probably asking itself, "Am I not hatred?" — If we once — — —[118]

Do we not do the same thing awake as we do in our dreams? We always first invent and poetically imagine the people we associate with — and in the next instant we have already forgotten this.[119]

When will man and woman stop misunderstanding each other? Their passions walk with different strides, — they measure time according to different measures.[120]

In order to see *far away*, we need to learn to see beyond ourselves.[121]

And those who believe in their life after death surely have also learned to be dead in life.[122]

People of faith[123] do not hate freethinkers the most, but rather new thinkers that have a new faith.

Ponderous, melancholic people become more lighthearted through hate and love: here they rise to their surface.[124]

The matter is clarified: now it does not concern us anymore. Beware of becoming too enlightened about yourself!

Compassion for the entire race — this leads to hard-heartedness against every individual.[125]

Terrible experiences seek out terrible people.

I, too, am the ore with an iron destiny: this is how I felt whenever you mentioned destiny.

He has his own god for himself: but ever since I saw that god, I have seen in him only the ape[126] of his god.

There is a degree of inherent mendacity that we call "good conscience."

They chase after anyone who convinces them that they have lost their way. It flatters them to hear that they had a way at all.[127]

The great thoughts that come from the heart and the petty ones that come from the head — both are badly conceived.[128]

You want to be judged by your intentions and not by your effect? But where do you get your intentions anyway? From your effect![129]

Those who haven't known how to find the way to their goal live more brazenly and more frivolously than those who have no goal: they want to laugh it off and get over their loss.[130]

The danger for sages is to become infatuated with foolishness.[131]

They sacrifice themselves, not out of compassion, but rather out of abundance: they reward others, they reward them with *themselves*![132]

The devil, a friend of knowledge, stays away from God: only from far away is it possible to develop an eye for gods.[133]

Love brings what is superior and unusual in someone to light: this is how it beautifies — through deception about someone (most of all self-deception!) But pay attention to what happens when people are aware of being loved but do *not* love back: there the soul itself reveals its sediments.[134]

Not only the herd, but also the shepherd, has need of a bellwether.[135]

Why so apart? — I find no one else I could obey and no one I would even like to command.[136]

An elephant that tries to *stand* on its head.[137]

You think everything has been accomplished when you have rendered lightning harmless? But *I* want it to work for me. — This is how I think of all the evil in you and in me.[138]

The innocence in a lie is the sign of sincere belief in something.[139]

We always love only our desire and not what we desire.[140]

Time feels different in the dark than in the light.

And wherever I see the sticky fingers of hucksters, I prefer to draw the short straw.[141]

There before you lies the black sad sea — you must cross that, too! Zarathustra 3.[142]

Crumpled houses, absurdly resembling a child's toy: if only a child would shove them back in the box again! — crumpled souls
Intimate and inclusive, but lowly, like doors which let in only lower things.[143]

Spoiled by many puny triumphs — he has always had it easy: he never became familiar with the best kind of seriousness.[144]

Human beings must become more evil — this is the greatest sorrow of the one who knows! And anyone who wants to create superior humans must make them even more evil — this is the suffering of those who create and are benevolent!

Oh Zarathustra advocate of life! You must also be the advocate of suffering! I cannot exempt you from hell — the underworld must rise up against you, the shades must still bear witness: "Life is torture."

A lustful eye — nourishment for a bilious soul[145]

When a big city expands into the country, it does not bring fertilizer to the land but rather corruption and horror.

Where have I witnessed the schooling and upbringing of people who are one day supposed to command? With doctrines of obedience, they had to flatter and feign their way into the company of those who obey.

Your virtues do not suit your bodies: your bodily ailments accuse the virtues that you gloat about.

Sickened as much by street talking as by street walkers: and precisely these are your most secret sicknesses.

There is great hypocrisy among you: those who command pretend to have the virtues of those who obey.

I try to persuade where I should be in command: this is what my bad education wants. This kind of persuasion is no better than flattery — here superior people are flattering their inferiors.

When everything goes as we will, it also goes as we wish.[146]

Everything from the past is a text with a hundred meanings and interpretations and truly! a path into *many* futures! yet those who give the future a single meaning also determine the single meaning of the past.

"It is not yet time for me to play the fool" says Zarathustra, when the fool says: "Throw everything away, dance and act as a human being would toward yourself and us."

For some, solitude is a sick person fleeing, for others, solitude is fleeing from a sick person.

These people drive the masses insane and make them puff themselves up so that their barrels overflow — they serve tyrants: and those people make tyrants puff themselves up and jump around until they burst — thus do they serve the masses.

This man laughs like a lightning bolt — but afterward he rumbles for a long time, like thunder

Contented sows or dying gladiators — don't you have any other options?

Gravediggers dig themselves into illness; deadly vapors rest beneath old excavated earth. It is not good to stir up a morass.

They imitate themselves — this is their second childhood.

The compassion of the greatest people is firm,[147] like the handshake of a giant.

Doesn't the sun lament: "I wanted to be a light to them, but I put out their eyes — I blinded them!

"How do I get through the city gate? I have unlearned what it is like to live among dwarves."

The greatest thing about great people is what is maternal in them. — The father — this is always only a matter of chance.

My fury still obeys me.

Beneath my peak and my snows I find all the regions of the living.

and little children do not always come to him who suffers them to come.

You cough and think that this is an objection to strong winds.

"We want food" you roar: your bellies add "Lots!" to this, your lusting eye adds: "Good!"

What is the basest of all base things? A conclusion, the oldest and most recent conclusion: "It hurts, therefore it is *bad*."

Since I have understood this "therefore" and this origin of bad things, I have laughed at all your "good and bad"! My laughter resounds beyond your "good and bad."

Beauty *hides* the man.[148]

To become smooth and hard-hearted we must go into the crowd, but also we must take along our secret solitude.

Strewn from star to star like the seed of life?

Terrible dithyramb of life in Zarathustra 4.

Suffer chance to come to me! It is innocent like a little child.

To outwit chance and lead it around by the hand.

Only those who know where they are going also know what wind is at their back.

Two new virtues — wise forgetfulness and the art of setting sails according to the wind.[149]

Women are becoming more manly: there are too few men.[150]

In kindness there is a lot of contempt for people, but no trace of hate and love for people.[151]

When the devil sheds his skin, his name also falls away.

The bite of conscience[152] a bite from God and if this God is a God of love — a love bite?

I see *their* star and I am delighted: but now they actually think of it as *my* star.

Don't listen to what they say — but look at the set of their jaws! They may lie with their tongues, but they are still speaking the truth with their mouths![153]

And what was the point of all nature being created if not that I might have signs I can use to *speak* with souls!

Now everything is just great! For now hucksters are wearing swords and walrus mustaches, and the regiment itself has gone over to the bowlegged.[154]

This is the black sad sea, like my destiny it lies before me —
Alas this pregnant listlessness at night! An open eye, but still drunk with sleep and still alien, it looks in my direction.
The sea breathes its warm breath on me, like my destiny, and tosses and turns on the pillow of its crags, it groans as though its expectations were evil —
I am sad for you, you dark monster, and for your sake I bear a grudge against myself. Alas, that I do not possess enough strength to deliver you from evil dreams!
What are you doing, Zarathustra? Do you want to comfort the sea with your song? Have you already become a compassionate spectator and harbinger of your own future?
What are you doing, love-sick fool, you superblissful trusting man? But, full of trust, you have always walked right up to all terrible things, even wanting to caress every monster.
A breath of warm air, a bit of soft fur around the claws: — and already seductive tones were pouring from your flute, with great yearning you always approached everything that was alive.
Now you must get to know this monster for my sake!

Better to trust your destiny, even if it roars from 1000 maws like a sea, better still if it bares its teeth at you in a storm than such pregnant sullenness each night.[155]

There is nothing more evil than a sleeping ocean and a pregnant destiny: how will you get over these black depths if you don't want to be more evil and more black than they are?

Whatever you might still encounter will come to you as your destiny: the time has passed when you could also still encounter a coincidence!

If you can't pray, then why can't you at least curse?

I fear you because you laugh while we fight for our lives: you look like someone who is certain that he will live.

Live or die — said Zarathustra.

And if we get out of this, I want to say: "God is not, and Zarathustra taught me this."

I forgive you your mistrust, yet I would not give a plug nickel[156] for your trust.

You still believe in wonders and wonderworkers, true need would also teach you how to pray. The ancient counterfeiters of the mind have also minted a counterfeit of your intellect[157] —

Disgust grips me, I am still only 3 days away from — — —

Cheerfulness as the secret foretaste of *death* — it lifts the great burden of our task from our shoulders.[158]

Zarathustra: Where is Zarathustra from? Who are father and mother to him? "Destiny and laughter are Zarathustra's father and mother; cruel destiny and loving laughter have together spawned a scion like that."[159]

The sky is on fire, the sea spits at it[160]

a puny community in the middle of nowhere and mist and conceit of all Bible-thumpers[161]

22 [4][162]

Scene on the ship.

Impression that human beings are becoming diminished. His *fear* increases.

Death and downfall of the isles.

Zarathustra seeks himself in the tumult:[163]

> with the contrarians (evil people)
>> the violent ones
>> the sculptors
>> the discoverers
>> the fools

22 [5][164]

For did I come to warn against pickpockets and to vilify vice?[165]

You are being pursued.

Keep it up: this is a good way to pursue me: up to now success has only come to those who are most relentlessly pursued.[166]

They are getting fed up with their hating and raging and they have visions of light on lonely roads that say to them: "Why not try loving!" —

There is a raging love that is so sweet!"

A shipwreck spat him toward land, on the crest of a wave he came riding into his promised land.[167]

By all that is bright and strong and good — this God — — —[168]

Next to every warehouse I saw an alehouse: their souls are chilled, they would like to find warmth in spiced wine or even in spicy women.[169]

Know this, for someone who creates, wisdom and goodness is[170] not a characteristic, but rather a means and condition

a contrarian, to himself a bad — spouse

"By accident" — not a good nobleman, even if he is of the oldest line.[171]

Trumpeters and other butterflies

"Your fate has soured you somewhat — now you rise and swell up beyond all bounds" — says the fool to Zarathustra.

You call them stilts — but they are pride's strong feet — long feet!

Servile and supine, obsequious and obnoxious, queasy and querulous

"how could I not be like oil and water when I am with you — always on top! — we would have to be vigorously shaken up together before it would be otherwise" says Zarathustra to the captain, who is surprised at his cheerfulness.[172]

whatever lives around you soon becomes part of what lives in you: it becomes customary. And where you customarily sit becomes the seat of customs.

ill people and obsessed people

"Thus do I praise myself for my part, and that should be enough for me. Now it was your turn to praise me."[173]

There are people with skills and people with jobs — but there are also those who stand on their own, who must stand up for themselves — or else they fall.[174]

— they fall on top of you, like monuments of demigods!

I am Zarathustra the Godless: who speaks here: who is more godless than I am? then I want to become his disciple.[175]

people like that have always had to crown themselves — they always found the priests too cowardly

Telling stories around the evening campfire[176]

against noise — it strikes thoughts dead[177]

with a voice like a stonemason's chisel

they creep around everywhere it is diseased and disgusting, like lice — why shouldn't we crack them!

the greatest danger lies behind us — there in that direction, where the blessed isles are. We set forth at just the right time. "Or too late" said Zarathustra.

to curse all the cowardly devils within you who love to whimper and fold their hands and who would like to pray to something.

goats geese and other crusaders, led by the holy spirit[178]

"they will slit you open, Zarathustra: you look like someone who has swallowed gold"

Pity those who would want to entertain others, if this were no longer their livelihood?

They must fight against the wild animal, hunger — otherwise their entertainment would be that of a wild animal — aimed at us.[179]

Their boredom would be a brood hen here

Common and limited enough for even the smallest of advantages, they read the rubbish of good fortune like tea leaves
Yes, they are rich — but their eyes are still thieves' eyes. Rag dealers. Vultures.[180]

My curse — the brotherhood of hatred and lightning bolts.

I went in search of origins: there I cut myself off from all reverence — all around me it became strange and lonely.
But whatever is reverent in me — blossomed secretly; there a tree sprang forth for me, I sit in its shadow, the tree of the future.[181]
"I am one who reveres the future"

relentlessly pursued, never caught[182]

putrid tepid rancid blood[183]

You made wolves into dogs and humans themselves into human pets[184]

22 [6]
I respect virtue when it is the caution of those who are pregnant: but your virtues are the virtues of those who will never give birth.[185]

All great things walk crooked paths: but these great things must be seen from a wider perspective: this was their courage, to take a crooked path toward a single goal.

Great people and great rivers take crooked paths toward their goal: crooked, but toward *their* goal. This is what is most courageous about them, that they still fear what is crooked.

22 [7]

stalwart in war, stalwart in birth: that's what I want in men and women:

The best taste is not the one that knows how to taste everything: I love contrary choosy palates and tongues, the ones that say "I".

No one wants her as a gift: so she already needs to sell herself![186]

To rule — and no longer to be the servant of a god — this has survived as a means of ennobling humans

22 [8][187]

On the Will to Suffering.
On the Vision and the Riddle.
On Unchosen Bliss.
Before Sunrise.
On the Virtue That Diminishes.
On Passing By.
The Wintersong.
On Apostates.
The Return Home.
On the Three Evils.
On the Spirit of Gravity.
The Summoning
The Convalescent.
On the Great Longing.
On Old and New Tablets
And One More Time!
The Other Dance Song.
On the Ring of Rings.

[23 = Z II 4. End 1883]

23 [1][1]

A brief innocent story that nevertheless has caused a lot of mischief: I'll tell it to you — you can tell the part about the mischief to yourselves!

There once was a boy who was told with looks and speeches: "whatever your father is, this is not your real father!"

This troubled the child and caused him to reflect; and finally he said to himself in his heart of hearts, completely in secret: "is there nothing finer in the world than a real father?

And when the child learned to pray, his first prayer was: "God, please give me a real father!"

Yet the child grew older and his secret love and prayer grew older with him: the teenage boy grew up among women and priests: —

A teenage boy, living among women and priests, grew profound and shy about love, and even about the word "love"

growing profound and thirsty for the dew of love, just like thyme in the night —

thirsty and shivering with thirst and a friend of the night because the night is full of shame and fragrant incense —

His soul itself took on the fragrance of the priests' incense and the women's innocence: yet it was still ashamed of this fragrance.

And just as a typical teenage boy prayerfully desires that a woman love him, so too he prayerfully desired the love of a father and was ashamed even of his prayer.

And so it came to pass that one day his prayer floated away into clouds of light, and words descended from the clouds of light: "Behold, this is my beloved son in whom I am well pleased."[2]

Is this possible! the teenage boy said. I, the beloved son of him, to whom I just prayed for a father? God my father! Is this possible?

This ancient all-powerful Jewish god with furrowed brow and parted lips — is my father! Can this be possible?

But he says it himself, and he has never yet lied: what can I do! I have to believe him!

Yet if I am his son, then I am God: yet if I am God, how am I human? — It is not possible — but I have to believe him!

The human in me — this is surely nothing but God's need for love: for just as I have thirsted for a father, so he has surely thirsted for his children.

That I am human, this is surely because of humans: I am meant to lure them to my father —

— to lure them into loving: oh these fools who have to be lured into loving!

They must love God: this is an easy doctrine and a pleasant one — to us children of God, a light yoke is given to bear: we must do what we most like to do.

This doctrine and wisdom is easy to grasp: even the poor in spirit may reach out their hands to it

Many things about humans aren't very divine: if we take a shit,[3] how are we supposed to be God in that moment?

But ⟨it⟩ is even worse with the other kind of shit called sin: humans want to keep it with them always and not to let go of it.

But I guess I have to believe it: it is possible to be God and still to take a shit: so I shall teach them to let go of their shit and become gods.

23 [2]

I recently drank of ancient wisdom, an unimaginably ancient heady wine of wisdom.

23 [3]⁴

On Fame.

Sensuality is one thing, giving birth something else. Ask women! Having a good time is not the point of giving birth.[5]

Pain makes hens and artists cluck. Sensuality stammers —: now hear me stammer my words on fame.

It is sensual, to press our hand into millennia as if into wax. Sensual, to write on the will of millennia as if on bronze.

It is sensual to melt stars of the future in the goblet of our will: sensual, reverently to shake out worlds on the rugs of eternity beneath us.

23 [4]⁶

One! Midnight begins! Wafting from afar, from the deep world below — does midnight's word seek its final resting place where I am, the hermit's place?

Two! The final resting place of the deep world — for is it really a hermit's pinnacle?[7] When it resounds through *my* ears and blood and marrow, does it seek — does it seek and still find *its* peace?

Three!

23 [5]⁸

On the Ways of the One Who Knows.

"How did you, oh Zarathustra, come to your wisdom: did you fly there? — this you ask of me — so that we may learn from you how we can fly to our wisdom?"

You asked well: you should also be taught well. Anyone who asks a good question is already more than halfway to an answer.

I have come to my wisdom through many ways and means, I did not climb to the pinnacle on a ladder and staircase, to this place where my eyes roamed into the distance that is mine.

And I never asked people: I asked and tried out the ways for myself. My entire journey was trying things out and asking.

Among people I was always the well-concealed one: whether I climbed or flew or stood and paused: they did not see me with their eyes.

They did not hear me with their ears: and often I listened for an echo but I heard only — praise.[9]

I spoke directly into their ears when I embarked on to new terrifying seas: is that how I concealed it? Yet now, when I wandered into new terrifying deserts before their very eyes — who *saw* me wander?

And whenever I climbed rope ladders into many a window, whenever I rode many a mast with nimble legs: I remained well concealed from them, along with my wicked deeds and adventures.

It often seemed to me to be malicious bliss, to sit on the highest masts, like a flame: maybe a tiny light, but still a great comfort for exhausted voyagers and castaways.[10]

I learned another kind of blissfulness and wickedness whenever a thawing wind blew: so that my torrent rose ever higher and my ice built up to towering heights — then I rejoiced.

I found enough weak and gentle people — they call themselves good and deal gently even with virtue; I found enough hypocrites as well, who misuse the name of justice.

I heard self-deceivers speak to me, whose lies rest innocently on hearts and tongues; even many parasites greedily pushed their way in to join the feast of my wisdom.

23 [6]

You should not drink until you are thirsty: and you should not dance until the spirit moves you. And only learn how to lie so that you understand what truth-telling is!

You should not be driven back to the truth until you are hungry for it: and when you have drunk your fill of the good wines of truth, then you will also want to dance.

23 [7][11]

Prelude.

Oh my brothers! That you first learned silence from me! And solitude!

23 [8][12]

On the Ultimate Consolation.

Behold, how everything was set up to be a workshop for creative souls: everything *indispensable* to creative souls is there in *abundance*: even including **pain**.

23 [9][13]

3. On Self-Diminution
The Wintersong.
On Passing By.
On Rulers.
On Those Who Enjoy.
On Image-Shapers.
On Evil People.
On Lawgivers
On Discoverers.
Before Sunrise (Vow)
On the Vision of the Most Solitary One.
The Other Dance Song.
On Solitude.
On the Great Longing.
On Laughing and Flying.
Conversation with Lightning.
On Eternity.
On Free Will. (Below!)

1. On the Will to Suffer
2. On Unchosen Bliss.
On Passing By.
Before Sunrise.
Yes! And Amen!
On the Great Longing.
The Other Dance Song.
Below!
The Wintersong.

On Pregnancy.
On Solitude.
On Fame.
On Rulers.
On (Teachers) Image-Shapers.
On Evil People.
Conversation with Lightning.
On the Vision of the Most Solitary One.
On Laughing (and the Spirit of Gravity).
Song of the One Who Flies.
On Lawgivers (Breaking of the Tablets)
On Those Who Enjoy.
On Discoverers (Chance)

23 [10]¹⁴

  1. On the Will to Suffer.
  2. On Examined Riddles.
  3. On Unchosen Bliss.
  4. Before Sunrise.
  5. On the Virtue That Diminishes ("Powerful People").
  6. On Apostates.
  7. On Passing By.
  8. On the Single Victory.
  9. On the Ways of the One who Knows.
10. The Wintersong.
11. On the Great Longing.
12. The Return Home.
13. On the Three Evils.
14. The Other Dance Song.
15. The New Tablets.
16. On the Spirit of Gravity.
17. On Convalescence.
21. And One More Time!
22. On the Ring of Rings.
(18–20 are missing)¹⁵

— On the Will to Suffer.
   On Examined Riddles.
— On Unchosen Bliss
— Before Sunrise.
— On the Virtue That Diminishes
— On Apostates.
— On Passing By.
   On the Will to Victory.
— The Wintersong.
   On the Great Longing.
— The Return Home.
— On the Three Evils.
— The Other Dance Song.
— The New Tablets
— On the Spirit of Gravity.
— The Convalescent.
   And One More Time!
   On the Ring of Rings.

the Summoning Up
On the Vision of the Most Solitary One.
On the Will for the Ring.
On the Great Longing.
And One More Time!
On the Ring of Rings.

On Consolation in Magnanimity ("Pain")
Abolition of *Sin* (because no God)
   (only a parable)

On the Ultimate Consolation
Without Sin.
On Princes and Peoples —

[24 = Mp XVII 1b. Winter of 1883–1884]

24 [1][1]

That it is difficult to get close to the Greeks, that after study-ing them for a long time we feel even more distant from them: this is the proposition and the entirely personal frustration with which I wish to begin my observations about the Greeks as connoisseurs of human nature. We can live with them for a good while, while holding beliefs that are opposite to theirs

and we learn that our alienation[2] is more instructive than our feeling of familiarity

perhaps a Greek would experience the way we have delved deeply in uncovering what is human to be an impiety against nature, a shameless act. Conversely, we feel alienated —γνώμη;[3] to hear "where there is knowledge, action must follow" and that virtue should be bliss, this sounds so strange and implausible to us that we do a double take to see if it was meant as a joke. It is as if they had given the intellect another layer of skin.

24 [2]

philosophical legacy of *classical antiquity*:

— "purpose"

— God and human (the point of view **before** Copernicus)

— pleasure as motive

— logic, the overvaluing of consciousness.

— the soul

there is no "thing in itself" any more than there can be "absolute knowledge."

I replace fundamental truths with fundamental probabilities — *provisionally accepted* **guidelines** by which to live and think

these guidelines not arbitrary but rather correspond to an *average degree of habituation*.

Habituation is the result of a *selection* made by my various affects, all of which, during this process, *wanted to have a sense of well-being* and *to preserve* themselves.

24 [3]

to observe creative power
  how much it sacrifices of the organism (often destructive)
  how it, when impregnating, transforms another organism
    and puts it into greatest danger.
The degrees of creative power
  1) actors, creating figures out of themselves, e.g., la Faustin[4]
  2) poets
    sculptors
    painters
  3) teachers — Empedocles
  4) conquerors
  5) lawgivers (philosophers)

generally, the type has yet to be found, except in the lowest levels: the history of suffering and joy has yet to be documented. *False* positions e.g., philosophers who position themselves *externally* — but this is only a *temporary* condition and is necessary for being pregnant.

24 [4][5,6]

The Eternal Recurrence.
A Book of Prophecy.

1. Presentation of the doctrine and of its *theoretical* presuppositions and consequences.
2. Proof of the doctrine.

3.   Potential consequences of it being *believed* (it brings
     everything to the *point of upheaval*)
     a) Means of enduring it
     b) Means of eliminating it
4.   Its place in history, as a *midpoint*.
     Time of greatest danger.
     Founding of an oligarchy *above* the peoples and their
     interests: education for the sake of a universally human
     politics.
     Counterpart of Jesuitism.

24 [5]

On the emergence of *logic*
original chaos of ideas
ideas that fit together remained, most of them perished —
and are perishing.[7]

Creating — as *selection* and *finishing* of what has been selected.
(*This* is what is *essential* in every act of will[8]

24 [6]

I have always felt a sense of *decline* in regard to German
culture.

this often made me treat the *entire* phenomenon of European culture *unfairly*, because I had become familiar with a
culture in decline.

the sound of Kant('s) senile and Chinese-like music is fading *out*,

The Germans are always a little late in arriving: they make
things *profound*, e.g.

dependence on foreign countries (how polyphonic!): e.g.,
Kant — Rousseau — sensualists Hume — Swedenborg
Schopenhauer — Indic peoples and Romanticism, Voltaire.
Wagner — French cult of ghastliness and great opera, *Paris*
and escape back to *original conditions*. (sister-marriage
Law of *latecomers* (province after Paris, Germany after France,
such that, of all people, *Germans discovered what is Greek*

the more we develop the strength of a drive, the **greater the inclination** to try to **hurl ourselves** into its *opposite*.[9]

Wagner's **style** of **decadence**: the single *phrase* becomes *sovereign*, subordination and orientation become random. Bourget p. 25.[10]

24 [7]

both of the greatest philosophical points of view (discovered by Germans)

that of *becoming*, of *evolution*

that is oriented around the *value* of *existence* (but the pathetic form of German pessimism must first be overcome!

brought together by me in a *decisive* way

everything becomes and eternally returns

— *slipping away* is not *possible*!

Supposing we *could* judge value, what would be the result?

the thought of r⟨ecurrence⟩ as principle *of selection*, in service to *force* (and barbarism!!)

Humankind's *ripeness* for *this* thought.[11]

Enlightenment concerning the fact that there is *no thing in itself* and

| The great nega-tions. | } | 1) no *knowledge in itself*!
2) *no good and evil in itself*!
3) *no goal and no origin*![12] |

The essence of the *organic* is the least slippery concept.

Purposes as accompanying phenomena of *needs*. Even the philosophies: *our* need right now is to *de*-moralize the world: otherwise we could not to live anymore. The absolute "unfreedom of the w⟨ill⟩," interpreted *morally*, arouses *resistance*.

24 [8]

With respect to the feeling of power, humans can be divided into

A) pitiful people: those for whom the smallest satisfaction is already enough. Proud people, even "good people."

B) dissatisfied people, who want satisfaction outside themselves

C) Those who believe themselves to be full of power

D) etc.

24 [9]

Psychology of Error[13]

Whenever we do something, a *feeling of force* emerges, often preceding what is done, in envisioning what is to be done (as when we catch sight of an enemy, an obstacle that we believe we are *capable of dealing with*): always accompanying this feeling. We instinctively think that this feeling of force ought to be the cause of the action, that it ought to be "the force." Our belief in causality is the belief in force and its effect; a transference of our experience; whereby we identify force with the feeling of force. — Yet nowhere does the force move things, the force that is felt "does not set the muscles in motion." "We have no idea, no experience, of such a process." — "We experience just as little of the *necessity* of a movement as of the force as something that makes things move." Force ought to be that which compels! "We only experience that one thing follows another — we experience neither the compulsion, nor the choice, that one thing follows another." Causality is first created through the projection of compulsion into the process of following. A certain "comprehension" emerges thereby, i.e., we have anthropomorphized the process for ourselves, made it "more familiar": that which is familiar is the habitual familiarity of *a feeling of force that is conjoined to human compelling*[14,15]

24 [10]

It is true that "necessity{"} can also mean "every time when A occurs, B will follow. Degree of probability (certainty) whereby the occurrence of what follows may be expected. This certainty rests on experience: B has always followed A, there has never been a non-B that has followed A. Conceptual support through the fact that processes of following, which are *of a nature similar* to AB, are cited to produce the certainty that B will follow A."[16]

"It is also the case that the sensation[17] of force cannot be derived from motion. Sensation in general cannot be derived from motion.[18]

Also supporting this is merely an illusory experience: in a substance (brain), sensation is engendered by transferred movement (stimuli). But engendered? Would that then have proved that the sensation did *not* yet exist there at all? so that its arising would have to be understood as a *creative act* of the motion that has taken place? The state of this substance, in which there is no sensation, is only a hypothesis! no experience![19] — therefore sensation as *property* of substance: there are sensing substances."[20]

"Do we have experience of certain substances *not* having sensation? No, it is just that we do not experience that they have it. It is impossible to derive sensation from non-sensing substances."[21] — Oh such hastiness![22]

24 [11]

"I want to go": but 1) I *have to* go, and the *willing*[23] is only something incidental which produces no motion at all, a prior image. 2) This image is unbelievably raw and indeterminate compared to what happens, it is conceptual and completely general, so that innumerable realities overlap underneath it. Therefore it cannot be the cause of what happens. — *Purposes are to be eliminated.*

24 [12]

When an officer gives the order "present arms," the soldiers do it. He commands, they want to do it now. In reality, what they do now is something *different* for each one of them: but to crude organs *it looks the same.* Those who act purposefully often find those purposes fulfilled: i.e., they see crudely and do not at all recognize what truly happens. That the world of what happens *corresponds to our incomplete image of what happens, overlaps* with it, this is the faith of teachers of purpose. The less that is known, the easier it is to maintain this faith.

24 [13][24]

"In the development of thought there must have come a point when it became conscious, such that whatever were designated as properties of things were sensations of the perceiving subject: at this point, the properties ceased to belong to the thing. "The thing in itself" remained. The distinction between things in themselves and the thing for us was based on the ancient naïve perception that projected energy into the thing: but analysis has shown that even force was imaginatively ascribed to the thing, and in the same way — substance. "The thing affects a subject?" Root of the idea of substance in language, not in that which is external to us! The thing in itself is no problem at all![25]

What exists should be thought of as sensation that has, as its foundation, nothing else lacking in sensation.[26]

In motion no new *content* is given to sensation. With respect to content, what exists[27] cannot be motion: therefore *form* of existence.[28,29]

NB. The *explanation* of events can be attempted, first: by representing images of events that *precede* the events (purposes)

second: by representing images that *follow* the events (the mathematical-physical explanation.

These approaches should not be confused with each other. Therefore: the physical explanation, which is the picturing of the world out of sensation and thought, cannot itself derive sensation and thought again and make them emerge: rather, physics must *consistently* construe even the sensing world **as lacking sensation and purpose** — all the way up to the most superior humans. And the teleological explanation is only a history *of purposes* and is *never* physicalist!

24 [14]

A multiplicity of forces, conjoined through a common nutritive process, is what we call "life." All so-called feeling, representing, thinking is part of this nutritive process as a means of making it possible, i.e., 1) a resistance to all other forces 2) an arrangement of these according to shapes and rhythms 3) an evaluation in regard to incorporation or separation.[30]

1. Humans are *form-building* creatures.

Humans believe in "being" and in things because they are form-building and rhythm-making creatures.

The shapes and forms that we see, and in which we believe we have things contained, are all absent. We simplify ourselves and we conjoin some "impressions" through figures that *we* create.

Those who close their eyes discover that a form-building drive continues to function and that innumerable things are attempted that do not correspond to any reality.

2. Humans are *rhythm-making creatures*. They project all events into these rhythms, it is a way of gaining control of the "impressions."

3. Humans are *resistant* forces: in regard to all other forces

The way they *nourish* themselves and acquire things is to shape them into "forms" and rhythms: *comprehension* is at first only *creation* of "things." *Knowledge a means of nourishment.*

24 [15]

Science does *not* ask what drove us to this willing: *in fact,* it *denies that willing has occurred* and thinks that something entirely different has happened — simply put, that the belief in will and purpose is an illusion. It does not inquire into the *motivations* for an action, as if these had already existed in our consciousness prior to the action: rather, it first divides the action into a mechanical group of appearances and seeks the prehistory of this mechanical movement — but *not* in feeling perceiving thinking. **That is why** it can never accept the explanation: perception is what was *supposed to be explained* in the first place. — Its problem is really this: to explain the world without resorting to perceptions as causes: for that would certainly mean: seeing perceptions as causes of perceptions. Its task is in no way accomplished.

Thus: either no will — the hypothesis of science — or free will. Latter assumption the prevailing feeling that is inescapable for us, even if the hypothesis were *proved*.

The popular belief in cause and effect rests on the presupposition that free will is *the cause of every effect*: before this we do not have the feeling of causality. Thus, this presupposition underlies even the feeling that every cause is *not* an effect but rather in the first place always a cause — if the will is the cause. "Our acts of will are *not necessary*" — this *is contained* in the concept "*will*." The effect *after* the cause is what is necessary — that's how we feel. —That even our willing must absolutely be like that, is a *hypothesis*.[31] But willing: = purposeful willing. Purpose contains a value judgment. Where do value judgments come from? Is the basis a consistent standard of "pleasant and painful"?

But in innumerable cases we do not *make* something painful until we project our value judgment into it.

Range of moral value judgments: they play a role in almost every sense impression. The world is *colored* for us through them.

We have projected the purpose and the value: through this we have within us an immense *latent force*: but *comparing* values reveals that opposing things were seen ⟨as⟩ valuable, that many codes of values have existed.

therefore nothing valuable "in itself"

the analysis of codes of values reveals their establishment as the establishment of *conditions of existence* for narrowly defined groups (and often mistakenly): for the sake of preservation.

in observing *contemporary* humans, it becomes obvious that we apply *widely differing* value judgments, and that there is no more creative force left in there — the basis: "the condition of existence" is now absent from moral judgments. The judgments are much more superfluous. They have not been this painful in a long time. —They are becoming *arbitrary*. Chaos.

Who creates *the goal* that remains ascendant above humankind and also above the individual? In earlier times, the point of morality was *preservation*. But now no one wants to *preserve* anything anymore, there is nothing left there to preserve. Therefore an *experimental morality, to give* ourselves a goal.[32]

species-preserving

24 [16][33]

About the Origin[34] of our
Value Judgments.

We can spatially analyze our own bodies, and then we get exactly the same representation of them that we do of the solar system, and we no longer notice the distinction between the organic and the inorganic

Hymn to value judgment.

In earlier times, the movements of the stars and planets were explained as effects of consciously purposeful beings: we don't need this anymore, and it has been a long time since we have regarded purpose-setting consciousness as adequate for explaining even bodily movements and personal transformations.[35] The vast majority of movements have nothing whatsoever to do with consciousness: *also nothing to do with perception*. Perceptions and thoughts are *very limited* and *rare* in relation to the countless number of events in every moment. Conversely, we perceive that a *purposefulness* prevails in the smallest event, for which our best knowledge is inadequate, a cautiousness, a selection, a collation, compensation etc. In short, we discover an activity that would have to be attributed to a *vastly superior* and more comprehensive *intellect* than the one of which we are conscious. We learn *to think less highly* of all consciousness: we unlearn how to make ourselves responsible for ourselves, since *we*, as conscious, purpose-setting beings, are only the smallest part of this process. We perceive almost nothing of the numerous influences in every moment, e.g., air electricity: enough forces could exist that continuously influence us, even though they never enter into our perception. Pleasure and pain are such rare and limited phenomena compared with the countless stimuli that a cell transmits, or an organ transmits, to another cell, or to another organ.

It is a phase of *modesty in respect to consciousness*. We finally understand the conscious I itself merely as a tool in service to that superior, more comprehensive intellect: and here we can ask whether all conscious *willing*, all *conscious purposes*, all *value judgments* are not perhaps just **means** through which something essentially *different* must be *achieved* than what appears within consciousness. We *tend to think*: it has to do with our *pleasure* and *displeasure* — — — but pleasure and displeasure could be the means by which we would have to *accomplish something* that lies outside our consciousness — — — It is to be demonstrated how much all that is conscious remains *on the surface*: how action, and the image of action, *differ*, how *little* is known of what *pre*cedes an action: how fanciful our feelings "freedom of the will" "cause and effect" are: how thoughts are only images, just as words are only signs of thoughts: the impossibility of explaining every action: the superficiality of all praise and blame: *how essential* **invention** and **imagination** are, in the place where we consciously live, how we speak in all of our phrases about inventions (including affects), and how *h⟨uman⟩ connections* rest upon a transmission and continual re-creation of these inventions: while fundamentally the real connections (through procreation) continue on their unknown path. Are human beings really *changed* by this belief in common inventions? Or is the complete system of ideas and value judgments merely *itself an expression* of unknown changes? So, do willing, purposes, thoughts, values really *exist*? Is all of conscious life perhaps only a *mirror image*? And even when a value judgment appears to *define* a human, does essentially something entirely different happen? In short: assuming we could successfully explain that which is purposeful in the workings of nature without assuming a purpose-setting I: could ultimately *our* purpose-setting, our willing, etc. perhaps be only a *sign language* for something essentially different — namely something not-willing and unconscious?[36] Merely the *most subtle impression* of this natural purposefulness of the organic, but nothing different from it?

And briefly put: perhaps the entire development of the mind has to do with the *body*: it is its *history that is becoming* **tangible**, a history of a *superior body being formed*. The organic is still ascending to higher levels. Our craving for knowledge of nature is a means by which the body wants to perfect itself. Or rather: hundreds of thousands of experiments are performed, in order to change nutrition, ways of living, lifestyles of the body: consciousness and the value judgments it contains, all kinds of pleasure and displeasure, are *signs of these changes* and *experiments. In the end, this has nothing at all to do with humans: they must be overcome.*[37]

24 [17][38]

They think of themselves as being *present* at the emergence of organisms: what is it about this process that has been perceivable through sight and touch? What can be rendered in numbers? Which rules manifest themselves in the movements? Thus: humans want to categorize every event as an *event for sight and touch*, consequently as movements: and they want to find *formulas* that will *simplify* the enormous mass of these experiences. *Reduction of all events* to something that can be measured by human senses[39] and mathematicians.

This has to do with an *inventory of human experiences*: assuming that humans, or rather the *human eye* and *conceptual ability*, might have been eternal witnesses to all things.

24 [18]⁴⁰

Science — this has been up to now the elimination of the complete confusion of things by means of hypotheses which "explain" everything — therefore motivated by the intellect's aversion to chaos. — This same aversion possesses me when I observe *myself*: I, too, would like to imaginatively represent to myself the inner world by means of a *schema* and move beyond intellectual confusion. Morality was just this sort of *simplification*: it taught that humans were *recognizable, familiar.* — Now we have destroyed morality — we have again become *completely obscure* to ourselves! I know that I know nothing *of myself. Physics* reveals itself as an *act of charity* for the emotions:⁴¹ science (*path to knowledge*) gains a new allure after morality has been eliminated — and *because here alone* we find consistency, we have to *orient* our lives around it in order to *preserve* consistency for ourselves. This results in a kind of *practical contemplation* about **the conditions of our existence** as those who know.

24 [19]⁴²

Morality of *truthfulness* in the herd. "You should be knowable,⁴³ express what is within you through clear and constant signs — otherwise you are dangerous: and if you are evil, the worst thing for the herd is your ability to disguise yourself. We despise what is secret what is unknowable. — *Consequently* you must consider yourself to be knowable, you must not be *concealed* from yourself, you must *not* believe in your *ability to change*." Thus: the demands of truthfulness presuppose a person's *knowability* and *stability*. Actually, the point of education is to bring a member of the herd to a *particular belief* concerning the essence of human beings: it *first creates this belief* and in addition it demands "truthfulness."

24 [20][44]

The Faith in **"Affects."** Affects are a construction of the intellect, a *fictional account of causes* that do not exist. All corporeal *general feelings*[45] that we do not understand are intellectually interpreted, i.e., a *reason* is sought as to why we feel this or that way, in persons, experiences etc. thus, something deleterious dangerous foreign is *assumed* as if it were the cause of our bad mood: actually it is *added* to the bad mood for the sake of *being able to think* about our condition. — Frequent blood flows to the brain accompanied by the feeling of suffocation are **interpreted** as *anger*: people and things that enrage us are triggers for the physiological state. — After the fact, once we have grown accustomed to them, certain processes and *general feelings* are associated so regularly that the sight of certain processes incites this same state of *general feeling* and accompanies any kind of circulation blockage, production of semen etc.: thus through proximity: we then say "the affect is triggered."

Judgments are already present in "pleasure" and "displeasure": stimuli are differentiated according to whether they do or don't enhance the feeling of power.

24 [21][46]

The faith in willing. It is a faith in miracles to posit a thought as the cause of a mechanical movement. *The consistency of science* demands that, after we have made the world *conceivable* for ourselves through tiny images, we also make affects desires willing etc. *conceivable* to ourselves, i.e., we **reject** them and we *treat them as mistakes of the intellect.*

24 [22][47]

Denunciation did not become a part of punishment until certain penalties were attached to *despicable* people (e.g., slaves). Those who were punished *most often* were despicable people and *finally* there was something to denounce in punishment itself. —

24 [23][48]

We believe *thinking* to be the strongest and most consistent activity at all levels of life, in every perception and apparent suffering as well! In this way, thinking obviously becomes *most powerful* and *most demanding*, and in time tyrannizes all other forces. In the end, it becomes "the passion in itself."

24 [24]

— — — thus selflessness would *further* evil. Virtue would be foolishness and self-contradiction. Those who would want to *make* human beings better could not do so by means of their goodness but rather by resisting their charitable inclinations.

24 [25][49]

supreme fairness and generosity as state of *weakness* (the New Testament and the early Christian community)

(revealing itself as complete *bêtise*[50] in the Englishmen Darwin, Wallace).

Those of you with superior natures, *your fairness* is driving you to *suffrage universel*[51] etc., your "humanity" is driving you to generosity in response to crimes and stupidity. *In time you will make possible the victory of stupidity and of thoughtless people*

(Comfort and stupidity —*the means*) (e.g., Bismarck —

Externally: age of brutal wars, revolutions, explosions

Internally: ever growing weakness of human beings. *Events* as *triggers*. Parisians as the European extreme.[52]

Consequence.

1) *Barbarians*,

first, of course, in shaping culture up to now (e.g., Dühring)

2) *Sovereign individuals* (where *concentrations* of barbarian *force* are combined with a lack of restraint regarding everything that has come before)

Age of the greatest stupidity, brutality and misery of the *masses*, and *of the most superior individuals*.

24 [26][53]

At our core:[54] not knowing, which way out? *Emptiness.*
Attempt to get beyond this through intoxication.

Intoxication as music

Intoxication as cruelty in the tragic enjoyment of the
downfall of what is most noble.

Intoxication as blind fervor for individual *people* (or *ages*)
(as hatred, etc.)

Attempt to work mindlessly as a tool of science.

to open our eyes to the many small pleasures e.g., even as
someone who knows. Modesty in regard to ourselves.

to generalize modesty concerning ourselves into a kind of
pathos

mysticism, the lustful *enjoyment* of the eternal void.

art for its own sake "*le fait,*"[55] "pure knowing" as narcotics
for disgust with *ourselves.*[56]

some sort of regular work, *some* sort of small stupid fanaticism

the confusion of all means — illness through universal
immoderation. (Debauchery kills pleasure.)

1) weakness of the will as result.

2) *having felt,* by contrast, extreme pride and the humiliation of minor weaknesses.

24 [27][57]

Morality for Moralists.

1 Little knowledge of our effect
   false presuppositions concerning our motivations

2 Exchange of moral labels; good people not wanting to see.

3 Motives of moralists, self-knowers, confessors etc.

4 Health and illness and their manifestations in good and
   evil people. The body as master teacher. Morality as sign
   language.[58]

5 Evil as organic function. Good people as degeneration,
   stagnation etc. "Altruism."

6 Conscience of the community and of the individual. At
the end, the individual as majority.

7 The future of morality. Religions.

24 [28]

My Innovations.

Further development of pessimism

the pessimism of the *intellect.*

mor⟨al⟩ criticism, disintegration of the final consolation
knowing the signs of *decline*

veiled by delusion every strong action

culture isolated, unjust, thereby strong

1.) My *ambition* to counter the decline and the increasing
weakness of personality. I sought a new *center.*

2.) Impossibility of this ambition *recognized*!

3.) **After this** *I went further along the path of disintegration,*
— there I **found new** *sources of strength* for *individuals.* We
must be *destroyers*! — —

I recognized that the state of *disintegration* in which **individual** *beings* **can** *perfect themselves* **as never before** — **is** a reflection and **exemplary case** of **universally shared existence.**[59]
Theory of **chance**, *the soul a selective and self-nourishing being*
exceptionally clever and **continuously** creative (this *creative*
power usually overlooked! understood only as "*passive*")

I recognized the *active force* that which is creative in the
midst of chance

— chance is itself *merely the collision of creative impulses*[60]

I held up *eternal recurrence against* the numbing feeling of
general disintegration and imperfection![61]

24 [29]

Fear of death as an *European illness.*[62]

Fear easy to instill,

even in stupid fish

Herd animals mainly *fearful,*

hearing highly attuned to alarm signals.

Moral judgments (fear and aversion) very different, inculcated early. The art of rendering judgments **against** others, something all teachers of virtue have in common.

24 [30]

to connect skepticism with *heroic* feelings

Skepticism of weakness and skepticism of courage

To imagine a human being *without morals*, who everywhere brings forth even the opposite judgment

Napoleon.

24 [31][63]

Compassion and love for humankind as development of the sex drive.

Justice as development of the drive for revenge.

Virtue as pleasure in resistance, will to power.

Honor as public recognition of that which has affinity and equal power.

aversion to the calculating *frogs*

All virtues physiological *states* namely the main organic functions perceived as necessary, as good.

All virtues are actually refined *passions* and intensified states.

24 [32]

Unfreedom or freedom of the will? There is *no will*.[64]

The individual is something completely *novel* and *someone who creates novelty*.[65]

24 [33][66]

Individuals are something absolute, all actions entirely *their* own.

In the end, they take the values for judging their actions from within themselves: this is because even those words that have been passed down must be *interpreted by them in a completely individual way for themselves*. The *interpretation* of the formula is at least personal, even if it creates no formula: as *interpreters* they are still *creative*.

24 [34]⁶⁷

All actions must first be prepared in as mechanical a way as possible, before they are willed. Or: "*purpose*" does not appear in the brain until, *for the most part*, everything is prepared for its completion. Purpose an "inner" "stimulus" — nothing more.

There is no "will": this is merely the understanding's simplifying concept, like "matter."

24 [35]

Our sense organs as causes of the external world? But *they* themselves are indeed also nothing but effects of our "senses." — Our image of the eye is a product of the *eye*.

24 [36]⁶⁸

1) There is no *matter*⁶⁹ — no atom p. 53

2) There is no *space*. (The prejudgment "empty of matter" is what created the assumption of spaces in the first place.

3) There is also no cause and effect. Rather: if a tension occurs here, a release of tension *must* occur in the whole rest of the world. (*That* the tension occurs is in turn the "*consequence*" of a release of tension elsewhere.) But it cannot *possibly* be a sequence: rather, *simultaneously*, tension increases here and decreases *there*. The processes that are actually connected to each other must transpire *absolutely simultaneously*. We single out a point as "effect," e.g., when a person falls over after being shot. But this is an immense chain of connected "effects." If time were necessary for the sake of the "effect," then *there would be* a *plus* **without** the corresponding minus, at least for moments: i.e., the force would sometimes wax sometimes wane

Vogt p. 654

we should presuppose a *living rhythm*, *not* cause and consequence!

4) we must not assume *any absolute creation*, because nothing can be comprehended with this "concept." To create force, that is not there, suddenly out of nothing: this is no *hypothesis* at all! (contra *Vogt* p. 2 etc.)

5) We can recognize the emergence of the organism from the "moral drives" of humans, reasoning from this developing process back to the development of the lowest organisms. Moral drives are the history of self-regulation and function-building of a whole (state community): how is the individual given a *feeling of function*?

The individual is an egg. Colony-building is the task of every individual

24 [37][70]

Omnia naturalia facienti sunt indifferentia, sed abstinenti vel neganti bona aut mala.[71]

Reference Matter

Notes

The following symbols are used throughout the text and notes:

[ ]	Deletion by Nietzsche	
| |	Addition by Nietzsche	
{ }	Addition by the translators	
⟨ ⟩	Addition by the editors (Colli and Montinari)	
— — —	Unfinished or incomplete sentence or thought	
Italics	Underlined once by Nietzsche	
Bold	Underlined twice or more by Nietzsche	
NL	Books in Nietzsche's personal library	

Variants and editions of Nietzsche's works are referred to by the following abbreviations:

CW	*The Complete Works of Friedrich Nietzsche*
KGB	*Briefwechsel: Kritische Gesamtausgabe*
KGW	*Werke: Kritische Gesamtausgabe*
KSA	*Werke: Kritische Studienausgabe*
Le	Twenty-volume 1894 Leipzig edition of Nietzsche's works (*Großoktav-Ausgabe*)
Pd	Preliminary draft
Pm	Printer's manuscript (clean final copy of handwritten MS)

Sd	Second draft
Se	Subsequent emendation

Titles of Nietzsche's works are referred to by the following abbreviations:

AC	*The Anti-Christian*
BGE	*Beyond Good and Evil*
BT	*The Birth of Tragedy*
D	*Dawn*
DD	*Dionysus Dithyrambs*
DS	*David Strauss the Confessor and the Writer*
EH	*Ecce Homo*
GM	*On the Genealogy of Morality*
HAH	*Human, All Too Human*
HL	*On the Utility and Liability of History for Life*
JS	*The Joyful Science*
MM	*Mixed Opinions and Maxims*
NCW	*Nietzsche Contra Wagner*
SE	*Schopenhauer as Educator*
TI	*Twilight of the Idols*
UO	*Unfashionable Observations*
WA	*The Wagner Case*
WB	*Richard Wagner in Bayreuth*
WP	*The Will to Power*
WS	*The Wanderer and His Shadow*
Z	*Thus Spoke Zarathustra*

Unless another volume of the Complete Works is indicated, all cross-references to fragments are ones that appear in this volume. References to the following works will also appear in the notes:

Flügel   Felix Flügel, *A Practical Dictionary of the English and German Languages in Two Parts/Praktisches Englisch-Deutsches und Deutsch-Englisches Wörterbuch in zwei Theilen.* Leipzig: Julius E. Richter; Hamburg: John Augustus Meissner, 1852. This is an expanded edition of his father Johann Gottfried Flügel's *A Complete Dictionary of the English and German and German and English Languages in Two Volumes/Vollständige Englisch-Deutsches und Deutsch-Englisches Wörterbuch in zwei Theilen*, first published in 1830.

Grimm *Deutsches Wörterbuch von Jacob und Wilhelm Grimm.* 16 Bde. in 32 Teilbänden. Leipzig 1854–1961. Quellen-verzeichnis Leipzig 1971. Online version at http://www.woerterbuchnetz.de/DWB.

Pfeiffer *Friedrich Nietzsche — Paul Rée — Lou von Salomé: Die Dokumente ihrer Begegnung.* Auf der Grundlage der einstigen Zusammenarbeit mit Karl Schlechta und Erhart Thierbach ("The documentation of their meetings." Based on previous collaboration with Karl Schlechta and Erhart Thierbach). Edited by Ernst Pfeiffer. Frankfurt on Main: Insel Verlag, 1970.

[1 = N V 9a. N VI 1a.]

1. *"solitudo continuata dulcescit"]* "Continued solitude grows sweet" {Cf. Luigi Boniforti (1817–1909), *Il lago Maggiore e suoi dintorni: Corografia e guida storica, artistica, industriale* ("Lake Maggiore and its surroundings: Chorography and historical, artistic, industrial guide") (Milan: Brigola, 1871), 239.}

2. *Madonna del Sasso. (Locarno)]* The Pilgrimage Church above the city of Locarno.

3. {See our notes on the translation of the pronoun *man* in the Translators' Afterword, 726–27.}

4. {These notes are based in part on books by the physicists Johann Karl Friedrich Zöllner (1834–82), *Über die Natur der Cometen: Beiträge zur Geschichte und Theorie der Erkenntniss* ("On the nature of comets: Contributions to the history and theory of knowledge") (Leipzig: Engelmann, 1872); and Johann Gustav Vogt (1843–1920), *Die Kraft: Eine real-monistische Weltanschauung* ("Force: A real-monistic worldview") (Leipzig: Haupt & Tischler, 1878).}

5. *unlearn] verlernen* {N has in mind here the deliberate and systematic attempt to discard or forget erroneous habits and opinions.}

6. Cf. 5[1] 60; {12[1] 184}.

7. Cf. 1[10]; 3[1] 2; *Z* I "On Freely-Chosen Death."

8. *"Suaviter in re, fortiter in me."]* "Gentle in action, resolute in me." A paraphrase of *Fortiter in re, suaviter in modo* ("Resolute in action, gentle in manner"), saying of the Jesuit general Claudio Aquaviva, *Industriae ad curandos animae morbos* ("Curing the illnesses of the soul"), Venice 1606 (according to Büchmann).

9. Cf. *JS* 262; 3[1] 224; {3[1] 34; 22[3]_563}.

10. Cf. 3[1] 34; {1[9]; 3[1] 224; 22[3]_563; *JS* 262. {Here and throughout these notebooks, wherever Nietzsche uses singular inflection to describe all members of a species (*wer*/"anyone who"), an ethnicity (*der Chinese*), or a vocation (*der Dichter*), we have pluralized the nouns and their possessive referents in order to preserve gender neutrality. For a detailed explanation of our approach, with examples, please see the section "Singular Universals" in the Translators' Afterword, 730–32.}

11. Cf. note to 1[6].

12. Cf. 3[1] 264.

13. Cf. *JS* 7; *CW* 13, 4[313].

14. *Vademecum. Vadetecum]* "Go with me. Go with you" {A vade mecum is a handbook for ready reference that someone can carry around.}

15. Cf. 1[101]; 3[1] Motto; 3[4]; *JS* "Toward New Seas."

16. *Friend!] Freundin!* {The poetic I is addressing a female friend.}

17. Freundin! — sprach Columbus — traue
Keinem Genueser mehr!
Immer starrt er in das Blaue,
Fernstes lockt ihn allzusehr!

*

Muth! Auf offnem Meer bin ich,
Hinter mir liegt Genua.
Und mit dir im Bund gewinn ich
Goldland und Amerika.

*

Stehen fest wir auf den Füßen!
Nimmer können wir zurück.
Schau hinaus: von fernher grüßen
Uns Ein Tod, Ein Ruhm, Ein Glück!

18. *Pd*: Toward New Seas
Friend take this book and do not trust*
a Genoese ever again!
What is farthest draws him all too much!

I was as one, I am as two,
Behind us lies Genoa,
And with golden threads I spin
A fortune for myself — Hallelujah!**

    *Read this book and do not trust {variant to the starred line above}
    **the future and America {variant to the double-starred line above}
    19. Verse from Lou von Salomé's "Prayer to Life"; she gave N this poem when she left Tautenburg, Cf. Pfeiffer 450.
    20. *sub specie trecentorum annorum?]* {A play on the Latin phrase *sub specie aeternitatis*, literally "under the aspect of eternity," which since Spinoza has meant "universally true." Here N means "under the aspect" or "within the timeframe of 300 years."}
    21. A later addition, in part, of already treated or yet to be treated topics.
    22. *neighborliness] Nächstensucht* {N means "neighbor" here in the sense of Jesus's second great commandment, "Love your neighbor as yourself" (Matthew 22:39); cf. 1[22]; 17[30].}
    23. *The "I" . . . feet.]* {*WP* 768.}
    24. Dies ist kein Buch: was liegt an Büchern!
Was liegt an Särgen und Leichentüchern!
Dies ist ein Wille, dies ist ein Versprechen,
Dies ist ein letztes Brücken-Zerbrechen,
Dies ist ein Meerwind, ein Ankerlichten,
Ein Räderbrausen, ein Steuer-Richten,
Es brüllt die Kanone, weiß dampft ihr Feuer,
Es lacht das Meer, das Ungeheuer —
    25. {Cf. 1[19]; 17[30].}
    26. Cf. *Z* I "On the Way of Those Who Create"; 3[1] 222.
    27. Cf. 3[1] 223; 5[1] 59.

28. Cf. 3[1] 282.

29. Cf. 3[1] 26; {see the Translators' Afterword, 743–44, for notes on the translation of N's *Gemüth*}.

30. Dated by Peter Gast "2 October 1882" in the notebook; actually to be dated beginning of August 1882, which may be concluded from Paul Rée's letter of 6 August 1882 to Lou von Salomé (in Tautenburg); cf. Pfeiffer 177.

31. {N's use of the masculine singular universal includes both men and women. We do not pluralize "medium" here for the sake of clarity.}

32. *Buckle]* {Henry Thomas Buckle (1821–62), English historian.}

33. *Advocatus diaboli]* "Devil's advocate" {Underlined by N.} Cf. 1[65]; {3[1] 10}.

34. *choice] Willkür* {We believe that "choice" best captures these allusions to Kant's technical term in his moral theory.}

35. Cf. 1[60].

36. {Cf. 3[1] 226.}

37. *state] Zustand* {The negation of the German term in this context indicates the impossibility of isolating any phase within a process}.

38. {Cf. 5[1] 54.}

39. *death] der Tod* {Here in nominative case, which we are assuming was meant to be *den Tod* (in the accusative).}.

40. {Cf. 1[78]; 5[1] 53.}

41. *Choice] Willkür*

42. Cf. 1[109].

43. *"Faites . . . terre."]* "Get married out of friendship in order to have children. Love has little to do with progeny. If you see a human being in front of you that you love more than yourself, you will be happy. But it is not the woman that one can love more than oneself, it is the child, it is the innocent being, it is the divine type that vanishes more or less while growing up, but, in the course of some years, brings us back to the perception of an ideal on earth." {Maxime du Camp cites this letter from George Sand of 21 June 1868 in his "Souvenirs littéraires. XIII: Lui et Elle; intérieur de journal," published in *Revue des deux mondes* 52 (15 August 1882): 729.}

44. Cf. 3[1] 20; *BGE* 86.

45. Cf. 3[1] 47; 12[1] 115, 27.

46. {Cf. 1[111]; 3[1] 16.}

47. *imperiousness] Herrschsucht* {Which N sometimes contrasts with *Selbstsucht* ("selfishness").}

48. {Cf. 1[111]; 3[1] 17; *BGE* 139.}

49. *women] Frauen* {Cf. 3[1] 351c; 1[50]; 12[1] 92.}.

50. *On the Reemergence] Zur Wieder-Entstehung* {In not distinguishing between *zu* and *von* in N's titles, we follow the usage of the Stanford edition.}

51. Cf. 3[1] 15; *Z* I "Zarathustra's Preface" 4.

52. Cf. 5[1] 43.

53. Cf. 3[1] 48.

54. Cf. 3[1] 14; *Z* I "On Friends."

55. Cf. 3[1] 13; {4[226]; 12[1] 147; 13[14]; 16[7]}.

56. Cf. 1[37].

57. Cf. 5[1] 68.

58. Cf. 3[1] 12; {22[3]_562}.

59. Cf. 5[1] 67; 3[1] 11; 4[29]; {3[1] 445; *BGE* 91}.

60. Cf. 1[32]; 3[1] 10.

61. *advocatus diaboli]* "devil's advocate"

62. Cf. 3[1] 9; *Z* I "Zarathustra's Preface" 2; {5[1] 245}.

63. *Heroic . . . God:]* Cf. 1[70]; 3[1] 222.

64. Cf. 1[32].

65. Cf. 1[24, 67]; 3[1] 122; 5[1] 66; 1[43, 108]; 3[1] 50, 49, 8; 1[72, 73]; *BGE* 129, 133.

66. *we know them through and through] ihre Maaße und Gewichte kennen*

67. *repeating beings] periodische Wesen*

68. {Cf. 3[1] 50; 22[3]_564; *BGE* 129.}

69. {Cf. 3[1] 49; 22[3]_564.}

70. Cf. 1[70]; 5[1] 65.

71. {Cf. 1[88]; 5[1] 61; 1[108].}

72. {Cf. 3[1] 8.}

73. *will for power] Machtwille*

74. Cf. 1[70]; 3[1] 8; 5[1] 64.

75. Cf. 3[1] 7.

76. Cf. 3[1] 7.

77. {Cf. 3[1] 29; 22[3]_563.}

78. *A person of faith] Der gläubige Mensch*

79. Cf. 5[1] 53; {1[43]}.

80. Cf. 1[34, 80]; 3[1] 51, 60.

81. *men and women] Männer und Frauen*

82. Cf. 4[39]; *CW* 13, 11[195].

83. Cf. 1[108] 1.

84. Cf. 12[1] 193.

85. Cf. 1[108] 2; 5[1] 63.

86. Cf. 1[108] 4; 5[1] 62; *BGE* 114.

87. *women] Frauen*

88. Cf. 1[108] 5–6; 5[1] 61.

89. {Cf. 1[73]; 5[1] 61; 1[108]. We translate *Untergang* as "downfall" in this volume, but we have changed the verb here to accommodate the transitive meaning.}

90. Cf. 3[1] 6; *Z* I "On Loving Thy Neighbor."

91. Cf. 5[1] 19.

92. Cf. 3[1] 4; 12[1] 120; *BGE* 275.

93. Cf. 3[1] 3; 12[1] 121; *BGE* 130.

94. *Schilling . . . Glockner.]* {Cf. Julius Karl Josef Schilling, *Spanische Grammatik* (Leipzig: Verlag G. A. Gloeckner, 1882); N misspells the name of Schilling's publisher.}

95. Cf. 3[1] 51; 12[1] 72; *BGE* 140.

96. Soll das Band nicht reißen,
Mußt du mal drauf beißen.

97. {These works are cited in Friedrich von Hellwald, *Kulturgeschichte in ihrer natürlichen Entwicklung bis zur Gegenwart* ("Cultural history in its natural development to the present") (Augsburg: Lampart, 1876), 8, 9, 13, 65. Hellwald's text was an important source for N of information concerning Zarathustra; in fact, N's first reference to Zarathustra (cf. *CW* 13, 11[195]) follows closely from this text, p. 169. N's connection with Hellwald's text was first discovered by Paolo D'Iorio; cf. "Beiträge zur Quellenforschung," *Nietzsche-Studien* 22 (1993): 395–97.}

98. {Cf. Eduard Hitzig, *Untersuchungen über das Gehirn: Abhandlungen physiologischen und pathologischen Inhalts* ("Studies

of the brain: Treatises with physiological and pathological content") (Berlin: August Hirschwald, 1874).}

99. *Animal . . . Science]* {In English in the original.}

100. {Cf. Paul von Lilienfeld, *Gedanken über die Socialwissen-
schaft der Zukunft* ("Thoughts on the social science of the future"), 2 vols. (Mitau: E. Behre, 1873).}

101. *Cosa . . . dura!!!]* {"Beautiful and mortal things/Pass away
and do not last!!!" Underlined by N. A verse from Sonnet 248 of the
Canzoniere, also called *Rarum vulgarium fragmenta*, by Petrarch.}

102. Cf. 1[15]; 3[1] Motto; 3[4].

103. *Columbus novus.]* "The New Columbus."

104. Dorthin will ich, und ich traue
Mir fortan und meinem Griff!
Offen ist das Meer: in's Blaue
Treibt mein Genueser Schiff.
                    **
Alles wird mir neu und neuer
Hinter mir liegt Genua.
Muth! Stehst du doch selbst am Steuer,
Lieblichste Victoria!

105. *Pd* in N V 9, 20 {Montinari's comments are within brackets
preceded by MM}:

Unmoved heart, a mute
hand at the helm.

There [to
that place]
{I} want
to go

Genoa — that sank, that disappeared!

[is] [that disappeared, is]
Genoa — have I already
forgotten it?

Heart, stay unmoved! Hand,   [Gloria] stands at my
    Hold the helm, hand!   Who stands there at the helm
                                    for me?

Ocean and fame [— and death] before me!
            — and Land! Gloria — and
                        Gloria! You stand at the helm

I want — to go there! Friend
                                    [Gloria]
Do not trust a Genoese ever again!

He is always staring into the blue   To there — or toward death!
What is farthest draws him all
    too much!
What is most foreign is dear to me today
Genoa lies far[s] behind

[MM: According to the drafts and attempts cited above, the fol-
lowing transitional version seems possible:]
That's the way I want to go! Friend, do not trust
A Genoese ever again!
He is always staring into the blue
What is farthest draws him all too much!
What is most foreign is dear to me today
Genoa lies far behind
Gloria! You stand at the helm
To there — or toward death!

N V 9, 18–17:
Open is the sea: into the blue
Drives my Genoese ship
To there, and I trust
Myself from now on and my grip.

Everything becomes new and newer to me
Genoa lies behind me:
And you yourself stand at the helm,
Dearest Victoria!

N V 9, 19:
To L.
I *want to go there*, and I trust
Myself and my grip from now on!
Open is the ocean: into the blue
Drives my Genoese ship.

Everything becomes new and newer to me
Genoa lies behind me
And you yourself stand at the helm*
Dearest Victoria!

*Courage! You yourself stand at the helm {Variant to the starred
line above.}

[MM: On the same page is the following variant to the second
strophe:]
What is most foreign is now dear to me
Genoa lies behind me
Courage! She herself stands at the helm.
[MM: This variant was rejected, yet it inspired the change in the
third line of the second strophe that is depicted above.]
    106. Cf. 3[2].
    107. *Der Baum spricht.*
Zu einsam wuchs ich und zu hoch:
Ich warte: worauf wart' ich doch?
              **
Zu nah ist mir der Wolken Sitz:
Ich warte auf den ersten Blitz.
    108. *An das Ideal.*
Wen liebt ich so wie dich, geliebter Schatten!
Ich zog dich an mich, in mich — und seitdem
Ward ich beinah zum Schatten, du zum Leibe.
Nur daß mein Auge unbelehrbar ist,
Gewöhnt, die Dinge außer sich zu sehen:
Ihm bleibst du stets das ew'ge "Außer-mir".
Ach, dieses Auge bringt mich außer mich!
    109. *Pd*: To the Ideal.
Whom have I loved as I love you, beloved shadow!
I pulled you to me, into me — and ever since
I am more shadow than I was before*
You more body than ever before and everyone [sees] [wonders]
    says:**

[Two became one, a shadow and a body
only that my own eye refuses to believe it
This is so] And still — that I for you

*Did I almost become a shadow [forever] only and you
**[Almost became] a body: no longer two, [only] our transfor-
   mation continues
   {Variants to the two starred lines above.}
   110. Cf. 1[21].
   111. *(Sanctus Januarius)]* ("Holy January"). {A pun on Saint
Januarius, the patron saint of Naples.}
   112. *"Die fröliche Wissenschaft."*
         (Sanctus Januarius)
Dies ist kein Buch: was liegt an Büchern!
An diesen Särgen und Leichentüchern!
Vergangnes ist der Bücher Beute:
Doch hierin lebt ein ewig *Heute.*
   113. *hold on]* Pd: cling
   114. *To whatever . . . hold!]* Pd: Whatever {will let} me cling to
my happiness
   115. *Im Gebirge.*
         (1876.)
Nicht mehr zurück? Und nicht hinan?
Auch für die Gemse keine Bahn?
                    **
So wart'ich hier und *fasse* fest,
Was Aug' und Hand mich fassen läßt!
                    **
Fünf Fuß breit Erde, Morgenroth,
Und *unter* mir — Welt, Mensch und — Tod!
{*KSA/KGW* failed to include the closing exclamation point.}
   116. *An die Freundschaft.*
Heil dir, Freundschaft!
Meiner höchsten Hoffnung
Erste Morgenröthe!
Ach, ohn' Ende
Schien oft Pfad und Nacht mir,
Alles Leben

Ziellos und verhaßt!
Zweimal will ich leben,
Nun ich schau' in deiner Augen
Morgenglanz und Sieg,
Du liebste Göttin!
    117. *Pd*: Hail to you, Friendship!
First guarantor
Of my last hope
Defiance and consolation
Of tired souls despairing
Guarantee and prelude
Of distant triumph
I want to live twice
To look twice into your eyes'
Morning splendor and midday peace
[Oh] Friendship! (N V 9, 14)

Hail to You, Friendship
First guarantor
Of my highest hope
Defiance and consolation
[After] in starless nights,
When struggle and life [seemed] [meant] to me [to be in vain]
[nothing]
I want to live twice,
To look twice into your eyes'
Morning splendor, oh Goddess Friendship!
Friendship! (N V 9, 13)

    118. *phrase] Wort* {*Wort* can also be translated as "word." We find "phrase" more appropriate to this context.}
    119. *Das Wort*
Lebend'gem Worte bin ich gut:
Das springt heran so wohlgemuth,
Das grüßt mit artigem Genick,
Ist lieblich selbst im Ungeschick,
Hat Blut in sich, kann herzhaft schnauben,
Kriecht dann zum Ohre selbst den Tauben,

Und ringelt sich und flattert jetzt,
Und was es thut — das Wort ergetzt.
Doch bleibt das Wort ein zartes Wesen,
Bald krank und aber bald genesen.
Willst ihm sein kleines Leben lassen,
Mußt du es leicht und zierlich fassen,
Nicht plump betasten und bedrücken,
Es stirbt oft schon an bösen Blicken —
Und liegt dann da, so ungestalt,
So seelenlos, so arm und kalt,
Sein kleiner Leichnam arg verwandelt,
Von Tod und Sterben mißgehandelt.
Ein todtes Wort — ein häßlich Ding,
Ein klapperdürres Kling-Kling-Kling.
Pfui allen häßlichen Gewerben,
An denen Wort und Wörtchen sterben!
   120. See following *Pd*:
If you grasp at it with an icy glance
Then it quickly closes its eyes.
How can you then
With its little shadow-corpse
How can you bind word to word

I'm a friend of [the German] lively phrase
That jumps out at us with such good faith,
[That has its endearing clumsiness
Its hearty eye]
That greets us with an artful curt[skill]sy
Endearing even in its clumsiness
[And wants you . . . it]
[It has] Has blood within, [an eager creature]
can sniff heartily [eagerly] (N V 9, 180)

[And] Creeps |then| even into deaf ears
Yet it always will remain a [W] delicate creature,
[Quickly]
Soon sick and yet soon well
[And] if you |wish| to let it live its fleeting life:*

Don't crudely grab and crush it,
It often dies merely from an evil [cold] eye.
[You may do that, you deformers,
With its little shadow-corpse]
[And lies then]
[And] there lies there then so [deformed] deformed,
So soulless, so poor and cold
Its little corpse [completely] terribly transformed,
brutalized through death and dying
[You] How ugly is a dead phrase]
You see it lying there and run away:
How ugly is a dead phrase!

Your grip [with hands] must be refined |and light| {Variant to the
starred line above.}
(N V 9, 179)

And shame on every ugly business,
Through [which little animal-phrases die]
[the phrase-beasts]
Through which the friendly [P] animals die!
To bookbinders and day laborers
[The phrase, a marvelous beast
winged, small]

A dead phrase — an ugly thing
a bone-on-bony cling-cling-cling;
And cursed be the ugly business
[Through] [Through which friendly little animals]
Through which phrases and phrase lets die,
[through bookbinders and day laborers]

|That| They fight among themselves without renown
The little men those swine
And call it "style" and take pride in it

and now it curls up and flutters,
And what it does — the phrase delights, (N V 9, 178)
    121. Cf. Pfeiffer.

122. Pfeiffer 211; cf. 1[84, 86, 87, 88]; 5[1] 63, 62, 61.

123. *women]* *Frauen*

124. *women]* *Frauen*

125. {Cf. 2[46]; 3[1] 53; 5[17].}

126. Pfeiffer 212; cf. 1[45].

127. Pfeiffer 214.

128. *women]* *Frauen*

129. *women]* *Frauen*

130. *power]* *Kraft* {We usually translate *Kraft* as "force," espe-cially in passages related to his concept of drives, but here "power" seems to be a more suitable rendering.}

131. Pfeiffer 215; cf. 1[50]; 3[1] 17; *BGE* 139; {22[3]_568}.

[2 = N V 9b.]

1. "On the occasion of Buddha's prophecy about Metteyya, the next Buddha, who will appear on the earth in the distant fu-ture, it reads: 'He will be the leader of a multitude of hundreds of thousands of disciples, just as I am now the leader of a multitude *of hundreds*' (Cakkavattisihanada Sutta)." Hermann Oldenberg, *Buddha: Sein Leben, seine Lehre, seine Gemeinde* (Berlin{: Hertz,} 1897), 162n1 (the 1881 edition in *NL*, 144n1).

2. {Carl Gustav Carus, *Vergleichende Psychologie oder Geschichte der Seele in der Reihenfolge der Tierwelt* ("Comparative psychology or history of the soul in the hierarchy of the animal kingdom") (Vienna: Brownmüller, 1866).}

3. Apparently copied out of a card catalogue.

4. *Vogt]* {Johann Gustav Vogt; cf. notebook 24, note 68.}

5. *Lindau]* {Paul Lindau}

6. *Wilbrandt]* {Adolf von Wilbrandt}

7. {Cf. 7[1, 73]; 9[36].}

8. Crossed out by N; cf. 3[1] 27.

9. Cf. 3[1] 307; *BGE* 103.

10. *And . . . blind.]* |And| yet proclaim to me, you animals: Is [not] the sun already at its noon height? Is [not] the serpent [|in its light|] [called] eternity |called?| already coiling itself [, in its light? Thus Zarathustra's hour had |already| come.] Zarathustra goes blind.

11. Cf. 5[1] 109; 12[1] 185.

12. Cf. 3[1] 209.

13. Cf. 3[1] 210.

14. Cf. 3[1] 199; *Z* I "On Little Women, Old and Young."

15. Cf. 3[1] 200.

16. Cf. 3[1] 198; *Z* I "On Friends."

17. Cf. 3[1] 197.

18. Cf. 3[1] 196; *Z* I "On War and Warrior-Peoples."

19. Cf. 3[1] 195.

20. Cf. 3[1] 192; *Z* I "On Chastity"; first crossed-out version: Sensuality rears its head like a dog that wants to have a bite of meat, even in the most cerebral interaction of the 2 sexes with each other. [MM: Similar thoughts in Lou Salomé's journals from this time: cf. Pfeiffer 208, 239.]

21. Cf. 5[1] 110. {The expanded context of 5[1] 110 indicates that N is talking about cats.}

22. Cf. 3[1] 190.

23. Cf. 3[1] 191, 194; *BGE* 160.

24. Cf. 3[1] 193; *BGE* 161.

25. Cf. 3[1] 189; *Z* I "Zarathustra's Preface" 4; paraphrase of Hebrews 12:6; cf. also Proverbs 13:24; Revelation 3:19.

26. Cf. 3[1] 221.

27. Cf. 3[1] 188.

28. Cf. 3[1] 180.

29. Cf. 3[1] 187.

30. Cf. 3[1] 178; *Z* I "On the Viper's Bite."

31. Cf. 3[1] 179.

32. Cf. 3[1] 177.

33. Cf. 5[29].

34. *necessary*] {In this case N italicizes *noth* in *nothwendige* because it is a compound word, but there is no way to render this in English except by italicizing part of the word.}

35. Cf. 3[1] 212; *Z* I "On the Viper's Bite."

36. {N is punning on the proverb *Geteiltes Leid ist halbes Leid,* i.e., "A problem shared is a problem halved."}

37. Refers to the following aphorisms: *HAH* 237, *Renaissance and Reformation*; *D* 88, *Luther the great benefactor*; *JS* 149, *The failure of reformations.*

38. Cf. 3[1] 66; 12[1] 114; *CW* 15, 31[52]; 32[9]; *Z* IV "The Festival of the Ass."

39. Cf. 3[1] 73; 5[1] 57.

40. *to ultimate knowledge] zur letzten Erkenntnis*

41. *wall of knowledge] Zaun der Erkenntnis*

42. Crossed out by N; cf. 3[1] 65; {4[44]; 22[3]_564}.

43. *it doesn't look so bad an ele(phant] es sieht da nicht übel aus ein Ele(phant* {This reflects the ungrammatical sentence in the original.}

44. Cf. 3[1] 61; *BGE* 92.

45. Cf. 3[1] 52.

46. Cf. 1[108] 6: "*Love* is completely . . . shrouded deity"; 3[1] 53.

47. Cf. 3[1] {64}: "It is not *how* . . . to be loved"; 3[1] 72; {22[3] _564}; *BGE* 79.

48. Cf. 3[1] 54.

49. Cf. 3[1] 55; {22[3]_564}.

[3 = Z I 1.]

1. *On the . . . eternity!" —]* Cf. 1[15]; 1[101]; 3[4]. 3[4] is an earlier version; motto and title added later.

2. "Dorthin will ich! Und ich traue
"Mir fortan und meinem Griff.
"Offen ist das Meer, ins Blaue
"Treibt mein Genueser Schiff.
"Alles wird mir neu und neuer,
"Weit hinaus glänzt Raum und Zeit —
"Heil dir, Schiff! Heil deinem Steuer!
"Um dich braust die Ewigkeit!" —

3. *"Beyond . . . Sentences.]* From: "Desayuno" {"Breakfast"}/"Disillusionment." {These were possible alternative titles; *die Ernüchterung* ("Disillusionment") could also be translated as "Sobriety."}

4. *"il sait . . . plaisirs."]* "Those who know how to enjoy life are sensible sluggards brooding over their pleasures." {Cf. Guillaume Amfrye de Chaulieu, *Oeuvres de Chaulieu, d'après les manuscrits de l'auteur: Tome premier* (La Haye: Bleuet, 1774), 59–60. N might also have come across this line from the Duc de Nevers in an article by Amédée Renée, "Les nièces de Mazarin. Troisième partie:

La Duchesse de Mercoeur, La Princesse de Conti, La Duchesse de Modène. — Le Duc de Nevers," in *Revue contemporaine,* Fourth year, Vol. 22 (Paris: Bureaux de la Revue Contemporaine, 1855): 150.}

5. Cf. *Z* I "On the Viper's Bite."

6. Cf. 1[6, 10]; *Z* I "On Freely-Chosen Death."

7. Cf. 1[93]; 12[1] 121; *BGE* 130.

8. *superior qualities] das Hohe*

9. *base qualities] dessen Niedriges*

10. Cf. 1[92]; 12[1] 120; *BGE* 275.

11. Cf. *Z* III "The Wanderer; {22[1]_561}.

12. Cf. 1[90]; *Z* I "On Love of One's Neighbor."

13. Cf. 1[75, 76].

14. Cf. 1[73].

15. Cf. 1[66]; 5[1] 245; *Z* I "Zarathustra's Preface" 2.

16. Cf. 1[32, 65].

17. Cf. 1[64]; 3[1] 445; 4[29]; 5[1] 67; *BGE* 91.

18. Cf. 1[63]; {22[3]_562}.

19. Cf. 1[59]; 12[1] 147; {2[226]; 13[14]; 16[7]}.

20. Cf. 1[58]; *Z* I "On Friends."

21. Cf. 1[52]; *Z* I "Zarathustra's Preface" 4.

22. *their neighbors] ihre Nächsten* {Not in the Christian or "neighborhood" sense, but rather "those to whom they are closest."}

23. Cf. *BGE* 148; 1[52]; {cf. 1[50, 111]}.

24. Cf. 1[50, 111]; *BGE* 139.

25. Cf. 4[43].

26. Cf. *BGE* 143; {4[43]}.

27. Cf. 1[47]; *BGE* 86; first version: Behind all the feelings a man has for a woman there still lies *contempt* for the female sex.

28. *superiority] Höhe*

29. Cf. 4[37]; *Z* I "On the Flies of the Marketplace."

30. {Cf. 22[3]_562.}

31. Cf. 1[50, 111]; *BGE* 85; {cf. 22[3]_562}.

32. *poetically imagined] erdichten*

33. Cf. *BGE* 138; {22[3]_562}.

34. Cf. *BGE* 132; {4[31]; 16[88]; 18[24]; 22[1]_546}.

35. Cf. 1[29].

36. Cf. 2[8].

37. Cf. *Z* I "On Little Women, Old and Young."

38. *People of faith] der gläubige Mensch* {cf. 1[77]; 22[3]_563.}

39. Cf. *Z* I "Zarathustra's Preface" 9.

40. Cf. *BGE* 135.

41. Cf. *Z* I "On Reading and Writing."

42. Cf. 1[9]; 12[1] 65; *Z* I "On Professorships of Virtue."

43. Cf. 1[9]; {3[1] 224; 22[3]_563}.

44. Cf. N to Heinrich von Stein, beginning December 1882 {*KGB* III:1, 288}.

45. Cf. *Z* I "On the Way of Those Who Create."

46. Cf. 12[1] 118; *Z* III "The Wanderer"; {22[3]_563}.

47. Cf. 12[1] 119; *Z* II "On Scholars"; "On Tarantulas"; {9[48]; 12[42, 43]; 13[6]}.

48. *We . . . explained.]* First version: Something is often considered to be absurd only because the conventional explanations for it are absurd: a deceptive work of art is the result. {N switches from passive voice in the first version to the singular universal pronoun *man* in the final version, which we render here as "we."}

49. Cf. *BGE* 90; {22[3]_563}.

50. Cf. *Z* I "On Reading and Writing."

51. *genius gravitationis]* "spirit of gravity" or "demon of gravity"

52. Cf. *Z* I "On Reading and Writing."

53. Cf. 12[1] 117; *BGE* 82.

54. *brought to light] sich aufklärt* {N's wordplay is between *sich aufklären* ("brought to light") as a passive substitute and *aufgeklärt sein* ("enlightened").}

55. Cf. *BGE* 80.

56. Cf. *Z* I "On Loving Thy Neighbor."

57. Cf. 1[49]; 12[1] 115, 27; *BGE* 97.

58. Cf. 1[57]; *BGE* 136.

59. Cf. 1[70]; *BGE* 133; {22[3]_564}.

60. Cf. 1[70]; *BGE* 129; {22[3]_564}.

61. Cf. 1[97]; 12[1] 72; *BGE* 140.

62. Cf. 3[1] 60; 1[34, 79, 80]; 4[44]; 5[1] 46; 12[1] 200.

63. Cf. 2[45]; {22[3]_564}.

64. Cf. 1[108]; 2[46]; 5[17]; *Z* I "On Children and Marriage."

65. Cf. 2[49]; N to Elisabeth N, Beginning of {9} September 1882 {*KGB* III:1, 252}.

66. Cf. 2[50]; {22[3]_564}.

67. {Cf. 22[3]_564.}

68. Cf. *Z* I "On the Flies of the Marketplace."

69. Cf. *BGE* 89.

70. Cf. note 62 above.

71. Cf. 2[44]; *BGE* 92.

72. *Those . . . enemy.] Pd*: If people have never been against you, you will [never subjugate them] never become their ruler.

73. Cf. 22[3]{_563}; *CW* 18, 20[31].

74. Cf. Vauvenargues: "Les grandes penseés viennent du coeur" {"Great thoughts come from the heart"}, quoted in Arthur Schopenhauer, *Parerga and Paralipomena*, vol. 2, trans. Adrian Del Caro and Christopher Janaway (Cambridge: Cambridge University Press, 2015), 12; cf. 22[3]{_563}; *CW* 18, 20[29].

75. Cf. *Z* I "On the Way of Those Who Create."

76. *It is not how . . . loved.]* Cf. 2[47]; 3[1] 72; {22[3]_564}; *BGE* 79.

77. Cf. 2[43]; 4[44]; 22[3]{_563}; *Z* IV "On Superior Humans" 19.

78. Cf. 2[41]; 12[1] 114; *CW* 15, 31[52]; 32[9]; *Z* IV "The Festival of the Ass."

79. Cf. 4[42]; *BGE* 164.

80. Cf. 22[3]{_564}.

81. Cf. 22[3]{_564}; *BGE* 165.

82. Cf. 2[47]; 3[1] {64}; 22[3]{_564}; *BGE* 79.

83. *by means of truthfulness] über seine Wahrhaftigkeit*

84. Cf. 2[42]; 5[1] 57.

85. Cf. 22[3]{_564}; *CW* 15, 31[38]; 32[9]; *Z* IV "On Superior Humans" 7.

86. Cf. *BGE* 149.

87. Cf. 12[1] 112; *Z* I "On the Viper's Bite." N crossed out this first version: Behind every person who judges stands the executioner.

88. First version: When we are sublimely above good and evil, we see all tragedies as unintended comedies and are far from granting tragic natures the greatest significance.

89. Cf. *BGE* 6; N to Lou von Salomé, 16 September 1882 {*KGB* III:1, 259}.

90. Cf. 22[3]{_565}; *BGE* 180.

91. Cf. *Z* I "On Friends."

92. Cf. *Z* I "On the Flies of the Marketplace."

93. Cf. 3[1] 149; *Z* I "On the Flies of the Marketplace." First version: Cowardice in the face of a neighbor is a basic character trait of very loveable people.

94. *grab . . . neck] am Schöpfe fassen*

95. Cf. 12[1] 113; *BGE* 179.

96. Cf. *Z* I "On Friends."

97. Cf. *Z* II "On Compassionate People."

98. Cf. *Z* I "On the Tree on the Mountainside."

99. Cf. 12[1] 192; *BGE* 150.

100. *an appendage]* From: the embodiment

101. *as an appendage . . . action] als Zubehör einer einzigen Tat*

102. *a chalk line drawn around a hen] der Kreidestreich um die Henne* {Refers to a trick used by hypnotists, whereby a hen would refuse to step across a chalk line, even though it was capable of doing so.}

103. Cf. *Z* I "On the Pale Criminal."

104. Cf. *Z* I "On the Way of Those Who Create."

105. First version: A. "What you are teaching here is not yet your philosophy!" B. Why not? A. "If it were yours |my friend,| you would (1) demand nothing more except to dance — at least once a day. (2) walk differently: you should be seen dancing at ⟨least⟩ once a day! Dancing is the proof [since] of truth for me, the proof of force." Later version: Our stride reveals whether we have found our path. Cf. *Z* IV "On Superior Humans" 17.

106. Cf. *BGE* 176.

107. Cf. 22[3]{_565}; *BGE* 175.

108. Cf. *Z* I "On Little Women, Old and Young."

109. *"One person . . . around"] "Einer ist doch noch zuviel um mich"* {A play on the proverb *Drei sind einer zu viel,* or "Two's company, three's a crowd."}

110. Cf. Z I "On Friends."

111. Cf. *BGE* 174.

112. Cf. *Z* I "On Friends."

113. Cf. *Z* I "On the Pale Criminal."

114. *to each my own] jedem das Meine* {A play on the saying *jedem das Seine,* or "to each his own."}

115. Cf. *Z* I "On the Viper's Bite."

116. Cf. *BGE* 65a.

117. Cf. 5[17]; 12[1] 111; *Z* I "On the Flies of the Marketplace."

118. Cf. 5[1] 209; 12[15]; 13[15].

119. *Pd*: We believe in things that do not exist e.g., selfless-ness, always at the cost of things that exist, e.g., selfishness.

120. Cf. *Z* I "On Little Women, Old and Young." {Cf. 4[38]; 5[1] 73b.}

121. Cf. *Z* I "On Friends."

122. Cf. 4[104]; 5[1] 166; *Z* I "Zarathustra's Preface" 4.

123. Cf. *CW* 15, 31[52]; 32[8]; *BGE* 65.

124. Cf. *BGE* 64.

125. *"All women] "Alle Frauen*

126. *"All women . . . one.]* Cf. *Z* I "On Friends."

127. Cf. *BGE* 152.

128. Cf. *Z* I "On Reading and Writing."

129. Cf. *Z* II "On Compassionate People"; {12[1] 107; 13[8]}. {English speakers feel pangs of conscience, Germans "bites" of conscience, so the pun on *Gewissensbisse/Beißen* is lost here.}

130. Cf. 12[1] 109; {3[1] 193}; *CW* 15, 31[53]; 32[9]; *BGE* 178.

131. *The . . . animals.]* Cf. 12[1] 110; *Z* II "On Compassionate People."

132. Cf. *BGE* 155.

133. Cf. 12[1] 108; *BGE* 170.

134. First version: with some decent will to live — there is lit-tle suffering on account of the "Will to Live."

135. Cf. 5[25]; *BGE* 154.

136. Cf. 5[1] 167; *BGE* 151.

137. Cf. 3[1] 85; *Z* I "On the Flies of the Marketplace."

138. Cf. *BGE* 63.

139. Cf. *Z* I "On Friends."

140. Cf. *Z* I "On the Virtue of Gift-Giving" 3.

141. Cf. *Z* I "Zarathustra's Preface" 9.

142. Cf. *Z* I "On Reading and Writing."

143. Cf. *BGE* 156.

144. First version: Nothing is more pathetic than to see good people straining to prove that superior h⟨uman beings⟩ were cre-ated in the image of their god.

145. Cf. *Z* I "On Reading and Writing."

146. Cf. *Z* I "On Reading and Writing."

147. Cf. 5[33].

148. {Pluralization was not possible here because of the discussion of two individuals.}

149. Cf. 12[1] 187.

150. Cf. *Z* I "On Reading and Writing."

151. *and . . . will stink]* and morality is removed from the world, namely, talked to death

152. Cf. *Z* I "On Chastity."

153. Cf. 12[1] 106; 13[8]; *Z* II "On Tarantulas."

154. Cf. *Z* I "On Reading and Writing."

155. Cf. *Z* I "On Reading and Writing."

156. Cf. *Z* I "On Reading and Writing."

157. Cf. *BGE* 157.

158. Cf. *Z* I "On the Way of Those Who Create." First version: Every sensation that doesn't kill us is killed by us.

159. Cf. *BGE* 158.

160. Cf. 2[35].

161. Cf. *Z* I "On the Viper's Bite"; {2[33]}.

162. Cf. 2[34]; *Z* I "On the Viper's Bite."

163. Cf. 2[31].

164. *women]* Frauen

165. *three-eyed]* dreiäugig {A metaphor of supernatural vision or insight from the iconography of Zeus in Greek mythology.}

166. Cf. 4[229]; *Z* I "On the Pale Criminal."

167. Cf. *Z* I "On the Pale Criminal."

168. Cf. *BGE* 159.

169. Cf. *Z* I "On the Viper's Bite."

170. Cf. 2[32]; *Z* I "On Love of One's Neighbor."

171. Cf. 2[30].

172. Cf. 2[28]; 5[17]; *Z* I "Zarathustra's Preface" 4; paraphrase of Hebrews 12:6; cf. also Proverbs 13:24; Revelation 3:19.

173. Cf. 2[25].

174. Cf. 2[26]; 3[1] 194; *BGE* 160.

175. Cf. 2[22]; *Z* I "On Chastity."

176. Cf. 2[27]; *BGE* 161.

177. Cf. note 174 above.

178. Cf. 2[21].

179. Cf. 2[20]; *Z* I "On War and Warrior Peoples."

180. Cf. 2[19].

181. Cf. 2[18]; *Z* I "On Friends."

182. Cf. 2[16]; *Z* I "On Little Women, Old and Young."

183. Cf. 2[17].

184. Cf. 12[1] 104; *BGE* 162. {The wordplay here is between *Nächster*, the biblical designation for a fellow human being, and *Nachbar*, someone living in close proximity; both are translated by "neighbor."}

185. Cf. *Z* I "On Friends."

186. Cf. *BGE* 100.

187. Cf. 12[1] 105; *Z* II "On Compassionate People."

188. Cf. *Z* I "On Loving Thy Neighbor."

189. Cf. 2[13].

190. Cf. 2[14].

191. Cf. 4[96]; 5[17]; *Z* I "On the Viper's Bite."

192. Cf. 2[38]; *Z* I "On the Viper's Bite."

193. Cf. *BGE* 67.

194. Cf. *CW* 15, 31[53]; 32[9]; *Z* IV "On Superior Humans" 9.

195. Cf. *Z* I "On Chastity."

196. *females] Weibchen* {With no attributive to provide the pejorative nuance implied by the diminutive, we chose what some regard as a pejorative form in American usage.}

197. *The "I" . . . its feet.]* Cf. 1[20].

198. Cf. 2[29].

199. Cf. 1[24]; *Z* I "On the Way of Those Who Create."

200. Cf. 1[25]; 5[1] 59.

201. Cf. 1[8]; {1[9]; 3[1] 34}; 22[3]_563; *JS* 262}.

202. Cf. 1[38]; 25[171].

203. Cf. 1[40]; *BGE* 66.

204. Cf. *CW* 15, 31[53]; 32[9]; *BGE* 69.

205. Cf. *CW* 15, 31[53]; 32[9]; *Z* IV "On Superior Humans."

206. Cf. 12[1] 151; *Z* II "The Prophet."

207. Cf. *Z* I "On War and Warrior Peoples."

208. Cf. *BGE* 68.

209. Cf. *CW* 15, 31[53]; 32[9]; *Z* IV "On Superior Humans."

210. Cf. *CW* 15, 31[53]; 32[9].

211. Cf. 12[1] 101; 13[16]; 16[7]; 23[5]; *CW* 15, 31[35, 36]; 32[10]; *BGE* 99.

212. Cf. *BGE* 102.

213. {Cf. 4[165]; 5[2]; 11[8]; 18[43, 49, 56]; 21[6]; 24[16].}

214. *aside from the ten thousand people who have superior spirits.]* *abseits von dem oberen Zehntausend des Geistes*; cf. *GM* II 7.

215. Cf. 12[1] 100; *BGE* 101.

216. Cf. 12[1] 101.

217. Cf. 12[1] 102.

218. *feeling] Empfindung* {We translate this as "feeling" when N doesn't mean sensation or perception. Elsewhere we also use "feeling" to translate *Gefühl*.}

219. Cf. *BGE* 72.

220. Cf. *D* 556.

221. *the stars . . . "above you,"]* {This is an allusion to Kant's famous conclusion to the *Critique of Practical Reason* that is now inscribed on his tombstone: "Zwei Dinge erfüllen das Gemüt mit immer neuer und zunehmender Bewunderung und Ehrfurcht, je öfter und anhaltender sich das Nachdenken damit beschäftigt: *der bestirnte Himmel über mir, und das moralische Gesetz in mir.*" ("Two things fill the mind with ever new and increasing admiration and reverence, the more often and more steadily one reflects on them: *the starry heavens above me and the moral law within me.*") (Immanuel Kant, *Critique of Practical Reason*, rev. ed., trans. Mary Gregor [Cambridge: Cambridge University Press, 2015], 129.)}.

222. Cf. *BGE* 71.

223. Cf. *BGE* 70.

224. *Precisely . . . lover.]* Cf. 4[70].

225. Cf. 12[1] 163.

226. Cf. 12[1] 97; *BGE* 73.

227. Cf. *Z* I "On the Way of Those Who Create."

228. Cf. 12[1] 98; *BGE* 73a.

229. Cf. 4[104]; *Z* I "On the Viper's Bite"; *BGE* 181.

230. Cf. 12[1] 99; 13[8]; 16[7]; *CW* 15, 31[36]; 32[9]; *Z* IV "On Superior Humans."

231. Cf. *BGE* 75.

232. *intellect] Geist* {Which can also mean "spirit."}

233. Cf. *BGE* 77.

234. Cf. *Z* I "On the Viper's Bite."

235. Cf. *BGE* 78.

236. Cf. 1[26].

237. Cf. 4[200]; 4[42]; 12[1] 96; 13[19]; *Z* IV "No Longer in Service"; *Z* II "On Compassionate People."

238. Cf. *BGE* 76.

239. Cf. *Z* I "On Reading and Writing."

240. Cf. *Z* I "On Reading and Writing."

241. Cf. *BGE* 95.

242. Cf. 12[1] 146; 13[14]; *Z* III "On Unchosen Bliss."

243. Cf. *Z* I "On the Tree on the Mountainside."

244. Cf. *Z* I "On Loving Thy Neighbor."

245. Cf. *Z* I "On Little Women, Old and Young"; {cf. 4[161]}.

246. Cf. *Z* I "On Reading and Writing."

247. *humans] Menschen* {N juxtaposes humans with women in this passage.}

248. Cf. 2[9]; *BGE* 103.

249. Cf. *Z* I "Zarathustra's Preface" 4.

250. Cf. *BGE* 94; {cf. 4[13]; 5[1] 113}.

251. *"Ella guardava suso, ed io in lei"]* "She looked upward, and I at her"; cf. *Divina Commedia, Paradiso II*, 22: "Beatrice in suso, ed io in lei guardava" ("Beatrice looked upward, and I at her").

252. Cf. *BGE* 236

253. *compulsion] Trieb* {Which we usually translate as "drive."}

254. Cf. 4[42].

255. Cf. *BGE* 173.

256. Cf. *BGE* 172.

257. {Cf. Matthew 18:3.}

258. Cf. *BGE* 96.

259. Cf. 12[1] 148; 13[14]; 16[7]; *Z* IV "On Superior Humans" 11. {We translate *der Nächste* (neighbor or fellow human being in the Christian sense) as "neighbor" and in this case pluralize it to preserve gender neutrality.}

260. Cf. *Z* I "On Loving Thy Neighbor."

261. Cf. *Z* I "On the Pale Criminal."

262. Cf. *BGE* 98. {Germans speak of the "bites of conscience" (*Gewissensbisse*); cf. note 129 above.}

263. Cf. 12[1] 93.

264. Cf. 12[1] 95.

265. Cf. *BGE* 182.

266. Cf. 5[35].

267. Cf. 5[35]; 12[1] 53; 13[12]; *Z* II "On Compassionate People."

268. Cf. 12[1] 94; 5[35].

269. Cf. 5[35].

270. Cf. 5 [35]; *Z* I "On Matters of Joy and Passion."

271. Cf. 5[35, 33]; 12[1] 142; *BGE* 183.

272. Cf. 5[33].

273. Cf. 12[1] 90; 13[16]; 16[7]; *BGE* 169.

274. Cf. 5[33].

275. Cf. 5[35].

276. *women] Frauen*

277. *Women . . . as such.]* Cf. 1[50]; 12[1] 92.

278. *I . . . persons.]* Cf. *Z* I "On Friends."

279. Cf. *Z* I "On Freely-Chosen Death."

280. Cf. *BGE* 104.

281. Cf. 12[1] 91; *Z* II "On Virtuous People."

282. Cf. *D* 275.

283. Cf. *BGE* 97.

284. Cf. *BGE* 185.

285. N skips over number 363 in his notebook.

286. Cf. *Z* I "On War and Warrior-Peoples."

287. Cf. *Z* I "On Little Women, Old and Young."

288. Cf. 4[95, 110]; 5[1] 29; *Z* I "On Chastity." {We render *er* as "he" because it is a reference to Zarathustra.}

289. Cf. *BGE* 106.

290. Cf. *BGE* 107.

291. *general feelings] Gemeingefühle* {The term *gemein* has two meanings, one of which is "general" or "shared in common," the other "base." N might have either of these in mind because morality refers to a shared phenomenon but also to base feelings like *ressentiment*.}

292. Cf. *BGE* 108.

293. Cf. *BGE* 109; *Z* I "On the Pale Criminal."

294. *pia fraus]* "pious fraud" {In the Catholic dogma of the "pious fraud," Jesus is presented as the bait on the hook of the cross with which Leviathan (the demon of the deep, i.e., the devil) is taken and made to render up the souls he has seized.}

295. *impia fraus]* "impious fraud"

296. Cf. *BGE* 105.

297. *sancta simplicitas]* "holy simplicity"

298. Cf. *Z* I "On the Way of Those Who Create."

299. Cf. *Z* I "On the Pale Criminal."

300. *So . . . him.]* Cf. *BGE* 113.

301. {See the Translators' Afterword, 748–93, for our arguments in favor of translating *Übermensch* as "superhumans."}

302. Cf. 12[1] 136; *Z* II "On Compassionate People."

303. Cf. 12[1] 179.

304. Cf. 12[1] 109; *BGE* 88.

305. Cf. *BGE* 112; {12[1] 89; 13[8]}.

306. Cf. 5[1] 127; *BGE* 184, 111.

307. Cf. 12[1] 180; *Z* II "On Compassionate People."

308. Cf. *Z* I "Zarathustra's Preface" 3.

309. Cf. 12[1] 87.

310. Cf. *BGE* 171.

311. Cf. 12[1] 181.

312. Cf. *Z* I "On Chastity"; {cf. Matthew 8:31, Mark 5:12, and Luke 8:32}.

313. Cf. 12[1] 144; *Z* III "On the Virtue That Diminishes."

314. Cf. 12[1] 149.

315. Cf. *BGE* 123.

316. Cf. *BGE* 168.

317. Cf. *BGE* 167.

318. Cf. *BGE* 122.

319. *with our mouths and faces]* mit Munde und Maule {N is playing off the idiom *ein Maul machen*, "to pout."}

320. Cf. 12[1] 88; 22[3]_569; *BGE* 166.

321. Cf. *BGE* 120.

322. Cf. *Z* I "On War and Warrior-Peoples."

323. Cf. *BGE* 125.

324. Cf. 22[3]{_568}; *BGE* 93.

325. Cf. *Z* I "On the Virtue of Gift-Giving" 3.

326. Cf. *Z* I "On the Tree on the Mountainside."

327. Cf. *BGE* 126.

328. Cf. *Z* I "On Loving Thy Neighbor."

329. Cf. *Z* I "On War and Warrior-Peoples."

330. Cf. *Z* I "On War and Warrior-Peoples."

331. *If God . . . love.]* Cf. 22[3]{_568}. {We preserve N's word-play on the "bites of conscience"; cf. note 129 above.}

332. Cf. *Z* I "On Reading and Writing"; {cf. *GM* III}.

333. Cf. *Z* I "On War and Warrior-Peoples"; {cf. 4[4]; 5[1] 94}.

334. Cf. *Z* I "On Little Women, Old and Young."

335. Cf. *Z* I "On Little Women, Old and Young."

336. Cf. *Z* I "On Little Women, Old and Young."

337. *those who darn its socks] Strumpfwirker* {*Strumpfwirker* were weavers of socks, the bottom caste of what was considered to be one of the lower professions.}

338. Cf. 12[1] 86; *Z* II "On Scholars."

339. *There are . . . manly.]* Cf. *Z* III "On the Virtue That Diminishes"; {cf. 22[3]_568}.

340. Cf. *BGE* 121.

341. *This thinker . . . red hot.]* Cf. 3[1] 11; *BGE* 91; {1[64]; 4[29]; 5[1] 67}.

342. Cf. *Z* I "On the Tree on the Mountainside"; {1[102]}.

343. *Pinie und Blitz.*

Hoch wuchs ich über Mensch und Thier;
Und sprech ich — Niemand spricht mit mir.

**

Zu einsam wuchs ich und zu hoch:
Ich warte: warauf wart' ich doch?

**

Zu nah ist mir der Wolken Sitz,—
Ich warte auf den ersten Blitz.

**

344. Cf. *JS* "Songs of Prince Vogelfrei": Sils Maria.

345. Cf. 1[101]; 1[15]; 3[1]; Motto; *JS* "Songs of Prince Vogelfrei":
On to New Seas.

346. *Auf hohem Meere.*

Freundin — sprach Columbus — traue
Keinem Genuesen mehr!
Immer start er in das Blaue,
Fernstes zieht ihn allzusehr!

**

Wen er liebt, den lockt erg erne
Weit hinaus aus Raum und Zeit — —
Über uns glänzt Stern bei Sterne,
Um uns braust die Ewigkeit.

**

[4 = N V 9c. N VI 1b. N V 8.]

1. {Cf. N to Heinrich von Stein, beginning December 1882,
KGB III:7/1, 312.}

2. Cf. 5[1] 92, 93, 94, 72, 95, 96.

3. {Cf. 5[1] 92.}

4. {Cf. 3[1] 438; 5[1] 94.}

5. {Cf. 4[38]; 5[1] 72.}

6. {Cf. 5[1] 96.}

7. Cf. 5[1] 97, 98.

8. Cf. 5[1] 99, 106, 103, 104; {5[1] 102}.

9. *god-humans]* Gottmensch {We use this rendering when N
refers to polytheistic systems; we use "God-made-human" when
N uses *Gottmensch* to refer to Jesus.}

10. Cf. 5[1] 105.

11. Cf. 4[13].

12. Cf. 5[1] 113.

13. *bustle]* Lärm ("noise")

14. {Cf. Hermann Oldenberg, *Buddha: Sein Leben, seine Lehre,
seine Gemeinde* (Berlin: Hertz, 1881), 375, *NL*; translated by William Hoey as *Buddha: His Life, His Doctrine, His Order* (London:
Williams and Norgate, 1882): 367.}

15. {Cf. 4[9].}

16. {Cf. 3[1] 313; 5[1] 113; *BGE* 94.}

17. Cf. 5[1] 100.

18. Cf. 5[1] 101, 117, 116.

19. *woman] Frau*

20. *I am . . . go away.]* Like Socrates; cf. Plato, *Phaedo* 60a.

21. Cf. 17[6]; *Z* II "On Priests."

22. *love me(a)ls Liebesma(h)le* {A reference to the Eucharist and perhaps to Wagner's opera *Das Liebesmahl der Apostel* (1843).}

23. {Cf. 4[32, 115, 249]; 5[1] 175.}

24. Cf. 5[1] 118; *Z* I "On Little Women, Old and Young."

25. Cf. 4[22, 204, 213]; 5[32]; *Z* I "Zarathustra's Preface" 5; "On a Thousand and One Goals."

26. Cf. 4[20, 204].

27. *tool] Mittel* {The standard translation is "means," but "tool" captures it better in this context.}

28. *superhumans]* {One of the few times N uses the term *Übermenschen* in the plural; see also 4[254], 5[32], 10[37, 41], and 13[26].}

29. Cf. *BGE* 135; 5[1] 56; *BGE* 116.

30. Cf. 5[1] 120.

31. Cf. 5[1] 119.

32. Cf. 5[1] 67.

33. Cf. *BGE* 132; {cf. 3[1] 25; 16[88]; 18[24]; 22[1]_546}.

34. Cf. {4[17, 32, 115, 249]}; 5[1] 175; *Z* II "On Priests."

35. Cf. 5[1] 91, 90, 89; *Z* I "On Friends"; "On War and Warrior-Peoples."

36. Cf. *Z* I "On the Flies of the Marketplace."

37. *creative] Schaffende* {Usually translated as "those who create."}

38. Cf. 3[1] 21; *Z* I "On the Flies of the Marketplace"; 5[1] 87, 86, 88; *BGE* 119.

39. Cf. 5[1] 69, 70, 71, 72, 73, 75, 78, 76, 74, 73, 77; 5[1] 95; 3[1] 128; *Z* I "On War and Warrior-Peoples"; "On Little Women, Old and Young."

40. *blessed? Be blessed] selig werde? Sei selig* {The standard English translation of *selig werden* is "to be saved" or "to find salvation," whereas the standard English translation of *selig sein*, as in the Beatitudes, is "Blessed is/are . . . " We translate *selig* as "blessed" in both clauses to preserve the wordplay; cf. Matthew 19:16.}

41. {Cf. 4[4]; 5[1] 72.}

42. {Cf. 3[1] 128; 5[1] 73b.}

43. Cf. 1[83]; *CW* 13, 11[195].

44. Cf. 5[1] 85, 84, 83, 82, 81, 80, 79.

45. {Cf. 5[1] 83; 12[1] 195.}

46. Cf. 5[1] 122, 121.

47. {Cf. 3[1] 68.}

48. *ancient]* alt

49. {Cf. 3[1] 287; 4[200]; 12[1] 96; 13[19].}

50. {Cf. 3[1] 317.}

51. Cf. *BGE* 143; 5[1] 48, 47; {3[1] 19}.

52. {Cf. 3[1] 18.}

53. *abolish]* aufheben {N could also have a Hegelian term in mind here, in which case "supersede" might be a more natural translation.}

54. *ignorance]* Unkenntnis {As opposed to the standard term *Unwissen*.}

55. Cf. 3[1] 65; 5[1] 45, 46.

56. {Cf. 2[43]; 3[1] 65; 22[3]_564.}

57. {Cf. 3[1] 51, 60; 1[34, 79, 80]; 4[44]; 5[1] 46; 12[1] 200.}

58. Cf. 3[1] 109.

59. *distress]* Noth {N could also have "hardship," "adversity," "misery," or "want" in mind.}

60. *escort]* Geleit {N omits the verb here.}

61. Cf. 4[139, 75]; *Z* I "Zarathustra's Preface" 3.

62. Cf. 4[169].

63. Cf. 12[1] 124.

64. Cf. 12[1] 127, 126.

65. {François duc de La Rochefoucauld, *De la Rochefoucault's Sätze aus der höhern Welt- und Menschenkunde* ("De la Rochefoucauld's phrases from the study of the higher world and human beings"), trans. from the French by Friedrich Schulz (Breslau: Wilhelm Gottlieb Korn, 1793), 77. *NL. De la Rochefoucaulds Maximen und Reflexionen*, trans. from the French by Friedrich Hörlek (Leipzig: Philipp Reclam, 1875), 26, nr. 183. *NL.*}

66. Cf. 12[1] 125, 128; *Z* II "On Great Events."

67. Cf. 12[1] 130, 131.

68. Cf. 12[1] 139.

69. Cf. 12[1] 132; 5[1] 36, 37.

70. *utile . . . dulce] utile* = useful; *dulce* = sweet {Cf. Horace, *Ars poetica*, lines 343–44: *Omne tulit punctum qui miscuit utile dulci, lectorem delectando pariterque monendo.* ("He wins every hand who mingles the useful with sweet, by delighting and instructing the reader at the same time.") These lines are annotated by N in his copy of *Des Q. Horatius Flaccus Sämmtliche Werke. Zweiter Theil: Satiren und Episteln; Für den Schulgebrauch*, ed. Georg Theodor August Krüger (Leipzig: B. G. Teubner, 1853).}

71. *sit tibi terra levis]* "May the earth rest lightly on you" {A benediction for the dead, often inscribed on tombstones or other gravestones, and commonly abbreviated STTL.}

72. Cf. 5[1] 39, 40, 38.

73. *mosquitoes] Mücken* {The "bloodsucking" context here indicates that N probably had mosquitoes (Culicidae) rather than gnats (Nematocera) in mind. Our nineteenth-century desk encyclopedia also attributes a bloodsucking function to *Mücken*. The strictness of the distinction *Mücken/Stechmücken* also varies regionally.}

74. Cf. 12[1] 134.

75. *just . . . avenged]* {This loses N's pun on *gerecht* ("just") and *gerächt* ("avenged").}

76. Cf. 12[1] 78, 150.

77. Cf. *Z* I "On War and Warrior-Peoples; 4[80]; 13[10].

78. {Cf. 5[33].}

79. Cf. 3[1] 259; *Z* I "On Reading and Writing."

80. Cf. 5[33]; 5[1] 27, 13, 14, 28; {12[1] 188; 12[1] 189}.

81. *drives me crazy] zum Aus-der-Haut fahren*

82. Cf. 5[1] 22, 23, 24, 25, 26.

83. *I don't . . . a meal.]* {This is a play on the German expression *der Appetit kommt beim Essen* ("appetite comes with eating"), itself derived from Rabelais's *"L'appétit vient en mangeant."*}

84. {Cf. 5[1] 24; 12[1] 156.}

85. *darkness . . . well."]* {A reference to the German proverb *Im Dunkeln ist gut munkeln* = "Darkness is good for whispering"; cf. 5[1] 26.}

86. Cf. 5[1] 33, 35, 34, 21.

87. *honorable men]* Biedermann {The term *Biedermann* was translated in N's time as man of honor, man of worth, gentleman, or worthy, and had not yet acquired the exclusively pejorative connotations that modern German has of a limited, provincial outlook.}

88. *until fame arrives]* zum Leuchten kommen {literally, until [one] becomes illustrious or famous}.

89. Cf. 5[I] 32, 31, 30.

90. *brakes]* Hemmschuh {*Hemmschuh* refers to a shoe-like device applied to the outside of the wheel of a carriage or other vehicle to provide braking ability.}

91. Cf. 5[I] 125; {4[49]}.

92. {Cf. 4[83].}

93. Cf. 5[I] 130, 129, 128, 160.

94. Cf. 5[I] 123, 117, 134, 136, 135, 137.

95. Cf. 5[I] 133, 138, 140, 143, 139.

96. Cf. 5[I] 145.

97. {Cf. 4[67].}

98. Cf. 5[I] 132, 142.

99. *Mémoires]* "memoirs"

100. *primum vivere]* "first live"

101. Cf. 4[75].

102. Cf. 5[I] 144, 143.

103. *mom]* Mütterchen

104. Cf. 5[I] 160; {4[76]}.

105. Cf. 5[I] 141.

106. Cf. 5[I] 131.

107. Cf. 5[I] 147, 150, 148, 159.

108. *bon goût]* "good taste"

109. Cf. 5[I] 149.

110. Cf. 5[I] 158, 157.

111. *reason]* (die) Vernunft {The definite article *die* appears in brackets in the original German and is not translated in the English equivalent.}

112. Cf. 5[I] 155, 156.

113. {Cf. 5[I] 155; 22[5] 572.}

114. *Someone profound.]* Der Tiefe

115. Cf. 5[1] 161, 162.

116. {Cf. 5[1] 153.}

117. {Cf. 5[33].}

118. Cf. 5[1] 151, 152.

119. Cf. 5[1] 160, 164.

120. {Cf. 3[1] 368; 4[110]; 5[1] 29.}

121. Cf. 5[1] 162; {3[1] 211}.

122. Cf. *Z* I "On Little Women, Old and Young"; "On the Virtue of Gift-Giving."

123. {Cf. 4[210, 228]; 5[7, 17].}

124. *At least . . . eclipsed in time.]* Dafür versinkt ihr nicht ganz in der Zeit.

125. Cf. 5[1] 104, 166, 151; *BGE* 181.

126. {Cf. 3[1] 130; 5[1] 166.}

127. {Cf. 3[1] 272.}

128. Cf. 5[1] 165, 29.

129. {Cf. 3[1] 368; 4[95]; 5[1] 29.}

130. *"Freethinking"] "Freigeist"* {The context of this word indicates intellectual and cognitive, not affective, improvement, thus pointing to "freethinking" rather than "free spirit."}

131. Cf. 4[116]; 5[1] 162, 5; *Z* I "On the Virtue of Gift-Giving."

132. Cf. 5[1] 177.

133. {Cf. 5[1] 176; {5[17]; 16[9]; 22[3]_563}.

134. Cf. {4[17, 32, 249];} 5[1] 175.

135. Cf. 4[112]; 5[1] 174.

136. Cf. 5[1] 172, 173, 188.

137. Cf. 9[57]; 15[8]; 15[60].

138. *Moldenhauer]* {E. F. Theodor Moldenhauer, nineteenth-century German astronomer and cosmologist, author of *Die Axendrehung der Weltkörper: Beitrag zur Lösung einer naturwissenschaftlichen Frage* ("The axial rotation of the world body: Contribution to solving a scientific question") (Berlin: Weber, 1871), and *Das Weltall und seine Entwicklung: Darlegung der neuesten Ergebnisse der kosmologischen Forschung* ("The universe and its evolution: Presentation of the latest results of cosmological research") (Cologne: Mayer, 1882).}

139. *Mainländer]* {Philip Mainländer (1841–76), German poet and philosopher. N was familiar with his central philosophical work, *Die Philosophie der Erlösung* ("The philosophy of redemption"). *NL.*}

140. Cf. 5[1] 171.

141. {Cf. 4[145].}

142. *in-and-for-itself] An-und-für-sich* {Although this has become a standard phrase in German, its origin is Hegelian and N no doubt recognizes this.}

143. Cf. 5[1] 171.

144. Cf. 5[1] 170, 169, 168.

145. *heal, savior]* {In German, "heal" (*heilen*) and "savior" (*Heiland*) are cognate.}

146. Cf. 5[1] 183.

147. Cf. 5[1] 184, 185.

148. *primum mobile]* "first moved" {The *primum mobile* in Ptolemaic astronomy was the outermost sphere of the heavens, which was the first mover of the universe. It is also associated with Aristotle's "prime mover," as in 4[138].}.

149. Cf. 5[1] 178.

150. {Cf. 4[49].}

151. Cf. 5[1] 181, 182; {5[1] 7}.

152. *moralis]* {Cf. Charlton T. Lewis and Charles Short, *A New Latin Dictionary* (Oxford: Clarendon Press, 1879): of or belonging to manners or morals, moral (a word formed by Cicero). "Illness" is underlined by N, "*moralis*" is not.}

153. Cf. 5[1] 180.

154. Cf. 5[1] 179.

155. {Cf. 4[122].}

156. *ends] Zweck* {N is playing off the distinction between means and ends in this fragment, so we translate *Zweck* here as "end" rather than "purpose."}

157. *codes of goodness] Gütertafel*

158. Cf. 5[1] 220, 191, 216.

159. *peach] Apfel* ("apple") {*Apfel* is translated here as "peach," since in N's time it could refer to any kind of juicy fruit. See Grimm 1:532–43.}

160. *sensibility]* Gemüth {See the Translators' Afterword, 743–44, for how we translate *Gemüth*.}

161. Cf. 5[1] 222.

162. *most intellectual]* die Geistigsten {Another possibility is "most spiritual"; we chose "most intellectual" because the preceding fragment is concerned with reason.}

163. Cf. 5[1] 246.

164. Cf. 5[1] 247, 248; {12[6]; 13[17]}.

165. *this timelessness]* dies ohne Zeit

166. *everything . . . straight]* {Cf. Isaiah 45:2; Luke 3:5.}

167. {Cf. 3[1] 303.}

168. Cf. 5[1] 267.

169. {Cf. 3[1] 245; 11[8]; 18[43, 49, 56]; 21[6]; 24[16].}

170. *laugh and weep]* {An allusion to Franz Schubert's song "Lachen und Weinen" ("Laughter and Weeping"), composed in 1822, D. 777 in Otto Erich Deutsch's catalogue.}

171. Cf. 5[1] 249; {5[23]; 12[7]}.

172. {Cf. 4[51].}

173. Cf. 5[1] 250, 251.

174. *one]* {As we explain in the Afterword, the singular reference to what has been created refers to a single category or species that includes a plurality of instances or members; see 732–34.}

175. Cf. 5[1] 252; {5[24]}.

176. Cf. 5[1] 266.

177. *golden bowl]* {Cf. Ecclesiastes 12:6.}

178. Cf. 5[1] 253.

179. Cf. 5[1] 254.

180. {Cf. 5[1] 254; 5[22]; 12[5]; 13[7]; 16[7].}

181. Cf. 5[1] 255.

182. Cf. 5[1] 256.

183. Cf. 5[1] 257.

184. Cf. 5[1] 219.

185. Cf. 5[1] 258.

186. {Cf. 5[1] 158.}

187. Cf. 5[1] 273.

188. *charcoal burners]* Kohlenbrenner {Charcoal burning was known for being a low-paying, dirty, dangerous profession. Burners

were forced to travel constantly to gain employment. The joke here is that the Church is approaching people who experience hell on earth with threats about the hell to come.}

189. Cf. 5[1] 265.

190. Cf. 5[1] 260.

191. *shoo-fly] Fliegenwedel* {A device associated with horseback riding; could be attached to saddle or harness.}

192. Cf. 5[1] 261.

193. Cf. 5[1] 263, 264; {12[1] 199; *KSA* mistakenly notes fragment 4[198]}.

194. {Cf. 3[1] 287; 4[42]; 12[1] 96; 13[19].}

195. Cf. 5[1] 265.

196. *coincidence] Zufall* {The standard rendering, "chance," does not work here.}

197. {Cf. 4[20, 22].}

198. *minds] Geister* {In this context, this could also be "spirits."}

199. *a little old lady] das alte Weibchen* {N does not mean any particular "little old lady," hence the change to the indefinite article.}

200. *rattle . . . drum]* {In English, drums roll; in German, they rattle.}

201. Cf. 5[8].

202. *I teach you about the superhumans] Ich lehre Euch den Übermenschen* {Here N means the subject to be taught, not the audience. See 5[8] and 16[89], where "superhumans" are also the subject matter.}

203. Cf. 5[10].

204. Cf. 5[9, 7]; {13[1]_388}.

205. {Cf. 4[100, 228]; 5[7, 17].}

206. Cf. 5[4, 5].

207. Cf. 5[3].

208. Cf. 5[32].

209. Cf. 5[13, 17].

210. Cf. 5[12].

211. {Cf. 5[18].}

212. Cf. 5[17].

213. {Cf. 1[59]; 3[1] 13; 12[1] 147; 13[14]; 16[7].}

214. Cf. 5[7, 17].

215. *bring] richtet* {The verb is singular, the subject plural here.}

216. {Cf. 4[100, 210].}

217. Cf. 5[13, 16, 17, 20, 32].

218. *ingenuity] Geist*

219. {Cf. 3[1] 182.}

220. {Cf. 4[266]; 5[14, 32].}

221. Cf. 5[1] 260.

222. *out of . . . into the fire] aus dem Regen . . . unter die Traufe* {The German equivalent of "out of the frying pan into the fire" is literally "out of the rain into the drainpipe."}

223. Cf. *Z* I "On the Three Transformations."

224. Cf. *Z* I "On the Viper's Bite."

225. Cf. *Z* I "On Despisers of the Body."

226. Cf. *Z* I "On the Three Transformations."

227. *{they}]* {The antecedent of "they" in the phrase "If they did" in the following sentence is missing in the German.}

228. Cf. *Z* I "On Freely-Chosen Death."

229. Cf. {4[17, 32, 115];} 5[1] 175.

230. Cf. *Z* I "On Professorships of Virtue."

231. Cf. 5 [32].

232. *lock, stock and barrel] Kost und Küche* {An obscure locution. Grimm 11:1847 cites *Kost und Kleidung* as analogous in English to "room and board."}

233. *after this position] nach dieser Seite*

234. Cf. *Z* I "On the Virtue of Gift-Giving."

235. Cf. 5[16, 20].

236. {Cf. 4[230]; 5[14].}

237. *noxious] böse* {Here adapted to the herbal metaphor.}

238. Cf. 5[32].

239. *knowing one] die Wissenden* {As opposed to *die Erkennenden* ("the ones who know").}

240. Cf. 4[279]; {5[21]}; *Z* I "On the Hinterworldly."

241. *The belly of existence] Der Bauch des Seins*

242. *good] Nutzen* {Translated as "good" here in the context of utilitarianism.}

243. Arrangement of *Z* I.

[5 = Z I 2a. Mp XV 3a.]

1. Collection of sayings from the early manuscripts (especially N V 9, N VI 1, N V 8); numbered by N.

2. Cf. *Z* II "On Self-Overcoming."

3. Cf. 12[1] 153; {4[112, 116]}.

4. Cf. 4[142].

5. *consumption] Schwindsucht* {The term in N's time for consumption (tuberculosis).}

6. Cf. 12[1] 155. {*KSA* 14 incorrectly refers to 12[1] 55.}

7. Cf. 4[71].

8. Cf. 4[71]; 12[1] 189.

9. Cf. *Z* I "On Reading and Writing."

10. Cf. 1[91].

11. Cf. 12[1] 141.

12. Cf. 4[73]; *Z* I "On Reading and Writing."

13. Cf. 4[72]; *Z* I "On Reading and Writing."

14. Cf. 4[72]; *Z* I "Zarathustra's Preface" 8.

15. Cf. 4[72]; 12[1] 56; *BGE* 18.

16. Cf. 4[72].

17. *darkness . . . well."]* {A reference to the German proverb *Im Dunkeln ist gut munkeln* = "Darkness is good for whispering"; cf. 4[72].}

18. Cf. 4[71].

19. Cf. 4[71]; *Z* I "On Freely-Chosen Death."

20. Cf. 3[1] 368; 4[95, 100]; *Z* I "On Chastity."

21. Cf. 4[74].

22. Cf. 4[74].

23. Cf. 4[74].

24. *"Honorable men"] "Biedermännerei"* {*Biedermann* or "honorable man" was an ideal in Nietzsche's time. By using the pejorative suffix *-erei*, he is saying that anyone who lives up to this ideal is contemptible.}

25. Cf. 4[73].

26. Cf. 1[85]; 4[73]; 12[1] 193; 16[49].

27. Cf. 4[73].

28. Cf. 4[59].

29. Cf. 4[59]; *Z* I "On Little Women, Old and Young."

30. {Cf. 4[62].}

31. {Cf. 4[62].}

32. {Cf. 4[62].}

33. Cf. 1[55].

34. Cf. 4[44]; *Z* I "On the Way of Those Who Create."

35. Cf. 4[44]; 12[1] 200; {cf. 3[1] 51, 60}.

36. Cf. 4[43].

37. {Cf. 4[43].}

38. Cf. *Z* I "On Friends."

39. Cf. 1[43, 78].

40. Cf. 12[1] 182.

41. Cf. 4[26]; *BGE* 116.

42. Cf. 3[1] 73; {2[42]}.

43. Cf. *BGE* 117.

44. Cf. 1[25]; 3[1] 223.

45. Cf. 1[5]; 12[1] 184.

46. Cf. 1[67, 70, 88]; {1[73, 108]}.

47. Cf. 1[87]; 1[108]4; 12[1] 194; *BGE* 114.

48. Cf. 1[86]; 1[108] 2.

49. *"Perish . . . ocean!"] Gehe unter in diesem Meer* {*Untergehen* has the literal sense here of disappearing under the waves.}

50. Cf. 1[72].

51. *temperaments] Naturen*

52. Cf. 1[70].

53. Cf. 4[29]; {1[64]; 3[1] 11; 3[1] 445; 4[29]; *BGE* 91}.

54. Cf. 1[62].

55. *become blessed . . . be blessed] selig werde . . . sei selig* {The standard English translation of *selig werden* is "to be saved" or "to find salvation," whereas the standard English translation of *selig sein*, as in the Beatitudes, is "Blessed is/are . . . " We translate *selig* as "blessed" in both clauses to preserve the wordplay. Cf. Matthew 19:16.}

56. Cf. 4[38].

57. Cf. 5[1] 95, 4[38]; cf. N to Heinrich von Stein, early December 1882 {*KGB* III:1, 287}.

58. Cf. *Z* I "On War and Warrior-Peoples"; {4[38]}.

59. Cf. 4[38]; {4[4]}.

60. Cf. 4[38].

61. *Everything . . . pregnancy.]* Cf. *Z* I "On Little Women, Old and Young"; cf. 3[1] 128; 4[38].

62. Cf. 4[38].

63. Cf. 4[38].

64. Cf. 4[38].

65. Cf. 4[38].

66. Cf. 4[38].

67. Cf. 4[40].

68. Cf. *Z* I "On War and Warrior-Peoples."

69. Cf. 4[40].

70. Cf. 4[40].

71. Cf. 4[40]; 12[1] 195; *Z* IV "On Superior Humans" 11.

72. Cf. 4[40].

73. Cf. 4[40].

74. Cf. 4[37]; *BGE* 119.

75. Cf. 4[37].

76. Cf. 4[37].

77. Cf. 4[34]; *Z* I "On War and Warrior-Peoples."

78. Cf. 4[34].

79. Cf. 4[34]; *Z* I "On Friends."

80. Cf. 4[4].

81. Cf. 4[4]; 5[1] 116.

82. Cf. 4[4]; *Z* I "On War and Warrior-Peoples."

83. Cf. note to 5[1] 70.

84. Cf. 4[4]; *Z* I "On War and Warrior-Peoples."

85. Cf. 4[5].

86. Cf. 4[5].

87. Cf. 4[6].

88. Cf. 4[14]; *Z* I "On War and Warrior-Peoples."

89. Cf. 4[15].

90. Cf. 4[6]; *Z* I "On Matters of Joy and Passion."

91. Cf. 4[6]; {5[30]}.

92. Cf. 4[6, 104].

93. Cf. 4[8].

94. Cf. 4[6].

95. Cf. 2[10]; 12[1] 185; *Z* II "On Compassionate People."

96. Cf. 2[23].

97. Cf. *Z* II "On Priests."

98. Cf. 12[1] 196; *BGE* 118.

99. Cf. 4[13]; {cf. 3[1] 313}.

100. *your] sein* {The context indicates that this probably refers back to "you."}

101. Cf. 4[15]; *Z* I "On Matters of Joy and Passion."

102. Cf. 4[15, 77]; *Z* I "On Little Women, Old and Young."

103. Cf. 4[18]; *Z* I "On Little Women, Old and Young."

104. Cf. 4[28].

105. {Cf. 4[27].}

106. Cf. 4[41].

107. Cf. 4[41].

108. Cf. 4[77]; 12[1] 197.

109. Cf. 4[49, 75]; *Z* I "Zarathustra's Preface" 3.

110. Cf. 3[1] 95; *BGE* 184.

111. Cf. 4[76].

112. Cf. 4[76]; *Z* I "On Preachers of Death."

113. Cf. 4[76].

114. Cf. 4[87]; 12[1] 198; *Z* II "The Stillest Hour."

115. Cf. 4[82]; 5[1] 142.

116. Cf. 4[78].

117. Cf. 4[77].

118. Cf. 4[77].

119. Cf. 4[77].

120. *The point must be reached] So weit soll es kommen*

121. Cf. 4[5, 77].

122. Cf. 4[78].

123. Cf. 4[78]; *Z* I "On the Flies of the Marketplace."

124. Cf. 4[78]; *Z* I "Zarathustra's Preface" 3.

125. Cf. 4[86]; *Z* I "On Matters of Joy and Passion"; "On the Tree on the Mountainside."

126. Cf. 4[82]; 5[1] 132.

127. Cf. 4[78, 84].

128. Cf. 4[84].

129. Cf. 4[79].

130. Cf. *Z* I "On Little Women, Old and Young."

131. Cf. 4[88].
132. Cf. 4[88].
133. Cf. 4[89].
134. Cf. 4[93]; *Z* I "On the Viper's Bite"; {4[104]}.
135. Cf. 4[93].
136. Cf. 4[92].
137. Cf. 4[92]; 5[33]; *Z* I "On the Viper's Bite."
138. Cf. 4[91].
139. Cf. 4[91]; 5[33].
140. Cf. 4[90].
141. Cf. 4[90, 186].
142. Cf. 4[88].
143. Cf. 4[76]; {4[85]; cf. Heraclitus, Diels-Kranz fragment B91: "It is not possible to step twice into the same river"}.
144. Cf. 4[92].
145. Cf. *Z* I "On the Three Transformations"; 4[92, 96, 112].
146. Cf. 4[94].
147. Cf. 4[110].
148. Cf. 3[1] 130; 4[104]; *Z* I "Zarathustra's Preface" 4.
149. Cf. 3[1] 146; *BGE* 151.
150. Cf. 4[129]; *Z* I "Zarathustra's Preface" 3.
151. Cf. 4[129].
152. Cf. 4[129]; *Z* I "On the Preachers of Death."
153. Cf. 4[120, 128]; *Z* I "On the Flies of the Marketplace."
154. Cf. 4[117]; *Z* I "Zarathustra's Preface" 2.
155. Cf. 4[117]; *Z* I "On the Pale Criminal."
156. Cf. 4[116]; *Z* I "Zarathustra's Preface" 3.
157. Cf. 4[17, 32, 115, 249]; *Z* II "On Priests."
158. Cf. 4[114]; 5[17]; {16[9]; 22[3]_563}.
159. {Cf. 4[113].}
160. Cf. *Z* I "On the Three Transformations."
161. Cf. 4[144].
162. Cf. 4[143].
163. *moral drives] sittlichen Triebe* {N uses *sittlich* to refer to the morality of customs; see *GM* II. Cf. 4[142].}
164. Cf. 4[142].
165. {Cf. 4[135].}

166. {Cf. 4[136].}

167. Cf. *Z* I "On the Pale Criminal."

168. Cf. *Z* I "On the Pale Criminal."

169. {Cf. 4[117].}

170. Cf. 4[148] {and note to 5[1] 170}; 12[20].

171. Cf. 12[21].

172. Cf. *Z* I "On Preachers of Death."

173. Cf. 5[19, 30]; *Z* I "Zarathustra's Preface" 3.

174. Cf. 12[18].

175. Cf. *Z* I "On Preachers of Death."

176. *knowledge] das Wissen*

177. *you . . . dozing.*] Cf. *Z* I "On the Pale Criminal."

178. Cf. 12[16]; *Z* I "On the Pale Criminal."

179. Cf. 3[1]124; 12[15]; 13[15].

180. Cf. 12[13].

181. Cf. 12[14]; {5[1] 214; 10[17]; 12[1] 171; 12[13]; 13[1]_375}.

182. *knowing . . . being known] Wissen und Erkanntsein*

183. Cf. 12[13, 14]; {5[1] 213; 10[17]; 12[1] 171; 13[1]_375}.

184. Cf. 4[148]; 5[1] 221.

185. Cf. 4[184]; *Z* I "On Preachers of Death."

186. Cf. 4[148].

187. Cf. 4[148]; 5[1] 216.

188. Cf. 4[152].

189. Cf. 5[27].

190. Cf. *Z* II "Upon the Blessed Isles."

191. {Cf. Ralph Waldo Emerson, *Versuche (Essays)*, trans. G. Fabricius (Hanover: Carl Meyer, 1858), 361, cited in the Preliminary Note by Mazzino Montinari to the Reference Matter to *Z* in *CW* 7; cf. also *Z* I "Zarathustra's Preface" 2.}

192. Cf. 12[11].

193. Cf. 1[72]; 5[1]65; *Z* I "On Preachers of Death."

194. Cf. *Z* I "On Preachers of Death."

195. Cf. 12[9].

196. Cf. *Z* I "On Preachers of Death" {N repeats the number 234 for this fragment.}

197. {Cf. Gustav Teichmüller, *Die wirkliche und die scheinbare Welt: Neue Grundlegung der Metaphysik* ("The real and the appar-

ent world: New foundation of metaphysics") (Breslau: Koebner, 1882), 131–32.}

198. *I am too full] Ich bin zu voll* {cf. 5[17]; *Z* I "Zarathustra's Preface" 4}.

199. Cf. 12[8]. {N is quoting from Teichmüller, *Die wirkliche und die scheinbare Welt*, 132.}

200. {N here misquotes from Teichmüller, *Die wirkliche und die scheinbare Welt*, 246. The original — "Was werden soll und werden wird, ist der Grund dessen, was wird" — would be translated: "What should become and what will become is the basis for what will be."}

201. Cf. 5[26]; 12[8].

202. Cf. 1[66]; 3[1] 9; *Z* I "Zarathustra's Preface" 2.

203. Cf. 4[155].

204. Cf. 4[160]; 12[6]; 13[17]; *Z* I "Upon the Blessed Isles"; {cf. Isaiah 40:4, Luke 3:5}.

205. Cf. 4[160].

206. Cf. 4[168]; 5[23]; 12[7].

207. Cf. 4[171].

208. Cf. 4[171]; *Z* I "Zarathustra's Preface" 3.

209. Cf. 4[172]; 5[24].

210. Cf. 4[175]; 5[17]; *Z* I "Zarathustra's Preface" 4.

211. Cf. 4[176]; 5[22]; 12[5]; 13[7]; 16[7]; *CW* 15, 31[6]; 32[9]; *Z* IV "The Leech."

212. Cf. 4[181]; *Z* I "Zarathustra's Preface" 3.

213. Cf. 4[182].

214. Cf. 4[183]; 12[4].

215. Cf. 4[186]; *Z* I "Zarathustra's Preface" 2.

216. Cf. 4[186]. {N repeats the fragment number here.}

217. Cf. 4[193, 234]; *Z* I "On the Flies of the Marketplace."

218. Cf. 4[196].

219. Cf. 12[2].

220. Cf. 4[199].

221. Cf. 4[199]; 12[1] 199.

222. Cf. 4[202]; 4[191]; 5[32].

223. Cf. 4[174]; *Z* I "On Loving Thy Neighbor."

224. Cf. 4[164]; *Z* I "On Chastity."

225. *moments of great contempt]* die großen Verachtungen

226. Cf. 4[188].

227. Cf. 4[165]; *Z* I "Zarathustra's Preface" 3; {3[1] 245]}.

228. Cf. 4[212]; 13[10]; *Z* II "The Dance Song."

229. Cf. 4[211].

230. Cf. 4[211].

231. Cf. 4[210, 228]; 5[17]; *Z* I "Zarathustra's Preface" 4.

232. *them]* ihn {Refers to those being taught rather than the superhumans; cf. 4[208].}

233. Cf. 4[210]; 13[1]{_388}; *Z* II "On Great Events."

234. *icons]* Bilder

235. Cf. 4[209].

236. Cf. 12[1] 138; 13[8]; *BGE* 81.

237. Cf. 4[215].

238. Cf. 4[214, 229]; 5[17]; 10[44].

239. Cf. 4[230]; {4[266]; 5[32]}.

240. Cf. 5[13].

241. *news]* Wort

242. Cf. 4[229]; 5[20].

243. Cf. 4[229, 210, 228, 96, 224, 214, 175, 114]; *Z* I "Zarathustra's Preface" 4; "On the Viper's Bite"; "On the Flies of the Marketplace"; "On Child and Marriage."

244. {Cf. 4[100, 210, 228]; 5[7].}

245. {Cf. 3[1] 211; 4[96]; *Z* I "On the Viper's Bite."}

246. {Cf. 4[175]; 5[1] 253.}

247. {Cf. 4[114]; 5[1] 176; 16[9]; 22[3]_563.}

248. {Cf. 3[1] 122; 12[1] 111.}

249. *neighbors]* der Nächste {N uses the biblical term for "fellow human being," as in "Love thy neighbor as thyself."}

250. Cf. 4[223].

251. Cf. 5[1] 197; 5[30]; *Z* I "On the Virtue of Gift-Giving"; "Zarathustra's Preface" 3.

252. *beyond this earth]* überirdisch {We do not have one English term that renders the "super" of N's intended meaning, so we paraphrase here.}

253. Like 5[16]; {cf. 4[229]}.

254. Cf. 13[8].

255. Cf. note to 5[1] 254.

256. Cf. 4[168]; 5[1] 249; 12[7].

257. Cf. 5[1] 252; 4[172].

258. Cf. 3[1] 143; *BGE* 154.

259. *reveals]* verrätht

260. Cf. 12[8]; 5[1] 244.

261. Cf. 5[1] 223.

262. Cf. *Z* I "Zarathustra's Preface" 7.

263. *clown]* Hanswurst {The clown-buffoon of German and Austrian improvisational theatre, with roots in the Italian *commedia del'arte*. By Luther's time, the name had become a pejorative term for anyone of unsophisticated and clownish demeanor.}

264. Cf. 2[36].

265. Cf. 5[1] 197; 5[19]; *Z* I "Zarathustra's Preface" 3; {4[6]; 5[1] 103}.

266. *terra incognita]* "unknown land"

267. Arrangement of *Z* I.

268. {Cf. 4[271].}

269. Cf. 3[1] 164, 350, 347; 4[91, 72, 92]; 5[1] 156, 154; 12[1] 142; *BGE* 183; *Z* I "On the Viper's Bite."

270. {Cf. 5[17].}

271. {Cf. 4[68].}

272. {Cf. 4[71].}

273. {Cf. 4[92].}

274. Cf. 4[137].

275. Cf. 3[1] 340, 341, 342, 345, 351, 346, 347.

[6 = M III 3b.]

1. Cf. 6[2, 3, 4]; the dating determined on the basis of the draft of a letter from N to Lou von Salomé (M III 3, 18–19) {*KGB* III:1, 295–96}; cf. Pfeiffer 263 *et passim*. {The organization of the fragments in this notebook have been altered to follow the organization as found in N's handwritten notebook.}

2. *Asceticism]* Ascetism {N appears to use the terms *Ascetism* and *Ascetismus* interchangeably.}

3. *one]* {*KSA/KGW* mistakenly underline *eine*; see http://www.nietzschesource.org/DFGA/M-III-3,10.}

4. {Cf. 4[51] and the corresponding note. This fragment has been reformatted in accordance with the notebook; see http://www.nietzschesource.org/DFGA/M-III-3,11.}

5. *to renouncing]* *aufzugeben* {*KSA/KGW* mistakenly fails to underline *aufzugeben*; see http://www.nietzschesource.org/DFGA/M-III-3,8.}

[7 = M III 4b.]

1. Draft of "Morality for Moralists"; cf. N to Overbeck in the summer {14 August} of 1883 {*KGB* III:1, 427}: "In the meantime the outline for a 'Morality for Moralists' completed." 7[201]; 24[27]; *CW* 15, 25[2]; *CW* 16, 34[213].

2. *egoist(ic) principle]* {Cf. Eduard von Hartmann, *Phänomenologie des sittlichen Bewusstseins: Prolegomena zu jeder künftigen Ethik* ("Phenomenology of moral consciousness: Prolegomena to every future ethics"), pt. 1: "Das pseudomoralische Bewusstsein" ("Pseudomoralistic consciousness") (Berlin: C. Duncker's Verlag, 1879), 1–102. *NL*.}

3. Critical retrospective on *BT*, N's notes on the first edition (1872). {Where N cites from *BT*, we have used the language that appears in the translation by Sean D. Kirkland and Andrew J. Mitchell in *CW* 1.}

4. *innocence of becoming]* Plans with this title also exist dating back to this time; cf. 8[26]; 14[1].

5. *principium individuationis]* "principle of individuation"

6. *art . . . being]* {Cf. *BT* "Foreword to Richard Wagner."}

7. {N incorrectly writes "p. 54"; the line quoted appears on p. 34, *BT* 7.}

8. *p. 82 . . . existence]* *BT* 15.

9. *"which stares . . . inscrutable"]* {*BT* 15.}

10. *p. 92 Quintessence.]* *BT* 17 (Beginning).

11. *p. 102 . . . art.]* *BT* 18.

12. *Belief . . . 117.]* *BT* 20.

13. *"another . . . 120.]* *BT* 21.

14. *Only . . . 132.]* *BT* 23.

15. *p. 136 . . . sense,]* *BT* 23 (Conclusion).

16. *p. 142 . . . hope]* *BT* 24 (Conclusion).

17. *Lecky I 199.]* {William Edward Hartpole Lecky,} *Geschichte des Ursprungs und Einflusses der Aufklärung in Europa* (*History of the Rise and Influence of the Spirit of Rationalism in Europe*), 2 vols. (London: Longmans, Green, 1865)}, trans. H. Jolowicz, 2 vols. (Leipzig/Heidelberg{: C. F. Winter,} 1873), 1:199. *NL.*

18. {"Reference to chap. 4 of Johann Joachim Winckelmann, *Gedanken über die Nachahmung der griechischen Werke in der Malerei und Bildhauerkunst* ("Thoughts on the imitation of Greek works in painting and sculpture") (1755).}

19. *the image of the sufferer] das Bild Leidenden* {The genitive article is missing.}

20. *Hartmann]* Cf. Hartmann, *Phänomenologie des sittlichen Bewusstseins*, 776.

21. *evil conscience] böses Gewissen* {As opposed to "bad conscience"/*schlechtes Gewissen.*}

22. *Rée]* On the critical dialogue with Paul Rée, cf. 7[24, 48, 137]; 15[47]; 16[15]; 16[18]; 17[49]; *CW* 15, 25[259]; 26[202, 218]; *CW* 16, 35[34]; 38[18]; *GM* Preface 4–7; *EH* "Books" HAH6.

23. *intérêt]* "interest"

24. *plaisir]* "pleasure"

25. *moral theory] Moralistik* {A pun on *Optik*, giving the nuance of an academic subject, e.g., *Germanistik.*}

26. *noblesse]* "nobility"

27. *superpowerful] Übermächtiger*

28. Cf. *BGE* 260.

29. {Following Leopold Schmidt, *Die Ethik der alten Griechen* ("The ethics of the ancient Greeks"), 2 vols. (Berlin: Wilhelm Hertz [Bessersche Buchhandlung], 1882), vol. 1. *NL.*}

30. *women] Frauen*

31. *Reverence for elders . . . modern]* Cf. Schmidt, *Die Ethik der alten Griechen*, 2:304: "in the Greek world elders were revered about as much as women are revered in the modern world."

32. ἀμύνεσθαι *. . . revenge]* {Cf. Schmidt, *Die Ethik der alten Griechen*, 2:314.}

33. {Cf. Menander's play *Farmer*: "The best man, Gorgias, is the man who knows/How to take many unrequited blows;/This quickness to resent things, this excess/Of virulence, prove littlemindedness."

See John Maxwell Edmonds, *The Fragments of Attic Comedy*, vol. 2 (Leiden: E. J. Brill, 1961), 587.}

34. *unfreedom of the will]* Unfreiheit des Willens

35. *What would the commonalities . . . (Tertullian)]* {These paragraphs were 7[23] in *KSA*, but were moved by Montinari to the end of 7[22] in the revised later edition of *KGW*.}

36. *Tertullian]* Cf. *GM* I 15.

37. *That which . . . itself.]* {This paragraph was included at the end of 7[22] in *KSA*, but was made 7[23] by Montinari in the revised later edition of *KGW*.}

38. Cf. note to 7[17]. {Cf. Paul Rée, *Der Ursprung der moralischen Empfindungen* (*The Origin of Moral Sensations*) (Chemnitz: Schmeitzner, 1877), §4, 52–58. *NL*.}

39. Written following the reading of Hartmann's *Phänomenologie*, cf. note to 7[10].

40. {Cf. *WP* 1026.}

41. {Cf. *WP* 1026.}

42. *those who are not self-interested]* des Uneigennützigen

43. {Cf. Spinoza, *Ethics*, Proposition 26: "Whatsoever we endeavor in obedience to reason is nothing further than to understand; neither does the mind, in so far as it makes use of reason, judge anything to be useful to it, save such things as are conducive to understanding." Cf. also Hartmann, *Phänomenologie des sittlichen Bewusstseins*, 12.}

44. Perhaps in conjunction with the reading of Wilhelm Roux's *Kampfe der Theile im Organismus* {: *Ein Beitrag zur Vervollständigung der mechanischen Zweckmässigkeitslehre* ("Struggle of the parts within the organism: A contribution to the completion of the doctrine of mechanical expediency") (Leipzig: Engelmann, 1881), *NL*.}; cf. note to *CW* 13, 11[128].

45. *"he is . . . collected"]* {Cf. Paul Deussen, *Das System des Vedânta nach den Brahma-sûtra's des Bâdarâyaṇa und dem commentare des Çaṅkara* (Leipzig: F. A. Brockhaus, 1883), 444. *NL*; translated by Charles Johnston as *The System of the Vedânta According to Bâdarâyana's Brahma-sûtras and Çaṅkara's Commentary Thereon Set Forth as a Compendium of the Dogmatics of Brahmanism from the Standpoint of Çaṅkara* (Chicago: Open Court, 1912), 411; translation modified.}

46. {Cf. Hartmann, *Phänomenologie des sittlichen Bewusstseins*, 10.}

47. {Cf. Hartmann, *Phänomenologie des sittlichen Bewusstseins*, 181–82.}

48. *that's . . . thought]* Looking back to the time period 1869–75.

49. *prudential morality]* {Cf. Hartmann, *Phänomenologie des sittlichen Bewusstseins*, 15ff.}

50. *"Hints . . . philosophy."]* Cf. *CW* 13, 11[195].

51. *moral insanity]* {In English in the original. Cf. Henry Maudsley, *Zurechnungsfähigkeit der Geisteskranken* (Leipzig: Brockhaus, 1875), 164–67. *NL*. Authorized German translation of *Responsibility in Mental Disease* (New York: D. Appleton, 1875), 170–73.}

52. *"No one . . . herself!"]* {N's translation of the line from Stendhal quoted in 7[46]. This is also how Stendhal's line appears in the German translation, *Über die Liebe*, in Stendhal, *Gesammelte Werke*, ed. and trans. Friedrich von Oppeln-Bronikowski (Berlin: Im Propyläen, 1921), 4:54.}

53. *Napoleon . . . century.]* {According to *KGW Nachbericht*, this line belongs in 7[45]. *KSA* 10 had this as the entirety of 7[46].}

54. *Stendhal . . . donner."]* {According to *KGW Nachbericht*, this is a separate fragment. *KSA* 10 had this as the first paragraph of 7[43]: "If a lady doesn't succeed in finding someone willing to take her, she will still succeed in finding someone she can sell herself to." Cf. Stendhal, *De l'amour* (Paris: Michel Lévy Frères, 1857), 38. *NL*.}

55. Cf. 7[60]; {cf. 7[58, 62, 125]; 8[26]; 24[16, 27].

56. Cf. note to 7[17].

57. *Lecky]* Cf. note to 7[8].

58. Cf. Z IV "Conversation with the Kings."

59. {*WP* 725.}

60. *The time of kings has passed]* {Cf. Friedrich Hölderlin, *The Death of Empedocles*, 1st version, 1417. See *The Death of Empedocles: A Mourning-Play*, trans. David Farrell Krell (Albany: State University of New York Press, 2009), 87.}

61. {Cf. 7[47, 62, 125]; 8[26]; 24[16, 27].}

62. {Cf. 7[47, 58, 62, 125]; 8[26]; 24[16, 27].}

63. *is experienced]* wird . . . durchgemacht

64. *Feelings] Empfindung*

65. *feeling!] Gefuhl!*

66. {This line from Ihering is cited in J. J. Baumann, *Handbuch der Moral nebst Abriß der Rechtsphilosophie* ("Handbook of morality along with an outline of the philosophy of jurisprudence") (Leipzig: S. Hirzel, 1879), 387–88. *NL.* Cf. Rudolf von Ihering, *Der Zweck im Recht* ("The purpose of law") (Leipzig: Breitkopf & Härtel, 1883), 2:191, 212, 226.}

67. *An act . . . etc.]* {Cf. Albert Hermann Post, *Bausteine für eine allgemeine Rechtswissenschaft auf vergleichend-ethnologischer Basis* ("Building blocks for a general jurisprudence on a comparative-ethnological basis"), 2 vols. (Oldenburg: Schultz, 1880/1), 1:224. *NL.*

68. *Desire for revenge] Rachegefühl*

69. *moralize] moralisiren* {*Moralisiren* has a broader meaning in German, beyond "sermonizing" or "preaching," having to do with "thinking morally" or "exercising moral categories."}

70. *consequences . . . feelings] Folgen . . . Empfindung* {We usually render *Empfindung* as "sensation" when *Gefühl* is present in the same fragment, but here the context calls for "feelings."}

71. {Cf. note 67 above.}

72. *sur l'amour v. p. 252.]* N's copy no longer extant in N's Library. {Cf. Stendhal, *De l'amour*, 252, where he refers to Helvétius.}

73. *"le plaisir"]* "pleasure"

74. Cf. Eugen Dühring, *Kursus der Philosophie als streng wissenschaftlicher Weltanschauung und Lebensgestaltung* ("Course of philosophy as strictly scientific worldview and guide to life") (Leipzig{: Koschny,} 1875), 147. *NL.* {Nietzsche misquotes Dühring, whose text reads: "sein mechanischer Zustand stets ein Theilzustand der universellen Mechanik des Kosmos ist" (its [the body's] mechanical state is always a partial condition of the universal mechanics of the cosmos).}

75. {According to Roux.}

76. {Cf. Schmidt, *Die Ethik der alten Griechen*, 2:403ff.}

77. Cf. note to *CW* 13, 11[128]; {cf. Roux, *Der Kampf der Theile im Organismus*, 73–89}.

78. *Struggle . . . stimuli]* Cf. ibid., 73–81 (Summary).

79. *Direct . . . weaker.]* Cf. ibid., 87: "Other than through the struggle of parts for space in the exchange of materials, or the

struggle for nutrients in cases of shortages thereof with or without the effect of stimuli, newly developing characteristics can win out and spread in direct ways, namely in direct competition with the old ones, whereby the latter are either directly destroyed or consumed, assimilated (assimilation itself is certainly most universal and progressive process)."

80. *the . . . weaker]* Cf. ibid., 91.

81. *the advantage . . . rule]* Cf. ibid., 76–78.

82. *When . . . nourishment.]* Cf. ibid., 75: "If there is a lack of nutrients for an extended time, then it is true that struggle for space can take place, but only those connections will remain which *cet. par.* [all other things being equal] use the least material for replication, whereas other processes are simply starved out, thus disappearing by means of self-elimination."

83. *Advantage . . . overcompensation.]* Cf. ibid., 78–79.

84. ira] "wrath"

85. Probably building on ibid., 77.

86. Cf. ibid., 39–46.

87. Cf. ibid., 63: "Furthermore, the position seems to me to be justified that Darwin articulates in an outstanding example, without developing the underlying principle, when he mentions that, with increasing age, people's handwriting sometimes comes to resemble that of their father. The basis for this lies in the thought that inherited acquired characteristics of ancestors, instead of reestablishing themselves after youth and adolescence, can be suppressed by means of shaping influences of the outside world on impressionable youth still capable of assimilation, and not until ripe old age, when this interaction with the outside world has become less extensive, do they become more and more prevalent. Correspondingly, I believe I have observed that family characteristics in men, especially psychological ones, sometimes develop and appear more and more in old age, after they have been suppressed by pedagogical influences outside the family."

88. *Rivalry . . . exist.]* Cf. ibid., 107, 110.

89. *inequality] Ungleichheit* {This could also be "dissimilarity."}

90. *When . . . parts.]* Cf. ibid., 76.

91. *Processes . . . fructification.]* Cf. ibid., 79; in places copied word for word.

92. *The . . . stimulus.]* Cf. ibid., 81: "in the process of which the more reactive substance took on relatively more stimuli."

93. *Processes emerge . . . supreme processes.]* Cf. ibid.

94. *All of . . . individuals.]* Cf. ibid., 83.

95. *Selection . . . whole individual.]* Cf. ibid., 84.

96. *forms]* Arten

97. *The "real meaning" behind]* Die "höhere Vernunft" in

98. *are not superfluously "prudent":]* überflüssiger Weise "klug" ist:

99. *it is our custom]* bei uns {In German this can refer to national, regional, or ethnic customs and practices.}

100. *Public-spiritedness]* Gemeinsucht {This appears to be N's coinage, occurring only in this notebook.}

101. *Great men]* Große Menschen {translated here in deference to the "great man" theory of N's time; cf. Thomas Carlyle, *Heroes, Hero-Worship, and the Heroic in History* (London: Fraser, 1841), 47: "The History of the world is but the Biography of great men"}.

102. *un-noble]* unnoble

103. *to those who have ears to hear it.]* {Cf. Matthew 11:15, Mark 4:9.}

104. {Cf. 7[47, 58, 62]; 8[26]; 24[16, 27].}

105. *advantage and ulterior advantage]* Nutzen und Hinternutzen

106. *Mainländer]* Philipp Mainländer, *Die Philosophie der Erlösung* ("The philosophy of redemption"), 2nd ed. (Berlin{: Grieben,} 1876), 64. *NL.*

107. *"the gleam . . . themselves."]* {Cf. ibid., 65.}

108. *"comparable . . . temperaments)"]* {Cf. ibid., 58.}

109. {This list of qualities is copied from ibid., 57–58.}

110. {Cf. ibid., 59, for these modifications.}

111. Cf. note to 7[17].

112. *debate]* Kampf {Usually translated as "struggle"}.

113. *"The condition . . . limb."]* {Citation from Ernst Heinrich Weber, *Untersuchungen über den Erregungsprozess im Muskel- und Nervensystem* ("Investigations of the process of stimulation in the muscle and nervous system") (Leipzig, 1870). Cf. Michael Foster, *Lehrbuch der Physiologie*, trans. Nicolaus Kleinenberg (Heidelberg: Winter, 1881), 502; originally published as *A Textbook of Physiology* (London: Macmillan, 1877), 413: "And in all the movements of

our body we are conscious, even to an astonishingly accurate degree, as is well seen in the discussions concerning vision, of the amount of the contraction to which we are putting our muscles. In some way or other we are made aware of what particular muscles or groups of muscles are being thrown into action, and to what extent that action is being carried." (It should be noted that Kleinenberg's German translation differs significantly from Foster's English text.) Foster draws heavily upon Weber's work.}

114. *Cold . . . Weber)]* {Cf. Foster, *Lehrbuch der Physiologie,* 499; *A Textbook of Physiology,* 410: "And Weber has pointed out that cold bodies feel heavier than hot bodies of the same weight."}

115. *When 2 . . . skin.]* {Cf. Foster, *Lehrbuch der Physiologie,* 497; *A Textbook of Physiology,* 409: "When two sensations follow each other in the same spot at a sufficiently short interval they are fused into one; . . . When sensations are generated at points of the skin too close together they become fused into one."}

116. {Cf. Mainländer, *Die Philosophie der Erlösung,* 60–62.}

117. *"which call . . . solitude"]* {Cf. Ralph Waldo Emerson, *Versuche (Essays),* trans. G. Fabricius (Hanover: Carl Meyer, 1858), 393. *NL.* Originally published in English as *The Collected Works of Ralph Waldo Emerson,* vol. 3: *Essays, Second Series* (Cambridge, MA: Belknap Press of Harvard University Press, 1983), 100.}

118. *"these delights . . . sober."]* {Cf. Emerson, *Versuche,* 392; *Essays, Second Series,* 100. The full sentence, which Nietzsche truncates, reads in the original "These enchantments are medicinal, they sober and heal us."}

119. {Cf. *WP* 941.}

120. *everlasting] das Unvergängliche* {Probably a reference to the conclusion of Goethe's *Faust* II.}

121. {*WP* 61.}

122. {Cf. Gustav Teichmüller, *Die wirkliche und die scheinbare Welt: Neue Grundlegung der Metaphysik* ("The real and the apparent world: New groundwork of metaphysics") (Breslau: Koebner, 1882), 204.}

123. {Cf. Emerson, *Versuche,* 410; *Essays, Second Series,* 112: "To the intelligent, nature converts itself into a vast promise."}

124. {Cf. Schmidt, *Die Ethik der alten Griechen,* 1:232.}

125. *the work of the gods] Werk der Götter* {The verb is omitted.}

126. *Aidos]* "reverence," "shame" {Underlined by N}

127. {Cf. Schmidt, *Die Ethik der alten Griechen*, 1:168ff.}

128. {Cf. ibid., 170.}

129. {Cf. ibid., 267–68; κόρος = surfeit; ὕβρις = hubris.}

130. {Cf. ibid., 261.}

131. {Cf. ibid., 260.}

132. {Cf. Homer, *Iliad* 18.107–110.}

133. {Cf. Schmidt, *Die Ethik der alten Griechen*, 266.}

134. {Cf. ibid., 281.}

135. {Cf. ibid.}

136. {*WP* 758.}

137. *otium]* "leisure"

138. *feeling] Empfindung* {This could also be "perception."}

139. {Cf. Schmidt, *Die Ethik der alten Griechen*, 274.}

140. *Origin] Herkunft* {Usually translated as "descent."}

141. {Cf. Karl Semper, *Die natürlichen Existenzbedingungen der Thiere* ("The natural conditions of existence of animals"), 2 vols. (Leipzig: Brockhaus, 1880), 1:18–19, 236–37, 241–42, 218–19; 2:222–23, 257. *NL.*}

142. *the creator] die Schöpferin* {N uses the term *Schöpferin* ("female creator"), which refers back to the feminine noun *Sympathie* ("sympathy").}

143. {Cf. Alfred Espinas, *Die tierischen Gesellschaften: Eine vergleichend-psychologische Untersuchung* ("Animal societies: A comparative-psychological examination"), trans. W. Schlosser (Braunschweig: Vieweg, 1879), 367–68. *NL.*}

144. {Cf. Hartmann, *Phänomenologie des sittlichen Bewusstseins*, 591.}

145. {Cf. Roux, *Der Kampf der Theile im Organismus*, 37.}

146. {Cf. Léon Dumont, *Vergnügen und Schmerz: Zur Lehre von den Gefühlen* ("Pleasure and pain: On the doctrine of the feelings") (Leipzig: Brockhaus, 1876), 30–31. *NL.*}

147. {Cf. Schmidt, *Die Ethik der alten Griechen*, 269.}

148. {Cf. Hartmann, *Phänomenologie des sittlichen Bewusstseins*, chap. 1.}

149. *competition] Kampf*

150. {Cf. Schmidt, *Die Ethik der alten Griechen*, 2:273.}

151. {Cf. ibid., 274.}

152. {Cf. ibid., 342.}

153. {Cf. ibid., 353.}

154. {Cf. ibid., 358.}

155. {Cf. ibid., 357.}

156. {Cf. ibid.}

157. {Cf. ibid., 361.}

158. {Cf., ibid., 362.}

159. {Cf. Roux, *Der Kampf der Theile im Organismus*, 96–97.}

160. {Cf. ibid., 98.}

161. {Cf. ibid., 102.}

162. {Cf. ibid., 110.}

163. {Cf. ibid.; altered quote.}

164. *open-mindedness] Freisinnigkeit*

165. {Cf. ibid., 149.}

166. {Cf. ibid., 151.}

167. Georg Heinrich Schneider, *Der thierische Wille: Systematische Darstellung und Erklärung der thierischen Triebe und deren Entstehung, Entwickelung und Verbreitung im Thierreiche als Grundlage zu einer vergleichenden Willenslehre* ("The animal will: Systematic description and analysis of the animal drives and their emergence, development, and distribution in the animal world as the basis of a comparative study of the will") (Leipzig{: Abel,} 1880), 29. *NL.* In the passage cited by N, Schneider gives a definition of the rudimentary organs as no longer functional; they "once had a purpose": this is true — according to N in this fragment and in other passages — of "evil people."

168. *a person's ability to know absolutely (be known absolutely)] an der absoluten Erkenntniß (Erkanntheit)*

169. Cf. note to 7[1].

170. {Cf. Hartmann, *Phänomenologie des sittlichen Bewusstseins*, 567ff.}

171. {Cf. ibid., 607ff.}

172. Cf. ibid., 3.

173. Cf. ibid., 5–6.

174. *φρόνησις]* "practical wisdom"

175. *ἀταραξία]* "tranquility"

176. {Cf. ibid., 5ff.}

177. Cf. ibid., 26.

178. Cf. ibid.

179. Cf. ibid., 28.

180. *confidently expect a lot of ourselves] von uns viel versprechen können* {N is playing with different meanings of the verb *versprechen*.}

181. Cf. ibid., 35.

182. Cf. ibid., 36.

183. {Cf. ibid., 39.}

184. {Cf. Arthur Schopenhauer, *Sämmtliche Werke*, vol. 3: *Der Welt als Wille und Vorstellung*, vol. 2, ed. Julius Frauenstädt (Leipzig: F. A. Brockhaus, 1877), 731. *NL*. Translated in English by Judith Norman, Alistair Welchman, and Christopher Janaway as *The World as Will and Representation* (Cambridge: Cambridge University Press, 2017), 652.}

185. {Schopenhauer, *Parerga and Paralipomena* 2, §172, cited in Hartmann, *Phänomenologie des sittlichen Bewusstseins*, 43.}

186. Cf. ibid., 27.

187. Cf. Teichmüller, *Die wirkliche und die scheinbare Welt*, {82–83}.

188. Concerning a critique of Hartmann's *Phänomenologie des sittlichen Bewusstseins*.

189. {Cf. Hartmann, *Phänomenologie des sittlichen Bewusstseins*, 26.}

190. *facta]* "facts"

191. {*WP* 698.}

192. *sull'indole del piacere e del dolore)]* "On the Nature of Pleasure and Pain"

193. *il solo principio . . . essere positivo.]* {"the only moving principle of man is pain. Pain precedes every pleasure[.] Pleasure is not a positive state." Cf. Dumont, *Vergnügen und Schmerz*, 35–36. Kant notes this endorsement of the Milanese philosopher Count Pietro Verri (1728–97), whose words he paraphrases, in §58 of *Anthropology from a Pragmatic Point of View*. Kant was familiar with Verri's work *Idee sull'indole del piacere* (1774) in its German translation by Christoph Meiners, *Gedanken über die Natur des Vergnügens* ("Thoughts on the nature of pleasure") (Leipzig: Weygand, 1777).}

194. *chronic] wiederkehrender* {Cf. Dumont, *Vergnügen und Schmerz*, 36.}

195. {Cf. ibid., 37.}

196. {Cf. ibid., 32.}

197. {Cf. Schneider, *Der thierische Wille*, 58.}

198. On the concept "Jesuitism," cf. Hartmann, *Phänomenologie des sittlichen Bewusstseins*, 567–69, {645–48}.

199. *The highest principle] Der höchste Gesichtspunkt*

200. {Cf. 16[41].}

201. Summary taken from Schneider, *Der thierische Wille*, 65–75.

202. *robs] beraubt* {N added a period after *beraubt* and then continues with its genitive objects.}

203. *noblest] höchsten* {In most cases, we translate the adjective *höchst* as "supreme." Here we prefer "noblest" to reflect English usage with "end."}

204. Cf. Espinas, *Die tierischen Gesellschaften*, 159.

205. Cf. ibid., {162}.

206. {Cf. ibid.}

207. Cf. Post, *Bausteine für eine allgemeine Rechtswissenschaft*, 1:201.

208. {Cf. ibid., 214.}

209. Baumann, *Handbuch der Moral*, {32}.

210. *center of gravity] Schwergewicht*

211. Cf. Hartmann, *Phänomenologie des sittlichen Bewusstseins*, 605.

212. Cf. Baumann, *Handbuch der Moral*, {18}.

213. *voluntary] willkürlich*

214. Cf. ibid., 22.

215. Extrapolating from Baumann.

216. Cf. Baumann, *Handbuch der Moral*, 31.

217. Cf. 8[26]; 14[1].

218. Cf. Emerson, *Versuche*, 99; *The Collected Works of Ralph Waldo Emerson*, vol. 2: *Essays, First Series* (Cambridge, MA: Harvard University Press, 1979), 78: "There is less intention in history than we ascribe to it."

219. Cf. Hartmann, *Phänomenologie des sittlichen Bewusstseins*, 599.

220. Cf. ibid., 593.

[8 = Mp XVII 1a.]

1. {Cf. Gustav Klemm, *Allgemeine Cultur-Geschichte der Menschheit, Band 4: Die Urzustände der Berg- und Wüstenvölker der activen Menschheit und deren Verbreitung über die Erde* ("Universal cultural history of humanity, vol. 4: The primordial states of the nomadic mountain and desert peoples and their expansion over the earth") (Leipzig: B. G. Teubner, 1845), 370.}

2. {Cf. Oscar Peschel, *Völkerkunde* ("Ethnology") (Leipzig: Duncker & Humblot, 1874): 176–77.}

3. {Cf. Gustav Klemm, *Allgemeine Cultur-Geschichte der Menschheit, Band 6: China und Japan* (Leipzig: B. G. Teubner, 1847), 130–31.}

4. {Cf. Peschel, *Völkerkunde*, 454.}

5. {Cf. John Lubbock, *Die Entstehung der Zivilisation und der Urzustand des Menschengeschlechtes, erläutert durch das innere und äußere Leben der Wilden*, trans. A. Passow (Jena: H. Costenoble, 1875), 15–16. *NL*. Originally published as *The Origin of Civilization and the Primitive Condition of Man: Mental and Social Condition of Savages*, 3rd ed. (London: Longmans, Green, 1875.}

6. *The Siamese . . . rice.]* {Cf. David Kaltbrunner, *Der Beobachter: Allgemeine Anleitung zu Beobacthungen über Land und Leute für Touristen, Exkursionisten, und Forschungsreisende* ("The observer: General guide for tourists, hikers, and researchers on making observations about a land and its people") (Zurich: J. Wurster, 1881), 676–78. *NL*.}

7. *— just as . . . mist]* {Cf. James Bell Pettigrew, *Die Ortsbewegung der Thiere: Nebst Bemerkungen über Luftschifffahrt* (Leipzig: Brockhaus, 1875), 8; originally published as *Animal Locomotion: or Walking, Swimming and Flying, with a Dissertation on Aeronautics* (London: Henry S. King, 1873).}

8. *— just as . . . its wings)]* {Cf. ibid., 177.}

9. {Cf. 16[63, 83], 18[3], 20[3, 16], 21[1, 2], 23[9].}

10. Cf. *CW* 13, 7[37] and corresponding note; {cf. also Pettigrew, *Die Ortsbewegung der Thiere*, 7ff.}.

11. Cf. *GM* III 17.

12. {Cf. William Shakespeare, *Was ihr wollt*, trans. August Wilhelm von Schlegel, in *Shakespeare's dramatische Werke in 9 Bänden*, vol. 4, trans. August Wilhelm von Schlegel und Ludwig Tieck (Berlin:

Georg Reimer, 1854), act 1, scene 3, 133. *NL*. N cites the standard German translation and refers to "Sir Andrew Aguecheek" by his character name in the Schlegel-Tieck translation: "Junker Christopxh."}

13. Cf. *GM* II 3.

14. {Many of N's notes here and in the remainder of this notebook can be traced to his reading of Albert Hermann Post, *Bausteine für eine allgemeine Rechtswissenschaft auf vergleichend-ethnologischer Basis* ("Building blocks for a general jurisprudence on a comparative-ethnological basis"), vol. 1 (Oldenburg: Schulz, 1880); vol. 2 (Oldenburg: Schulz, 1881). *NL*.}

15. {Cf. ibid., 1:191.}

16. {Cf. ibid., 1:58, 73–74, 77, 81, 82, 85, 92–98, 103, 104, 108–13, 122–24; 2:37–38, 46–47, 55.}

17. *jus primae noctis]* "the right of the first night" {Often referred to by medievalists writing in English as the "droit du seigneur." It refers to the putative right of the lord to sleep with any peasant bride on her wedding night.}

18. *young females] Weibchen* {This is the standard German term for the female of the species in animals.}

19. *in our culture] bei uns*

20. *separatio quoad thorum et mensam]* "separation from bed and table" {An ecclesiastical decree that allowed husband and wife to live separate lives without annulling the marital bond.}

21. πόλις] "polis," i.e., "city-state"

22. {Cf. Post, *Bausteine für eine allgemeine Rechtswissenschaft*, 2:55.}

23. *even old Don Quixote!] noch der Don Quixote!* {We provide an equivalent for N's use of the definite article with a proper name, associated in German with provincial or dialect usage.}

24. {Cf. Post, *Bausteine für eine allgemeine Rechtswissenschaft*, 2:76–77, 88, 119–21, 217.}

25. *blood debts] Blutgeld* {The traditional English term for *Blutgeld* is the Old English term "wergild," or literally, "man-money," the amount of compensation paid by a person committing an offense to the injured party. We translate it as "blood debt" to make the term accessible to modern readers and to distinguish it from "blood money," which has a different sense.}

26. *Type . . . relatives.]* {Cf. ibid., 2:18–26.}

27. *Any place . . . perpetrator.]* {Cf. ibid., 2:143–45.}

28. *Presupposition . . . involved.]* {Cf. ibid., 1:153.}

29. *Outlawing: . . . father.]* {Cf. ibid., 1:64–65, 72–73.}

30. *Therefore: . . . communities.]* {Cf. ibid., 1:176.}

31. *In particular . . . here.]* {Cf. ibid., 1:178.}

32. *The more surely . . . the group.]* {Cf. Alfred Victor Espinas, *Die thierischen Gesellschaften: Eine vergleichend-psychologische Untersuchung* ("Animal societies: A comparative-psychological investigation"), trans. W. Schloesser (Braunschweig: Vieweg, 1879), 525–27. *NL.* Originally published in French as *Des sociétés animales: Étude de psychologie comparée*, 2nd ed. (Paris: Baillière, 1878).}

33. *To use . . . all.]* {Cf. ibid., 541.}

34. {*WP* 771.}

35. *sacrificio dell'intelletto]* "sacrifice of the intellect" {N underlines *sacrificio*}.

36. *what is there, still so good]* das Vorhandene noch so gute {N places two phrases here side by side, with the probable meaning of "no matter how good."}

37. Cf. 24[1]; *CW* 17, 5[96, 98].

38. {N's page references here and below are to Leopold Schmidt, *Die Ethik der alten Griechen* ("The ethics of the ancient Greeks"), vol. 2 (Berlin: Verlag von Wilhelm Hertz [Bessersche Buchhandlung], 1882). *NL.*}

39. *refuted]* gefälscht.

40. {On Baltasar Gracián, cf. N's letter to Heinrich Köselitz of 20 September 1884, *KGB* III:1, 535.}

41. *ὕβρις]* "hubris," extreme pride or self-confidence

42. *they]* man {A better rendering than "we" here, because N is referring to all Greeks.}

43. *γνῶθι σαυτόν]* "know thyself"

44. *subtext]* Hintergedanken {See Grimm 10, 1503.}

45. *πρόσθε . . . Χίμαιρα.]* "Plato in front, Plato in back, Chimaera in the middle." Paraphrase of *Iliad* 6.181, where the chimaera is described as "lion-fronted and snake behind, a goat in the middle." Cf. *BGE* 190.

46. {*WP* 787.}

47. {Cf. 7[7] and corresponding note.}

48. {*WP* 372.}

49. *good people]* Heading added in the summer of 1888.

50. {*WP* 418.}

51. {*WP* 574; cf. *BGE* Preface, 16, 17, 54.}

52. Cf. 7[268].

53. {Cf. 7[7] and corresponding note.}

54. {Cf. 16[33].}

55. {Cf. 7[47, 58, 62, 125]; 24[16, 27].}

56. {*WP* 1012.}

[9 = N VI 2.]

1. Collection of sayings and turns of phrase related to *Z* II; for the most part adopted in 13[1].

2. {Cf. 12[43]; 13[1]_373; 13[9].}

3. {Cf. 13[1]_373.}

4. {Cf. 13[1]_373.}

5. {Cf. 13[1]_374.}

6. {Cf. 13[1]_374.}

7. *I you and he.]* Ich Du und Er {N capitalizes the pronouns here.}

8. {Cf. 13[1]_371; 13[11]; 16[4]; 22[1]_548.}

9. {Cf. 13[1]_372.}

10. Cf. *Z* II "The Prophet"; {cf. 13[1]_373}.

11. *snored]* röchelte {*Röcheln*, to snore, to wheeze, to snuffle, has connotations of a death rattle.}

12. Cf. 13[1{_382}; 13[20].

13. Arrangement of *Z* II.

14. As in 9[1]; {cf. 13[1]_380}.

15. *to convert to my cause]* euch zu mir *bekehren*

16. *"Party liner"] "Mensch der Partei"*

17. *surge]* Brandung {As in the sense of surf or the ocean; cf. 13[1]_380; 16[7]; 22[1]_550.}

18. Cf. 13[1]{_396; 13[6]}; *Z* II "On Virtuous People."

19. Cf. 13[1]{_376}; *Z* II "The Child with the Mirror."

20. Cf. 13[1]{_376; 13[12]}.

21. Cf. *Z* II "On Virtuous People."

22. *I thirst for it.] ihn dürste ich* {Could also mean "it thirsts for me."}

23. Cf. 13[1]{_371}; *Z* II "The Stillest Hour."

24. Cf. 13[1]{_372; 10[17].}

25. {Cf. 13[1]_378.}

26. Cf. 13[1]{_389–90}.

27. {Cf. 13[1]_389, 13[12]; 16[7].}

28. *bark] Kahn* {A larger, open river- or sea-going vessel, usually with one mast, used for cargo on rivers or in coastal trade; in N also a general term for sea-going vessel.}

29. {Cf. 13[1]_389; 16[7]; 22[1]_550.}

30. {Cf. 13[1]_389; 16[7]; 22[1]_550.}

31. Cf. 13[1]{_389}.

32. {Cf. 13[1]_390; 16[7]; 22[1]_549.}

33. {Cf. 9[18]; 13[1]_389.}

34. Cf. 13[1]{_390; 13[18]; 16[7]}.

35. Cf. 13[1]{_392}.

36. {Cf. 13[1]_393; 13[8]; 16[7]; 22[1]_549.}

37. Cf. 13[1]{_392}.

38. *La vie . . . qui pense.]* "Life is a tragedy for those who feel, and a comedy for those who think." {The line "The world is a comedy to those that think; a tragedy to those that feel" appears often in Walpole's letters; the line "La vie est une tragédie pour ceux qui sentent, et une comédie pour ceux qui pensent" is also attributed to Jean de la Bruyère.}

39. Cf. 13[1]{_387–88; 13[6]}.

40. *removing mountains] Berge versetzen* {An allusion to Paul's words on love from 1 Corinthians 13:2.}

41. Cf. 13[1]{_386; 13[15]}.

42. Cf. 13[1]{_391}.

43. *grace] Anmuth*

44. Key terms referring to earlier fragments.

45. Cf. 13[1]{_375; 12[43]; 13[12]}.

46. Cf. 13[1, 21].

47. Cf. 13[1{_391}, 16, 20].

48. {Cf. *BGE* 260.}

49. Cf. 13[3]{_401–2}.

50. Cf. 13[2].

51. *Purification . . . world.]* Cf. 12[42].

52. Cf. 12[42].

53. Cf. 13[1{_372}, 20].

54. *they shoot off their mouths; we are supposed to think that this is out of the abundance of their hearts.] sie nehmen den Mund voll; man soll meinen, das Herz gehe ihnen über.* {N is playing off the biblical passage in Matthew 12:34, "for out of the abundance of the heart the mouth speaketh," which Luther translates as "Wes das Herz voll ist, des geht der Mund über." In substituting the idiom *den Mund vollnehmen*, meaning "to shoot off one's mouth," N puts the hypocrisy in the worst possible light. Luther was particularly proud of this translation, and cites it in his 1530 *Open Letter on Translating.*}

55. {Cf. 12[42]; 13[20].}

56. {Cf. 13[1]_372; 16[4]; 22[1]_549.}

57. *Fear . . . spring!]* Cf. 13[1{_373}].

58. *Workers . . . power.]* {Cf. *WP* 764.} Cf. 12[42].

59. Cf. 12[42].

60. {Cf. 3[1] 49; 12[1] 119; 12[42, 43]; 13[6].}

61. *Individuum est aliquid novum]* "The individual is something new"

62. {The addition of the definite article is needed to render the clarity of N's German.}

63. {Cf. 12[42].}

64. Cf. 12[42]; 13[1]{_373}.

65. Cf. 13[1]; *Z* II "The Stillest Hour."

66. Cf. *Z* II "The Night Song."

67. Nacht ist es — nun reden
lauter alle springenden Brunnen
— und auch du, meine Seele
bist ein springender Brunnen.
Nacht ist es — nun erst erwachen
alle Lieder der Liebenden.
Und auch du, meine Seele, bist
das Lied eines Liebenden.

68. *knowledge] Wissen*

69. Arrangement of *Z* II.

70. {Cf. Daniel Darc, *Petit bréviaire du Parisien* (Paris: Paul Ollendorff, 1883). N misspells Ollendorff's name.}

[10 = N VI 3.]

1. Cf. 13[3]{_402}.

2. Cf. 13[3]{_404}.

3. Key terms in *Z* II (from earlier fragments).

4. {Cf. 16[90].}

5. *my I] mein Ich* {The I is the subject of the sentence doing the dreaming. Cf. 10[10].}

6. Cf. 13[3]{_403}.

7. *hound of hell] Höllenhund* {See the Translators' Afterword, 740–41, on the translation of *Höllenhund*.}

8. {Cf. 13[3]_400.}

9. Cf. 13[3]{_403}.

10. As in 10[3].

11. Cf. 13[3]{_405}; 10[41]; 13[17, 25]}.

12. {Cf. 10[35]; 17[56]; 22[1]_552.}

13. Cf. *Z* II "The Prophet."

14. Cf. 13[3]{_405}.

15. *the Corsican] {Napoleon}

16. Cf. *Z* II "The Prophet."

17. As in 10[3]; cf. 13[3].

18. {An allusion to Kant; cf. 10[40]; 13[24, 27]; 16[84]; 21[3].}

19. Cf. 12[42]; 13[3]{_405–6}.

20. *aging virgins] alter Mädchen* {The term for "old maid" was *alte Jungfer* in N's time, which survives in modern German. Cf. Flügel 551.}

21. Cf. 13[3]_405; 16[7].

22. Cf. *Z* II "The Prophet."

23. Cf. 13[3]. {We found no parallel passage in 13[3]; but cf. *DD* "Amidst Birds of Prey."}

24. {Cf. 9[15]; 13[1]_372.}

25. Cf. 13[18]; {5[1] 213, 214; 12[1] 171; 12[13, 14]; 13[1]_375; allusion to the end of Goethe's *Faust* II, lines 12104–5}.

26. Cf. 13[1]{_377}.

27. Cf. 13[3]{_406}.

28. Cf. 13[3]{_402}.

29. Cf. 13[18]; 12[43].

30. Cf. 13[9].

31. Cf. 13[3]{_406}.

32. Cf. *Z* II "Upon the Blessed Isles" {cf. note to 10[17]}.

33. Cf. *Z* II "On Great Events."

34. Cf. *Z* II "On the Famously Wise."

35. *your neck is too stiff]* *zu gerade im Rücken sein*

36. Arrangement of *Z* II; cf. 13[3].

37. *Taine]* {Hippolyte Taine, French literary critic and historian.}

38. *Twilight of the gods]* *Götterdämmer* {Not *Götterdämmerung*, which would be the title of the fourth and final opera in Wagner's *Der Ring des Nibelungen*.}

39. Cf. 13[3]{_406}.

40. Cf. 13[3]{_406}.

41. {Cf. 13[3]_407.}

42. Cf. *Z* II "The Tomb Song"; "The Stillest Hour"; {cf. 10[8]; 17[56]; 22[1]_552}.

43. *word]* *Wort* {We keep this in the singular in order to reflect "word" in the sense of John 1:1.}

44. Cf. 13[13].

45. Cf. 13[1]{_383}.

46. Cf. 13[1]{_374; 13[16]}.

47. Arrangement of *Z* II.

48. *Those who speak freely]* *Freisprecher* {N could also be referring to acts of exoneration, but the context of the list indicates otherwise.}

49. Arrangement of *Z* II.

50. Cf. 13[24].

51. Arrangement of a Zarathustra drama (like a version of *Z* II); fragments 10[46, 47] are also included.

52. {Cf. 16[4].}

[11 = N VI 4.]

1. Arrangement of *Z* II.

2. *What is . . . vanity.]* Cf. 12[44]; *Z* II "On Human Prudence."

3. Cf. *Z* II "The Child with the Mirror."

4. {Cf. 3[1] 245; 4[165]; 18[43, 49, 56]; 21[6]; 24[16].}

5. {Cf. 9[48]; 18[55].}

6. Refers to a third part of *Z* (immediately following or during the writing of *Z* II).

7. {Cf. 22[1]_558.}

8. Cf. *BGE* 83.

9. Arrangement of *Z* II.

10. Cf. 13[14].

11. Cf. 13[13].

12. Arrangement of *Z* II.

13. Arrangement of *Z* II.

[12 = Z I 3.]

1. Published for the first time as an annual issue (1975/76) for "Authors and Friends of the House of De Gruyter." Collection of sayings from *HAH, MM, WS, D,* and *JS,* as well as from earlier notebooks from the period 1882/83; with emendations and changes; used for *Z* II, III, IV, *BGE.* {In an effort to follow the editorial decision to maintain translation consistency across the *CW* volumes, we have used the language of the already published translations by Gary Handwerk of *HAH, MM,* and *WS,* by Brittain Smith of *D,* and by Adrian Del Caro of *BGE,* making changes only where we deemed it necessary in order to maintain consistency with our global translation decisions.}

2. {Cf. *HAH* 482.}

3. {Cf. *HAH* 483.}

4. {Cf. *HAH* 494.}

5. {Cf. *HAH* 498.}

6. {Cf. *HAH* 504.}

7. {Cf. *HAH* 506.}

8. {Cf. *HAH* 508.}

9. {Cf. *HAH* 515.}

10. {Cf. *HAH* 514.}

11. {Cf. *HAH* 529.}
12. {Cf. *HAH* 544.}
13. {Cf. *HAH* 564.}
14. {Cf. *HAH* 310.}
15. {Cf. *HAH* 582.}
16. {Cf. *HAH* 580.}
17. {Cf. *HAH* 575.}
18. {Cf. *HAH* 402.}
19. {Cf. *HAH* 391.}
20. {Cf. *HAH* 388.}
21. {Cf. *HAH* 320.}
22. {Cf. *HAH* 308.}
23. {Cf. *HAH* 301.}
24. {Cf. *HAH* 295.}
25. {Cf. *MM* 6.}
26. {Cf. *MM* 406.}
27. {Cf. *MM* 402.}
28. {Cf. *MM* 390.}
29. {Cf. *MM* 378.}
30. {Cf. *MM* 381.}
31. {Cf. *MM* 368.}
32. {Cf. *MM* 362.}
33. {Cf. *MM* 357.}
34. *spirit] Geist* {This could also be understood as "mind."}
35. {Cf. *MM* 353.}
36. {Cf. *MM* 348.}
37. {Cf. *MM* 341.}
38. {Cf. *MM* 313; John 12:14.}
39. {Cf. *MM* 309.}
40. {Cf. *MM* 274.}
41. {Cf. *MM* 267.}
42. {Cf. *MM* 255.}
43. {Cf. *MM* 240.}
44. {Cf. *MM* 202.}
45. {Cf. *MM* 168.}
46. {See note 34 above.}
47. {Cf. *MM* 160.}

48. {Cf. *MM* 136.}

49. {Cf. *MM* 140.}

50. {Cf. *MM* 128.}

51. {Cf. *MM* 120.}

52. {Cf. *MM* 34.}

53. {Cf. *MM* 36.}

54. {Cf. *MM* 65.}

55. {Cf. 3[1] 341; 5[35]; 13[12].}

56. {Cf. *MM* 77.}

57. {Cf. *MM* 82.}

58. {Cf. *WS* 340.}

59. {Cf. *WS* 335.}

60. {Cf. *WS* 325.}

61. {Cf. *WS* 290.}

62. {Cf. *WS* 240.}

63. {Cf. *WS* 254.}

64. {Cf. *WS* 18. N here alludes to a saying of Diogenes the Cynic; cf. Diogenes Laertius, *Lives of Eminent Philosophers* 6.2, 6, 41.}

65. {Cf. *WS* 55.}

66. {Cf. *WS* 120.}

67. {Cf. *HAH* 83.}

68. {Cf. *HAH* 76.}

69. {Cf. *HAH* 66.}

70. {Cf. *HAH* 186.}

71. {Cf. *HAH* 187.}

72. {Cf. *HAH* 560; cf. Matthew 25:14–30.}

73. {Cf. *HAH* 568.}

74. *"Should . . . into it."]* "Soll das Band nicht reißen — mußt du mal drauf beißen."

75. {Cf. 1[97]; 3[1] 51; *BGE* 140.}

76. {Cf. *D* 574.}

77. {Cf. *D* 557.}

78. {Cf. *D* 447.}

79. {Cf. *D* 438.}

80. {Cf. *D* 406.}

81. {Cf. *D* 415.}

82. {Cf. *D* 399.}

83. {Cf. *D* 380.}

84. {Cf. *D* 391.}

85. {Cf. *D* 299.}

86. {Cf. *D* 249.}

87. {Cf. *D* 208.}

88. {Cf. *D* 185.}

89. {Cf. 3[1] 444.}

90. {Cf. 3[1] 404.}

91. {Cf. 3[1] 422; 22[3]_569; *BGE* 166.}

92. {Cf. 3[1] 394; 12[1] 89; 13[8].}

93. {Cf. 3[1] 349; 13[16]; 16[7]; *BGE* 169.}

94. {Cf. 3[1] 356.}

95. *Women] Frauen*

96. {Cf. 1[50]; 3[1] 351.}

97. {Cf. 3[1] 336.}

98. {Cf. 3[1] 342; 5[35].}

99. {Cf. 3[1] 338.}

100. {Cf. 3[1] 287; 4[42, 200]; 13[19].}

101. {Cf. 3[1] 264; *BGE* 73.}

102. {Cf. 3[1] 270; *BGE* 73a.}

103. {Cf. 3[1] 273; 13[8]; 16[7]; *CW* 15, 31[36]; 32[9].}

104. {Cf. 3[1] 249; *BGE* 101.}

105. {Cf. {3[1] 243}; 13[16]; 16[7]; 23[5]; *CW* 15, 31[35, 36]; 32[10]; *BGE* 99.}

106. {Cf. 3[1] 251.}

107. {Cf. 13[16], *JS* 214.}

108. {Cf. 3[1] 202; *BGE* 162; the wordplay is between *Nächster*, Jesus's designation for a fellow human being, and, in the latter two, *Nachbar*, the term for someone living in close proximity.}

109. {Cf. 3[1] 206.}

110. {Cf. 3[1] 170; 13[8].}

111. {Cf. 3[1] 138.}

112. {Cf. 3[1] 141; *BGE* 170.}

113. {Cf. 3[1] 139; 3[1] 393.}

114. {Cf. 3[1] 139.}

115. {Cf. 3[1] 122; 5[17].}

116. {Cf. 3[1] 77.}

117. *grab us by the scruff of the neck]* am Schopfe fassen {Cf. 3[1] 86; *BGE* 179.}

118. {Cf. 2[41]; 3[1] 66; *CW* 15, 31[52]; 32[9].}

119. {Cf. 1[49], 3[1] 47.}

120. {Cf. *BGE* 141.}

121. {Cf. 3[1] 44.}

122. {Cf. 3[1] 38; 22[3]_563.}

123. {Cf. 3[1] 49; 9[48]; 12[42, 43]; 13[6].}

124. *superior qualities . . . base qualities]* das Hohe . . . dessen Niedriges {Cf. 1[92].}

125. {Cf. *GM* II 1.}

126. {Cf. 4[53].}

127. {Cf. 4[56].}

128. {Cf. 4[54].}

129. {Cf. 4[54].}

130. {Cf. 4[56].}

131. {Cf. 4[57].}

132. {Cf. 4[57].}

133. *utile]* "useful"

134. *dulce]* "sweet" {Cf. 4[59] and note 70 in Nb 4 on Horace's *Ars poetica*.}

135. *Dulciarier]* {"Dulciaries" is an archaic English word for "sweetening things."}

136. {Cf. 13[6]; 16[7].}

137. {Cf. 4[64]; N is playing with the distinction between *gerecht* (just) and *gerächt* (avenged).}

138. {Cf. 3[1] 389.}

139. {Cf. 3[1] 217.}

140. {Cf. 5[11]; 13[8]; *BGE* 81.}

141. {Cf. 4[58].}

142. {Cf. 13[9].}

143. {Cf. 5[1] 20.}

144. {Cf. 3[1] 347; 5[33, 35]; *BGE* 183.}

145. {Cf. 25[301].}

146. {Cf. 3[1] 414.}

147. {Cf. 3[1] 300; 13[14].}

148. {Cf. 1[59]; 3[1] 13; 4[226]; 13[14]; 16[7].}

149. {Cf. 3[1] 328; 13[14]; 16[7].}

150. {Cf. 3[1] 415.}

151. {Cf. 3[1] 234.}

152. {Cf. 4[112]; 5[1] 5.}

153. {Cf. 4[131].}

154. {Cf. 5[1] 12.}

155. {Cf. 4[72]; 5[1] 24.}

156. {Cf. 5[1] 193.}

157. {Cf. 13[10]; *D* 48.}

158. {Cf. 3[1] 260.}

159. *error veritate simplicior]* "error is simpler than truth" {Cf. *D* 168.}

160. *Ubi pater sum, ibi patria.]* "Wherever I am father, there is the fatherland." {Reworking of the Latin expression *ubi panis, ibi patria* (where there is bread, there is [my] country).}

161. {Cf. *D* 235.}

162. *Here where we live]* Bei uns {This idiom locates the action or experience within a country, a region, or a community.}

163. {Cf. *D* 236.}

164. {Cf. *D* 535.}

165. {Cf. *D* 537.}

166. {Cf. {5[1] 213, 214; 10[17, 24]; 12[13, 14]; 13[1]_375; 13[18]; cf. lines 12104–11 of Goethe's *Faust* II.}

167. {Cf. *MM* 325.}

168. {Cf. *WS* 131.}

169. {Cf. *WS* 132.}

170. {Cf. 3[1] 392.}

171. {Cf. 3[1] 402.}

172. {Cf. 3[1] 411.}

173. {Cf. 5[1] 55.}

174. {Cf. 1[5]; 5[1] 60.}

175. {Cf. 2[10]; 5[1] 109.}

176. {Cf. 3[1] 167.}

177. {Cf. 4[71]; 5[1] 14.}

178. {Cf. 3[1] 300.}

179. {Cf. 3[1] 94; *BGE* 150.}

180. {Cf. 1[85].}

181. {Cf. 1[87, 108]; 5[1] 62; *BGE* 114.}

182. {Cf. 4[40]; 5[1] 83.}

183. {Cf. 5[1] 112; *BGE* 118.}

184. {Cf. 4[77]; 5[1] 123.}

185. {Cf. 4[87].}

186. *advocate] Anwalt*

187. {Cf. 4[199]; 5[1] 264.}

188. {Cf. 3[1] 51, 60; 1[34, 79, 80]; 4[44]; 5[1] 46.}

189. Cf. 5[1] 262.

190. Cf. 5[1] 257.

191. Cf. *Z* IV "The Leech"; {4[176]; 5[1] 254; 5[22]; 13[7]; 16[7]; *CW* 15, 31[6, 9]}.

192. Cf. *Z* II "Upon the Blessed Isles."

193. {Cf. 4[160]; 5[1] 247; 13[17]; Isaiah 40:4.}

194. Cf. 4[168]; 5[1] 249; 5[23].

195. Cf. 5[1] 239, 244.

196. Cf. 5[1] 234; *Z* II "On Those Who Are Sublime."

197. Cf. 5[1] 229.

198. Cf. 13[11].

199. Cf. 5[1] 214; 12[14].

200. Cf. 5[1] 213, 214; 13[1]{_375; 10[17]; 12[1] 171}.

201. Cf. 5[1] 209; 13[15]; {3[1] 124}.

202. Cf. 5[1] 207.

203. Cf. 5[1] 198.

204. Cf. 5[1] 191.

205. *peach] Apfel* {We switched the fruit (from "apple") in order to preserve the wordplay with "fuzz."}

206. Cf. 5[1] 195.

207. Cf. 5[1] 183.

208. *effect at a distance]* {This is N's translation of *actio in distans*; cf. *JS* 60.}

209. *the arc of the motion] Bewegungskurve*

210. Source unknown.

211. *secondary manifestation] Nebenäußerung*

212. *Euryanthe]* {*Euryanthe* is an opera by Carl Maria von Weber (1786–1826), first performed 25 October 1823 in Vienna.}

213. Key terms for *Z* II.

214. {Cf. 3[1] 49; 9[48]; 12[1] 119; 12[43]; 13[6].}

215. {Cf. 9[48].}

216. Collection of fragments, used mostly for Z II "On Tarantulas"; cf. 13[1] as well.

217. {Cf. 3[1] 39; 9[48]; 12[1] 119; 12[42]; 13[6].}

218. {Cf. 9[1]; 13[1]_368; 13[9].}

219. {Cf. 13[1]_375.}

220. {Cf. 13[1]_379.}

221. {Cf. 13[1]_379.}

222. {Cf. 13[1]_379.}

223. {Cf. 13[1]_383.}

224. {Cf. 13[1]_382.}

225. {Cf. 9[17]; 13[1]_390.}

226. {Cf. 13[1]_397; 16[7]; 17[48]; 23[5]; 22[1]_553.}

227. {Cf. 10[21].}

228. Arrangement of Z II.

[13 = Z I 4.]

1. Collection of sayings and turns of phrase for the most part from Notebook 9 (N VI 2), and in part from Notebook 10 (N VI 3); enhanced by emendations; used for Z II and early drafts 13[6–9, 11, 12, 14–19].

2. {Cf. 9[14, 36, 56]; 13[20].}

3. {Cf. 9[14].}

4. {Cf. 9[14].}

5. {Cf. 9[1]; 13[11]; 16[4]; 22[1]_375}

6. {Cf. 9[1].}

7. {Cf. 9[45]; 16[4]; 22[1]_375}

8. {Cf. 13[8].}

9. {Cf. 9[45].}

10. {Cf. 13[14].}

11. {Cf. 9[15, 45]; 10[17]; 16[4].}

12. {Cf. 9[49].}

13. {Cf. 9[3].}

14. {Cf. 9[13]; 13[1]_375; 13[11].}

15. {Cf. 16[4]; 22[1].}

16. {Cf. 9[46].}

17. {Cf. 9[1]; 12[43]; 13[9].}

18. {Cf. 9[1].}

19. {Cf. 9[1].}

20. {Cf. 9[1].}

21. *"Black on White"*] {Probably a reference to a game similar to mahjong.}

22. queen] *Herrin* {*Herrin* = "mistress," but this meaning in English is now obsolete, so we have opted for a different term for a female figure of authority.}

23. {Cf. 10[38].}

24. {Cf. 9[1].}

25. {Cf. 9[1].}

26. {Cf. 13[8].}

27. *mere woman*] *Weibchen*

28. {Cf. Genesis 2: 21–27}

29. {Cf. 9[30]; 13[11].}

30. {Cf. 9[30].}

31. *in the tree "Future"*] *auf dem Baume Zukunft* {The quotation marks are not in the German but are inserted here to indicate N's suggestion that this is the name of the tree.}

32. {Cf. 9[30]; 12[43].}

33. {Cf. 9[30].}

34. {Cf. 10[23, 24]; 12[1] 171.}

35. *floating around right now*] *jetzt in der Luft liegen*

36. {Cf. 9[11]; 13[12].}

37. {Cf. 9[10].}

38. {Cf. 9[10].}

39. {Cf. 9[10].}

40. {Cf. 9[10].}

41. {Cf. 13[11].}

42. {Cf. 16[4]; 22[1]_376.}

43. {Cf. 16[4]; 22[1]_377.}

44. {Cf. 10[18].}

45. *Every intellect . . . my intellect.*] *Aller Geist . . . mein Geist* {This could also be "spirit" or "mind."}

46. {Cf. 9[10].}

47. {Cf. 9[16].}

48. {Cf. 13[7].}

49. {Cf. 16[4]; 22[1]_549.}

50. {Cf. 9[23]; 13[1]_386.}

51. {Cf. 16[4]; 22[1]_549.}

52. {Cf. 13[11].}

53. {Cf. 12[9, 43].}

54. {Cf. 16[7]; 22[1]_550.}

55. {Cf. 13[12]; 16[7]; 22[1]_550.}

56. {Cf. 9[6].}

57. {Cf. 9[6].}

58. {Cf. 9[6].}

59. {Cf. 9[6]; 16[7]; 22[1].}

60. {Cf. 9[6].}

61. {Cf. 16[7]; 22[1]_549.}

62. {Cf. 9[52].}

63. {Cf. 9[53].}

64. {Cf. 13[7].}

65. *Via Appia]* {The Appian Way was one of the first and most important Roman roads, stretching 350 miles from the Roman Forum to modern-day Brindisi. Cf. 9[4]; 13[20].}

66. {Cf. 13[11]; 16[7]; 17[58]; 22[1]_551.}

67. {Cf. 13[6].}

68. {Cf. 12[43].}

69. {Cf. 12[43].}

70. *boat] Nachen* {An open vessel, about the size of a gondola, propelled by oars or a longer oar, used for light cargo on rivers or for transporting passengers to ships at anchor; in a letter written 1 June 1859 (*KGB* I:1, 66) from his first year at Schulpforta to his childhood friend Wilhelm Pinder, N includes a poem in which he uses this term for the boat in which Charon transports the dead to the Underworld.}

71. {Cf. 13[10, 14]; 16[7]; 22[1]_550.}

72. {Cf. 13[23].}

73. {Cf. 16[7]; 22[1].}

74. *intellect . . . intellect.] Geist . . . Geist* {This could also be rendered as "spirit."}

75. {Cf. 13[8].}

76. *son of man]* Menschensohn {Reflects the standard biblical term.}

77. {Cf. 9[24].}

78. {Cf. 9[24].}

79. {Cf. 9[24].}

80. {Cf. 9[24].}

81. {Cf. 9[24].}

82. {Cf. 9[23].}

83. {Cf. 9[23]; 1 Corinthians 13:2.}

84. {Cf. 9[23].}

85. {Cf. 9[23]; 13[6].}

86. {Cf. 9[23]; 13[6].}

87. {Cf. 16[7]: 22[1]_549.}

88. {Cf. 4[210]; 5[9].}

89. *make better forecasts of human weather]* daß sie die Wetter-
zeichen des Menschen besser reden machen

90. {Cf. 9[18].}

91. {Cf. 9[18]; 16[7]; 22[1]_550; a reference to Pentecost. See Acts 2:3.}

92. *this gold dances leaps and crouches]* es hebt und senkt sich der
Tanz dieses Gold {Our paraphrase reflects the more extensive description in 9[18]; see also 16[7]; 22[1]_550.}

93. {Cf. 9[18], 13[12]; 16[7].}

94. {Cf. 9[17].}

95. {Cf. 9[17]; 13[12].}

96. {Cf. 9[17]; 13[12].}

97. {Cf. 9[17].}

98. {Cf. 9[17]; 12[43].}

99. {Cf. 9[19]; 13[18]; 16[7].}

100. {Cf. 9[19]; 16[7]; 22[1]_549.}

101. *Did not cry out No!]* Riefen nicht Nein! {There is no subject
referent for the verb "Riefen."}

102. {Cf. 9[32].}

103. {Cf. 9[32].}

104. {Cf. 9[32].}

105. {Cf. 9[31].}

106. {Cf. 9[31].}

107. {Cf. 9[31].}
108. {Cf. 13[8].}
109. {Cf. 9[21]; 13[8].}
110. {Cf. 9[21].}
111. {Cf. 9[21].}
112. {Cf. 9[20]; 13[8]; 16[7]; 22[1]_549.}
113. {Cf. 13[7].}
114. {Cf. 13[8].}
115. {Cf. 13[18].}
116. {Cf. 16[7].}
117. {Cf. 16[7].}
118. *dressing and disguises] Kleider und Verkleidung*
119. {Cf. 16[7].}
120. {Cf. 9[15].}
121. {Cf. 9[7]; 13[6].}

122. *driver and beater] Treiber und Dränger* {Hunting terms that characterize the men who drive the hunted animals into a place where they may be killed.}

123. {Cf. 12[43]; 16[7]; 17[48]; 23[5]; 22[1]_553.}
124. {Cf. 16[7].}
125. Cf. 10[45, 46, 47].

126. Collection of sayings and turns of phrase, only some of which are from earlier notebooks (Notebook 10 = N VI 3 in particular); used sparingly for *Z* II.

127. {Cf. 13[14]; 16[7].}
128. {Cf. 10[4]; 13[3]_403.}
129. {Cf. 13[18]; 16[7].}
130. {Cf. 9[34].}
131. {Cf. 9[34].}
132. {Cf. 9[34].}
133. {Cf. 9[34].}
134. {Cf. 9[34].}
135. {Cf. 9[34].}
136. {Cf. 13[7].}
137. {Cf. 10[1].}
138. {Cf. 10[1].}
139. {Cf. 10[4].}

140. {Cf. 10[4]; 13[3]_400.}

141. {Cf. 10[4].}

142. {Cf. 10[4].}

143. {Cf. 10[5].}

144. {Cf. 10[7].}

145. {Cf. 10[9].}

146. {Cf. 10[9].}

147. {Cf. 10[14], 16[7].}

148. *ties up hearts until they shatter]* die herzzerschnürende

149. {Cf. 10[19].}

150. {Cf. 10[19].}

151. {Cf. 10[23].}

152. {Cf. 10[32].}

153. {Cf. 10[33].}

154. {Cf. 10[34].}

155. *binders and tamers]* Binder und Bändiger {We read *binden* in the sense of "binding and loosing," the power given by God.}

156. *you should be given that]* {N uses the idiom *das soll man euch zu Ehren sagen*, literally, "in all fairness, that should be said to you." Cf. 10[34].}

157. *buckets of love]* händevoll Liebe

158. {Cf. 10[25; 10[35].}

159. {Cf. 16[7]; 22[1]_549.}

160. Not used for *Z.*

161. *that those who create]* das den Schaffenden {The verb is omitted; the inflection indicates that the worm is doing something to those who create.}

162. Excised chapter, for the most part comprising earlier fragments; {cf. 9[23]; 13[1]_387–88}.

163. {Cf. 3[1] 49; 9[48]; 12[1] 119; 12[42]; 12[43].}

164. {Cf. 9[7]; 13[1]_397.}

165. {Cf. note to 12[1] 135.}

166. {Cf. 12[1] 133; 16[7].}

167. {Cf. 13[1]_382.}

168. Like note 162 above.

169. {Cf. 13[1]_377.}

170. {Cf. 13[1]_378; 22[1]_549.}

171. {Cf. 13[1]_378.}
172. {Cf. 13[1]_382.}
173. {Cf. 13[1]_393.}
174. {Cf. 13[1]_393.}
175. {Cf. 4[176]; 5[1] 254; 5[22]; 12[5]; 16[7]; *CW* 15, 31[6, 9].}
176. {Cf. 13[3]_402.}
177. {Cf. 13[1]_398.}
178. Like note 162 above.
179. {Cf. 13[1]_372.}
180. {Cf. 13[1]_374.}
181. {Cf. 13[1]_385.}
182. {Cf. 9[21]; 13[1]_393.}
183. {Cf. 9[20]; 13[1]_393; 16[7]; 22[1]_549.}
184. {Cf. 13[1]_394.}
185. {Cf. 13[1]_395.}
186. {Cf. 13[1]_392.}
187. {Cf. 5[11]; 12[1] 138; *BGE* 81.}
188. {Cf. 3[1] 170; 12[1] 106.}
189. {Cf. 3[1] 138 and corresponding note; 12[1] 107.}
190. {Cf. 3[1] 273; 12[1] 99; 16[7]; *CW* 15, 31[36]; 32[9].}
191. {Cf. 3[1] 394; 12[1] 89.}
192. {Cf. 4[275, 279]; 5[21].}
193. Like note 162 above.
194. {Cf. 12[43]; 13[1]_373.}
195. {Cf. 10[22].}
196. {Cf. 13[1]_381.}
197. Collection, used for the most part for *Z* II "On Self-Overcoming."
198. {Cf. 12[1] 160.}
199. {Cf. 4[67, 79].}
200. Like note 162 above.
201. {Cf. 9[30]; 13[1]_375.}
202. {Cf. 5[1] 227.}
203. {Cf. 12[12].}
204. {Cf. 13[1]_397.}
205. {Cf. 13[1]_382; 16[7]; 17[58]; 22[1]_551.}
206. {Cf. 13[1]_379.}

207. {Cf. 9[13]; 13[1] 373.}
208. {Cf. 9[1]; 13[1]_371; 16[4]; 22[1].}
209. {Cf. 13[1]_379.}
210. Like note 162 above.
211. {Cf. 13[1]_379; 16[7]; 22[1]_550.}
212. {Cf. 9[24]; 13[1]_386.}
213. {Cf. 9[11]: 13[1]_376].}
214. {Cf. 9[23]; 13[1]_386.}
215. {Cf. 9[18], 13[1] ; 16[7].}
216. {Cf. 9[17]; 13[1]_390.}
217. {Cf. 9[17]; 13[1]_390.}
218. {Cf. 3[1] 80; 5[35]; 12[1] 53.}
219. Like note 162 above; {cf. 10[36]}.
220. {Cf. 10[36].}
221. {Cf. 13[1]_387.}
222. {Cf. 11[16].}
223. Like note 162 above.
224. {Cf. 13[1]_372.}
225. {Cf. 13[1]_384; 13[10]; 16[7]; 22[1]_550.}
226. {Cf. 13[3]; 16[7].}
227. {Cf. 3[1] 300; 12[1] 146.}
228. {Cf. 1[59]; 3[1] 13; 4[226]; 12[1] 147; 16[7].}
229. {Cf. 3[1] 328; 12[1] 148; 16[7].}
230. {Cf. 13[1]_377.}
231. {Cf. 11[15].}
232. Like note 162 above; {cf. 9[24]; 13[1]_386}.
233. {Cf. 3[1] 124; 5[1] 209; 12[15].}
234. Like note 162 above.
235. {Cf. 13[1]_373.}
236. {Cf. 13[1]_391.}
237. {Cf. 10[38]; 13[1]_374.}
238. {Cf. 10[38]; 13[1]_374.}
239. {Cf. 12[1] 103.}
240. {Cf. 3[1] 243; 12[1] 101; 16[7]; 23[5]; *BGE* 99.}
241. {Cf. 3[1] 349; 12[1] 90; 16[7]; *BGE* 169.}
242. Like note 162 above; {cf. 13[1]_398}.
243. {Cf. 13[1]_392.}

244. {Cf. 4[160]; 5[1] 247; 12[6].}

245. Like note 162 above; {cf. 10[17]}.

246. {Cf. 9[19]; 13[1]; 16[7].}

247. {Cf. 13[1]_394.}

248. {Cf. 13[3, 18]; 16[7].}

249. {Cf. 3[1] 342; 12[1] 94.}

250. *old wives] alte Weiber* {Translated here as "wives" because of the connection in English to "old wives' tales."}

251. *young and female] junge Weibchen*

252. {Cf. 10[21].}

253. Like note 162 above.

254. {Cf. 13[29, 31].}

255. {Cf. 13[1]_382.}

256. {Cf. 3[1] 287; 4[42, 200]; 12[1] 96.}

257. Arrangement of Z II.

258. {Cf. 9[32].}

259. {Cf. 9[14, 36, 56]; 13[1]_396; 13[20].}

260. {Cf. 9[4]; 13[1]_382.}

261. Outline of Z.

262. Plan for a sequel to Z, dated just before the completion of Z II.

263. Outline of Z.

264. *Stromboli]* {Small volcanic island off the north coast of Sicily.}

265. {Cf. 13[1]_383.}

266. Key terms for Z.

267. Key terms for Z.

268. Arrangement of Z II.

269. Arrangement of Z II.

270. Arrangement of Z II.

271. Arrangement of Z II.

272. Arrangement of Z II.

273. Arrangement of Z II.

274. Arrangement of Z II.

275. Arrangement of Z II.

276. Arrangement of Z II.

277. Arrangement of Z II.

[14 = M III 2b.]

  1. Cf. 7[268].

  2. *impetus]* "passions" {This is the Latin plural, not our English translation.}

[15 = N VI 5.]

  1. The writings of this notebook constitute an attempt that N abandoned to continue his Zarathustra work after the completion of *Z* II with a third and a fourth part; these writings were given little attention later during the writing of *Z* III.

  2. *not to . . . of life!]* {Cf. *BGE* 4.}

  3. List of books or authors that N planned to read.

  4. {Cf. Sir Walter Scott, *The Monastery: A Romance* (1820) and *The Abbot* (1820), a sequel to *The Monastery*.}

  5. {Cf. Joseph Haller, *Altspanische Sprichwörter und sprichwörtliche Redensarten aus den Zeiten vor Cervantes* ("Old Spanish proverbs and proverbial phrases from the times before Cervantes") (Regensburg: Manz, 1883).}

  6. {Cf. Wilhelm Leopold Colmar Freiherr von der Goltz, *Das Volk in Waffen: Ein Buch über Heerwesen und Kriegführung unserer Zeit* ("The People in arms: A book on military affairs and warfare of our time") (Berlin: Decker, 1883). *NL*.}

  7. {Cf. 16[86]; 22[1]_546.}

  8. {Cf. 22[1]_546.}

  9. *suspends . . . in favor]* aufhebt

  10. {Cf. 16[86].}

  11. *agon]* "contest," "struggle"

  12. *ancestry]* Herkunft

  13. *Emerson p. 237.]* N refers to the following passage in *Versuche (Essays)*, {trans. G. Fabricius (Hanover: Carl Meyer, 1858), *NL*; originally published in English as *The Collected Works of Ralph Waldo Emerson*, vol. 2: *Essays, First Series*, ed. Alfred Riggs Ferguson, Joseph Slater, and Jean Ferguson Carr (Cambridge, MA: Harvard University Press, 1971), 190}: "The one thing which we seek with insatiable desire is to forget ourselves, to be surprised out of our propriety, to lose our sempiternal memory, and to do something without knowing how or why; in short, to draw

a new circle. Nothing great was ever achieved without enthusiasm. The way of life is wonderful: it is by abandonment. The great moments of history are the facilities of performance through the strength of ideas, as the works of genius and religion. 'A man,' said Oliver Cromwell, 'never rises so high as when he knows not whither he is going.' Dreams and drunkenness, the use of opium and alcohol are the semblance and counterfeit of this oracular genius, and hence their dangerous attraction for men. For the like reason, they ask the aid of wild passions, as in gaming and war, to ape in some manner these flames and generosities of the heart." {Although *KSA* 14 notes that the Cromwell quote "was underlined by N," this is not in fact correct; although the entire page was repeatedly highlighted, these particular lines are uniquely highlighted by seven marginal lines.} On Cromwell's quote, cf. *SE* 1, *CW* 2, 174.

14. *then you **must** bring them up, bring them up to you!]* so **mußt** *du erziehen, zu Dir hinaufziehen*! {N's wordplay is on *erziehen*, meaning "to raise" or "to educate."}

15. {These lines were copied by N from Wilhelm Leopold Colmar Freiherr von der Goltz, "Feldherren und Feldherrenthum" ("Field marshals and their domain"), *Deutsche Rundschau* 31 (April–June 1882): 378–402.}

16. *rooted in the earth]* wachse aus der Erde

17. {Cf. ibid., 390; said about Alexander.}

18. {Cf. ibid., 399; the quote is from Thomas Carlyle, *Geschichte Friedrichs II: Von Preußen, genannt Friedrich der Große* (*History of Friedrich II of Prussia, Called Frederick the Great*), first published in English in 1858 (the sentence quoted appears in vol. 4, p. 168), trans. J. Neuberg (Berlin: Verlag der Königlichen Geheimen Oberhofbuchdr., 1866), 178: "Ich will es vollbringen oder sterben!" ("I will achieve it or die!").}

19. {Cf. Goltz, "Feldherren und Feldherrenthum," 387; the quote is from Aristotle: "Der Zorn ist nothwendig, ohne ihn triumphirt man in Nichts" ("Anger is necessary, without it there is no victory"). Cf. Seneca, *De ira* ("On anger") 1.9.2: "Ira, inquit Aristoteles, necessaria est, nec quidquam sine illa expugnari potest." English translation: "On Anger," in Seneca, *Moral and*

Political Essays, ed. and trans. John M. Cooper and J. F. Procopé (Cambridge: Cambridge University Press, 1995), 27: "Anger," says Aristotle, "is needful; no fight can be won with it."}

20. {Cf. Goltz, "Feldherren und Feldherrenthum," 388; the quote is from Carl von Clausewitz, *Vom Kriege* (Berlin: Dümmlers Verlag, 1832), 4: "in so gefährlichen Dingen, wie der Krieg eins ist, sind die Irrthümer, welche aus Gutmüthigkeit entstehen, gerade die schlimmsten." English translation: *On War*, trans. Michael Howard and Peter Paret (Princeton, NJ: Princeton University Press, 1984), 75: "war is such a dangerous business that the mistakes which come from kindness are the very worst."}

21. {Cf. Goltz, "Feldherren und Feldherrenthum," 383.}

22. {Cf. ibid., 384; the quote is attributed to Tamerlane: "Wie klein ist diese Erde für den Ehrgeiz eines großen Fürsten" ("This earth is too small for the ambition of a great prince").}

23. *measure]* *Verdienst*

24. {Cf. ibid.; cf. also Theobald Chauber, *Friedrich der Große, König von Preusen: Sein Leben und Wirken* (Stuttgart: Scheible's, 1834), 277: "Das wahre Verdienst eines Fürsten besteht in der aufrichtigen Neigung zum allgemeinen Besten in seiner Liebe zum Vaterlande und zum Ruhm" ("The true merit of a prince consists in the sincere affection for the general good in his love of country and glory").}

25. {Cf. Goltz, "Feldherren und Feldherrenthum," 386.}

26. {Cf. ibid., 379–83.}

27. {Cf. ibid., 382, where this remark is attributed to Alcibiades.}

28. {Cf. ibid., where this remark is attributed to Xenophon.}

29. {Cf. ibid., 383, where this remark is attributed to Napoleon in reference to war. Cf. Bruno Colson, ed., *Napoleon on War*, trans. Gregory Elliott (Oxford: Oxford University Press, 2015), 126: "in war, morale and opinion are more than half of reality."}

30. {Cf. Goltz, "Feldherren und Feldherrenthum," 380.}

31. {Cf. ibid.; this remark is taken from Napoleon's letter of 26 September 1797 to the Minister of Foreign Affairs: "Tous les grands événements ne tiennent jamais qu'à un cheveu." (*Correspondance de Napoléon Ier: Publiée par ordre de l'empereur Napoléon III* [Paris: 1859], 3:342).}

32. {Cf. Goltz, "Feldherren und Feldherrenthum," in reference to the Prophet Mohammed.}

33. *is stewing in his own juices]* in *seinem eigenen Saft kochen* {Or literally, "to boil in one's own juice."}

34. {Cf. *JS* 341}

35. Cf. note to 7[17].

36. *To know]* erkennen {Cf. the Translators' Afterword, 739–40, on the rendering of *wissen* and *erkennen*.}

37. *mimicry]* {In English in the original. N is almost certainly referring to British naturalist Alfred Russel Wallace (1823–1913), who discussed mimicry in animals as a form of "protective resemblance." Cf. *D* 26; *TI* "Forays" 14.}

38. Cf. 15[8].

39. {Cf. Eduard von Hartmann, *Gesammelte Studien und Aufsätze gemeinverständlichen Inhalts* ("Collected studies and essays for a more general audience") (Berlin: Duncker, 1876).}

40. {Cf. Leopold von Ranke, *Die römischen Päpste, ihre Kirche und ihr Staat im sechszehnten und siebzehnten Jahrhundert* ("The Roman popes, their church and their state in the sixteenth and seventeenth centuries"), 3 vols. (Berlin: Duncker und Humblot, 1834–36).}

41. {Cf. Julius Wellhausen, *Prolegomena zur Geschichte Israels* ("Prolegomena to the history of Israel"), 2nd ed. (Berlin: Reimer, 1883). *NL*.}

42. {Cf. Eugen Dreher, *Der Darwinismus und seine Consequenzen in wissenschaftlicher und socialer Beziehung* ("Darwinism and its consequences in relation to science and society") (Halle: Pfeffer, 1882). *NL*; *Ton und Wort mit Bezugnahme auf das Musik-Drama R. Wagners* ("Tone and word with reference to the musical drama of R. Wagner") (Halle: Pfeffer, 1880).}

43. {Cf. Jeremy Bentham, *Grundsätze der civil- und criminalgesetzbegung* ("Principles of civil and criminal legislation"), German trans. by Friedrich Eduard Beneke (Berlin: C. F. Amelang, 1830) of *Traité de legislation civile et pénale*, ed. and trans. Étienne Dumont (Paris: Bossange, Masson, et Besson, 1802).}

44. {Hendrik Kern, *Der Buddhismus und seine Geschichte in Indien: Eine Darstellung der Buddhistischen Kirche* ("Buddhism

and its history in India: A presentation of the Buddhist church"),
2 vols., trans. from Dutch by Hermann Jacobi (Leipzig: Schulze,
1882, 1884).}

[16 = Z II 1a.]

    1. Plan for a Zarathustra drama (after the completion of *Z* II).

    2. Collection of sayings and turns of phrase, drawn completely
from earlier notebooks, especially 9, 10, and 13.

    3. {Cf. 9[1]; 13[1]_371; 13[11]; 22[1]_548.}

    4. {Cf. 9[45]; 13[1]_372; 22[1]_549.}

    5. {Cf. 9[15]; 10[17]; 13[1]_372.}

    6. {Cf. 13[1]_373; 22[1]_548.}

    7. {Cf. 13[1]_376; 22[1]_549.}

    8. {Cf. 13[1]_377; 22[1]_549.}

    9. {Cf. 13[1]_378; 22[1]_549.}

    10. {Cf. 13[1]_378; 22[1]_549.}

    11. A later addition from early 1888.

    12. Like 16[4].

    13. {Cf. 13[1]_379; 22[1]_550.}

    14. {Cf. 13[1]_379; 13[12]; 22[1]_550.}

    15. {Cf. 9[6]; 13[1]_380; 22[1]_550.}

    16. {Cf. 13[1]_381; 22[1]_549.}

    17. {Cf. 13[1]_382; 13[11]; 17[58]; 22[1]_551.}

    18. {Cf. 13[1]_383; 13[10, 14]; 22[1]_550.}

    19. {Cf. 13[1]_384; 22[1]_549.}

    20. {Cf. 13[1]_388; 22[1]_549.}

    21. {Cf. 9[18]; 13[1]_389; 22[1]_550.}

    22. {Cf. 9[18]; 13[1]_389; 22[1]_550.}

    23. {Cf. 9[18], 13[1]_389; 13[12].}

    24. {Cf. 9[19]; 13[1]_390; 13[18].}

    25. {Cf. 9[19]; 13[1]_390; 22[1]_549.}

    26. {Cf. 9[20]; 13[1]_393; 13[8]; 22[1]_549.}

    27. {Cf. 13[1]_394.}

    28. {Cf. 13[1]_394.}

    29. {Cf. 13[1]_395.}

    30. {Cf. 12[43]; 13[1]_397; 17[48]; 23[5]; 22[1]_553.}

    31. {Cf. 13[1]_397.}

32. {Cf. 13[3]_399; 13[14].}

33. {Cf. 13[3]_400; 13[18].}

34. {Cf. 10[14], 13[3]_405.}

35. {Cf. 13[3]_407; 22[1]_549.}

36. {Cf. 3[1] 243; 12[1] 101; 13[16]; 23[5]; *CW* 15, 31[35, 36]; 32[10]; *BGE* 99.}

37. {Cf. 3[1] 349; 12[1] 90; 13[16]; *BGE* 169.}

38. {Cf. 1[59]; 3[1] 13; 4[226]; 12[1] 147; 13[14].}

39. {Cf. 3[1] 328; 12[1] 148; 13[14].}

40. {Cf. 3[1] 273; 12[1] 99; 13[8].}

41. {Cf. 4[176]; 5[1] 254; 5[22]; 12[5]; 13[7]; *CW* 15, 31[6, 9].}

42. {Cf. 12[1] 133; 13[6].}

43. {Cf. 22[1]_547.}

44. Draft of a plan before the completion of *Z* III; in conjunction with this, see the plans and drafts 21[1–6].

45. Like 16[8].

46. {Cf. 4[114]; 5[1] 176; 5[17]; 22[3]_563.}

47. *"they . . . life."]* Cf. *BT* 7.

48. *The message: . . . "hinterworld")]* {Cf. *HL* 9 on Eduard von Hartmann's *Philosophie des Unbewussten* ("Philosophy of the Unconscious").}

49. *"pessimist of the intellect."]* According to J. Burckhardt's *Definition der Griechen* ("Definition of the Greeks"), cf. *CW* 12, 5[70] and accompanying note; {cf. *MM* 11, *CW* 4, 16}.

50. *"what . . . honor.]* Cf. *MM* 26, *CW* 4, 21.

51. Cf. 22[1]{_547}.

52. Cf. 22[1]{_547}.

53. *history of origins] Enstehungs-Geschichte*

54. {Cf. *SE* 5, *CW* 2, 214, lines 25–28.}

55. Cf. note to 7[17].

56. *origin] Herkommen* {Also later in this fragment.}

57. *HAH* 96, 97.

58. N's quotes from Paul Rée, *Der Ursprung der moralischen Empfindungen* (Chemnitz{: Schmeitzner,} 1877), *NL*. {Translated by Robin Small as *The Origin of the Moral Sensations*, in Paul Rée, *Basic Writings*, ed. Robin Small (Urbana: University of Illinois Press, 2003): 81–167.}

59. {Cf. Rée, "The Origin of the Moral Sensations," 114: "But if nothing in the punishments carried out reminds one that they are a means of deterrence for the future, it must come to seem that they are a retribution for the past."}

60. {Cf. ibid., 115: "Actions that are necessary cannot be subjected either to attribution of responsibility or to retribution for what has occurred."}

61. *Will-o'-the-wisp]* Irrlicht {Phantom lights engendered by decaying plants in swamps and wetlands, associated in myth with beings that lead travelers astray.}

62. Cf. note to 7[17].

63. {*WP* 760.}

64. *Jesuitism . . . civilization.]* {Cf. Eduard von Hartmann, *Phänomenologie des sittlichen Bewusstseins: Prolegomena zu jeder künftigen Ethik* ("Phenomenology of moral consciousness: Prolegomena to any future ethics") (Berlin: Duncker, 1879), 646. *NL.*}

65. {*WP* 769.}

66. *Because everything . . . has been done.]* {Cf. *GM* II 4.}

67. As in 16[8].

68. *The others . . . "principles."]* {Cf. *WP* 764.}

69. *Organic-moral]* organisch-moralisch {Cf. 1[19, 22]; 17[30].}

70. *competition . . . intellect]* {*WP* 613.}

71. Cf. 22[1]{_547}.

72. Cf. 22[1]{_547}.

73. As in 16[8]; the same is true without exception for the fragments that immediately follow, all the way to the end: 16[38–90].

74. N is referring to the following passage in Emerson's *Versuche* {*Essays: Second Series,* "Politics"}: "To educate the wise man, the State exists; and with the appearance of the wise man, the State expires. The appearance of character makes the State unnecessary. The wise man is the State. He needs no army, fort, or navy, — he loves men too well; no bribe, or feast, or palace, to draw friends to him; no vantage ground, no favorable circumstance. He needs no library, for he has not done thinking; no church, for he is a prophet; no statute book, for he has the lawgiver; no money, for he is value; no road, for he is at home where he is; no experience, for the life of the creator shoots through him, and looks from his eyes. He has no personal friends, for he

who has the spell to draw the prayer and piety of all men unto him, needs not husband and educate a few, to share with him a select and poetic life. His relation to men is angelic; his memory is myrrh to them; his presence, frankincense and flowers." {Much of this} excerpt was underlined by N, the entire passage highlighted several times.

75. *completely in harmony with the truth] vollkommen der Wahrheit* {We attempt to capture the strangeness of the phrasing.}

76. {Cf. 7[238].}

77. {Cf. 22[1]_547.}

78. {Cf. the third movement of Beethoven's penultimate string quartet (String Quartet No. 15 in A Minor, Op. 132), subtitled "Heiliger Dankgesang eines Genesenden an die Gottheit" ("Holy Song of Thanksgiving to the Deity from a Convalescent").}

79. *Beatitude] Seligpreisung* {A reference to the Beatitudes in the Sermon on the Mount (Matthew 5:3–11).}

80. *sub specie aeterni]* "under the aspect of the eternal" {That is, in its essential or eternal form. Phrase associated with Spinoza.}

81. *unified by power] Einheit des* { . . . } *in der Macht* {The inflection makes it clear that all three groups are included.}

82. {Cf. 16[59, 84]; 21[3]; 22[1]_547.}

83. {Cf. 16[59, 84]; 21[3]; 22[1]_547.}

84. *ripeness and tenderness] Reife und Mürbe* {We use "ripeness" and "tenderness" here instead of the more conventional translations "maturity" and "mellowing" in order to maintain N's botanical analogy.}

85. *exuberance] Übermuth*

86. {Cf. 16[50]; 21[3]; 22[1]_547.}

87. *Zarathustra . . . nothing else!]* {An allusion to Luther's remark in Worms: "Here I stand. I can do nothing else."}

88. *Determinism]* {N uses the English term here, and the German term *Determinismus* below.}

89. *fatum]* "fate," "one's lot" {N here underlines the Latin *fatum*.}

90. *that can't be missing] die nicht fehlen darf*

91. *audience] die Empfänger*

92. *Or?] Oder?* {Cf. the conclusion to *D*.}

93. {*WP* 974.}

94. {Cf. 17[29]; 22[3]_623.}

95. {Cf. 17[29]; 18[4]; 20[1]; 22[1]_548; 22[1]_562.}

96. {Cf. 16[50, 59]; 22[1]_547.}

97. {Cf. 17[29].}

98. {Cf. Gustav Teichmüller, *Neue Studien zur Geschichte der Begriffe, Heft 3: Die praktische Vernunft bei Aristoteles* ("New studies on the history of concepts, vol. 3: Practical reason according to Aristotle") (Gotha: Perthes, 1879); Teichmüller mentions "selfishness" on p. 130, not 131.}

99. {Cf. 17[27].}

100. {Cf. 17[27, 29, 40].}

101. {Cf. 15[21].}

102. {Cf. 15[18]; 22[1]_546.}

103. {Cf. 15[18]; 22[1]_546.}

104. {Cf. 22[1]_545.}

105. {Cf. 3[1] 25; 4[31]; 16[88]; 18[24]; 22[1]_546; *BGE* 132.}

106. *teach about the superhumans]* den Übermenschen lehren {Cf. 4[208] and 5[8], where "superhumans" are also the subject matter.}

107. {Cf. 10[3].}

[17 = N VI 6.]

1. Cf. 22 [1]{_555}.

2. *huckster-virtues]* Krämer-Tugenden {We have chosen the term "huckster" for *Krämer* because the usual term, "shopkeeper," is not pejorative enough to capture N's meaning.}

3. *money-grubbing]* geldklebrige

4. Outline still predates the composition of *Z* III.

5. *they all deserve each other]* sie sind alle einander wert {Cf. 17[9]; 18[19]; 22[2].}

6. {Cf. 22[1]_555.}

7. Like 17[2].

8. Cf. 22[1]{_556}.

9. {Cf. 22[1]_556.}

10. {Cf. 22[1]_556.}

11. Cf. 22[5]_573.

12. *mortar]* Mörser {As in mortar and pestle, here used for mixing herbs, as opposed to "on a bible or altar."}

13. {Cf. 4[17].}

14. Cf. 22[1]{_556}.

15. {Cf. 22[1]_561.}

16. Arrangement predates the composition of *Z* III.

17. {Cf. 17[2]; 18[19]; 22[2].}

18. {Cf. 22[1]_562; 22[2].}

19. *the way I wish] wie ich Lust habe* {We here deviate from the usual rendering of *Lust* ("desire" or "pleasure") to preserve the wordplay.}

20. Cf. 22[1]{_560}.

21. {Cf. 22[1]_561.}

22. {Cf. 17[10, 26]; 22[1]_556; 22[1]_560.}

23. {Cf. 22[1]_560.}

24. Cf. 22[2].

25. {Cf. 22[1]_560.}

26. Cf. 22[1]{_560}.

27. {Except for the second phrase, cf. 22[3]_567.}

28. {Cf. 22[3]_565.}

29. *firm] hart* {We chose the equivalent adjective for "handshake" in English.}

30. {Cf. Matthew 19:14; Mark 10:14; Luke 18:16. For the next three phrases, cf. 22[3]_567.}

31. {Cf. 22[3]_565.}

32. {For the next four fragments, cf. 22[3]_566.}

33. {For the next five fragments, cf. 22[3]_565.}

34. {Cf. 17[15]; 22[3]_565; 22[3]_569.}

35. {Cf. 20[12]; 22[3]_565.}

36. {Cf. 22[3]_568.}

37. {Cf. 22[3]_568.}

38. {Cf. 22[3]_568.}

39. {For the final three fragments, cf. 22[3]_568.}

40. *aloneness] Alleinsein*

41. {Cf. 17[14]; 17[15]; 22[3]_569.}

42. *So why, then, . . . dreaming.]* Cf. *Z* III "The Wanderer."

43. Cf. *Z* III "The Wanderer"; {17[14]; 22[3]_569}.

44. Cf. 22[3, 5] {Included in this fragment are a series of clever phrases and wordplay, some of which are repeated or revised in later notebooks.}

45. {Cf. 22[3]_569.}

46. {Cf. 17[17]; 18[2]; 22[5].}

47. {Cf. 20[12]; 22[5].}

48. {Cf. 17[20]; 22[5].}

49. *entertain others]* *ihnen Unterhaltung schaffen* {The wordplay is between *Unterhaltung* ("entertainment") and *Unterhalt* ("livelihood").}

50. *"by accident"]* *"von Ohngefähr"*

51. {Cf. 20[12]; 22[5].}

52. Cf. 22[5].

53. {Cf. 17[16]; 18[2]; 22[5].}

54. Concerning a fourth part of *Z* before the composition of *Z* III.

55. Cf. 22[3, 5].

56. {Cf. 18[46]; 22[3]_571.}

57. {Cf. 17[16]; 22[5].}

58. {Cf. 17[25, 56]; 18[34]; 22[1]_552; 22[5]_571; 22[5]_574.}

59. Cf. 22[3{_570}].

60. {N here alludes to the opening scene of Wagner's *Siegfried* (first performed in Bayreuth 16 August 1876), where the hero asks his foster father Mime: "Wer is mir Vater und Mutter?" ("Who are father and mother to me?").}

61. Like 17[9].

62. {Cf. 22[4].}

63. {Cf. 18[18]; 22[5].}

64. Cf. 22[3]{_571}.

65. Cf. 22[5]; {18[46]}.

66. {Cf. 17[20, 56]; 18[34]; 22[1]_552; 22[5]_571; 22[5]_574.}

67. Title part of the plans from before the composition of *Z* III; {cf. 17[10]; 22[1]_556; 22[1]_560}.

68. Like 17[2]; {cf. 16[84]; 17[29]; 17[40]}.

69. Like 17[2]; {cf. 22[1]_556}.

70. Like 17[2].

71. {Cf. 16[84].}

72. {Cf. 16[84]; 17[29].}

73. {Cf. 16[84]; 17[27, 40].}

74. {Cf. 16[84]; 18[4]; 20[1]; 22[1]_548; 22[1]_556.}

75. {Cf. 20[1]; 22[1]_548.}

76. {Cf. 17[48]; 20[1]; 22[1]_547.}

77. *finger] Zehe* {We switch from "toe" to "finger" to render the idiom.}

78. Cf. 22[1]{_556}.

79. {Cf. 1[19, 22].}

80. New comprehensive plan from before the composition of *Z* III; cf. also the plans in Group 21.

81. {Cf. 22[1]_557.}

82. Cf. 22[1]{_547}.

83. Like 17[9].

84. {Cf. 22[1]_557.}

85. {Cf. Herbert Spencer, *Die Thatsachen der Ethik* (*The Data of Ethics*, part 1 of vol. 1 of *The Principles of Ethics*), trans. Benjamin Vetter (Stuttgart: Schweizerbart, 1879), 269. *NL.*}

86. Cf. 22[1]{_557}.

87. Cf. 22[1]{_557}.

88. Like 17[26].

89. *akrasia]* "weakness of will"

90. Cf. 22[1]{_557}.

91. Like 17[9].

92. {Cf. Ralph Waldo Emerson, *Versuche (Essays)*, trans. G. Fabricius (Hanover: Carl Meyer, 1858), *NL*; "Manners," in *The Collected Works of Ralph Waldo Emerson*, vol. 3: *Essays, Second Series* (Cambridge, MA: Belknap Press of Harvard University Press, 1983), 89–90.}

93. {Cf. 19[5]; 20[10].}

94. *enjoyment of self abolishing] Selbst-Aufhebung-Genuß* {See our notes on *Aufhebung* in the Translators' Afterword, 738; cf. 20[10].}

95. Like 17[9]; {cf. 16[84]; 17[27, 29]}.

96. {Cf. 20[10].}

97. {Cf. 22[1]_557.}

98. Like 17[18]; cf. *Z* III "On the Virtue That Diminishes."

99. {Cf. 22[1]_557.}

100. Apparently out of a book catalogue.

101. Like 17[2].

102. *to fall apart] zu Grunde gehn*

103. Like 17[2]; cf. 22[1]{_557}.

104. {Cf. 22[3]_565.}
105. Cf. 22[1]{_557}.
106. {Cf. 12[43]; 13[1]_397; 16[7]; 22[1]_553; 23[5].}
107. {Cf. 17[30]; 20[1]; 22[1]_547.}
108. {Cf. 22[1]_553.}
109. Cf. note to 7[17].
110. {Cf. 22[1]_552.}
111. {Cf. 17[52, 60]; 18[1]; 20[9]; 22[1]_557.}
112. Like 17[2]; cf. 22[1]{_552}.
113. Like 17[2] and 17[18].
114. {Cf. 17[50, 60]; 18[1]; 20[9]; 22[1]_557.}
115. *Moravians] Herrenhuter* {The Moravian Church or *Unitas Fratrum* had a threefold ideal of faith, fellowship, and freedom, and a strong emphasis on practical Christian life rather than on doctrine or tradition. First founded at the end of the sixteenth century, it experienced revival under the leadership of Nikolaus Ludwig, Count Zinzendorf, in the town of Herrenhut in Saxony in the eighteenth century.}
116. Like 17[18].
117. Like 17[18]; cf. 22[1]{_552}.
118. Like 17[9]; cf. 22[1]{_552}.
119. Cf. 22[1]{_552}.
120. {Cf. 17[20, 25]; 18[34]; 22[1]_552; 22[5]_571; 22[5]_574.}
121. {Cf. 10[8, 35]; 22[1]_552.}
122. {Cf. 22[1]_552.}
123. Cf. 17[18].
124. Cf. 22[1]{_551}.
125. {Cf. 13[1]_382; 13[11]; 16[7]; 22[1]_551.}
126. Cf. 22[1]{_551; 17[67]; 20[9]}.
127. Cf. {20[9] (characteristics of friendship)}; 22[1]{_557}.
128. {Cf. 17[50, 52]; 18[1]; 20[9]; 22[1]_557.}
129. *your] seinen* {We use the second-person form to convey the context of advice; cf. 20[9]; 22[1]_557.}
130. Cf. 22[1]{_554}.
131. Like 17[9].
132. Cf. 22[1]{_557}.
133. Cf. 22[1]{_554}.

134. *novelty] Neubegierde* {Cf. Grimm 13:656–57.}

135. Cf. 22[1]{_558}.

136. Cf. 22[1]{_553}.

137. Cf. 22[1]{_554}.

138. {Cf. 17[59]; 20[9]; 22[1]_551.}

139. *in his supreme right] an sein höheres Recht* {This could also refer to the supreme right of the people.}

140. {Cf. 22[1]_554.}

141. Concerning a third and fourth part dating before the composition of *Z* III.

142. {Cf. 22[1]_560.}

143. {Cf. 20[9].}

144. Cf. 22[1]{_554}.

145. Cf. 22[1]{_554}.

146. Cf. 22[1]{_558}.

147. {Cf. Mark 10:14.}

148. {Cf. 22[1]_558}; N's term is *Händler*, which means "merchants." We try to preserve the wordplay on Handel's name here.}

149. In this book, Auguste Blanqui argued for a notion close to thoughts of eternal return of the same; cf. Henri Lichtenberger, *Die Philosophie Friedrich Nietzsches*, {trans. into German from the French by Elisabeth Förster-Nietzsche (Dresden and} Leipzig{: Carl Reissner,} 1899), 204–9.

150. {Cf. Louis-Auguste Blanqui, *L'éternité par les astres (*Paris: Librairie Germer Baillière, 1872); translated by Frank Chouraqui as *Eternity by the Stars* (New York: Contra Mundum Press, 2013).}

151. Cf. 22[1]{_558}.

152. {Cf. 22[1]_558.}

153. Like 17[2].

154. {Cf. 22[1]_558.}

155. *future generations] die zukünftigen Menschen*

156. *women] Frauen* {N uses *Weiber* in 18[15, 23]; 22[1]_558; 23[3].}

157. Cf. 22[1]{_559}.

158. *obsession . . . hits home]* {We try here to re-create N's wordplay with *Sucht* ("obsession"), *mein Heim suchen* ("sought . . . my home"), and *Heimsuchung* ("hit home").}

159. Cf. 22[1]{_559}.
160. {Cf. Exodus 33:3.}
161. Cf. 22[1]{_559}.
162. {Cf. 22[1]_559.}

[18 = N VI 7.]

1. Cf. 22[3]{_570}.

2. *"God is not]* *"es ist kein Gott* {Here as in 22[3], N varies his usual phrase *es gibt keinen Gott* ("there is no God"). The meaning is essentially the same.}

3. {Cf. 17[50, 52, 60]; 20[9]; 22[1]_557.}

4. {Cf. 20[14].}

5. Like 17[18].

6. {Cf. 17[16, 17]; 22[5].}

7. {Cf. 16[84]; 17[29]; 20[1]; 22[1]_548; 22[1]_556.}

8. *that's where the spice is]* *hier ist der Pfeffer* {Literally, "here is the pepper."}

9. *This now over there]* *Dieses Jetzt da*

10. {Cf. 17[78]; 18[23]; 22[1]_558; 23[3].}

11. *rasped]* *röchelte*

12. {Cf. 17[22]; 22[5].}

13. Cf. 21[3].

14. {Cf. 13[3]_402.}

15. {Cf. 17[78]; 18[15]; 22[1]_558; 23[3].}

16. *in the family way]* *gesegneten Leibes* {A "proper" euphemism for pregnancy.}

17. {Cf. 3[1] 25; 4[31]; 16[88]; 22[1]_546; *BGE* 132.}

18. Cf. 18[34].

19. Arrangement of *Z* III.

20. Cf. *Z* III "The Return Home."

21. {Cf. 17[20, 25, 56]; 22[1]_552; 22[5]_571; 22[5]_574.}

22. Cf. *Z* III "On Apostates."

23. *word]* *das Wort* {"Word" has the dual meaning in English of "individual word" and "saying."}

24. {Cf. 18[57, 59].}

25. *sealing]* *Besiegelung*

26. {Cf. 3[1] 245; 4[165]; 11[8]; 18[49, 56]; 21[6]; 24[16].}

27. Cf. *Z* III "On the Vision and the Riddle."

28. *loving refreshment] Liebsal* {A pun on the German *Labsal*, meaning "refreshment."}

29. Cf. 22[5]; {17[24]}.

30. *Bible-thumpers] Betbrüder* {We think "Bible-thumpers" is the closest equivalent; cf. 17[20]; 22[3]_571.}

31. {Cf. 22[1]_554.}

32. Cf. 22[8]; 23[10].

33. {Cf. 3[1] 245; 4[165]; 11[8]; 18[43, 56]; 21[6]; 24[16].}

34. Ich fand auf meinem Gange
seine langen Esels-Ohren —
ich fand auch meine Schlange,
die hatte den Kopf verloren.

35. Cf. 9[48]; 11[9].

36. *junkyard dog] Kettenhund* {Literally "dog on a chain."}

37. {Cf. 3[1] 245; 4[165]; 11[8]; 18[43, 49]; 21[6]; 24[16].}

38. {Cf. 18[38, 59].}

39. Cf. *Z* III "The Other Dance Song"; {18[38, 57].}

[19 = N VI 8.]

1. *to break] zerbrechen* {Consistent with the wording in Exodus 32:19, KJV.}

2. Cf. *Z* III "The Return Home."

3. Cf. *Z* III "On Apostates."

4. Cf. *Z* III "On Old and New Tablets."

5. {Cf. 17[39]; 20[10].}

6. Cf. *Z* IV "The Sign."

7. Arrangement of *Z* III.

8. Cf. *Z* III "The Convalescent."

9. *rasp] röchelst* {Has connotations of a death rattle.}

10. Cf. *Z* III "On Old and New Tablets" 29.

11. Cf. 16[49]; 21[3].

12. *my soul, the prophet] meine Seele, die Wahrsagerin* {The feminine inflection does not necessarily indicate that N thinks of the soul as female, so we have not translated *Wahrsagerin* as "prophetess."}

[20 = Z II 2.]

   1. Cf. *Z* III "The Wanderer"; 22[1]{_548}.

   2. {Cf. 17[30, 48]; 22[1]_547.}

   3. {Cf. 17[30]; 22[1]_547.}

   4. {Cf. 16[84]; 18[4]; 22[1]_548; 22[1]_556.}

   5. Cf. 20[3].

   6. Before the composition of *Z* III; cf. 21[1–6].

   7. *tartuffery] Tartufferie* {From the character in Molière's *Tartuffe* (1664).}

   8. {Cf. Herbert Spencer, *Einleitung in das Studium der Sociologie* ("Introduction to the study of sociology"), ed. Heinrich Marquardsen (Leipzig: Brockhaus, 1875), 2:110. *NL*.}

   9. *abolition] Aufhebung*

   10. *Teichmüller p. 55]* Cf. note to 7[153]; {cf. Gustav Teichmüller, *Neue Studien zur Geschichte der Begriffe, Heft 3: Die praktische Vernunft bei Aristoteles* ("New studies on the history of concepts, vol. 3: Practical reason according to Aristotle") (Gotha: Perthes, 1879).}

   11. {Cf. ibid., 65.}

   12. *"The courageous . . . done"]* {Cf. ibid., 76.}

   13. Cf. note to 20[3]; 21[1–6].

   14. Cf. 21[1–6].

   15. {Cf. 17[59, 67]; 22[1]_551.}

   16. {Cf. 17[60]; 22[1]_557.}

   17. {Cf. 17[50, 52, 60]; 18[1]; 22[1]_558.}

   18. Cf. 21[1–6].

   19. {Cf. 17[40].}

   20. {Cf. 17[39].}

   21. Cf. *DD* "Last Will."

   22. *you my necessity]* {Here Zarathustra's invocation "Du meine Notwendigkeit" ("You my necessity") recalls and inverts Siegfried's invocation to his sword Notung in act 1, scene 3 of Wagner's opera. N also puns on *Wende* ("cusp") and *Nothwendigkeit* ("necessity").}

   23. Cf. 22[3, 5].

   24. {Cf. 17[16]; 22[5].}

   25. {Cf. 17[13]; 22[3]_565.}

26. Cf. *Z* III "On Apostates."

27. *toy trumpeters] Schnurrpfeifer* {Flügel 847 defines *Schnurrpfeife/Schnurrpfeiferei* as a vulgar term for frivolous or meaningless things or activities, here a reference to the abysmal quality of their message.}

28. {Cf. 18[1].}

29. Cf. *Z* III "On the Spirit of Gravity."

30. Arrangement of *Z*.

[21 = Mp XV 3b.]

1. Cf. 20[3].

2. *temptation] Versuchung* {This could also be rendered as "experiment."}

3. Cf. 20[10].

4. {Cf. 16[50, 59, 84]; 22[1]_547.}

5. *order] der Orden* {In the sense of a fraternity or religious order.}

6. Cf. 20[3].

7. {Cf. 3[1] 245; 4[165]; 11[8]; 18[43, 49, 56]; 24[16].}

8. *bien public]* "public good," something available for the common good (e.g., clean air).

9. {N noted the link between socialism, Jesuitism, and eudaimonistic ethics in Eduard von Hartmann's *Phänomenologie des sittlichen Bewusstseins: Prolegomena zu jeder künftigen Ethik* (Berlin: C. Duncker, 1879), 649–50. *NL*.}

10. *actions] Handeln* {N means "acting" here, as in engaging in activity or action.}

[22 = Z II 3a.]

1. Revised copy from the earlier notebooks (13, 15, 16, 17, 18) containing sayings and turns of phrase that were adopted in part for *Z* III.

2. {Cf. 16[88].}

3. {Cf. 3[1] 25; 4[31]; 16[88]; 18[24]; *BGE* 132.}

4. {Cf. 15[18]; 16[86].}

5. {Cf. 15[18]; 16[86].}

6. {Cf. 16[50, 59, 84]; 21[3].}

7. {Cf. 16[46].}

8. {Cf. 16[36].}

9. {Cf. 16[35].}

10. {Cf. 16[13].}

11. {Cf. 16[12].}

12. {Cf. 16[7].}

13. {Cf. 17[32].}

14. {Cf. 17[30]; 20[1].}

15. {Cf. 17[30, 48]; 20[1].}

16. {Cf. 20[1]; 22[1]_547.}

17. {Cf. 16[84]; 17[29]; 18[4]; 20[1]; 22[1]_548.}

18. *You go the way . . . last refuge.]* {Cf. 20[1].}

19. *coincidence] Zufall* {Here N adds the modifier *jeden* ("every"), so our shift from "chance" to "coincidence" refers to a single instance.}

20. {Cf. 9[1]; 13[1]_371; 13[11]; 16[4].}

21. {Cf. 13[1]_373; 16[4].}

22. {Cf. 13[3]; 16[7].}

23. {Cf. 13[1]_378; 16[4].}

24. {Cf. 13[1]_376; 16[4].}

25. {Cf. 13[1]_377; 16[4].}

26. {Cf. 13[1]_378; 16[4].}

27. {Cf. 9[45]; 13[1]_372; 16[4].}

28. {Cf. 13[1]_384; 16[7].}

29. {Cf. 13[1]_381; 16[7].}

30. {Cf. 13[1]_388; 16[7].}

31. {Cf. 9[19]; 13[1]_390; 16[7].}

32. {Cf. 9[20]; 13[1]_393; 13[8]; 16[7].}

33. {Cf. 13[1]_379; 16[7].}

34. {Cf. 13[1]_379; 13[12]; 16[7].}

35. {Cf. 13[1]_383; 13[10, 14]; 16[7].}

36. {Cf. 9[6]; 13[1]_380; 16[7].}

37. {Cf. 9[18]; 13[1]_389; 16[7].}

38. {Cf. 9[18]; 13[1]_389; 16[7].}

39. *We should only steal . . . taking notice.]* {Cf. 17[59].}

40. {Cf. [17[67]; 20[9].}

41. {Cf. 17[58].}

42. {Cf. 13[11]; 16[7]; 17[58].}

43. {Cf. 17[58].}

44. {Cf. 17[20, 25]; 18[34]; 22[5]_571; 22[5]_574.}

45. *It is still . . . watch!]* {Cf. 10[8, 35]; 17[56].}

46. {Cf. 17[55].}

47. {Cf. 17[54].}

48. *is just to]* soll nur . . . sein

49. {Cf. 17[51].}

50. {Cf. 17[51].}

51. {Cf. 17[49].}

52. {Cf. 17[48].}

53. {Cf. 12[43]; 13[1]_397; 16[7]; 17[48]; 23[5].}

54. *divine lightness-skill]* göttliche Leicht-Fertigkeit {N's word-play here is between *leichtfertig* "taking things lightly" and *Leicht-Fertigkeit* "being adept at making ourselves light."}

55. {Cf. 17[66].}

56. {Cf. 17[64].}

57. *I do not . . . you]* {Cf. 17[61].}

58. {Cf. 17[70]; 22[1]_558.}

59. {Cf. 17[70, 71].}

60. *are your own incidents and accidents!]* was euch zufällt und auf euch fällt! {Cf. 17[68].}

61. {Cf. 17[67].}

62. {Cf. 17[67].}

63. {Cf. 18[46].}

64. *happiness]* Glück {This could also be "good fortune."}

65. *And if . . . great wealth.]* {Cf. 17[1].}

66. {Cf. 17[3].}

67. {Cf. 17[3].}

68. *And we often . . . breeders.]* {Cf. 17[5].}

69. *Oh these narrow . . . tenth generation]* Oh diese engen . . . ins zehnte Geschlecht {Cf. 17[7].}

70. {Cf. 17[10, 26]; 22[1]_560.}

71. {Cf. 17[9]; 22[2].}

72. {Cf. 17[29].}

73. {Cf. 16[84]; 17[29]; 18[4]; 20[1]; 22[1]_548.}

74. *in my little finger]* in der linksten Zehe {We switch from "toe" to "finger" to render the idiom; cf. 17[30].}

75. {Cf. 17[28, 31].}

76. *our]* seinen {We are translating this as a singular universal ("*man*"), but N might intend it as referring to Z himself or some individual in the narrative; cf. 17[32].}

77. {Cf. 17[34].}

78. {Cf. 17[34].}

79. {Cf. 17[35].}

80. {Cf. 17[38].}

81. {Cf. 17[40].}

82. {Cf. 17[41].}

83. {Cf. 17[45].}

84. {Cf. 17[46].}

85. {Cf. 17[60]; 20[9].}

86. {Cf. 17[50, 52, 60]; 18[1]; 20[9].}

87. {Cf. 17[63].}

88. {Cf. 17[63].}

89. {Cf. 17[65].}

90. {Cf. 11[10].}

91. {Cf. 17[70]; 22[1]_544.}

92. *Corpse robbers . . . fingers."]* {Cf. 17[72].}

93. {Cf. 17[74].}

94. {Cf. 17[74].}

95. {Cf. 17[76].}

96. {Cf. 17[78].}

97. {Cf. 17[78]; 18[15, 23]; 23[3].}

98. {See 17[80], note 157.}

99. *It wants to command . . . hard-heartedness.]* {Cf. 17[80].}

100. {Cf. 17[82].}

101. {Cf. 17[85].}

102. {Cf. 17[85].}

103. *"The worst . . . virtues]* {Cf. 17[85].}

104. {Cf. 17[10].}

105. {Cf. 17[69].}

106. {Cf. 17[12].}

107. {Cf. 17[12].}

108. {Cf. 17[11].}

109. {Cf. 17[26]; 22[1]_556.}

110. {Cf. 17[10].}

111. *"Let us be modest . . . snore.]* {Cf. 17[10].}

112. {Cf. 17[8].}

113. {Cf. 3[1] 5.}

114. Shortly before the final composition of *Z* III. {This section includes what appear to be possible titles for *Z*, but the parenthetical comments and the outlines convinced us not to capitalize these items as we have done for the items in 22[8] below.}

115. *fatum]* "fate"

116. Like 22[1].

117. {Cf. 1[63]; 3[1] 12.}

118. {Cf. 3[1] 22.}

119. {Cf. 3[1] 24.}

120. {Cf. 3[1] 23.}

121. {Cf. 3[1] 38; 12[1] 118.}

122. {Cf. 1[8, 9]; 3[1] 34; 3[1] 224.}

123. *People of faith]* der gläubige Mensch {Cf. 1[77]; 3[1] 29.}

124. {Cf. 3[1] 42.}

125. {Cf. 4[114]; 5[1] 176; 5[17]; 16[9].}

126. *ape] Affen* {Cf. *Z* III "On Passing By," where N uses the same play on words between "ape" and "imitator."}

127. {Cf. 3[1] 62.}

128. {Cf. 3[1] 63.}

129. {Cf. 3[1] 57.}

130. {Cf. 1[70]; 3[1] 49}; *BGE* 133.}

131. {Cf. 2[45]; 3[1] 52.}

132. {Cf. 2[50]; 3[1] 55.}

133. {Cf. 1[70]; 3[1] 50}; *BGE* 129.}

134. {Cf. 2[47]; 3[1] {64}, p. 61, 3–8; 3[1] 72.}

135. {Cf. 3[1] 71.}

136. {Cf. 3[1] 70.}

137. {Cf. 2[43]; 3[1] 65; 4[44].}

138. {Cf. 3[1] 74.}

139. {Cf. 3[1] 82.}

140. {Cf. 3[1] 105.}

141. *Time feels . . . short straw.]* {Cf. 17[13].}

142. {Cf. 17[15]; 22[3]_569.}

143. {Cf. 16[84]; 17[29].}

144. {Cf. 17[43]: 20[12].}

145. *Crumpled houses . . . bilious soul]* {Cf. 17[13].}

146. *Where have I witnessed . . . as we wish.]* {Cf. 17[13].}

147. *firm]* hart

148. {Cf. 20[19].}

149. *Contented sows . . . to the wind.]* {Cf. 17[13].}

150. {Cf. 3[1] 444.}

151. {Cf. 3[1] 429.}

152. *bite of conscience]* Gewissensbiss {We speak of "pangs of conscience," whereas the Germans speak of "bites of conscience." We preserve N's wordplay here; cf. 3[1] 436.}

153. {Cf. 3[1] 422; 12[1] 88.}

154. {Cf. 17[16].}

155. *This is the black sad sea . . . each night.]* {Cf. 17[14, 15]; 22[3]_565.}

156. *not give a plug nickel]* keinen Heller geben {A "Heller" was a small copper coin worth about half a penny.}

157. *If you can't pray, . . . intellect]* {Cf. 18[1].}

158. *lifts . . . from our shoulders]* enthebt {Cf. 17[21].}

159. {Cf. 17[21].}

160. {Cf. 17[23].}

161. *Bible-thumpers]* Betbruderei {Cf. 17[20]; 18[46].}

162. Like 22[2].

163. {Cf. 18[2].}

164. Like 22[1].

165. {Cf. 17[22]; 18[18].}

166. {Cf. 17[20, 25, 56]; 18[34]; 22[1]_552.}

167. {Cf. 17[16, 17]; 18[2].}

168. {Cf. 17[17].}

169. {Cf. 17[17].}

170. *is]* ist {N uses the third-person singular *ist* to match "characteristic" with "means and condition."}

171. {Cf. 20[12].}

172. *a contrarian, . . . cheerfulness.]* {Cf. 17[16].}

173. {Cf. 17[16].}

174. *ill people . . . fall.]* {Cf. 17[16].}

175. {Cf. 17[20].}

176. {Cf. 17[16].}

177. {Cf. 17[6]}

178. {Cf. 20[12].}

179. *with a voice . . . at us.]* {Cf. 17[16].}

180. {Cf. 17[24]; 18[46].}

181. *I went in search . . . the future.]* {Cf. 17[24].}

182. {Cf. 17[20, 25, 56]; 18[34]; 22[1]_552; 22[5]_571.}

183. {Cf. 17[25].}

184. {Cf. 17[25].}

185. {Cf. 17[13].}

186. {Cf. 7[43].}

187. Arrangement of *Z* III.

[23 = Z II 4.]

1. Not used in *Z*.

2. {Cf. Matthew 3:17; Luke 3:22, 9:35.}

3. *if we take a shit]* wenn man Koth läßt {N's wordplay is between *Koth* (shit or filth) *lassen* — "to take a shit" — and, in the next sentence, *Koth halten* — "to keep it."}

4. A chapter from *Z* III that was not completed; {cf. 18[23]}.

5. {Cf. 18[15, 23]; 23[3].}

6. Cf. *Z* III "The Other Dance Song."

7. {Cf. 18[57].}

8. Compilation for a chapter from *Z* III that was never completed.

9. {Cf. 3[1] 243; 12[1] 101; 13[16]; 16[7].}

10. {Cf. 12[43]; 13[1]_397; 16[7]; 17[48]; 22[1]_553.}

11. Not completed.

12. Not completed.

13. Arrangement of *Z* III.

14. Arrangement of *Z* III.

15. {This annotation is N's.}

[24 = Mp XVII 1b.]

1. On the Greeks as connoisseurs of humanity; cf. 8[15]; *CW* 17, 5[96, 98].

2. *alienation]* Befremden

3. γνώμη] "sign" "mark" "mind" "intelligence" "opinion" {The Greek is obscure here, and it is quite possible that there was an error when N's manuscript was transcribed.}

4. *la Faustin*] {Parisian actress and eponymous protagonist of Edmond de Goncourt's 1882 novel.}

5. {*WP* 1057.}

6. Cf. *CW* 15, 25[1, 6, 227, 323]; 26[259, 465]; 27[58, 80, 82]; *CW* 16, 34[191].

7. *original chaos . . . perishing.*] {*WP* 508.}

8. *Creating . . . of will*] {*WP* 662.}

9. *in regard to . . . its opposite.*] {Cf. *WP* 92.}

10. *Bourget p. 25.*] A reference to Paul Bourget, *Essais de psychologie contemporaine* ("Essays on contemporary psychology") (Paris{: Lemerre,} 1883); cf. *WA* 7 note 66.

11. *both of the greatest . . . this thought.*] {*WP* 1058.}

12. *origin*] *Herkunft* {In *CW*, *Ursprung* is usually translated as "origin" and *Herkunft* as "descent," but we believe that the context dictates this rendering. Cf. note 34 below.}

13. *Psychology of Error*] Title added later (August 1888) according to the plan in *CW* 18, 18[17].

14. *Whenever we do something . . . human compelling*] {*WP* 664.}

15. {Cf. Richard Avenarius, *Philosophie als Denken der Welt gemäss dem Princip des kleinsten Kraftmasses: Prolegomena zu einer Kritik der reinen Erfahrung* ("Philosophy as thinking of the world in accordance with the principle of the least amount of energy: Prolegomena to a critique of pure experience") (Leipzig: Fues's Verlag (R. Reisland), 1876), 45–46.}

16. {Cf. ibid., 46.}

17. *sensation*] *Empfindung* {In this fragment, and in 24[13], we have departed from our usual translation of *Empfindung* as "perception" or "feeling" so as to reflect the fact that N is quoting from the positivist philosopher Avenarius.}

18. {Cf. ibid., 47.}

19. {Cf. ibid., 47–48.}

20. {Cf. ibid., 49.}

21. {Cf. ibid., 50.}

22. *"It is also the case that . . . such hastiness!*] {*WP* 626.}

23. *the willing] das Wollen* {In German, this could be either "wanting" or "willing," and here N is referring to the nature of the will and free will.}

24. {*WP* 562.}

25. *"In the development . . . at all!]* {Cf. Avenarius, *Philosophie als Denken der Welt*, 58–59.}

26. *What . . . sensation.]* {Cf. ibid., 59.}

27. *what exists] Das Seiende*

28. *form of existence] Form des Seins*

29. *In motion . . . existence.]* {Cf. ibid., 60.}

30. *A multiplicity . . . or separation.]* {*WP* 641.}

31. *Science does not ask . . . hypothesis.]* {*WP* 667.}

32. *But willing: = . . . a goal.]* {Cf. *WP* 260.}

33. {Cf. *WP* 676.}

34. *Origin] Herkunft*

35. *personal transformations] sich-Verändern*

36. {Cf. 7[47, 58, 62, 125]; 8[26]; 24[27].}

37. {Cf. 3[1] 245; 4[165]; 11[8]; 18[43, 49, 56]; 21[6].}

38. {*WP* 640.}

39. *measured by human senses] auf den Sinnenmenschen*

40. {*WP* 594.}

41. *emotions] Gemüth* {See the Translators' Afterword, 738–44.}

42. {*WP* 277.}

43. *knowable] erkennbar*

44. {Cf. *WP* 670.}

45. *general feelings] Gemeingefühle* {Grimm defines this term as meaning sense impressions that have to do with the body in general, such as pain and hunger.}

46. {Cf. *WP* 670.}

47. {*WP* 741.}

48. {*WP* 611.}

49. {Cf. *WP* 130.}

50. *bêtise]* "stupidity" {Underlined by N.}

51. *suffrage universel]* "universal suffrage"

52. {Cf. Bourget, *Essais de psychologie contemporaine*, 152–53.}

53. {Cf. *WP* 29.}

54. *At our core] im Innersten* {"in our heart of hearts," "at the core of our being"}.

55. *"le fait"]* "the fact"

56. *art . . . ourselves.]* {Cf. Bourget, *Essais de psychologie contem-poraine*, 158–59, 209.}

57. Cf. note to 7[1].

58. {Cf. 7[47, 58, 62, 125]; 8[26]; 24[16].}

59. *My Innovations. . . . universally shared existence.]* {Cf. WP 417.}

60. *Theory of chance, . . . creative impulses]* {Cf. WP 673.}

61. *against . . . imperfection!]* {Cf. WP 417.}

62. {Cf. Francis Galton, *Inquiries into Human Faculty and Its Development* (London: Macmillan, 1883), 213: "There is an Oriental phrase, as I have been told, that the fear of the inevitable approach of death is a European malady."}

63. {Cf. WP 255.}

64. *Unfreedom . . . no will.]* {Cf. WP 671.}

65. *The individual . . . novelty.]* {Cf. WP 767.}

66. {Cf. WP 767.}

67. {Cf. WP 671.}

68. Quotations from J. G. Vogt, *Die Kraft: Eine real-monistische Weltanschauung* ("Force: A real-monistic worldview") (Leipzig{: Haupt und Tischler,} 1878). *NL.*

69. *matter] Stoff* {We also render *Materie* as "matter" in the concluding sentence of 24[34].}

70. {Cf. *CW* 6: 19[3].}

71. *Omnia naturalia . . . mala.]* "All natural things are indifferent to the person who is acting; (it is) to the person who is holding back, or denying, that they are good or evil."

Translators' Afterword

Paul S. Loeb and David F. Tinsley

The fragments and notes contained in this volume, which Nietzsche wrote while composing *Thus Spoke Zarathustra* (*Z*), cover the period from July 1882 through the winter of 1883–84. We begin by providing a biographical sketch for this time in Nietzsche's life. We then discuss briefly the philosophical works he produced, as well as the principal authors and thinkers Nietzsche was reading. The bulk of this Afterword is devoted to issues of translation. We start by explaining our philosophy and then illustrate our approach by providing examples of global translation decisions that could not be addressed in the endnotes. We then focus our attention on the proper translation of Nietzsche's crucial terms *Mensch* and *Übermensch*, in light of Nietzsche's evolving philosophical concept of superhumans.

Nietzsche's Life, 1882–1884: A Biographical Sketch[1]

Other than occasional visits to his mother and sister in Naumburg in Thuringia, Nietzsche's pattern of residence had taken on a certain regularity. Supported by his pension from the

1. For this section, we draw upon the *Chronicle of Nietzsche's Life* by Colli and Montinari (*KSA* 15 / *CW* 19); Ronald Hayman, *Nietzsche: A Critical Life* (Harmondsworth, UK: Penguin Books, 1982); Curtis Cate, *Friedrich Nietzsche* (New York: Overlook Press, 2002); and Julian Young, *Friedrich Nietzsche: A Philosophical Biography* (Cambridge: Cambridge University Press, 2010). Thanks to Daniel Blue for helpful feedback regarding this section.

University of Basel, as well as by his mother's generous ship-
ments of clothing and his favorite foods, he would spend the
summers in his "cave," a dark room in the second story of the
Durisch family home in the mountain village Sils Maria in
southeastern Switzerland, and his winters in search of healthy
air in a series of Mediterranean port towns, first in Genoa,
then in Rapallo, and finally in Nice.

1882 marked a time of turmoil and transition in Nietzsche's
life. Never robust, his health had worsened significantly during
the previous year. His growing blindness had reached a critical
stage, and he struggled, with limited success, to control, by
means of diet, exercise, and self-diagnosis, his frequent bouts of
debilitating nausea and seizures. *Persona non grata* in Bayreuth
after his break with Wagner in 1877, Nietzsche also experienced
two significant periods of estrangement from his own family.
The first rift with his sister Elisabeth and his mother came as a
result of his catastrophic relationship with Lou Salomé, which
reached its greatest intensity in Tautenberg in the summer of
1882 and imploded in Leipzig in November of the same year.
His friendship with Paul Rée was a further casualty of this
failed relationship. A second major rift with his family followed
Elisabeth's announcement, in September 1883, that she planned
to marry the Prussian super-patriot and anti-Semite Bernhard
Förster. Nietzsche found support and understanding in visits
and correspondence with Franz and Ida Overbeck in Basel, as
well as in his friendship with the composer Heinrich Köselitz,
a.k.a. Peter Gast, who also served as Nietzsche's proofreader
and sometime scribe.

In 1882 Nietzsche felt a semblance of good health restored, a
return of energy and optimism, which brought renewed productivity in his philosophical writing. The winter and spring
of 1882 had seen him complete *The Joyful Science*, in which he
proclaimed the death of God. During his summer sojourn in
Tautenberg, the only summer during these years he did not
spend in Sils Maria, he was correcting the final proofs of *JS*.
Having conceived the doctrine of eternal recurrence the previ-

ous summer at "The Rock" near Sils Maria, he finished part I of *Z* during a ten-day stretch of good weather in Rapallo in January 1883, part II in Sils Maria the following July, and part III in Nice in January 1884. According to his own account, he had taken up work on part IV, finishing it in February 1885. Although he would not begin the actual writing of *Beyond Good and Evil* until June 1885 in Sils Maria, Notebooks 4, 7, and 24 document how much the topics of that later book already occupied him during his writing of *Z*.

Notebook 1 is dedicated to Lou Salomé, who visited Nietzsche in Tautenberg, a scenic forested region south of Naumburg, beginning on 7 August, for three weeks of daily walks and intense conversations. Its tone reflects Nietzsche's exhilaration in anticipation of her visit. He had made her acquaintance through his friend Paul Rée, the German moral philosopher and Darwinist, whose *Psychologische Beobachtungen* (*Psychological Observations*)[2] had inspired Nietzsche and broadened his exposure to British and French thinking. Salomé eventually proposed that the three of them live together, chastely, for a year in an informal "monastery of free spirits." This idealized community of minds provided a facade for the ruthless competition between the two men for an exclusive and less than chaste relationship with Salomé. Both of them unsuccessfully proposed marriage. Notebooks 2 and 3 stem from the last few days in Tautenberg with Salomé and from Nietzsche's time in Leipzig, where Rée and Salomé visited him after he had fled his family's enmity. His sister Elisabeth, who had turned against Salomé since their visit in Bayreuth, did all she could to turn Nietzsche's mother and Nietzsche himself against Salomé.[3]

Notebooks 4–6 reflect a period of extreme isolation and depression in the winter of 1882–83, when Nietzsche considered

2. *Psychologische Beobachtungen* (Berlin: Duncker, 1875); translated and edited by Robin Small as *Psychological Observations*, in Paul Rée, *Basic Writings* (Urbana: University of Illinois Press, 2003), 1–80.

3. For an extended and insightful account, see Rudolph Binion, *Frau Lou: Nietzsche's Wayward Disciple* (Princeton, NJ: Princeton University Press, 1968).

suicide following the implosion of his relationship with Salomé. Nietzsche recovered enough to finish part I of Z.[4] Notebooks 7 and 9 stem from the late spring and early summer that
Nietzsche spent in Genoa and Rome, a time of reconciliation
with his family. Notebook 8 and Notebooks 10–14 were composed in the productive summer of 1883 in Sils Maria, where
Nietzsche completed part II of Z. They coincide with his final
break with Rée and his coming to terms with the end of his
relationship with Salomé.

Notebooks 15–21 contain notes from the late summer of
1883 in Sils Maria and the early fall, when Nietzsche was
intensely occupied with part III of Z. Nietzsche also visited his
family in Naumburg for a few weeks until the second rift with
his sister. Notebooks 22 and 23 reflect Nietzsche's productivity
following the move to his new winter home in Nice; Notebook 24 stems from early January and February of 1884, when
he completed part III of Z and resumed his work on part IV.

Nietzsche's Notes on Secondary Sources[5]

The years 1881–83 marked a time of transition in Nietzsche's
studies as well, from his self-described "middle" period to his
"late" period, and featured a review and rereading of authors
he had first consulted in the mid-1870s, including Schopenhauer, Emerson, Eugen Dühring, Philipp Mainländer, and F.
A. Lange.[6] His creative focus for most of this period was on Z,

4. Cf. Mazzino Montinari, "*Thus Spoke Zarathustra* I through IV," in
CW 7, on the different stages in Nietzsche's composition of Z.

5. In this section we offer a brief look at the principal sources that Nietzsche cites, quotes, or paraphrases in the notebooks of this volume. A more
complete list of references to his source material may be found in the endnotes. See Thomas H. Brobjer, *Nietzsche's Philosophical Context: An Intellectual Biography* (Urbana: University of Illinois Press, 2008), 222–26, for a
comprehensive list of sources, organized by year and by notebook. For more
detailed analysis of Nietzsche's sources, organized by topic, see Robin
Small, *Nietzsche in Context* (Aldershot, UK: Ashgate, 2001).

6. Cf. Brobjer, *Nietzsche's Philosophical Context*, 90.

but there are also many preparatory notes that find later application in *BGE*. Notebook 7 even features an early version of *BGE* 260, in which the notions of master- and slave-morality are presented for the first time.

The notes that Nietzsche took while developing his thoughts on the status of the self, the genealogy of morality, and the relationship of rational thought to the physiological functions of drives are found mainly in Notebooks 7, 15, and 16. In Notebook 7, where Nietzsche is writing on egoism and morality, we find notes on the German philosopher Eduard von Hartmann, whose *Phänomenologie des sittlichen Bewusstseins* ("Phenomenology of moral consciousness")[7] was an important source on Spinoza. Nietzsche's critique of metaphysics and of the "I" as a foundation of epistemology had many sources. Later in these notes he refers specifically to the German philosopher Gustav Teichmüller's *Die wirkliche und die scheinbare Welt* ("The real and the apparent world"),[8] the dualism of Teichmüller's title being one of the fundamental concepts that Nietzsche wished to refute. Although Nietzsche's friendship with Rée ended with the Salomé debacle, his reception and rejection of Rée's ideas on moral philosophy continue in these notebooks (see Notebook 7n22). Nietzsche reread Dühring's *Kursus der Philosophie* ("The course of philosophy")[9] during this period. It is from Dühring that Nietzsche appropriated and modified the term *ressentiment* that would occupy such a key place in *BGE* and *On the Genealogy of Morality*.[10] Many of Dühring's works are among the most heavily annotated in Nietzsche's personal library.

7. Eduard von Hartmann, *Phänomenologie des sittlichen Bewusstseins: Prolegomena zu jeder künftigen Ethik* ("Phenomenology of moral consciousness: Prolegomena to every future ethics") (Berlin: C. Duncker's Verlag, 1879).

8. Gustav Teichmüller, *Die wirkliche und die scheinbare Welt: Neue Grundlegung der Metaphysik* ("The real and the apparent world: New groundwork of metaphysics") (Breslau: Koebner, 1882).

9. Eugen Dühring, *Kursus der Philosophie als streng wissenschaftlicher Weltanschauung und Lebensgestaltung* ("A course in philosophy as strictly scientific worldview and guide to life") (Leipzig{: Koschny,} 1875).

10. Cf. Brobjer, *Nietzsche's Philosophical Context*, 68.

The physiological bases of sense impressions and the dynamic of competing drives were another point of focus and study for Nietzsche during this period. There is frequent reference to the German zoologist and founder of experimental embryology, Wilhelm Roux. For the images of the body as source of expansion of energy and joy, Nietzsche draws upon the works of Mainländer (né Philipp Batz), the German poet and philosopher, particularly Mainländer's *Die Philosophie der Erlösung* ("The philosophy of redemption").[11] One source on feelings of pleasure and pain that Nietzsche consulted at this time was the French philosopher and psychologist Léon Dumont's *Vergnügen und Schmerz: Zur Lehre von den Gefühlen* ("Pleasure and pain: On the doctrine of feelings").[12] For the physiological mechanisms informing sense impressions, Nietzsche appears to have relied upon Michael Foster's *A Textbook of Physiology*, in the Nicolaus Kleinenberg German translation,[13] which drew substantially upon the work of Leipzig professor Ernst Heinrich Weber, who explored the connections between human physiology and psychology. Nietzsche also references three sources on animal physiology and drives that he consulted during this time, by the German ethnologist and animal ecologist Karl Semper, the French philosopher Alfred Espinas, and the German zoologist Georg Heinrich Schneider.

Nietzsche's eclectic interests in aesthetics, cultural history, and law find mention elsewhere in these notebooks. He cites from the Irish historian William Lecky on architecture as well as from the German classical art historian and archaeologist Johann Winckelmann's famous essay on depictions of suffering. Nietzsche's continuing fascination with the ancient Greeks

11. Philipp Mainländer, *Die Philosophie der Erlösung* (Berlin{: Grieben,} 1876),

12. Léon Dumont, *Vergnügen und Schmerz: Zur Lehre von den Gefühlen* (Leipzig: Brockhaus, 1876).

13. Michael Foster, *Lehrbuch der Physiologie*, German trans. by Nicolaus Kleinenberg (Heidelberg: Winter, 1881).

is especially evident in Notebooks 8 and 24, reflecting in part his reading of German classicist Leopold Schmidt's *Die Ethik der alten Griechen* ("The ethics of the ancient Greeks").[14] Nietzsche's interest in Eastern philosophy and Hinduism from his early period, which came from Schopenhauer, was revitalized in part by his rereading the translations and works of his friend Paul Deussen, the German Indologist and professor of philosophy at the University of Kiel. His references to guilt and innocence in light of judicial punishment quote the German legal scholar Rudolf von Ihering.

Our Philosophy of Translation

Our goal in translating Nietzsche's unpublished notebooks is not only to provide a precise English translation of each word or phrase but also to capture the style and spirit of what Nietzsche was trying to say, as Nietzsche might have formulated it in English.[15] For Nietzsche, language is everything. How cleverly Nietzsche expressed a thought was often as important to him as what he was saying. Thus, in searching for English equivalents for Nietzsche's German, we have sought to recapture at least some of the wordplay, wit, and clever phrasing (*Schlagfertigkeit*) that permeate his writing.

Communicating the sense of Nietzsche's text to readers who do not read German poses challenges rarely encountered when translating the philosophical writing of other authors. Some of Nietzsche's formulations in these notebooks draw as much upon literary traditions, for example, the rhetoric of the aphorism — looking back to Goethe, Lichtenberg, Montaigne, and

14. Leopold Schmidt, *Die Ethik der alten Griechen*, vol. 1 (Berlin: Wilhelm Hertz [Bessersche Buchhandlung], 1882).

15. Our approach has much in common with that of R. Kevin Hill and Michael A. Scarpitti in their translation of the material known as *The Will to Power*. See their "Note on the Text and Translation" in *The Will to Power* (London: Penguin Books, 2017), xxvii–xxxiii.

beyond — as they do upon the rhetoric of traditional philosophical argument. Many formulations anticipate the incredible range of rhetoric and genre that characterizes *Z*. As Clancy Martin rightly observes,

> [a]nother problem with translating *Z* — perhaps the thorniest of all — is that Nietzsche imitates so many different kinds of writing in the book. As a philologist and nineteenth-century German, he is often classical: sometimes Thucydidean, sometimes Platonic, sometimes satirical after Juvenal or Persius, sometimes as clear, precise and methodical as Aristotle. As a minister's son and a parodist and opponent of Christianity his style is often biblical, and specifically Lutheran. And, finally, as German's greatest stylist yet, he is innovative and above all modern: modern in the sense that we more commonly associate with French and English writers in the early twentieth century.[16]

Our approach to translating Nietzsche set in motion a continuous process of linguistic exploration and return, analogous to that of expatriates, who, having been immersed in another language and culture, are confronted, after returning home, with the challenge of communicating the otherness of the experience in a language with a different vocabulary and different cultural norms and expectations. The Latin-derived English term "translate" and its inseparably-prefixed German equivalents *übersetzen/übertragen* connote this sense of carrying something over or across a barrier or divider — in this case, to use one of Nietzsche's favorite metaphors, the vast ocean that divides Nietzsche's nineteenth-century German and our twenty-first-century American English.

Navigating this "ocean" required continuous attention to the historical context of Nietzsche's language, which meant taking into

16. Clancy Martin, review of *Thus Spoke Zarathustra*, comparing the translations of Adrian Del Caro and Graham Parkes, *Notre Dame Philosophical Reviews: An Electronic Journal*, 2008.02.06, http://ndpr.nd.edu/news/thus-spoke-zarathustra/.

account semantic developments in German — and in English — since Nietzsche's time. We therefore found it essential to consult works such as Flügel's *Praktisches Englisch-Deutsches und Deutsch-Englisches Wörterbuch in zwei Theilen* ("Practical dictionary of the English and German languages in two volumes") from 1852, Grieb's *Deutsch-Englisches und Englisch-Deutsches Wörterbuch* ("Dictionary of the English and German languages") from 1885, Kürschner's *Universal-Konversations-Lexikon* ("Universal encyclopedia for conversations") from 1900, and Büchmann's *Geflügelte Worte: Der Citatenschatz des deutschen Volkes* ("Dictums: A treasury of quotations for the German people") from 1882 and 1910, along with the *Nietzsche Wörterbuch* from the De Gruyter Nietzsche Online resource, the indispensable online *Grimm Wörterbuch* (Grimm), and the condensed print and online editions of the *OED*.[17] Although we did not view reference works contemporary with Nietzsche as definitive in themselves, they did help us decide, for example, whether *vergewaltigen* ("to rape" in modern German) was to be understood predominantly in sexual terms, how positively the image of a *Biedermann* ("man of honor" or "upright citizen") was viewed in Wilhelminian society, and how *Übermensch* and *übermenschlich* were translated before Nietzsche. The descriptions and illustrations in Kürschner helped us to reimagine the science, technology, and fashion of the nineteenth century. Büchmann allowed us to identify the sources and specific phrasing of famous quotations and literary allusions, as they were understood in Nietzsche's time. In the endnotes, we provide translations of quotations in French, Latin, and Greek; we document Nietzsche's frequent references and allusions to events and proverbs of the Luther Bible;

17. See Felix Flügel, *Praktisches Englisch-Deutsches und Deutsch-Englisches Wörterbuch in zwei Theilen* (Leipzig: Julius E. Richter; Hamburg: Meissner, 1852); Christoph Fr. Grieb, *Deutsch-Englisches und Englisch-Deutsches Wörterbuch*, 2 vols. (Stuttgart: Neff, 1885); Joseph Kürschner, *Universal-Konversations-Lexikon* (Berlin: Hermann Hilger Verlag, 1900?); and Georg Büchmann, *Geflügelte Worte: Der Citatenschatz des deutschen Volkes* (Berlin: F. Weidling, 1882, 1910).

we identify philosophers and authors prominent in Nietzsche's time, some of whom remain largely unknown to nonspecialists; and we define obscure technical terms from proto-industrial Wilhelminian society such as *Nachen* ([jolly] boat) or *Fliegenwedel* (shoe-fly/fly whisk).

Notes on Some Common Grammatical Constructions

Because of their origins as West Germanic dialects of Indo-European, as well as the structural and pedagogical influence of Latin on the development of the written languages, German and English have many grammatical constructions in common. However, divergent patterns of usage mean that some constructions flow more naturally in one language than in the other, even when both languages accept them as grammatical. That's why we sometimes choose alternatives that we think read better in American English, in order to capture the fluency and impact of Nietzsche's German.[18]

A salient illustration of this approach involves how we render the third-person singular universal pronoun *man*. Following Walter Kaufmann, a few translators still render *man* by using the universal impersonal third-person English pronoun "one." Although grammatical, the usage of "one" as an impersonal universal is disappearing from American English, replaced by pronominal universals such as "you" or "we." The challenge is that Nietzsche uses *man* continually in his writing, and such usage flows naturally in Nietzsche's prose. But when one uses "one" to render *man*, one often finds that one's prose no longer flows quite so well. That's why we chose to substitute the pronominal plural universal "we" for *man*, along with its possessive pronoun "our" for *sein*.

18. Hill and Scarpitti follow a similar approach: "[T]here are many grammatical constructions which, while equally possible in both languages, are far more natural in German than in English." Thus, they prefer not to "reproduce such constructions at the price of making Nietzsche's writing appear far clunkier in the original that it actually is" (*Will to Power*, xxix).

Man liebt immer nur seine   We always love only our desire
Begierde und nicht das Begehrte.   and not what we desire. (3[1] 105)

This use of first-person plural can introduce a nuance of inclu-
sion between narrator and readers that is not conveyed by *man*.
We adjust our phrasing wherever this nuance conflicts with
what we think Nietzsche was trying to say. The pronoun *man*
can also function as a passive substitute in German, something
that has no real equivalent in English. When Nietzsche uses
man in this way, we render it in the passive whenever possible.

Personen, die man zu einem   People who were employed for an
Unternehmen benutzt hat,   enterprise which has *failed* should
welches *mißrathen* ist, soll man be doubly compensated. (1[5])
doppelt belohnen.

Inflection

The fact that German is more highly inflected than English
influenced our basic approach in decisive ways.

(1) We add the noun "people" to adjectival constructions in
which the nominal form is omitted in order to distinguish
between *das Gute* (the good, what is good) and *die Guten*
(good people). We realize that in doing so we are moving away
from usage that has been accepted since Kaufmann. But
translating both *das Gute* and *die Guten* as "the good" introduces ambiguity that is not there in the German, where inflection makes it clear whether the reference is to a quality or to a
person. Thus, when we translate *die Guten* as "good people,"
the chapter title *Von den Tugendhaften* in *Z* as "On Virtuous
People," and so on, we are not adding anything to what Nietzsche says. His formulations make it clear which one he means;
we are merely preserving the clarity of the original.

(2) Differing levels of inflection also mean that word order is
used more often to convey emphasis in German, whereas English
typically uses word order to identify subject and object functions
and must therefore rely upon adverbial phrases or clauses to convey emphasis. Nietzsche often begins declarative clauses with the

accusative object or a prepositional phrase, a standard syntactical device to convey emphasis in German. Retaining such inversion in the English sentence results in clunky phrasing or even ambiguity. We therefore prefer to use standard English word order and try to convey Nietzsche's emphasis in other ways.

Über jedes Leiden sind wir *empört*, wenn es sinnlos ist, "*unverdient*" . . .	We are *outraged* by each act of suffering, when it is senseless, "*undeserved*" . . . (7[9])

(3) In German, inflection allows readers to identify most pronominal antecedents through gender, number, and case agreement; in English, readers must rely on number agreement and syntax. In cases where the antecedent of "it" is not clear in English, we replace "it" with the nominal form of the antecedent to preserve the clarity of Nietzsche's prose, as with our substitution of "the ocean" (in bold) in the following passage

Ich blicke hinab in das Meer: still steht *es* und tückisch blickt mir aus ihm ein Bild entgegen.	I look down into the ocean: it lies placidly and out of it an image looks treacherously back at me.
Ein kostbares Bild mit weißen Brüsten hält *es* in seinen Armen: träge und tückisch schleicht *es* über den Sand, daß — — —	In its arms **the ocean** holds a priceless image with white breasts: it steals languidly and treacherously across the sand, so that — — — (9[11])

Flavoring Particles (Modalpartikeln)

German and English both use adverbial flavoring particles to convey nuances of the speaker's intentions or expectations. But different flavoring particles have emerged in the historical development of each language, and even where cognates have survived (*denn*/"then"; *nämlich*/"namely,"), it is not always preferable to use the cognate or even one equivalent word to express what Nietzsche was trying to convey. The semantic diversity of the flavoring particle *doch* and the temporal connotations of the flavoring particle *erst* pose particular challenges, and we provide the following examples to illustrate our approach. The ubiquitous *doch* occurs almost four thousand times in Nietzsche's writings and functions not only to convey greater emphasis but also as the principal particle of contradiction for negations and of contrast for diminutions. The context determines that we render *doch* as "still" (7[25]), as "but" (7[30]), as "yet" (7[44] and 7[52]), and as "and yet" to begin a clause (7[75]).

The particle *erst* has two principal contexts in Nietzsche's notes:

(1) As a synonym for *zuerst* ("first" or "initially"), for example, marking the first time an action or event occurs.

(2) In combination with adverbs or conjunctions, *jetzt erst*, *dann erst*, *erst wenn*, or by itself, as a synonym for *erst recht*, for example, when the action or event is occurring for the first time but not until or only after an initial condition has been met. The challenge is to find an equivalent in English that expresses this nuance of conditional temporality. We think that negating the resulting action or event, as in the following example, conveys the conditional aspect and allows the English to flow as naturally as Nietzsche's German.

Erst wenn ihr dürstet, sollt ihr trinken: und erst wenn der Geist euch treibt, sollt ihr tanzen. Und lernt erst lügen, damit ihr versteht, was Wahrheit-reden ist! Der Hunger erst soll euch zur Wahrheit zurücktreiben: und wenn ihr voll seid der guten Weine der Wahrheit, werdet ihr auch tanzen wollen.	You should not drink until you are thirsty: and you should not dance until the spirit moves you. And only learn how to lie so that you understand what truth-telling is! You should not be driven back to the truth until you are hungry for it: and when you have drunk your fill of the good wines of truth, then you will also want to dance. (23[6])

To render *Erst wenn ihr dürstet, sollt ihr trinken* as "you should drink only when you are thirsty" conveys the restrictive nuance but misses the nuance of "not until" implicit in Nietzsche's use of this construction.

Gerundive and Standard Nouns of Creativity or Cognition

Nietzsche makes extensive use of attributive and nominal gerundives to designate cognitive or creative activity. For example, he is careful to differentiate between the standard noun for "creator," *der Schöpfer*, and its gerundive variant, "someone who creates," *der Schaffende*, with the latter term occurring in variants over two hundred times in his works, notes, and letters. To render both *Schöpfer* and *Schaffender* as "creator" obliterates a key semantic distinction in Nietzsche's German. Therefore, we maintain the distinction by using "one who creates" or "someone who creates" in the singular and "those who create" whenever we pluralize to preserve gender neutrality (see below). We follow the same approach with analogous pairs such as *Kenner/Erkennende* (connoisseur/someone who knows), *Lehrer/Lehrende* (teacher/someone who teaches), and so on.

Singular Universals

Nietzsche frequently uses masculine singular inflection in his discussions of species (*der Mensch*), ethnicity (*der Chinese*), or vocation (*der Dichter*). Take, for example, his claim "der Mensch wird durch seine Instinkte geleitet" (7[239]), which has traditionally been translated as "man is guided by his instincts." When Nietzsche uses masculine singular inflection in such contexts, he does not have an individual in mind, but rather a universal prototype that embodies all of the qualities typically associated with humanity. In choosing *Mensch* instead of *Mann*, Nietzsche clearly has a universal prototype in mind that includes men and women. But as soon as a possessive pronoun is required, German and traditional English usage both call for masculine inflection (*sein*/"his").

We decided to move away from traditional English usage for two reasons: (1) our desire to preserve gender neutrality — we no longer wanted to allow masculine inflection to stand for the universal prototype; (2) we were concerned about the potential that contemporary readers less fluent in German might confuse the gendered connotations of "man" and "his" with the universal connotations of these pronouns. We then weighed some contemporary translators' alternatives for rendering such universality. We decided against universalizing the possessive pronoun itself by pluralizing it (*der Dichter/sein* = "the poet"/"their") for two reasons: (1) it is ungrammatical; (2) there is the potential for overlap with pronouns associated with emerging gender-neutral usage in the US. We also decided against using feminine inflection *ihr/*"her" consistently or alternating the gender of the possessive pronoun (sein = "his," then "her," then "his," etc.). Any of these approaches would obscure or even destroy the complexly consistent gendering that is one of the foundations of Nietzsche's worldview. In the end, we settled upon the option of pluralizing nominal forms as a grammatical alternative that preserves the sense of prototypical universality. Thus, we render "der Mensch wird durch seine Instinkte geleitet"as "human beings are driven by their instincts."

We extend this pluralization model to include ethnic designations:

Der Chinese ißt sehr viel Gerichte in sehr kleinen Portionen.	The Chinese eat very many dishes in very small portions. (8[1])

as well as to vocations,

Wer als Dichter mit baarem Golde zahlen will, muß mit *seinen* Erlebnissen zahlen: deshalb verbittet sich aber der Dichter seine nächsten Freunde als Interpreten — sie errathen, indem sie *zurück* rathen.	Those who, as poets, want to pay with pure gold must pay with *their* experiences: for this reason, though, poets refuse to tolerate having their closest friends as interpreters — their closest friends figure things out by giving them *feedback*. (7[111])

as well as to masculine singular interrogative universals:

Wer seinen Gegner tödten will, mag erwägen, ob er ihn nicht gerade dadurch bei sich verewigt.	Those who want to kill their enemies should consider whether this act will immortalize their enemies for them. (12[1] 77)

and even to some neuter singular gender designations:

Vom Weibe	On Women {*not*: "On the Woman"} {title of 1[111]}

As soon as a singular modifier is added, either an adjective (*der christliche Gott*/"the Christian God") or a restrictive phrase or clause (*die Unschuld der Lüge*/"the innocence of a lie"), the singular definite article is called for in English. In the plural, the definite article is often dropped: *die weiblichen Affecte* = "female affects." In general, when a masculine possessive universal is called for, we pluralize.

Punctuation

Translators of Nietzsche still struggle with the issue of rendering his punctuation. We have tried to preserve Nietzsche's original punctuation wherever possible. This works well, for the most part, with colons, semicolons, dashes, and exclamation points. However, the rules dictating comma usage differ to such a degree between German and English, especially in regard to dependent clauses, that we do occasionally delete Nietzsche's commas where English usage does not call for them. We also add commas where their absence would result in ambiguity or lack of clarity in rendering Nietzsche's original.

Translating Unpublished Fragments

Translating Nietzsche's unpublished fragments meant taking several issues into account that surface less often when translating his published works.

Issues of Genre

Nietzsche used these notebooks for many different purposes. He composed *Z* between 1883 and 1885, and large portions of the notebooks served as a laboratory for working on outlines and phrasing for *Z*. Our readers can follow his different plans for organizing the material, changes in the titles of the different sections, and early versions of passages that are among his most famous. There is even a brief outline for a *Z* drama. There is also a good deal of material relating to the composition of *BGE*, notably in Notebooks 3, 7, 12, and 15; *BGE* appeared in 1886. The notebooks in this volume also contain a small collection of poems, Nietzsche's notes on authors and works he was reading, and commentary on philosophical topics and issues of the day.

Issues of Style

A significant challenge involved translating the frequent ellipses. Often Nietzsche chose not to complete a thought, substituting three long dashes, which could indicate that he considered the conclusion to be foregone or else that he believed he still had work to do.

Eure Krankheiten treten gegen euch auf und verklagen euch ob der Tugenden, deren ihr euch brüstet: und was euch nicht auf den Leib paßt, wie sollte das ein — — —	Your ailments set themselves against you and accuse you on account of the virtues you gloat about: and what doesn't suit your body, how should this — — — (17[13])

Nietzsche also frequently abbreviated words for which Colli and Montinari supplied emendations. Here, on occasion, we adjusted the angle-bracketing of the words to make the English as comprehensible as the German:

So w⟨enig⟩ V⟨ernunft⟩ a⟨ls⟩ m⟨öglich⟩ — das ist, artiger geredet: Zufall. Auf den Füßen des Zufalls laufen alle Dinge hinweg und zurück — — —	As l⟨ittle⟩ r⟨eason⟩ a⟨s⟩ p⟨ossible⟩ — this is, more delicately phrased: chance. All things run there and back on the feet of chance — — — (18[30])

As a general rule, we tried to convey rather than to resolve ambiguities in Nietzsche's original phrasing. We preserved the ellipses, kept fragments fragmentary, found English equivalents for his abbreviations, and retained ungrammatical usage. We only provided emendations when it seemed to us that the text of our translation would appear incomprehensible to the English reader in a way that Nietzsche's original text would not appear to the German reader.

We also learned to be alert to Nietzsche's use of appositives, generally a series of two or more unpunctuated, equivalent nouns or phrases. Rendering these appositives differs from rendering a grammatical series, that is, three or more nouns or phrases joined by commas and a concluding conjunction (usually *und*/"and" or *oder*/"or") that signals whether they are to be considered as alternatives or as synonyms within a collective concept. Unless the lack of punctuation renders the fragment incomprehensible, we provide an English equivalent for each appositive without punctuation in order to maintain the ambiguity of relationship conveyed by Nietzsche's German.

Zarathustra 3. *einsam gottlos furchtbar fürchterlich* soll Zarathustra dem Einsiedler erscheinen —	Zarathustra 3. *alone godless terrible terrifying*, Zarathustra should appear this way to the hermit — (17[75])

Our readers will also notice that Nietzsche repeats or revises particular thoughts, turns of phrase, or even entire fragments within the body of our twenty-four notebooks, a process that will extend into volume 15 of *The Complete Works* and, in some cases, into *Z* (*CW* 7) itself. Some changes involve as little as substituting a semicolon for a comma. In other places, Nietzsche undertakes minor revisions; see, for example, the four variations at 13[1]_379, 13[12], 16[7], and 22[1]_550. Colli and Montinari note many of these variants, but they also miss a substantial number of them. We provide what we hope are comprehensive lists of these passages, with the goal of allowing readers to follow how Nietzsche's phrasing and thoughts evolved during the three-year period covered by this volume.[19]

Issues of Content

Our approach to translating the content of the fragments and notes collected in this volume has been influenced by the existing translations of *Z* and of other works that Nietzsche would subsequently publish, especially *BGE*. The history of translating *Z* into English extends back more than a century, generating not only a working English vocabulary for *Z* but also a range of possibilities for the translation of each fragment. We sometimes break with precedent, most notably in our translation of *Mensch* and *Übermensch*, but also in translating some other key terms (see below). Once we determine the translation of an individual term in a particular context, we use that translation in all of Nietzsche's notes to *Z* and in our translation of *Z*.

We do not document which specific fragments Nietzsche chose or adapted for *Z*, beyond those already noted by Colli and Montinari. In our view, making such connections is in itself an interpretive act. The De Gruyter Nietzsche Online website provides the most complete documentation of *Z* references in the unpublished material. Any repetition of a term or even a particular phrase can easily be documented by an online search. We document repetitions or adaptations of individual fragments within the notes themselves. For the longer fragments, such as 13[1], 13[3], and 22[1], we provide the page number within this volume as a convenience to our readers.

Our volumes also contain material that Nietzsche chose *not* to use for *Z*, for example, in Notebooks 13 and 15. This presents a different challenge for translators. Although we have the published version of *Z* to document Nietzsche's final decisions

---

19. Locating such parallel passages is done most efficiently through online searches on websites such as NietzscheSource and De Gruyter's Nietzsche Online.

regarding diction and phrasing, there is no way of knowing what decision he had made at the time he recorded a particular note or a particular version of a fragment. The absence of a term, such as *Pergament*, or a character, such as Pana (13[3]_ 401), or a scene, such as Zarathustra's conversation with the king in 13[4], in the published version of *Z*, or conversely, its presence in abandoned material, is not necessarily evidence against its validity as part of the process of development in Nietzsche's phrasing and thought. Therefore, even if all translators agree on the rendering of a term or phrase in the published version of *Z*, this does not guarantee that such a rendering is valid for Nietzsche's notes.

There are also extended sections that contain the actual notes that Nietzsche took on works by authors such as Emerson, von Hartmann, and Roux, most notably in Notebooks 7, 15, 16 and 24. Where Nietzsche quotes from German translations of works written originally in English or French, our editors, Alan D. Schrift and Duncan Large, assisted us in finding existing English versions of those works. Where Nietzsche appears to be paraphrasing or rendering the content in his own words, we provide our own translation.

Other sections, most notably "Böse Weisheit"/"Wicked Wisdom," the collection of aphorisms at the beginning of Notebook 12, consist of excerpts or revisions from earlier works such as *The Birth of Tragedy*, *Dawn*, and *Human, All Too Human*, plus material that would be included in *BGE*. In such cases, passages are noted and the sources are identified wherever possible. Some notebooks contain material subsequently incorporated into the text edited by Nietzsche's sister and published as *The Will to Power*. If the work Nietzsche is quoting has already appeared in the Stanford edition of Nietzsche's *Complete Works*, we use the existing Stanford translation of the passage, although we do standardize the rendering of grammatical constructions like *man* (see above) as a courtesy to our readers.

Translating Nietzsche's Poetry

The period from 1882 to 1885 also marks Nietzsche's return to poetry after a five-year hiatus.[20] Indeed, in the eleven-year period between the publication of "An die Melancholie" ("To Melancholy") in 1871 and the poems of *JS*, Nietzsche published only three poems, "Der Wanderer" ("The Wanderer"), "Am Gletscher" ("At the Glacier"), and "Der Herbst" ("Autumn").[21]

Nevertheless, as Philip Grundlehner has noted, Nietzsche "believed poetry to be a vital and inseparable part of his production as philosopher."[22] The "New Columbus" variants included in this volume illustrate the fact that Nietzsche "revised many of his poems sometimes over a period of years," which is further evidence that he took his poetry seriously.[23] And unlike Schopenhauer, Nietzsche's "poetry is not separate from philosophy" but rather "it adds a dimension that prose does not permit."[24]

We attempt to convey the beauty and profundity of Nietzsche's poetry, but we do not attempt to duplicate his rhyme schemes, thereby privileging accuracy in content over the aesthetic effects of form. In regard to word order, German inflection allows for even greater latitude in poetry than it does in prose. This is also true of English, to a more limited degree. Hence, we do maintain German word order in some lines whenever we think that doing so preserves the integrity or the flow of a particular poem.

20. In translating the poems that appear in these notes, we drew upon several insights presented by Philip Grundlehner, *The Poetry of Friedrich Nietzsche* (Oxford: Oxford University Press, 1986).

21. "The Wanderer" was included in a letter to Erwin Rohde (18 July 1876, *KGB* II:5, 177): "At the Glacier" and "Autumn" were both composed during Nietzsche's ill-fated but productive stay in Rosenlauibad above Bern in August 1877. For the original text and an English translation, along with extensive analysis, see Grundlehner, *The Poetry of Friedrich Nietzsche*, 63–88.

22. Ibid., xiv.

23. Ibid., xv.

24. Karl Jaspers, quoted in ibid., xxvii.

A Glossary of Standardized Terms

In the glossary that follows, we discuss our choices for some important terms in *Z* and the notebooks that are associated with it, especially in cases where we diverge from precedent. In our endnotes, we briefly state our reasons for rendering other less common or more obscure terms.

aufheben — The word fields divide in English among (1) the standard meaning of the verb *aufheben*, which we render as "abolish"; (2) specialized meanings in conjunction with particular accusative objects (we "lift" a ban, we "set aside" a judgment, we "repeal" a law); (3) the reflexive verb *sich aufheben*, which we render as "cancel themselves out" or "nullify themselves"; (4) and variants of the reflexive noun *Selbst-Aufhebung*, which we don't think Nietzsche intended in a Hegelian sense and which we render as "self-abolishing," to mirror the form of Nietzsche's key term *Selbstüberwindung* ("self-overcoming").

Bildner (der) — Here we follow Gary Handwerk in *HAH* and *HAH* II, rendering *Bildner* as "sculptor" (Handwerk also uses "shaper"), except for the hyphenated noun *Götzen-Bildner*, where we follow the standard English locution "idol-makers." Nietzsche generally prefers *Künstler* for "artist" (almost a thousand occurrences in his works, notes, and letters) and reserves *Bildner* as a special metaphor of creation through destruction.

Empfindung (die) — At B376 in the *Critique of Pure Reason*, Kant translates *Empfindung* with the Latin *sensatio* and *Wahrnehmung* with the Latin *perceptio*. Following this suggestion, English-speaking translators of Kantian and post-Kantian German philosophical texts have usually chosen to render these two terms as "sensation" and "perception." But Kant is idiosyncratic in this respect and is not following any generally accepted usage in the German language. In fact, as these notes show, Nietzsche uses the term *Empfindung* in a much wider sense that actually does follow the generally accepted use of this term and does not adhere to the very technical and restricted use proposed by Kant for use in philosophy discussions related to his preferred topics. It is true that post-Kantian philosophers such as Hegel and Schopenhauer attempt to follow Kant's usage in this respect (hence the similar translation of their use of these two terms), but it is certainly not the case that all German philosophers continued to follow Kant's proposed meanings. Nietzsche did not; in fact, as our translation shows, he most often had in mind the affective sense of the term *Empfindung* that is best captured by our English term "feeling." Moreover, when Nietzsche does have in mind the more cognitive associations of the term *Empfindung* (as in 7[198] and 24[13, 15, 16]), he usually has a wider sense in mind that is best captured by our English term "perception." When Nietzsche clearly has something like sensation in mind (as in 7[139] and 7[223]), we have not hesitated to render *Empfindung* as "sensation." In short, we should not always apply Kant's severely restricted and technical distinction between *Empfindung* and *Wahrnehmung* to Nietzsche's use of these terms unless we are positive that Nietzsche is quoting or discussing some Kantian or neo-Kantian text or topic (as in 5[1]239 and 7[223]). Our translation looks closely at each place where Nietzsche uses these two terms and makes a case-by-case contextual decision that we think best captures his meaning.

erkennen/Erkenntnis (die)/Erkennende(r) — In contrast to the fundamental verbs of knowing, *wissen* and *kennen*, which describe a situation, condition, or result, *erkennen* and its variants describe a process through which knowledge is gained. Of the semantic variants for *erkennen* cited in the *Deutsches Wörterbuch von Jacob und Wilhelm Grimm*, we distinguish in Nietzsche's notes between the mundane sense of "to recognize" or "to realize" and the epistemological process paraphrased in Grimm as *geistiges erkennen und einsehen*, which can include knowledge or insights gained through reason or experience.

Rather than attempt to generate an artificial vocabulary that could do justice not only to distinctions within standard German usage but also to philosophical discourse then and now, we decided to render *Erkenntnis/Erkennen* as "knowledge/knowing." We opted for this conventional rendering for three reasons: (1) it reflects actual English usage in the epistemological debates among Kant's British interlocutors such as Locke, Berkeley, and Hume, of which Nietzsche was aware and which he took into account; (2) it has been preserved and sustained in contemporary philosophical discourse about Nietzsche's epistemology; (3) it better reflects Nietzsche's semantic preferences in the unpublished notes, where *erkennen* predominates over *wissen*. We document a few exceptions in the endnotes.

Erlösung/erlösen — We translate *Erlösung* as "redemption" in most passages, rendering Nietzsche's litany *Erlösung von Erlösern* as "redemption from redeemers." We believe that "liberation" is closest to N's meaning in 16[11] and 16[33], and we use this to render his other litany, *Man soll das Weib im Weibe erlösen* as "Woman must be liberated from women." In some contexts, we prefer the biblical phrasing "to deliver ourselves" or "to deliver us from" because of the potential confusion with the therapeutic connotations of "redeeming ourselves."

Feuerhund (der)/Höllenhund (der) — *Feuerhund* and *Höllenhund* designate the same being in Nietzsche's notebooks, where images of hell predominate (cf. 13[2], 13[3]_400 and 13[3]_403), as well as in *Z* II and IV, where there is more emphasis on classical mythology and on Zarathustra's quest for essential minerals from the center of the earth. Translators from Kaufmann onward have chosen the literal rendering "firehound/fire-hound/fire hound" for *Feuerhund*, which we did not adopt for three reasons: (1) "firehound" is a neologism that has no place in the English vocabulary of the underworld or hell; (2) in English, compound nouns beginning with "fire" usually connote beings, tools, or structures that prevent fire, not embody it; (3) "firehound" does not resonate with the political connotations that most commentators see in Nietzsche's *Feuerhund*. The word *Feuerhund* can also mean "andiron," but this sense of the word has a separate etymology.[25] The American English equivalent of *Feuerhund* is not "firehound" but rather the regional southern variant "firedog," further evidence that *Hund* should not be translated here by its cognate. *Höllenhund* is the German equivalent of the English word "hellhound," used in folklore studies to designate any mythical dog with supernatural powers. As a category, hellhounds include Cerberus, the three-headed monster dog that guards the gates of the Underworld in Greek mythology; Garmr, the bloodstained guardian of Hel's gate in Old Norse mythology; and the ravening wolf/dogs that accompany Wotan or Graf Hackelberg in the Germanic mythology of "The Wild Hunt" (*Die wilde Jagd*), popularized by Jacob Grimm and adapted by several composers in Nietzsche's time. We render *Höllenhund* as "hound of hell" and *Feuerhund* as "hound of fire" to preserve the semantic distinction while retaining the parallels in form.

Freigeist [der]/Freigeisterei [die] — After consultation with our editors and with translators across *CW*, we have translated this term as "free spirit(s)" when the context indicates Nietzsche's positive position vis-à-vis what he is saying about these figures, as in 1[42] and 20[3]. We have translated the term as "free thinker(s)" when the context indicates that Nietzsche is voicing criticism vis-à-vis these figures, as in 4[16], 6[1], and 6[4]. We provide an endnote whenever the context calls for a departure from this general principle.

Frau [die]/Weib [das]/Weibchen [das] — *Weib* was the prevalent gender designation in Nietzsche's time, referring to women of every age, social status, and class. As the generic

25. See Grimm. Similar citations will subsequently be referred to according to the URL provided by Grimm for the term, in this case, http://www.woerterbuchnetz.de/DWB?bookref=3,1594,56. Both of our nineteenth-century German-English dictionaries translate it as "andiron" or "firedog."

term, its connotations were neutral, and designations could venerate or disparage, depending on its modifiers.[26] Readers accustomed to *Frau/Ehefrau* as the primary designation for gender and social function in modern standard German must come to terms with the different semantic emphasis of Nietzsche's time, as illustrated by Nietzsche's comment in an early letter to Erwin Rohde (9 December 1868; *KGB* I:2, 351): "Übrigens auch mit seiner Frau, die ein ganz unmenschlich verdienstvolles Weib sein soll" (By the way, the same thing is true of his wife, who they say is an admirable woman in every way).

The translator's dilemma lies in finding equivalents for the above reversal of nuance, since the singular noun "woman" is not only the generic term in English for an adult female, paired with "man," but also can designate, in the singular without an article, the entire gender. We believe "women" is the best term for universal gender designations (see above), since the plural can stand for Nietzsche's pronouncements about the entire gender. In the case of Nietzsche's mantra "Das Weib im Weibe erlösen!" (To redeem the woman in women!; 16[50]), we use both the singular and the plural to preserve the distinction Nietzsche has in mind.

We searched long and hard for an English term that could convey the misogynist etymology associated with *Weib*, the literary motif of misogynist disparagement, *das böse Weib*, and the expletive *Weiber!* in German. Contemporary slang ("bitch," "witch," "wench," etc.) is too transitory and fails to resonate with the entire English-speaking community. American women colleagues whom we consulted suggested the technical generic term "female" in its colloquial form as the best misogynist equivalent, so we have made use of that.

26. http://www.woerterbuchnetz.de/DWB?bookref=28,329,25: "an sich gilt weib für die frau jedes alters und standes, für die ledige, verheirathete, verwitwete, lebende und tote, für jungfrauen und mutter" (*weib* is a valid designation for a woman of any age and social class, for unmarried, married, widowed, living and dead women, for virgins and mothers).

Nietzsche's love of supercilious diminutives such as *ein altes Weibchen* or *ein junges Weibchen* further complicates the process. "Little old lady" is a fair rendering of the former term, but there is no good equivalent in English for "little young lady." The *Z* I chapter title "Von alten und jungen Weiblein" presents a particularly interesting challenge. We follow Kaufmann, Del Caro, and Parkes with some minor variations in rendering it as "On Little Women, Old and Young."

Geist (der) — Most scholars agree that this term is one of the most difficult to translate, because there is no single word in English that captures everything that is meant by the German word. Accordingly, we have chosen to translate this word in different ways depending on the context. Where we think that Nietzsche is emphasizing the cognitive, rational, and intellectual aspects of the term, we have rendered it as "mind" or "intellect." Where we think that he is emphasizing the term's affective nuances having to do with emotion, feeling, pleasure, and value, we have rendered it as "spirit." This is not to say, however, that either of these aspects is meant to exclude the other. For example, a *freier Geist* is a "free spirit" in the sense of being an independent and morally unconstrained person who is liberated on both cognitive and noncognitive levels.[27]

Gemüth (das) — Our translation of *Gemüth* reflects its transitional status in Nietzsche's time.[28] In early translations from the Latin, *Gemüth* could be equated with either *mens* (the mind) or *animus* (the spirit). In the eighteenth century, *Gemüth* designated the home of all mental faculties, including perception and concepts or thoughts, "the total unity of our inner being," of which *Geist* (mind) was just a part. In the late eighteenth and early nineteenth centuries, *Gemüth* became more narrowly associated with *Empfindungen* (feelings/sense

---

27. Thanks to Matthew Meyer for his advice on this entry.
28. http://www.woerterbuchnetz.de/DWB?bookref=5,3293,72.

impressions/sensations) and came to be understood as the repository for emotions and even sensuality. By the middle of the nineteenth century, the tendency was to distinguish between *Geist*, the mind as repository of reason and understanding, and *Gemüth*, the faculty of feeling and perception.

Gleichniss/Gleichniß (das) — Nietzsche makes frequent ironic reference in these notebooks to the concluding rhymes of Goethe's *Faust* II, "Alles Vergängliche ist nur ein Gleichnis" (All that is transitory is only a symbol). In passages where the allusion to *Faust* is clear, we render *Gleichnis* as "symbol," following almost all *Faust* translators. In biblical contexts, we render it as "parable." Elsewhere the context dictates whether we translate it as "metaphor," "simile," or "analogy."

hart/Härte (die) — Although most translators have chosen to render these terms with the English cognate in all contexts, we see a clear distinction in American English usage between "hard" as an attributive for objects versus "hard" as an attributive for persons. Flügel, one of our nineteenth-century sources, preserves the distinction between "rough, harsh, severe" conditions and "callous, fierce, inhuman" attitudes. The same problem exists for "hardness." We don't say "he showed great hardness in his dealings with others." We don't believe Nietzsche is restricting *hart* to a physical characteristic. He means "hardened," "callous," or "unyielding." Our solution is to render *hart*, when meant as a personal attribute, as "hard-hearted." We add attributes to the nominal variants that specifically signal that Nietzsche has personal characteristics in mind, such as "hardness of feeling" or "hardness of heart." For example, we render the key phrase from *Z* III, "The Wanderer," *Gelobt sei, was hart macht*, as "Praise be to whatever makes us hard-hearted." For descriptive predicate adjectives, we prefer "hardened."

höhere Menschen — With the exception of Graham Parkes, all *Z* translators use the English cognate "higher" in this context. We do not follow precedent here, because we do not believe that "higher men" or "higher human beings" conveys what Nietzsche is trying to say. The standard English equivalent adjective expressing connotations of "greater" or "more significant" is the Latin term "superior," not "higher," and that is what we use, except when English usage of the nominal form dictates something else, such as "more lofty feelings," "greater pleasure," or "higher purposes."

kleine Menschen — Here we choose alternatives to the English phrasing "small people" or "little people," in which there is too much potential for ambiguity between connotations of stature and connotations of social significance. We settled upon "puny" as the adjective that best conveys Nietzsche's contempt. We settled upon "smallness" as the best equivalent of the nominal form, *Kleinheit*.

klug/Klugheit (die) — In Nietzsche it is necessary to distinguish between cleverness and prudence. For example, we render *ihre dreiäugige Klugheit* as "her three-eyed cleverness" (3[1] 181), but *die Moral der Klugheit* as "the morality of prudence" (7[38]) and the chapter title in *Z* II, "Von der Menschenklugheit," as "On Human Prudence."

Kraft (die) — In most cases Nietzsche uses *Kraft* in scientific contexts to mean something like "force." There are a few passages in Nietzsche's notes where *Kraft* is better rendered as "power." We note these exceptions.

Nächste (der)/Nächstenliebe (die) — The challenge here is to render the biblical phrasing that Nietzsche has in mind, translated in the most current version of the New Revised Standard Version of the Bible as "neighbor," while avoiding confusion with the American English designation "neighbor" as "someone living close by." Nietzsche himself plays with these connotations in 3[1] 202: "'Unser Nächster ist nicht unser Nachbar': so denken alle Politiker und Völker." We render it as "'Our neighbor doesn't live in the neighborhood': this is how all politicians and peoples think." We choose to render the nominal form *Nächstenliebe* in biblical terms as "loving thy neighbor," as in Jesus's second great commandment, "Love thy neighbor as thyself."

Selbstsucht (die)/Herrschsucht (die) — Nietzsche uses the term *Selbstsucht* in contrast to several antonyms, in order to refute the negative connotations traditionally associated with this term. We render *Selbstsucht* as "selfishness" throughout our volumes, in contrast to *Herrschsucht* ("imperiousness"), *Nächstensucht* ("neighborliness"), *Gemeinsucht* ("public-spiritedness"), and *Selbstlosigkeit* ("selflessness").

sollen/wollen — Nietzsche uses the dichotomy between the modal verbs *du sollst* and *ich will* repeatedly in these notebooks. This is his shorthand for the kind of human transformation he desires, moving from obedience before an external omnipotent God (*du sollst*) toward the internal imperative of the individual's will to power (*ich will*). To highlight the biblical context, we render the phrase *du sollst*, the basis for the Ten Commandments in German, in the archaic language of the King James Bible: "thou shalt."[29] Translators since Thomas Common have rendered *ich will* in Nietzsche as "I will," which is problematical for several reasons. (1) *Ich will* without an infinitive verb is transitive and connotes either desire or present-tense volition, rendered most accurately as "I want (to)." The English equivalent "I will" is also transitive but connotes either future intention or present willing, not the modality of wanting. (2) If Nietzsche intended to render both as modal verbs, omitting the infinitive because it is irrelevant, then "I want to" and not "I will" is the proper rendering. (3) In placing the spirit of the lion above the gold-scaled dragon in "On the Three Transformations," Nietzsche is reversing the ideal modeled by Jesus in the Garden of Gethsemane. In the King James version of Luke's gospel this passage reads: "Saying,

29. The New Revised Standard translation of the Bible renders this as "you shall."

Father, if thou be willing, remove this cup from me: neverthe-less, not my will, but thine, be done." Luther rendered this as "und sprach: Vater, willst du, so nehme diesen Kelch von mir, doch nicht mein, sondern dein Wille geschehe!" By contrast, Nietzsche advocates a transformation whereby humans will act according to the imperative "*My* will be done," that is, "What-ever I want to happen, shall happen!" The English phrase "I will" with no accusative object does not convey this; most read-ers would understand this phrase as meaning "I will do this." Thus, to communicate the essential nuance of volition, we translate *ich will* as "I will this."

Tafel (die) — For the nominal root, we distinguish between biblical contexts, in which we render *Tafel* as "tablet," and the contemporary context of moral philosophy, in which we ren-der the term as "code." This differentiation allows us to pre-serve the traditional rendering of the *Z* III chapter as "On Old and New Tablets."

Zufall (der) — We translate the phenomenon as "chance" and an individual instance as a "coincidence" or an "accident."

We now move from a general discussion of our translation choices to a specific discussion of how we translate Nietzsche's crucial terms *Mensch* and *Übermensch*.

Translating *Mensch* and *Übermensch*
From Man to Humans

In German, the etymology of equivalents for "man" diverges into a masculine singular term for the male gender, *der Mann*, and a masculine singular term for the human species, *der Mensch*.[30] *Der Mensch* has its origins in the adjectival form of *Mann*, but even the earliest sources show *der Mensch* and a neuter variant *das Mensch*[31] signifying "in general, a human being, of both genders and of any age . . . and this general meaning occurs frequently in the singular as well as in the plural."[32] The degree to which this contrast between the masculine singular form and the universal connotations became entrenched is evident in the surviving sixteenth-century singular idiom, *das alle Menschen*, as in "so wird dein alle menschen lachen" (then what is completely human in you [literally, what you share with all humans] will laugh). The flexibility of *Mensch* in connoting universality extends to an interchangeability of definite and indefinite articles (*der Mensch* can have the same connotation as *ein Mensch*). Species designations can occur in both the singular and the plural, thus making the pluralization of *Mensch* less significant than is usually the case.

Grimm documents the three principal occurrences of the masculine singular noun *Mensch*: (1) the metaphysical distinction between God the Creator and his human creations — "der Mensch, der Schöpfung Ruhm und Preis" (Gellert; human beings, the crown and prize of creation); (2) the mythological distinction between gods and humans — "je mehr du fühlst ein Mensch zu sein, desto ähnlicher bist du den Göttern"

30. There is a parallel etymology for the universal usage of the singular noun *Mann* in German, but *Mensch* dominates the word fields surrounding this usage.

31. The modern German slang variant *das Mensch*, i.e., a "woman of easy virtue," is a later development.

32. http://www.woerterbuchnetz.de/DWB?bookref=12,2021,16.

(Goethe; the more you feel yourself to be human, the more you resemble the gods); and (3) the hierarchical distinction between angels, humans, and animals — "Was ist der Mensch? Halb Tier, halb Engel" (Haller; What are human beings? Half animal, half angel).[33] As we might expect, the metaphysical dimension evoked by Haller in the third example is absent in these two volumes of notes and in *Z*. Humans are most often designated by the masculine singular noun *Mensch* with the masculine definite article *der*. In contrast, the representative animal that Nietzsche most often chooses is the ape, designated by the singular noun *Affe* with the masculine definite article *der*.

Up until twenty years ago, given our philosophy of translation, the English equivalent designation "man" with the possessive pronoun "his" would have been our choice. But twenty-first-century English usage requires that *Mensch* be rendered in its nongendered form, as "human" or "human being." The first possibility we considered was to maintain the singular universal in English, in this case "the human being" or "the human." But as soon as Nietzsche uses a possessive, the required form in English is "his," which violates the universal meaning of *Mensch* in German as well as our aim of gender neutrality. For reasons that we reviewed at the start of this Afterword, we rejected switching to a gender-neutral pronoun such as "its" in such cases, or to an ungrammatical plural possessive such as "their." But when we pluralized the *Mensch* occurrences, we found that the English reads well and that Nietzsche's intended meaning is preserved: "Human beings are something that must be overcome."

Pluralizing *der Mensch*, as we pluralize *der Chinese* or *der Dichter*, not only preserves gender neutrality whenever singular possessive pronouns are used, it is also consistent with the meaning and etymology of *Mensch*, even as it preserves the universalizing effect of its idiomatic usage. In the history of

33. http://www.woerterbuchnetz.de/DWB?bookref=12,2021,16.

the German language, what is meant is not one individual but a universal prototype that stands for the entire human species, men, women, and children. Moreover, Nietzsche talks about human beings in two, largely distinct contexts. When Nietzsche's context is the human species, we render *Mensch* as "humans" or "human beings," depending on what reads better. When Nietzsche's context is universal human behavior or psychology, we render *Mensch* as "person" or "people." Notice that, in this latter context, the singular with a definite article, "the person" or even "a person," does not convey the same degree of prototypical universality.

The Modifier übermenschlich

Most striking within the etymology of *Übermensch* and its variants is the predominance of the adjectival and adverbial form *übermenschlich*, beginning in the sixteenth century, when the German theologian Wendelin Steinbach defined it by reference to the Latin adjective *supernaturalis* in terms of qualities that are beyond humanity, such as immortality.[34] A digital search of texts published before 1850 contained in Projekt Gutenberg yields scores of citations of the adjectival form or its nominal derivations (*das Übermenschliche*/"the superhuman" or "what is superhuman"; *etwas Übermenschliches*/"something superhuman").[35] By Nietzsche's time, *übermenschlich* had become a standard term to describe powers or abilities that exceed human capacity or capability, as in E. T. A. Hoffmann's *Die Elixiere des Teufels* (*The Devil's Elixir*; 1815–16): " . . . ja ich fühlte in dem Augenblick eine übermenschliche Kraft in mir emporkeimen . . . " ("indeed, in that moment I felt within myself a burgeoning superhuman strength"). Moreover, the standard English translation for the term *übermenschlich* was well established by the

34. http://www.woerterbuchnetz.de/DWB?bookref=23,418,75.

35. Nietzsche's earlier works demonstrate that he was accustomed to using the adjectival and adverbial forms. Cf. *BT* 1; *Philosophy in the Tragic Age of the Greeks* 8; *HL* 6 (*CW* 2, 122, l. 24); *SE* 6 (*CW* 2, 229, l. 36); *WB* 11 (*CW* 2, 327, l. 27); *HAH* 111, 143, 164, 441, 461; *WS* 73, 190; *D* 27, 60, 113, 548.

mid-nineteenth century: it was "superhuman." The 1852 edition of Flügel (p. 966) and the 1885 edition of Christoph Grieb's *Deutsch-Englisches Wörterbuch* (p. 879) both translate *übermenschlich* exclusively as "superhuman."[36] And there is almost universal agreement among translators today that "superhuman" is the best rendering of *übermenschlich*.[37]

From Superman to Overman

The etymology of the noun *Übermensch* demonstrates how Nietzsche took a word that had been in common usage since the Reformation and reshaped it for his own purposes. First documented in Dominican correspondence from 1527, *Übermensch* was used to describe the followers of Luther.[38] Although Nietzsche did not coin the term, *Übermensch* came to be associated with Nietzsche. In the 1882 edition of Büchman's *Geflügelte Worte*, the German equivalent of *Bartlett's Familiar Quotations*, there is no mention of Nietzsche or *Übermensch*. Yet, according to the 1910 edition, "The particular way that *Übermensch* is understood today was first developed through Nietzsche" (p. 424). Before Nietzsche, the adjectival/adverbial form *übermenschlich* was the much more common term. After Nietzsche, the nominal form *Übermensch* achieved greater notoriety and usage. Nietzsche himself uses *übermenschlich* only a few times in this volume of notes, out of a total of nearly fifty occurrences in his works, notes, and letters. By contrast, *Übermensch* occurs almost two hundred times in his ouevre, with almost one third of these occurrences documented in this volume.

36. Bilingual dictionaries, by their very nature, tend to focus on well-established terms and more conventional usage. Both dictionaries appeared before Nietzsche's publications during the period of this volume and before those publications were well or very widely known. Furthermore, of the four German adjectival synonyms immediately cited in Grimm, the two containing the prefix *über* are also translated in modern English through the Latin variant: *übernatürlich* as "supernatural" and *überirdisch* as "supernal" or "superlunary."

37. This includes Smith, *D* §27 (*CW* 5); Del Caro, *BGE* §294 (*CW* 8); Handwerk, *HAH* §111 (*CW* 3).

38. http://www.woerterbuchnetz.de/DWB?bookref=23,417,31.

The translation history of *Übermensch* as a Nietzschean concept is much more contentious than that of its adjectival and adverbial variant, *übermenschlich*. For more than a half century, the standard translation of *Übermensch* was the upper-case noun "Superman." In 1903 George Bernard Shaw translated Nietzsche's term *Übermensch* in this way in his famous and influential play *Man and Superman*. "Superman" was also Thomas Common's choice in his 1909 revision of the first English translation of *Z* (in 1896) by Alexander Tille (who had chosen "beyond-man"). Although Shaw and Common capitalized the term "Superman," this is not required by the German text any more than Nietzsche's parallel term *Mensch* calls for capitalization of the English translation "human."

"Superman" remained the standard translation of *Übermensch* until Kaufmann coined the term "overman" in 1954 and convinced most scholars to follow his lead. Kaufmann offered historical, morphological, and etymological arguments in favor of "overman." We will summarize these arguments and then explain briefly why we chose not to accept them. Faced with the monumental task of rehabilitating Nietzsche as a philosopher for American readers less than a decade after World War II, Kaufmann argued against the term "Superman" because he thought it brought to mind politically charged reminders of Nazi eugenics propaganda. But of course the term *Übermensch* brings to mind the same associations and reminders for speakers of the German language. Other translators have expressed reservations about the potential for contamination by the name "Superman" in popular literature, comics, and film. But in fact Nietzsche's concept has had a significant influence on these popular references.[39] In any case, the shift in translation preference for *Mensch* from "man" to "human" (see above) puts these reservations to rest.

39. Cf. Adam Barkman, "Superman: From Anti-Christ to Christ-Type," in *Superman and Philosophy: What Would the Man of Steel Do?*, ed. Mark D. White (Malden, MA: Blackwell, 2013), 111–20.

Kaufmann's morphological arguments focused upon the proper rendering of the prefix *über*. English offers two possibilities for the context in question, one derived from Latin, "super," and the English cognate derived from West Germanic, "over." Translators who have recently followed Kaufmann in rendering *Übermensch* with the term "overman" or the ungendered and capitalized term "Overhuman" cite Kaufmann's argument that this term best conveys Nietzsche's associations with other *über* terminology that is usually rendered by means of "over," such as *Überfluss* ("overflow"), *überwinden* ("overcome"), and *übergehen* ("to pass over").[40] They also cite Kaufmann's reference to Nietzsche's knowledge of Ralph Waldo Emerson's concept of the Over-Soul in his 1841 *Essays*. But we think that the Latinate prefix "super" carries with it many of the same connotations of elevation and preserves enough of the wordplay with Nietzsche's parallel "over" locutions and contrasting "under" locution. Also, we don't think there is any conceptual connection between Nietzsche's concept of the *Übermensch* and Emerson's idealistic concept of the Over-Soul. In any case, the fact that Nietzsche did not coin *Übermensch* renders moot the argument that "over" is a more felicitous translation than "super" because Nietzsche was familiar with Emerson's notion of the Over-Soul. Finally, as we mentioned above, the Latinate prefix "super" is quite naturally and standardly used to translate the adjectival and adverbial form *übermenschlich*, and we think it more important to capture this grammatical relation than the associations with other *über* terminology. Nietzsche uses the modifying form frequently in *Ecce Homo*, in association with the nominal form (*EH* "Destiny" 5).[41]

40. Friedrich Nietzsche, *Thus Spoke Zarathustra: A Book for All and None*, ed. Adrian Del Caro and Robert B. Pippin, trans. Adrian Del Caro (Cambridge: Cambridge University Press, 2006); Friedrich Nietzsche, *Thus Spoke Zarathustra: A Book for Everyone and Nobody*, trans. Graham Parkes (Oxford: Oxford University Press, 2005).

41. Cf. Jill Marsden, "Sensing the Overhuman," *Journal of Nietzsche Studies* 30 (2005): 102–14, 103.

In his etymological arguments for rendering *Übermensch* as "overman," Kaufmann claims he is going back to an "older term, 'overman,' which has been reinstated."[42] But by "older" he does not mean the English Nietzschean term used by previous translators such as George Bernard Shaw or Thomas Common (who both chose "Superman"); instead, he means an archaic English term that referred to a labor foreman, supervisor, or overseer. Obviously, this archaic term has nothing to do with Nietzsche's term.[43] We think it is time to dispense with Kaufmann's neologism. Whereas Nietzsche's term *Übermensch* has a history and a place in the German language prior to his influential use of it, the term "overman" in a Nietzschean sense has no history or place in the English language at all.

From Overman to Superhumans

Our choice was therefore between "superhuman" and an ungendered modification of Kaufmann's neologism, "overhuman." We found "superhuman" to be the better choice because it corresponds to current standard English usage in its word field and because it is part of a tradition of translating *Übermensch* that extends back to the beginning of the sixteenth century. Moreover, in standard usage the universally accepted equivalent for *Untermensch* draws upon the Latin tradition: we say "subhuman." To maintain consistency, rendering *Übermensch* as "overhuman" would thus require a second neologism, "underhuman." In *GM* I 16, Nietzsche describes Napoleon as "diese Synthesis von *Unmensch* und *Übermensch*"(this synthesis of an *inhuman* and a *superhuman*). Here again, the standard term "superhuman" fits perfectly in this context, without

42. Walter Kaufmann, *Nietzsche: Philosopher, Psychologer, Antichrist*, 4th ed. (Princeton, NJ: Princeton University Press, 1974), 115.

43. A further counterargument to Kaufmann's morphological and etymological justifications for "overman" can be found in his translation of *JS* 382 in *The Gay Science* (New York: Vintage Books, 1974). If his arguments are valid for the noun, they should be equally valid for the adjective, yet Kaufmann renders the hyphenated adjective *menschlich-übermenschlichen* as "human, superhuman."

us resorting to the neologism "overhuman."[44] Certainly, the original meaning of Kaufmann's archaic term does not lend itself at all to the ungendered modification "overhuman," which has now become a completely invented English word. And we find it telling that Kaufmann does not follow his own arguments but translates this passage as "this synthesis of the inhuman and superhuman."

Once we agreed on the term "superhuman" for *Übermensch* in the *Z* volumes, we were confronted with the same challenges discussed above concerning how to translate *Mensch*. To translate *der Übermensch* in the singular introduces the same ambiguity between the adjectival, "the superhuman," referring to qualities or behavior, and the nominal, "the superhuman," referring to beings. More important, when Nietzsche uses the term in its masculine singular form with the definite article, in most cases he is using the term as a masculine singular universal. As with the identical use of *Mensch*, Nietzsche does not have a single individual in mind but rather the universal prototype of an entire species.

Ich liebe den, der lebt, damit er erkenne und der erkennen will, damit der *Übermensch* lebe.	I love those who live to know and who want to know so that the superhumans may live. (5[17])

Here Nietzsche's singular demonstrative *den* does not stand for one individual but rather for *any* individual who lives to know, and Nietzsche asserts that the purpose of these individuals living to know is so that the superhumans may live. As with *Mensch*, we did not want to render universal possessive pronouns in the singular with the masculine pronoun "his." In pluralizing both the demonstrative and the noun in the

44. When we experimented with rendering the adjectival form, the prefix "over" seemed particularly out of place; "superhuman virtues," for example, simply sounds better than "overhuman virtues" (25[80]). There is also the potential for confusion with adjectives like "overeager" between "over" and "overly," where readers wonder whether Nietzsche means "over and above" or "excessively."

above passage and elsewhere, we achieve Nietzsche's desired meaning, maintain gender neutrality, and avoid the misleading masculine singular inflection that has led some commentators to see *der Übermensch* as a single (male) individual.

Many translators and scholars have concluded that *der Übermensch* refers to a special kind of male individual because Nietzsche uses the singular noun with a masculine definite article along with the associated masculine pronouns (*ihn* and *sein*) (see, e.g., 4[171], 4[224], 5[1], 12[17], 13[1], 18[56]). But Nietzsche makes identical and parallel uses of his term *der Mensch* —a term that translators and scholars routinely and correctly translate as a collective singular universal that means "humans" or "human beings." Moreover, Nietzsche will often move back and forth, with no contextual difference, between the singular noun, *Mensch*, and the equivalent plural noun, *Menschen*, and there are several passages in which he does the same thing with *Übermensch* and *Übermenschen* (see, e.g., 4[254], 5[32], 10[37], 10[41], and 13[26]). The fact that Nietzsche sometimes uses the plural nonuniversal inflection *Übermenschen* is not evidence that he is using the singular *Übermensch* to refer to an individual but rather further grammatical evidence that he is using the singular universal inflection to refer to a category, group, or prototype. There is no place in these notes, or in *Z*, where the context shows that Nietzsche is using *Übermensch* to refer to specific individuals. Nor is there any such place for Nietzsche's contrasting expressions, *der letzte Mensch* (the last human beings) and *der kleine Mensch* (puny human beings). These should be compared with Nietzsche's use of the term *der höhere Mensch* (superior human beings), especially in part IV of *Z*, where the context clearly shows his intent to refer to specific individuals (such as the sorcerer, or the ugliest man, or the one-eyed pope).

Finally, some have argued that it is best to leave the term *Übermensch* untranslated because it is well known by Nietzsche scholars and even to some extent in the culture at large.[45] However, a general editorial decision was made that the entire *Complete Works* would leave no German words untranslated. Also it would be odd to leave just the single term *Übermensch* untranslated in the whole *Z* book and in all the associated notebook material. More to the point, it would also be excessive to leave all of the associated adjectival and adverbial locutions (*übermenschlich*) untranslated; but if they are translated, the reader will lose the connection to the untranslated *Übermensch*.

Our decision to translate the masculine singular universal *Übermensch* as "superhumans" obviates the reasons usually given in favor of capitalizing or gendering the English translation of *Übermensch*. It also avoids a potential typographical confusion between the nominal and modifying forms of this term ("superhuman"), and it removes the misleading suggestion, implicit in the term "Superman" and the associated male pronouns, that Nietzsche's term refers to a male individual. Beyond these etymological and morphological arguments, we believe that there are compelling exegetical and philosophical arguments, rooted in the *Z* notebook material and in *Z* itself, for understanding *Übermensch* in terms of a species and not an individual. We now turn to these arguments.

Nietzsche's Philosophical Concept of Superhumans

Throughout his career, Nietzsche uses the philosophical concept of superhumans in three different ways. We will call these the *supernatural* use, the *superior-individual* use, and the *superior-species* use. He inherited the first two uses from earlier traditions in German writing, one having to do with philological investigations of validating mythological narratives, and the other having to do with the Romantic valorization of heroic

45. Friedrich Nietzsche, *Thus Spoke Zarathustra: A Book for All and None*, trans. Clancy Martin (New York: Barnes and Noble Classics, 2005).

individuals. But he invented the third use in response to Darwin's theory of the origin of the human species. This particular use did not exist in the German language at all, not even in Nietzsche's own published texts, prior to its introduction in 1883 with the publication of the first part of Z.[46]

The Supernatural Use

Nietzsche's first published use of the concept of superhumans occurs in the first edition of *JS*, §143, titled "Greatest Advantage of Polytheism." This is the key passage:

> The invention of gods, heroes, and superhumans of all kinds, as well as near-humans and subhumans [*Uebermenschen aller Art, sowie von Neben- und Untermenschen*], of dwarves, fairies, centaurs, satyrs, demons, and devils was invaluable training for justifying the selfishness and sovereignty of the individual: the freedom granted to one god in relation to other gods was in turn granted to oneself in relation to laws and customs and neighbors.[47]

Read contextually within the rest of §143, this passage relates the concept of superhumans to the idea of polytheism. For this reason, the concept might be called a theistic concept. But this passage also relates the concept of superhumans to a group of invented supernatural beings who, like the gods, live above and outside human beings, in some distant superworld (*über sich und ausser sich, in einer fernen Ueberwelt*). These beings are associated with gods but are not themselves gods. They include heroes, near-humans, subhumans, dwarfs, fairies, centaurs, satyrs, demons, and devils. This is why we have called this first published mention a supernatural use of the concept of superhumans. Nietzsche also

---

46. Our discussion below focuses on the nominal form, *Übermensch*. But it applies as well to the more common adjectival and adverbial form, *übermenschlich* — as, for example, Nietzsche's supernatural use of this form in *BT* §1, his superior individual use of this form in *D* §548, and his superior species use of this form in *JS* §382.

47. In this passage, Nietzsche uses the alternative spellings, *Uebermensch* and *Ueberwelt*.

contrasts his term *Uebermenschen* with the linguistically related terms *Nebenmenschen* and *Untermenschen*, in this way positioning human beings at the center of a hierarchy of invented supernatural beings.[48] The supernatural beings who are superior to human beings would seem to be the gods, heroes, and superhumans; those who are semi-equal to human beings would seem to be the dwarfs, fairies, centaurs, and satyrs; and those who are inferior would seem to be the demons and devils. The superhumans thus belong among the superior and elevated beings in Nietzsche's supernatural catalogue, along with the gods and the heroes. But even the heroes are not actually existing human beings, only invented mythological beings (like Odysseus or Siegfried). There is thus an important contrast to be drawn here with Nietzsche's second use of the concept of superhumans, a use that refers to actually existing figures such as Borgia and Napoleon.

Nietzsche's supernatural use of the concept of superhumans is not original to him. He inherited this use from a tradition of philologists and historians who were seeking to discover the linguistic and mythological sources that could be used to define and validate what it meant to be German. These scholars applied the term when they were describing the hierarchies of invented gods and humans in their discussions of Greek, Roman, and Old Norse mythologies. Here is a representative example from Jacob Grimm's discussion of the sagas' representation of the "idisî" or wise women:

> Yet from the earliest times it [the term *idisî*], like the gr. νύμφη, appears to have been applied primarily to superhuman beings, who were seen to be lower than goddesses, higher than earthly women, taking the middle level that is under discussion here.[49]

48. Our decision to use "human" in place of the traditional English designation, "man," automatically shaped our choices for the variants of *Mensch* that Nietzsche uses in his works, notes, and letters: *Gottmensch*/"god-humans"; *Halbmensch*/"half-humans"; *Mitmensch*/"fellow humans"; *Nebenmensch*/"near-humans"; *Übermensch*/"superhumans"; *Unmensch*/"inhumans"; and *Unter-mensch*/"subhumans."

49. Jacob Grimm, *Deutsche Mythologie*, 3rd ed., vol. 1 (Göttingen: Dieterichsche Buchhandlung, 1854), 372.

It is noteworthy that in this first published mention of the concept of superhumans, Nietzsche uses the plural term *Uebermenschen* instead of the collective singular term *Uebermensch*. This is because, as we argue below, Nietzsche's later use of the concept no longer refers to a mere plurality of individuals (whether supernatural or actually existing) but rather to a single new species that could emerge sometime in the future and would be superior to the human species.

In the unpublished preparatory notes collected in this volume, Nietzsche never mentions this supernatural use of his concept except in the very indirect and metaphorical sense that the members of this new species will relate to human beings as if they were indifferent Epicurean gods (7[21], 16[85]). However, in the published *Z* he does allude back to his earlier supernatural use when he has Zarathustra describe what poets have typically believed about this concept. Here is the key passage:

> Yet this is what all poets believe: that those who prick up their ears while lying in the grass or on secluded slopes experience some aspect of the things that are between heaven and earth.
>
> And if tender stirrings come to them, then the poets always think that nature herself is in love with them:
>
> And she creeps up to their ears to tell them secrets and enamored flatteries: the like of which makes them boastful and bloated before all mortals!
>
> Oh, there are so many things between heaven and earth of which only poets have allowed themselves to dream!
>
> And especially *above* heaven: for all gods are poetic metaphor, poetic plunder!
>
> Truly, we are lifted ever higher — namely to the kingdom of the clouds: it is there that we place our motley young fools and then call them gods and superhumans [*Götter und Übermenschen*]: —
>
> Still, they weigh just enough for these thrones! — all these gods and superhumans [*alle diese Götter und Übermenschen*].

> Oh, how weary I am of all these things that don't measure
> up, that are supposed to be must-see events! Oh, how weary I
> am of poets! (*Z* II "On Poets")

This passage is important because it includes the book's only pejorative and dismissive mention of the concept of superhumans. For this reason, it is often cited as Nietzsche's critique of his own new Zarathustran concept of superhumans.[50] However, a closer reading shows that this particular mention overlaps with Nietzsche's earlier use of the plural "*Uebermenschen*" in *JS* §143 in the following ways: superhumans are invented and false; they are supernatural and associated with gods; and they dwell above human beings in distant, cloudy heavens. By contrast, Zarathustra teaches that his own goal of creating superhumans can only be realized once all gods are dead; that these superhumans will be the natural fruit of thousands of years of selective breeding among the descendants of his disciples; and that these superhumans will inhabit the earth and constitute the meaning of the earth. Thus, Nietzsche's actual point in this passage is to highlight the uniqueness and originality of his own Zarathustran use of the concept of superhumans. He does so by contrasting it with the supernatural use of this concept by earlier scholars of mythology such as Jacob Grimm. Of special interest to Nietzsche is the influence of these scholars on the poetic compositions of Wagner in which he dreamed up colorful fantasies of airy, imperfect, and quasi-divine superhumans. It is true that Zarathustra begins his speech by including himself among the poets who lie too much. Yet at this point in the speech where he has reviewed the lies that poets tell about superhumans, he has also declared that he is weary of such lies and indeed that he is weary of all poets, old and new, because they are all superficial, muddled, and vain.

50. Cf. Tom Stern, "Nietzsche on Context and the Individual," *Nietzsche-forschung* 15 (2008): 299–315.

The Superior-Individual Use

Following the publication of *Z*, Nietzsche uses the term *Übermensch* only six times in the texts that he published or prepared for publication. For the reader's convenience, we have collected these passages in the Appendix below. He uses the term once in *On the Genealogy of Morality* (*GM* I 16), once in *Twilight of the Idols* (*TI* "Forays" 37), once in *The Anti-Christian* (*AC* 6), and three times in *EH* (*EH* "Books" 1, Z6, "Destiny" 5).[51] These published passages are noteworthy, especially when considered together, because they reflect Nietzsche's appropriation of an earlier Romantic use of the concept of superhumans that is distinct from the philological use outlined above as well as from his new and original Darwinist use in *Z*.

In these passages Nietzsche expresses his view that there exist certain individual human beings who possess such extraordinary abilities that they should be regarded as superior in value to most other human beings. One of the most famous and enduring presentations of this view can be found in Machiavelli's *Prince*, where the *virtù*-laden Cesare Borgia is glorified as the best example of such a superior individual. This is why Nietzsche repeatedly mentions this lesser-known Renaissance figure in these passages. Following Machiavelli, Nietzsche is concerned to pit his admiration of Borgia against the socially sanctioned "idealistic" type of superior individuals, that is, individuals who are usually regarded as superior in value to most others on account of their saintly and moral qualities. To Machiavelli's Renaissance Borgia, Nietzsche adds Napoleon as his own age's very best instance of a superior individual. Moreover, as Machiavelli did with Borgia and as he himself does with Borgia (*BGE* 197), Nietzsche emphasizes Napoleon's terrible, monstrous, and inhuman aspects as contributing to his superior value: "*Napoleon*: one comprehends that the higher human being and the terrible

---

51. In *EH*, Nietzsche also quotes two places in *Z* where he uses the term *Übermensch* (*EH* "Books" Z8, "Destiny" 5).

human being necessarily belong together" (*CW* 17, 10[5]). More abstractly, Nietzsche writes:

> The human is the beastly animal and super animal; the higher human being is the inhuman and superhuman being: these belong together. [*Der Mensch ist das Unthier und Überthier; der höhere Mensch ist der Unmensch und Übermensch: so gehört es zusammen.*] With each increase in the greatness and stature of the human being, so increases the depth and terribleness as well: one ought not will the one without the other — or rather: the more fully the one is willed, so then does one more fully achieve precisely the other. (*CW* 17, 9[154]).[52]

Notice that in *TI* "Forays" 37 (see Appendix), Nietzsche refers to Cesare Borgia only as a *kind* of superhuman being (*eine Art Übermensch*), and then only when considered *in relation to* human-kind as a whole (*im Verhältniss zur Gesammt-Menschheit*). Nietzsche's point is that Borgia was only superhuman in an analogical and comparative sense. Nietzsche reinforces this last point when he also describes Borgia in these passages as a superior human being (*ein höherer Mensch*) or as a superior kind of human being (*eine höhere Art Mensch*) — meaning that, despite his superior abilities and his superior value, he was still human.

This latter description is especially significant because it alludes back to Nietzsche's Zarathustran concept and narrative theme of superior human beings (*höhere Menschen*). In his speech devoted to this concept, Zarathustra tells the assembled superior men that God is dead and that they should no longer feel constrained by the prevailing dogma of human equality. He instructs them that the time has come for them to overthrow the long rule of the rabble and to take charge of the world (*Z* IV "On Superior

52. We cite this from George Leiner's translations from *CW* 17: *Unpublished Fragments: Summer 1886–Fall 1887* (Stanford, CA: Stanford University Press, forthcoming), which at times differ from our own translation decisions in this and our other volumes, most notably here with respect to *höher*, which we translate as "superior."

Humans" 1–3). Nevertheless, Zarathustra emphasizes, because the very greatest human beings are still failed and half-broken, and because they all contain the rabble within themselves, they are not his true concern. They can only prepare the way, and eventually sacrifice themselves, for the sake of his only true concern, the future superhumans. Here are the two key passages:

> "You may indeed be superior humans, collectively," Zarathustra continued. "But for me — you are not superior and strong enough [. . .]
>
> Nor are you beautiful enough for me and wellborn. I need clean, smooth mirrors for my teachings; on your surfaces my own image is still distorted.
>
> Your shoulders are weighed down by many a burden, many a memory; in your corners many a wicked dwarf crouches. There is hidden rabble in you as well.
>
> And even if you are superior and of a superior kind: much in you is crooked and deformed. There's no smith in the world who could hammer you smooth and straight for me." (*Z* IV "The Welcoming")

> Those who care the most ask today: "how will human beings survive?" But Zarathustra is the only one and the first to ask: "how shall human beings be *overcome*?"
>
> The superhumans are dear to me, *they* are my first and only concern, — and *not* humans [*Der Übermensch liegt mir am Herzen, der ist mein Erstes und Einziges, — und nicht der Mensch*]: not our neighbors, not the poorest people, not those who suffer the most, not the best people —
>
> Oh my brothers, what I am able to love in humans is that they are a passing-over and a passing-away [*Oh meine Brüder, was ich lieben kann am Menschen, das ist, dass er ein Übergang ist und ein Untergang*]. (*Z* IV "On Superior Humans" 3).

Thus, when we read Nietzsche's post-*Zarathustra* remarks about superior individuals like Borgia who actually existed in the past, we should keep in mind his sharp distinction between any such human beings and future superhumans. This sharp distinction applies even to Nietzsche's suggestion in *AC* 4 (see Appendix) that superior human individuals like Borgia may continue to emerge in the future. And it applies as well to his suggestion in the same text that such cases of great success may even consist in whole families (like the Renaissance Borgias), tribes (like the Huns or the Visigoths), or peoples (like the ancient Greeks and Romans). Whether emerging in the future or consisting of more than just a single individual, the bull's-eye will still be human and is therefore excluded from Nietzsche's new and original philosophical concept of superhumans.

Although Nietzsche does not similarly qualify his description in *GM* I 16 (see Appendix) of Napoleon as a synthesis of inhuman and superhuman qualities, he does explicitly introduce him as the most late-born human being (*Mensch*). This careful description should be contrasted with Zarathustra's prevision of a figure who is no longer human (*nicht mehr Mensch*) and who laughs with a laughter that is not human (*das keines Menschen Lachen war*) (*Z* III "On the Vision and Riddle" 2). This description of Napoleon should also be read alongside Zarathustra's crucial claim that a superhuman being has never yet existed (*Niemals noch gab es einen Übermenschen*; *Z* II "On Priests").[53] This is a point that Nietzsche brings up several times

53. Here and below, we follow Nietzsche's interpretive instruction in *GM* II 24–25 and in *EH* that he designed his character Zarathustra's speeches and life story to express important and difficult truths that he himself was not strong or healthy enough to express in his own voice in his later nonfictional works. See chapter 8 of Paul S. Loeb, *The Death of Nietzsche's Zarathustra* (Cambridge: Cambridge University Press, 2010); and Paul S. Loeb, "Ecce Superhomo: How Zarathustra Became What Nietzsche Was Not," in *Nietzsche's "Ecce Homo,"* ed. Duncan Large and Nicholas Martin (Berlin: Walter de Gruyter, forthcoming).

in his preparatory notes (10[37], 10[41], 13[26]). In the immediate context of this claim, Zarathustra concedes to his disciples that great men have certainly existed in the past. But he warns his disciples to free themselves of their influence because, when seen stripped of their moral pretensions, even these greatest of individuals are all-too-human (*allzumenschlich*) and therefore still too closely related to the rabble and the puniest of human beings. This is why Nietzsche has Zarathustra cry out in despair toward the end of the published book:

> I had once seen them both naked, the greatest human beings and the puniest human beings: all too similar to one another, — even the greatest still all too human!
> The greatest all too puny! — This is how I became sick and tired of human beings! (*Z* III "The Convalescent" 2)

Some of Nietzsche's other remarks about Napoleon provide evidence that he includes even him in this observation. For example:

> There are manners of the spirit by which even great spirits betray that they stem from rabble or semi-rabble: — for it is the gait and stride of their thoughts that betray them; they cannot *walk*. Thus, to his deep frustration, Napoleon himself could not walk like a prince and "legitimately" on those occasions when one really must know how, as in great coronation processions and the like: even there he was always merely the lead in a column — proud and hasty at the same time and very self-conscious of it. (*JS* 282)

In this way, then, Nietzsche is actually employing his new and original Zarathustran use of the term *Übermensch* to criticize the historically earlier tradition of using this term to refer to individual human beings who have superior abilities and superior value in relation to most other human beings. Indeed, it is noteworthy that Nietzsche singles out the figure of Napoleon as the best instance his age has to offer of a superior individual who is a kind of superhuman compared to all other human beings. Here Nietzsche lets his readers know that he is inheriting and superseding an earlier Romantic tradition that valorized heroic individuals — especially the contemporaneous Napoleon. In particular, Nietzsche is concerned to appropriate and criticize the language and ideas of two of the most important figures in this earlier tradition: Thomas Carlyle and Johann Wolfgang von Goethe.

The British author Carlyle was best known in Nietzsche's time for his 1841 collection of lectures, *On Heroes, Hero-Worship, and the Heroic in History*. In this book, Carlyle inaugurated what is now called the great man theory of history, which he introduces as follows:

> For, as I take it, Universal History, the history of what man has accomplished in this world, is at bottom the History of the Great Men who have worked here. They were the leaders of men, these great ones; the modellers, patterns, and in a wide sense creators, of whatsoever the general mass of men contrived to do or to attain; all things that we see standing accomplished in the world are properly the outer material result, the practical realization and embodiment, of Thoughts that dwelt in the Great Men sent into the world: the soul of the whole world's history, it may justly be considered, were the history of these.[54]

Having claimed that the history of the world is the biography of great men (p. 13), Carlyle argues that these great men have always been worshipped in the past and that this hero worship is the bedrock of all human life:

> Yes, from Norse Odin to English Samuel Johnson, from the divine Founder of Christianity to the withered Pontiff of Encyclopedism, in all times and places, the Hero has been worshipped. It will ever be so. We all love great men; love, venerate and bow down submissive before great men: nay can

54. Thomas Carlyle, *On Heroes, Hero-Worship, and the Heroic in History* (Berkeley: University of California Press, 1993), 3.

we honestly bow down to anything else? Ah, does not every true man feel that he is himself made higher by doing reverence to what is really above him? No nobler or more blessed feeling dwells in man's heart. And to me it is very cheering to consider that no sceptical logic, or general triviality, insincerity and aridity of any Time and its influences can destroy this noble inborn loyalty and worship that is in man. In times of unbelief, which soon have to become times of revolution, much down-rushing, sorrowful decay and ruin is visible to everybody. For myself in these days, I seem to see in this indestructibility of Hero-worship the everlasting adamant lower than which the confused wreck of revolutionary things cannot fall. The confused wreck of things crumbling and even crashing and tumbling all round us in these revolutionary ages, will get down so far; no farther. It is an eternal corner-stone, from which they can begin to build themselves up again. That man, in some sense or other, worships Heroes; that we all of us reverence and must ever reverence Great Men: this is, to me, the living rock amid all rushings-down whatsoever;—the one fixed point in modern revolutionary history, otherwise as if bottomless and shoreless.[55]

In response to this argument, and also to Carlyle's concluding account of Napoleon as the most recent heroic great man, Nietzsche wrote an extended critique of what he called "the hero-cult and its fanatics" (*Der Heroen-Cultus und seine Fanatiker*). In the final remarks of this critique, Nietzsche associates Napoleon, Carlyle, and Romanticism:

People of this sort lived, for example, around *Napoleon*: indeed, perhaps it was precisely he who introduced into the soul of our century the Romantic prostration before the "genius" and the "hero," a prostration alien to the spirit of the Enlightenment, he of whom a Byron was not ashamed to say, he was a "worm compared with such a being." (The formulas for such prostration were founded by that presumptuous old muddle- and surly-head,

55. Ibid., 14–15.

> Thomas Carlyle, who spent a long life trying to make reason
> romantic for his fellow Englishmen: to no avail!) (*D* 298)

Unlike Carlyle, Nietzsche is not inspired by Napoleon's existence to go along with his century's Romantic idea of worshipping superior individuals. Indeed, this is the whole point of
his new philosophical concept of superhumans, and this is
why, in the passage from *EH* ("Books" 1; see Appendix), Nietzsche dismisses those readers who have recognized Carlyle's "hero
cult" in his word *Übermensch*.[56]

The other crucial figure regarded by Nietzsche as playing a
key role in the earlier Romantic tradition is Goethe. He was
almost universally venerated in Nietzsche's time as the greatest
German poet.[57] It is an interesting fact that Goethe thought
highly of Carlyle and of his hero-worship lectures, whereas
Nietzsche dismissed Carlyle but had the greatest admiration
for Goethe. Indeed, it is obvious that Nietzsche considered
Goethe to be one of the superior individuals (*TI* "Forays" 48–
51). So when Nietzsche writes about Goethe's admiration for
Napoleon, he makes it clear that this is not some kind of prostration or hero worship but rather the kind of respect that one
great man extends another:

> What is certain is that it was not the "Wars of Liberation" that
> caused him to perk up, no more so than the French Revolu-
> tion — no, the event for whose sake he *rethought* his *Faust* and
> in fact the whole problem of being "human" [*das ganze Problem
> "Mensch"*] was the appearance of Napoleon. (*BGE* 244)

56. For a useful discussion of Nietzsche's understanding and criticisms
of Carlyle's lecture series, see William Meakins, "Nietzsche, Carlyle, and
Perfectionism," *Journal of Nietzsche Studies* 45 (2014): 258–78.

57. We use the term "Romantic" in the sense that Nietzsche understood
it. British Germanists and some prominent American Goethe scholars, such
as Jane K. Brown, see Goethe as a Romantic poet. But German Germanists
and some of their American students use Goethe's life as the template for the
literary periodization of his time, whereby he moves from "Storm and Stress"
(*Sturm und Drang*) in his early work through (neo)classical to his status as
one of the great poets of the Western tradition. According to the German
scheme, Goethe rejects both early and late Romanticism as pathological.

And similarly:

> In the midst of an age disposed to unreality, Goethe was a
> convinced realist: he said yes to all that was related to him in
> this respect — he had no greater experience than that *ens
> realissimum* called Napoleon. (*TI* "Forays" 50)

Nevertheless, and this is a point missed by most scholars, it is
Nietzsche's considered view that Goethe, like Napoleon and
like all other great men, was still human-all-too-human and
therefore not so different after all from the puniest of human
beings. Just as Nietzsche ridicules Napoleon's ignoble gait in *JS*
§282, cited above, so too he repeatedly makes fun of Goethe's
penchant for having his heroic figures, such as Werther or Faust,
fall into worshipful Romantic prostration before some puny
embodiment of "the Eternal Feminine" (*das Ewig-Weibliche*; *Z*
II "On Poets"; *BGE* 236). For example:

> This century loves to ascribe to its most intellectual men a
> taste for immature, mentally deficient and modest little girls
> of the people, Faust's taste for Gretchen — this speaks against
> the taste of the century and its most intellectual men. (5[1] 17;
> see also *Z* I "On Child and Marriage")

Hence, Nietzsche explains, Goethe's *Faust*, which is supposed to
be a tragedy of knowledge, actually makes him laugh (3[1] 406):

> *The Faust idea.* — A little seamstress is seduced and made
> unhappy; a great scholar of all four branches of learning is the
> evil-doer. Can such unnatural things happen: No, certainly
> not! Without the assistance of the devil in person, the great
> scholar would not have brought it about. — Is this really
> supposed to be the greatest German "tragic idea," as we hear
> the Germans say? (*WS* 124)

Thus, when Nietzsche deploys his new philosophical concept of
superhumans, we should notice that this is his way of criticiz-
ing and dismissing even the figure of Goethe, who as a young
man loomed so large in the proto-Romantic "Storm and Stress"

movement and whose turn toward classical genres was signaled, in part, by the versification and completion of *Faust* I. What this means more specifically is that Nietzsche intends his new Zarathustran concept as a *criticism* of Goethe's ironic use of the term *Übermensch* in the "study" scene of *Faust* I. Some scholars have argued that Nietzsche's Zarathustran concept of superhumans is a conscious adaptation of Goethe's *Urfaust* invention.[58] But a more careful analysis shows that Nietzsche regards Goethe's concept as applying merely to a superior individual, someone like Borgia or Napoleon or even Goethe himself, who is only a *kind* of superhuman *when compared* to most other human beings. Obviously Goethe wants his readers to marvel at Faust's stupendous abilities and superior value, which is why he has Faust take seriously the Earth Spirit's mocking description of him as a superhuman (*Faust* I:489–90). But Nietzsche points to Goethe's taste in women and his ridiculous "Faust-Idea" as a demonstration of Goethe's own failed and puny human nature and as further proof that even the greatest of human beings who have been called superhuman must now be overcome and superseded by true superhumans.

The evidence we have presented here contradicts in many ways the reading of Nietzsche's term *Übermensch* that was first proposed by Walter Kaufmann in his extremely influential study of Nietzsche's philosophy (first published in 1950).[59] According to Kaufmann, Nietzsche's Zarathustran concept of superhumans is identical to his concept of superior individuals and is best exemplified by the figure of Goethe. But in arguing for this claim, Kaufmann ignores the development in Nietzsche's thinking and interprets the Zarathustran concept by appeal to his earliest writings and to his final writings. Eliding the fact that Nietzsche had not yet conceived his concept of the superhumans, Kaufmann simply identifies it with the idea in *Unfashionable Observations* that the goal of humankind lies in its scattered and accidentally

58. Cf. Adrian Del Caro, "Zarathustra vs. Faust, or Anti-Romantic Rivalry among Superhumans," in *Nietzsche on Art and Life*, ed. Daniel Came (Oxford: Oxford University Press, 2014), 143–62.

59. Kaufmann, *Nietzsche: Philosopher, Psychologist, Antichrist*, 307–16.

emerging highest specimens and single great men (*On the Utility and Liability of History for Life* §9, [*CW* 2, 151]; *Schopenhauer as Educator* §6 [*CW* 2, 215]). And dismissing the important qualifications and distinctions we have summarized above as "mattering little," Kaufmann simply identifies Nietzsche's Zarathustran concept of superhumans with his later discussion in *GM*, *TI*, *AC*, and *EH* (see Appendix) about scattered and accidentally emerging superior human beings (such as Goethe, Napoleon, and Caesar). With these identifications in mind, Kaufmann then offers his translation and interpretation of Nietzsche's Zarathustran use of the term *Übermensch*. According to Kaufmann, it means "overman" in the sense that it refers to a great man like Goethe who has overcome (mastered, sublimated) his animality (his passions, instincts, impulses) and thereby attained self-mastery and become *truly human*. But this interpretation belongs more properly in a discussion of the concept of freedom proposed by Rousseau and Kant. It has nothing to do with Nietzsche's insistence that even the best human beings like Goethe are not good enough and must be superseded by future superhumans.

As a final point for this section, we would like to note that there is some overlap between Nietzsche's supernatural and superior-individual uses of his concept of superhumans. This is because *JS* §143 aims to explain how the invention of superhumans and other supernatural beings was the medium whereby superior individuals were able to express their own idiosyncratic ideals in the social context of a hostile central morality that declared a single human norm for everyone. As Nietzsche writes:

> But beyond oneself and outside, in a distant superworld, one was permitted to see a *plurality of norms*: one god was not the denial or blasphemy against another god! Here for the first time individuals were allowed, here for the first time the rights of individuals were respected. (*JS* 143)

According to Nietzsche's theory, then, supernatural superhumans were actually a projection of superior individuals. When people worshipped these fantastical supernatural figures, they were indirectly worshipping existing human beings in their midst. This is why superior individuals and their superior abilities seemed to acquire a supernatural aura. Nietzsche had already made a similar point in his earlier books about the widespread tendency to attribute a supernatural status to superior individuals (the saint, the genius, the prince) who displayed superhuman (*übermenschlich*) qualities (*HAH* I 143, 164, 441, 461; *WS* 73, 190).

The Superior-Species Use

Nietzsche publicly unveiled his new and original concept of superhumans in August 1883 in the preface to part I of *Z*. He published this part on its own before he published parts II and III in late 1883 and 1884, respectively, and before he published the first collected edition of parts I–III in 1886. He had a private printing of part IV distributed to a select group of individuals in 1885 (which he later attempted to recall), but he never published this part IV for the public and he did not include it in the 1886 collected edition of the book.[60]

At the start of the narrative in this preface, Zarathustra descends from his mountain cave in order to impart the wisdom he has gathered in solitude for the past ten years. On the

60. In his influential commentary on *Z*, *Nietzsche's Teaching* (New Haven, CT: Yale University Press, 1986), 19–22, 181, 204, 257–58, Laurence Lampert argues that Zarathustra abandons his *Übermensch* teaching as the narrative of *Z* progresses and that this teaching plays no role in Nietzsche's post-*Zarathustra* works. But Lampert draws a mistaken contrast between the introductory "linear" teaching of superhumans and the final "circular" teaching of eternal recurrence and fails to understand Nietzsche's account of the internal coherence between these two teachings. He also ignores important textual evidence from part IV of *Z* (which he calls an "afterthought") and from later texts such as *GM* (II:12, 16, 24–25) and *EH* ("Books" Z6, Z8, "Destiny" 5). See Loeb, *The Death of Nietzsche's Zarathustra*, 203–6 and chap. 8.

way down, he encounters a hermit saint, and he is surprised
to learn that the hermit hasn't yet heard the news that God
is dead. Immediately following this important revelation, Zarathustra proceeds to the town marketplace so as to begin his
public teaching. In the first sentence of his first speech, Zarathustra announces his new doctrine of superhumans. We have
included the original German passages here, and in a few places
below, so that readers can follow Nietzsche's innovations:

Ich lehre euch den Übermenschen.
Der Mensch ist Etwas, das
überwunden werden soll. Was
habt ihr gethan, ihn zu
überwinden?

    Alle Wesen bisher schufen
etwas über sich hinaus: und ihr
wollt die Ebbe dieser grossen
Flut sein und lieber noch zum
Tiere zurückgehn, als den
Menschen überwinden?

    Was ist der Affe für den
Menschen? Ein Gelächter oder
eine schmerzliche Scham. Und
ebendas soll der Mensch für den
Übermenschen sein: ein Gelächter
oder eine schmerzliche Scham.

    Ihr habt den Weg vom
Wurme zum Menschen
gemacht, und Vieles ist in euch
noch Wurm. Einst wart ihr
Affen, und auch jetzt ist der
Mensch mehr Affe, als irgend
ein Affe.

I teach you about the superhumans.
Humans are something that
must be overcome. What
have you done to overcome
them?

    All creatures so far have
created something beyond themselves: and you want to be the ebb
of this great flood and would even
prefer to go back to being animals
than to overcome humans?

    What are apes to humans?
A laughing stock or a painful
embarrassment. And that is
precisely what humans will be to
superhumans: a laughing stock
or a painful embarrassment.

    You have made your way from
worms to humans, and much in
you is still worm. Once you were
apes, and even now humans are
more ape than any apes. (*Z* I
"Preface" 3; see also 4[181] and 5[1]
255 in this volume)

There are many clear indications in this key opening passage
that Nietzsche is using the term *Übermenschen* to mean a new

and future species that will be superior to the human species. He compares superhumans to the human species as well as to two animal species, apes and worms. Just as humans have made their way from apes and worms, so, too, superhumans might make their way from humans. Just as all creatures so far have created something beyond themselves, so, too, humans should aim to create something beyond themselves, namely, superhumans. If they do not choose this goal or if they do not succeed in this goal, humans will be the ebb in the great flood of creation, and they will go back to being animals. In order to achieve this goal, humans will have to overcome themselves. At this future point in time, superhumans will be superior to humans, just as humans are now superior to the two animal species, apes and worms. Superhumans will regard humans as a laughingstock or a painful embarrassment, just as humans (who are even now more ape than any apes) regard apes in this way.

Although this passage does not explicitly refer to superhumans as a species (in the sense that humans, apes, or worms are usually characterized as species), there is a place later in the book where Zarathustra again warns his disciples about the possibility that humans might go back to being animals. He calls this potential movement "degeneration" (*Entartung*) — a term that for him signifies the stagnation and decay of the species (*Art*). By contrast, he says, he is concerned to teach them about an upward movement from species (*Art*) to super-species (*Über-Art*) — an obvious reference back to his introductory teaching of an upward movement from humans to superhumans:

> Tell me, my brothers: what do we regard as bad and most bad? Is it not *degeneration*? — And where the bestowing soul is lacking we always infer degeneration.
>
> Upward goes our way, from species over to super-species. (*Z* I "On the Virtue of Gift-Giving" I)

Even more explicitly, Nietzsche wrote the following preparatory note in which he envisioned the future coexistence of the
human species with a new godlike superhuman species. Here
he calls the superhumans a species (*Art*) in the same sense that
humans are a species:

Meine Forderung: Wesen
hervorzubringen, welche über
der ganzen Gattung "Mensch"
erhaben dastehen: und diesem
Ziele sich und "die Nächsten"
zu opfern.

Die bisherige Moral hatte
ihre Grenze innerhalb der
Gattung: alle bisherigen Moralen
waren nützlich, um der Gattung
zuerst unbedingte Haltbarkeit zu
geben: *wenn* diese erreicht ist,
kann das Ziel höher genommen
werden.

Die *eine* Bewegung ist
unbedingt: die Nivellirung der
Menschheit, große Ameisen-
Bauten usw. (Dühring zu
charakterisiren als außerorden-
tlich ärmlich und typisch-*gering*,
trotz seinen pathetischen Worten)

Die *andere* Bewegung: meine
Bewegung: ist umgekehrt die
Verschärfung aller Gegensätze
und Klüfte, Beseitigung
der Gleichheit, das Schaffen
Über-Mächtiger.

Jene erzeugt den letzten
Menschen. *Meine* Bewegung den
Übermenschen.

Es ist *durchaus* **nicht** das
Ziel, die letzteren als die Herren
der Ersteren aufzufassen:

My demand: to produce
beings who stand sublimely
above the entire species "human
being": and who sacrifice
themselves and "their neighbors"
for this goal.

Morality up to now has had
its boundaries dictated by the
species: all moralities up to now
were useful for establishing *first
and foremost* the unconditional
stability of the species: *when* this
has been achieved, the goal can
be set higher.

The *one* movement is
unconditional: the leveling of
humankind, giant ant hills etc.
(Dühring to be characterized as
extraordinarily impoverished
and typically *narrow*, despite his
lofty words)

The *other* movement: my
movement: is conversely the
intensification of all oppositions
and divisions, elimination of
equality, the creation of the
superpowerful.

The *former* generates last
humans. *My* movement,
superhumans.

The goal is **not** *at all* to
conceive of the latter as the
masters of the former: but

sondern: es sollen zwei Arten neben einander bestehen — möglichst getrennt; *die eine wie die epikurischen Götter, sich um die andere nicht kümmernd.*

rather: the two species should exist alongside one another — as segregated as possible; *the one, like the Epicurean gods, having no concern for the other.* (7[21]; see also 16[85], 35[73])

In this passage, Nietzsche distinguishes between two kinds of movement available to the still-fluid and as-yet-indeterminate human species (*BGE* 62; *GM* III 13). The first is a leveling and equalizing movement driven by human herd instincts that aim to stabilize and fix the human species as much as possible. The endpoint of this movement will be the "last humans" (*der letzte Mensch*) — meaning that humans will stop evolving because there will no longer be any chaos left within the species driving it to create something beyond itself (*Z* I "Preface" 3). Humans will have gone back to being animals because they will have the same fixed species nature as all other extant animal species that no longer aim at anything beyond their own herd survival and herd reproduction. In a preparatory note, Nietzsche explains this movement as a decision on the part of humans to come to a standstill as super-apes and as an image of the last eternal humans: "Der Mensch bestimmt stehen zu bleiben, als der *Überaffe*, Bild des letzten Menschen, der der ewige ist" (4[163]). It is noteworthy that he describes the no-longer-evolving humans as "super-apes" — thus suggesting again that the further evolution of humans will create a new species, the superhumans. This other movement is the one Nietzsche advocates on behalf of superior individuals like himself who still feel this chaos within themselves and therefore aim to destabilize the species as much as possible by intensifying any existing hostilities, inequalities, and power struggles (see also *Z* II "On Tarantulas"). This movement will be upward in the sense of producing superpowerful *human* beings who will stand above the whole human species and sacrifice themselves and others for the sake of creating a new and superior, godlike species, the *superhumans*.

Although Nietzsche draws an analogy here between superhumans and Epicurean gods, this passage and others like it show that Nietzsche's Zarathustran concept of superhumans has nothing in common with his earlier philological concept of supernatural superhumans. Indeed, as we have seen, Nietzsche contrasts these two concepts within the text of *Z*. In the chapter on poets, Zarathustra ridicules the poetic invention of fantastic superhuman beings living in castles on the clouds. But in this preface he articulates a completely immanent and naturalistic concept of superhumans. He has Zarathustra teach that superhumans will really exist in the future on the actual earth and that they will represent a further and superior stage in the development that has already taken place on the way from actually existing animal species like worms and apes to the actually existing human species.

It is also significant that Nietzsche introduces his new concept of superhumans with Zarathustra's revelation that God is dead. Later in *Z* Nietzsche extends this idea to all gods and presumably to all the supernatural entities that were associated with divinity in *JS* §143:

> "All gods are dead: now we want superhumans to live." [*"Todt sind alle Götter: nun wollen wir, dass der Übermensch lebe."*] (*Z* I "On the Virtue of Gift-Giving" 3; see also *Z* IV "On Superior Humans" 2)

Thus, according to Nietzsche, the end of all belief in divinity and in supernatural superhumans is a precondition for the emergence of a new belief in the possibility of humans overcoming themselves and creating a superior species of superhumans. In an especially helpful later passage, Nietzsche contrasts humanity's very real ability to conceive and create this new species with the impossible task of conceiving and creating divinity:

Einst sagte man Gott, wenn man auf ferne Meere blickte; nun aber lehrte ich euch sagen: Übermensch.	People used to say God when they gazed out over distant seas; yet now I have taught you to say: superhumans.

Gott ist eine Muthmaassung; aber ich will, dass euer Muthmaassen nicht weiter reiche, als euer schaffender Wille.

God is a conjecture; but I don't want your conjecturing to extend further than your creating will.

Könntet ihr einen Gott *schaffen*? — So schweigt mir doch von allen Göttern! Wohl aber könntet ihr den Übermenschen schaffen.

Could you *create* a god? — Then don't you dare speak to me of any gods! But you could certainly create superhumans.

Nicht ihr vielleicht selber, meine Brüder! Aber zu Vätern und Vorfahren könntet ihr euch umschaffen des Übermenschen: und Diess sei euer bestes Schaffen! —

Perhaps not you yourselves, my brothers! But you could recreate yourselves into fathers and forefathers of superhumans: and let this be your best creating! —

Gott ist eine Muthmaassung: aber ich will, dass euer Muthmaassen begrenzt sei in der Denkbarkeit.

God is a conjecture: but I want your conjecturing to be limited to what is conceivable.

Könntet ihr einen Gott *denken*? — Aber diess bedeute euch Wille zur Wahrheit, dass Alles verwandelt werde in Menschen-Denkbares, Menschen-Sichtbares, Menschen-Fühlbares! Eure eignen Sinne sollt ihr zu Ende denken!

Could you *conceive* a god? — But this is what the will to truth should mean to you, that everything be transformed into what is humanly conceivable, humanly visible, humanly tangible! You should think your own senses all the way through to their conclusion! (*Z* II "Upon the Blessed Isles")

Nietzsche comments here that people used to dream about impossible supernatural beings. But now they need to be taught to think realistically about how they can re-create themselves into ancestors of a future superhuman species. In a couple of brief preparatory notes, he goes further than this and suggests that previous human dreams of supernatural beings were actually a product of humankind's dissatisfaction with itself and of its resulting desire to create a superior species of superhumans:

Unsere Verachtung des M⟨enschen⟩ trieb uns hinter die Sterne. Religion, Metaphysik, als Symptom einer Begierde, den Übermenschen zu schaffen.	Our contempt for h⟨umans⟩ drove us beyond the stars. Religion, metaphysics, as symptom of a desire to create superhumans. (4[214])
Ich betrachte alle metaphysischen und religiösen Denkweisen als Folge einer Unzufriedenheit am Menschen eines Triebes nach einer höheren, *übermenschlichen* Zukunft — nur daß die Menschen sich in's Jenseits flüchten wollten: statt an der Zukunft zu bauen. Ein Mißverständniß der höheren Naturen, die am häßlichen Bilde des Menschen leiden.	I regard all metaphysical and religious modes of thought as results of a dissatisfaction with humans, of a drive for a superior, *superhuman* future — except that humans wanted to flee into the beyond: instead of building on the future. A misunderstanding on the part of superior natures who suffer on account of the ugly image of human beings. (*CW* 11, 27[74])

These unpublished fragments are especially interesting because they offer Nietzsche's background thinking when he has Zarathustra declare, right after announcing his new teaching, that his listeners should want superhumans to be the meaning of the earth:

> I implore you, my brothers, *remain faithful to the earth* and do not believe those who speak to you of extraterrestrial hopes! [. . .]
> I love those who do not first seek behind the stars for a reason to perish and be a sacrifice: who instead sacrifice themselves for the earth, so that the earth may one day belong to superhumans [*dass die Erde einst der Übermenschen werde*]. (*Z* I "Preface" 3–4; cf. also *Z* I "On the Virtue of Gift-Giving" 2 and 5[17])

These collected passages also show that Nietzsche's new Zarathustran concept of superhumans has nothing to do with the Romantic concept of superior individuals. Whereas the former is entirely directed toward the far future, the latter is inspired by the historical past. Whereas the former envisions something that has never yet existed, the latter idolizes famous instances of past existence. And whereas the former imagines a new species that will be superior to all human beings, the latter glorifies the greatest human specimens, who are nevertheless still puny by virtue of being human. Again, Nietzsche contrasts these two concepts within the text of *Z*.

Niemals noch gab es einen Übermenschen. Nackt sah ich Beide, den grössten und den kleinsten Menschen: —

Allzuähnlich sind sie noch einander. Wahrlich, auch den Grössten fand ich — allzumenschlich!

A superhuman being has never yet existed. I saw both naked, the greatest and the puniest human beings: —

They are all too similar to one another. Truly, I found even the greatest — all too human! (*Z* II "On Priests")

Ihr höchsten Menschen, denen mein Auge begegnete! das ist mein Zweifel an euch und mein heimliches Lachen: ich rathe, ihr würdet meinen Übermenschen — Teufel heissen!

Ach, ich ward dieser Höchsten und Besten müde: aus ihrer "Höhe" verlangte mich hinauf, hinaus, hinweg zu dem Übermenschen!

Ein Grausen überfiel mich, als ich diese Besten nackend sah: da wuchsen mir die Flügel, fortzuschweben in ferne Zukünfte.

In fernere Zukünfte, in südlichere Süden, als je ein Bildner träumte: dorthin, wo Götter sich aller Kleider schämen!

You most superior human beings whom I have ever laid eyes on! this is my doubt about you and my secret laughter: I suspect you would call my superhumans — devils!

Oh, I became weary of these most superior and best human beings: from their "pinnacle" I was compelled upward, outward, and away to superhumans!

I was overcome with dread when I saw these best human beings naked: then I sprouted wings to soar away into distant futures.

Into more distant futures, into more southern souths than any artist ever dreamed: there, where gods are ashamed of all clothing! (*Z* II "On Human Prudence")

In part IV, Nietzsche depicts Zarathustra's interactions with a collection of diverse superior men who are modeled on actual men who were famous during Nietzsche's time, some of whom played an important role in his own development: Napoleon (the kings), Tolstoy (the voluntary beggar), Schopenhauer (the soothsayer), Wagner (the sorcerer), Paul Rée (the leech-brain expert), Lord Byron (the shadow), and David Strauss (the ugliest man). Here Nietzsche offers an extensive catalogue of all the various ways in which these superior men are lacking because aspects of them still belong to the herd, the mob, and the rabble (as symbolized by their long-eared companion, the ass). In his speech welcoming these superior men to his mountain cave, Zarathustra tells them that they are not strong, healthy, beautiful, or wellborn enough for him and that they are not the ones to whom his heritage and name belong. Only his chosen disciples, the ones he calls his children, the ones who will become ancestors of the superhumans, the ones he calls his new beautiful species (*meine neue schöne Art*), are entitled to his name and his heritage (*Z* IV "The Welcoming"). Similarly, in his speech to the assembled superior men about his concept of superior human beings, Zarathustra urges them to help him create superhumans, since these are his first and only concern — not humans, not even the very best among them (*Z* IV "On Superior Humans" 1–2).

In these passages, then, Nietzsche invents a new use for the term *Übermensch* that had never before appeared in his own writings or in the history of German thought. Looking back at his introduction of this new use in part I of *Z*, it is not difficult to guess the stimulus for this invention. As commentators have noted from the start, what is most striking about this introduction is Nietzsche's clear and direct allusion to Darwinism, which he later calls "the last great scientific movement" (*JS* 357).[61]

61. For a useful survey of Nietzsche's engagement with Darwinism, see Thomas Brobjer, *Nietzsche and the "English": The Influence of British and American Thinking on His Philosophy* (New York: Humanity Books, 2008), 235–71.

Most obviously, Nietzsche writes that humans were once apes and that as a consequence they now regard apes with a feeling of painful embarrassment. This is the most famous image associated with Darwinism at the time Nietzsche was writing. Ten years earlier, in his first published text after *BT,* Nietzsche had alluded to this image in his polemical confrontation with David Friedrich Strauss's influential book *The Old Faith and the New: A Confession.*[62] Although Strauss claimed to replace Christianity with Darwinism, Nietzsche argued that he refused to acknowledge the radical consequences of Darwinism. Referring to Strauss's chapter titled "Apes and Humans: Darwin on the Descent of Humans from Apes" ("Affe und Mensch: Darwin über die Affenabstammung des Menschen"), Nietzsche wrote:

> With a certain crude contentment [Strauss] covers himself with the shaggy cloak of our ape-genealogists and praises Darwin as one of humankind's greatest benefactors . . . (*HL* 7, *CW* 2, 39, lines 1-4)

In later years, Nietzsche encountered this same famous image in some of his most closely studied readings. For example, his philosophical partner, Paul Rée, had singled out this image in his brief introduction to *The Origin of Moral Feelings.*[63] After writing that Darwin's discovery of the theory of evolution now enabled us to trace moral phenomena back to natural causes, Rée summarized this theory in a single proposition:

> This natural explanation is fundamentally based on the proposition: The higher animals have evolved from the lower by means of natural selection, humans from apes.

Writing during his stay with Rée in Sorrento, Nietzsche includes the following observation in *HAH*. Here Nietzsche anticipates

62. David Friedrich Strauss, *Der Alte und der Neue Glaube: Ein Bekenntnis* (Leipzig: S. Hirzel, 1872).

63. Paul Rée, *Der Ursprung der moralischen Empfindungen* (Chemnitz: Ernst Schmeitzner, 1877).

Zarathustra's claim that humans once were apes and might even return to being animals — unless they act to avoid this fate:

> The whole of humanity is perhaps only a developmental phase of a certain animal species of limited duration: so that human beings came from apes and will again become apes, while there is nobody who takes any interest whatsoever in this wonderful comic ending [. . .] the decline of universal world culture might some day lead to an even more heightened repulsiveness and eventual bestialization of humanity to the point of apishness. — Precisely because we can envision this perspective, we are perhaps in a position to prevent the future from reaching such an end. (*HAH* 247)

Finally, writing just a few years later, Nietzsche anticipates Zarathustra's remark that humans feel painful embarrassment when confronted with the news of their evolutionary origins in apes and other animals. But he is much less optimistic about the possibility of humans achieving any kind of grandeur in their evolutionary future:

> *The new fundamental feeling: our permanent transitoriness.* — Formerly one tried to get a feel for the majesty of human beings by pointing backward toward their divine descent: this has now become a forbidden path, because before its gate stands the ape along with other heinous beasts, grinning knowingly as if to say: no farther here in this direction. So, one has a go of it now from the opposite direction: the path humanity *pursues* shall serve as proof of its majesty and kinship to God. Alas, this too leads nowhere! At the end of this path stands the funeral urn of the *last* human and gravedigger (with the inscription "*nihil humani a me alienum puto*"). However high humanity may have evolved — and perhaps at the end it will be standing even lower than at the beginning! — there is in store for humanity no more a transformation into a higher order than for the ant and the earwigs, which, at the end of their "earthly days," will not

ascend to kinship with God and eternal life. The Becoming drags the Has Been along behind it: why should an exception to this eternal spectacle be made for some little planet and again for some little species on it! Away with such sentimentalities! (*D* 49)

On a more abstract level, Nietzsche's introduction of his new concept of superhumans at the start of part I of *Z* includes several background principles that he regards as advances made by the Darwinist scientific movement:

- No living species, not even the human species, has been divinely created.

- No living species, not even the human species, is eternal or immutable.

- Instead, all living species, including the human species, are a product of natural evolution.

- All living species, including the human species, are transitory, impermanent, and subject to flux. They have an evolutionary origin, are capable of evolutionary change, and may be subject to evolutionary extinction.

- All living species, including the human species, are interrelated and evolutionarily descended from other living species.

- The human species is an animal species.

- The human species is evolutionarily descended from an ancestor that is shared by the simpler and more primitive ape species. Therefore, the human species shares traits with the ape species.

- In terms of geological chronology, all the animal species, including the human species, share evolutionary ancestors with far simpler and more primitive animal species, such as invertebrate animal species like the worm. Therefore, the human species shares traits with the worm species.

Clearly, then, Nietzsche's invention of a new philosophical concept of superhumans was made possible by his sympathetic
reception of the contemporaneous Darwinist movement. Because
of this movement, he was able to conceive the idea that humans
might be capable of further evolution and even create a better
species.[64]

However, this doesn't mean that Nietzsche's new concept
is Darwinist. In fact, when reviewing his accomplishments
in *EH*, Nietzsche singles out for scorn the "learned cattle"
who suspect him of Darwinism on account of his concept of
superhumans (*EH* "Books" 1; see Appendix). The reason for
this is, again, easy to find in his introduction of this concept in
part I of *Z*.[65] For nowhere here does Nietzsche mention Darwin's theory, cited above by Paul Rée, that natural selection is
the means whereby species evolve. Instead, Zarathustra says
that all living creatures so far, except humans, have created
something beyond themselves and that they have done so by
overcoming themselves. Whereas all other living creatures are
clearly exceeded by humans, humans are not exceeded by anything else on earth (*Z* III "On Old and New Tablets" 23). So in

64. Nevertheless, there are scholars who write about the topic of Nietzsche and Darwinism but continue to interpret the *Übermensch* as a kind of
superior (male) individual. Cf. Dirk R. Johnson, *Nietzsche's Anti-Darwinism*
(Cambridge: Cambridge University Press, 2010), 57–60, 64–66, 77; John
Richardson, *Nietzsche's New Darwinism* (Oxford: Oxford University Press,
2004), 209.

65. In his commentary, Kaufmann acknowledges "the plain fact" that,
despite Nietzsche's remark in *EH*, his introduction of Zarathustra's
Übermensch teaching invites a Darwinist interpretation (*Nietzsche: Philosopher, Psychologist, Antichrist*, 311–13). But instead of exploring this connection further, Kaufmann resorts to Nietzsche's much earlier text, *UO*, in order to claim that this teaching concerns only his admiration for superior
individuals like Goethe. In an especially far-fetched exegetical argument,
Kaufmann claims that the reason Nietzsche dismissed the Darwinist interpretation is that he expected his readers to construe Zarathustra's simile of
the ape by recalling his much earlier remark that "the philosophers, artists,
and saints" are "truly human beings and no-longer-animals" (*SE* 5).

order for humans to create something that exceeds them, that is, the superhumans, they will have to overcome themselves.

Here Nietzsche anticipates the new teaching that Zarathustra will unveil in part II of the book, in the key chapter titled "On Self-Overcoming." In this chapter, Nietzsche simply dismisses what was then the most famous aspect of Darwin's theory of natural selection, indeed the aspect mentioned in the title of his book — namely, his doctrine of the struggle for existence or the struggle for life (*Kampf um's Dasein, Kampf um's Leben*).[66] He then replaces it with his own new doctrine of the struggle for power:

> "He who shot at the truth with the phrase 'will to existence' certainly did not hit it: this will — does not exist!
>
> "For: that which is not cannot will; yet what is in existence, how could this still will to exist!
>
> "Only where there is life, is there also will: but not will to live, instead — thus I teach you — will to power
>
> "Much is esteemed more highly by the living than life itself; yet out of esteeming itself there speaks — the will to power!" (See also *BGE* 13; *JS* 349; *TI* "Forays" 14)

In this speech, Nietzsche argues against Darwin that living creatures do not compete for survival; they do so in order to gain power. But this raises the question as to how Nietzsche can offer an alternative naturalistic explanation of the newly demonstrated fact that species evolve. In Darwin's view, the struggle for existence plays an essential role. Those living creatures whose randomly acquired heritable variations do not offer them an advantage in adapting to their environment will lose this struggle against their competitors and will *be selected* out of existence — thus leaving their competitors to flourish and evolve. For Nietzsche, however, the answer lies in his claim that living

66. Charles Darwin, *On the Origin of Species by Means of Natural Selection, or the Preservation of Favored Races in the Struggle for Life* (London: John Murray, 1859).

creatures value power more than survival. This means that they are even willing to risk their survival and *select themselves* out of existence, if this will make them feel more powerful. Nietzsche calls this process "life's self-overcoming":

> Wherever I found living creatures, there I found will to power; and even in the will of those serving I found the will to be master.
>
> That the weaker should serve the stronger, of this they are persuaded by their will, which wants to be master over what is weaker still: this is the one pleasure they cannot renounce.
>
> And just as the lesser surrender to the greater, in order that they may take pleasure in their power over the least: in this way even the greatest may still surrender and for the sake of power wager — life itself [. . .]
>
> The surrender of the greatest is this, that there is risk and danger and a death-defying roll of the dice [. . .]
>
> And life itself told me this secret. "Behold," it spoke, "I am that *which must always overcome itself.*
>
> "Of course you call it will to reproduce or drive to a purpose, to something higher, more distant, more manifold: but all this is one, and one secret.
>
> "I will rather perish than renounce this one thing; and truly, wherever there is downfall and the falling of leaves, behold, there life sacrifices itself — for power!" (*Z* II "On Self-Overcoming")

It is important to notice that Nietzsche's argument here focuses only on those living creatures that are the most powerful and whose dominance has left them no viable competitors in the universal struggle for power. But they want to feel more power still, and so they are driven to create something greater beyond themselves, that is, a future species that will be much more powerful than they are. They must therefore breed stronger offspring and then select themselves out of existence by seeking the greatest risks and dangers — thus leaving their descendants to flourish and repeat the same cycle until eventually a new species has emerged. In this way, they are able to gain a pleasurable feeling that their power extends far beyond the limits of their own short lives and their current sphere of control.

In the preface to part I of *Zarathustra*, published twenty-four years after the appearance of Darwin's *On the Origin of Species*, Nietzsche has his protagonist announce to humans that it is time for them to set a goal and plant the seed of their highest hope. This is because they have now attained their state of maximum power and no longer have any viable competitors on earth. As Zarathustra tells the superior men: "What is farthest, deepest, highest to the stars in humans, their monstrous power [*Des Menschen Fernstes, Tiefstes, Sternen-Höchstes, seine ungeheure Kraft*]" (*Z* IV "On Superior Humans" 15). But they still have the drive for more power, or as Zarathustra puts it in more poetic terms: their soil is still rich enough to grow the tallest tree; the string of their bow is still tense enough to launch the arrow of their longing beyond the human; they still have enough chaos within them to give birth to a dancing star; and their cloud is still dark enough to discharge a bolt of lightning. According to Nietzsche, what will motivate the most powerful human beings into setting this goal is their dissatisfaction with humankind in general and even with themselves. So Zarathustra encourages the most powerful human beings to intensify their feelings of self-contempt as much as possible. First, he asks them to construct as their greatest experience the hour in which they feel contempt for all those aspects of themselves that they have previously valued: their happiness, reason, virtue, justice, and compassion. All of these should now be regarded as poverty, filth, and wretched contentment. Second, in a long passage modeled on the Bible's Sermon on the Mount, Zarathustra asks the most powerful human beings to convert their intensified feelings of self-contempt into an overwhelming desire to perish and to sacrifice themselves for the sake of superhumans. And finally, recognizing that his recently educated audience may now feel too proud to accept his first two lessons, Zarathustra describes for them the most contemptible kind of humans, the future last humans, those whose will to power has declined to the point where they are no longer able to feel any self-contempt, where they merely want to live as long and as contentedly as possible, and where they merely blink at the idea of creating something beyond themselves.

Nietzsche doesn't specifically mention the selective-breeding aspect of his evolution theory in the "Preface" or in the "On Self-Overcoming" chapter of *Z*. Instead, he dwells on this aspect when applying his theory to the human species in the rest of the book and in his preparatory notes: "the humans who were overcome were themselves the fathers of superhumans [*der überwundene Mensch selber war der Vater des Übermenschen*]" (18[56]; cf. also 15[4], 16[86]). Speaking to his chosen disciples, who have been repeatedly instructed that humans must be overcome, Zarathustra teaches them to think of love, marriage, and children as necessary steps on their way to becoming ancestors of superhumans. Here are the relevant passages:

Bitterniss ist im Kelch auch der besten Liebe: so macht sie Sehnsucht zum Übermenschen, so macht sie Durst dir, dem Schaffenden!

Durst dem Schaffenden, Pfeil und Sehnsucht zum Über- menschen: sprich, mein Bruder, ist diess dein Wille zur Ehe?

Heilig heisst mir solch ein Wille und solche Ehe. —

There is bitterness in the cup of even the best love: thus it causes longing in you for super- humans, thus it causes thirst in you, the one who creates!

Thirst of the one who creates, arrow and longing for superhu- mans: speak, my brother, is this your will to marriage?

Such a will and such a marriage, I call these holy. — (*Z* I "On Child and Marriage")

Also rathe ich allen Redlichen; und was wäre denn meine Liebe zum Übermenschen und zu Allem, was kommen soll, wenn ich anders riethe und redete!

Thus I counsel all honest people; and what then would my love for superhumans be, and for all that is to come, if I counseled and spoke otherwise!

Nicht nur fort euch zu pflanzen, sondern *hinauf* — dazu, oh meine Brüder, helfe euch der Garten der Ehe!	Not only to propagate yourselves further, but rather *upward* — oh my brothers, may the garden of marriage help you in this! (*Z* III "On Old and New Tablets" 24)
Der Strahl eines Sternes glänze in eurer Liebe! Eure Hoffnung heisse: "möge ich den Übermenschen gebären!"	Let the ray of a star shine in your love! Let your hope be called: "may I give birth to superhumans!" (*Z* I "On Little Women, Old and Young"; see also 4[100])
Ihr Einsamen von heute, ihr Ausscheidenden, ihr sollt einst ein Volk sein: aus euch, die ihr euch selber auswähltet, soll ein auserwähltes Volk erwachsen: — und aus ihm der Übermensch.	You solitary ones of today, you withdrawing ones, one day you shall be a people: from you who have chosen yourselves a chosen people shall grow: — and from them the superhumans. (*Z* I "On the Virtue of Gift-Giving" 2)

Many scholars have criticized Nietzsche for not understanding Darwin's theory of evolution, or for offering flawed arguments against this theory, or for proposing an implausible alternative to this theory.[67] But they don't really investigate his new Zarathustran concept of superhumans as a superior species, and they don't see how this concept was his first and most important public response to Darwin's theory. This concept would not have been possible without Darwin's destruction of previous theologically based theories of eternal and immutable species. It is true, of course, that in Darwin's account of environmentally adaptive fitness there is no room for the idea of superior and inferior species. But this point is also the inspiration for Nietzsche's rejection of the previous theologically based consensus that humankind is the peak of evolution (*AC* 14). By

67. Cf. Gregory Moore, *Nietzsche, Biology and Metaphor* (Cambridge: Cambridge University Press, 2002), 21–55.

arguing against Darwin that living creatures struggle for power instead of survival, Nietzsche is able to envision a species that will be superior to humankind because it will be more powerful. He is also able to modify Darwin's theory that species evolve through natural selection with his claim that supremely dominant species may risk their survival and select themselves out of existence for the sake of obtaining still greater power. And whereas Darwin often depicts nature as a kind of agent of artificial selection, Nietzsche locates this agency in the individual members of these supremely dominant species as they aim to extend their power through their artificially selected progeny.

Because Nietzsche claims that his theory of evolution can explain everything that Darwin's theory explains (*BGE* 13), as well as cases of self-sacrificing organisms that Darwin had trouble explaining, critics might want to respond that he is offering the wrong *kind* of explanation.[68] In particular, they might concede that Nietzsche's theory of evolution through self-overcoming and artificial selection could be a plausible account of how human beings would choose to create a superior species. However, because it appears to attribute purposive long-term planning to all living creatures, Nietzsche's theory would seem to be nothing more than an anthropomorphic projection onto nature. Nietzsche's rebuttal to this serious charge would explain how he is actually following Darwin in offering a strictly naturalistic account of future human evolution. He is not imbuing nature with mind but rather translating the human mind back into nature.[69] Just as Darwin proposes that all seemingly species-specific human behavior can be explained in terms of instincts that are shared with all other animal species, so too Nietzsche argues that the human longing to create superhumans

68. See Darwin's famous discussion of eusocial insects in chapter 7 of *The Origin of Species*: "I confine myself to one special difficulty, which at first appeared to me insuperable, and actually fatal to my whole theory."

69. See Paul S. Loeb, "Nietzsche's Place in the Aristotelian History of Philosophy," in *Nietzsche and the Philosophers*, ed. Mark Conard (New York: Routledge, 2017), 9–39.

should be explained in terms of an unconscious and irrational drive for power that they share with all other living creatures. This is why, for example, Nietzsche chooses the zoological language of "breeding" (*Züchtung*) to describe the human creation of superhumans. Indeed, he argues in his later works, it was actually Darwin who anthropomorphically projected into nature the struggle for existence that permeated his own Malthusian milieu of restricted will to power, overpopulation, and scarce resources (*JS* 349; *TI* "Forays" 14).[70]

Conclusion

Our goal in this Afterword has been to offer some helpful advice on Nietzsche's writing and philosophy in his 1882–84 notes. This advice is intended for English-speaking readers who are not fluent in German and are obliged to accept the expertise and wisdom of his translators. In terms of Nietzsche's writing, we have aimed to show in more detail than usual how he used the German language and how translators like us convert this stylistically complex and innovative usage into an accurate and readable English. We hope to have communicated the many complicated issues that any translator of Nietzsche must take into account and also to have demonstrated, through summary and examples, the principles that underlie our approach. In terms of his philosophy, we have concentrated on Nietzsche's invention in these notes of a new use for the German term *Übermensch*. Walter Kaufmann's vastly influential translations

70. A separate interpretive question concerns Nietzsche's view that no superhumans have ever existed despite the fact that human beings have always been engaged in practices of selective breeding. Why does Nietzsche think that this same practice, along with a focus on self-overcoming, should now lead to the creation of a superhuman species? The answer to this important question lies in Nietzsche's emphasis on Zarathustra's new teaching of eternal recurrence. See chapters 7 and 8 of Loeb, *The Death of Nietzsche's Zarathustra*; and Paul S. Loeb, "Nietzsche's Transhumanism: Evolution and Eternal Recurrence," in *Nietzsche and Transhumanism: Precursor or Enemy*, ed. Yunus Tuncel (Newcastle, UK: Cambridge Scholars, 2017), 83–100.

and interpretations have led generations of translators and readers to suppose that Nietzsche's new use of this term referred merely to his admiration for extraordinary human individuals like Napoleon and Goethe. But we have argued here that close attention to the linguistic, textual, and philosophical context of Nietzsche's new use of the term *Übermensch* shows that he was inspired by Darwin's discoveries to conceive of the idea that human beings might be driven by their tremendous will to power into creating a superior species that would relate to all human beings, no matter how extraordinary, in the same way that humans now relate to apes.

Appendix

Appearances of the term *Übermensch* in Nietzsche's published works following the publication of *Thus Spoke Zarathustra*

Like a final sign pointing to the *other* way Napoleon appeared, the most singular and late-born human being [*Mensch*] there ever was, and in him the incarnate problem of the *noble ideal in itself* — and consider well *what* kind of problem it is: Napoleon, this synthesis of an *inhuman* and a *superhuman* [*diese Synthesis von Unmensch und Übermensch*] . . . (*GM* I 16)

As was to be expected, the whole *ferocity* of moral stultification that, as we all know, passes for morality itself in Germany, was mobilized against my concept of "beyond good and evil"—: I could tell some pretty tales about that. Above all, I was asked to reflect on the "undeniable superiority" of our time in its ethical judgment, the genuine *progress* we have made here: in comparison with *us*, a Cesare Borgia should not be presented as a "superior human being" at all, as a kind of *superhuman* being [*als ein "höherer Mensch," als eine Art* Übermensch], as I present him . . . (*TI* "Forays" 37)

Humanity does *not* represent a development for the better
or the stronger or the superior in the way this is believed
today. "Progress" is merely a modern idea, which is to say a
false idea. The European of today remains, in terms of value,
deeply inferior to the European of the Renaissance; further
development is absolutely *not*, by any form of necessity,
enhancement, intensification, strengthening.

In another sense, in individual cases there is continual
success in the most diverse places in the world and from the
most diverse cultures where a *superior type* does in fact present
itself: something that is a kind of superhuman in relation to
humanity as a whole [*etwas, das im Verhältniss zur Gesammt-
Menschheit eine Art Übermensch ist*]. Such serendipities of great
success have always been possible and perhaps will always be
possible. And even whole families, tribes, and peoples can in
certain circumstances represent just such a *lucky hit*. (*AC* 4)

In the final analysis, this is my typical experience and, if you
prefer, the *originality* of my experience. Those who thought
they had understood something by me fashioned something
of me in their own image — not infrequently the opposite of
me, for example, an "idealist"; those who understood nothing
of me denied that I came into consideration at all. — The
word "*superhumans*" [*Das Wort* "Übermensch"] to designate
the type that has turned out best, in contrast to "modern"
humans, to "good" humans, to Christians and other nihilists
— a word that becomes, in the mouth of a Zarathustra, that
destroyer of morality, a most thought-provoking word, is
almost invariably, and completely innocently, understood in
the sense of those values whose opposite was manifested in the
figure of Zarathustra, in other words, as the "idealistic" type
of a superior kind of human, half "saint," half "genius" . . .
This has caused other learned cattle to suspect me of Darwinism; they have even recognized in it the "hero cult," so
wickedly rejected by me, of Carlyle, that great unconscious,
unintentional counterfeiter. When I whispered in someone's

ear that he should look around for a Cesare Borgia rather
than a Parsifal, he could not believe his ears.[71] (*EH* "Books" 1)

Here, at every moment, human beings are overcome, here the
concept "superhumans" has become the highest reality — at
an infinite distance *beneath* him lies everything that was ever
found great in the human being. [*Hier ist in jedem Augenblick
der Mensch überwunden, der Begriff "Übermensch" ward hier
höchste Realität, — in einer unendlichen Ferne liegt alles das,
was bisher gross am Menschen hiess,* unter *ihm.*] (*EH* "Books" Z6)

Zarathustra, the first psychologist of the good, is — therefore
— a friend of evil. When a *décadence*-kind of human has
climbed to the rank of the most superior kind, this could only
happen at the expense of their opposite kind, the strong kind
of human confident about life. When the herd animal glows
in the radiance of the purest virtue, the exceptional human
must have been devalued into evil. When mendacity at any
price appropriates the word "truth" for its perspective, a really
truthful person must be relegated to the worst of names.
Here, Zarathustra leaves no doubt: he says that his recognition of the good, the "best," was exactly the thing that
aroused his horror at the human in general; through *this*
dislike, his wings had grown ready "to soar off to distant
futures," — he does not conceal the fact that *his* type of
human, a relatively superhuman type, is superhuman precisely
in relation to the *good people*, and that the good and the just
people would call his superhumans *devils* . . . [*dass sein Typus*

71. See also Nietzsche's letter to Malwida von Meysenbug (20 October
1888, *KGB* III:5, 458): "— — for your own purposes, you have again — something I never forgive — made my concept 'superhumans' [*meinem Begriff
"Übermensch"*] into a 'more sophisticated sham,' into something resembling
sibyls and prophets: whereas every serious reader of my texts has to know
that the one type of human being that cannot disgust me is a type completely antithetical to the ideal-idols of yesteryear, a thousand times more
similar to Cesare Borgia than to a Christ."

*Mensch, ein relativ übermenschlicher Typus, gerade im Verhält-
niss zu den* Guten *übermenschlich ist, dass die Guten und
Gerechten seinen Übermenschen* Teufel *nennen würden . . .*]

You most superior human beings whom I have ever
laid eyes on! this is my doubt about you and my secret
laughter: I suspect you would call my superhumans —
devils! [*ich rathe, ihr würdet meinen Übermenschen —
Teufel heissen!*]

You are so alienated from greatness with souls like
yours, that you would find superhumans *terrifying* in
their goodness . . . [*So fremd seid ihr dem Grossen mit
eurer Seele, dass euch der Übermensch* furchtbar *sein
würde in seiner Güte . . .*] (*EH* "Destiny" 5, quoting *Z*
II "On Human Prudence")

Index of Persons

Page numbers followed by n and nn indicate notes.

Subject Index

Page numbers followed by n and nn indicate notes.

The Complete Works of Friedrich Nietzsche

IN NINETEEN VOLUMES

Library of Congress Cataloging-in-Publication Data

Names: Nietzsche, Friedrich Wilhelm, 1844–1900, author. | Loeb, Paul S.,
  translator, writer of afterword. | Tinsley, David F., translator, writer of
  afterword. | Nietzsche, Friedrich Wilhelm, 1844–1900. Works. English.
  1995 ; v. 14–15.
Title: Unpublished fragments from the period of Thus spoke Zarathustra /
  Friedrich Nietzsche ; translated, with an afterword, by Paul S. Loeb and
  David F. Tinsley.
Description: Stanford, California : Stanford University Press, 2019– |
  Series: The complete works of Friedrich Nietzsche ; volume 14–15 |
  "Translated from Friedrich Nietzsche, Sämtliche Werke: Kritische
  Studienausgabe, ed. Giorgio Colli and Mazzino Montinari, in 15 vols.
This book corresponds to Vol. 10." | Includes bibliographical references
and indexes. Contents: I. Summer 1882–winter 1883/84 — II. Spring 1884–
winter 1884/85.
Identifiers: LCCN 2018019454| ISBN 9780804728874 (v. 1 : cloth : alk.
paper)
  | ISBN 9781503607521 (v. 1 : pbk. : alk. paper)
Subjects: LCSH: Nietzsche, Friedrich Wilhelm, 1844–1900—Notebooks,
  sketchbooks, etc.
Classification: LCC B3312.E5 L58 2019 | DDC 193—dc23
LC record available at https://lccn.loc.gov/2018019454

Typeset by Classic Typography in 10.5/12 Adobe Garamond